HUMAN WORTH

RICHARD PAUL JANARO
DARWIN E. GEARHART

HOLT, RINEHART AND WINSTON, INC.

New York   Chicago   San Francisco   Atlanta   Dallas

PREFACE

The need for this anthology has grown out of what the editors consider to be the new humanism. Unlike the older variety, which believed in learning about and venerating a few outstanding representatives of the "very best" that mankind could produce, today's humanism concerns itself with all people.

A humanistic collection of readings, therefore, should be one that presents writers who have something to say and say it well whether they have attained "classic" stature or not. The criteria we have used in making our selections have been varied, except that in every piece we have found something that deserves attention because it has style or grace, or there is something startling and controversial or perhaps something simple and touching about it.

Over and above readability and stimulation, we asked of each selection that it contribute in some way to the understanding of the overall theme of Human Worth. Every reading suggests some way in which Human Worth can be defined and recognized. If our age needs anything, top priority must surely be given to the affirmation of the inherent value of existence, of the things that have made it possible for mankind not only to survive, but, as Faulkner so emphatically declared, "to prevail."

We have sought, also, to present fairly writings from the past and present, from Western and non-Western viewpoints, by women and men, and to explore fully the spectrum of possibilities inherent in the phrase Human Worth. Our procedure was to be altogether casual about the whole arrangement: to accept the humanity of these writers without regard to who they are, when they lived, or what they believed, as long as they had an important statement to make and a vital way of making it. This broad base of significance is what we believe the new humanism is all about.

We have organized the theme of Human Worth in terms of three major aspects, corresponding to the order in which each of us might investigate his/her own Worth: *Orientations, Boundaries,* and *The Unbounded Self.*

In *Orientations* we find a variety of attitudes on subjects such as education and the sex roles and we explore the effect these have on us. In *Boundaries* the reader has an opportunity to consider whether it is power, money, and status that determine Human Worth; whether it is the capacity for being disciplined, or the capacity for rejecting or changing the system that seeks to control us; and whether we derive Worth from civilization and culture, or from living the natural life. In the final section *The Unbounded Self* the reader explores the possibility that, no matter what happens to us in society, we are free to develop inwardly as we wish, free to pursue the rational life or to attempt to go beyond that into the uncharted areas of consciousness; and finally, free to respond emotionally to life as we will—free to feel optimistic or cynical about it—free not to want to live it at all, or to find hope in the most unexpected places.

The possible meanings of Human Worth lie not only in ideas, however, but in their modes of expression as well. For this reason we have been concerned with introducing readers to multiple forms of expression. There are essays, short stories, poems, and a play. In some cases nearly identical statements are made through very different literary genres, and this will show the reader how form and style can effect final impact. A life-denying poem, charged with passion and excitement, filled with sensuous language and imagery, may still come across as life-affirming, even though the intellectual intentions of the poet may have been far different.

At the end of the prose and drama selections the reader will find a number of suggested Responses. These are questions which can help him make a start toward understanding the author's statement, its relevance to the matter of Human Worth, and, the light it may shed upon his/her own self-explorations. The Responses may also prove useful as points of departure for the reader's own writing.

For instructors and students who enjoy experimentation in the classroom, we have provided an Appendix of Actions. The Action designed for each selection is intended to help the group as a whole achieve a learning experience over and above that which each reader will discover for himself. Actions allow classes to test out an author's stated thesis or implied meaning; to investigate possible ramifications of what the author has said; or to find out how a certain principle, or ideal, might work out if someone actually tried to live it.

But editorial assistance in a humanistic anthology must be supplementary. If it proves unnecessary, so much the better. Our best hope is that the selections presented in this book will help the readers consider the many aspects and varieties of Human Worth and lead them to see themselves and others in new ways.

November 1972

R. P. J.
D. E. G.

An Instructor's Manual, containing rhetorical questions on the prose selections, is available from the publisher on request.

To
Jane and Jessie with love

CONTENTS

I. ORIENTATIONS

II. BOUNDARIES

III. THE UNBOUNDED SELF

I saw a man pursuing the horizon;
Round and round they sped.
I was disturbed at this;
I accosted the man.
"It is futile," I said,
"You can never—"
"You lie," he cried,
And ran on.

Stephen Crane

Orientations

I

Is it learning that gives us Worth?

                        But learning what?

Perhaps it's whatever sex we are.

                        But what is a sex?

Maybe it's the capacity to love.

Or else it's the fact that man has a moral nature.

                        Whose morality?

                            yours or MINE?

                            Someone Else's?

                    WHO DECIDES?

EDUCATION
AND
HUMAN DIGNITY

Few people deny the existence of that quality we have labeled Human Worth, but fewer still agree on how it ought to be defined or the places it can be found or the extent to which this individual or that exemplifies its meaning. For some it is a universal commodity or characteristic, something all people have at birth—whether from God or the natural scheme of things—and retain throughout their existence. It is as fundamental as man's biological nature, as his spirit, as the breath of life itself. For some Human Worth is a precious, fragile essence that is slowly and systematically stifled and diminished the older one grows—a victim of government, law, science and technology, and other "dehumanizing" institutions. But a classic argument has been made and is still being made for the fact that Human Worth is something that does not exist at birth, but can only be acquired through the long and laborious process of "humanization" which the institutions of man, notably education, make possible.

The traditional defense of a planned and rigorous education is that without it people would be self-centered, aggressive, narrow-minded, without skills, without perspective, and, above all, without the subtle capacity to enjoy life's higher moments. How would people gain the concrete knowledge they need in order to survive in this world? Where would they find the models of human behavior upon which to pattern their lives? their moral systems?

There was a time when almost nobody questioned the need for education or the right of the educational establishment to decide for each person what he needed to fulfill his humanity. But disenchantment with traditional approaches and requirements has been steadily growing. It is pointed out, for example, that much of the knowledge people will need to survive in the world of the future hasn't been discovered yet. It is being said that history— once a solid basis for all true education—is an embarrassing anthology of Western civilization's colossal blunders.

The following selections offer a variety of ideas about what education—*and* Human Worth—ought to be all about. The first, a letter by Thomas Jefferson outlining his plan for a public education system, takes what many would no doubt consider a highly conservative view. Though Jefferson is revered as the architect of American democracy, he advocates here a selective policy, planned and administered by "the most enlightened individuals" and certainly not accessible to all people. The enlightened interpret in advance the potential of aspiring students and decide which ones may enter certain fields and which ones will have less educational opportunity.

Though it is written in a twentieth-century context and serves in one respect as a response to contemporary student activism, the report from Harvard's Committee on Governance reaffirms the traditional function of higher learning in our society. *Before* they are educated, how many people know what education is supposed to do for them? The university—administrators and faculty—must remain the best judge of its services and obligations to students.

But the Harvard Report is more than counterbalanced by a number of recently published, severe indictments of academic traditionalism. Neil Postman and Charles Weingartner, author of *Teaching as a Subversive Activity*, are dedicated teachers who confess their disenchantment with the system of higher education as it currently exists, and their book offers a blueprint of how the system can be undermined in order to turn out realistically educated people who have learned how to cope with life's actualities. In our selection the authors see education not as something which elevates the student upward toward theoretical levels or standards but as something which facilitates self-awareness and sensitivity to one's environment. Theirs represents the approach of the new humanism, which says that everyone can learn.

If Postman and Weingartner want education to take the student as he is and help him to develop his unique potential, the behavioral psychologist B.F. Skinner proposes a dramatically different kind of education in the chapter we have included from *Walden Two*. The book as a whole creates a scientific utopia in which people lead an ideal existence through careful conditioning designed by experts on the human mind. Education is thus of paramount importance, its function being not only to increase intellectual capacity but to systematically root out all of the undesirable traits with which people are born. In this selection we discover how young children at Walden Two are trained to be socially rather than competitively oriented.

THE IDEAL CURRICULUM
Thomas Jefferson

The life and accomplishments of **Thomas Jefferson** (1743–1826), and his importance to the ideology of this country are too well known to require a restatement here. We are, rather, specifically concerned with his contributions to the philosophy of education in a free society, the impact of which is still being felt and the humane elements of which are still debated.

The Jefferson plan for public education is a diversified one that becomes highly stratified in its upper stages, in sharp contrast to the belief of many educators today that an open-door policy must be maintained at all levels of the system. It provides for:

1. A three-year elementary training, open to everyone without cost
2. A secondary school to prepare students for university education, free to qualified children of the poor, and open to any children whose parents can afford it
3. University education of a professional, liberal-arts, or vocational nature, depending upon aptitude, free to a highly select few who qualify but have no means—these to use their knowledge in the service of the state, and open to those who can both pay the tuition and pass the entrance examinations.

As you can see, the higher we go, the more selective Jefferson's proposal becomes, until, at the university level, nobody is admitted solely as a matter of democratic course or as a courtesy to the upper-classes.

Those who contend that "higher" education frequently misses out altogether in its avowed intention of developing each student's potential are fond of making derisive references to Jefferson's nonequalitarian approach. The University of Virginia, established through Jefferson's persistent efforts to found a publically supported university which the deserving might attend even if they lacked the financial means, is, for example, bitterly criticized by the poet Karl Shapiro. Looking back upon his undergraduate days there in his poem "University," he remembers the institution as being snobbish and racist; he sees its founder, a "true nobleman, once a democrat" sleeping "on his private mountain." The University, for Shapiro, is a symbol of all that denies rather than contributes to Human Worth.

> In whited cells, on lawns equipped for peace,
> Under the arch, and lofty banister,
> Equals shake hands, unequals blankly pass;
> The exemplary weather whispers "Quiet, quiet . . ."[1]

But Jefferson would no doubt have defended his views against the charge of elitism or exclusiveness. He would no doubt have pointed out that all human beings are equal in their *right* to education, but not in the degree to which they begin to manifest the effects of education. And many still basically agree with his advocacy of an open-door policy for those who deserve to come in.

Beyond the divergence of viewpoints, however, is the undeniable unorthodoxy of Jefferson's theories. For their time they were radical indeed and established a model unheard of in American or European academic circles which future educators in this country could use as a point of departure. Jefferson resolutely fought against both legislative and civic resistance to his idea of education-by-merit rather than education-by-blood-line. By any standards the opening of The University of Virginia in 1825 must be considered a milestone event in the history of institutions and Human Worth in America.

The Ideal Curriculum

To Peter Carr

Monticello, September 7, 1814

Dear Sir,—On the subject of the academy or college proposed to be established in our neighborhood, I promised the trustees that I would prepare for them a plan, adapted, in the first instance, to our slender funds, but susceptible of being enlarged, either by their own growth or by accession from other quarters.

I have long entertained the hope that this, our native State, would take up the subject of education, and make an establishment, either

From *The Letters of Thomas Jefferson.*

[1] "University" from *Selected Poems* by Karl Shapiro. Copyright 1940 by Karl Shapiro and reprinted by permission of Random House, Inc.

with or without incorporation into that of William and Mary, where every branch of science, deemed useful at this day, should be taught in its highest degree. With this view, I have lost no occasion of making myself acquainted with the organization of the best seminaries in other countries, and with the opinions of the most enlightened individuals, on the subject of the sciences worthy of a place in such an institution. In order to prepare what I have promised our trustees, I have lately revised these several plans with attention; and I am struck with the diversity of arrangement observable in them—no two alike. Yet, I have no doubt that these several arrangements have been the subject of mature reflection, by wise and learned men, who, contemplating local circumstances, have adapted them to the conditions of the section of society for which they have been framed. I am strengthened in this conclusion by an examination of each separately, and a conviction that no one of them, if adopted without change, would be suited to the circumstances and pursuit of our country. The example they set, then, is authority for us to select from their different institutions the materials which are good for us, and, with them, to erect a structure, whose arrangement shall correspond with our own social condition, and shall admit of enlargement in proportion to the encouragement it may merit and receive. As I may not be able to attend the meetings of the trustees, I will make you the depository of my ideas on the subject, which may be corrected, as you proceed, by the better view of others, and adapted, from time to time, to the prospects which open upon us, and which cannot be specifically seen and provided for.

In the first place, we must ascertain with precision the object of our institution, by taking a survey of the general field of science, and marking out the portion we mean to occupy at first, and the ultimate extension of our views beyond that, should we be enabled to render it, in the end, as comprehensive as we would wish.

1. Elementary schools.

It is highly interesting to our country, and it is the duty of its functionaries, to provide that every citizen in it should receive an education proportioned to the condition and pursuits of his life. The mass of our citizens may be divided into two classes—the laboring and the learned. The laboring will need the first grade of education to qualify them for their pursuits and duties; the learned will need it as a foundation for further acquirements. A plan was formerly proposed to the legislature of this State for laying off every county into hundreds of wards of five or six miles square, within each of which should be a school for the education of the children of the ward, wherein they should receive three years' instruction gratis, in reading, writing, arithmetic as far as fractions, the roots and ratios, and geography. The Legislature at one time tried an ineffectual expedient for introducing this plan, which having failed, it is hoped they will some day resume it in a more promising form.

2. General schools.

At the discharging of the pupils from the elementary schools, the two classes separate—those destined for labor will engage in the business of agriculture, or enter into apprenticeships to such handicraft art as may be their choice; their companions, destined to the pursuits of science, will proceed to the college, which will consist, 1st of general schools; and, 2d, of professional schools. The general schools will constitute the second grade of education.

The learned class may still be subdivided into two sections: 1, Those who are destined for learned professions, as means of livelihood; and, 2, The wealthy, who, possessing independent fortunes, may aspire to share in conducting the affairs of the nation, or to live with usefulness and respect in the private ranks of life. Both of these sections will require instructions in all the higher branches of science; the wealthy to qualify them for either public or private life; the professional section will need those branches, especially, which are the basis of their future profession, and a general knowledge of the others, as auxiliary to that, and necessary to their standing and association with the scientific class. All the branches, then, of useful science, ought to be taught in the general schools, to a competent degree, in the first instance. These sciences may be arranged into three departments, not rigorously scientific, indeed, but sufficiently so for our purposes. These are, I. Language; II. Mathematics; III. Philosophy.

I. Language. In the first department, I would arrange a distinct science. 1, Languages and History, ancient and modern; 2, Grammar; 3, Belles Lettres; 4, Rhetoric and Oratory; 5, A school for the deaf, dumb and blind. History is here associated with languages, not as a kindred subject, but on the principle of economy, because both may be attained by the same course of reading, if books are selected with that view.

II. Mathematics. In the department of Mathematics, I should give place distinctly: 1, Mathematics pure; 2, Physico-Mathematics; 3, Physics; 4, Chemistry; 5, Natural History, to wit: Mineralogy; 6, Botany; and 7, Zoology; 8, Anatomy; 9, the Theory of Medicine.

III. Philosophy. In the Philosophical department, I should distinguish: 1, Ideology; 2, Ethics; 3, the Law of Nature and Nations; 4, Government; 5, Political Economy.

But, some of these terms being used by different writers, in different degrees of extension, I shall define exactly what I mean to comprehend in each of them.

I. 3. Within the term of Belles Lettres I include poetry and composition generally, and criticism.

II. 1. I consider pure mathematics as a science of, 1, Numbers, and 2, Measure in the abstract; that of numbers comprehending Arithmetic, Algebra and Fluxions; that of Measure (under the general appellation of Geometry), comprehending Trigonometry, plane and spherical, conic sections, and transcendental curves.

II. 2. Physico-Mathematics treat of physical subjects by the aid of mathematical calculation. These are Mechanics, Statics, Hydrostatics, Hydrodynamics, Navigation, Astronomy, Geography, Optics, Pneumatics, Acoustics.

II. 3. Physics, or Natural Philosophy (not entering the limits of Chemistry) treat of natural substances, their properties, mutual relations and action. They particularly examine the subjects of motion, action, magnetism, electricity, galvanism, light, meteorology, with an etc. not easily enumerated. These definitions and specifications render immaterial the question whether I use the generic terms in the exact degree of comprehension in which others use them; to be understood is all that is necessary to the present object.

3. Professional Schools.

At the close of this course the students separate; the wealthy retiring, with a sufficient stock of knowledge, to improve themselves to any degree to which their views may lead them, and the professional section to the professional schools, constituting the third grade of education, and teaching the particular sciences which the individuals of this section mean to pursue, with more minuteness and detail than was within the scope of the general schools for the second grade of instruction. In these professional schools each science is to be taught in the highest degree it has yet attained. They are to be the

1st Department, the fine arts, to wit: Civil Architecture, Gardening, Painting, Sculpture, and the Theory of Music; the

2d Department, Architecture, Military and Naval; Projectiles, Rural Economy (comprehending Agriculture, Horticulture and Veterinary), Technical Philosophy, the Practice of Medicine, Materia Medica, Pharmacy and Surgery. In the

3d Department, Theology and Ecclesiastical History; Law, Municipal and Foreign.

To these professional schools will come those who separated at the close of their first elementary course, to wit:

The lawyer to the law school.

The ecclesiastic to that of theology and ecclesiastical history.

The physician to those of medicine, materia medica, pharmacy and surgery.

The military man to that of military and naval architecture and projectiles.

The agricultor to that of rural economy.

The gentleman, the architect, the pleasure gardener, painter and musician to the school of fine arts.

And to that of technical philosophy will come the mariner, carpenter, shipwright, pumpmaker, clockmaker, machinist, optician, metallurgist, founder, cutler, druggist, brewer, vintner, distiller, dyer, painter, bleacher, soapmaker, tanner, powdermaker, saltmaker, glassmaker, to learn as much as shall be necessary to pursue their art understandingly, of the sciences of geometry, mechanics, statics, hydrostatics, hydraulics, hydrodynamics, navigation, astronomy, geography, optics, pneumatics, physics, chemistry, natural history, botany, mineralogy and pharmacy.

The school of technical philosophy will differ essentially in its functions from the other professional schools. The others are instituted to ramify and dilate the particular sciences taught in the schools of the second grade on a general scale only. The technical school is to abridge those which were taught there too much *in extenso* for the limited wants of the artificer or practical man. These artificers must be grouped together, according to the particular branch of science in which they need elementary and practical instruction; and a special lecture or lectures should be prepared for each group. And these lectures should be given in the evening, so as not to interrupt the labors of the day. The school, particularly, should be maintained wholly at the public expense, on the same principles with that of the ward schools. Through the whole of the collegiate course, at the hours of recreation on certain days, all the students should be taught the manual exercise; military evolutions and manœuvers should be under a standing organization as a military corps, and with proper officers to train and command them.

A tabular statement of this distribution of the sciences will place the system of instruction more particularly in view:

1st or Elementary Grade in the Ward Schools.
Reading, Writing, Arithmetic, Geography.
2d, or General Grade.
1. Language and History, ancient and modern.
2. Mathematics, viz: Mathematics pure, Physico-Mathematics, Physics, Chemistry, Anatomy, Theory of Medicine, Zoology, Botany and Mineralogy.
3. Philosophy, viz: Ideology, and Ethics, Law of Nature and Nations, Government, Political Economy.
3d, or Professional Grades.
Theology and Ecclesiastical History; Law, Municipal and Foreign; Practice of Medicine; Materia Medica and Pharmacy; Surgery; Architecture, Military and Naval, and Projectiles; Technical Philosophy; Rural Economy; Fine Arts.

On this survey of the field of science, I recur to the question, what portion of it we mark out for the occupation of our institution? With the first grade of education we shall have nothing to do. The sciences of the second grade are our first object; and, to adapt them to our slender beginnings, we must separate them into groups, comprehending many sciences each, and greatly more, in the first instance, than ought to be imposed on, or can be competently conducted by a single professor permanently. They must be subdivided from time to time, as our means increase, until each professor shall have no more under his care than he can attend to with advantage to his pupils and ease to himself. For the present, we may group the sciences into professorships, as follows, subject, however, to be changed, according to the qualifications of the persons we may be able to engage.

I. Professorship.
Languages and History, ancient and modern.
Belles-Lettres, Rhetoric and Oratory.
II. Professorship.
Mathematics pure, Physico-Mathematics.
Physics, Anatomy, Medicine, Theory.
III. Professorship.
Chemistry, Zoology, Botany, Mineralogy.
IV. Professorship.
Philosophy.

The organization of the branch of the institution which inspects its government, police and economy, depending on principles which have no affinity with those of its institution, may be the subject of separate and subsequent consideration.

With this tribute of duty to the board of trustees, accept assurances of my great esteem and consideration.

RESPONSES: Questions for Writing and Discussion

1. Are students in the best position to know what education should be doing for them? Or do you agree with Jefferson's having sought "the opinions of the most enlightened individuals, on the subject of the sciences worthy of a place in such an institution"? The crux of the matter is similar to the old question of how one can know that a certain exotic food will make him sick until he has eaten it.

2. Jefferson's educational system revolves around the conviction that the education to which each American is entitled should be "proportioned to the conditions and pursuits of his life." This conflicts with the open-door policy which many colleges observe today, whereby one

is admitted on the basis of a high-school diploma and nominal tuition fees, waived for the needy. Critics of this policy sometimes argue that all it does is clutter up the classroom with people who "should not" be there, create the need for a larger, hence inferior, faculty, and inevitably "lower the standards." Was Jefferson's policy better? Or is open-door education the only answer in a democratic society?

3. Put yourself back into the Virginia of Jefferson's day. Indicate how each of the following cases might have fared under his educational plan:

a. A book-reading, philosophically oriented son of a farm laborer
b. A philandering son of a plantation owner with little taste for studying
c. A poor boy with a genius for political theory
d. The son of a farm-equipment mechanic who isn't sure what he can do best

4. A wealthy young person who wished to "live with usefulness and respect in the private ranks of life" would have had quite a curriculum to pursue in the General School. Do you agree that it would have been necessary? (Are the required courses of today pertinent to the declared later-life goals of all students? If your answer is negative why do you suppose they are required? Is the thinking of curriculum planners similar to Jefferson's on this subject?)

5. The introduction to this selection noted, as the letter does not, that a needy person with intelligence and motivation could make it all the way through university training in Jefferson's system. Thus, theoretically, no one is excluded. Is this true?

6. Jefferson encountered much resistance to his "radical" plan. Why do you think the Virginia legislators were upset by it?

7. Higher education in America today is suffering from financial strains. State legislatures are cutting away more funds every year. This would seem to suggest they have the backing of the people, that the love affair between the American public and the school system is ending. Attacks on education are coming from both left and right: the former, because the schools are hopelessly outmoded; the latter, because the schools are becoming dangerously radical and experimental. You are a student. Are the charges well founded? Can you make any of your own? Are there additional reasons for the waning of public support that you believe are not being stated? Or do you believe the decline in support is unjustified? If so, how would you try to reverse the trend?

THE VALUES AND PURPOSES OF THE UNIVERSITY

The Harvard Committee on Governance

Prior to World War II "going to college" was regarded as one of life's higher privileges, expected of the sons (but not always the daughters) of those who could afford it. The less affluent but no less ambitious applied for scholarships or waited on tables. But after the war a great change in the college population took place. Within ten years the idea had become fixed in the public consciousness that "you'll never get anywhere without a degree." At first the students jammed inside lecture halls and tended to comply silently with university regulations and course requirements. But within another decade there were signs of growing unrest and dissatisfaction. The new breed of student and, in many cases, faculty began to complain about unrealistic and outmoded practices in education. By the late sixties sit-ins, demonstrations, and marches on campuses throughout the country served notice that not only the practices but now *the very concepts* of higher education were being challenged.

In a number of instances college administrations acceded without much resistance to demands for new courses and integrated faculties. In other cases long hours of negotiations produced uneasy truces and tense compromises on both sides. But some institutions, notably those with the deepest roots and proudest traditions, began to take firm and resolute stands against the pressures being exerted by the students for control of the establishment.

In 1969 the Harvard Committee on Governance was organized for the purpose of reviewing the "management and allocation" of the University's resources and of clearly articulating the interrelationship among the administration, faculty, and student body. The end product of the Committee's deliberations was a pamphlet which not only states Harvard's decision not to be pressured into policy and curriculum changes, but reexamines and defines the entire philosophy behind higher education.

We have included what we believe to be the crucial section of the pamphlet. Here the Committee clearly sets forth the context within which they feel any university of higher learning must operate. Without an atmosphere of academic freedom in which he is guaranteed the right to pursue intellectual and scientific interests often beyond "practical" concerns, the university professor, in the opinion of the Committee, cannot fulfill his proper function in society.

The Values and Purposes of the University

Traditionally, the pursuit of truth and learning is the central value of the university. This value unites the university's primary functional purpose of providing education with the supporting purposes of generating knowledge, serving the community, and preserving our cultural heritage. The justification of special academic freedom rests ultimately on its being a necessary condition for the pursuit of truth. But in many quarters today the ideal of an institution devoted to the search for truth by open inquiry has lost credibility. Why?

Has this ideal lost credibility within the university because too many university men have been diverted from the search for truth? To be blunt—the answer is yes. To put it more judiciously—we need to ask ourselves some difficult questions.

One such question is, have the ever-increasing demands of the buyers of our products caused faculties to abdicate their responsibility for determining the course of teaching and inquiry? Our modern industrial society has a voracious appetite for young people trained for professional, managerial, and technological careers. The demand generates pressure upon the academic community to turn out, and upon students to become, the "products" in greatest demand in the existing social order. The current runs so strongly in this direction that there is danger of neglecting the basic question: Education for what larger purposes? A legitimate part of the educational function is to accommodate the needs of many students to learn to play a constructive role within the current social structure, but often the search for truth also requires both him and his teacher to question that same social structure. The function of the university community in educating the young for vocations useful to society must be kept in constant tension with its role in providing a forum for social and moral criticism.

The buyer's market extends to the provision of knowledge through research, reports, consultations, and, sometimes, active participation in the conduct of affairs. The demand generates countless indirect and subtle pressures affecting the conduct of the whole academic enterprise: course enrollments, research grants, consultation fees, public and professional kudos, promotions, and smaller perquisites. The government is the largest single buyer of knowledge, perhaps larger than all others combined; thus, its demands put its stamp upon the academic community. To the extent that the consumers of knowledge are indifferent to suffering or injustice, its providers help to perpetuate the wrong. This circumstance, probably more than any other, has eroded

From *The Nature and Purposes of the University: A Discussion Memorandum*, The University Committee on Governance, Harvard University, January 1971.

13

confidence in the plea that university men are impartial seekers of truth. Again, one must note a measure of ambivalence. The uses to which knowledge will be put cannot be known in advance, nor is the use always constant. The purposes of the buyers of knowledge are seldom as sharply right or wrong as those of the heroes and rogues of television. In some areas one may even cherish the hope that the provision of knowledge and understanding is the best way to change a mistaken government policy. But we must ask ourselves, to what extent do the purchasers of our products, rather than our own sense of where we should reach for truth, presently determine the direction of our corporate and individual endeavors?

This question is pressed more urgently because of current intellectual fashions. For instance, the idea that knowledge should lead to wisdom has been considered old-fashioned. Instead, the "positivist, technocratic" view of knowledge has insisted that all learning and intellectual effort must base itself on what it conceives to be the paradigm of the natural sciences. In this view the central role of the university is to advance the frontiers of knowledge through distinct, autonomous disciplines. The positivist technocrat insists upon separating the world of "fact" from the sphere of "value" and asserts a somewhat simple-minded and unproblematic notion of objectivity. This tendency to look to the systematization and perfection of disciplines has not been confined to the social and natural sciences. In the humanities, in the law, in philosophy, there is so much sheer professional expertise as to make it natural enough to forget the sustaining ideal of the education of individual character and the slow persuasion of public conscience. But this tendency toward specialism, if unbridled, serves to split research efforts away from teaching and both teaching and research away from a concern with the large-scale issues of our times. It downgrades the importance of excellence in teaching with an over-emphasis on techniques and facts.

This argument is not meant to belittle the values of technology, the importance of internal coherence, or the need for every sort of knowledge. Still less is it intended to fly to the opposing pole of subjectivism, which discovers absolute truths by revelation—or pure intuition. The point is simply this: intellectual concerns that become divorced from the great moral issues, from the aspirations of humanity and goals of the enterprise are inadequate. University men deserve criticism if our inquiries and teaching are value-free, detached from the great issues such as racial justice, relief of poverty, pollution of the environment, and war and peace. A university should be not only an institution that preserves culture and advances the frontiers of knowledge; it should also be a place where the conflicting social, intellectual and spiritual tendencies of an age confront each other in the classroom on the common ground of respect for the relevance of sustained rational endeavor. Have we enmeshed ourselves in too narrow a conception of the scientific method?

To sharpen our question further, we can compare Harvard with two models that have been put forward to clarify the choice that exists concerning the relation between the university and its surrounding social order. The "classical" model would have the university stand outside, detached from society. Such a university would be peopled with scholars holding all varieties of creeds and beliefs who are set free to question and criticize all areas and aspects of human experience. The primary role is that of critic. The second type is the "pragmatic" model, in which the primary function is one of service to the needs of the contemporary social system. Such service centers around the education of large numbers of people, with additional contributions in the form of the generation and application of knowledge. The emphasis here is on direct involvement. Each model has its own price. If one chooses the first, then one is barred in the role of teacher and researcher, though not as a citizen, from going beyond theory into active advocacy. If one chooses the second, one must acknowledge the right of outside groups to influence the nature of the services to be rendered.

Both of these types, while extreme, have their proponents at Harvard as well as at other universities. While Harvard has represented a mix of these two models, it seems that in recent years, it has drifted toward the pragmatic model. Perhaps the question is not which type is best but rather how to achieve a better balance and, beyond that, how to transcend the dilemma by enhancing the qualities of both detachment and involvement. After all, both tendencies can be seen in the behavior of the major campus groups. Students are not only drawn outward toward involvement with current social issues but also inward toward the detached acquisition of knowledge and learning. Faculty are pulled both outward toward the development of new knowledge and inward to reflection and the classroom. Administrators are involved outward in the search for resources and also inward in the coordination of academic affairs. In appropriate amounts, these dichotomies in interaction can generate the creative tension that can develop greatness in a university. A lack of balance can also destroy it.

In the last analysis all individual and institutional commitment to a search for truth through the process of reason has rested on faith— upon the belief that man is a rational and social being endowed with a sense of justice that enables him to choose between good and evil; that he must choose for himself; that there are circumstances that best facilitate that choice; and that we must do what we can to bring this to pass. This traditional faith is less easily defended now than fifty years ago. For one thing, we have learned that reasoning is a less simple process than was once supposed. We are more mindful of the darker, frightening side of man. On the brighter side, we are more ready to agree that spontaneity, intuition, love—all the life of feeling that we associate with the ways of the poet and artist—may save the processes of the intellect from sterility and desiccation. The insight of the social sciences and the honesty of the arts have taught us to look at ourselves stripped of pretense and what we see is less than lovely. It takes honesty and courage to see ourselves as we are; but perhaps we should strive to regain the greater Hellenic courage to see man stumble and fall, yet avow his nobler capacity. In the long run, mankind needs some institution dedicated to the search for truth and the value of intellectual inquiry. The university has undertaken the job, and although it may have been diverted, it has a greater potential for fulfilling the role than any other human institution. We must reaffirm our commitment to the search for truth as the central value of the university. We must rekindle our faith in the capacity of people to choose wisely for themselves within a climate of honest search. We must renew our dedication to a university community wherein the dialectic of detached inquiry and passionate involvement is safeguarded and preserved.

RESPONSES: Questions for Writing and Discussion

1. From your knowledge of the recent history of student unrest and perhaps in terms of your own attitudes, do you agree with the committee's analysis of the causes of the crisis? Explain why you do or do not.

2. The committee's recommendation of the need for university autonomy in directing the course of higher education is based on the three general functions cited at the outset: "generating knowledge, serving the community, and preserving our cultural heritage." Can you define what is intended by each of these? Do you agree that each should be an aim of education in this country?

3. A dichotomy or polarity is set up in the report between the classical and the pragmatic models of a university. Explain in your own words what each one is and how it operates. If a choice were forced on you, which one would you use in establishing your own college?

4. A further dualism is suggested—between "excellence in teaching" and an "overemphasis on techniques and facts," the latter an outgrowth of what the committee sees as university preoccupation with technological training. Do you find such a separation in your own experience? Can you cite examples of excellent teachers who did not emphasize "techniques and facts"? What seemed to be their purpose?

When, by contrast, is a teacher of techniques and facts not a good one? Summarize your thinking on the subject in a concise statement of what actually does constitute a good teacher.

5. Reread the paragraph on p. 14, beginning "This argument is not meant to belittle the values of technology. . . ." Can you find fault with its central idea of a university? Why or why not? Some points to consider here are:

    a. What "culture" do you think the committee is talking about?

    b. What is "sustained rational endeavor"?

    c. How does it differ from the "too narrow conception of the scientific method," which the committee finds evident in the classroom?

6. Summarize the concluding paragraph in your own words. (What, in particular, is the "Hellenic courage to see man stumble and fall, yet avow his nobler capacity"?) Is the substance of this paragraph empty rhetoric? Is it unbridled idealism? A dangerous regression into outmoded principles? A practicable blueprint for good education, which you would like to see implemented immediately?

THE TEACHER AS SUBVERSIVE
Neil Postman and Charles Weingartner

Neil Postman and **Charles Weingartner** are representative of those educators who understand the causes of student dissatisfaction and sympathize with many of the demands for sweeping educational reforms. They believe that they and their "subversive" colleagues, from their vantage point behind the lectern, may know even more than the students about what they consider to be the inadequacies of the educational establishment. They see their purpose as being far more than to put new methods into practice. They want to counsel others on how to undermine academic bureaucracy from within the system itself, hopefully changing it for the better. *Teaching as a Subversive Activity*, directed toward faculty members, has been followed by another book *The Soft Revolution*, described as a student guide "for turning schools around." The authors look toward a utopian future when both educational groups become powerful allies in a common cause. They are in obvious disagreement with the position taken in the Harvard report.

the preceding selection, which argues for the right of the administration to have the final say in determining and implementing a university's philosophy and methods.

The selection which follows outlines the role of tomorrow's teacher. Here the authors are not making a negative assault on the educational system so much as they are looking at how society works, and from this they derive one concept of how schools ought to function.

The essay is particularly detailed in its treatment of the dehumanizing effects of mass media and some of the methods whereby the ordinary citizen in today's world is systematically brainwashed. They make abundantly evident what the student ought to expect (and demand) from the school: help in learning how in later life to discover and then defend himself against the "crap" of cultural traditions and the neatly packaged "crap" he gets from the TV set when he is not getting it from the boss.

The Teacher as Subversive

"In 1492, Columbus discovered America. . . ." Starting from this disputed fact, each one of us will describe the history of this country in a somewhat different way. Nonetheless, it is reasonable to assume that most of us would include something about what is called the "democratic process," and how Americans have valued it, or at least have said they valued it. Therein lies a problem: one of the tenets of a democratic society is that men be allowed to think and express themselves freely on any subject, even to the point of speaking out against the idea of a democratic society. To the extent that our schools are instruments of such a society, they must develop in the young not only an awareness of this freedom but a will to exercise it, and the intellectual power and perspective to do so effectively. This is necessary so that the society may continue to change and modify itself to meet unforeseen threats, problems, and opportunities. Thus, we can achieve what John Gardner calls an "ever-renewing society."

So goes the theory.

In practice, we mostly get a different story. In our society, as in others, we find that there are influential men at the head of important institutions who cannot afford to be found wrong, who find change inconvenient, perhaps intolerable, and who have financial or political interests they must conserve at any cost. Such men are, therefore, threatened in many respects by the theory of the democratic process and the concept of an ever-renewing society. Moreover, we find that there are obscure men who do *not* head important institutions who are similarly threatened because they have identified themselves with certain ideas and institutions which they wish to keep free from either criticism or change.

Such men as these would much prefer that the schools do little or nothing to encourage youth to question, doubt, or challenge any part of the society in which they live, especially those parts which are most vulnerable. "After all," say the practical men, "they are *our* schools, and they ought to promote *our* interests, and *that* is part of the democratic process, too." True enough; and here we have a serious point of conflict. Whose schools are they, anyway, and whose interests should they be designed to serve? We realize that these are questions about which any self-respecting professor of education could write several books, each one beginning with a reminder that the problem is not black or white, either/or, yes or no. But if you have read our introduction, you will not expect us to be either professorial or prudent. We are, after all, trying to suggest strategies for survival as they may be developed in our schools, and the situation requires emphatic responses. We believe that the schools must serve as the principal medium for developing in youth the attitudes and skills of social, political, and cultural criticism. No. That is not emphatic enough. Try this: In the early 1960s, an interviewer was trying to get Ernest Hemingway to identify the characteristics required for a person to be a "great writer." As the interviewer offered a list of various possibilities, Hemingway disparaged each in sequence. Finally, frustrated, the interviewer asked, "Isn't there any one essential ingredient that you can identify?" Hemingway replied, "Yes, there is. In order to be a great writer a person must have a built-in, shockproof crap detector."

It seems to us that, in his response, Hemingway identified an essential survival strategy and the essential function of the schools in today's world. One way of looking at the history of the human group is that it has been a continuing struggle against the veneration of "crap." Our intellectual history is a chronicle of the anguish and suffering of men who tried to help their contemporaries see that some part of their fondest beliefs were misconceptions, faulty assumptions, superstitions, and even outright lies. The mileposts along the road of our intellectual development signal those points at which some person developed a new perspective, a new meaning, or a new metaphor. We have in mind a new education that would set out to cultivate just such people—experts at "crap detecting."

There are many ways of describing this function of the schools, and many men who have. David Riesman, for example, calls this the "counter-cyclical" approach to education, meaning that schools should stress values that are not stressed by other major institutions in the culture. Norbert Wiener insisted that the schools now must function as "anti-entropic feedback systems," "entropy" being the word used to denote a general and unmistakable tendency of all systems—natural and man-made—in the universe to "run down," to reduce to chaos and uselessness. This is a process that cannot be reversed but that can be slowed down and partly controlled. One way to control it is through "maintenance." This is Eric Hoffer's term, and he believes that the quality of maintenance is one of the best indices of the quality of life in a culture. But Wiener uses a different metaphor to get at the same idea. He says that in order for there to be an anti-entropic force, we must have adequate feedback. In other words, we must have instruments to tell us when we are running down, when maintenance is required. For Wiener, such instruments would be people who have been educated to recognize change, to be sensitive to problems caused by change, and who have the motivation and courage to sound alarms when entropy accelerates to a dangerous degree. This is what we mean by "crap detecting." It is also what John Gardner means by the "ever-renewing society," and what Kenneth Boulding means by "social self-consciousness." We are talking about the schools' cultivating in the young that most "subversive" intellectual instrument—the anthropological perspective. This perspective allows one to be part of his own culture and, at the same time, to be out of it. One views the activities of his own group as would an anthropologist, observing its tribal rituals, its fears, its conceits, its ethnocentrism. In this way, one is able to recognize when reality begins to drift too far away from the grasp of the tribe.

We need hardly say that achieving such a perspective is extremely difficult, requiring, among other things, considerable courage. We are, after all, talking about achieving a high degree of freedom from the intellectual and social constraints of one's tribe. For example, it is generally assumed that people of other tribes have been victimized by indoctrination from which our tribe has remained free. Our own outlook seems "natural" to us, and we wonder that other men can perversely persist in believing nonsense. Yet it is undoubtedly true that, for most people, the acceptance of a particular doctrine is largely attributable to the accident of birth. They might be said to be "ideologically interchangeable," which means that they would have accepted any set of doctrines that happened to be valued by the tribe to which they were born. Each of us, whether from the American tribe, Russian tribe, or Hopi tribe, is born into a symbolic environment as well as a physical one. We become accustomed very early to a "natural" way of talking, and being talked to, about "truth." Quite arbitrarily, one's perception of what is "true" or real is shaped by the symbols and symbol-manipulating institutions of his tribe. Most men, in time, learn to respond with fervor and obedience to a set of verbal abstractions which they feel provides them with an ideological identity. One word for this, of course, is "prejudice." None of us is free of it, but it is the sign of a competent "crap detector" that he is not completely captivated by the arbitrary abstractions of the community in which he happened to grow up.

In our own society, if one grows up in a language environment which includes and approves such a concept as "white supremacy," one can quite "morally" engage in the process of murdering civil-rights workers. Similarly, if one is living in a language environment where the term "black power" crystalizes an ideological identity, one can engage, again quite "morally," in acts of violence against any nonblack persons or their property. An insensitivity to the unconscious effects of our "natural" metaphors condemns us to highly constricted perceptions of how things are and, therefore, to highly limited alternative modes of behavior.

Those who *are* sensitive to the verbally built-in biases of their "natural" environment seem "subversive" to those who are not. There is probably nothing more dangerous to the prejudices of the latter than a man in the process of discovering that the language of his group is limited, misleading, or one-sided. Such a man is dangerous because he is not easily enlisted on the side of one ideology or another, because he sees beyond the words to the processes which give an ideology its reality. In his *May Man Prevail?*, Erich Fromm gives us an example of a man (himself) in the process of doing just that:

> The Russians believe that they represent socialism because they talk in terms of Marxist ideology, and they do not recognize how similar their system is to the most developed form of capitalism. We in the West believe that we represent the system of individualism, private initiative, and humanistic ethics, because we hold on to *our* ideology, and we do not see that our institutions have, in fact, in many ways become more and more similar to the hated system of communism.

Religious indoctrination is still another example of this point. As Alan Watts has noted: "Irrevocable commitment to any religion is not only intellectual suicide; it is positive unfaith because it closes the mind to any new vision of the world. Faith is, above all, openness—an act of trust in the unknown." And so "crap detecting" requires a perspective on what Watts calls "the standard-brand religions." That perspective can also be applied to knowledge. If you substitute the phrase "set of facts" for the word "religion" in the quotation above, the statement is equally important and accurate.

The need for this kind of perspective has always been urgent but never so urgent as now. We will not take you again through that painful catalogue of twentieth-century problems we cited in our Introduction. There are, however, three particular problems which force us to conclude that the schools must consciously remake themselves into training centers for "subversion." In one sense, they are all one problem but for purposes of focus may be distinguished from each other.

The first goes under the name of the "communications revolution," or media change. As Father John Culkin of Fordham University likes to say, a lot of things have happened in this century and most of them plug into walls. To get some perspective on the electronic plug, imagine that your home and all the other homes and buildings in your neighborhood have been cordoned off, and from them will be removed all the electric and electronic inventions that have appeared in the last 50 years. The media will be subtracted in reverse order, with the most recent going first. The first thing to leave your house, then, is the television set—and everybody will stand there as if they are attending the funeral of a friend, wondering, "What are we going to do tonight?" After rearranging the furniture so that it is no longer aimed at a blank space in the room, you suggest going to the movies. But there won't be any. Nor will there be LP records, tapes, radio, telephone, or telegraph. If you are thinking that the absence of the media would only affect your entertainment and information, remember that, at some point, your electric lights would be removed, and your refrigerator, and your heating system, and your air conditioner. In short, you would have to be a totally different person from what you are in order to survive for more than a day. The chances are slim that you could modify yourself and your patterns of living and believing fast enough to save yourself. As you were expiring, you would at least know something about how it was before the electric plug. Or perhaps you wouldn't. In any case, if you had energy and interest enough to hear him, any good ecologist could inform you of the logic of your problem: a change in an environment is rarely only additive or linear. You seldom, if ever, have an old environment *plus* a new element, such as a printing press or an electric plug. *What you have is a totally new environment requiring a whole new repertoire of survival strategies.* In no case is this more certain than when the new elements are technological. Then, in no case will the new environment be more radically different from the old than in political and social forms of life. When you plug something into a wall, someone is getting plugged into you. Which means you need new patterns of defense, perception, understanding, evaluation. You need a new kind of education.

It was George Counts who observed that technology repealed the Bills of Rights. In the eighteenth century, a pamphlet could influence an entire nation. Today all the ideas of the Noam Chomskys, Paul

Goodmans, Edgar Friedenbergs, I. F. Stones, and even the William Buckleys, cannot command as much attention as a 30-minute broadcast by Walter Cronkite. Unless, of course, one of them were given a prime-time network program, in which case he would most likely come out more like Walter Cronkite than himself. Even Marshall McLuhan, who is leading the field in understanding media, is having his ideas transformed and truncated by the forms of the media to fit present media functions. (One requirement, for example, is that an idea or a man must be "sensational" in order to get a hearing; thus, McLuhan comes out not as a scholar studying media but as the "Apostle of the Electronic Age.")

We trust it is clear that we are not making the typical, whimpering academic attack on the media. We are not "against" the media. Any more, incidentally, than McLuhan is "for" the media. You cannot reverse technological change. Things that plug in are here to stay. But you can study media, with a view toward discovering what they are doing to you. As McLuhan has said, there is no inevitability so long as there is a willingness to contemplate what is happening.

Very few of us have contemplated more rigorously what is happening through media change than Jacques Ellul, who has sounded some chilling alarms. Without mass media, Ellul insists, there can be no effective propaganda. With them, there is almost nothing but. "Only through concentration of a large number of media in a few hands can one attain a true orchestration, a continuity, and an application of scientific methods of influencing individuals." That such concentration is occurring daily, Ellul says, is an established fact, and its results may well be an almost total homogenization of thought among those the media reach. We cannot afford to ignore Norbert Wiener's observation of a paradox that results from our increasing technological capability in electronic communication: as the number of messages increases, the amount of information carried decreases. We have more media to communicate fewer significant ideas.

Still another way of saying this is that, while there has been a tremendous increase in media, there has been, at the same time, a decrease in available and viable "democratic" channels of communication because the mass media are entirely one-way communication. For example, as a means of affecting public policy, the town meeting is dead. Significant community action (without violence) is increasingly rare. A small printing press in one's home, as an instrument of social change, is absurd. Traditional forms of dissent and protest seem impractical, e.g., letters to the editor, street-corner speeches, etc. No one can reach many people unless he has access to the mass media. As this is written, for example, there is no operational two-way communication possible with respect to United States policies and procedures in Vietnam. The communication is virtually all one way: from the top down, via the mass media, especially TV. The pressure on everyone is to subscribe without question to policies formulated in the Pentagon. The President appears on TV and clearly makes the point that anyone who does not accept "our policy" can be viewed only as lending aid and comfort to the enemy. The position has been elaborately developed in all media that "peaceniks" are failing in the obligation to "support our boys overseas." The effect of this process on all of us is to leave no alternative but to accept policy, act on orders from above, and implement the policy without question or dialogue. This is what Edgar Friedenberg calls "creeping Eichmannism," a sort of spiritless, mechanical, abstract functioning which does not allow much room for individual thought and action.

As Paul Goodman has pointed out, there are many forms of censorship, and one of them is to deny access to "loudspeakers" to those with dissident ideas, or even *any* ideas. This is easy to do (and not necessarily conspiratorial) when the loudspeakers are owned and operated by mammoth corporations with enormous investments in their proprietorship. What we get is an entirely new politics, including the possibility that a major requirement for the holding of political office be prior success as a show-business personality. Goodman writes in *Like a Conquered Province:*

> The traditional American sentiment is that a decent society cannot be built by dominant official policy anyway, but only by grassroots resistance, community cooperation, individual enterprise, and citizenly vigilance to protect liberty. . . . *The question is whether or not our beautiful libertarian, pluralist, and populist experiment is viable in modern conditions.* If it's not, I don't know any other acceptable politics, and I am a man without a country.

Is it possible that there are millions becoming men without a country? Men who are increasingly removed from the sources of power? Men who have fewer and fewer ideas available to them, and fewer and fewer ways of expressing themselves meaningfully and effectively? Might the frustration thus engendered be one of the causes of the increasing use of violence as a form of statement?

We come then to a second problem which makes necessary a "subversive" role for the schools. This one may appropriately be called the "Change Revolution." In order to illustrate what this means, we will use the media again and the metaphor of a clock face. Imagine a clock face with 60 minutes on it. Let the clock stand for the time men have had access to writing systems. Our clock would thus represent something like 3,000 years, and each minute on our clock 50 years. On this scale, there were no significant media changes until about nine minutes ago. At that time, the printing press came into use in Western culture. About three minutes ago, the telegraph, photograph, and locomotive arrived. Two minutes ago: the telephone, rotary press, motion pictures, automobile, airplane, and radio. One minute ago, the talking picture. Television has appeared in the last ten seconds, the computer in the last five, and communications satellites in the last second. The laser beam—perhaps the most potent medium of communication of all—appeared only a fraction of a second ago.

It would be possible to place almost any area of life on our clock face and get roughly the same measurements. For example, in medicine, you would have almost no significant changes until about one minute ago. In fact, until one minute ago, as Jerome Frank has said, almost the whole history of medicine is the history of the placebo effect. About a minute ago, antibiotics arrived. About ten seconds ago, open-heart surgery. In fact, within the past ten seconds there probably have been more changes in medicine than is represented by all the rest of the time on our clock. This is what some people call the "knowledge explosion." It is happening in every field of knowledge susceptible to scientific inquiry.

The standard reply to any comment about change (for example, from many educators) is that change isn't new and that it is easy to exaggerate its meaning. To such replies, Norbert Wiener had a useful answer: the difference between a fatal and a therapeutic dose of strychnine is "only a matter of degree." In other words, change isn't new; what is new is the *degree of change*. As our clock-face metaphor was intended to suggest, about three minutes ago there developed a qualitative difference in the character of change. Change changed.

This is really quite a new problem. For example, up until the last generation it was possible to be born, grow up, and spend a life in the United States without moving more than 50 miles from home, without ever confronting serious questions about one's basic values, beliefs, and patterns of behavior. Indeed, without ever confronting serious challenges to anything one knew. Stability and consequent predictability—within "natural cycles"—was the characteristic mode. But now, in just the last minute, we've reached the stage where change occurs so rapidly that each of us in the course of our lives has continuously to work out a set of values, beliefs, and patterns of behavior that are viable, or *seem* viable, to each of us personally. And just when we have identified a workable system, it turns out to be irrelevant because so much has changed while we were doing it.

Of course, this frustrating state of affairs applies to our education as well. If you are over twenty-five years of age, the mathematics you were taught in school is "old"; the grammar you were taught is obsolete and in disrepute; the biology, completely out of date, and the history, open to serious question. The best that can be said of you, assuming that you *remember* most of what you were told and read, is that you are a walking encyclopedia of outdated information. As Alfred North Whitehead pointed out in *The Adventure of Ideas:*

> Our sociological theories, our political philosophy, our practical maxims of business, our political economy, and our doctrines of education are derived from an unbroken tradition of great thinkers and of practical examples from the age of Plato . . . to the end of the last century. The whole of this tradition is warped by the vicious assumption that each generation will substantially live amid the conditions governing the lives of its fathers and will transmit those conditions to mould with equal force the lives of its children. *We are living in the first period of human history for which this assumption is false.*

All of which brings us to the third problem: the "burgeoning bureaucracy." We are brought there because bureaucracies, in spite of their seeming indispensability, are by their nature highly resistant to change. The motto of most bureaucracies is, "Carry On, Regardless." There is an essential mindlessness about them which causes them, in most circumstances, to accelerate entropy rather than to impede it. Bureaucracies rarely ask themselves Why?, but only How? John Gardner, who as President of the Carnegie Corporation and (as of this writing) Secretary of Health, Education, and Welfare has learned about bureaucracies at first hand, has explained them very well:

> To accomplish renewal, we need to understand what prevents it. When we talk about revitalizing a society, we tend to put exclusive emphasis on finding new ideas. But there is usually no shortage of new ideas; the problem is to get a hearing for them. And that means breaking through the crusty rigidity and stubborn complacency of the *status quo*. The aging society develops elaborate defenses against new ideas—"mind-forged manacles," in William Blake's vivid phrase. . . . As a society becomes more concerned with precedent and custom, it comes to care more about how things are done and less about *whether* they are done. The man who wins acclaim is not the one who "gets things done" but the one who has an ingrained knowledge of the rules and accepted practices. Whether he accomplishes anything is less important than whether he conducts himself in an "appropriate" manner.
>
> The body of custom, convention, and "reputable" standards exercises such an oppressive effect on creative minds that new developments in a field often originate outside the area of respectable practice.

In other words, bureaucracies are the repositories of conventional assumptions and standard practices—two of the greatest accelerators of entropy.

We could put before you a volume of other quotations—from Machiavelli to Paul Goodman—describing how bureaucratic structures retard the development and application of new survival strategies. But in doing so, we would risk creating the impression that we stand with Goodman in yearning for some anarchistic Utopia in which the Army, the Police, General Motors, the U.S. Office of Education, the Post Office, et al. do not exist. We are not "against" bureaucracies, any more than we are "for" them. They are like electric plugs. They will probably not go away, but they do need to be controlled if the prerogatives of a democratic society are to remain visible and usable. This is why we ask that the schools be "subversive," that they serve as a kind of anti-bureaucracy bureaucracy, providing the young with a "What is it good for?" perspective on its own society. Certainly, it is unrealistic to expect those who control the media to perform that function. Nor the generals and the politicians. Nor is it reasonable to expect the "intellectuals" to do it, for they do not have access to the majority of youth. But schoolteachers do, and so the primary responsibility rests with them.

The trouble is that most teachers have the idea that they are in some other sort of business. Some believe, for example, that they are in the "information dissemination" business. This was a reasonable business up to about a minute or two ago on our clock. (But then, so was the horseshoe business and the candle-snuffer business.) The signs that their business is failing are abundant, but they keep at it all the more diligently. Santayana told us that a fanatic is someone who redoubles his efforts when he has forgotten his aim. In this case, even if the aim has not been forgotten, it is simply irrelevant. But the effort has been redoubled anyway.

There are some teachers who think they are in the "transmission of our cultural heritage" business, which is not an unreasonable business if you are concerned with the whole clock and not just its first 57 minutes. The trouble is that most teachers find the last three minutes too distressing to deal with, which is exactly why they are in the wrong business. Their students find the last three minutes distressing—and confusing—too, especially the last 30 seconds, and they need *help*. While they have to live with TV, film, the LP record, communication satellites, and the laser beam, their teachers are still talking as if the only medium on the scene is Gutenberg's printing press. While they have to understand psychology and psychedelics, anthropology and anthropomorphism, birth control and biochemistry, their teachers are teaching "subjects" that mostly don't exist anymore. While they need to find new roles for themselves as social, political, and religious organisms, their teacher (as Edgar Friedenberg has documented so painfully) are acting almost entirely as shills for corporate interests, shaping them up to be functionaries in one bureaucracy or another.

Unless our schools can switch to the right business, their clientele will either go elsewhere (as many are doing) or go into a severe case of "future shock," to use a relatively new phrase. Future shock occurs when you are confronted by the fact that the world you were educated to believe in doesn't exist. Your images of reality are apparitions that disappear on contact. There are several ways of responding to such a condition, one of which is to withdraw and allow oneself to be over-come by a sense of impotence. More commonly, one continues to act *as if* his apparitions were substantial, relentlessly pursuing a course of action that he knows will fail him. You may have noticed that there are scores of political, social, and religious leaders who are clearly suffering from advanced cases of future shock. They repeat over and over again the words that are supposed to represent the world about them. But nothing seems to work out. And then they repeat the words again and again. Alfred Korzybski used a somewhat different metaphor to de-scribe what we have been calling "future shock." He likened one's language to a map. The map is intended to describe the territory that we call "reality," i.e., the world outside of our skins. When there is a close correspondence between map and territory, there tends to be a high degree of effective functioning, especially where it relates to survival. When there is little correspondence between map and territory, there is a strong tendency for entropy to make substantial gains. In this context, the terrifying question What did you learn in school today? assumes immense importance for all of us. We just may not survive another generation of inadvertent entropy helpers.

What is the necessary business of the schools? To create eager consumers? To transmit the dead ideas, values, metophors, and informa-tion of three minutes ago? To create smoothly functioning bureaucrats? *These* aims are truly subversive since they undermine our chances of surviving as a viable, democratic society. And they do their work in the name of convention and standard practice. We would like to see the schools go into the anti-entropy business. Now, that is subversive, too. But the purpose is to subvert attitudes, beliefs, and assumptions that foster chaos and uselessness.

RESPONSES: Questions for Writing and Discussion

1. On the whole, has your educational experience tended to sup-port the authors' contention that the majority of teachers are dealing only with the first fifty-seven minutes of the civilization clock? Share some specific instances with the rest of the class.

2. If it is true that what students most desperately need is help in coping with the last three minutes of this clock, how, in your opinion, are teachers to function in such a capacity? Consider such questions as where teachers will get the necessary training when they themselves

have been taught mostly by fifty-seven minute people. Try to draw a profile of the three-minute teacher of the future.

3. The authors mention Marshall McLuhan, who has perhaps done more than any one person to analyze and inform us of what the media, especially television, are doing to us. The classroom sometimes makes abundant use of television. What has been your experience with the electronic dimension of education? Has your learning been enhanced or impeded by it?

4. One major function of education, the one the authors deal with in this selection, is to find ways of helping students to detect the "crap" in the social environment within which they must live. Whatever use may be made of television in the classroom, it is continually affecting us outside as well—and seldom with a conscious educational purpose in mind. The long paragraph about the effect of electric things on our lives makes a powerful point about "crap" and the electric media, especially the statement, "When you plug something into a wall, someone is getting plugged into you." What is "television crap"? How can we recognize it? defend ourselves against it? Mention some positive benefits that can be derived from noneducational television—that is, what do you consider to be the most desirable use one can make of this medium?

5. Do you agree with the authors that there are few channels available to *you personally* through which to voice your protests and make known your views about education? What about the campus newspaper or closed-circuit television station? Is there a place on your campus where students are allowed to assemble without close super- vision, where a speaker's stand and PA system are accessible to anyone who has something to say? Are available channels on your campus controlled? By the faculty? the administration? student cliques? How do you feel about unlimited freedom of speech on the campus without anyone's exercising the power of censorship?

6. The selection concludes with two different uses of the term "subversive"—one to define the conditions presently existing in most classrooms, the other, conditions as they should be. Distinguish be- tween the two.

TRAINING CHILDREN FOR SELF-CONTROL

B. F. Skinner

B. F. Skinner (b. 1904) enjoys a distinction few may achieve: recognition in two widely separated fields. He is one of America's leading psychologists, and he is the author of *Walden Two*, the novel from which the following selection is taken and which has stirred up as much controversy as almost any other published in the mid-twentieth century. That *Walden Two* will take its place in the library of utopian novels seems undeniable.

Utopianism has a long history, beginning with Plato's *Republic*. The word "utopia" itself was coined by Sir Thomas More in 1516 (from the Greek, meaning "not a place"), who used it as the title of a book about an imaginary land with a perfect political and social order. Aristotle, St. Augustine, Machiavelli, Hobbes, Marx, and Thoreau have all entertained visions of ideal communities whose principle of rule and whose institutions exist in the best interests of the people and, *whether they know it or not*, provide for them the happiest possible life.

Skinner's *Walden Two* is a long way from Thoreau's simple hut, and doubtless many readers would deny that it represents an ideal way of life at all. It is a thriving metropolis, predesigned and carefully managed by behavioral psychologists (who believe that man can be understood as any other animal can be understood—in terms of responses conditioned by the environment). Skinner's spokesman in the novel, T. E. Frazier, believes that, by deliberately producing an environment that generates desirable intellectual and moral qualities, behavioral science can bring into existence that better world of which men and women have long dreamed. Frazier's view is that Human Worth in the highest sense is something that *can* be created.

Those who object to Skinner's ideas—and his detractors are many—tend to take the position that Human Worth does not exist without the freedom to decide upon and follow one's own destiny. They see the behaviorists in control of Walden Two as a new breed of absolute dictators. If such a society were to come about, who would guarantee, they ask, that those making the decisions will themselves possess the ideal intellectual and moral qualities they seek to engender through laboratory techniques? But Skinner's most recent work, *Beyond Freedom and Dignity*, denies the importance men have traditionally attributed to liberty as something worth having for its own sake. Freedom, Skinner argues, is a vastly misunderstood commodity; left to themselves, men and women will remain the slaves of their irrational passions. Prejudice, hatred, and war will persist. Greed, competitiveness, and crime will continue unabated. Trust in the disinterested and superior skills of science is the only logical answer.

The following selection from *Walden Two* deals with the training of children to possess that self-control which, Frazier reminds his guests, Jesus himself once taught long before the world was ready for so radical a doctrine. It is a scientific plan to educate human beings to understand and use the power of love. Readers may decide for themselves whether the stated objective is a sound one and whether the desired end product—the non-competitive individual—justifies the lack of personal choice open to those whom Walden Two seeks to shape and mold.

Training Children for Self-Control

"Each of us," Frazier began, "is engaged in a pitched battle with the rest of mankind."

"A curious premise for a Utopia," said Castle. "Even a pessimist like myself takes a more hopeful view than that."

"You do, you do," said Frazier. "But let's be realistic. Each of us has interests which conflict with the interests of everybody else. That's our original sin, and it can't be helped. Now, 'everybody else' we call 'society.' It's a powerful opponent, and it always wins. Oh, here and there an individual prevails for a while and gets what he wants. Sometimes he storms the culture of a society and changes it slightly to his own advantage. But society wins in the long run, for it has the advantage of numbers and of age. Many prevail against one, and men against a baby. Society attacks early, when the individual is helpless. It enslaves him almost before he has tasted freedom. The 'ologies' will tell you how it's done. Theology calls it building a conscience or developing a spirit of selflessness. Psychology calls it the growth of the super-ego.

"Considering how long society has been at it, you'd expect a better job. But the campaigns have been badly planned and the victory has never been secure. The behavior of the individual has been shaped according to revelations of 'good conduct,' never as the result of experimental study. But why not experiment? The questions are simple enough. What's the best behavior for the individual so far as the group is concerned? And how can the individual be induced to behave in that way? Why not explore these questions in a scientific spirit?

"We could do just that in Walden Two. We had already worked out a code of conduct—subject, of course, to experimental modification.

Reprinted with permission of The Macmillan Company from *Walden Two* by B. F. Skinner. Copyright 1948 by B. F. Skinner.

The code would keep things running smoothly if everybody lived up to it. Our jobs was to see that everybody did. Now, you can't get people to follow a useful code by making them into so many jacks-in-the-box. You can't foresee all future circumstances, and you can't specify adequate future conduct. You don't know what will be required. Instead you have to set up certain behavioral processes which will lead the individual to design his own 'good' conduct when the time comes. We call that sort of thing 'self-control.' But don't be misled, the control always rests in the last analysis in the hands of society.

"One of our Planners, a young man named Simmons, worked with me. It was the first time in history that the matter was approached in an experimental way. Do you question that statement, Mr. Castle?"

"I'm not sure I know what you are talking about," said Castle.

"Then let me go on. Simmons and I began by studying the great works on morals and ethics—Plato, Aristotle, Confucius, the New Testament, the Puritan divines, Machiavelli, Chesterfield, Freud— there were scores of them. We were looking for any and every method of shaping human behavior by imparting techniques of self-control. Some techniques were obvious enough, for they had marked turning points in human history. 'Love your enemies' is an example—a psychological invention for easing the lot of an oppressed people. The severest trial of oppression is the constant rage which one suffers at the thought of the oppressor. What Jesus discovered was how to avoid these inner devastations. His technique was to *practice the opposite emotion*. If a man can succeed in 'loving his enemies' and 'taking no thought for the morrow,' he will no longer be assailed by hatred of the oppressor or rage at the loss of his freedom or possessions. He may not get his freedom or possessions back, but he's less miserable. It's a difficult lesson. It comes late in our program."

"I thought you were opposed to modifying emotions and instincts until the world was ready for it," said Castle. "According to you, the principle of 'love your enemies' should have been suicidal."

"It would have been suicidal, except for an entirely unforeseen consequence. Jesus must have been quite astonished at the effect of his discovery. We are only just beginning to understand the power of love because we are just beginning to understand the weakness of force and aggression. But the science of behavior is clear about all that now. Recent discoveries in the analysis of punishment—but I am falling into one digression after another. Let me save my explanation of why the Christian virtues—and I mean merely the Christian techniques of self-control—have not disappeared from the face of the earth, with due recognition of the fact that they suffer a narrow squeak within recent memory.

"When Simmons and I had collected our techniques of control, we had to discover how to teach them. That was more difficult. Current educational practices were of little value, and religious practices scarcely any better. Promising paradise or threatening hell-fire is, we assumed, generally admitted to be unproductive. It is based upon a fundamental fraud which, when discovered, turns the individual against society and nourishes the very thing it tries to stamp out. What Jesus offered in return for loving one's enemies was heaven *on earth*, better known as peace of mind.

"We found a few suggestions worth following in the practices of the clinical psychologist. We undertook to build a tolerance for annoying experiences. The sunshine of midday is extremely painful if you come from a dark room, but take it in easy stages and you can avoid pain altogether. The analogy can be misleading, but in much the same way it's possible to build a tolerance to painful or distasteful stimuli, or to frustration, or to situations which arouse fear, anger or rage. Society and nature throw these annoyances at the individual with no regard for the development of tolerances. Some achieve tolerances, most fail. Where would the science of immunization be if it followed a schedule of accidental dosages?

"Take the principle of 'Get thee behind me, Satan,' for example," Frazier continued. "It's a special case of self-control by altering the environment. Subclass A 3, I believe. We give each child a lollipop which has been dipped in powdered sugar so that a single touch of the tongue can be detected. We tell him he may eat the lollipop later in the day, provided it hasn't already been licked. Since the child is only three or four, it is a fairly diff—"

"Three or four!" Castle exclaimed.

"All our ethical training is completed by the age of six," said Frazier quietly. "A simple principle like putting temptation out of sight would be acquired before four. But at such an early age the problem of not licking the lollipop isn't easy. Now, what would you do, Mr. Castle, in a similar situation?"

"Put the lollipop out of sight as quickly as possible."

"Exactly. I can see you've been well trained. Or perhaps you discovered the principle for yourself. We're in favor of original inquiry wherever possible, but in this case we have a more important goal and we don't hesitate to give verbal help. First of all, the children are urged to examine their own behavior while looking at the lollipops. This helps them to recognize the need for self-control. Then the lollipops are concealed, and the children are asked to notice any gain in happiness or any reduction in tension. Then a strong distraction is arranged—say, an interesting game. Later the children are reminded of the candy and encouraged to examine their reaction. The value of the distraction is generally obvious. Well, need I go on? When the experiment is repeated a day or so later, the children all run with lollipops to their lockers and do exactly what Mr. Castle would do—a sufficient indication of the success of our training."·

"I wish to report an objective observation of my reaction to your story," said Castle, controlling his voice with great precision. "I find myself revolted by this display of sadistic tyranny."

"I don't wish to deny you the exercise of an emotion which you seem to find enjoyable," said Frazier. "So let me go on. Concealing a tempting but forbidden object is a crude solution. For one thing, it's not always feasible. We want a sort of psychological concealment— covering up the candy by paying no attention. In a later experiment the children wear their lollipops like crucifixes for a few hours."

> " 'Instead of the cross, the lollipop,
>   About my neck was hung,' "

said Castle.

"I wish somebody had taught me that, though," said Rodge, with a glance at Barbara.

"Don't we all?" said Frazier. "Some of us learn control, more or less by accident. The rest of us go all our lives not even understanding how it is possible, and blaming our failure on being born the wrong way."

"How do you build up a tolerance to an annoying situation?" I said.

"Oh, for example, by having the children 'take' a more and more painful shock, or drink cocoa with less and less sugar in it until a bitter concoction can be savored without a bitter face."

"But jealousy or envy—you can't administer them in graded doses," I said.

"And why not? Remember, we control the social environment, too, at this age. That's why we get our ethical training in early. Take this case. A group of children arrive home after a long walk tired and hungry. They're expecting supper; they find, instead, that it's time for a lesson in self-control: they must stand for five minutes in front of steaming bowls of soup.

"The assignment is accepted like a problem in arithmetic. Any groaning or complaining is a wrong answer. Instead, the children begin at once to work upon themselves to avoid any unhappiness during the delay. One of them may make a joke of it. We encourage a sense of humor as a good way of not taking an annoyance seriously. The joke won't be much, according to adult standards—perhaps the child will simply pretend to empty the bowl of soup into his upturned mouth.

Another may start a song with many verses. The rest join in at once, for they've learned that it's a good way to make time pass."

Frazier glanced uneasily at Castle, who was not to be appeased.

"That also strikes you as a form of torture, Mr. Castle?" he asked.

"I'd rather be put on the rack," said Castle.

"Then you have by no means had the thorough training I supposed. You can't imagine how lightly the children take such an experience. It's a rather severe biological frustration, for the children are tired and hungry and they must stand and look at food; but it's passed off as lightly as a five-minute delay at curtain time. We regard it as a fairly elementary test. Much more difficult problems follow."

"I suspected as much," muttered Castle.

"In a later stage we forbid all social devices. No songs, no jokes—merely silence. Each child is forced back upon his own resources—a very important step."

"I should think so," I said. "And how do you know it's successful? You might produce a lot of silently resentful children. It's certainly a dangerous stage."

"It is, and we follow each child carefully. If he hasn't picked up the necessary techniques, we start back a little. A still more advanced stage"—Frazier glanced again at Castle, who stirred uneasily—"brings me to my point. When it's time to sit down to the soup, the children count off—heads and tails. Then a coin is tossed and if it comes up heads, the 'heads' sit down and eat. The 'tails' remain standing for another five minutes."

Castle groaned.

"And you call that envy?" I asked.

"Perhaps not exactly," said Frazier. "At least there's seldom any aggression against the lucky ones. The emotion, if any, is directed against Lady Luck herself, against the toss of the coin. That, in itself, is a lesson worth learning, for it's the only direction in which emotion has a surviving chance to be useful. And resentment toward things in general, while perhaps just as silly as personal aggression, is more easily controlled. Its expression is not socially objectionable."

Frazier looked nervously from one of us to the other. He seemed to be trying to discover whether we shared Castle's prejudice. I began to realize, also, that he had not really wanted to tell this story. He was vulnerable. He was treading on sanctified ground, and I was pretty sure he had not established the value of most of these practices in an experimental fashion. He could scarcely have done so in the short space of ten years. He was working on faith, and it bothered him.

I tried to bolster his confidence by reminding him that he had a professional colleague among his listeners. "May you not inadvertently teach your children some of the very emotions you're trying to eliminate?" I said. "What's the effect, for example, of finding the anticipation of a warm supper suddenly thwarted? Doesn't that eventually lead to feelings of uncertainty, or even anxiety?"

"It might. We had to discover how often our lessons could be safely administered. But all our schedules are worked out experimentally. We watch for undesired consequences just as any scientist watches for disrupting factors in his experiments.

"After all, it's a simple and sensible program," he went on in a tone of appeasement. "We set up a system of gradually increasing annoyances and frustrations. against a background of complete serenity. An easy environment is made more and more difficult as the children acquire the capacity to adjust."

"But *why?*" said Castle. "Why these deliberate unpleasantnesses— to put it mildly? I must say I think you and your friend Simmons are really very subtle sadists."

"You've reversed your position, Mr. Castle," said Frazier in a sudden flash of anger with which I rather sympathized. Castle was calling names, and he was also being unaccountably and perhaps intentionally obtuse. "A while ago you accused me of breeding a race of softies," Frazier continued. "Now you object to toughening them up. But what you don't understand is that these potentially unhappy situations are never very annoying. Our schedules make sure of that. You wouldn't understand, however, because you're not so far advanced as our children."

Castle grew black.

"But what do your children get out of it?" he insisted, apparently trying to press some vague advantage in Frazier's anger.

"What do they get out of it!" exclaimed Frazier, his eyes flashing with a sort of helpless contempt. His lips curled and he dropped his head to look at his fingers, which were crushing a few blades of grass.

"They must get happiness and freedom and strength," I said, putting myself in a ridiculous position in attempting to make peace.

"They don't sound happy or free to me, standing in front of bowls of Forbidden Soup," said Castle, answering me parenthetically while continuing to stare at Frazier.

"If I must spell it out," Frazier began with a deep sigh, "what they get is escape from the petty emotions which eat the heart out of the unprepared. They get the satisfaction of pleasant and profitable social relations on a scale almost undreamed of in the world at large. They get immeasurably increased efficiency, because they can stick to a job without suffering the aches and pains which soon beset most of us. They get new horizons, for they are spared the emotions characteristic of frustration and failure. They get—" His eyes searched the branches of the trees. "Is that enough?" he said at last.

"And the community must gain their loyalty," I said, "when they discover the fears and jealousies and diffidences in the world at large."

"I'm glad you put it that way," said Frazier. "You might have said that they must feel superior to the miserable products of our public schools. But we're at pains to keep any feeling of superiority or con- tempt under control, too. Having suffered most acutely from it myself, I put the subject first on our agenda. We carefully avoid any joy in a personal triumph which means the personal failure of somebody else. We take no pleasure in the sophistical, the disputative, the dialectical." He threw a vicious glance at Castle. "We don't use the motive of domination, because we are always thinking of the whole group. We could motivate a few geniuses that way—it was certainly my own motivation—but we'd sacrifice some of the happiness of everyone else. Triumph over nature and over oneself, yes. But over others, never."

"You've taken the mainspring out of the watch," said Castle flatly.

"That's an experimental question, Mr. Castle, and you have the wrong answer."

Frazier was making no effort to conceal his feeling. If he had been riding Castle, he was now using his spurs. Perhaps he sensed that the rest of us had come round and that he could change his tactics with a single holdout. But it was more than strategy, it was genuine feeling. Castle's undeviating skepticism was a growing frustration.

"Are your techniques really so very new?" I said hurriedly. "What about the primitive practice of submitting a boy to various tortures before granting him a place among adults? What about the disciplinary techniques of Puritanism? Or of the modern school, for that matter?"

"In one sense you're right," said Frazier. "And I think you've nicely answered Mr. Castle's tender concern for our little ones. The unhappi- nesses we deliberately impose are far milder than the normal unhappi- nesses from which we offer protection. Even at the height of our ethical training, the unhappiness is ridiculously trivial—to the well-trained child.

"But there's a world of difference in the way we use these annoy- ances," he continued. "For one thing, we don't punish. We never administer an unpleasantness in the hope of repressing or eliminating undesirable behavior. But there's another difference. In most cultures the child meets up with annoyances and reverses of uncontrolled magnitude. Some are imposed in the name of discipline by persons in authority. Some, like hazings, are condoned though not authorized. Others are merely accidental. No one cares to, or is able to, prevent them.

"We all know what happens. A few hardy children emerge, particularly those who have got their unhappiness in doses that could be swallowed. They become brave men. Others become sadists or masochists of varying degrees of pathology. Not having conquered a painful environment, they become preoccupied with pain and make a devious art of it. Others submit—and hope to inherit the earth. The rest—the cravens, the cowards—live in fear for the rest of their lives. And that's only a single field—the reaction to pain. I could cite a dozen parallel cases. The optimist and the pessimist, the contented and the disgruntled, the loved and the unloved, the ambitious and the discouraged —these are only the extreme products of a miserable system.

"Traditional practices are admittedly better than nothing," Frazier went on. "Spartan or Puritan—no one can question the occasional happy result. But the whole system rests upon the wasteful principle of selection. The English public school of the nineteenth century produced brave men—by setting up almost insurmountable barriers and making the most of the few who came over. But selection isn't education. Its crops of brave men will always be small, and the waste enormous. Like all primitive principles, selection serves in place of education only through a profligate use of material. Multiply extravagantly and select with rigor. It's the philosophy of the 'big litter' as an alternative to good child hygiene.

"In Walden Two we have a different objective. We make every man a brave man. They all come over the barriers. Some require more preparation than others, but they all come over. The traditional use of adversity is to select the strong. We control adversity to build strength. And we do it deliberately, no matter how sadistic Mr. Castle may think us, in order to prepare for adversities which are beyond control. Our children eventually experience the 'heartache and the thousand natural shocks that flesh is heir to.' It would be the cruelest possible practice to protect them as long as possible, especially when we *could* protect them so well."

Frazier held out his hands in an exaggerated gesture of appeal.

"What alternative *had* we?" he said, as if he were in pain. "What else could we do? For four or five years we could provide a life in which no important need would go unsatisfied, a life practically free of anxiety or frustration or annoyance. What would *you* do? Would you let the child enjoy this paradise with no thought for the future—like an idolatrous and pampering mother? Or would you relax control of the environment and let the child meet accidental frustrations? *But what is the virtue of accident?* No, there was only one course open to us. We had to *design* a series of adversities, so that the child would develop the greatest possible self-control. Call it deliberate, if you like, and accuse us of sadism; there was no other course." Frazier turned to Castle, but he was scarcely challenging him. He seemed to be waiting, anxiously, for his capitulation. But Castle merely shifted his ground.

"I find it difficult to classify these practices," he said. Frazier emitted a disgruntled "Ha!" and sat back. "Your system seems to have usurped the place as well as the techniques of religion."

"Of religion and family cultures," said Frazier wearily. "But I don't call it usurpation. Ethical training belongs to the community. As for techniques, we took every suggestion we could find without prejudice as to the source. But not on faith. We disregard all claims of revealed truth and put every principle to an experimental test. And by the way, I've very much misrepresented the whole system if you suppose that any of the practices I've described are fixed. We try out many different techniques. Gradually we work toward the best possible set. And we don't pay much attention to the apparent success of a principle in the course of history. History is honored in Walden Two only as entertainment. It isn't taken seriously as food for thought. Which reminds me, very rudely, of our original plan for the morning. Have you had enough of emotion? Shall we turn to intellect?"

Frazier addressed these questions to Castle in a very friendly way and I was glad to see that Castle responded in kind. It was perfectly clear, however, that neither of them had ever worn a lollipop about the neck or faced a bowl of Forbidden Soup.

RESPONSES: Questions for Writing and Discussion

1. Frazier refers to but does not explain "the weakness of force and aggression." In terms of his behavioristic utopia, aggression may logically seem undesirable, but what, in your opinion, makes an aggressive person *weak*?

2. Castle is an outside visitor whose remarks indicate that he is far from sold on behavioral science. Do you agree with him that the lollipop experiment is a case of "sadistic tyranny"? Do you believe it is better to indulge children a bit more at an age (three or four, remember?) when they may not understand what is happening to them?

3. Frazier's justification is that children of this age are much hardier than adults imagine. Consider the case of a permissive parent (perhaps your own or one you know). Is there a possibility that over-kindness, that continually "giving in" represents the path of least resistance for the adult? is actually harmful to the child? represents a long-delayed wish fulfillment on the part of the adult?

4. Skinner's belief is that in real life an individual is subjected to far more objectionable forms of behavioral conditioning than is the case at Walden Two. He cites punishment as an especially sad case in point. In Walden Two punishment is replaced by self-imposed discipline. Do you agree that this is feasible? (If you are a parent, do you

regularly employ punishment as a conditioning factor? If you become a parent, do you think you will? If the answer in either case is yes, indicate the harshest degree of punishment you believe in using. If the answer is no, explain why you are against such measures.)

5. Was severe punishment administered in the lower grades you attended? What purpose do you think it was intended to serve? (Jerry Farber, an exponent of radical educational reform in America, points out that schools often are filled with sadists, who do nothing so much as enjoy themselves at the students' expense and that their methods often succeed in graduating sadists to carry on the tradition. Do you agree?)

6. Other than being punished in one form or another, have you had any earlier educational experiences that seem now to have been designed deliberately to evoke negative reactions, or even a kind of suffering? What was *their* purpose? Do you think it worked?

7. Frazier argues that the people who learn self-control at all, as things stand, normally do so "by accident." We presume he means through the suffering that follows unpleasant experiences. Is there anything to be said for allowing someone to do battle with life unarmed, as it were; to take his chances and be faced with the uncertainty over what new torments each day may bring?

8. Another phase of the program at Walden Two is the training of children to "avoid any joy in a personal triumph which means the personal failure of somebody else."

    a. Does the school system in real life, according to your own experiences, encourage such joy?

    b. Do you agree it should be avoided?

ON FIRST LOOKING INTO CHAPMAN'S HOMER

John Keats

In his short life of less than twenty-six years **John Keats (1795–1821)** wrote more enduring poetry than many who lived three times as long. The desire to create and the constant recognition of life's brevity gave him not only motivation but much of his subject matters as well. Many of his finest poems are about creativity and the artistic imagination through which one escapes from time. "Chapman's Homer" expresses also the deep respect Keats had for education, enriching oneself by learning from what others have done—in contrast to the way in which some of Keats' contemporaries scorned their literary and historical heritage.

The poem is a fine example of the Italian sonnet, a demanding form which normally is better suited to the abundant rhyming possibilities of the Italian language. The poet must find enough words to satisfy the rhyme scheme—abba abba cdcdcd—without making his efforts seem obvious or forced. In this poem not only do the rhymes seem to fall naturally in place, but what Keats has to say seems almost accidentally to need no more than fourteen lines.

On First Looking Into Chapman's Homer

Much have I travell'd in the realms of gold,
    And many goodly states and kingdoms seen;
    Round many western islands have I been
Which bards in fealty to Apollo hold.
Oft of one wide expanse had I been told
    That deep-brow'd Homer ruled as his demesne;
    Yet did I never breathe its pure serene
Till I heard Chapman speak out loud and bold:
Then felt I like some watcher of the skies
    When a new planet swims into his ken;
Or like stout Cortez when with eagle eyes
    He star'd at the Pacific—and all his men
Look'd at each other with a wild surmise—
    Silent, upon a peak in Darien.

WHEN I HEARD
THE LEARN'D ASTRONOMER
Walt Whitman

As a consciously American poet, **Walt Whitman (1819–1892)** rebelled against the traditional poetic forms of his English and European predecessors. In poetic technique, as in his thinking, Whitman is guided and inspired by nature itself. Instead of measured iambics and the artificiality of rhyme, Whitman utilizes "natural" rhythms such as those of the rising and falling of the tides or the sweep of wind along the prairies.

Each poem, Whitman believed, has its own peculiar style, rhythm, and form. Whitman allows his theme or subject to give the final shape to the work, so that he is neither restricted to a certain number of lines or required to expand on an idea in order to fill up, say, fourteen lines. In the following poem poetic form and theme become almost inseparable. The poet refuses to be confined by his own craft or by the astronomer's formal, dull lecture.

When I Heard the Learn'd Astronomer

When I heard the learn'd astronomer;
When the proofs, the figures, were ranged in columns before me;
When I was shown the charts and the diagrams, to add, divide, and
measure them;
When I, sitting, heard the astronomer, where he lectured with much
applause in the lecture-room,
How soon, unaccountable, I became tired and sick;
Till rising and gliding out, I wander'd off by myself,
In the mystical moist night-air, and from time to time,
Look'd up in perfect silence at the stars.

THE STUDENT
Marianne Moore

In 1961 Marianne Moore (1887–1971) was asked to be Poet of Honor for the Poetry Day Celebration of *Poetry* magazine. This was interpreted by many as an acknowledgement that America's reigning poet was about to be honored. Marianne Moore had the credentials for it: a lifetime of memorable utterances and compassionate observations on all aspects of American life. There is a poem in the Moore canon for almost every profession or stage of living. As an editor summarized it, the poet's scope covers "people, animals, flowers, music, and sports pages"; her favorite subjects are "saints and baseball players . . . buffaloes and basilisks . . . moral triumphs and mechanical marvels." Her one constant expression, however, is a deep affection for human beings caught in the throes of living.

It would have been surprising indeed if Marianne Moore had overlooked the American undergraduate, under pressure from society to "get that degree," under pressure from lecturers to take notes from them and do well on tests ("we have not knowledge, just opinions"), but struggling all the while to nurture the wolf inside him.

The Student

"In America," began
the lecturer, "everyone must have a
degree. The French do not think that
all can have it, they don't say everyone
            must go to college." We
incline to feel
            that although it may be unnecessary

to know fifteen languages,
one degree is not too much. With us, a
school—like the singing tree of which
the leaves were mouths singing in concert—
            is both a tree of knowledge
and of liberty—
            seen in the unanimity of college

mottoes, *Lux et veritas,*
Christo et ecclesiae, Sapient
felici. It may be that we
have not knowledge, just opinions, that we
            are undergraduates,
not students; we know
            we have been told with smiles, by expatriates

of whom we had asked "When will
your experiment be finished?" "Science
is never finished." Secluded
from domestic strife, Jack Bookworm led a
            college life, says Goldsmith;

and here also as
  in France or Oxford, study is beset with

dangers,—with bookworms, mildews,
and complaisancies. But someone in New
England has known enough to say
the student is patience personified,
  is a variety
of hero, "patient
  of neglect and of reproach"—who can "hold by

himself." You can't beat hens to
make them lay. Wolf's wool is the best of wool,
but it cannot be sheared because
the wolf will not comply. With knowledge as
  with the wolf's surliness,
the student studies
  voluntarily, refusing to be less

than individual. He
"gives his opinion and then rests on it";
he renders service when there is
no reward, and is too reclusive for
  some things to seem to touch
him, not because he
  has no feeling but because he has so much.

THEME FOR ENGLISH B
Langston Hughes

Unlike the student who narrates the following poem, **Langston Hughes**
(1902–1967) emerged from the midwestern background of Kansas and
Missouri. But a year at Columbia University and then a succession of odd
jobs in Eastern cities gave Hughes a perspective on what Black America
was all about. He was one of the first literary voices communicating black
experience. In 1925, when he was twenty-three, he received the first award
ever given by *Opportunity* magazine to a black poet and then went on to

publish a dozen volumes in his career, which includes the writing of fiction and literary criticism. He became most closely identified with the Harlem scene through his stories about life in the inner city revolving around the central figure of Jesse B. Simple.

The poet's message to his black brothers is expressed here as in most of his work: the pride of black identity must not be sacrificed. The "page for English B" is what the student chose to make it. But is the poet perhaps saying something also for "other folks who are other races"? And a little something for teachers as well?

Theme For English B

The instructor said,

> Go home and write
> a page tonight.
> And let that page come out of you—
> Then, it will be true.

I wonder if it's that simple?

I am twenty-two, colored, born in Winston-Salem.
I went to school there, then Durham, then here
to this college on the hill above Harlem.
I am the only colored student in my class.
The steps from the hill lead down into Harlem,
through a park, then I cross St. Nicholas,
Eighth Avenue, Seventh, and I come to the Y,
the Harlem Branch Y, where I take the elevator
up to my room, sit down, and write this page:

It's not easy to know what is true for you or me
at twenty-two, my age. But I guess I'm what
I feel and see and hear, Harlem, I hear you:
hear you, hear me—we two—you, me, talk on this page.
(I hear New York, too.) Me—who?
Well, I like to eat, sleep, drink, and be in love.
I like to work, read, learn, and understand life.
I like a pipe for a Christmas present,

or records—Bessie, bop, or Bach.
I guess being colored doesn't make me *not* like
the same things other folks like who are other races.
So will my page be colored that I write?
Being me, it will not be white.
But it will be
a part of you, instructor.
You are white—
yet a part of me, as I am a part of you.
That's American.
Sometimes perhaps you don't want to be a part of me.
Nor do I often want to be a part of you.
But we are, that's true!
As I learn from you,
I guess you learn from me—
although you're older—and white—
and somewhat more free.

This is my page for English B.

NATURAL IDENTITY AND SOCIAL ROLES

A number of years ago a humorous book was written about men and women; it was titled *Is Sex Necessary?* For most readers this was an academic question only. But the underlying theme of the book was quite serious: are the pleasures of sexual experience compensation enough for the agonizing games men and women must play for each other's and for society's sake? Sex, as everyone knows, is more than anatomy. It is more than a biological interaction. It also involves the complex interweaving of roles, the part in life's drama that men and women are expected to play by virtue of their sex. As our society has evolved, sex has become more than a designation; it is also a *definition*—of traits, qualities, behavior, attitudes, and feelings. The definition in turn raises certain expectations about a person and his worth and serves to influence the way people think about themselves and about others. Thus it is not at all uncommon to hear "he took it like a man" or "that's just like a woman." Such sentiments assume the fact of relative value, of *superior* and *inferior*, often assessed with no direct knowledge about the human being in question.

The selections in this group all relate to the vital question of the degree to which estimations of individual worth are or ought to be based upon a person's sex. No attempt has been made to cover the intricate history of sex roles, but most of these readings suggest that the ideas of the roles *are* rooted in history far more than they are in nature. They also suggest that objectivity about sex roles is difficult at best, and usually impossible for most people.

This is not hard to believe when one considers how many people do in fact relate the value differences between the sexes to natural or even divine law. The idea is seldom entertained—or entertained by few—that a man might weep in public if only he dared or that a woman might decide she would rather become president of the United States than marry and bear children without having to be accused of unwomanly and unnatural aspirations.

The excerpt from John Stuart Mill's *The Subjection of Women*, one of the earliest studies of male-female inequality from the standpoint of social custom rather than scientific truth, points out how men and women are trained from childhood to behave in certain ways and to think of themselves as better or worse than the opposite sex.

The extracts from the diaries of Adam and Eve, as Mark Twain has whimsically imagined them for us, endeavor to view the events in Eden from the masculine and the feminine points of view. They offer insights into what the natural lines of sexual difference might have been before woman, symbolized by Eve, decided to accept her status of inferiority because of her "fatal curiosity" and her part in the fall of the human race—an ancient sin which in the Western cultural heritage has no doubt had much to do with history's definition of woman.

Dealing less with theological and more with professional matters, Virginia Woolf is no less whimsical than Mark Twain when, to prove her point, she concocts a mythical sister for Shakespeare, a girl named Judith with as much genius as her brother. She then shows us what might have happened to Judith while William was becoming the toast of London.

Bringing us into our own times, Marya Mannes' "Female Intelligence: Who Wants It?" continues the investigation of the role of women in professional life. But now we become aware of an even more subtle anxiety that must be endured. With increased freedom of mobility, with educational opportunities now available to her, woman today often is forced to make an anguished choice between her traditional role as wife and mother and the newly allowed fulfillment of her creative potential, and to feel pangs of remorse in later life no matter which decision she makes.

A study of sex roles and Human Worth would not be complete if the reader believed that women have always been and continue to be the only ones who suffer from the traditional guidelines for the proper conduct of life. Irwin Shaw's "The Eighty-Yard Run" explores the masculine image—football player, aggressive lover, successfully competitive businessman—which Americans inherit and are taught to look upon with approval. Though it mentions speakeasies and the stock market crash of 1929, this short story traces the still possible deterioration of a human life that cannot find any excuses for its failure to measure up to the expectations society entertains about the male of the species.

THE NATURAL EQUALITY OF THE SEXES

John Stuart Mill

The demand for equalizing the worth of men and women is not a passing fad that has arisen in the last decade. Belief in sexual equality has had its supporters in the past.

To John Stuart Mill (1806–1873), one of liberty's stoutest champions and authors of statements which even now would strike some as being ultra-radical and unrealistic in the extreme, reason made it clear that those who believed in natural inequality between men, nations, races, religions, and the sexes failed to perceive the differences between social customs and nature itself. How could nature create an inferior being?

On the other hand, as the following selection points out, exponents of the concept of natural inequality are able to look with some justification to the prevalence of orders of beings in virtually all of the societies of the world. Nowhere can one find a classless society or one in which men and women enjoy the same rights and privileges. Thus it *appears* that, if left to his own devices, man is by nature opposed to the concept of freedom and equality for all.

But such apparently natural hierarchies also stem from custom. They represent the way people tended to do things in the long-ago past when "the law of force" existed and before the "moral education of mankind" could take place. What shocks Mill is that, despite modern society's claims, it is no further advanced in the matter of "moral cultivation." It is reason that tells us of natural equality, but natural equality will not exist so long as ancient tradition, which operates to the benefit of the powerful, the affluent, and to men, is allowed to suppress rationality.

The selection also bears down hard upon Christianity, which, according to Mill, advocated equality of the sexes in theory but not in practice. Even where the church does not discriminate against women directly, it supports the existence of institutions which operate in terms of "an arbitrary prefer-ence of one human being over another."

Apparently liberated women did exist in Mill's time. The selection makes reference to those "whom equality of consideration will not satisfy." They are women who protest that they are legally denied all rights, make themselves heard, and are then allowed to take full advantage of their martyrdom. But Mill again blames the law and social custom for such cases. They can, he warns, be expected to continue their powerful assaults against a male-oriented society until that society redefines their role with reason and justice.

If one allows reason to guide him, he must recognize, Mill continues, that women have already proved themselves equal to men—and in the field of politics at that, precisely the area in which the law has forbidden them to intrude. He refers to the first Queen Elizabeth, Joan of Arc, and Queen Victoria, who were able to transcend the law and do their jobs at least as well as men. Mill also points out that, paradoxically, no law prohibits a woman from becoming another Shakespeare or Beethoven.

Several years after this selection was written, there appeared Charles Darwin's *The Origin of Species* (1859). This work became a biological bible for many who would argue—presumably from an equally rational ap-proach—that inequality was indeed the law of nature and both reason and social institutions must accept and implement the fact. Many interpreters of Darwin defined Human Worth in terms of the higher value of those fittest to survive. Darwin-oriented males used nature, not custom, as the basis for an articulation of sex roles.

The Natural Equality of the Sexes

A pertinacious adversary, pushed to extremities, may say, that husbands indeed are willing to be reasonable, and to make fair concessions to their partners without being compelled to it, but that wives are not: that if allowed any rights of their own, they will acknowledge no rights at all in any one else, and never will yield in anything, unless they can be compelled, by the man's mere authority, to yield in everything. This would have been said by many persons some generations ago, when satires on women were in vogue, and men thought it a clever thing to insult women for being what men made them. But it will be said by no one now who is worth replying to. It is not the doctrine of the present day that women are less susceptible of good feeling, and con-sideration for those with whom they are united by the strongest ties, than men are. On the contrary, we are perpetually told that women are

From *The Subjection of Women.*

better than men, by those who are totally opposed to treating them as if they were as good; so that the saying has passed into a piece of tiresome cant, intended to put a complimentary face upon an injury, and resembling those celebrations of royal clemency which, according to Gulliver, the king of Lilliput always prefixed to his most sanguinary decrees. If women are better than men in anything, it surely is in individual self-sacrifice for those of their own family. But I lay little stress on this, so long as they are universally taught that they are born and created for self-sacrifice. I believe that equality of rights would abate the exaggerated self-abnegation which is the present artificial ideal of feminine character, and that a good woman would not be more self-sacrificing than the best man: but on the other hand, men would be much more unselfish and self-sacrificing than at present, because they would no longer be taught to worship their own will as such a grand thing that it is actually the law for another rational being. There is nothing which men so easily learn as this self-worship: all privileged persons, and all privileged classes, have had it. The more we descend in the scale of humanity, the intenser it is; and most of all in those who are not, and can never expect to be, raised above any one except an unfortunate wife and children. The honourable exceptions are proportionally fewer than in the case of almost any other human infirmity. Philosophy and religion, instead of keeping it in check, are generally suborned to defend it; and nothing controls it but that practical feeling of the equality of human beings, which is the theory of Christianity, but which Christianity will never practically teach, while it sanctions institutions grounded on an arbitrary preference of one human being over another.

There are, no doubt, women, as there are men, whom equality of consideration will not satisfy; with whom there is no peace while any will or wish is regarded but their own. Such persons are a proper subject for the law of divorce. They are only fit to live alone, and no human beings ought to be compelled to associate their lives with them. But the legal subordination tends to make such characters among women more, rather than less, frequent. If the man exerts his whole power, the woman is of course crushed: but if she is treated with indulgence, and permitted to assume power, there is no rule to set limits to her encroachments. The law, not determining her rights, but theoretically allowing her none at all, practically declares that the measure of what she has a right to, is what she can contrive to get.

The equality of married persons before the law is not only the sole mode in which that particular relation can be made consistent with justice to both sides, and conducive to the happiness of both, but it is the only means of rendering the daily life of mankind, in any high sense, a school of moral cultivation. Though the truth may not be felt or generally acknowledged for generations to come, the only school of genuine moral sentiment is society between equals. The moral education of mankind has hitherto emanated chiefly from the law of force, and is adapted almost solely to the relations which force creates. In the less advanced states of society, people hardly recognize any relation with their equals. To be an equal is to be an enemy. Society, from its highest place to its lowest, is one long chain, or rather ladder, where every individual is either above or below his nearest neighbour, and wherever he does not command he must obey. Existing moralities, accordingly, are mainly fitted to a relation of command and obedience. Yet command and obedience are but unfortunate necessities of human life: society in equality is its normal state.

. . . . Let us at first make entire abstraction of all psychological considerations tending to show, that any of the mental differences supposed to exist between women and men are but the natural effect of the differences in their education and circumstances, and indicate no radical differences, far less radical inferiority, of nature. Let us consider women only as they already are, or as they are known to have been; and the capacities which they have already practically shown. What they have done, that at least, if nothing else, it is proved that they can do. When we consider how sedulously they are all trained away from, instead of being trained towards, any of the occupations or objects reserved for men, it is evident that I am taking a very humble ground for them, when I rest their case on what they have actually achieved. For, in this case, negative evidence is worth little, while any positive evidence is conclusive. It cannot be inferred to be impossible that a woman should be a Homer, or an Aristotle, or a Michael Angelo, or a Beethoven, because no woman has yet actually produced works comparable to theirs in any of those lines of excellence. This negative fact at most leaves the question uncertain, and open to psychological discussion. But it is quite certain that a woman can be a Queen Elizabeth, or a Deborah, or a Joan of Arc, since this is not inference, but fact. Now it is a curious consideration, that the only things which the existing law excludes women from doing, are the things which they have proved that they are able to do. There is no law to prevent a woman from having written all the plays of Shakespeare, or composed all the operas of Mozart. But Queen Elizabeth or Queen Victoria, had they not inherited the throne, could not have been entrusted with the smallest of the political duties, of which the former showed herself equal to the greatest.

. . . . Is it reasonable to think that those who are fit for the greater functions of politics, are incapable of qualifying themselves for the less? Is there any reason in the nature of things, that the wives and sisters of princes should, whenever called on, be found as competent as the princes themselves to *their* business, but that the wives and sisters of statesmen, and administrators, and directors of companies, and managers of public institutions, should be unable to do what is done by their brothers and husbands? The real reason is plain enough; it is that princesses, being more raised above the generality of men by their rank than placed below them by their sex, have never been taught that it was improper for them to concern themselves with politics; but have been allowed to feel the liberal interest natural to any cultivated human being, in the great transactions which took place around them, and in which they might be called on to take a part. The ladies of reigning families are the only women who are allowed the same range of interests and freedom of development as men; and it is precisely in their case that there is not found to be any inferiority. Exactly where and in proportion as women's capacities for government have been tried, in that proportion have they been found adequate.

This fact is in accordance with the best general conclusions which the world's imperfect experience seems as yet to suggest, concerning the peculiar tendencies and aptitudes characteristic of women, as women have hitherto been. I do not say, as they will continue to be; for, as I have already said more than once, I consider it presumption in any one to pretend to decide that women are or are not, can or cannot be, by natural constitution. They have always hitherto been kept, as far as regards spontaneous development, in so unnatural a state, that their nature cannot but have been greatly distorted and disguised; and no one can safely pronounce that if women's nature were left to choose its direction as freely as men's, and if no artificial bent were attempted to be given to it except that required by the conditions of human society, and given to both sexes alike, there would be any material difference, or perhaps any difference at all, in the character and capacities which would unfold themselves.

RESPONSES: Questions for Writing and Discussion

1. Women, according to Mill, are said to be "better than men" when it comes to "self-sacrifice for those of their own family." But he adds, self-sacrifice is what women are taught they are born for. Does this tend to be the general experience of women today? That is, in families having children of both sexes, are the girls taught the virtue of self-abnegation and "letting Brother come first"? Are boys still being raised to "worship their own will"?

2. Mill admits that many women are not satisfied with merely attaining "equality of consideration," but "there is no peace while any will or wish is regarded but their own." He sees such women as not

fit for marriage. Still, he explains such aggressiveness as an outgrowth of the suppression of the feminine sex. What does he mean? Do his sentiments apply to some male-female relationships today? In homes where the wife "wears the pants" and greets her night-prowling husband at the door with a rolling pin, which marriage partner deserves to be considered oppressed and long suffering?

3. If life in its normal state is "society in equality" but command by men and obedience by women are "unfortunate necessities," how may we account for this development? Why did such necessities ever arise in the first place if they were not the "normal state"? To discuss this intriguing question, it is helpful to run through some of the reasons often advanced for the "natural" inferiority of women, such as:

    a. Woman's role in the fall of man.

    b. The Darwinian theory of natural selection.

    c. Male rationality versus female intuitiveness and emotionalism.

    d. "If women had had the capacity for leadership when it was up for grabs, why didn't they assume it then?"

4. Mill points to women like Queen Elizabeth and Joan of Arc who made their way in a man's world and rose to positions of authority. But he also cites the often-advanced argument that there exists in the history of the arts no female Homer, Michelangelo, Shakespeare, or Beethoven. If women were able to assert themselves in the field of politics despite great obstacles, why not in the humanities?

5. Throughout his philosophical career Mill based his liberal views squarely on the doctrine of natural rights, just as Thomas Jefferson had done before him. How do you feel about natural rights? Does reason guarantee such things? Why, or why not? Do you believe that people were born to be free? That they must achieve freedom? If so, is it just as natural to "achieve" the suppression of others?

6. Are those women of today who labor long and hard in the cause of feminine liberation using the tooth and claw methods which many call the "law of the jungle" and believe to be the natural condition of mankind? Or are they, like Mill, appealing to reason? And, if so, are we once again facing the agonizing question of whether natural rights are guaranteed by reason or by the law of possession? (If women are "fighting back" in a struggle for survival which bears out Darwin's theory of natural selection, are they justified in speaking of the "unfair" or "unjust" treatment of women in the past?)

PASSAGES FROM THE DIARIES OF ADAM AND EVE

Mark Twain

Samuel Langhorne Clemens (1835–1910) was born in Missouri, a state for which he remains the official literary spokesman and in which he passed through adolescence in much the manner described in *Tom Sawyer* and *Huckleberry Finn*. His preparation for a writing career is almost a classic example of how an American literary figure is groomed. He worked as a printer's apprentice at the age of twelve, his father's death having forced him to drop out of school and earn a living. By the time he was eighteen he had been independent for so long and become so restless that he left the relatively uncosmopolitan confines of Hannibal and set out for the excitement of the big cities. In 1857 he found the ideal existence for a wandering American youth eager to encounter new adventures every day: he became an apprentice pilot on a Mississippi river boat.[1]

Twain's writings are many-sided. They mirror faithfully the excitement and vitality of an expanding America of the mid-nineteenth century. They are also rich in satiric commentary on that same America. *Huckleberry Finn* is more than a boy's adventure story, though it is justly famous in that regard. It has much to say about law and order versus individual rights, about the immorality of racism in America, about religious absolutism, out-moded educational systems, marriage, the lack of culture and aesthetic dimensions in frontier country, and the evils of American materialism.

Much of Twain's strength as a writer lies in the range of his concerns and the fact that he shows more than one side of his subject. True, in late works like the 1899 short story "The Man That Corrupted Hadleyburg" and the posthumously published novel *The Mysterious Stranger*, he narrows the focus to an abject despair over mankind's depravity. But the following selection, taken from the less familiar *Private Life of Adam and Eve* (1869), reveals Twain as the humane satirist, attempting to display human frailties as justly as he can. We are shown the story of Eden and the fall from both the male and female viewpoints. If Eve is the first to devour the forbidden apples, she feels she *must* understand things because Adam is not very advanced intellectually. If Adam is cautious and afraid to disobey the rules, he has a premonition of what death must be, and he recognizes the need for having laws and adhering to them. Above all, each views the other in ways

---

[1] The depth of the water in any given place was marked by a kind of sing-song chant from the measurer. One of the most frequently heard chants was adopted by Clemens for a pen name: Mark Twain.

that help us to understand the limitation of vision all of us share by virtue of the sex roles we play.

But in addition to these insights, Twain's handling of the story forces us to come to grips with a view of woman with deep roots in both Christian and popular belief. Eve herself—as countless women no doubt have done in her name—willingly renounces her self-confidence and accepts male domination as being appropriate to God's scheme of things. This ancient devaluation of feminine status bears reexamination at a time when all of us are becoming conscious of many past inequalities in the assessment of Human Worth.

Passages from the Diaries of Adam and Eve

Extracts from Adam's Diary

Translated from the original ms.

Monday

This new creature with the long hair is a good deal in the way. It is always hanging around and following me about. I don't like this; I am not used to company. I wish it would stay with the other animals. . . . Cloudy to-day, wind in the east; think we shall have rain. . . . *We?* Where did I get that word? . . . I remember now—the new creature uses it.

Monday

The new creature says its name is Eve. That is all right. I have no objections. Says it is to call it by when I want it to come. I said it was superfluous, then. The word evidently raised me in its respect; and indeed it is a large, good word, and will bear repetition. It says it is not an It, it is a She. This is probably doubtful; yet it is all one to me; what she is were nothing to me if she would but go by herself and not talk.

Thursday

She told me she was made out of a rib taken from my body. This is at least doubtful, if not more than that. I have not missed any rib. . . . She is in much trouble about the buzzard; says grass does not agree with it; is afraid she can't raise it; thinks it was intended to live on decayed flesh. The buzzard must get along the best it can with what is provided. We cannot overturn the whole scheme to accommodate the buzzard.

From *The Private Life of Adam and Eve.*

Tuesday

She has taken up with a snake now. The other animals are glad, for she was always experimenting with them and bothering them; and I am glad, because the snake talks, and this enables me to get a rest.

Friday

She say the snake advises her to try the fruit of that tree, and says the result will be a great and fine and noble education. I told her there would be another result, too—it would introduce death into the world. That was a mistake—it had been better to keep the remark to myself; it only gave her an idea—she could save the sick buzzard, and furnish fresh meat to the despondent lions and tigers. I advised her to keep away from the tree. She said she wouldn't. I foresee trouble. Will emigrate.

Eve's Diary

Translated from the original

Saturday

I am almost a whole day old, now. I arrived yesterday. That is as it seems to me. And it must be so, for if there was a day-before-yesterday I was not there when it happened, or I should remember it. It could be, of course, that it did happen, and that I was not noticing. Very well; I will be very watchful, now, and if any day-before-yester-days happen I will make a note of it. It will be best to start right and not let the record get confused, for some instinct tells me that these details are going to be important to the historian some day. For I feel like an experiment, I feel exactly like an experiment; it would be impossible for a person to feel more like an experiment than I do, and so I am coming to feel convinced that that is what I *am*—an experiment; just an experiment, and nothing more. . . .

Stars are good. I wish I could get some to put in my hair. But I suppose I never can. You would be surprised to find how far off they are, for they do not look it. When they first showed, last night, I tried to knock some down with a pole, but it didn't reach, which astonished me; then I tried clods till I was all tired out, but I never got one. It was because I am left-handed and cannot throw good. Even when I aimed at the one I wasn't after I couldn't hit the other one, though I did make some close shots, for I saw the black blot of the clod sail right into the midst of the golden clusters forty or fifty times, just barely missing them, and if I could have held out a little longer maybe I could have got one.

So I cried a little, which was natural, I suppose, for one of my age, and after I was rested I got a basket and started for a place on the extreme rim of the circle, where the stars were close to the ground and I could get them with my hands, which would be better, anyway, because I could gather them tenderly then, and not break them. But it was farther than I thought, and at last I had to give it up; I was so tired I couldn't drag my feet another step; and besides, they were sore and hurt me very much.

I couldn't get back home; it was too far, and turning cold; but I found some tigers, and nestled in among them and was most adorably comfortable, and their breath was sweet and pleasant, because they live on strawberries. I had never seen a tiger before, but I knew them in a minute by the stripes. If I could have one of those skins, it would make a lovely gown.

To-day I am getting better ideas about distances. I was so eager to get hold of every pretty thing that I giddily grabbed for it, sometimes when it was too far off, and sometimes when it was but six inches away but seemed a foot—alas, with thorns between! I learned a lesson; also I made an axiom, all out of my own head—my very first one: *The scratched Experiment shuns the thorn.* I think it is a very good one for one so young.

I followed the other Experiment around, yesterday afternoon, at a distance, to see what it might be for, if I could. But I was not able to make out. I think it is a man. I had never seen a man, but it looked like one, and I feel sure that that is what it is. I realize that I feel more curiosity about it than about any of the other reptiles. If it is a reptile, and I suppose it is; for it has frowsy hair and blue eyes, and looks like a reptile. It has no hips; it tapers like a carrot; when it stands, it spreads itself apart like a derrick; so I think it is a reptile, though it may be architecture.

I was afraid of it at first, and started to run every time it turned around, for I thought it was going to chase me; but by-and-by I found it was only trying to get away, so after that I was not timid any more, but tracked it along, several hours, about twenty yards behind, which made it nervous and unhappy. At last it was a good deal worried, and climbed a tree. I waited a good while, then gave it up and went home.

To-day the same thing over. I've got it up the tree again.

Wednesday

We are getting along very well indeed, now, and getting better and better acquainted. He does not try to avoid me any more, which is a good sign, and shows that he likes to have me with him. That pleases me, and I study to be useful to him in every way I can, so as to increase his regard. During the last day or two I have taken all the work of naming things off his hands, and this has been a great relief to him, for he has no gift in that line, and is evidently very grateful. He can't think of a rational name to save him, but I do not let him see that I am aware of his defect. Whenever a new creature comes along, I name it before he has time to expose himself by an awkward silence. In this way I have saved him many embarrassments. I have no defect like this. The minute I set eyes on an animal I know what it is. I don't have to reflect a moment; the right name comes out instantly, just as if it were an inspiration, as no doubt it is, for I am sure it wasn't in me half a minute before. I seem to know just by the shape of the creature and the way it acts what animal it is.

Thursday

My first sorrow. Yesterday he avoided me and seemed to wish I would not talk to him. I could not believe it, and thought there was some mistake, for I loved to be with him, and loved to hear him talk, and so how could it be that he could feel unkind towards me when I had not done anything? But at last it seemed true, so I went away and sat lonely in the place where I first saw him the morning that we were made and I did not know what he was and was indifferent about him; but now it was a mournful place, and every little thing spoke of him, and my heart was very sore.

Sunday

It is pleasant again, now, and I am happy; but those were heavy days; I do not think of them when I can help it.

I tried to get him some of those apples, but I cannot learn to throw straight. I failed, but I think the good intention pleased him. They are forbidden, and he says I shall come to harm; but so I come to harm through pleasing him, why shall I care for that harm?

After the Fall

When I look back, the Garden is a dream to me. It was beautiful, surpassingly beautiful, enchantingly beautiful; and now it is lost, and I shall not see it any more.

The Garden is lost, but I have found *him*, and am content. He loves me as well as he can; I love him with all the strength of my passionate nature, and this, I think, is proper to my youth and sex. If I ask myself why I love him, I find I do not know; so I suppose that this kind of love is not a product of reasoning and statistics, like one's love for other reptiles and animals. I think that this must be so. I love certain birds because of their song; but I do not love Adam on account of his singing —no, it is not that; the more he sings the more I do not get reconciled to it. Yet I ask him to sing, because I wish to learn to like everything he is interested in. I am sure I can learn, because at first I could not stand it, but now I can. It sours the milk, but it doesn't matter; I can get used to that kind of milk.

It is not on account of his brightness that I love him—no, it is not that. He is not to blame for his brightness, such as it is, for he did not make it himself; he is as God made him, and that is sufficient. There was a wise purpose in it; *that* I know. In time it will develop, though I think it will not be sudden; and, besides, there is no hurry; he is well enough just as he is.

It is not on account of his gracious and considerate ways and his delicacy that I love him. No, he has lacks in these regards, but he is well enough just so, and is improving.

It is not on account of his industry that I love him—no, it is not that. I think he has it in him, and I do not know why he conceals it from me. It is my only pain. Otherwise he is frank and open with me, now. I am sure he keeps nothing from me but this. It grieves me that he should have a secret from me, and sometimes it spoils my sleep, thinking of it, but I will put it out of my mind; it shall not trouble my happiness, which is otherwise full to overflowing.

It is not on account of his education that I love him—no, it is not that. He is self-educated, and does really know a multitude of things, but they are not so.

It is not on account of his chivalry that I love him—no, it is not that. He told on me, but I do not blame him; it is a peculiarity of sex, I think, and he did not make his sex. Of course I would not have told on him, I would have perished first; but that is a peculiarity of sex, too, and I do not take credit for it, for I did not make my sex.

Then why is it that I love him? *Merely because he is masculine,* I think.

At bottom he is good, and I love him for that, but I could love him without it. If he should beat me and abuse me, I should go on loving him. I know it. It is a matter of sex, I think.

He is strong and handsome, and I love him for that, and I admire him and am proud of him, but I could love him without those qualities. If he were plain, I should love him; if he were a wreck, I should love him; and I would work for him, and slave over him, and pray for him, and watch by his bedside until I died.

Yes, I thing I love him merely because he is *mine* and is *masculine.* There is no other reason, I suppose. And so I think it is as I first said: that this kind of love is not a product of reasoning and statistics. It just *comes*—none knows whence—and cannot explain itself. And doesn't need to.

It is what I think. But I am only a girl, and the first that has examined this matter, and it may turn out that in my ignorance and inexperience I have not got it right.

Forty Years Later

It is my prayer, it is my longing, that we may pass from this life together—a longing which shall never perish from the earth, but shall have place in the heart of every wife that loves, until the end of time; and it shall be called by my name.

But if one of us must go first, it is my prayer that it shall be I; for he is strong, I am weak, I am not so necessary to him as he is to me—life without him would not be life; how could I endure it? This prayer is also immortal, and will not cease from being offered up while my race continues. I am the first wife; and in the last wife I shall be repeated.

RESPONSES: Questions for Writing and Discussion

1. In examining both sets of entries, we find that Eve appears to have been intellectually more precocious than Adam (in fact, in her eyes he is a bit on the dumb side) and that, in finally placing herself in a subordinate's role, she brings into the world a self-sacrificing kind of love by way of compensating for also having introduced death. What do Adam's special strengths appear to be? Does he deserve the role of lord and master? Or to put the question in another way: Does Eve deserve to have bowed her head?

2. In considering the above question, did you find yourself involved with religion? Natural law? Logic? None of these things? Anything else?

3. If all you had to go on was the insight provided by Mark Twain, how would you define the words "masculine" and "feminine"? (Perhaps the class as a whole could reach an agreement and then decide whether the definitions were fair and accurate.)

4. Twain, as we indicated in the introduction to this selection, tries to show both sides of the story. But since he himself is a male, does a male orientation show up in the treatment of either character?

5. Eve, for all that she sees herself as Adam's intellectual superior, is lonely without him and finally would rather have his love than Eden *or* the wisdom she has attained by eating the apples. In your opinion, do women gain something by having the love and protection of men even if they must give up many things in exchange? Does Eve "come to her senses" in her final statements, especially the one she makes forty years after the fall? Or has she been sold a bill of goods?

6. Eve's negative view of herself at the end reminds one of the lyrics for many popular songs of the thirties and forties, all written by men, in which a female narrator admits her unworthiness and willingness to suffer at the hands of a dominating male. Some examples are

"My Man," "What's the Use of Wonderin'," and "Something Wonderful." Find a copy of the lyrics of these and similar songs and analyze the portrait they offer of the "ideal" woman and her function in life.

7. Women are today expressing themselves in fields once denied to them, including that of the popular song. Buffy Sainte-Marie, Joni Mitchell, Joan Baez, and Judy Collins are but a few of the talented singers and composers who allow men to see the world through the eyes of sensitive women. Investigate some of the lyrics of their songs— or those of other feminine composers. What is the impression each song conveys of the feminine psyche? Compare a few feminine lyrics with a few masculine lyrics (especially if you can find parallel subject matter).

IF SHAKESPEARE'D HAD A BRILLIANT SISTER
Virginia Woolf

It is easy enough to find feminine authors today who speak out loud and clear on the subject of sexism (the conviction that not only do qualitative differences separate the sexes but that one's own sex was intended by nature —or God—to predominate). Books like Betty Friedan's *The Feminine Mystique* (1963) and Germaine Greer's *The Female Eunuch* (1971) not only became instant best sellers, not only made their authors celebrated figures, but, even more important, brought out into the open what Betty Friedan labeled "The Problem That Has No Name."

Earlier in this century, however, most of the women who were outspoken on the subject, either in print or on the rostrum, were considered radicals and oddballs, definite exceptions to the norm. Though there are a number of prominent female literary figures throughout the nineteenth century and the early decades of the twentieth, one seldom finds them directly confronting "The Problem That Has No Name." Pioneers like the Brontës, George Eliot, and George Sand even hid behind male pseudonyms. Rare was the female author of literary "reputability" who dared to use the power of her pen to stir the conscience of male readers and bring out into the open the facts of sexual oppression. **Virginia Woolf (1882–1941)** was just such a pioneer.

That her views might prove unpopular scarcely deterred her at all. She had already taken considerable risks by helping to develop the genuine psychological novel, which presented situations from the complex vantage point of the inner life. In novels like *Mrs. Dalloway, To the Lighthouse,* and *The Waves,* Virginia Woolf forced readers to come to her on her own terms and make their way through an oblique and demanding style.

That the risk proved worth the effort, that she won ready acceptance by her male peers and critics did not keep Virginia Woolf from recognizing that others of her sex in the past and present had not been so fortunate. In *A Room of One's Own* (1929), the author analyzes the whole question of women's relative lack of participation in the arts and answers those readers who might invoke the old argument (also used about blacks and other minorities), "If they had what it takes, why didn't *they* create a culture?"

In this selection Miss Woolf suggests what fate might have befallen a mythical sister of Shakespeare, assuming that "Judith" possessed every bit as much genius as her brother. Those readers who are tempted to protest that what is being said applies to the remote past but is not relevant to the contemporary scene should go immediately from this selection to Marya Mannes' "Female Intelligence: Who Wants It?," which follows in quite coincidentally.

If Shakespeare'd Had a Brilliant Sister

It was disappointing not to have brought back in the evening some important statement, some authentic fact. Women are poorer than men because—this or that. Perhaps now it would be better to give up seeking for the truth, and receiving on one's head and avalanche of opinion hot as lava, discoloured as dish-water. It would be better to draw the curtains; to shut out distractions; to light the lamp; to narrow the enquiry and to ask the historian, who records not opinions but facts, to describe under what conditions women lived, not throughout the ages, but in England, say in the time of Elizabeth.

For it is a perennial puzzle why no woman wrote a word of that extraordinary literature when every other man, it seemed, was capable of song or sonnet. What were the conditions in which women lived, I asked myself; for fiction, imaginative work that is, is not dropped like a pebble upon the ground, as science may be; fiction is like a spider's web, attached ever so lightly perhaps, but still attached to life at all four

From *A Room of One's Own* by Virginia Woolf, copyright, 1929, by Harcourt Brace Jovanovich, Inc.; renewed, 1957 by Leonard Woolf. Reprinted by permission of the publishers.

corners. Often the attachment is scarcely perceptible; Shakespeare's plays, for instance, seem to hang there complete by themselves. But when the web is pulled askew, hooked up at the edge, torn in the middle, one remembers that these webs are not spun in mid-air by incorporeal creatures, but are the work of suffering human beings, and are attached to grossly material things, like health and money and the houses we live in.

I went, therefore, to the shelf where the histories stand and took down one of the latest, Professor Trevelyan's *History of England*. Once more I looked up Women, found "position of," and turned to the pages indicated. "Wife-beating," I read, "was a recognised right of man, and was practised without shame by high as well as low. . . . Similarly," the historian goes on, "the daughter who refused to marry the gentle-man of her parents' choice was liable to be locked up, beaten and flung about the room, without any shock being inflicted on public opinion. Marriage was not an affair of personal affection, but of family avarice, particularly in the 'chivalrous' upper classes. . . . Betrothal often took place while one or both of the parties was in the cradle, and marriage when they were scarcely out of the nurses' charge." That was about 1470, soon after Chaucer's time. The next reference to the position of women is some two hundred years later, in the time of the Stuarts. "It was still the exception for women of the upper and middle class to choose their own husbands, and when the husband had been assigned, he was lord and master, so far at least as law and custom could make him. Yet even so," Professor Trevelyan concludes, "neither Shakespeare's women nor those of authentic seventeenth-century memoirs, like the Verneys and the Hutchinsons, seem wanting in per-sonality and character." Certainly, if we consider it, Cleopatra must have had a way with her; Lady Macbeth, one would suppose, had a will of her own; Rosalind, one might conclude, was an attractive girl. Professor Trevelyan is speaking no more than the truth when he remarks that Shakespeare's women do not seem wanting in personality and character. Not being a historian, one might go even further and say that women have burnt like beacons in all the works of all the poets from the beginning of time—Clytemnestra, Antigone, Cleopatra, Lady Macbeth, Phèdre, Cressida, Rosalind, Desdemona, the Duchess of Malfi, among the dramatists; then among the prose writers: Millamant, Clarissa, Becky Sharp, Anna Karenine, Emma Bovary, Madame de Guermantes—the names flock to mind, nor do they recall women "lacking in personality and character." Indeed, if women had no existence save in the fiction written by men, one would imagine her a person of the utmost importance; very various; heroic and mean; splendid and sordid; infinitely beautiful and hideous in the extreme; as great as a man, some think even greater.[1] But this is woman in fiction. In fact, as Professor Trevelyan points out, she was locked up, beaten and flung about the room.

A very queer, composite being thus emerges. Imaginatively she is of the highest importance; practically she is completely insignificant. She pervades poetry from cover to cover; she is all but absent from history. She dominates the lives of kings and conquerors in fiction; in fact she was the slave of any boy whose parents forced a ring upon her finger. Some of the most inspired words, some of the most profound thoughts in literature fall from her lips; in real life she could hardly read, could scarcely spell, and was the property of her husband.

It was certainly an odd monster that one made up by reading the historians first and the poets afterwards—a worm winged like an eagle; the spirit of life and beauty in a kitchen chopping up suet. But these monsters, however amusing to the imagination, have no existence in fact. What one must do to bring her to life was to think poetically and prosaically at one and the same moment, thus keeping in touch with fact—that she is Mrs. Martin, aged thirty-six, dressed in blue, wearing a black hat and brown shoes; but not losing sight of fiction either— that she is a vessel in which all sorts of spirits and forces are coursing and flashing perpetually. The moment, however, that one tries this method with the Elizabethan woman, one branch of illumination fails; one is held up by the scarcity of facts. One knows nothing detailed, nothing perfectly true and substantial about her. History scarcely mentions her. And I turned to Professor Trevelyan again to see what history meant to him. I found by looking at his chapter headings that it meant—

"The Manor Court and the Methods of Openfield Agriculture . . . The Cistercians and Sheepfarming . . . The Crusades . . . The University . . . The House of Commons . . . The Hundred Years' War . . .

---

[1] "It remains a strange and almost inexplicable fact that in Athena's city, where women were kept in almost Oriental suppression as odalisques or drudges, the stage should yet have produced figures like Clytemnestra and Cassandra, Atossa and Antigone, Phèdre and Medea, and all the other heroines who dominate play after play of the 'misogynist' Euripides. But the paradox of this world where in real life a respectable woman could hardly show her face alone in the street, and yet on the stage woman equals or surpasses man, has never been satisfactorily explained. In modern tragedy the same predominance exists. At all events, a very cursory survey of Shakespeare's work (similarly with Webster, though not with Marlowe or Jonson) suffices to reveal how this dominance, this initiative of women, persists from Rosalind to Lady Macbeth. So too in Racine; six of his tragedies bear their heroines' names; and what male characters of his shall we set against Hermione and Andromaque, Bérénice and Roxane, Phèdre and Athalie? So again with Ibsen; what men shall we match with Solveig and Nora, Hedda and Hilda Wangel and Rebecca West?"—F. L. Lucas, Tragedy, pp. 114-15.

The Wars of the Roses . . . The Renaissance Scholars . . . The Dissolution of the Monasteries . . . Agrarian and Religious Strife . . . The Origin
of English Sea-power . . . The Armada . . ." and so on. Occasionally an
individual woman is mentioned, an Elizabeth, or a Mary; a queen or a
great lady. But by no possible means could middle-class women with
nothing but brains and character at their command have taken part in
any one of the great movements which, brought together, constitute
the historian's view of the past. Nor shall we find her in any collection
of anecdotes. Aubrey hardly mentions her. She never writes her own
life and scarcely keeps a diary; there are only a handful of her letters
in existence. She left no plays or poems by which we can judge her.
What one wants, I thought—and why does not some brilliant student
at Newnham or Girton supply it?—is a mass of information; at what
age did she marry; how many children had she as a rule; what was her
house like; had she a room to herself; did she do the cooking; would
she be likely to have a servant? All these facts lie somewhere, presumably, in parish registers and account books; the life of the average
Elizabethan woman must be scattered about somewhere, could one
collect it and make a book of it. It would be ambitious beyond my
daring, I thought, looking about the shelves for books that were not
there, to suggest to the students of those famous colleges that they
should re-write history, though I own that it often seems a little queer
as it is, unreal, lop-sided; but why should they not add a supplement
to history? calling it, of course, by some inconspicuous name so that
women might figure there without impropriety? For one often catches
a glimpse of them in the lives of the great, whisking away into the background, concealing, I sometimes think, a wink, a laugh, perhaps a tear.
And, after all, we have lives enough of Jane Austen; it scarcely seems
necessary to consider again the influence of the tragedies of Joanna
Baillie upon the poetry of Edgar Allan Poe; as for myself, I should
not mind if the homes and haunts of Mary Russell Mitford were closed
to the public for a century at least. But what I find deplorable, I continued, looking about the bookshelves again, is that nothing is known
about women before the eighteenth century. I have no model in my
mind to turn about this way and that. Here am I asking why women did
not write poetry in the Elizabethan age, and I am not sure how they were
educated; whether they were taught to write; whether they had
sitting-rooms to themselves; how many women had children before they
were twenty-one; what, in short, they did from eight in the morning
till eight at night. They had no money evidently; according to Professor Trevelyan they were married whether they liked it or not before
they were out of the nursery, at fifteen or sixteen very likely. It would
have been extremely odd, even upon this showing, had one of them
suddenly written the plays of Shakespeare, I concluded, and I thought

of that old gentleman, who is dead now, but was a bishop, I think, who declared that it was impossible for any woman, past, present, or to come, to have the genius of Shakespeare. He wrote to the papers about it. He also told a lady who applied to him for information that cats do not as a matter of fact go to heaven, though they have, he added, souls of a sort. How much thinking those old gentlemen used to save one! How the borders of ignorance shrank back at their approach! Cats do not go to heaven. Women cannot write the plays of Shakespeare.

Be that as it may, I could not help thinking, as I looked at the works of Shakespeare on the self, that the bishop was right at least in this; it would have been impossible, completely and entirely, for any woman to have written the plays of Shakespeare in the age of Shakespeare. Let me imagine, since facts are so hard to come by, what would have happened had Shakespeare had a wonderfully gifted sister, called Judith, let us say. Shakespeare himself went, very probably—his mother was an heiress—to the grammar school, where he may have learnt Latin—Ovid, Virgil and Horace—and the elements of grammar and logic. He was, it is well known, a wild boy who poached rabbits, perhaps shot a deer, and had, rather sooner than he should have done, to marry a woman in the neighborhood, who bore him a child rather quicker than was right. That escapade sent him to seek his fortune in London. He had, it seemed, a taste for the theatre; he began by holding horses at the stage door. Very soon he got work in the theatre, became a successful actor, and lived at the hub of the universe, meeting everybody, knowing everybody, practising his art on the boards, exercising his wits in the streets, and even getting access to the palace of the queen. Meanwhile his extraordinarily gifted sister, let us suppose, remained at home. She was as adventurous, as imaginative, as agog to see the world as he was. But she was not sent to school. She had no chance of learning grammar and logic, let alone of reading Horace and Virgil. She picked up a book now and then, one of her brother's perhaps, and read a few pages. But then her parents came in and told her to mend the stockings or mind the stew and not moon about with books and papers. They would have spoken sharply but kindly, for they were substantial people who knew the conditions of life for a woman and loved their daughter—indeed, more likely than not she was the apple of her father's eye. Perhaps she scribbled some pages up in an apple loft on the sly, but was careful to hide them or set fire to them. Soon, however, before she was out of her teens, she was to be betrothed to the son of a neighbouring wool-stapler. She cried out that marriage was hateful to her, and for that she was severely beaten by her father. Then he ceased to scold her. He begged her instead not to hurt him, not to shame him in this matter of her marriage. He would give her a chain of beads or a fine petticoat, he said; and there were tears in his eyes. How could she disobey him? How could she break his heart? The force of her own gift alone drove her to it. She made up a small parcel of her belongings, let herself down by a rope one summer's night and took the road to London. She was not seventeen. The birds that sang in the hedge were not more musical than she was. She had the quickest fancy, a gift like her brother's, for the tune of words. Like him, she had a taste for the theatre. She stood at the stage door; she wanted to act, she said. Men laughed in her face. The manager—a fat, loose-lipped man— guffawed. He bellowed something about poodles dancing and women acting—no woman, he said, could possibly be an actress. He hinted— you can imagine what. She could get no training in her craft. Could she even seek her dinner in a tavern or roam the streets at midnight? Yet her genius was for fiction and lusted to feed abundantly upon the lives of men and women and the study of their ways. At last—for she was very young, oddly like Shakespeare the poet in her face, with the same grey eyes and rounded brows—at last Nick Greene the actor- manager took pity on her; she found herself with child by that gentle- man and so—who shall measure the heat and violence of the poet's heart when caught and tangled in a woman's body?—killed herself one winter's night and lies buried at some cross-roads where the omnibuses now stop outside the Elephant and Castle.

That, more or less, is how the story would run, I think, if a woman in Shakespeare's day had had Shakespeare's genius. But for my part, I agree with the deceased bishop, if such he was—it is unthink- able that any woman in Shakespeare's day should have had Shake- speare's genius. For genius like Shakespeare's is not born among labour- ing, uneducated, service people. It was not born in England among the Saxons and the Britons. It is not born today among the working classes. How, then, could it have been born among women whose work began, according to Professor Trevelyan, almost before they were out of the nursery, who were forced to it by their parents and held to it by all the power of law and custom?

RESPONSES: Questions for Writing and Discussion

1. In the course of her investigation Virginia Woolf makes us aware of the number of imposing female characters which men have added to the annals of fiction and drama. From Clytemnestra to Madame de Guermantes—she stopped with Proust, but surely each of us could add to her list—there exists a succession of enduring portraits of women. Woman in literature acquires the reputation of being "heroic and mean; splendid and sordid; infinitely beautiful and

hideous in the extreme; as great as a man, some think even greater." Select one such characterization from any form of fiction or drama, including movies and television. The only requirement is that the character is given great stature by a male author. Describe your choice to the class, commenting on whether you believe this writer really wishes to be fair to women; has guilt feelings about men's crimes against women and wants to compensate; creates a strong but essentially ugly character so as to remind us of woman's moral inferiority; wants to point out how women have made men miserable; secretly admires the female sex and would like to identify with it; is actually creating a man but calling the character a woman; and so on.

2. Do you agree with the author "that nothing is known about women before the eighteenth century" except for a few fleeting shreds of information and the sort of fanciful reconstruction of an era in which she herself is indulging? Is she overstating the case? Why not jot down things you think you know about women in other periods and other countries? Perhaps four or five facts would do. Next to each one indicate, as well as you can remember, the source of your knowledge. A history teacher? A magazine? Books? (Published where and when?) Share your list with the class as a whole or with one or two others; then discuss what you have derived from the exercise.

3. Have each person consult what an historian has to say about "Woman, position of . . ." in some time and place other than Elizabethan England. The information should be arranged as a series of statements cast in this kind of form: "In seventeenth-century Salem, she . . ." Go up and down the rows or around the circle or whatever, letting each participant read aloud one of his sentences. (If possible, tape the session and replay it several weeks later.) The effects should be that of a spoken collage.

4. Close your eyes and move forward in time to our own period, carrying William and Judith Shakespeare with you. Project them into a contemporary setting. Assume that the mother, if not an heiress, is sufficiently endowed to afford the best education for both of them. What happens to Judith now? Does she end up as the equal of her brother? Or must she cope with new versions of old problems?

FEMALE INTELLIGENCE: WHO WANTS IT?

Marya Mannes

During the thirties and forties actresses like Rosalind Russell and Katharine Hepburn were fond of playing the role of an aggressive, sharp-witted career woman piledriving her way through the Madison Avenue male-oriented executive world. Though she has meteoric success in business, she is made to discover late in the film that she has gained the whole world but suffered the loss of a man's love—"the only thing that really counts." Inevitably she is tamed by the hero, usually Cary Grant or Spencer Tracy, and looks forward to a life of docile domestic bliss.

This constant film theme reflected changes that were taking place in America. No matter what contrite sentiments Russell or Hepburn spoke at the fadeout to her lord and master she herself was a highly paid performer. World War II required the services of women in countless highly professional positions once considered the exclusive property of men. Women became war correspondents, radio commentators, and politicians. When the war came to an end, it was unthinkable that the game of sex roles could ever be played in precisely the same way as it had been before the war: at least not for many women who were enjoying their newly attained status.

But along with the professional woman there arose the professional woman's *problem*, summed up in a song Rosalind Russell sang in a musical comedy of the early fifties. "Just be as well informed as he," she warned the feminine members of the audience who might aspire to liberation, "you'll never hear 'O Promise Me.'"

By 1960, the date of publication of the selection that follows, there was clearly a crisis brewing. Television commentators warned dolefully of "soaring" divorce rates. A succession of unhappy children, pawns in the sex-role game, trudged nervously to their weekly appointment with the psychiatrist. Even suicides (both sexes) were attributed to woman's desperate choice between "marriage and a career." Hollywood stars with their unending string of husbands, "children by a previous marriage," and divorces continued to serve as "cases in point." Experts on domesticity—both male and female—pleaded for sanity and a return to a more stable way of life.

Marya Mannes (b. 1904), author of our selection, sees the crisis in terms of the possibility that too many women of real potential and creative talent were still being held back by the social taboos on woman's aggressiveness in presuming to compete in a man's world. By 1960 the ratio of women to men in college had shown a steady rise, but so had the number of female dropouts. The divorce rates, too, continued to rise. Something was obviously wrong, but Miss Mannes isn't so sure the fault lies with women.

Her own career resembles a Rosalind Russell movie: feature editor of *Vogue* from 1933 to 1936 and *Glamour* from 1946 to 1947; then columnist for *McCall's* and *The New York Times*, and finally TV commentator. Currently, she is active on the intellectual scene in America through her books, her many articles, and her television appearances. Long an established professional woman, Marya Mannes is no longer fighting for "equal rights." Instead she looks for the emergence of totally liberated human beings who have transcended their bounded sex roles.

Female Intelligence: Who Wants It?

Every now and then there is a resounding call for a national resource—largely untapped and unmustered—referred to as the intelligence of women, or the female brain. Editorial writers, tired of outer space, say· that if we are to win the race of survival and keep up with the Russians we must not squander this precious resource but rather press it into service.

Commenting on the number of women doctors, engineers, physicists and laboratory technicians in the Soviet Union compared to our paltry own, citing the desperate shortages in fields where productive intellect is essential, they cry: "To the drawing-board, to the laboratories, to the computers!" And presidents of women's colleges beseech their students: "Use this brain you've got and we're training: society need it!"

Gratifying though it may be to have the female intelligence not only publicly acknowledged but officially sought, these calls are met by a massive wave of indifference emanating from women even more than from men. We do not really believe either the acknowledgment or the demand for the kind of intelligence they speak of and claim they want, nor do we see any signs of a public attitude which would make its application either welcome or practical on a national scale.

The college presidents, the editorialists, the recruiters of resources are talking not of the intelligence which every woman needs to be a successful wife and mother or even a competent worker in office or factory or civic affairs. They are talking of the kind of free and independent intelligence which can analyze, innovate and create: the mind of the scientist and the artist, at liberty to roam in the world of abstractions and intangibles until, by will and effort, a concrete and tanglible pattern is made clear.

Are women capable of this kind of intelligence? If they are not to the degree of genius—and the long history of man has produced no female Bachs or Shakespeares or Leonardos or Galileos—and although Madame Curie is in lonely company, women have in every time given to the mainstream of the arts, letters and sciences. And when even a Jesuit priest-sociologist, Father Lucius F. Cervantes—whose recent book "And God Made Man and Woman" is a long and satisfied re-iteration of the sacred differences between the two sexes—writes, "As far as has been ascertained there is no inherent intellectual capacity differential between men and women," then surely women are not by nature denied the ability to think creatively and abstractly.

It is rather that this ability is unpopular with women because it is unpopular with men. Our prior need, in short, is to be loved. And if the possession of this kind of intelligence is a deterrent to love, then it is voluntarily restricted or denied by women themselves.

I have seen enough of this deterrence and this denial, since my youth, to believe it the common experience. And although it has not always been mine (I am fortunate in a happy marriage), I recognize only too well the signal of alarm in the eyes of men when a woman of intellect challenges their own.

It flashed even before I recognized it: boys at dances would for-sake me soon for others, not—in Marty's language—because I was a "dog," but because I talked to them of sonnets or senses instead of about themselves. Used to a family where ideas were as much a part of the dinner table as food, I knew of no special kind of talk geared to men rather than to women. Worse, I thought that to be interesting one had to say interesting things. This was possibly the greatest miscalcula-tion since the Charge of the Light Brigade.

For most men, I duly discovered, prefer the woman whose interest lies not in her thoughts nor her speech nor her talents, but in her interest in them. Mind, they believe, interferes with this attention, and to some extent they are right. Right or wrong, the average American male is uneasy in the presence of markedly intelligent women; and the woman who wishes to change this unease into love must spend a good part of her life reining in her wits in the reluctant admission that they do her more harm than good.

Now there is a great paradox in all this. On the one hand, more girls go to college than ever before, and more colleges are equipped to develop their minds toward whatever intellectual goals they might aspire to. On the other hand, as President Thomas C. Mendenhall of Smith College recently—and sharply—deplored, there is a 60 per cent dropout of women students before graduation and most of this is due to their early marriage and almost immediate proliferation of the species.

In an open forum recently, I asked Millicent C. McIntosh, president of Barnard, and Dr. George N. Shuster of Hunter what they considered the purpose of higher education for women if they left the campus in droves for a career of total domesticity. Their answer, roughly, was this: "Our main aim is to turn out women who can apply a trained intelligence to the problems of daily living, and whose intellectual resources can enrich their lives and those of their children."

They agreed that only a small proportion of girls manifested a genuine drive toward intellectual excellence, or a sustained dedication necessary to the mastery of any art or science, and they deplored this. But the shared opinion seemed to be that a girl who went to college would not only be a more intelligent wife and mother than the girl who did not, but that in later life and increased freedom she could draw on greater reserves of mind and spirit.

And yet an English teacher at one of the Eastern universities said: "There is a terrible waste here. I've taught girls with as much, if not more, talent than many of the boys I've had in my classes: first class writers and thinkers. And what do they do when they leave here? Work? Not on your life. They marry and have four children, and that's that."

The argument, widely used, that a woman so trained can always return to her field when her children are grown and her time is her own, is specious, to say the least. In the sciences, if not in the arts, advances in theory and techniques are so rapid that a fifteen-year gap becomes unbreachable. Quite apart from that, the muscle of intellect degenerates with lack of use. The servantless young mother with small children has not the time, the place or the isolation necessary for any orderly process of thought or any sustained practice of the imagination.

Yet society—including most of the young women involved in this early and long domesticity—does not consider this condition even remotely tragic. On the contrary, there appears to be wide-spread approval of the return of women from the spurious and aggressive "independence" of their mothers to their prime function as the creators and guardians of the family.

Young girls themselves in countless numbers have chosen the security and closeness of a full household rather than the lonely road of individual fulfillment as creative identities. And although many young women work out of the home before and even after marriage, it is less for love of work than for love of a home in which a standard of living is more important than a standard of thinking.

Only a few seem to work because of an urgent need to be for once —if only part of every day—out of context and into their own skin, applying their intelligence singly toward matters not concerned with their personal lives.

Even this need, usually condoned for economic reasons ("She has to work to make ends meet") is criticized by those professionally concerned with allocating roles to the sexes, as an evasion of woman's prime responsibility and an indication either of maladjustment or of a false sense of values. And, although the country is full of educators charged with the development of the female intelligence, every social pressure is exerted on women from their childhood on toward one goal: marriage—the earlier the better—and babies, the more the better. And the girl who feels that she has something to give beyond her natural functions as a wife and mother is lonely, indeed—pitied even when she succeeds.

If television drama serials and mass magazine fiction are any indication of the national temper, there is only one "right" fulfillment for all women. The "career woman" may be admired for her success, but her absorption in her work—whether it be medicine, law, letters or art—is a tacit admission of her lack of fulfillment as a woman. And even if she marries and bears children, the assumption prevails that both her husband and her offspring will suffer from her preoccupation with the world outside.

Many housewives may secretly long for their independence, but they are secure in the knowledge that their own absorption in the home and the community is a guarantee against a continual conflict of loyalties and, indeed, against the natural hostility of men; a resentment, however covert, against the competition of the kind of female intelligence which, precisely because of its independence, is still called "masculine."

If it is true that this kind of intelligence is undesirable to the majority of men, accustomed as they are to the "liberated" woman of today, what are the reasons?

I suspect that in the stormy sea of "equality," men are uncertain of the extent and nature of their dominance—if, indeed, they believe in it—and that they need a constant reassurance of their superiority in one field at least, that of the creative intellect.

They need not look far to see that it is they who formulate national policies, send rockets into space and govern the world of business, art and science. The challenge from women in these fields is still negligible, but it exists; a source of discomfort rather than satisfaction. And although many men are generous in their admiration of a few women who have achieved distinction in the laboratory or in letters or in scholarship, most men have no desire to be married to them. They take too much trouble.

And here we come, I think, to the root of the matter: a masculine laziness in the ways of love which inclines them to avoid rather than surmount this particular kind of challenge. It is far easier to choose the relaxed and compliant woman than one who makes demands on the intelligence. They may be intrigued by the brilliant woman, but they rarely want her for themselves.

For the qualities that form a creative intellect are hard to live with. The woman cursed with them can retain the love of men and the approval of society only if she is willing to modify and mute them as much as she can without reducing them to impotence. As one so cursed, however modestly, I herewith submit some hard-won suggestions:

I would counsel the woman of intellect to watch her wit. Though it need not be tinged with malice, it has of necessity an astringency which many people find disconcerting. In a bland society, the un-sheathed dart can draw blood, if only from vanity. And after the tide of laughter at a woman's wit has ebbed, the wrack left in the public mind is a sort of malaise: "She has a sharp tongue" or "I wouldn't want to tangle with her."

Candor is a second danger. The woman who is honest with men is so at her own risk if this honesty requires either criticism or skepticism of their position. And if she has convictions opposed to those of the man she speaks with she will be wise to withhold them or speak them so softly that they sound like concurrence.

She must, above all, have no conviction that what she has to say is of importance, but train herself instead to listen quietly to men no more knowledgeable in a given subject than herself and, what is more, to defer to their judgment. This is not always easy, but a woman cannot afford the luxury of declarations, however pertinent, if she seeks— and what woman does not?—to attract.

A man who is intense or excited about his work can be highly attractive, but woe to the woman who is either. Most people cannot distinguish between the tiresome garrulity of a woman preoccupied with her affairs and the purely abstract passion of a woman concerned with the process of thought. A state of tension is inseparable from active intelligence, but it is socially unpermissible in women.

If such women are artists—and I use this to cover all forms of creative expression—and particularly if they have achieved any stature as such, they may have the attraction of rarity. There are even men who are mature enough and secure enough to cherish in them the capacity to create abstractly as well as biologically.

But they are rarer still, for the care and cultivation of an artist is a job that wives are trained for and few husbands want. The woman artist who has a husband and children must then, to quote Phyllis McGinley, have "three hands"—a mutation still infrequent but which the irradiation of women's minds may yet produce.

Is this irradiation really desirable? Are the full resources of the feminine intelligence really needed? And if they are to be mobilized for the national good, what is to be done about a climate of opinion satisfied with the overwhelming emphasis, on the part of the younger generation, on domesticity and large families? Do we need more babies or do we need more doctors and scientists and thinkers and innovators? Is it enough that we have a great pool of college graduates applying their intelligence to the problems of their homes and towns, or do we really need more women able to come to grips with the major issues of our time?

If we do, changes will have to be made, many of which may well be unattainable at this time. But if the nation's leaders really want and need this kind of woman, the opinion molders of the mass media will have to start right now giving her an honorable place in society, and men will have to start giving her an honorable place in their hearts as well as in their professions.

For one thing, parents with daughters who show a genuine intellectual talent and aspiration in any field should not feel compelled to enter her in the infantile mating-marathon that pushes a girl toward marriage from the age of 12 on. It should be possible for such a girl to prefer an exciting book to a dull date without the censure of her family or her peers, and to continue her training through her twenties without courting celibacy.

Much has been said about the new sense of responsibility shown by the young in their early acceptance of marriage and parenthood. But time may show that the cocoon of a large-familied home is—like that of a large corporation—the best protection from the loneliness of thought and a voluntary abdication of the burdens of personal freedom.

If a woman wishes to resume her chosen work after marriage and the bearing of children, there should be no stigma attached if she can afford to hire outside help for either home tasks or the care of the young. And we might begin to consider a pattern of community-supported nurseries which would permit the woman who can afford help to pursue her profession at least partially free from the continuous demands of child care.

A few months ago a delegation of Russian professional women visited this country, and one of them remarked in amazement at the lack of any such service. Our profusion of labor-saving gadgets did not, it seems, blind her eyes to the domestic entrapment of the young American woman.

As for college education, there should, I believe, be a division made between students merely marking time before marriage and girls seriously bent on a career or profession, confining the domestic-minded to a two-year course of liberal arts and reserving the four-year, degree-granting course for the latter. After these have graduated, their entrance into the laboratories and offices of the country should be made on the same basis as that for equally qualified men—not, that is, as an interim occupation but as a chosen, sustained career.

And here, of course, is where the woman herself must be prepared to pay a fairly high price. If work is important to her she cannot allow herself the luxury of a large family or the kind of man who insists on one. Nor can she afford the close, and often cozy, community huddle in which women share their domestic preoccupations daily with one another. She must be prepared to fight for the freedom she wants at the risk of loneliness and the denial of a number of things dear to any woman.

As for men, they will have to stop thinking in terms of competition and think in terms af alliance instead: the alliance of companion intellects toward similar goals. If they can bring themselves to consider women primarily as human beings, they will be able to treat them intellectually as men and emotionally as women. If they do that, they will find the brilliant woman surprisingly docile and far from unfeminine.

If, however, men continue to subscribe to the prevailing belief that the American heroine must never be too intelligent for her own good and their own comfort, the cry for female brains will go largely unheeded—unless a national emergency makes it clear that we have for years been wasting one of the resources on which our strength depends and which other civilizations are using to their advantage.

RESPONSES: Questions for Writing and Discussion

1. If, as the author states, women abdicate willingly from their own potential because "our prior need is to be loved," can it be argued that women are happy being the objects of men's love and care and therefore do not *need* a redefinition of their sex roles? Or, rather, that the goal of such happiness is imposed upon women long before they are able to make a free choice?

2. The author notes parenthetically that she is happily married. But it seems evident that so contemporary a person as Marya Mannes would hardly be involved in a typical American marriage. Draw a profile of the kind of relationship you think such a writer and her husband would have. Describe the ground rules of the marriage and the way a given crisis might be handled. Examples: the wife wants to take her vacation alone; the husband wants his own apartment for times of solitude; a teenaged daughter declares she is going to live with her

friend and gives no further details; a teenaged son brings his girl friend for dinner, and it begins to develop into an indefinite visit.

3. The experience of being forsaken at school dances because of a blatant display of erudition has probably happened to scores of women, perhaps in this very class. Who would like to describe some instances of rejection because of intelligence? And what male would like to take the position that *lack* of intelligence is not the prime factor a man considers when choosing a female partner for a date? What male would like to say it *is* and defend such a basis for selection? What female would like to agree that women ought to keep their knowledge strictly to themselves?

4. If "love of a home in which a standard of living is more important than a standard of thinking" is characteristic of girls who drop out of college for marriage, do you agree with the presidents of Barnard and Hunter, who urge women to complete their education in order to become better wives and mothers?

5. Marya Mannes cites the stereotype of the professional woman as she appears in the mass media: "her absorption in her work . . . is a tacit admission of her lack of fulfillment as a woman." Have you seen or read any recent popular stories involving a career woman? Share with the class your perceptions of the treatment of the character. Was she happy? If not, what were the underlying assumptions behind her unhappiness? How did your own sex role affect the manner in which you reacted to the character?

6. The author concludes her essay with a prescription for an intelligent woman's survival in today's world. Among other counsel, she states quite positively that "the luxury of a large family" is something the intelligent woman cannot afford if she wishes to work. In your opinion, would such a woman, one who "must be prepared to pay a fairly high price," be denying herself a woman's *natural* maternal fulfillment? Would she be doing this just to prove a point? Would she regret the decision later in life, especially if she decided to have no children at all? (Germane to this topic is the whole question of whether "being a true woman" also means being a mother; whether, in fact, society or nature is mainly responsible for the guilt experienced by many women who have not borne children.)

THE EIGHTY-YARD RUN
Irwin Shaw

From the preceding selections, one is likely to come away with the notion that sex roles as created and imposed by society are largely unfair to women but acceptable to men. That tradition has cast men in the role of superiors is undeniable, but it is not necessary to assume that every man of the past and present has been entirely happy with the way in which "superiority" is understood. Restrictions on one side can be matched by equally rigid boundaries on the other. To define one sex is indirectly to define the other as well.

The limitations of the male role have, however, come to the surface only recently. Perhaps writers of the past—such as Mill and Twain—who offer much valuable insight into the inequities suffered by women seldom turned the searching light of analysis upon *themselves as men*. The assumption is usually that the liberal male author is happily free from constraints and is therefore free to devote himself to the cause of helping others become liberated. The gradual emergence of the "new" woman—the enlightened woman, the woman who can compete with men on the open market—has perhaps been influential in bringing about a masculine reevaluation of the masculine circumstances.

Irwin Shaw (b. 1913) is one writer who has been fascinated by the psychology and the problems of men in contemporary America. "The Eighty-Yard Run" offers a pitiable—possibly "tragic" would be a better word—portrait of a man trapped and all but destroyed by the myth of what being a man is supposed to mean. It exposes to full view the specters that Shaw sees haunting the male in America: specters of aggressive and unconditional conquests on the playing field, around the business table, and in the bedroom. At the same time it probably has a good deal to say to girl friends and wives who continually strive to understand and play the proper parts for the benefit of similarly obsessed males.

Irwin Shaw was born in Brooklyn and attended Brooklyn College. His work vibrates with the rhythms of New York, and it has kept pace with the changing America from the late thirties, when he began his writing career, to the present moment, when he ranks as one of America's two or three foremost novelists. He will doubtless emerge as one of the important chroniclers of life in America throughout most of the twentieth century, and his close-ups (he has done much writing for the screen) of men and women struggling to cope with themselves, each other, and society will constitute an appreciable body of insights into some of the modern innings of the male-female game.

The Eighty-Yard Run

The pass was high and wide and he jumped for it, feeling it slap flatly against his hands, as he shook his hips to throw off the halfback who was diving at him. The center floated by, his hands desperately brushing Darling's knee as Darling picked his feet up high and delicately ran over a blocker and an opposing linesman in a jumble on the ground near the scrimmage line. He had ten yards in the clear and picked up speed, breathing easily, feeling his thigh pads rising and falling against his legs, listening to the sound of cleats behind him, pulling away from them, watching the other backs heading him off toward the sideline, the whole picture, the men closing in on him, the blockers fighting for position, the ground he had to cross, all suddenly clear in his head, for the first time in his life not a meaningless confusion of men, sounds, speed. He smiled a little to himself as he ran, holding the ball lightly in front of him with his two hands, his knees pumping high, his hips twisting in the almost girlish run of a back in a broken field. The first halfback came at him and he fed him his leg, then swung at the last moment, took the shock of the man's shoulder without breaking stride, ran right through him, his cleats biting securely into the turf. There was only the safety man now, coming warily at him, his arms crooked, hands spread. Darling tucked the ball in, spurted at him, driving hard, hurling himself along, his legs pounding, knees high, all two hundred pounds bunched into controlled attack. He was sure he was going to get past the safety man. Without thought, his arms and legs working beautifully together, he headed right for the safety man, stiff-armed him, feeling blood spurt instantaneously from the man's nose onto his hand, seeing his face go awry, head turned, mouth pulled to one side. He pivoted away, keeping the arm locked, dropping the safety man as he ran easily toward the goal line, with the drumming of cleats diminishing behind him.

How long ago? It was autumn then, and the ground was getting hard because the nights were cold and leaves from the maples around the stadium blew across the practice fields in gusts of wind, and the girls were beginning to put polo coats over their sweaters when they came to watch practice in the afternoons. . . . Fifteen years. Darling walked slowly over the same ground in the spring twilight, in his neat shoes, a man of thirty-five dressed in a double-breasted suit, ten pounds heavier in the fifteen years, but not fat, with the years between 1925 and 1940 showing in his face.

The coach was smiling quietly to himself and the assistant coaches were looking at each other with pleasure the way they always did when one of the second stringers suddenly did something fine, bringing credit to them, making their $2,000 a year a tiny bit more secure.

Darling trotted back, smiling, breathing deeply but easily, feeling wonderful, not tired, though this was the tail end of practice and he'd run eighty yards. The sweat poured off his face and soaked his jersey and he liked the feeling, the warm moistness lubricating his skin like oil. Off in a corner of the field some players were punting and the smack of leather against the ball came pleasantly through the afternoon air. The freshmen were running signals on the next field and the quarterback's sharp voice, the pound of the eleven pairs of cleats, the "Dig, now *dig!*" of the coaches, the laughter of the players all somehow made him feel happy as he trotted back to midfield, listening to the applause and shouts of the students along the sidelines, knowing that after that run the coach would have to start him Saturday against Illinois.

Fifteen years, Darling thought, remembering the shower after the workout, the hot water steaming off his skin and the deep soapsuds and all the young voices singing with the water streaming down and towels going and managers running in and out and the sharp sweet smell of oil of wintergreen and everybody clapping him on the back as he dressed and Packard, the captain, who took being captain very seriously, coming over to him and shaking his hand and saying, "Darling, you're going to go places in the next two years."

The assistant manager fussed over him, wiping a cut on his leg with alcohol and iodine, the little sting making him realize suddenly how fresh and whole and solid his body felt. The manager slapped a piece of adhesive tape over the cut, and Darling noticed the sharp clean white of the tape against the ruddiness of the skin, fresh from the shower.

He dressed slowly, the softness of his shirt and the soft warmth of his wool socks and his flannel trousers a reward against his skin after the harsh pressure of the shoulder harness and thigh and hip pads. He drank three glasses of cold water, the liquid reaching down coldly inside of him, soothing the harsh dry places in his throat and belly left by the sweat and running and shouting of practice.

Fifteen years.

The sun had gone down and the sky was green behind the stadium and he laughed quietly to himself as he looked at the stadium, rearing above the trees, and knew that on Saturday when the 70,000 voices roared as the team came running out onto the field, part of that enormous salute would be for him. He walked slowly, listening to the gravel crunch satisfactorily under his shoes in the still twilight, feeling his clothes swing lightly against his skin, breathing the thin evening air, feeling the wind move softly in his damp hair, wonderfully cool behind his ears and at the nape of his neck.

Louise was waiting for him at the road, in her car. The top was down and he noticed all over again, as he always did when he saw her, how pretty she was, the rough blonde hair and the large, inquiring eyes and the bright mouth, smiling now.

She threw the door open. "Were you good today?" she asked.

"Pretty good," he said. He climbed in, sank luxuriously into the soft leather, stretched his legs far out. He smiled, thinking of the eighty yards. "Pretty damn good."

She looked at him seriously for a moment, then scrambled around, like a little girl, kneeling on the seat next to him, grabbed him, her hands along his ears, and kissed him as he sprawled, head back, on the seat cushion. She let go of him, but kept her head close to his, over his. Darling reached up slowly and rubbed the back of his hand against her cheek, lit softly by a street lamp a hundred feet away. They looked at each other, smiling.

Louise drove down to the lake and they sat there silently, watching the moon rise behind the hills on the other side. Finally he reached over, pulled her gently to him, kissed her. Her lips grew soft, her body sank into his, tears formed slowly in her eyes. He knew, for the first time, that he could do whatever he wanted with her.

"Tonight," he said. "I'll call for you at seven-thirty. Can you get out?"

She looked at him. She was smiling, but the tears were still full in her eyes. "All right," she said. "I'll get out. How about you? Won't the coach raise hell?"

Darling grinned. "I got the coach in the palm of my hand," he said. "Can you wait till seven-thirty?"

She grinned back at him. "No," she said.

They kissed and she started the car and they went back to town for dinner. He sang on the way home.

Christian Darling, thirty-five years old, sat on the frail spring grass, greener now than it ever would be again on the practice field, looked thoughtfully up at the stadium, a deserted ruin in the twilight. He had started on the first team that Saturday and every Saturday after that for the next two years, but it had never been as satisfactory as it should have been. He never had broken away, the longest run he'd ever made was thirty-five yards, and that in a game that was already won, and then that kid had come up from the third team, Diederich, a blank-faced German kid from Wisconsin, who ran like a bull, ripping lines to pieces Saturday after Saturday, plowing through, never getting hurt, never changing his expression, scoring more points, gaining more ground than all the rest of the team put together, making everybody's

All-American, carrying the ball three times out of four, keeping every-body else out of the headlines. Darling was a good blocker and he spent his Saturday afternoons working on the big Swedes and Polacks who played tackle and end for Michigan, Illinois, Purdue, hurling into huge pile-ups, bobbing his head wildly to elude the great raw hands swinging like meat-cleavers at him as he went charging in to open up holes for Diederich coming through like a locomotive behind him. Still, it wasn't so bad. Everybody liked him and he did his job and he was pointed out on the campus and boys always felt important when they introduced their girls to him at their proms, and Louise loved him and watched him faithfully in the games, even in the mud, when your own mother wouldn't know you, and drove him around in her car keeping the top down because she was proud of him and wanted to show every-body that she was Christian Darling's girl. She bought him crazy presents because her father was rich, watches, pipes, humidors, an ice-box for beer for his room, curtains, wallets, a fifty-dollar dictionary.

"You'll spend every cent your old man owns," Darling protested once when she showed up at his rooms with seven different packages in her arms and tossed them onto the couch.

"Kiss me," Louise said, "and shut up."

"Do you want to break your poor old man?"

"I don't mind. I want to buy you presents."

"Why?"

"It makes me feel good. Kiss me. I don't know why. Did you know that you're an important figure?"

"Yes," Darling said gravely.

"When I was waiting for you at the library yesterday two girls saw you coming and one of them said to the other, 'That's Christian Darling. He's an important figure.'"

"You're a liar."

"I'm in love with an important figure."

"Still, why the hell did you have to give me a forty-pound dictionary?"

"I wanted to make sure," Louise said, "that you had a token of my esteem. I want to smother you in tokens of my esteem."

Fifteen years ago.

They'd married when they got out of college. There'd been other women for him, but all casual and secret, more for curiosity's sake, and vanity, women who'd thrown themselves at him and flattered him, a pretty mother at a summer camp for boys, an old girl from his home town who'd suddenly blossomed into a coquette, a friend of Louise's who had dogged him grimly for six months and had taken advantage of the two weeks that Louise went home when her mother died. Per-haps Louise had known, but she'd kept quiet, loving him completely, filling his rooms with presents, religiously watching him battling with the big Swedes and Polacks on the line of scrimmage on Saturday afternoons, making plans for marrying him and living with him in New York and going with him there to the night clubs, the theaters, the good restaurants, being proud of him in advance, tall, white-teethed, smiling, large, yet moving lightly, with an athlete's grace, dressed in evening clothes, approvingly eyed by magnificently dressed and famous women in theater lobbies, with Louise adoringly at his side.

Her father, who manufactured inks, set up a New York office for Darling to manage and presented him with three hundred accounts, and they lived on Beekman Place with a view of the river with fifteen thousand dollars a year between them, because everybody was buying everything in those days, including ink. They saw all the shows and went to all the speakeasies and spent their fifteen thousand dollars a year and in the afternoons Louise went to the art galleries and the matinees of the more serious plays that Darling didn't like to sit through and Darling slept with a girl who danced in the chorus of *Rosalie* and with the wife of a man who owned three copper mines. Darling played squash three times a week and remained as solid as a stone barn and Louise never took her eyes off him when they were in the same room together, watching him with a secret, miser's smile, with a trick of coming over to him in the middle of a crowded room and saying gravely, in a low voice, "You're the handsomest man I've ever seen in my whole life. Want a drink?"

Nineteen twenty-nine came to Darling and to his wife and father-in-law, the maker of inks, just as it came to everyone else. The father-in-law waited until 1933 and then blew his brains out and when Darling went to Chicago to see what the books of the firm looked like he found out all that was left were debts and three or four gallons of unbought ink.

"Please, Christian," Louise said, sitting in their neat Beekman Place apartment, with a view of the river and prints of paintings by Dufy and Braque and Picasso on the wall, "please, why do you want to start drinking at two o'clock in the afternoon?"

"I have nothing else to do," Darling said, putting down his glass, emptied of its fourth drink. "Please pass the whisky."

Louise filled his glass. "Come take a walk with me," she said. "We'll walk along the river."

"I don't want to walk along the river," Darling said, squinting intensely at the prints of paintings by Dufy, Braque and Picasso.

"We'll walk along Fifth Avenue."

"I don't want to walk along Fifth Avenue."

"Maybe," Louise said gently, "you'd like to come with me to some art galleries. There's an exhibition by a man named Klee. . . ."

"I don't want to go to any art galleries. I want to sit here and drink Scotch whisky," Darling said. "Who the hell hung those goddam pictures up on the wall?"

"I did," Louise said.

"I hate them."

"I'll take them down," Louise said.

"Leave them there. It gives me something to do in the afternoon. I can hate them." Darling took a long swallow. "Is that the way people paint these days?"

"Yes, Christian. Please don't drink any more."

"Do you like painting like that?"

"Yes, dear."

"Really?"

"Really."

Darling looked carefully at the prints once more. "Little Louise Tucker. The middle-western beauty. I like pictures with horses in them. Why should you like pictures like that?"

"I just happen to have gone to a lot of galleries in the last few years . . ."

"Is that what you do in the afternoon?"

"That's what I do in the afternoon," Louise said.

"I drink in the afternoon."

Louise kissed him lightly on the top of his head as he sat there squinting at the pictures on the wall, the glass of whisky held firmly in his hand. She put on her coat and went out without saying another word. When she came back in the early evening, she had a job on a woman's fashion magazine.

They moved downtown and Louise went out to work every morning and Darling sat home and drank and Louise paid the bills as they came up. She made believe she was going to quit work as soon as Darling found a job, even though she was taking over more responsibility day by day at the magazine, interviewing authors, picking painters for the illustrations and covers, getting actresses to pose for pictures, going out for drinks with the right people, making a thousand new friends whom she loyally introduced to Darling.

"I don't like your hat," Darling said, once, when she came in in the evening and kissed him, her breath rich with martinis.

"What's the matter with my hat, Baby?" she asked, running her fingers through his hair. "Everybody says it's very smart."

"It's too damned smart," he said. "It's not for you. It's for a rich, sophisticated woman of thirty-five with admirers."

Louise laughed. "I'm practicing to be a rich, sophisticated woman of thirty-five with admirers," she said. He stared soberly at her. "Now, don't look so grim, Baby. It's still the same simple little wife under the hat." She took the hat off, threw it into a corner, sat on his lap. "See? Homebody Number One."

"Your breath could run a train," Darling said, not wanting to be mean, but talking out of boredom, and sudden shock at seeing his wife curiously a stranger in a new hat, with a new expression in her eyes under the little brim, secret, confident, knowing.

Louise tucked her head under his chin so he couldn't smell her breath. "I had to take an author out for cocktails," she said. "He's a boy from the Ozark Mountains and he drinks like a fish. He's a Communist."

"What the hell is a Communist from the Ozarks doing writing for a woman's fashion magazine?"

Louise chuckled. "The magazine business is getting all mixed up these days. The publishers want to have a foot in every camp. And anyway, you can't find an author under seventy these days who isn't a Communist."

"I don't think I like you to associate with all those people, Louise," Darling said. "Drinking with them."

"He's a very nice, gentle boy," Louise said. "He reads Ernest Dowson."

"Who's Ernest Dowson?"

Louise patted his arm, stood up, fixed her hair. "He's an English poet."

Darling felt that somehow he had disappointed her. "Am I supposed to know who Ernest Dowson is?"

"No, dear. I'd better go in and take a bath."

After she had gone, Darling went over to the corner where the hat was lying and picked it up. It was nothing, a scrap of straw, a red flower, a veil, meaningless on his big hand, but on his wife's head a signal of something . . . big city, smart and knowing women drinking and dining with men other than their husbands, conversation about things a normal man wouldn't know much about, Frenchmen who painted as though they used their elbows instead of brushes, composers who wrote whole symphonies without a single melody in them, writers who knew all about politics and women who knew all about writers, the movement of the proletariat, Marx, somehow mixed up with five-dollar dinners and the best-looking women in America and fairies who made them laugh and half-sentences immediately understood and secretly hilarious and wives who called their husbands "Baby." He put the hat down, a scrap of straw and a red flower, and a little veil. He drank some whisky straight and went into the bathroom where his wife was lying deep in her bath, singing to herself and smiling from time to time like a little girl, paddling the water gently with her hands, sending up a slight spicy fragrance from the bath salts she used.

He stood over her, looking down at her. She smiled up at him, her eyes half closed, her body pink and shimmering in the warm, scented water. All over again, with all the old suddenness, he was hit deep inside him with the knowledge of how beautiful she was, how much he needed her.

"I came in here," he said, "to tell you I wish you wouldn't call me 'Baby.'"

She looked up at him from the bath, her eyes quickly full of sorrow, half-understanding what he meant. He knelt and put his arms around her, his sleeves plunged heedlessly in the water, his shirt and jacket soaking wet as he clutched her wordlessly, holding her crazily tight, crushing her breath from her, kissing her desperately, searchingly, regretfully.

He got jobs after that, selling real estate and automobiles, but somehow, although he had a desk with his name on a wooden wedge on it, and he went to the office religiously at nine each morning, he never managed to sell anything and he never made any money.

Louise was made assistant editor, and the house was always full of strange men and women who talked fast and got angry on abstract subjects like mural painting, novelists, labor unions. Negro short-story writers drank Louise's liquor, and a lot of Jews, and big solemn men with scarred faces and knotted hands who talked slowly but clearly about picket lines and battles with guns and leadpipe at mine-shaft-heads and in front of factory gates. And Louise moved among them all, confidently, knowing what they were talking about, with opinions that they listened to and argued about just as though she were a man. She knew everybody, condescended to no one, devoured books that Darling had never heard of, walked along the streets of the city, excited, at home, soaking in all the million tides of New York without fear, with constant wonder.

Her friends liked Darling and sometimes he found a man who wanted to get off in the corner and talk about the new boy who played fullback for Princeton, and the decline of the double wing-back, or even the state of the stock market, but for the most part he sat on the edge of things, solid and quiet in the high storm of words. "The dialectics of the situation . . . The theater has been given over to expert jugglers . . . Picasso? What man has a right to paint old bones and collect ten thousand dollars for them? . . . I stand firmly behind Trotsky . . . Poe was the last American critic. When he died they put lilies on the grave of American criticism. I don't say this because they panned my last book, but . . ."

Once in a while he caught Louise looking soberly and consider-ingly at him through the cigarette smoke and the noise and he avoided her eyes and found an excuse to get up and go into the kitchen for more ice or to open another bottle.

"Come on," Cathal Flaherty was saying, standing at the door with a girl, "you've got to come down and see this. It's down on Fourteenth Street, in the old Civic Repertory, and you can only see it on Sunday nights and I guarantee you'll come out of the theater singing." Flaherty was a big young Irishman with a broken nose who was the lawyer for a longshoreman's union, and he had been hanging around the house for six months on and off, roaring and shutting everybody else up when he got in an argument. "It's a new play, *Waiting for Lefty;* it's about taxi-drivers."

"Odets," the girl with Flaherty said. "It's by a guy named Odets."

"I never heard of him," Darling said.

"He's a new one," the girl said.

"It's like watching a bombardment," Flaherty said. "I saw it last Sunday night. You've got to see it."

"Come on, Baby," Louise said to Darling, excitement in her eyes already. "We've been sitting in the Sunday *Times* all day, this'll be a great change."

"I see enough taxi-drivers every day," Darling said, not because he meant that, but because he didn't like to be around Flaherty, who said things that made Louise laugh a lot and whose judgment she accepted on almost every subject. "Let's go to the movies."

"You've never seen anything like this before," Flaherty said. "He wrote this play with a baseball bat."

"Come on," Louise coaxed, "I bet it's wonderful."

"He has long hair," the girl with Flaherty said. "Odets. I met him at a party. He's an actor. He didn't say a goddam thing all night."

"I don't feel like going down to Fourteenth Street," Darling said, wishing Flaherty and his girl would get out. "It's gloomy."

"Oh, hell!" Louise said loudly. She looked cooly at Darling, as though she'd just been introduced to him and was making up her mind about him, and not very favorably. He saw her looking at him, knowing there was something new and dangerous in her face and he wanted to say something, but Flaherty was there and his damned girl, and anyway, he didn't know what to say.

"I'm going," Louise said, getting her coat. "I don't think Fourteenth Street is gloomy."

"I'm telling you," Flaherty was saying, helping her on with her coat, "it's the Battle of Gettysburg, in Brooklynese."

"Nobody could get a word out of him," Flaherty's girl was saying as they went through the door. "He just sat there all night."

The door closed. Louise hadn't said good night to him. Darling walked around the room four times, then sprawled out on the sofa, on top of the Sunday *Times.* He lay there for five minutes looking at the ceiling, thinking of Flaherty walking down the street talking in that booming voice, between the girls, holding their arms.

Louise had looked wonderful. She'd washed her hair in the afternoon and it had been very soft and light and clung close to her head as she stood there angrily putting her coat on. Louise was getting prettier every year, partly because she knew by now how pretty she was, and made the most of it.

"Nuts," Darling said, standing up. "Oh, nuts."

He put on his coat and went down to the nearest bar and had five drinks off by himself in a corner before his money ran out.

The years since then had been foggy and downhill. Louise had been nice to him, and in a way, loving and kind, and they'd fought only once, when he said he was going to vote for Landon. ("Oh, Christ," she'd said, "doesn't *anything* happen inside your head? Don't you read the papers? The penniless Republican!") She'd been sorry later and apologized for hurting him, but apologized as she might to a child. He'd tried hard, had gone grimly to the art galleries, the concert halls, the bookshops, trying to gain on the trail of his wife, but it was no use. He was bored, and none of what he saw or heard or dutifully read made much sense to him and finally he gave it up. He had thought, many nights as he ate dinner alone, knowing that Louise would some home late and drop silently into bed without explanation, of getting a divorce, but he knew the loneliness, the hopelessness, of not seeing her again would be too much to take. So he was good, completely devoted, ready at all times to go anyplace with her, do anything she wanted. He even got a small job, in a broker's office, and paid his own way, bought his own liquor.

Then he'd been offered the job of going from college to college as a tailor's representative. "We want a man," Mr. Rosenberg had said, "who as soon as you look at him, you say, 'There's a university man.'" Rosenberg had looked approvingly at Darling's broad shoulders and well-kept waist, at his carefully brushed hair and his honest, wrinkleless face. "Frankly, Mr. Darling, I am willing to make you a proposition. I have inquired about you, you are favorably known on your old campus, I understand you were in the backfield with Alfred Diederich."

Darling nodded. "Whatever happened to him?"

"He is walking around in a cast for seven years now. An iron brace. He played professional football and they broke his neck for him."

Darling smiled. That, at least, had turned out well.

"Our suits are an easy product to sell, Mr. Darling," Rosenberg said. "We have a handsome, custom-made garment. What has Brooks Brothers got that we haven't got? A name. No more."

"I can make fifty, sixty dollars a week," Darling said to Louise that night. "And expenses. I can save some money and then come back to New York and really get started here."

"Yes, Baby," Louise said.

"As it is," Darling said carefully, "I can make it back here once a month, and holidays and the summer. We can see each other often."

"Yes, Baby." He looked at her face, lovelier now at thirty-five than it had ever been before, but fogged over now as it had been for five years with a kind of patient, kindly, remote boredom.

"What do you say?" he asked. "Should I take it?" Deep within him he hoped fiercely, longingly, for her to say, "No, Baby, you stay right here," but she said, as he knew she'd say, "I think you'd better take it."

He nodded. He had to get up and stand with his back to her, looking out the window, because there were things plain on his face that she had never seen in the fifteen years she'd known him. "Fifty dollars is a lot of money," he said. "I never thought I'd ever see fifty dollars again." He laughed. Louise laughed, too.

Christian Darling sat on the frail green grass of the practice field. The shadow of the stadium had reached out and covered him. In the distance the lights of the university shone a little mistily in the light haze of evening. Fifteen years. Flaherty even now was calling for his wife, buying her a drink, filling whatever bar they were in with that voice of his and that easy laugh. Darling half-closed his eyes, almost saw the boy fifteen years ago reach for the pass, slip the halfback, go skittering lightly down the field, his knees high and fast and graceful, smiling to himself because he knew he was going to get past the safety man. That was the high point, Darling thought, fifteen years ago, on an autumn afternoon, twenty years old and far from death, with the air coming easily into his lungs, and a deep feeling inside him that he could do anything, knock over anybody, outrun whatever had to be outrun. And the shower after and the three glasses of water and the cool night air on his damp head and Louise sitting hatless in the open car with a smile and the first kiss she every really meant. The high point, an eighty-yard run in the practice, and a girl's kiss and everything after that a decline. Darling laughed. He had practiced the wrong thing, perhaps. He hadn't practiced for 1929 and New York City and a girl who would turn into a woman. Somewhere, he thought, there must have been a point where she moved up to me, was even with me for a moment, when I could have held her hand, if I'd known, held tight, gone with her. Well, he'd never known. Here he was on a playing field that was fifteen years away and his wife was in another city having dinner with another and better man, speaking with him a different, new language, a language nobody had ever taught him.

Darling stood up, smiled a little, because if he didn't smile he knew the tears would come. He looked around him. This was the spot. O'Connor's pass had come sliding out just to here . . . the high point. Darling put up his hands, felt all over again the flat slap of the ball. He shook his hips to throw off the halfback, cut back inside the center, picked his knees high as he ran gracefully over two men jumbled on the ground at the line of scrimmage, ran easily, gaining speed, for ten yards, holding the ball lightly in his two hands, swung away from the halfback diving at him, ran, swinging his hips in the almost girlish manner of a back in a broken field, tore into the safety man, his shoes drumming heavily on the turf, stiff-armed, elbow locked, pivoted, raced lightly and exultantly for the goal line.

It was only after he had sped over the goal line and slowed to a trot that he saw the boy and girl sitting together on the turf, looking at him wonderingly.

He stopped short, dropping his arms. "I . . . " he said, gasping a little, though his condition was fine and the run hadn't winded him. "I—once I played here."

The boy and the girl said nothing. Darling laughed embarrassedly, looked hard at them sitting there, close to each other, shrugged, turned and went toward his hotel, the sweat breaking out on his face and running down into his collar.

RESPONSES: Questions for Writing and Discussion

1. The value system of Christian Darling revolves around such things as evident masculinity (physical strength, muscular tightness despite the aging process, a continued youthful appearance, success in competition, and the adulation of a woman.) The story has enjoyed a high literary reputation for many years for its supposedly accurate portrait of a familiar American masculine type. But there are telltale allusions that cause its age to start showing: for example, the coaches' earning $2000 a year; the stock market collapse in 1929; and the fact that "you can't find an author under seventy these days who isn't a Communist." But a story becomes a classic if its truths outweigh its topical references. Does the portrait of Darling give this story the status of a classic?

2. Even if the feeling of the times is not what tends to cause a work of fiction or drama to endure, a "fringe benefit" of reading it is that we learn some things we may not have known about a particular period. Make a list of all the apparent facts you derived from Irwin Shaw about the twenties and thirties.

3. Describe an average day in Christian Darling's life at age

thirty-five, with his wife away at the office. Try to visualize everything he does from the moment he awakens. Relate each action to the male sex role, and, if possible, indicate its function within that role.

4. Women's liberationists frequently argue that they are working toward freeing both sexes from the constraints of their respective roles in life. Would Christian Darling have lived a happier life by being "liberated"? Imagine an encounter between him and a liberationist of today. What would she point out to him?

5. If the liberationist helped bring about a change in Darling's attitude toward himself, what effect might this have on Louise? Consider her character carefully, especially from the standpoint of relative sex roles. In the story's present reality—that is, with both characters in their mid-thirties—she is at the peak of her career; her husband has hit rock-bottom. True, she is a loyal and concerned wife, but is she that *primarily*? Would she be happier playing a subordinate role to a really strong Christian? Or as his equal but not his superior? Or in no other relationship but the one that exists?

6. Judging by rising attendance figures at major sporting events, there is no waning of interest in competitive athletics on the part of the American public. We are continually told that sports are part of the "American way of life." American males, in patricular, carry their love of athletic contests throughout their lives, though the number of women who attend football and baseball games as well as boxing matches keeps going up. This last fact comes at a time when the definition of the feminine sex role is changing. Is there a relationship between sports and the male sex role? Between the growing number of female fans and *their* roles?

FIE, FIE!

William Shakespeare

William Shakespeare's (1564–1616) most popular comedy of sex roles is *The Taming of the Shrew*. The following lines are spoken to the women in the audience by Kate, the heroine, after she has been beaten—physically as well as mentally—into "proper" submission by Petruchio, whom she now recognizes as her lord and master. Earlier in the play, however, Kate has proved a terror to the entire male population of Padua, crying out fierce revolutionary sentiments which would not be out of place in a demonstration march today. That the play was a comedy necessitated a "happy" ending in which all's right with the world, and the nature of the ending tells us much about the male-orientation of Shakespeare's public.

Elsewhere in his plays Shakespeare manifests ambivalent attitudes toward women. Some of his finest creations are "liberated" to the end. Portia, for example, dominates *The Merchant of Venice*, destroying Shylock in the famous court battle over the pound of flesh. Cleopatra, who wrecks half the civilized world through her infatuation for Antony, outwits the conquering Caesar by committing suicide before he can carry her back to Rome as a slave.

At any rate, it is not too hard to believe that what Kate has to say to the audience reflects what many wives in Shakespeare's day—and much, much later—believed, or thought they believed, or were told that they believed. They also represent the ideal image of wifely worth in the minds and hearts of millions of husbands.

Fie, Fie!

Kath. Fie, fie! unknit that threatening unkind
    brow,
And dart not scornful glances from those eyes,
To wound thy lord, thy king, thy governor.
It blots thy beauty as frosts do bite the meads,
Confounds thy fame as whirlwinds shake fair buds,
And in no sense is meet or amiable.
A woman mov'd is like a fountain troubled,
Muddy, ill-seeming, thick, bereft of beauty;
And while it is so, none so dry or thirsty
Will deign to sip or touch one drop of it.
Thy husband is thy lord, thy life, thy keeper,
Thy head, thy sovereign; one that cares for thee,
And for thy maintenance commits his body
To painful labour both by sea and land,
To watch the night in storms, the day in cold,
Whilst thou liest warm at home, secure and safe;
And craves no other tribute at thy hands
But love, fair looks, and true obedience—
Too little payment for so great a debt.
Such duty as the subject owes the prince
Even such a woman oweth to her husband;
And when she is forward, peevish, sullen, sour,

And not obedient to his honest will,
What is she but a foul contending rebel
And graceless traitor to her loving lord?
I am asham'd that women are so simple
To offer war where they should kneel for peace,
Or seek for rule, supremacy, and sway,
When they are bound to serve, love, and obey.
Why are our bodies soft and weak and smooth,
Unapt to toil and trouble in the world,
But that our soft conditions and our hearts
Should well agree with our external parts?
Come, come, you froward and unable worms!
My mind hath been as big as one of yours,
My heart as great, my reason haply more,
To bandy word for word and frown for frown;
But now I see our lances are but straws,
Our strength as weak, our weakness past compare,
That seeming to be most which we indeed least
    are.
Then vail your stomachs, for it is no boot,
And place your hands below your husband's foot;
In token of which duty, if he please.
My hand is ready; may it do him ease.

MEN MARRY WHAT THEY NEED
John Ciardi

There has never been a lack of poems filled with unconditional declarations of love for the opposite sex. By a strange coincidence the overwhelming majority of such poems have been written by male poets. By another strange coincidence the terms of the relationships do not evidently reflect how the lady in question might feel in each instance. She is usually described in poetic images that express what sort of love object the man believes he is adoring. Love poems are not therefore the best place to look for a realistic definition of sex roles. In fact, along with love songs they have greatly contributed to the romanticism of male-female experience, causing some true believers no end of unhappiness in later life.

One notable exception is the poem which follows. **John Ciardi (b. 1916)** —perhaps best known for his translation into a modern and distinctly American idiom of Dante's *Divine Comedy*—describes marriage as a clear-headed relationship between two partners rather than the traditional "husband" and "wife." They are not man and woman, but "man-woman, woman-man, and each the other."

Men Marry What They Need

i

Men marry what they need. I marry you,
morning by morning, day by day, night by night,
and every marriage makes this marriage new.

In the broken name of heaven, in the light
that shatters granite, by the spitting shore,
in air that leaps and wobbles like a kite,

I marry you from time and a great door
is shut and stays shut against wind, sea, stone,
sunburst, and heavenfall. And home once more

inside our walls of skin and struts of bone,
man-woman, woman-man, and each the other,
I marry you by all dark and all dawn

and have my laugh at death. Why should I bother
the flies about me? Let them buzz and do.
Men marry their queen, their daughter, or their mother

by hidden names, but that thin buzz whines through:
where reasons are no reason, cause is true.
Men marry what they need. I marry you.

THE HEART OF A WOMAN
Georgia Douglas Johnson

This poem is an early expression of feminine experience in America. Published in 1918, it is the work of a black poet who had already carved out a place for herself in professional and national life. Educated at the Oberlin Conservatory, she began her career as a composer, then turned to teaching. Her husband served as Recorder of Deeds under William Howard Taft, necessitating a move to the capital, where **Georgia Douglas Johnson (b. 1886)** became active in government agencies. The poem which follows affords some clue to the forces which drove her on, forces which required achievement rather than patient endurance of her woman's role in the America of half a century ago.

The Heart of a Woman

The heart of a woman goes forth with the dawn,
As a lone bird, soft winging, so restlessly on,
Afar o'er life's turrets and vales does it roam
In the wake of those echoes the heart calls home.

The heart of a woman falls back with the night,
And enters some alien cage in its plight,
And tries to forget it has dreamed of the stars,
While it breaks, breaks, breaks on the sheltering bars.

SUDDEN FROST
Hannah Kahn

Known for many years to poetry readers of South Florida, where she has lived since 1936, **Hannah Kahn** is finally beginning to achieve national and international recognition. She has been published in *American Scholar, Harper's, Saturday Review,* and *The New York Times*. She has been the recipient of numerous poetry awards. Currently she is poetry editor for the *Miami Herald.* At the same time she is busily pursuing the college degree she never received earlier in life!

Hannah Kahn's poetry has a special but unmistakable quality that distinguishes it from the work of other American poets. Perhaps this owes much to the fact that her background has been less academic than deeply and steadily involved in the day-to-day process of living. Her poems speak of both ordinary moments and of milestone events in everyone's existence (such as the recognition that comes to the wife in this poem). They are usually very short. Hannah Kahn has a distinct gift for capturing in a few words the elusive feelings shared by many but which often pass unnoticed into the buried life. Her special province is the feminine experience in America—not in circles where women have felt free to speak their minds, but in the routine environment of the home.

Sudden Frost

All the soft sounds of night are suddenly turned
Inward upon me. There is a murmurous drone,
A whisper, an echo, a language I have not learned,
Something inherent in silence that makes me alone.
Lying beside you, sensing that you are asleep,
Wanting to touch you, yet fearing that you might awaken,
I clasp my hands tightly, needing this moment to keep
Assurance that I am not lost and not forsaken.

Dawn comes slowly to women who wait for the night
To merge with the oncoming day, to focus again
On moonlight remembered, the throbbing pulse of light
That blurs with the simmering sound of falling rain.
And I become all women, lonely and lost
Who have no armor against sudden frost.

From *Eve's Daughter* by Hannah Kahn. Reprinted by permission of the author.

Robert Thomason

I clasp my hands tightly, needing
    this moment to keep
Assurance that I am not
    lost and forsaken.
        Hannah Kahn

KINDNESS
Sylvia Plath

The following poem expresses a feminine dilemma which innumerable women have been unable to solve. The poet is the mother of two children, and she has a husband who obviously respects and loves her. In truth she appears to have everything. Yet somehow the "kindness" becomes subtly oppressive, a prison from which no escape seems possible.

Before the tragic suicide which ended a promising life much too soon, **Sylvia Plath (1932–1963)** completed two extraordinary volumes of poems: *The Colossus* and *Ariel*. Reading the poems in the second book, written in the heat of creative fervor during the months preceding her death, one finds the record of a tormented search for a fulfillment which lacks a name. (But obviously "kindness" is not enough.)

In her work one finds a passion for something that lies beyond all inhibiting boundaries, whether imposed by marriage itself or by the poet's own mind. Robert Lowell describes her as being "a little like a racehorse, galloping relentlessly with risked, outstretched neck, death hurdle after death hurdle topped." In some poems, however, she recognizes the futility of her indefinable quest and the need all of us have for making compromises.

Kindness

Kindness glides about my house.
Dame Kindness, she is so nice!
The blue and red jewels of her rings smoke
In the windows, the mirrors
Are filling with smiles.

What is so real as the cry of a child?
A rabbit's cry may be wilder
But it has no soul.
Sugar can cure everything, so Kindness says.
Sugar is a necessary fluid,

Its crystals a little poultice.
O kindness, kindness

Sweetly picking up pieces!
My Japanese silks, desperate butterflies,
May be pinned any minute, anaesthetized.

And here you come, with a cup of tea
Wreathed in steam.
The blood jet is poetry,
There is no stopping it.
You hand me two children, two roses.

WIDENING CIRCLES
OF LOVE

Human Worth sometimes applies to what people are in themselves and sometimes to what happens when they are together—in other words, to the capacity for loving and making sacrifices for others. In some contexts, ego becomes the enemy of Human Worth, the force which must be overcome if true nobility is to shine through. In others, ego is a positive thing. The Greeks, for example, thought of Human Worth in terms of reaching one's full potential, but the Romans, while agreeing on this score, also added the idea that being worthily human meant doing one's duty for the state. Christianity made individualism much less important than altruism, but the Renaissance of the fourteenth, fifteenth, and sixteenth centuries said ego was respectable and beautiful. Michelangelo's statues, even his dome of St. Peter's, are strident expressions of a confident mortal exulting in his own being. Looking back over the history of the human adventure, it is hard to decide whether self or selflessness has made the difference and supplies us with the basic definition of Human Worth.

Just what "love" is can be debated more than almost any other single concern. One writer has suggested that people would never fall in love or commit actions said to express love if they had never heard of love.

Another has called love the thing that happens when two people are being selfish at the same time. Another considers love the ability to care for another as much as for oneself. History gives us the names of persons who seem to have transcended all self-interest and dedicated their lives to a higher cause: Christ, Joan of Arc, Gandhi, King—not to mention all the legendary heroes of wars who gave their own lives to save an entire company.

The readings in this section deal with varying kinds of love relationships which different writers view as helping to show what Human Worth really means. The complexity of married love is the theme of Carson McCullers' "A Domestic Dilemma." While most of the story reveals a marriage that a casual observer would call "on the rocks"—terrible arguments, the alcoholism of the wife, the neglect of the children—we somehow come away with a sense of affirmation that is hard to define. But we know it has something to do with the fact that the compromises and sacrifices which marriage sometimes wrings from people out of harsh necessity can be the very things that ennoble them.

Great Goodness of Life, a one-act play by Amiri Baraka (LeRoi Jones), defines love in broader terms than that of a man for a woman: the loyalty and responsibility of a man toward his brothers. Court Royal, the play's protagonist, is placed on trial by the brotherhood and made to face the agonizing truth that, in pursuing his own happiness, he has tragically betrayed the cause of black liberation.

Robert Frost's narrative poem "The Death of the Hired Man" sees love in matter-of-fact, unemotional terms that takes us directly to the facts of everyday living. Its uncomplicated incident raises one of the world's enduring questions: Are we responsible for each other? Are we made that way? Is it human fate for each of us at some time to undergo the anguish of having to care more for others than we do for ourselves whether we like it or not? And is this very anguish the thing which, in the end and after all the complaining, we do best of all?

No consideration of love would be complete, however, without giving some thought to the personality and philosophy of the man Jesus. It is hard to deny that the doctrine of loving one's neighbor, even when he is an enemy, has had a profound effect on the mind, imagination, and sometimes conscience of people for centuries. Kahlil Gibran's *Jesus: The Son of Man* offers a number of different viewpoints about Jesus as a human being, supposedly expressed by his contemporaries. Reading them side by side, one is impressed by the variety of possibilities and finds himself asking once again, "Could such a man have lived? Could he have been what so many believe he was? Is such an ideal of love within human grasp?"

A DOMESTIC DILEMMA
Carson McCullers

If one had to translate the special quality of the work of **Carson McCullers**
(1917–1967) into the sound of a musical instrument, it would have to be that
of a solitary and mournful flute. Few contemporary writers have focused so
intently on the theme of loneliness and the need of people to reach out for
each other. Her first novel *The Heart Is a Lonely Hunter,* published when
she was twenty-three, served as a clear indication that the American literary
scene had acquired a specialist in the perception of the isolated and sensitive
soul. The novel's mute hero was to be representative of a succession of
McCullers' characters—all eligible to be saved through love but peculiarly
susceptible to being rejected and misunderstood. Perhaps now that her
work is complete, she will emerge as the prophetess of a changing America
where the human potential for love remains unfulfilled and where real
communication between people is rare.

Of special concern to Carson McCullers is what happens to people living
in large urban areas like New York, which is the setting of "A Domestic
Dilemma." Born in Columbus, Georgia, she herself moved to New York
when she was seventeen and, while working, attending night schools, and
trying to find the time for writing, she may have had much of the same
fragmented and lonely existence experienced by her characters.

In "A Domestic Dilemma" the theme of loneliness within the crowded
city is heightened by the fact that the hero is married and has children. But
the loneliness is finally offset by the things which are available to all of us
and which, for the author, redeem and dignity human life, giving it the only
fulfillment most of us can ever expect to know: the stabilizing influence of
home and the family (especially important in the large cities), the deep ties
that bind the members together, and the sense of responsibility which those
ties awaken.

A Domestic Dilemma

On Thursday Martin Meadows left the office early enough to make the
first express bus home. It was the hour when the evening lilac glow was
fading in the slushy streets, but by the time the bus had left the Mid-

town terminal the bright city night had come. On Thursdays the maid had a half-day off and Martin liked to get home as soon as possible, since for the past year his wife had not been—well. This Thursday he was very tired and, hoping that no regular commuter would single him out for conversation, he fastened his attention to the newspaper until the bus had crossed the George Washington Bridge. Once on 9-W Highway Martin always felt that the trip was halfway done, he breathed deeply, even in cold weather when only ribbons of draught cut through the smoky air of the bus, confident that he was breathing country air. It used to be that at this point he would relax and begin to think with pleasure of his home. But in this last year nearness brought only a sense of tension and he did not anticipate the journey's end. This evening Martin kept his face close to the window and watched the barren fields and lonely lights of passing townships. There was a moon, pale on the dark earth and areas of late, porous snow; to Martin the countryside seemed vast and somehow desolate that evening. He took his hat from the rack and put his folded newspaper in the pocket of his overcoat a few minutes before time to pull the cord.

The cottage was a block from the bus stop, near the river but not directly on the shore; from the living-room window you could look across the street and opposite yard and see the Hudson. The cottage was modern, almost too white and new on the narrow plot of yard. In summer the grass was soft and bright and Martin carefully tended a flower border and a rose trellis. But during the cold, fallow months the yard was bleak and the cottage seemed naked. Lights were on that evening in all the rooms in the little house and Martin hurried up the front walk. Before the steps he stopped to move a wagon out of the way.

The children were in the living room, so intent on play that the opening of the front door was at first unnoticed. Martin stood looking at his safe, lovely children. They had opened the bottom drawer of the secretary and taken out the Christmas decorations. Andy had managed to plug in the Christmas tree lights and the green and red bulbs glowed with out-of-season festivity on the rug of the living room. At the moment he was trying to trail the bright cord over Marianne's rocking horse. Marianne sat on the floor pulling off an angel's wings. The children wailed a startling welcome. Martin swung the fat little baby girl up to his shoulder and Andy threw himself against his father's legs.

"Daddy, Daddy, Daddy!"

Martin sat down the little girl carefully and swung Andy a few times like a pendulum. Then he picked up the Christmas tree cord.

"What's all this stuff doing out? Help me put it back in the drawer.

You're not to fool with the light socket. Remember I told you that before. I mean it, Andy."

The six-year-old child nodded and shut the secretary drawer. Martin stroked his fair soft hair and his hand lingered tenderly on the nape of the child's frail neck.

"Had supper yet, Bumpkin?"

"It hurt. The toast was hot."

The baby girl stumbled on the rug and, after the first surprise of the fall, began to cry; Martin picked her up and carried her in his arms back to the kitchen.

"See, Daddy," said Andy. "The toast———"

Emily had laid the children's supper on the uncovered porcelain table. There were two plates with the remains of cream-of-wheat and eggs and silver mugs that had held milk. There was also a platter of cinnamon toast, untouched, except for one tooth-marked bite. Martin sniffed the bitten piece and nibbled gingerly. Then he put the toast into the garbage pail.

"Hoo—phui—What on earth!"

Emily had mistaken the tin of cayenne for the cinnamon.

"I like to have burnt up," Andy said. "Drank water and ran outdoors and opened my mouth. Marianne didn't eat none."

"Any," corrected Martin. He stood helpless, looking around the walls of the kitchen. "Well, that's that, I guess," he said finally. "Where is your mother now?"

"She's up in you alls' room."

Martin left the children in the kitchen and went up to his wife. Outside the door he waited for a moment to still his anger. He did not knock and once inside the room he closed the door behind him.

Emily sat in the rocking chair by the window of the pleasant room. She had been drinking something from a tumbler and as he entered she put the glass hurriedly on the floor behind the chair. In her attitude there was confusion and guilt which she tried to hide by a show of spurious vivacity.

"Oh, Marty! You home already? The time slipped up on me. I was just going down———" She lurched to him and her kiss was strong with sherry. When he stood unresponsive she stepped back a pace and giggled nervously.

"What's the matter with you? Standing there like a barber pole. Is anything wrong with you?"

"Wrong with *me*?" Martin bent over the rocking chair and picked up the tumbler from the floor. "If you could only realize how sick I am—how bad it is for all of us."

Emily spoke in a false, airy voice that had become too familiar to him. Often at such times she affected a slight English accent copying perhaps some actress she admired. "I haven't the vaguest idea what you mean. Unless you are referring to the glass I used for a spot of sherry. I had a finger of sherry—maybe two. But what is the crime in that, pray tell me? I'm quite all right. Quite all right."

"So anyone can see."

As she went into the bedroom Emily walked with careful gravity. She turned on the cold water and dashed some on her face with her cupped hands, then patted herself dry with the corner of a bath towel. Her face was delicately featured and young, unblemished.

"I was just going down to make dinner." She tottered and balanced herself by holding to the door frame.

"I'll take care of dinner. You stay up here. I'll bring it up."

"I'll do nothing of the sort. Why, whoever heard of such a thing?"

"Please," Martin said.

"Leave me alone. I'm quite all right. I was just on the way down——"

"Mind what I say."

"Mind your grandmother."

She lurched toward the door, but Martin caught her by the arm. "I don't want the children to see you in this condition. Be reasonable."

"Condition!" Emily jerked her arm. Her voice rose angrily. "Why, because I drink a couple of sherries in the afternoon you're trying to make me out a drunkard. Condition! Why, I don't even touch whiskey. As well you know. *I* don't swill liquor at bars. And that's more than you can say. I don't even have a cocktail at dinnertime. I only sometimes have a glass of sherry. What, I ask you, is the disgrace of that? Condition!"

Martin sought words to calm his wife. "We'll have a quiet supper by ourselves up here. That's a good girl." Emily sat on the side of the bed and he opened the door for a quick departure.

"I'll be back in a jiffy."

As he busied himself with the dinner downstairs he was lost in the familiar question as to how this problem had come upon his home. He himself had always enjoyed a good drink. When they were still living in Alabama they had served long drinks or cocktails as a matter of course. For years they had drunk one or two—possibly three drinks before dinner, and at bedtime a long nightcap. Evenings before holidays they might get a buzz on, might even become a little tight. But alcohol had never seemed a problem to him, only a bothersome expense that with the increase in the family they could scarcely afford. It was only after his company had transferred him to New York that Martin was aware that certainly his wife was drinking too much. She was tippling, he noticed, during the day.

The problem acknowledged, he tried to analyze the source. The change from Alabama to New York had somehow disturbed her; accustomed to the idle warmth of a small Southern town, the matrix of the family and cousinship and childhood friends, she had failed to accommodate herself to the stricter, lonelier mores of the North. The duties of motherhood and housekeeping were onerous to her. Homesick for Paris City, she had made no friends in the suburban town. She read only magazines and murder books. Her interior life was insufficient without the artifice of alcohol.

The revelations of incontinence insidiously undermined his previous conceptions of his wife. There were times of unexplainable malevolence, times when the alcoholic fuse caused an explosion of unseemly anger. He encountered a latent coarseness in Emily, inconsistent with her natural simplicity. She lied about drinking and deceived him with unsuspected stratagems.

Then there was an accident. Coming home from work one evening about a year ago, he was greeted with screams from the children's room. He found Emily holding the baby, wet and naked from her bath. The baby had been dropped, her frail, frail skull striking the table edge, so that a thread of blood was soaking into the gossamer hair. Emily was sobbing and intoxicated. As Martin cradled the hurt child, so infinitely precious at that moment, he had an affrighted vision of the future.

The next day Marianne was all right. Emily vowed that never again would she touch liquor, and for a few weeks she was sober, cold and downcast. Then gradually she began—not whiskey or gin—but quantities of beer, or sherry, or outlandish liqueurs; once he had come across a hatbox of empty crème de menthe bottles. Martin found a dependable maid who managed the household competently. Virgie was also from Alabama and Martin had never dared tell Emily the wage scale customary in New York. Emily's drinking was entirely secret now, done before he reached the house. Usually the effects were almost imperceptible—a looseness of movement or the heavy-lidded eyes. The times of irresponsibilities, such as the cayenne-pepper toast were rare, and Martin could dismiss his worries when Virgie was at the house. But, nevertheless, anxiety was always latent, a threat of undefined disaster that underlaid his days.

"Marianne!" Martin called, for even the recollection of that time brought the need for reassurance. The baby girl, no longer hurt, but no less precious to her father, came into the kitchen with her brother. Martin went on with the preparations for the meal. He opened a can of soup and put two chops in the frying pan. Then he sat down by the table and took Marianne on his knees for a pony ride. Andy watched them, his fingers wobbling the tooth that had been loose all that week.

"Andy-the-candyman!" Martin said. "Is that old critter still in your mouth? Come closer, let Daddy have a look."

"I got a string to pull it with." The child brought from his pocket a tangled thread. "Virgie said to tie it to the tooth and tie the other end to the doorknob and shut the door real suddenly."

Martin took out a clean handkerchief and felt the loose tooth carefully. "That tooth is coming out of my Andy's mouth tonight. Otherwise I'm awfully afraid we'll have a tooth tree in the family."

"A what?"

"A tooth tree," Martin said. "You'll bite into something and swallow that tooth. And the tooth will take root in poor Andy's stomach and grow into a tooth tree with sharp little teeth instead of leaves."

"Shoo, Daddy," Andy said. But he held the tooth firmly between his grimy little thumb and forefinger. "There ain't any tree like that. I never seen one."

"There *isn't* any tree like that and I never *saw* one."

Martin tensed suddenly. Emily was coming down the stairs. He listened to her fumbling footsteps, his arm embracing the little boy with dread. When Emily came into the room he saw from her movements and her sullen face that she had again been at the sherry bottle. She began to yank open drawers and set the table.

"Condition!" she said in a furry voice. "You talk to me like that. Don't think I'll forget. I remember every dirty lie you say to me. Don't you think for a minute that I forget."

"Emily!" he begged. "The children——"

"The children—yes! Don't think I don't see through your dirty plots and schemes. Down here trying to turn my own children against me. Don't think I don't see and understand."

"Emily! I beg you—please go upstairs."

"So you can turn my children—my very own children——" Two large tears coursed rapidly down her cheeks. "Trying to turn my little boy, my Andy, against his own mother."

With drunken impulsiveness Emily knelt on the floor before the startled child. Her hands on his shoulders balanced her. "Listen, my Andy—you wouldn't listen to any lies your father tells you? You wouldn't believe what he says? Listen, Andy, what was your father telling you before I came downstairs?" Uncertain, the child sought his father's face. "Tell me. Mama wants to know."

"About the tooth tree."

"What?"

The child repeated the words and she echoed them with unbelieving terror. "The tooth tree!" She swayed and renewed her grasp on the child's shoulder. "I don't know what you're talking about. But listen, Andy, Mama is all right, isn't she?" The tears were spilling down her face and Andy drew back from her, for he was afraid. Grasping the table edge, Emily stood up.

"See! You have turned my child against me."

Marianne began to cry, and Martin took her in his arms.

"That's all right, you can take *your* child. You have always shown partiality from the very first. I don't mind, but at least you can leave me my little boy."

Andy edged close to his father and touched his leg. "Daddy," he wailed.

Martin took the children to the foot of the stairs. "Andy, you take up Marianne and Daddy will follow you in a minute."

"But Mama?" the child asked, whispering.

"Mama will be all right. Don't worry."

Emily was sobbing at the kitchen table, her face buried in the crook of her arm. Martin poured a cup of soup and set it before her. Her rasping sobs unnerved him; the vehemence of her emotion, irrespective of the source, touched in him a strain of tenderness. Unwillingly he laid his hand on her dark hair. "Sit up and drink the soup." Her face as she looked up at him was chastened and imploring. The boy's withdrawal or the touch of Martin's hand had turned the tenor of her mood.

"Ma-Martin," she sobbed. "I'm so ashamed."

"Drink the soup."

Obeying him, she drank between gasping breaths. After a second cup she allowed him to lead her up to their room. She was docile now and more restrained. He laid her nightgown on the bed and was about to leave the room when a fresh round of grief, the alcoholic tumult, came again.

"He turned away. My Andy looked at me and turned away."

Impatience and fatigue hardened his voice, but he spoke warily. "You forget that Andy is still a little child—he can't comprehend the meaning of such scenes."

"Did I make a scene? Oh, Martin, did I make a scene before the children?"

Her horrified face touched and amused him against his will. "Forget it. Put on your nightgown and go to sleep."

"My child turned away from me. Andy looked at his mother and turned away. The children——"

She was caught in the rhythmic sorrow of alcohol. Martin withdrew from the room saying: "For God's sake go to sleep. The children will forget by tomorrow."

As he said this he wondered if it was true. Would the scene glide so easily from memory—or would it root in the unconscious to fester in the after-years? Martin did not know, and the last alternative sickened him. He thought of Emily, foresaw the morning-after humiliation: the shards of memory, the lucidities that glared from the obliterating darkness of shame. She would call the New York office twice—possibly three or four times. Martin anticipated his own embarrassment, wondering if the others at the office could possibly suspect. He felt that his secretary had divined the trouble long ago and that she pitied him. He suffered a moment of rebellion against his fate, he hated his wife.

Once in the children's room he closed the door and felt secure for the first time that evening. Marianne fell down on the floor, picked herself up and calling: "Daddy, watch me," fell again, got up, and continued the falling-calling routine. Andy sat in the child's low chair, wobbling the tooth. Martin ran the water in the tub, washed his own hands in the lavatory, and called the boy into the bathroom.

"Let's have another look at that tooth." Martin sat on the toilet, holding Andy between his knees. The child's mouth gaped and Martin grasped the tooth. A wobble, a quick twist and the nacreous milk tooth was free. Andy's face was for the first moment split between terror, astonishment, and delight. He mouthed a swallow of water and spat into the lavatory.

"Look, Daddy! It's blood. Marianne!"

Martin loved to bathe his children, loved inexpressibly the tender, naked bodies as they stood in the water so exposed. It was not fair of Emily to say that he showed partiality. As Martin soaped the delicate boy-body of his son he felt that further love would be impossible. Yet he admitted the difference in the quality of his emotions for the two children. His love for his daughter was graver, touched with a strain of melancholy, a gentleness that was akin to pain. His pet names for the little boy were the absurdities of daily inspiration—he called the little girl always Marianne, and his voice as he spoke it was a caress. Martin patted dry the fat baby stomach and the sweet little genital fold. The washed child faces were radiant as flower petals, equally loved.

"I'm putting the tooth under my pillow. I'm supposed to get a quarter."

"What for?"

"You know, Daddy. Johnny got a quarter for his tooth."

"Who puts the quarter there?" asked Martin. "I used to think the fairies left it in the night. It was a dime in my day, though."

"That's what they say in kindergarten."

"Who does put it there?"

"Your parents," Andy said. "You!"

Martin was pinning the cover on Marianne's bed. His daughter was already asleep. Scarcely breathing, Martin bent over and kissed her forehead, kissed again the tiny hand that lay palm-upward, flung in slumber beside her head.

"Good night, Andy-man."

The answer was only a drowsy murmur. After a minute Martin took out his change and slid a quarter underneath the pillow. He left a night light in the room.

As Martin prowled about the kitchen making a late meal, it occurred to him that the children had not once mentioned their mother or the scene that must have seemed to them incomprehensible. Absorbed in the instant—the tooth, the bath, the quarter—the fluid passage of child-time had borne these weightless episodes like leaves in the swift current of a shallow stream while the adult enigma was beached and forgotten on the shore. Martin thanked the Lord for that.

But his own anger, repressed and lurking, rose again. His youth was being frittered by a drunkard's waste, his very manhood subtly undermined. And the children, once the immunity of incomprehension passed—what would it be like in a year or so? With his elbows on the table he ate his food brutishly, untasting. There was no hiding the truth—soon there would be gossip in the office and in the town; his wife was a dissolute woman. Dissolute. And he and his children were bound to a future of degradation and slow ruin.

Martin pushed away from the table and stalked into the living room. He followed the lines of a book with his eyes but his mind conjured miserable images: he saw his children drowned in the river, his wife a disgrace on the public street. By bedtime the dull, hard anger was like a weight upon his chest and his feet dragged as he climbed the stairs.

The room was dark except for the shafting light from the half-opened bathroom door. Martin undressed quietly. Little by little, mysteriously, there came in him a change. His wife was asleep, her peaceful respiration sounding gently in the room. Her high-heeled shoes with the carelessly dropped stockings made to him a mute appeal. Her underclothes were flung in disorder on the chair. Martin picked up the girdle and the soft, silk brassière and stood for a moment with them in his hands. For the first time that evening he looked at his wife. His eyes rested on the sweet forehead, the arch of the fine brow. The brow had descended to Marianne, and the tilt at the end of the delicate nose. In his son he could trace the high cheekbones and pointed chin. Her body was full-bosomed, slender and undulant. As Martin watched the tranquil slumber of his wife the ghost of anger vanished. All thoughts of blame or blemish were distant from him now. Martin put out the bathroom light and raised the window. Careful not to awaken Emily he slid into the bed. By moonlight he watched his wife for the last time. His hand sought the adjacent flesh and sorrow paralleled desire in the immense complexity of love.

RESPONSES: Questions for Writing and Discussion

1. Her marriage to a man like Martin appears to be the thing that will save Emily Meadows from total surrender to alcoholism. But in the "immense complexity of love" marital and family obligations play a part in everyone's problems. Emily is plagued by feelings of guilt, and, though the author does not cite these as further motivations for her drinking, it isn't hard to imagine that this would be true of a real-life Emily. To determine the extent to which marriage saves or contributes to the anguish of Emily, imagine her as being a single girl from rural Alabama, moving to New York for a career. Imagine New York as it is today with its teeming streets, abundance of crimes, and hard-to-breathe air, but also with its sophistication, cultural events, and opportunities for women to advance themselves. Measure the pros against the cons and then decide whether a nonmarried Emily would have become an alcoholic.

2. The implied contrast between small-town and big-city America, which is used by the author to account for Emily's problems, was a recurrent theme in nineteenth-century fiction—so much so, in fact, that it became a sentimental cliché. Novels, plays, and stories abounded in which the innocent milkmaid or ploughboy leaves the farm and comes to grief in the cruel, callous, and amoral metropolis. Is the sentiment old-fashioned and no longer realistic? *Are* people better off on the farm?

3. As the story is presented, Emily and the children need have no fears because of the kind of husband and father that the author has created for them. (One cannot help wondering what would have happened if Martin had decided to start drinking himself as an escape from both the unfamiliarity of the New York scene and his wife's inability to cope with it.) An important fact to consider is that the author is a woman and her central character a man. In your opinion, would a real-life Martin be so domestically inclined, given the circumstances that prevail in the story? Is the characterization of Martin faithful to male psychology as you genereally perceive it? Or is he a female author's idealization of a man?

4. The "immense complexity of love," which causes this story to end on a life-affirming note, is given considerable assistance by the apparently comfortable economic condition of the family. (They *can* afford a maid, even though one may argue that Martin had no choice but to hire one.) One can only guess at the fate of a poor family in a

large urban area, with an alcoholic mother and a father who is away from the home all day. Do you believe that in cases of very modest to poor circumstances, family ties help or hinder people to achieve Human Worth?

5. The definition of love in the last sentence appears to apply only to Martin. Whether Emily "loves" him and, if so, whether the definition needs to be altered in her case are problems with which the author does not directly deal. There seems to be a world of difference between Martin's capacity for self-sacrifice and Emily's weakness and self-concern. In your opinion, does Martin's brand of love ennoble him? Or is he a fool?

6. Assuming for the moment that Martin does achieve a fair amount of human dignity by virtue of his love for Emily, how shall we assess the value of family life in terms of the children? Project them ahead into adolescence. If their mother continues to drink, how will they grow up? Will they understand and admire their father's dedication? Will they pity him and decide family life isn't worth it? Can adolescents cope with the "immense complexity" of their parents' relationships? In other words, do children generally profit or suffer from such a family environment? From the child's viewpoint, is the story pro- or anti-family?

GREAT GOODNESS OF LIFE (A COON SHOW)

Amiri Baraka (LeRoi Jones)

LeRoi Jones (b. 1934) first captured the attention of both black and white theater audiences with a one-act play *Dutchman*. On a deserted subway train Lula, a sensuous, apple-eating modern Eve, tempts and seduces a mild-mannered, apparently establishment black man named Clay into asserting his manhood and releasing his latent violence. When she realizes she cannot cope with him any longer, she kills him. The author was showing white America the shame and infamy of its false liberalism, which is really racism in disguise. He was also telling black America to beware, and to trust no longer, to believe no more in optimistic fantasies of a better future, and to be ready to act.

Now Amiri Baraka, the playwright addresses himself almost exclusively to a black audience, using the theater to shock, terrify, and arouse the con-science of his viewers. His is revolutionary drama in the fullest sense of the word, aiming not to entertain but to identify a cause and point out a direction.

Great Goodness of Life is representative of this latest phase of Baraka's work. But it does not sermonize; rather, it creates a spellbinding ritual, using some of the theater's most ancient conventions—such as masks and a chorus —to elicit basic emotional responses. Like many of his contemporaries in black theater, Baraka believes it is necessary to break from the white tradi-tion of the well-made play in order to force audiences to open their eyes and ears.

Like the father in the preceding story "A Domestic Dilemma" the play's hero Court Royal exists within the boundaries of family life. But for the playwright the family is only a small unit within much larger circles: the community in which one lives and, beyond that, the brotherhood of one's ethnic group. Royal has ignored higher loyalties in favor of security for him-self and his family. He may represent for Baraka a large cross section of that black America which has bought the American dream of success and material gain and has betrayed the black cause in pursuing it. Royal's son probably symbolizes a number of things—the future of the black man, the revolution by the poor and oppressed, Black Power itself. In creating a powerful reverse Oedipus myth in which this time the father murders the son, Baraka creates a new kind of tragedy. The catastrophe is no longer something the hero brings upon himself, but what he brings upon his people. The measure of Human Worth now becomes one's willingness to risk every-thing, even his life if necessary, for the brotherhood.

Great Goodness of Life (A Coon Show)

The Scene:
An old house, with morning frost letting up a little.

A VOICE

Court.
(*A man comes out, gray but still young looking. He is around 50. He walks straight, though he is nervous. He comes uncertainly. Pauses*)
Come on.
(*He walks right up to the center of the lights*)
Come on.

COURT

I don't quite understand.

VOICE

Shut up, nigger.

COURT

What?
(*Meekly, then trying to get some force up*)
Now what's going on? I don't see why I should . . .

VOICE

I told you to shut up nigger.

COURT

I don't understand. What's going on?

VOICE

Black lunatic. I said shut up. I'm not going to tell you again!

COURT

But . . . Yes.

VOICE

You are Court Royal, are you not?

COURT

Yes. I am. But I don't understand.

VOICE

You are charged with shielding a wanted criminal. A murderer.

COURT

What? Now I know you have the wrong man. I've done no such thing.
I work in the Post Office. I'm Court Royal. I've done nothing wrong.
I work in the Post Office and have done nothing wrong.

VOICE

Shut up.

COURT

But I'm Court Royal. Everybody knows me. I've always done everything . . .

VOICE

Court Royal, you are charged with harboring a murderer. How do you
plead?

COURT

Plead? There's a mistake being made. I've never done anything.

VOICE

How do you plead?

COURT

I'm not a criminal. I've done nothing . . .

VOICE

Then you plead "not guilty"?

COURT

Of course, I'm not guilty. I work in the Post Office.

(*Tries to work up a little humor*)

You know me, probably. Didn't you ever see me in the Post Office? I'm a supervisor, you know me. I work at the Post Office. I'm no criminal. I've worked at the Post Office for thirty years. I'm a supervisor. There must be some mistake. I've worked at the Post Office for thirty years.

VOICE

Do you have an attorney?

COURT

Attorney? Look you'd better check you got the right man. You're making a mistake. I'll sue. That's what I'll do.

(*The* VOICE *laughs long and cruelly*)

I'll call my attorney right now. We'll find out just what's going on here.

VOICE

If you don't have an attorney, the court will assign you one.

COURT

Don't bother. I have an attorney. John Breck's my attorney. He'll be down here in a few minutes—the minute I call.

VOICE

The court will assign you an attorney.

COURT

But I have an attorney. John Breck. See, it's on this card.

VOICE

Will the legal-aid man please step forward.

COURT

No. I have an attorney. If you'll just call, or adjourn the case until my attorney gets here.

VOICE

We have an attorney for you. Where is the legal-aid man?

COURT

But I have an attorney. I want my attorney. I don't need any legal-aid man. I have money, I have an attorney. I work in the Post Office. I'm a supervisor, here look at my badge.

(*A bald-headed smiling house slave in a wrinkled dirty tuxedo crawls across the stage; he has a wire attached to his back leading off stage. A huge key in the side of his head. We hear the motors "animating" his body groaning like tremendous weights. He grins, and slobbers, turning his head slowly from side to side. He grins. He makes little quivering sounds*)

VOICE

Your attorney.

COURT

What kind of foolishness is this?
   (*He looks at the* MAN)
What's going on? What's your name?

ATTORNEY

   (*His "voice" begins sometime after the question, the wheels churn out his answer, and the deliberating motors sound throughout the scene*)
Pul . . . lead . . . errrr . . .
   (*As if the motors are having trouble starting*)
Pul—pul— . . . lead . . . er . . . err Guilty!
   (*Motors get it together and move in proper synchronization*)
Pul—Plead Guilty, it's your only chance. Just plead guilty brother. Just plead guilty. It's your only chance. Your only chance.

COURT

Guilty? Of what? What are you talking about? What kind of defense attorney are you? I don't even know what I'm being charged with, and you say plead guilty. What's happening here?
   (*At* VOICE)
Can't I even know the charge?

VOICE

We told you the charge. Harboring a murderer.

COURT

But that's an obvious mistake.

ATTORNEY

There's no mistake. Plead guilty. Get off easy. Otherwise *thrrrrit.*
   (*Makes throat cutting gesture, then chuckles*)
Plead guilty, brother, it's your only chance.
   (*Laughs*)

VOICE

Plea changed to guilty?

COURT

What? No. I'm not pleading guilty. And I want my lawyer.

VOICE

You have your lawyer.

COURT

No, my lawyer is John Breck.

ATTORNEY

Mr. Royal look at me.
   (*Grabs him by the shoulders*)

I am John Breck.
> (*Laughs*)

Your attorney, and friend. And I say plead guilty.

COURT

John Bre . . . what?
> (*He looks at* ATTORNEY *closely*)

Breck. Great God, what's happened to you? Why do you look like this?

ATTORNEY

Why? Haha, I've always looked like this, Mr. Royal. Always.
> (*Now* ANOTHER VOICE, *strong, young, begins to shout in the darkness at* ROYAL)

YOUNG VOICE

Now will you believe me stupid fool? Will you believe what I tell you or your eyes? Even your eyes. You're here with me, with us, all of us, and you can't understand. Plead guilty you are guilty stupid nigger. You'll die they'll kill you and you don't know why, now will you believe me? Believe me, half-white coward. Will you believe reality?

VOICE

Get that criminal out of here. Beat him. Shut him up. Get him.
> (*Now sounds of scuffling come out of darkness. Screams. Of a group of men subduing another man*)

YOUNG VOICE

You bastard. And you Court Royal you let them take me. You liar. You weakling. You woman in the face of degenerates. You let me be taken. How can you walk the eartttttt . . .
> (*He is apparently taken away*)

COURT

Who's that?
> (*Peers into darkness*)

Who's that talking to me?

VOICE

Shut up Royal. Fix your plea. Let's get on with it.

COURT

That voice sounded very familiar.
> (*Caught in thought momentarily*)

I almost thought it was . . .

VOICE

Since you keep your plea of not guilty you won't need a lawyer. We can proceed without your services counselor.

ATTORNEY

As you wish your honor. Good-bye Mr. Royal.
> (*He begins to crawl off*)

Good-bye, dead sucker! Hahahaha . . .
   (*Waving hands as he crawls off and laughing*)
Hahahaha, ain't I a bitch . . . I mean ain't I?
   (*Exits*)

COURT

John, John. You're my attorney, you can't leave me here like this.
   (*Starts after him . . . shouts*)
JOHN!
   (*A siren begins to scream, like in jailbreak pictures . . . "Arrrrrrr."
   The lights beat off, on, in time with the metallic siren shriek.
   COURT ROYAL is stopped in his tracks, bent in anticipation, the
   siren continues. Machine guns begin to bang bang as if very close
   to him, cell doors slamming, whistles, yells "Break . . . Break," the
   machine guns shatter, COURT ROYAL stands frozen half bent arms
   held away from his body balancing him in his terror. As the
   noise, din, continues, his eyes grow until he is almost going to
   faint*)

COURT

Ahhhhhhhgggg. Please . . . Please . . . don't kill me. Don't shoot me,
I didn't do anything. I'm not trying to escape. Please . . . Please . . .
PLEEEEEAS . . .
   (*The VOICE begins to shriek almost as loud with laughter, as all
   the other sounds, and jumping lights stop as VOICE starts to laugh.
   The VOICE just laughs and laughs, laughs until you think it will
   explode or spit up blood it laughs long and eerily out of the
   darkness*)

COURT

   (*Still dazed and staggered. He looks around quickly, trying to
   get himself together. He speaks now very quietly, and shaken*)
Please. Please.
   (*The other VOICE begins to subside, the laughs coming in sharp
   cutoff bursts of hysteria*)

VOICE

You donkey.
   (*Laughs*)
You piece of wood. You shiny shuffling piece of black vomit.
   (*The laughter quits like the tide rolling softly back to silence.
   Now there is no sound, except for COURT ROYAL's breathing, and
   shivering clothes. He whispers:*)

COURT

Please?
   (*He is completely shaken and defeated frightened like a small
   animal, eyes barely rolling*)

Please. I won't escape.
(*His words sound corny tinny stupid dropped in such silence*)
Please, I won't try again. Just tell me where I am?
(*The silence again. For a while no movement,* COURT *is frozen, stiff, with only eyes sneaking, now they stop, he's frozen, cannot move, staring off into the cold darkness. A chain, slightly, more, now heavier, dragged bent, wiggled slowly, light now heavily in the darkness, from another direction. Chains. They're dragged, like things are pulling them across the earth. The chains. And now low chanting voices, moaning, with incredible pain and despair, the voices press just softly behind the chains, for a few seconds, so very very briefly then gone. And silence.* COURT *does not move. His eyes roll a little back and around. He bends his knees dipping his head bending. He moans . . .*)

COURT

Just tell me where I am?

VOICE

Heaven.
(*The* VOICE *is cool and businesslike.* COURT'S *eyes, head raise an imperceptible trifle. He begins to pull his arms slowly to his sides, and clap them together. The lights dim, and only* COURT *is seen in dimmer illumination. The* VOICE *again . . .*)
Heaven.
(*Pause*)
Welcome.

COURT (*Mumbling*)

I never understood . . . these things are so confusing.
(*His head jerks like he's suddenly heard Albert Ayler. It raises, his whole body jerks around like suddenly animate ragdoll. He does a weird dance like a marionette jiggling and waggling*)
You'll wonder what the devil-meant. A jiggedy bobbidy fool. You'll wonder what the devil-sent. Diggedy dobbidy cool. Ah man.
(*Singing*)
Ah man, you'll wonder who the devil-sent. And what was heaven heaven heaven.
(*This is like a funny joke-dance, with sudden funniness from* COURT, *then suddenly as before he stops frozen again, eyes rolling, no other sound heard. Now a scream, and white hooded* MEN *push a greasy-head nigger lady across in front of* COURT. *They are pulling her hair, and feeling her ass. One whispers from time to time in her ear. She screams and bites occasionally, occasionally kicking*)

HOOD 1

(*To the* VOICE) She's drunk.
  (*Now to* COURT)
You want to smell her breath?

COURT

(*Frightened also sickened at the sight, embarrassed*) N-no. I don't want to. I smell it from here. She drinks and stinks and brings our whole race down.

HOOD 2

Ain't it the truth!

VOICE

Grind her into poison jelly. Smear it on her daughter's head.

HOOD 1

Right, Your Honor. You got a break, sister.
  (*They go off*)
Hey, uncle, you sure you don't want to smell her breath?
  (COURT *shivers "No"*)

VOICE

Royal, you have concealed a murderer, and we have your punishment ready for you. Are you ready?

COURT

What? No. I want a trial. Please a trial. I deserve that. I'm a good man.

VOICE

Royal, you're not a man!

COURT

Please . . . .
  (*Voice breaking*)
Your Honor, a trial. A simple one, very quick, nothing fancy . . . I'm very conservative . . . no frills or loud colors, a simple concrete black toilet paper trial.

VOICE

And funeral.
  (*Now two* MEN IN HOODS, *white work gloves, and suits, very sporty, come in with a stretcher. A black man is dead on it. There is long very piped applause. "Yea. Yea."*)

HOOD 1

It's the Prince, Your Honor. We banged him down.

VOICE

He's dead?

HOOD 2

Yes. A nigger did it for us.

VOICE

Conceal the body in a stone. And sink the stone deep under the ocean.
Call the newspapers and give the official history. Make sure his voice
is in that stone too, or

(*Heavy nervous pause*)

. . . just go ahead.

HOOD 1

Of course Your Honor.

(*Looks to* COURT, *almost as an afterthought*)

You want to smell his breath?

(*They go out*)

COURT

(*Mumbling, still very frightened*) No . . . no . . . I have nothing to do
with any of this. I'm a good man. I have a car. A home.

(*Running down*)

A club.

(*Looks up pleading*)

Please there's some mistake. Isn't there? I've done nothing wrong. I
have a family. I work in the Post Office, I'm a supervisor. I've worked
for thirty years. I've done nothing wrong.

VOICE

Shut up whimpering pig. Shut up and get ready for sentencing. It'll be
hard on you, you can bet that.

COURT

(*A little life, he sees he's faced with danger*) But tell me what I've
done. I can remember no criminal, no murderer I've housed. I work
eight hours, then home, and television, dinner, then bowling. I've
harbored no murderers. I don't know any. I'm a good man.

VOICE

Shut up liar. Do you know this man?

(*An image is flashed on the screen behind him. It is a rapidly
shifting series of faces. Malcolm. Patrice. Robert Williams. Garvey.
Dead nigger kids killed by the police. Medgar Evers*)

COURT

What?

VOICE

I asked you do you know this man? I'm asking again, for the last time.
There's no need to lie.

COURT

But this is many men, many faces. They shift so fast I cannot tell who
they are . . . or what is meant. It's so confusing.

VOICE

Don't lie, Royal. We know all about you. You are guilty. Look at that face. You know this man.

COURT

I do?
(*In rising terror*)
No. No. I don't, I never saw that man, it's so many faces, I've never seen those faces . . . never . . .

VOICE

Look closer, Royal. You cannot get away with what you've done. Look more closely. You recognize that face . . . don't you? The face of the murderer you've sheltered all these years. Look, you liar, look at that face.

COURT

No, no, no . . . I don't know them. I can't be forced into admitting something I never did. Uhhh . . . I have worked. My God, I've worked. I've meant to do the right thing. I've tried to be a . . .
(*The faces shift, a long slow wail, like moan, like secret screaming has underscored the flashing faces . . . now it rises sharply to screaming point thrusts.* COURT *wheels around to face the image on the screen, directly. He begins shouting loud as the voices . . .*)

COURT

No, I've tried . . . please I never wanted anything but peace . . . please, I tried to be a man. I did. I lost my . . . heart . . . please it was so deep, I wanted to do the right thing, just to do the right thing. I wanted . . . everything to be . . . all right. Oh, please . . . please.

VOICE

Now tell me, whether you know that murderer's face or not. Tell me before you die!

COURT

No, no. I don't know him. I don't. I want to do the right thing. I don't know them.
(*Raises his hands in his agony*)
Oh, son . . . son . . . dear God, my flesh, forgive me . . .
(*Begins to weep and shake*)
my sons.
(*He clutches his body shaken throughout by his ugly sobs*)
Dear God . . .

VOICE

Just as we thought. You are the one. And you must be sentenced.

COURT

I must be sentenced. I am the one.
   (*Almost trancelike*)
I must be sentenced. I am the one.

VOICE

The murderer is dead. You must be sentenced alone.

COURT

(*As first realization*) The murderer . . . is . . . dead?

VOICE

And you must be sentenced. Now. Alone.

COURT

(*Voice rising, in panic, but catching it up short*) The murderer . . .
is dead.

VOICE

Yes. And your sentence is—

COURT

I must be sentenced . . . alone. Where is the murderer? Where is his
corpse?

VOICE

You will see it presently.

COURT

(*Head bowed*) God. And I am now to die like the murderer died?

VOICE

No.
   (*Long pause*)
We have decided to spare you. We admire your spirit. It is a compliment to know you can see the clearness of your fate, and the
rightness of it. That you love the beauty of the way of life you've
chosen here in the anonymous world. No one beautiful is guilty. So
how can you be? All the guilty have been punished. Or are being
punished. You are absolved of your crime, at this moment, because
of your infinite understanding of the compassionate God Of The Cross.
Whose head was cut off for you, to absolve you of your weakness. The
murderer is dead. The murderer is dead.
   (*Applause from the darkness*)

COURT

And I am not guilty now?

VOICE

No, you are free. Forever. It is asked only that you give the final
instruction.

COURT

Final instruction . . . I don't understand . . .

VOICE

Heroes! bring the last issue in.

(*The last two* HOODED MEN *return with a* YOUNG BLACK MAN *of about twenty. The boy does not look up. He walks stiff-legged to the center of* COURT. *He wears a large ankh around his neck. His head comes up slowly. He looks into* COURT's *face*)

YOUNG MAN

Peace.

(COURT *looks at his face; he begins to draw back. The* HOODED MAN *comes and places arms around* COURT's *shoulders*)

VOICE

Give him the instruction instrument.

(HOODED MAN *takes a pistol out of his pocket and gives it with great show to* COURT)

HOOD 1

The silver bullet is in the chamber. The gun is made of diamonds and gold.

HOOD 2

You get to keep it after the ceremony.

VOICE

And now, with the rite of instruction, the last bit of guilt falls from you as if it was never there, Court Royal. Now, at last, you can go free. Perform the rite, Court Royal, the final instruction.

COURT

What? No. I don't understand.

VOICE

The final instruction is the death of the murderer. The murderer is dead and must die, with each gift of our God. This gift is the cleansing of guilt, and the bestowal of freedom.

COURT

But you told me the murderer was dead, already.

VOICE

It *is* already. The murderer has been sentenced. You have only to carry out the rite.

COURT

But you told me the murderer was dead.

(*Starts to back away*)

You told me . . . you said I would be sentenced alone.

VOICE

The murderer *is* dead. This is his shadow. This one is not real. This is the myth of the murderer. His last fleeting astral projection. It is the murderer's myth that we ask you to instruct. To bind it forever . . . with death.

COURT

I don't . . . Why do . . . you said I was not guilty. That my guilt had fallen away.

VOICE

The rite must be finished. This ghost must be lost in cold space. Court Royal, this is your destiny. This act was done by you a million years ago. This is only the memory of it. This is only a rite. You cannot kill a shadow, a fleeting bit of light and memory. This is only a rite, to show that you would be guilty but for the cleansing rite. The shadow is killed in place of the killer. The shadow for reality. So reality can exist beautiful like it is. This is your destiny, and your already lived-out life. Instruct, Court Royal, as the centuries pass, and bring you back to your natural reality. Without guilt. Without shame. Pure and blameless, your soul washed

(*Pause*)

white as snow.

COURT

(*Falling to his knees, arms extended as in loving prayer, to a bright light falling on him, racing around the space*)

Oh, yes . . . I hear you. And have waited, for this promise to be fulfilled.

VOICE

This is the fulfillment. You must, at this moment, enter into the covenant of guiltless silence. Perform the rite, Court Royal.

COURT

Oh, yes, yes . . . I want so much to be happy . . . and relaxed.

VOICE

Then carry out your destiny . . .

COURT

Yes, yes . . . I will . . . I will be happy . . .

(*He rises, pointing the gun straight at the* YOUNG BOY's *face*)

I must be . . . fulfilled . . . I will . . .

(*He fires the weapon into* BOY's *face. One short sound comes from the* BOY's *mouth:*)

YOUNG BOY

Papa.

(*He falls.* COURT *stands looking at the dead* BOY *with the gun still up. He is motionless*)

VOICE

Case dismissed, Court Royal . . . you are free.

COURT

(*Now suddenly to life, the lights go up full. He has the gun in his hand. He drops, flings it away from him*)

My soul is as white as snow.
   (*He wanders up to the body*)
My soul is as white as snow.
   (*He starts to wander off the stage*)
White as snow. I'm free. I'm free. My life is a beautiful thing.
   (*He mopes slowly toward the edge of the stage, then suddenly a
   brighter mood strikes him. Raising his hand as if calling someone*)
Hey, Louise, have you seen my bowling bag? I'm going down to the
alley for a minute.
   (*He is frozen. The lights dim to . . .*)

                              BLACK

RESPONSES: Questions for Writing and Discussion

1. Reread the charge against Court Royal very carefully. He is
accused of harboring a murderer. What does this mean outside the
symbolic context of the play? What does it mean in terms of the
realities of black experience in America today? (Why does Court
keep insisting to the judge that he has done nothing and does not
understand why he should be on trial?)

2. The young man who is dragged in and said to be the murderer
in question cries "Papa" at the instant he is shot by Court. Do you
think he is really the hero's son? Or a symbol? Or perhaps both?
Relate this character and his death to your perceptions of the play's
possibilities of meaning.

3. Why is Court's attorney described as a house slave in a
wrinkled tuxedo? What does he mean when he tells his client that he
has always looked like this?

4. This play is by a black playwright who uses "A Coon Show"
as a subtitle, and the word "nigger" liberally appears throughout the
dialogue. In what context does Baraka employ such terms? Since, as
has been said, Baraka writes primarily for a black audience, what
effect does he want to have by such language?

5. Explain the final line of the play. Why is there such an abrupt
change in subject matter and locale? (If we place Court back in the
real world at this moment, what relevance to a real black family and
to bowling bags have the events which have transpired up to this
line?)

6. In your opinion, is there anything wrong with a man's wanting
to bowl or having a job and a wife named Louise and being afraid to
give up certain security for the uncertainties of the higher loyalties
the play suggests are being ignored?

7. We don't know very much about Louise, but, projecting the play's theme into real life, can you talk about the role of the black wife in terms of the liberation movement? Technically any black woman enjoys the status of "sister," just as any black man may call any other black man "brother." But in actuality a real-life Louise might have children who must be cared for and perhaps a job to which she must report each day in order to put food on the table. A real-life Louise might already have lost her husband to the movement. In the cause of black unity and nationalism what do you think is expected of the black woman?

8. Would some alternative to the present family model prove more effective in promoting the cause of black nationalism? If you believe so, describe your alternative; show how it would work and how things would be better because of it. If you do not believe so, show why (a) black nationalism is not an important or desirable goal or (b) the preservation of the family is vital if the movement is to succeed.

9. Sociologists and psychologists who are alarmed at the rising divorce rate throughout America and rising statistics on desertion and numbers of children brought into the world never to know their fathers, sometimes imply that the "breakdown" of the family (in both black and white America) is symptomatic of many disturbing things happening to our society. On the other hand, this play appears to say that, in order to preserve the family, one has to make too many compromises with the establishment and the present economic system. Do we have a vicious circle here? Do we need a strong family unit to make the system go? And does the system betray the Human Worth of those who faithfully serve it?

10. Look into the future—one in which the family has all but disappeared. What is it like? Are people happier? Why, or why not? Is something missing? Has something been gained that wasn't there before?

THE DEATH OF THE HIRED MAN
Robert Frost

It is an old claim that Human Worth is measured by the degree to which a person reaches out beyond ego and involves himself honestly and deeply in the concerns of others. Literature is filled with many declarations of such

selfless love. Often the words sound impressive but hollow. In a few instances, such as the following poem, the affirmation of human brotherhood
is made less as a glorious statement than as an unalterable matter of fact.

As in all of **Robert Frost's (1875–1963)** work, the meaning is hardly
insisted upon. It seems to be inseparable from the situation—as though just
waiting for both poet and reader to find it. What does one do when the
hired man comes "home" and one isn't sure that he likes it? The fact is
that Silas *is* there, in the kitchen, all the while husband and wife are discussing his fate. We are responsible for each other because we have to be.
Life forces it upon us. Frost doesn't glorify the concept. What would be the
point?

The quiet wisdom behind the poem's simple incident is an example of
the approach Robert Frost takes to the business of living. Carl Van Doren
has called his poetry "the sound of a Yankee voice," and in truth it embodies
the classic traits of the New England mind: restrained, shrewd, unsenti-
mental but not unfeeling, and, above all, realistic. Perhaps the life style
implicit in the poems derives from a centuries-old tradition of Yankee closeness to nature, being attuned to all her subtle changes, and growing a tough
and hardy outer skin that does not for all its hardships deny life. Frost's
fundamental statement to the world is that life after all is good; it is only
one's expectations that can be cruel.

The poetic style of Frost grows naturally out of the man himself, and
in this respect he may be taken as a pure example of the American poet.
That is, he writes of ordinary people and ordinary events in ordinary
language; and yet it is his gift that he is able to make memorable utterances
out of these ingredients. Probably no other poet in history has done more
with the simplest and most unliterary of words.

The Death of the Hired Man

Mary sat musing on the lamp-flame at the table,
Waiting for Warren. When she heard his step,
She ran on tiptoe down the darkened passage
To meet him in the doorway with the news
And put him on his guard. "Silas is back."   5
She pushed him outward with her through the door
And shut it after her. "Be kind," she said.
She took the market things from Warren's arms

And set them on the porch, then drew him down
To sit beside her on the wooden steps.   10

"When was I ever anything but kind to him?
But I'll not have the fellow back," he said.
"I told him so last haying, didn't I?
If he left then, I said, that ended it.
What good is he? Who else will harbor him   15
At his age for the little he can do?
What help he is there's no depending on.
Off he goes always when I need him most.
He thinks he ought to earn a little pay,
Enough at least to buy tobacco with,   20
So he won't have to beg and be beholden.
'All right,' I say, 'I can't afford to pay
Any fixed wages, though I wish I could.'
'Someone else can.' 'Then someone else will have to.'
I shouldn't mind his bettering himself   25
If that was what it was. You can be certain,
When he begins like that, there's someone at him
Trying to coax him off with pocket money—
In haying time, when any help is scarce.
In winter he comes back to us. I'm done."   30
"Sh! not so loud: he'll hear you," Mary said.

"I want him to: he'll have to soon or late."

"He's worn out. He's asleep beside the stove.
When I came up from Rowe's I found him here,
Huddled against the barn door fast asleep,   35
A miserable sight, and frightening, too—
You needn't smile—I didn't recognize him—
I wasn't looking for him—and he's changed.
Wait till you see."
                    "Where did you say he'd been?"
"He didn't say. I dragged him to the house,   40
And gave him tea and tried to make him smoke.
I tried to make him talk about his travels.
Nothing would do: he just kept nodding off."

"What did he say? Did he say anything?"

"But little."
              "Anything? Mary, confess   45
He said he'd come to ditch the meadow for me."

"Warren!"
      "But did he? I just want to know."

"Of course he did. What would you have him say?
Surely you wouldn't grudge the poor old man
Some humble way to save his self-respect.   50
He added, if you really care to know,
He meant to clear the upper pasture, too.
That sounds like something you have heard before?
Warren, I wish you could have heard the way
He jumbled everything. I stopped to look   55
Two or three times—he made me feel so queer—
To see if he was talking in his sleep.
He ran on Harold Wilson—you remember—
The boy you had in haying four years since.
He's finished school, and teaching in his college.   60
Silas declares you'll have to get him back.
He says they two will make a team for work:
Between them they will lay this farm as smooth!
The way he mixed that in with other things.
He thinks young Wilson a likely lad, though daft   65
On education—you know how they fought
All through July under the blazing sun,
Silas up on the cart to build the load,
Harold along beside to pitch it on."

"Yes, I took care to keep well out of earshot."   70

"Well, those days trouble Silas like a dream.
You wouldn't think they would. How some things linger!
Harold's young college-boy's assurance piqued him.
After so many years he still keeps finding
Good arguments he sees he might have used.   75
I sympathize. I know just how it feels
To think of the right thing to say too late.
Harold's associated in his mind with Latin.
He asked me what I thought of Harold's saying
He studied Latin, like the violin,   80
Because he liked it—that an argument!
He said he couldn't make the boy believe
He could find water with a hazel prong—
Which showed how much good school had ever done him.
He wanted to go over that. But most of all   85
He thinks if he could have another chance
To teach him how to build a load of hay——"

"I know, that's Silas' one accomplishment.
He bundles every forkful in its place,
And tags and numbers it for future reference,   90
So he can find and easily dislodge it
In the unloading. Silas does that well.
He takes it out in bunches like big birds' nests.
You never see him standing on the hay
He's trying to lift, straining to lift himself."   95

"He thinks if he could teach him that, he'd be
Some good perhaps to someone in the world.
He hates to see a boy the fool of books.
Poor Silas, so concerned for other folk,
And nothing to look backward to with pride,   100
And nothing to look forward to with hope,
So now and never any different."

Part of a moon was falling down the west,
Dragging the whole sky with it to the hills.
Its light poured softly in her lap. She saw it   105
And spread her apron to it. She put out her hand
Among the harplike morning-glory strings,
Taut with the dew from garden bed to eaves,
As if she played unheard some tenderness
That wrought on him beside her in the night.   110
"Warren," she said, "he has come home to die:
You needn't be afraid he'll leave you this time."

"Home," he mocked gently.

                    "Yes, what else but home?
It all depends on what you mean by home.
Of course he's nothing to us, any more
Than was the hound that came a stranger to us
Out of the woods, worn out upon the trail."

"Home is the place where, when you have to go there,
They have to take you in."

                    "I should have called it
Something you somehow haven't to deserve."

Warren leaned out and took a step or two,
Picked up a little stick, and brought it back
And broke it in his hand and tossed it by.
"Silas has better claim on us you think
Than on his brother? Thirteen little miles

As the road winds would bring him to his door.
Silas has walked that far no doubt today.
Why doesn't he go there? His brother's rich,
A somebody—director in the bank."

"He never told us that."

                "We know it though."

"I think his brother ought to help, of course.
I'll see to that if there is need. He ought of right
To take him in, and might be willing to—
He may be better than appearances.
But have some pity on Silas. Do you think
If he had any pride in claiming kin
Or anything he looked for from his brother,
He'd keep so still about him all this time?"

"I wonder what's between them."

                      "I can tell you.
Silas is what he is—we wouldn't mind him—
But just the kind that kinsfolk can't abide.
He never did a thing so very bad.
He don't know why he isn't quite as good
As anybody. Worthless though he is,
He won't be made ashamed to please his brother."

"*I* can't think Si ever hurt anyone."

"No, but he hurt my heart the way he lay
And rolled his old head on that sharp-edged chair-back.
He wouldn't let me put him on the lounge.
You must go in and see what you can do.
I made the bed up for him there tonight.
You'll be surprised at him—how much he's broken.
His working days are done; I'm sure of it."

"I'd not be in a hurry to say that."

"I haven't been. Go, look, see for yourself.
But, Warren, please remember how it is:
He's come to help you ditch the meadow.
He has a plan. You mustn't laugh at him.
He may not speak of it, and then he may.
I'll sit and see if that small sailing cloud
Will hit or miss the moon."

It hit the moon.
Then there were three there, making a dim row,
The moon, the little silver cloud, and she.

Warren returned—too soon, it seemed to her,
Slipped to her side, caught up her hand and waited.

"Warren?" she questioned.

"Dead," was all he answered.

RESPONSES: Questions for Writing and Discussion

1. What was the reason for the original dispute with Warren that sent Silas away, supposedly never to return? Given our society and its value system (especially the importance of sound business thinking), did Warren have a right to feel as he did about Silas' returning?

2. Have Mary and Warren been overly kind to Silas in the past? ("In winter time he comes back to us.") Have they "spoiled" Silas? Have they been doing a duty all people should perform? If your answer to this last question is yes, indicate who expects such kindness from people and by what right such expectations are entertained.

3. From what both husband and wife say, we learn a great deal about the personality of Silas. But the description of Silas' relationship with Harold Wilson, the school boy and part-time farm hand, shows this perhaps most clearly. Fill in the blanks about Silas from your own imagination. Describe the man as fully as possible. Can you think of any reason Frost would spend so much time giving information about Silas? Presumably the poem would be lacking something without it. What?

4. The key to an understanding of the poem may lie in the interchange between husband and wife on the subject of home, beginning with the line

"Home," he mocked gently.

and ending with the lines

"I should have called it
Something you somehow haven't to deserve."

What is Warren's view of home? Mary's? Yours?

5. Silas apparently has had a falling out some time ago with his rich brother—"A somebody—director at the bank." Can you fill in the details and offer an account of what was "between them"? Should the brother have put himself out to keep up with Silas and the state of his finances and health? Should Silas have demanded that his brother

take him in? Is Silas more his brother's responsibility than he is Mary's and Warren's?

6. Just before the climax of the poem—the revelation that Silas is dead—Frost has Mary casually say she intends to sit there and watch to see whether

> that small sailing cloud
> Will hit or miss the moon.

What in the world have clouds and the moon to do with what is going on in this poem?

7. While husband and wife have been debating and discussing the problem of Silas, the hired man is curled up by the stove, dying. Since Frost has used the world "Death" in the poem's title, we are prepared for the revelation and know from the outset that the argument is purely academic at this point anyway. What statement do you think Frost is making by the foregone certainty that Silas will die in that house whether Warren likes it or not?

JESUS THE MAN
Kahlil Gibran

Without going into questions of dogma, theology, or the historical validity of claims for his divinity, millions have simply accepted Jesus as a very real being. Millions have thought of Jesus as a personal friend and a loving brother. "He walks with me and he talks with me," goes the old hymn, and it tells much of the whole story of the appeal and popularity Jesus has exerted for centuries. In Jesus, Western man's idea of God many have acquired its most accessible and humanized personification. It could also be said that in Jesus Western humanity acquired its most godlike form—a lasting model of Human Worth.

If organized religion in the United States is having problems today keeping its flocks intact, the hold of Jesus seems to be as strong as ever. The perpetuation of war, poverty, and oppression have demonstrated to no few that the philosophy of Jesus may be the only solution for human ills. Advocates interpret the disasters that have blighted human history as sure signs of what happens when that philosophy is not heeded. For them Jesus points the way to the only possible world that can endure—one in which the individual finds fulfillment in loving and being loved by friend and stranger alike; a world in which there is no longer any reason for hostility or bloodshed, for either crime or a police state.

But interest in Jesus has been and continues to be varied indeed. For some Jesus never existed at all—or at least not as the perfect man Christian mythology has created. For some he *was* the son of God sent down to die for the sins of man, making redemption possible once and for all, with no further discussion necessary. For others the man Jesus must have been an impossible idealist, perhaps even a fool, preachng a gospel for which the world will never be ready. Still others are in two minds: Maybe there was an historical Jesus and maybe he said some of the things attributed to him; but can we really be certain of his motives? A recent study of the personality of Jesus (Hugh Schoenfield, *The Passover Plot*) even suggests that the crucifixion was a fraudulent attempt by a purely human being to prove to people that he was the promised Messiah.

Nearly half a century ago **Kahlil Gibran (1883–1931)**, a mystic and poet, born in Lebanon of Syrian parentage, well known for his collection of visionary poems *The Prophet*, recognized the fascination inherent in treating Jesus as a human being. *Jesus: The Son of Man*, from which our selections are taken, is a modern poet's version of the New Testament; it presents Jesus from a number of human viewpoints: some positive, some negative, some not so sure. These poems taken together offer a closeup of an astonishing phenomenon, seemingly captured as it actually took place. Gibran's poetic gifts bring to life the complexities of the Jesus question and allow the reader who so desires to reflect soberly and objectively on the subject.

Jesus the Man

Joseph of Arimathæa[1]

You would know the primal aim of Jesus, and I would fain tell you. But none can touch with fingers the life of the blessed vine, nor see the sap that feeds the branches.

And though I have eaten of the grapes and have tasted the new vintage at the winepress, I cannot tell you all.

I can only relate what I know of Him.

Our Master and our Belovèd lived but three prophet's seasons.

---

[1] A wealthy Israelite who begged Pilate for the body of Jesus and buried it in his own rock-hewn tomb.

Gene Mathis

He spoke of nought then but the other man—the neighbor, the roadfellow, the stranger, and our childhood's playmates.   *Kahlil Gibran*

They were the spring of His song, the summer of His ecstasy, and the autumn of His passion; and each season was a thousand years.

The spring of His song was spent in Galilee. It was there that He gathered His lovers about Him, and it was on the shores of the blue lake that He first spoke of the Father, and of our release and our freedom.

By the Lake of Galilee we lost ourselves to find our way to the Father; and oh, the little, little loss that turned to such gain.

It was there the angels sang in our ears and bade us leave the arid land for the garden of heart's desire.

He spoke of fields and green pastures; of the slopes of Lebanon where the white lilies are heedless of the caravans passing in the dust of the valley.

He spoke of the wild brier that smiles in the sun and yields its incense to the passing breeze.

And He would say, "The lilies and the brier live but a day, yet that day is eternity spent in freedom."

And one evening as we sat beside the stream He said, "Behold the brook and listen to its music. Forever shall it seek the sea, and though it is for ever seeking, it sings its mystery from noon to noon.

"Would that you seek the Father as the brook seeks the sea."

Then came the summer of His ecstasy, and the June of His love was upon us. He spoke of naught then but the other man—the neighbor, the road-fellow, the stranger, and our childhood's playmates.

He spoke of the traveller journeying from the east to Egypt, of the ploughman coming home with his oxen at eventide, of the chance guest led by dusk to our door.

And he would say, "Your neighbor is your unknown self made visible. His face shall be reflected in your still waters, and if you gaze therein you shall behold your own countenance.

"Should you listen in the night, you shall hear him speak, and his words shall be the throbbing of your own heart.

"Be unto him that which you would have him be unto you.

"This is my law, and I shall say it unto you, and unto your children, and they unto their children until time is spent and generations are no more."

And on another day He said, "You shall not be yourself alone. You are in the deeds of other men, and they though unknowing are with you all your days.

"They shall not commit a crime and your hand not be with their hand.

"They shall not fall down but that you shall also fall down; and they shall not rise but that you shall rise with them.

"Their road to the sanctuary is your road, and when they seek the wasteland you too seek with them.

"You and your neighbor are two seeds sown in the field. Together you grow and together you shall sway in the wind. And neither of you shall claim the field. For a seed on its way to growth claims not even its own ecstasy.

"Today I am with you. Tomorrow I go westward; but ere I go, I say unto you that your neighbor is your unknown self made visible. Seek him in love that you may know yourself, for only in that knowledge shall you become my brothers."

Then came the autumn of His passion.

And He spoke to us of freedom, even as He had spoken in Galilee in the spring of His song; but now His words sought our deeper understanding.

He spoke of leaves that sing only when blown upon the wind; and of man as a cup filled by the ministering angel of the day to quench the thirst of another angel. Yet whether that cup is full or empty it shall stand crystalline upon the board of the Most High.

He said, "You are the cup and you are the wine. Drink of yourselves to the dregs; or else remember me and you shall be quenched."

And on our way to the southward He said, "Jerusalem, which stands in pride upon the height, shall descend to the depth of Jahannum the dark valley, and in the midst of her desolation I shall stand alone.

"The temple shall fall to dust, and around the portico you shall hear the cry of widows and orphans; and men in their haste to escape shall not know the faces of their brothers, for fear shall be upon them all.

"But even there, if two of you shall meet and utter my name and look to the west, you shall see me, and these my words shall again visit your ears."

And when we reached the hill of Bethany, He said, "Let us go to Jerusalem. The city awaits us. I will enter the gate riding upon a colt, and I will speak to the multitude.

"Many are there who would chain me, and many who would put out my flame, but in my death you shall find life and you shall be free.

"They shall seek the breath that hovers betwixt heart and mind as the swallow hovers between the field and his nest. But my breath has already escaped them, and they shall not overcome me.

"The walls that my Father has built around me shall not fall down, and the acre He has made holy shall not be profaned.

"When the dawn shall come, the sun will crown my head and I

shall be with you to face the day. And that day shall be long, and the world shall not see its eventide.

"The scribes and the Pharisees say the earth is thirsty for my blood. I would quench the thirst of the earth with my blood. But the drops shall rise oak trees and maple, and the east wind shall carry the acorns to other lands."

And then He said, "Judea would have a king, and she would march against the legions of Rome.

"I shall not be her king. The diadems of Zion were fashioned for lesser brows. And the ring of Solomon is small for this finger.

"Behold my hand. See you not that it is overstrong to hold a sceptre, and over-sinewed to wield a common sword?

"Nay, I shall not command Syrian flesh against Roman. But you with my words shall wake that city, and my spirits shall speak to her second dawn.

"My words shall be an invisible army with horses and chariots, and without ax or spear I shall conquer the priests of Jerusalem, and the Caesars.

"I shall not sit upon a throne where slaves have sat and ruled other slaves. Nor will I rebel against the sons of Italy.

"But I shall be a tempest in their sky, and a song in their soul.

"And I shall be remembered.

"They shall call me Jesus the Anointed."

These things He said outside the walls of Jerusalem before He entered the city.

And His words are graven as with chisels.

Nathaniel[2]

They say that Jesus of Nazareth was humble and meek.

They say that though He was a just man and righteous, He was a weakling, and was often confounded by the strong and the powerful; and that when He stood before men of authority He was but a lamb among lions.

But I say that Jesus had authority over men, and that He knew His power and proclaimed it among the hills of Galilee, and in the cities of Judea and Phœnicia.

What man yielding and soft would say, "I am life, and I am the way to truth"?

---

[2] One of the first alleged disciples of Jesus from Cana in Galilee, though his name does not appear on the lists of the Twelve. The name itself means "God has given." Modern scholarship identifies him with Bartholomew, mentioned in John 1: 47.

What man meek and lowly would say, "I am in God, our Father; and our God, the Father, is in me"?

What man unmindful of His own strength would say, "He who believes not in me believes not in this life nor in the life everlasting"?

What man uncertain of tomorrow would proclaim, "Your world shall pass away and be naught but scattered ashes ere my words shall pass away"?

Was He doubtful of Himself when He said to those who would confound Him with a harlot, "He who is without sin, let him cast a stone"?

Did He fear authority when He drove the money-changers from the court of the temple, though they were licensed by the priests?

Were His wings shorn when He cried aloud, "My kingdom is above your earthly kingdoms"?

Was He seeking shelter in words when He repeated again and yet again, "Destroy this temple and I will rebuild it in three days"?

Was it a coward who shook His hand in the face of the authorities and pronounced them "liars, low, filthy, and degenerate"?

Shall a man bold enough to say these things to those who ruled Judea be deemed meek and humble?

Nay. The eagle builds not his nest in the weeping willow. And the lion seeks not his den among the ferns.

I am sickened and the bowels within me stir and rise when I hear the faint-hearted call Jesus humble and meek, that they may justify their own faintheartedness; and when the downtrodden, for comfort and companionship, speak of Jesus as a worm shining by their side.

Yea, my heart is sickened by such men. It is the mighty hunter I would preach, and the mountainous spirit unconquerable.

Thomas[3]

My grandfather who was a lawyer once said, "Let us observe truth, but only when truth is made manifest unto us."

When Jesus called me I heeded Him, for His command was more potent than my will; yet I kept my counsel.

When He spoke and the others were swayed like branches in the wind, I listened immovable. Yet I loved Him.

Three years ago He left us, a scattered company to sing His name, and to be His witnesses unto the nations.

---

[3] Called Didymus, he was one of the Twelve Apostles. According to John (20: 24-29) he doubted until he had received tangible proof of the resurrection. This was to place his hand on the wounds.

At that time I was called Thomas the Doubter. The shadow of my grandfather was still upon me, and always I would have truth made manifest.

I would even put my hand in my own wound to feel the blood ere I would believe in my pain.

Now a man who loves with his heart yet holds a doubt in his mind, is but a slave in a galley who sleeps at his oar and dreams of his freedom, till the lash of the master wakes him.

I myself was that slave, and I dreamed of freedom, but the sleep of my grandfather was upon me. My flesh needed the whip of my own day.

Even in the presence of the Nazarene I had closed my eyes to see my hands chained to the oar.

Doubt is a pain too lonely to know that faith is his twin brother.

Doubt is a foundling unhappy and astray, and though his own mother who gave him birth should find him and enfold him, he would withdraw in caution and in fear.

For Doubt will not know truth till his wounds are healed and restored.

I doubted Jesus until He made Himself manifest to me, and thrust my own hand into His very wounds.

Then indeed I believed, and after that I was rid of my yesterday and the yesterdays of my forefathers.

The dead in me buried their dead; and the living shall live for the Anointed King, even for Him who was the Son of Man.

Yesterday they told me that I must go and utter His name among the Persians and the Hindus.

I shall go. And from this day to my last day, at dawn and at eventide, I shall see my Lord rising in majesty and I shall hear Him speak.

A Widow in Galilee

My son was my first and my only born. He labored in our field and he was contented until he heard the man called Jesus speaking to the multitude.

Then my son suddenly became different, as if a new spirit, foreign and unwholesome, had embraced his spirit.

He abandoned the field and the garden; and he abandoned me also. He became worthless, a creature of the highways.

That man Jesus of Nazareth was evil, for what good man would separate a son from his mother?

The last thing my child said to me was this: "I am going with one of His disciples to the North Country. My life is established upon the Nazarene. You have given me birth, and for that I am grateful to you. But I needs must go. Am I not leaving with you our rich land, and all our silver and gold? I shall take naught but this garment and this staff."

Thus my son spoke, and departed.

And now the Romans and the priests have laid hold upon Jesus and crucified Him; and they have done well.

A man who would part mother and son would not be godly.

The man who sends our children to the cities of the Gentiles cannot be our friend.

I know my son will not return to me. I saw it in his eyes. And for this I hate Jesus of Nazareth who caused me to be alone in this un-ploughed field and this withered garden.

And I hate all those who praise Him.

Not many days ago they told me that Jesus once said, "My father and my mother and my brethren are those who hear my word and follow me."

But why should sons leave their mothers to follow His footsteps?

And why should the milk of my breast be forgotten for a fountain not yet tasted? And the warmth of my arms be forsaken for the North-land, cold and unfriendly?

Aye, I hate the Nazarene, and I shall hate Him to the end of my days, for He has robbed me of my first-born, my only son.

Jotham of Nazareth to a Roman

My friend, you like all other Romans would conceive life rather than live it. You would rule lands rather than be ruled by the spirit.

You would conquer races and be cursed by them rather than stay in Rome and be blest and happy.

You think but of armies marching and of ships launched into the sea.

How shall you then understand Jesus of Nazareth, a man simple and alone, who came without armies or ships, to establish a kingdom in the heart and an empire in the free spaces of the soul?

How shall you understand this man who was not a warrior, but who came with the power of the mighty ether?

He was not a god, He was a man like unto ourselves; but in Him the myrrh of the earth rose to meet the frankincense of the sky; and in His words our lisping embraced the whispering of the unseen; and in His voice we heard a song unfathomable.

Aye, Jesus was a man and not a god, and therein lies our wonder and our surprise.

But you Romans wonder not save at the gods, and no man shall surprise you. Therefore you understand not the Nazarene.

He belonged to the youth of the mind and you belong to its old age.

You govern us today; but let us wait another day.

Who knows but that this man with neither armies nor ships shall govern tomorrow?

We who follow the spirit shall sweat blood while journeying after Him. But Rome shall lie a white skeleton in the sun.

We shall suffer much, yet we shall endure and we shall live. But Rome must needs fall into the dust.

Yet if Rome, when humbled and made low, shall pronounce His name, He will heed her voice. And He will breathe new life into her bones that she may rise again, a city among the cities of the earth.

But this He shall do without legions, nor with slaves to oar His galleys. He will be alone.

Cyborea the Mother of Judas

My son was a good man and upright. He was tender and kind to me, and he loved his kin and his countrymen. And he hated our enemies, the cursèd Romans, who wear purple cloth though they spin no thread nor sit at any loom; and who reap and gather where they have not ploughed nor sowed the seed.

My son was but seventeen when he was caught shooting arrows at the Roman legion passing through our vineyard.

Even at that age he would speak to the other youths of the glory of Israel, and he would utter many strange things that I did not understand.

He was my son, my only son.

He drank life from these breasts now dry, and he took his first steps in this garden, grasping these fingers that are now like trembling reeds.

With these selfsame hands, young and fresh then like the grapes of Lebanon, I put away his first sandals in a linen kerchief that my mother had given me. I still keep them there in that chest, beside the window.

He was my first-born, and when he took his first step, I too took my first step. For women travel not save when led by their children.

And now they tell me he is dead by his own hand; that he flung himself from the High Rock in remorse because he had betrayed his friend Jesus of Nazareth.

I know my son is dead. But I know he betrayed no one; for he loved his kin and hated none but the Romans.

My son sought the glory of Israel, and naught but that glory was upon his lips and in his deeds.

When he met Jesus on the highway he left me to follow Him. And in my heart I knew that he was wrong to follow any man.

When he bade me farewell I told him that he was wrong, but he listened not.

Our children do not heed us; like the high tide of today, they take no counsel with the high tide of yesterday.

I beg you question me no further about my son.

I loved him and I shall love him forevermore.

If love were in the flesh I would burn it out with hot irons and be at peace. But it is in the soul, unreachable.

And now I would speak no more. Go question another woman more honored than the mother of Judas.

Go to the mother of Jesus. The sword is in her heart also; she will tell you of me, and you will understand.

RESPONSES: Questions for Writing and Discussion

"Joseph of Arimathæa"

1. Of all the doctrines in the philosophy of Jesus the love for one's neighbor is central and no doubt the most difficult to realize. For many the very idea of such a love is unrealistic because it is unnatural to man. But the words of Joseph are filled with allusions to nature, and Jesus' doctrine of love is seen as being in accordance with nature's law. (Example: "For a seed on its way to growth claims not even its own ecstasy.") What is your feeling about the naturalness of love on so broad a scale?

2. Joseph reports Jesus as having said of Jerusalem: "I shall not be her king. The diadems of Zion were fashioned for lesser brows." This would seem to indicate that Jesus did not have political motives. But many have refused to believe this. Jesus is sometimes viewed as a seeker of worldly power. Can you think of at least one argument for or against this notion?

"Nathaniel"

3. In this poem we find exception taken to the traditional words "meek" and "humble" applied to Jesus, but rather, a view of Jesus as a "mighty hunter" and a "mountainous spirit." (Nietzsche considered Jesus a prime example of the superman.) Which view seems to fit Jesus as you understand his philosophy?

"Thomas"

4. The classic position of the doubting Thomas is one many share. That is, they would like to think all they have heard about Jesus is true but find it difficult to accept it without proof. Does it come down to a choice between faith and doubt? May one accept some of the story but not all? How? Which part of the story? Is a halfway position possible?

"A Widow in Galilee"

5. This mother has lost her son in the service of Christ, whom she cannot forgive for it. This opens the door for yet another view of Jesus: as a fanatic with a fanatic's cause and fanatical followers. Today we are witnessing a widespread revival of Jesus and his teachings. How do you look upon today's followers of Jesus? As fanatics? As people who have seen the light? What is a fanatic? What is a truly Christian person?

"Jotham of Nazareth to a Roman"

6. "He belonged to the youth of the mind and you belong to its old age." What are the two outlooks polarized in this statement? Is the philosophy of Jesus still young? Or has it long since entered *its* "old age"?

7. A prophecy is made: "Rome must needs fall into the dust." Does any nation that will not live by the philosophy of Jesus run the same risk? What would it mean for a nation to follow that philosophy? Would it work?

"Cyborea the Mother of Judas"

8. Gibran may have considerable insight into what such a woman might really have believed about her son. What is your attitude toward Judas, based on the facts as you understand them? Has he been misunderstood? Is it possible that he was truly a patriot of Jerusalem? Does he deserve his reputation as the arch betrayer of all time?

9. If Jesus were the son of God and if God is all powerful and all knowing, is it possible that Judas could have been part of a heavenly plan? If so, was his suicide an act of justice?

10. Cyborea implies at the end of her poem that she and Mary have much in common. What is it? (Try writing an imaginary dialogue between them as they meet the day after the Crucifixion.)

TRUE LOVE
Judith Viorst

This poem appears in a collection whose title tells most of the story: *It's Hard To Be Hip Over Thirty and Other Tragedies of Married Life*. The poet is a New York suburbanite, sophisticated, very much the crusading woman of today. Her poems express one marital crisis after another. Some reflect the poet's resentment at the sex role she is forced to play. After all, she "was looking forward to orgiastic Village pot parties and fleeting moments of passion, but wound up, instead, in the suburbs with a washer-drier, a car pool, and Gerber's strained bananas in her hair." Two things appear to have saved her: a sense of humor and a sense of reality.

True Love

It's true love because
I put on eyeliner and a concerto and make pungent
 observations about the great issues of the day
Even when there's no one here but him,
And because
I do not resent watching the Green Bay Packers
Even though I am philosophically opposed to football,
And because
When he is late for dinner and I know he must be
 either having an affair or lying dead in the
 middle of the street,
I always hope he's dead.

It's true love because
If he said quit drinking martinis but I kept drinking
 them and the next morning I couldn't get out of
 bed,
He wouldn't tell me he told me,
And because
He is willing to wear unironed undershorts

Out of respect for the fact that I am philosophically
    opposed to ironing,
And because
If his mother was drowning and I was drowning and
    he had to choose one of us to save,
He says he'd save me.

It's true love because
When he went to San Francisco on business while I
    had to stay home with the painters and the
    exterminator and the baby who was getting the
    chicken pox,
He understood why I hated him,
And because
When I said that playing the stock market was
    juvenile and irresponsible and then the stock I
    wouldn't let him buy went up twenty-six points,
I understood why he hated me,
And because
Despite cigarette cough, tooth decay, acid indigestion,
    dandruff, and other features of married life that
    tend to dampen the fires of passion,
We still feel something
We can call
True love.

IF EVERYTHING HAPPENS
THAT CAN'T BE DONE

E. E. Cummings

It is almost impossible to try to capsule the nature and significance of **E. E. Cummings'** (1894–1960) poetry in a brief introduction. To elude categorization was probably one of his intentions, and to this extent he may also be labeled "representatively" American. He is the self-conscious non-conformist that all American writers want to be in theory, but, unlike such contemporaries as Frost and MacLeish, who say American things without altogether abandoning pre-established rhythm and rhyme patterns, Cummings rewrites the poetry handbooks to suit himself. Like many American writers, he recognizes the problems of language and the barrier it erects between the self and reality. One of his aims in poetry has been to employ words in strange and startling ways (nouns as verbs, adjectives as nouns, and so forth) to force the reader to see and feel with new eyes.

Behind the sometimes radical experimentation, however, one finds very basic and honest themes: the joy of living, the goodness of loving, and the intrinsic Worth of "little" people everywhere. One critic has even described Cummings' major theme as "the all-importance of being nobody." A criticism of his work is that it is self-consciously radical, the work of a show-off rather than a true poet. But for several generations many readers of Cummings have responded eagerly to his life-affirmations, which at times seem to be those of a human being who somehow managed to retain the exuberance most of us had as children but have long since lost.

if everything happens that can't be done

if everything happens that can't be done
(and anything's righter
than books
could plan)
the stupidest teacher will almost guess
(with a run
skip
around we go yes)
there's nothing as something as one

one hasn't a why or because or although
(and buds know better
than books
don't grow)
one's anything old being everything new
(with a what
which
around we come who)
one's everyanything so

so world is a leaf so tree is a bough
(and birds sing sweeter

than books
tell how)
so here is away and so your is a my
(with a down
up
around again fly)
forever was never till now

now i love you and you love me
(and books are shuter
than books
can be)
and deep in the high that does nothing but fall
(with a shout
each
around we go all)
there's somebody calling who's we

we're anything brighter than even the sun
(we're everything greater
than books
might mean)
we're everyanything more than believe
(with a spin
leap
alive we're alive)
we're wonderful one times one

BEAUTIFUL BLACK MEN
Nikki Giovanni

Any nation or any ethnic or religious group armed with a powerful cause
will inevitably do more than have an impact on history. It will produce an
impressive body of literature. Black America is today in ferment, not only
with movements aiming at profound social changes but with new directions
in fiction, drama, and poetry. The contemporary black author, unlike most of
his predecessors of twenty or thirty years ago, seldom feels the need to be

"accepted" by white America and therefore does not abandon characteristic black modes of expression. The syntax of much black poetry in no way resembles white reader's preconceptions of what poetry "ought" to sound like. It takes the rhythm and feel of black speech and creates a new kind of reading excitement.

Nikki Giovanni (b. 1943) writes of feminine experience, what it means to be a black woman in America, what it means to be black in America; she writes of revolution and the need for black unity. In the following poem she expresses that total acceptance of one's brothers and sisters, that broad and unconditional commitment to a people that the central character in *Great Goodness of Life* so conspicuously lacks.

Beautiful Black Men (with compliments and apologies to all not mentioned by name)

i wanta say just gotta say something
bout those beautiful beautiful beautiful outasight
black men
with they afros
walking down the street
is the same ol danger
but a brand new pleasure

sitting on stoops, in bars, going to offices
running numbers, watching for their whores
preaching in churches, driving their hogs
walking their dogs, winking at me
in their fire red, lime green, burnt orange
royal blue tight tight pants that hug
what i like to hug

jerry butler, wilson pickett, the impressions
temptations, mighty mighty sly
don't have to do anything but walk
on stage
and i scream and stamp and shout
see new breed men in breed alls
dashiki suits with shirts that match
the lining that compliments the ties

that smile at the sandals
where dirty toes peek at me
and i scream and stamp and shout
for more beautiful beautiful beautiful
black men with outasight afros

THE CLOD AND THE PEBBLE
William Blake

Though he lived a long life during which he wrote some of the most complex and philosophical poems in the English language, **William Blake (1757–1827)** somehow managed to hold tightly to the innocence of a child. Poems like the one which follows have that simplicity-yet-profundity one finds in the disarming statements children make or the rhymes children recite while playing games.

In point of fact, it is the child's philosophy that attracts Blake. He views the tragedy of human existence in terms of the gradual loss of unquestioning faith in life and people. He sees the human capacity for reason as being the true enemy of mankind; for rational thought and analysis do nothing but distort reality, rendering it back to the thinker piece by piece rather than as a beautiful whole that is to be accepted and lived more than understood. Reason, represented by the Pebble, separates people from each other, for the thinking life turns in upon itself; and people grow up caring only for themselves, having lost the child's natural affection for others. But the reader must decide for himself which viewpoint is the more realistic or desirable of the two.

The Clod and the Pebble

"Love seeketh not itself to please,
Nor for itself hath any care,
But for another gives its ease,
And builds a Heaven in Hell's despair."

So sang a little Clod of Clay
Trodden with the cattle's feet,

But a Pebble of the brook
Warbled out these metres meet:

"Love seeketh only Self to please,
To bind another to its delight,
Joy in another's loss of ease,
And builds a Hell in Heaven's despite."

BETWEEN THE WORLD AND ME
Richard Wright

Long before the advent of a concerted black nationalist movement **Richard Wright (1908–1960)** had distinguished himself as a literary spokesman against bigotry and racism. His autobiographical *Black Boy* remains a stirring recreation of what it was like to grow up black in the rural South. He achieved international fame with his novel *Native Son* (1940), one of the first works to deal in depth with the frustrated and angry inner life of a black man penned up in a sweltering ghetto. In 1945 Wright, following the pattern established by other black American artists, moved to Europe and lived there as an expatriate until his death in Paris fifteen years later.

The following poem first appeared in *Partisan Review* in 1935. It expresses the same rage against white America's inhumanity and incapacity for love which explode across the pages of Wright's fiction. But it makes its powerful point in only a few lines, once again demonstrating what poets do for readers. The poem bypasses the conscious mind, working instead on the reader's deeper states through a rapidly moving interior collage of images. In this way does the black poet seek to stir not consciousness, but conscience.

Between the World and Me

And one morning while in the woods I stumbled suddenly upon the
    thing,
Stumbled upon it in a grassy clearing guarded by scaly oaks and elms.

And the sooty details of the scene rose, thrusting themselves between the world and me. . . .

There was a design of white bones slumbering forgottenly upon a cushion of ashes.

There was a charred stump of a sapling pointing a blunt finger accusingly at the sky.

There were torn tree limbs, tiny veins of burnt leaves, and a scorched coil of greasy hemp;

A vacant shoe, an empty tie, a ripped shirt, a lonely hat, and a pair of trousers stiff with black blood.

And upon the trampled grass were buttons, dead matches, butt-ends of cigars and cigarettes, peanut shells, a drained gin-flask, and a whore's lipstick;

Scattered traces of tar, restless arrays of feathers, and the lingering smell of gasoline.

And through the morning air the sun poured yellow surprise into the eye sockets of a stony skull. . . .

And while I stood my mind was frozen with a cold pity for the life that was gone.

The ground gripped my feet and my heart was circled by icy walls of fear—

The sun died in the sky; a night wind muttered in the grass and fumbled the leaves in the trees; the woods poured forth the hungry yelping of hounds; the darkness screamed with thirsty voices; and the witnesses rose and lived:

The dry bones stirred, rattled, lifted, melting themselves into my bones.

The grey ashes formed flesh firm and black, entering into my flesh.

The gin-flask passed from mouth to mouth; cigars and cigarettes glowed, the whore smeared the lipstick red upon her lips,

And a thousand faces swirled around me, clamoring that my life be burned. . . .

And then they had me, stripped me, battering my teeth into my throat till I swallowed my own blood.

My voice was drowned in the roar of their voices, and my black wet body slipped and rolled in their hands as they bound me to the sapling.

And my skin clung to the bubbling hot tar, falling from me in limp patches.

And the down and quills of the white feathers sank into my raw flesh, and I moaned in my agony.

Then my blood was cooled mercifully, cooled by a baptism of gasoline.

And in a blaze of red I leaped to the sky as pain rose like water, boiling my limbs.

Panting, begging I clutched childlike, clutched to the hot sides of
   death.
Now I am dry bones and my face a stony skull staring in yellow
   surprise at the sun. . . .

THE MAN HE KILLED
Thomas Hardy

Thomas Hardy (1840–1928) is better known for his novels than his poetry,
but both reflect his pessimistic view of human existence. He saw the world
as a tragic place in which people make a pitiful attempt to fulfill themselves
and eke out a meager happiness but are always thwarted by some ironic
and disastrous turn of events or else betrayed by their own intellectual and
moral defects. At one point in his own life Hardy was tempted to think more
positively about human life, but World War I convinced him that humanity
was incapable of improving its lot. Men could not care about each other.
Egoism and greed would always conspire to keep the world in the shadow
of conflicts and deaths. The following poem is one of the enduring expressions of the futility of war, waged by those who would never have the
chance to reach out and touch each other.

The Man He Killed

"Had he and I but met
   By some old ancient inn,
We should have sat us down to wet
   Right many a nipperkin!

"But ranged as infantry,
   And staring face to face,
I shot at him as he at me,
   And killed him in his place.

Reprinted by permission of The Macmillan Company from *Collected Poems* by
Thomas Hardy.

"I shot him dead because—
Because he was my foe,
Just so: my foe of course he was;
That's clear enough; although

"He thought he'd 'list, perhaps,
Off-hand like—just as I—
Was out of work—had sold his traps—
No other reason why.

"Yes; quaint and curious war is!
You shoot a fellow down
You'd treat if met where any bar is,
Or help to half-a-crown."

HUMAN WORTH
AND MORAL VALUES

A moral value is the basis for a choice among alternatives. It is the underlying assumption about the rightness, appropriateness, or workability of something we do, especially when the action performed involves other people. Insofar as a person has a network of such values, in some way consistent with each other, he may be said to have a moral system or moral code.

In the history of Human Worth, morality has played an essential role, but not the same kind of role for everyone. At one end of the scale is *moral absolutism*, which maintains that the rightness or wrongness of an action must be the same for all people. Sometimes the standard of determination is reason itself; sometimes it is the belief in God and an acceptance of his commandments; sometimes it is what reason tells us society must require in order to exist. Sometimes it involves sanctions—rewards or punishments for those who do or fail to do the right thing, however it may be defined. Sometimes one is urged to do the right thing because it is the right thing, and for no other reason.

At the other end of the scale is *moral relativism*, which maintains that there can be no universal standard applicable to everyone, everywhere. If reason is invoked by the relativist, it is understood that what seems the rational course for one may not work for another. Expediency—the urgencies and priorities of the moment—is often the telling factor. The moral relativist may at times advocate behavior which seems to conform to rational or religious absolute norms, but he is distinguished from the absolutist in his belief that moral codes can, do, and *must* change as times and circumstances change. The extreme form of moral relativism is the position of amoralism, which views the individual as being the sole determinant of his actions and denies the validity of any considerations beyond self-interest.

Moral philosophers have pondered divergent possibilities for centuries. Some have seen moral absolutes as oppressive super-structures controlling the individual and making "free will" a myth, as life-denying forces, totally destructive to Human Worth. Others have argued that Human Worth becomes possible only when all people are willing to submit to a transcendent moral authority. The amoralists have demanded the freedom to make their own decisions, and they see the need for conformity as an encroachment upon Worth. And then there are "natural" moralists who believe humanity only realizes itself when it follows the natural laws of its being and that moral behavior can be nothing but whatever seems most instinctive and comfortable to an individual. They believe that selling out to forces which try to transcend nature is denying Human Worth altogether.

The first selection is taken from Plato's *Republic,* a series of complex dialogues which seek to answer the question of what makes someone's life a good and just one. Throughout the book Plato's spokesman, Socrates, is the upholder of reason as the universal, unchanging foundation of all action. For him moral or just deeds are committed for the sake of their rightness, not for convenience or personal benefit. The moral idealism of Socrates has remained for all times one of the most difficult positions for people to achieve, except in theory. For this reason we have included the "Classic Case for Injustice" presented by one of Socrates' listeners, who argue from a pragmatic viewpoint many readers will no doubt find more realistic: namely, that men are basically selfish and behave morally only because they are forced by society to do so. If there is a defense of moral absolutism beyond this—as Socrates maintained was the case—it is crucial to find a convincing answer to the question raised by the story of the magic rings.

Frank O'Connor's short story "The Idealist" tends to drama-tize the relativistic viewpoint. The foundation for it is often cited as the most powerful single determinant behind a person's deeds: the stark reality of "me or them." The hero discovers it is not the better part of human wisdom to cling to moral abso-lutes when everyone else is out for himself. Is it Human Worth, the story asks, to persist in folly? Is it not wiser in the long run to look out for oneself? What good will moral integrity be when one is repeatedly the loser in his encounters with the world? Still, the reader may detect an echoing note of sadness in this story, as a sweet ideal fades mournfully away; perhaps even the fragile hint that Human Worth *ought* to mean something less pragmatic if only it could.

Many who find themselves in agreement with O'Connor's hero are likely to do so without bothering to place a philosophical label on themselves or their actions. Still, a reading of Bernard Williams' "The Amoralist" can prove enlightening. It is one thing to do what seems to need doing without much more than a vague sense of self-righteousness, but it is quite something else to admit that one is acting as an amoralist and have to encounter the author's careful analysis of the illogic of the position. It is particularly imperative that the case against amoralism be carefully weighed when the amoralist is himself often the first person who argues for his right to do as he pleases on *un*analyzed grounds.

In John Steinbeck's "About Ed Ricketts," written in tribute to the memory of one of the author's closest friends, we find what will strike some readers as a portrait of the amoralist personified— a true libertine, a self-centered playboy who lived strictly on his own terms, regardless of what he did to others. But Steinbeck is not an amoralist. He is a naturalist. Ed Ricketts, in his eyes, was "half-goat, half-Christ," and Steinbeck offers him to us as the very symbol of the natural, hence moral, man—a beautiful person who lived as the inner law of his being dictated and who had the moral courage to resist being shaped and molded by the transcendent moralities of absolutism which for Steinbeck are violations of natural law.

A CLASSIC CASE FOR INJUSTICE
Plato

The Republic of **Plato** (427–346 B.C.) is his most popular work and one of the world's richest sources of ideas about what makes any life good, moral, and just. Plato's spokesman is Socrates, who in real life never wrote down a word of what he taught others but who had been Plato's mentor and spiritual guide. *The Republic,* like all of Plato's major writings, is in the form of dialogues between Socrates, who takes an uncompromising, rational approach in all matters, and his young followers, who advance more practical solutions, ideas many readers of today find to be more in keeping with contemporary attitudes. Though the Socratic view that what is right cannot vary with individuals and circumstances has haunted the human conscience for centuries, the practical view—represented in our selection by Glaucon— has been that a universal standard of morality makes no sense in a world whose people can't live by it.

In fact, Glaucon's hypothetical case of the two magic rings is advanced to illustrate how unjustly people would act if their deeds went undetected.

He poses a powerful argument, one that all proponents of absolute morality must be prepared to resist: namely, that each of us chooses the just course only because society demands it of him and he is afraid of the consequences of deviating from the norm. But this, the argument continues, is no proof of the real existence of an absolute morality. Where would such a thing be except in the actions of people? And if these are hypocritical, how may they be said to embody truly moral principles? Socrates is challenged to admit that morality must be a matter of convenience, that there is no such thing as "good in itself."

But Socrates cannot agree with the practical view. What people really do has no bearing on what they *should* do. His own life had offered an impressive illustration of what it meant to follow the dictates of reason not convenience. Imprisoned for alleged heresies against the state and religion and urged by his followers to escape, he absolutely refused on the grounds that one cannot fight injustice with further injustice. That a law is bad is one thing; to disobey a law, quite another. Reason is man's inner conscience, he taught, and there is no happiness for one who betrays himself. On the contrary, one who acts justly in all instances, regardless of personal consequences, learns the profound truth: *No evil can befall a good man.*

The Republic begins as a friendly conversation on the subject of why people want to be rich. Cephalus has invited Socrates and his friends to his home, which is very lavish. Asked why he feels wealth is important, he answers that it allows him to stay on good terms with the world, never being in any man's debt. Socrates then proceeds to inquire whether he believes the essence of the good and just life is to render to each what is his due. The debaters get into a complicated discussion about what justice really means and whether it is always the same or varies with circumstances. Many views are exchanged, and then Glaucon comes forth with his classic case for injustice.

At the conclusion of our selection Socrates is getting ready to answer the challenge which Glaucon and the others have put to him. The reader already knows what his response will be: Right is right, no matter what people may do or what their motives are. Here we have a crucial point which has plagued the human mind in its moral deliberations: If reason points the way to absolute moral standards but people tend not to be guided by reason, are we not dealing with the necessity for social or institutional controls? Morality imposed from without? And subject always to be defied whenever the opportunity arises? Do we gain Human Worth by living by uncompromising principles? Or lose Human Worth when, taking the just course, we fall victim to the injustice practiced by others?

A Classic Case for Injustice

I thought that, with these words, I was quit of the discussion; but it seems this was only a prelude. Glaucon, undaunted as ever, was not content to let Thrasymachus abandon the field.

Socrates, he broke out, you have made a show of proving that justice is better than injustice in every way. Is that enough, or do you want us to be really convinced?

Certainly I do, if it rests with me.

Then you are not going the right way about it. I want to know how you classify the things we call good. Are there not some which we should wish to have, not for their consequences, but just for their own sake, such as harmless pleasures and enjoyments that have no further result beyond the satisfaction of the moment?

Yes, I think there are good things of that description.

And also some that we value both for their own sake and for their consequences—things like knowledge and health and the use of our eyes?

Yes.

And a third class which would include physical training, medical treatment, earning one's bread as a doctor or otherwise—useful, but burdensome things, which we want only for the sake of the profit or other benefit they bring.

Yes, there is that third class. What then?

In which class do you place justice?

I should say, in the highest, as a thing which anyone who is to gain happiness must value both for itself and for its results.

Well, that is not the common opinion. Most people would say it was one of those things, tiresome and disagreeable in themselves, which we cannot avoid practising for the sake of reward or a good reputation.

From *The Republic of Plato*, tr. Francis Macdonald Cornford. Reprinted by permission of The Clarendon Press, Oxford.

I know, said I; that is why Thrasymachus has been finding fault with it all this time and praising injustice. But I seem to be slow in seeing his point.

Listen to me, then, and see if you agree with mine. There was no need, I think, for Thrasymachus to yield so readily, like a snake you had charmed into submission; and nothing so far said about justice and injustice has been established to my satisfaction. I want to be told what each of them really is, and what effect each has, in itself, on the soul that harbours it, when all rewards and consequences are left out of account. So here is my plan, if you approve. I shall revive Thrasymachus' theory. First, I will state what is commonly held about the nature of justice and its origin; secondly, I shall maintain that it is always practised with reluctance, not as good in itself, but as a thing one cannot do without; and thirdly, that this reluctance is reasonable, because the life of injustice is much the better life of the two—so people say. That is not what I think myself, Socrates; only I am bewildered by all that Thrasymachus and ever so many others have dinned into my ears; and I have never yet heard the case for justice stated as I wish to hear it. You, I believe, if anyone, can tell me what is to be said in praise of justice in and for itself; that is what I want. Accordingly, I shall set you an example by glorifying the life of injustice with all the energy that I hope you will show later in denouncing it and exalting justice in its stead. Will that plan suit you?

Nothing could be better, I replied. Of all subjects this is one on which a sensible man must always be glad to exchange ideas.

Good, said Glaucon. Listen then, and I will begin with my first point: the nature and origin of justice.

What people say is that to do wrong is, in itself, a desirable thing; on the other hand, it is not at all desirable to suffer wrong, and the harm to the sufferer outweighs the advantage to the doer. Consequently, when men have had a taste of both, those who have not the power to seize the advantage and escape the harm decide that they would be better off if they made a compact neither to do wrong nor to suffer it. Hence they began to make laws and covenants with one another; and whatever the law prescribed they called lawful and right. That is what right or justice is and how it came into existence; it stands half-way between the best thing of all—to do wrong with impunity—and the worst, which is to suffer wrong without the power to retaliate. So justice is accepted as a compromise, and valued, not as good in itself, but for lack of power to do wrong; no man worthy of the name, who had that power, would ever enter into such a compact with anyone; he would be mad if he did. That, Socrates, is the nature of justice according to this account, and such the circumstances in which it arose.

The next point is that men practise it against the grain, for lack of power to do wrong. How true that is, we shall best see if we imagine two men, one just, the other unjust, given full licence to do whatever they like, and then follow them to observe where each will be led by his desires. We shall catch the just man taking the same road as the unjust; he will be moved by self-interest, the end which it is natural to every creature to pursue as good, until forcibly turned aside by law and custom to respect the principle of equality.

Now, the easiest way to give them that complete liberty of action would be to imagine them possessed of the talisman found by Gyges, the ancestor of the famous Lydian. The story tells how he was a shepherd in the King's service. One day there was a great storm, and the ground where his flock was feeding was rent by an earthquake. Astonished at the sight, he went down into the chasm and saw, among other wonders of which the story tells, a brazen horse, hollow, with windows in its sides. Peering in, he saw a dead body, which seemed to be of more than human size. It was naked save for a gold ring, which he took from the finger and made his way out. When the shepherds met, as they did every month, to send an account to the King of the state of his flocks, Gyges came wearing the ring. As he was sitting with the others, he happened to turn the bezel of the ring inside his hand. At once he became invisible, and his companions, to his surprise, began to speak of him as if he had left them. Then, as he was fingering the ring, he turned the bezel outwards and became visible again. With that, he set about testing the ring to see if it really had this power, and always with the same result: according as he turned the bezel inside or out he vanished and reappeared. After this discovery he contrived to be one of the messengers sent to the court. There he seduced the Queen, and with her help murdered the King and seized the throne.

Now suppose there were two such magic rings, and one were given to the just man, the other to the unjust. No one, it is commonly believed, would have such iron strength of mind as to stand fast in doing right or keep his hands off other men's goods, when he could go to the market-place and fearlessly help himself to anything he wanted, enter houses and sleep with any woman he chose, set prisoners free and kill men at his pleasure, and in a word go about among men with the powers of a god. He would behave no better than the other; both would take the same course. Surely this would be strong proof that men do right only under compulsion; no individual thinks of it as good for him personally, since he does wrong whenever he finds he has the power. Every man believes that wrongdoing pays him personally much better, and, according to this theory, that is the truth. Granted full license to do as he liked, people would think him a miserable fool if they found him refusing to wrong his neighbours or to touch their belongings, though in public they would keep up a pretence of praising his conduct, for fear of being wronged themselves. So much for that.

Finally, if we are really to judge between the two lives, the only way is to contrast the extremes of justice and injustice. We can best do that by imagining our two men to be perfect types, and crediting both to the full with the qualities they need for their respective ways of life. To begin with the unjust man: he must be like any consummate master of a craft, a physician or a captain, who, knowing just what his art can do, never tries to do more, and can always retrieve a false step. The unjust man, if he is to reach perfection, must be equally discreet in his criminal attempts, and he must not be found out, or we shall think him a bungler; for the highest pitch of injustice is to seem just when you are not. So we must endow our man with the full complement of injustice; we must allow him to have secured a spotless reputation for virtue while committing the blackest crimes; he must be able to retrieve any mistake, to defend himself with convincing eloquence if his misdeeds are denounced, and, when force is required, to bear down all opposition by his courage and strength and by his command of friends and money.

Now set beside this paragon the just man in his simplicity and nobleness, one who, in Aeschylus' words, 'would be, not seem, the best.' There must, indeed, be no such seeming; for if his character were apparent, his reputation would bring him honours and rewards, and then we should not know whether it was for their sake that he was just or for justice's sake alone. He must be stripped of everything but justice, and denied every advantage the other enjoyed. Doing no wrong, he must have the worst reputation for wrong-doing, to test whether his virtue is proof against all that comes of having a bad name; and under this lifelong imputation of wickedness, let him hold on his course of justice unwavering to the point of death. And so, when the two men have carried their justice and injustice to the last extreme, we may judge which is the happier.

My dear Glaucon, I exclaimed, how vigorously you scour these two characters clean for inspection, as if you were burnishing a couple of statues!

I am doing my best, he answered. Well, given two such characters, it is not hard, I fancy, to describe the sort of life that each of them may expect; and if the description sounds rather coarse, take it as coming from those who cry up the merits of injustice rather than from me. They will tell you that our just man will be thrown into prison, scourged and racked, will have his eyes burnt out, and, after every kind of torment, be impaled. That will teach him how much better it is to seem virtuous than to be so. In fact those lines of Aeschylus I quoted are more fitly applied to the unjust man, who, they say, is a realist and does not live for appearances: 'he would be, not seem' unjust,

> reaping the harvest sown
> In those deep furrows of the thoughtful heart
> Whence wisdom springs.

With his reputation for virtue, he will hold offices of state, ally himself by marriage to any family he may choose, become a partner in any business, and, having no scruples about being dishonest, turn all these advantages to profit. If he is involved in a lawsuit, public or private, he will get the better of his opponents, grow rich on the proceeds, and be able to help his friends and harm his enemies.[1] Finally, he can make sacrifices to the gods and dedicate offerings with due magnificence, and, being in a much better position than the just man to serve the gods as well as his chosen friends, he may reasonably hope to stand higher in the favour of heaven. So much better, they say, Socrates, is the life prepared for the unjust by gods and men.

Here Glaucon ended, and I was meditating a reply, when his brother Adeimantus exclaimed:

Surely, Socrates, you cannot suppose that that is all there is to be said.

Why, isn't it? said I.

The most essential part of the case has not been mentioned, he replied.

Well, I answered, there is a proverb about a brother's aid. If Glaucon has failed, it is for you to make good his shortcomings; though, so far as I am concerned, he has said quite enough to put me out of the running and leave me powerless to rescue the cause of justice.

Nonsense, said Adeimantus; there is more to be said, and you must listen to me. If we want a clear view of what I take to be Glaucon's meaning, we must study the opposite side of the case, the arguments used when justice is praised and injustice condemned. When children are told by their fathers and all their pastors and masters that it is a good thing to be just, what is commended is not justice in itself but the respectability it brings. They are to let men see how just they are, in order to gain high positions and marry well and win all the other advantages which Glaucon mentioned, since the just man owes all these to his good reputation.

In this matter of having a good name, they go farther still: they throw in the favourable opinion of heaven, and can tell us of no

---

[1] To help friends and harm enemies, offered as a definition of Justice by Polemarchus, now appears as the privilege of the unjust.

end of good things with which they say the gods reward piety. There
is the good old Hesiod, who says the gods make the just man's oak-
trees 'bear acorns at the top and bees in the middle; and their sheep's
fleeces are heavy with wool,' and a great many other blessings of that
sort. And Homer speaks in the same strain:

> As when a blameless king fears the gods and upholds right judgment;
> then the dark earth yields wheat and barley, and the trees are laden
> with fruit; the young of his flocks are strong, and the sea gives abun-
> dance of fish.

Musaeus and his son Eumolpus[2] enlarge in still more spirited terms
upon the rewards from heaven they promise to the righteous. They
take them to the other world and provide them with a banquet of
the Blest, where they sit for all time carousing with garlands on their
heads, as if virtue could not be more nobly recompensed than by an
eternity of intoxication. Others, again, carry the rewards of heaven
yet a stage farther: the pious man who keeps his oaths is to have
children's children and to leave a posterity after him. When they have
sung the praises of justice in that strain, with more to same effect, they
proceed to plunge the sinners and unrighteous men into a pool of mud
in the world below, and set them to fetch water in a sieve. Even in
this life, too, they give them a bad name, and make out that the unjust suffer all those penalties which Glaucon described as falling upon
the good man who has a bad reputation: they can think of no others.
That is how justice is recommended and injustice denounced.

Besides all this, think of the way in which justice and injustice are
spoken of, not only in ordinary life, but by the poets. All with one
voice reiterate that self-control and justice, admirable as they may be,
are difficult and irksome, whereas vice and injustice are pleasant and
very easily to be had; it is mere convention to regard them as dis-
creditable. They tell us that dishonesty generally pays better than
honesty. They will cheerfully speak of a bad man as happy and load
him with honours and social esteem, provided he be rich and otherwise powerful; while they despise and disregard one who has neither
power nor wealth, though all the while they acknowledge that he is
the better man of the two.

Most surprising of all is what they say about the gods and virtue:
that heaven itself often allots misfortunes and a hard life to the good
man, and gives prosperity to the wicked. Mendicant priests and sooth-
sayers come to the rich man's door with a story of a power they possess
by the gift of heaven to atone for any offence that he or his ancestors

---

[2] Legendary figures, to whom were attributed poems setting forth the doctrines
of the mystery religion known as Orphism.

have committed with incantations and sacrifice agreeably accompanied by feasting. If he wishes to injure an enemy, he can, at a trifling expense, do him a hurt with equal ease, whether he be an honest man or not, by means of certain invocations and spells which, as they profess, prevail upon the gods to do their bidding. In support of all these claims they call the poets to witness. Some, by way of advertising the easiness of vice, quote the words: 'Unto wickedness men attain easily and in multitudes; smooth is the way and her dwelling is very near at hand. But the gods have ordained much sweat upon the path to virtue' and a long road that is rough and steep.

Others, to show that men can turn the gods from their purpose, cite Homer: 'Even the gods themselves listen to entreaty. Their hearts are turned by the entreaties of men with sacrifice and humble prayers and libation and burnt offering, whensoever anyone transgresses and does amiss.' They produce a whole farrago of books in which Musaeus and Orpheus, described as descendants of the Muses and the Moon, prescribe their ritual; and they persuade entire communities, as well as individuals, that, both in this life and after death, wrongdoing may be absolved and purged away by means of sacrifices and agreeable performances which they are pleased to call rites of initiation. These deliver us from punishment in the other world, where awful things are in store for all who neglect to sacrifice.

Now, my dear Socrates, when all this stuff is talked about the estimation in which virtue and vice are held by heaven and by mankind, what effect can we suppose it has upon the mind of a young man quick-witted enough to gather honey from all these flowers of popular wisdom and to draw his own conclusions as to the sort of person he should be and the way he should go in order to lead the best possible life? In all likelihood he would ask himself, in Pindar's words: 'Will the way of right or the by-paths of deceit lead me to the higher fortress,' where I may entrench myself for the rest of my life? For, according to what they tell me, I have nothing to gain but trouble and manifest loss from being honest, unless I also get a name for being so; whereas, if I am dishonest and provide myself with a reputation for honesty, they promise me a marvellous career. Very well, then; since 'outward seeming,' as wise men inform me, 'overpowers the truth' and decides the question of happiness, I had better go in for appearances wholeheartedly. I must ensconce myself behind an imposing façade designed to look like virtue, and trail the fox behind me, 'the cunning shifty fox'[3]—Archilochus knew the world as well as any man. You may say it is not so easy to be wicked without ever being found out. Perhaps not; but great things are never easy.

---

[3] An allusion to a fable by Archilochus.

Anyhow, if we are to reach happiness, everything we have been told points to this as the road to be followed. We will form secret societies to save us from exposure; besides, there are men who teach the art of winning over popular assemblies and courts of law; so that, one way or another, by persuasion or violence, we shall get the better of our neighbours without being punished. You might object that the gods are not to be deceived and are beyond the reach of violence. But suppose that there are no gods, or that they do not concern themselves with the doings of men; why should we concern ourselves to deceive them? Or, if the gods do exist and care for mankind, all we know or have ever heard about them comes from current tradition and from the poets who recount their family history, and these same authorities also assure us that they can be won over and turned from their purpose 'by sacrifice and humble prayers' and votive offerings. We must either accept both these statements or neither. If we are to accept both, we had better do wrong and use part of the proceeds to offer sacrifice. By being just we may escape the punishment of heaven, but we shall be renouncing the profits of injustice; whereas by doing wrong we shall make our profit and escape punishment into the bargain, by means of those entreaties which win over the gods when we transgress and do amiss. But then, you will say, in the other world the penalty for our misdeeds on earth will fall either upon us or upon our children's children. We can counter that objection by reckoning on the great efficacy of mystic rites and the divinities of absolution, vouched for by the most advanced societies and by the descendants of the gods who have appeared as poets and spokesmen of heavenly inspiration.

What reason, then, remains for preferring justice to the extreme of injustice, when common belief and the best authorities promise us the fulfilment of our desires in this life and the next, if only we conceal our ill-doing under a veneer of decent behaviour? The upshot is, Socrates, that no man possessed of superior powers of mind or person or rank or wealth will set any value on justice; he is more likely to laugh when he hears it praised. So, even one who could prove my case false and were quite sure that justice is best, far from being indignant with the unjust, will be very ready to excuse them. He will know that, here and there, a man may refrain from wrong because it revolts some instinct he is graced with or because he has come to know the truth; no one else is virtuous of his own will; it is only lack of spirit or the infirmity of age or some other weakness that makes men condemn the iniquities they have not the strength to practise. This is easily seen: give such a man the power, and he will be the first to use it to the utmost.

What lies at the bottom of all this is nothing but the fact from which Glaucon, as well as I, started upon this long discourse. We put it to you, Socrates, with all respect, in this way. All you who profess to sing the praises of right conduct, from the ancient heroes whose legends have survived down to the men of the present day, have never denounced injustice or praised justice apart from the reputation, honours, and rewards they bring; but what effect either of them in itself has upon its possessor when it dwells in his soul unseen of gods or men, no poet or ordinary man has ever yet explained. No one has proved that a soul can harbour no worse evil than injustice, no greater good than justice. Had all of you said that from the first and tried to convince us from our youth up, we should not be keeping watch upon our neighbours to prevent them from doing wrong to us, but everyone would keep a far more effectual watch over himself, for fear lest by wronging others he should open his doors to the worst of all evils.

That, Socrates, is the view of justice and injustice which Thrasymachus and, no doubt, others would state, perhaps in even stronger words. For myself, I believe it to be a gross perversion of their true worth and effect; but, as I must frankly confess, I have put the case with all the force I could muster because I want to hear the other side from you. You must not be content with proving that injustice is superior to injustice; you must make clear what good or what harm each of them does to its possessor, taking it simply in itself and, as Glaucon required, leaving out of account the reputation it bears. For unless you deprive each of its true reputation and attach to it the false one, we shall say that you are praising or denouncing nothing more than the appearances in either case, and recommending us to do wrong without being found out; and that you hold with Thrasymachus that right means what is good for someone else, being the interest of the stronger, and wrong is what really pays, serving one's own interest at the expense of the weaker. You have agreed that justice belongs to that highest class of good things which are worth having not only for their consequences, but much more for their own sakes—things like sight and hearing, knowledge, and health, whose value is genuine and intrinsic, not dependent on opinion. So I want you, in commending justice, to consider only how justice, in itself, benefits a man who has it in him, and how injustice harms him, leaving rewards and reputation out of account. I might put up with others dwelling on those outward effects as a reason for praising the one and condemning the other; but from you, who have spent your life in the study of this question, I must beg leave to demand something better. You must not be content merely to prove that justice is superior to injustice, but explain how one is good, the other evil, in virtue of the intrinsic effect each has on its possessor, whether gods or men see it or not.

RESPONSES: Questions for Writing and Discussion

1. For Socrates the good or just life, the life for which each of us ought to strive, is unrelated to " harmless pleasures and enjoyments that have no further result beyond the satisfaction of the moment." Presumably the values which serve as the basis for our choices would not be concerned with the "satisfaction of the moment." Presumably passing pleasures would sometimes have to be conscientiously avoided —chosen *against*—in the interest of doing the right or moral thing. In your opinion, do most people, when making their choices, think of their own immediate pleasures? Do you? If this is so, do you agree with Socrates that it is wrong?

2. Glaucon introduces the example of the magic rings to prove two important points: (1) that the just life is not the most satisfying life—that people do the right thing because they are forced into it, not because it is valued for its own sake; and (2) that "the life of injustice is much the better life of the two." What does Glaucon mean by injustice here? Do you agree that it is better than a life of justice? Better for whom?

3. As Glaucon states his classic case for injustice, he says that people tend not to do wrong because they wish to avoid having others do wrong to them. In other words, people make an agreement with each other (which takes the form of legal restrictions) not to inflict mutual harm. But this, claims Glaucon, is acting in self-interest, not in the interest of justice itself. Suppose these restrictions did not in fact exist? Do you think people would be basically decent and honest with each other? Do you believe people are basically selfish and would deal dishonestly with each other if not compelled to do otherwise? (If your answer to this last question is yes, do you think people have a right to complain about police power? If you think people are really good at heart and do not need legal supervision, imagine yourself living in a city with no law enforcement. What would it be like?)

4. What Glaucon thinks to prove by the story of the two rings is that nobody "would have such iron strength of mind as to stand fast in doing right or keep his hands off other men's goods, when he could go to the market-place and fearlessly help himself to anything he wanted . . ." and so on. But that men would act out of completely selfish motives if they had the chance does not necessarily say it is right to do so. Or does it? That is, in your opinion, should the *reality* of human experience be the guide in creating one's moral system? Or should one's guide be the *ideality*—the way things ought to be?

5. Glaucon believes the perfectly just man could not be happy, because he would be unable to possess anything but his own goodness. If he were a worldly success and had many material advantages,

people would think he had practiced goodness just for gain and would not then trust him. And in truth he would not know himself whether this had been his motive. The only possible course would be simple goodness itself with no possibility of profiting by it. Do you believe the life of simple goodness would be rewarding in itself? Do we need material advantages in order to be happy?

6. Adeimantus interjects the view that people are raised to value personal gains and advantages and to hold goodness in esteem only if they are somehow rewarded for it. He goes on to argue that nothing in human society *really* encourages people to want to do anything but to be thought just and honest so as to make out well in the world. Nothing in society offers anyone a reason for prizing a moral existence divorced from the idea of profit. Do you agree with him?

7. The selection ends with the challenge to Socrates to show how justice is as valuable for itself as are sight, hearing, knowledge, and health. While the total case for justice takes the rest of the book, the foundation on which it rests is reason. For Socrates the right or just course is the one that is always evident to people of reason. For example, if a man's family is hungry and in need of fuel and he has no funds to buy these things, he would not, if acted upon by reason, steal the money even on an occasion when he could do so very easily and without being detected. Reason would tell him that he *cannot* take what is not his. Using the example of this wretched soul, can you put yourself in Socrates' place and explain why it would be *better* for the man to resist the temptation to steal? What would "better" mean from the Socratic viewpoint?

8. Imagine that you are the man cited above in example #7. Imagine some specific circumstances of your life which, in your opinion, appear to prove that you have been the victim of an unjust social system, that you have been reduced to this condition of abject poverty because of the dishonesty and selfishness of others. Construct a strong argument in favor of the justice of fighting back against injustice *using its own tactics*—that is, deceit and self-interest. Now think of a counterargument Socrates might advance. Which seems more convincing? Which course is more desirable? Which is more profitable? Which will you take? (These are not necessarily going to be the same.)

THE IDEALIST
Frank O'Connor

Those who oppose moral absolutism are likely to do so on two grounds: first, because they find it personally inconvenient and far too demanding; or second, because they find it unrealistic and undescriptive of the way the world generally goes. An alternative is moral relativism, or the conviction that the moral value of any action committed by oneself or by another depends upon circumstances: the purpose of the action, the time and the place, the personalities involved, and the consequences of it. Presumably Brutus might have argued that, in murdering Caesar, he was benefiting the Roman Empire. Proponents of moral absolutism sometimes refer to the relativists as cowards. Proponents of moral relativism sometimes denounce the absolutists as dictators and destroyers of Human Worth.

"The Idealist" by **Frank O'Connor (1903–1966)** is more than a period piece about conditions in a grammar school in the Ireland of half a century ago. Though most of the characters are school boys and the gravest moment poses the question of whether or not a shilling has been taken from somebody's pocket, the issues involved relate to the ancient battle over moral codes and their application to reality. The young hero of the story is an "idealist" in the sense that he carries a precise and unwavering system of values with him into any situation that may arise. His way is the time-honored (but not necessarily time-tested) way of the absolutist. *Simply tell the truth* is the motto by which he lives. A moral action is one that is truthful and honest; an immoral action, one whose motive is the deliberate attempt to deceive for personal gains. As events work out, his code causes him nothing but pain and suffering. Is the uncompromising code the best in the long run? Is there satisfaction in knowing that one has performed morally regardless of what happens? And, if the consequences are unpleasant, is the deed immoral no matter how "pure" one's motives may have been? Is the narrator of the story a fool who straightens himself out? Or is he an admirable young man who sells himself out?

"Story-telling," O'Connor once wrote, "is the nearest thing one can get to the quality of a pure lyric poem. It doesn't deal with problems; it doesn't have any solutions to offer; it just states the human condition." But at the same time, the human condition is full of problems, most of them unsolved. A good work of fiction is bound to bring one or more of these into focus; if nothing else, it invites us to relate the issues to our own lives. None surely is more enduringly relevant and worth reexamining than the dilemma faced by the narrator of this story. All of us must decide whether to "go with the tide" and adapt our moral values to the circumstances that arise, always making certain that we're the ones who profit the most, or to stand fast on the side of "the right," never perhaps knowing how much harm or good we do to ourselves and others with our "moral courage." Does a person gain or lose his Worth as he gains or loses strong ideals?

The Idealist

I don't know how it is about education, but it never seemed to do anything for me but get me into trouble.

Adventure stories weren't so bad, but as a kid I was very serious and preferred realism to romance. School stories were what I liked best, and, judged by our standards, these were romantic enough for anyone. The schools were English, so I suppose you couldn't expect anything else. They were always called "the venerable pile," and there was usually a ghost in them; they were built in a square that was called "the quad," and, according to the pictures, they were all clock-towers, spires, and pinnacles, like the lunatic asylum with us. The fellows in the stories were all good climbers, and got in and out of school at night on ropes made of knotted sheets. They dressed queerly; they wore long trousers, short, black jackets, and top hats. Whenever they did anything wrong they were given "lines" in Latin. When it was a bad case, they were flogged and never showed any sign of pain; only the bad fellows, and they always said: "Ow! Ow!"

Most of them were grand chaps who always stuck together and were great at football and cricket. They never told lies and wouldn't talk to anyone who did. If they were caught out and asked a point-blank question, they always told the truth, unless someone else was with them, and then even if they were to be expelled for if they wouldn't give his name, even if he was a thief, which, as a matter of fact, he frequently was. It was surprising in such good schools, with fathers who never gave less than five quid, the number of thieves there were. The fellows in our school hardly ever stole, though they only got a penny a week, and sometimes not even that, as when their fathers were on the booze and their mothers had to go to the pawn.

I worked hard at the football and cricket, though of course we never had a proper football and the cricket we played was with a hurley stick against a wicket chalked on some wall. The officers in the barrack played proper cricket, and on summer evenings I used to go and watch them, like one of the souls in Purgatory watching the joys of Paradise.

Even so, I couldn't help being disgusted at the bad way things were run in our school. Our "venerable pile" was a red-brick building without tower or pinnacle a fellow could climb, and no ghost at all: we had no team, so a fellow, no matter how hard he worked, could never play for the school, and, instead of giving you "lines," Latin or any other sort, Murderer Moloney either lifted you by the ears or bashed you with a cane. When he got tired of bashing you on the hands he bashed you on the legs.

But these were only superficial things. What was really wrong was ourselves. The fellows sucked up to the masters and told them all that went on. If they were caught out in anything they tried to put the blame on someone else, even if it meant telling lies. When they were caned they snivelled and said it wasn't fair; drew back their hands as if they were terrified, so that the cane caught only the tips of their fingers, and then screamed and stood on one leg, shaking out their fingers in the hope of getting it counted as one. Finally they roared that their wrist was broken and crawled back to their desks with their hands squeezed under the armpits, howling. I mean you couldn't help feeling ashamed, imagining what chaps from a decent school would think if they saw it.

My own way to school led me past the barrack gate. In those peaceful days sentries never minded you going past the guardroom to have a look at the chaps drilling in the barrack square; if you came at dinnertime they even called you in and gave you plumduff and tea. Naturally, with such temptations I was often late. The only excuse, short of a letter from your mother, was to say you were at early Mass. The Murderer would never know whether you were or not, and if he did anything to you you could easily get him into trouble with the parish priest. Even as kids we knew who the real boss of the school was.

But after I started reading those confounded school stories I was never happy about saying I had been to Mass. It was a lie, and I knew that the chaps in the stories would have died sooner than tell it. They were all round me like invisible presences, and I hated to do anything which I felt they might disapprove of.

One morning I came in very late and rather frightened.

"What kept you till this hour, Delaney?" Murderer Moloney asked, looking at the clock.

I wanted to say I had been at Mass, but I couldn't. The invisible presences were all about me.

"I was delayed at the barrack, sir," I replied in panic.

There was a faint titter from the class, and Moloney raised his brows in mild surprise. He was a big powerful man with fair hair and blue eyes and a manner that at times was deceptively mild.

"Oh, indeed," he said, politely enough. "And what delayed you?"

"I was watching the soldiers drilling, sir," I said.

The class tittered again. This was a new line entirely for them.

"Oh," Moloney said casually, "I never knew you were such a military man. Hold out your hand!"

Compared with the laughter the slaps were nothing, and besides, I had the example of the invisible presences to sustain me. I did not flinch. I returned to my desk slowly and quietly without snivelling or squeezing my hands, and the Murderer looked after me, raising his brows again as though to indicate that this was a new line for him, too. But the others gaped and whispered as if I were some strange animal. At playtime they gathered about me, full of curiosity and excitement.

"Delaney, why did you say that about the barrack?"

"Because 'twas true," I replied firmly. "I wasn't going to tell him a lie."

"What lie?"

"That I was at Mass."

"Then couldn't you say you had to go on a message?"

"That would be a lie too."

"Cripes, Delaney," they said, "you'd better mind yourself. The Murderer is in an awful wax. He'll massacre you."

I knew that. I knew only too well that the Murderer's professional pride had been deeply wounded, and for the rest of the day I was on my best behaviour. But my best wasn't enough, for I underrated the Murderer's guile. Though he pretended to be reading, he was watching me the whole time.

"Delaney," he said at last without raising his head from the book, "was that you talking?"

" 'Twas, sir," I replied in consternation.

The whole class laughed. They couldn't believe but that I was deliberately trailing my coat, and, of course, the laugh must have convinced him that I was. I suppose if people do tell you lies all day and every day, it soon becomes a sort of perquisite which you resent being deprived of.

"Oh," he said, throwing down his book, "we'll soon stop that."

This time it was a tougher job, because he was really on his mettle. But so was I. I knew this was the testing-point for me, and if only I could keep my head I should provide a model for the whole class. When I had got through the ordeal without moving a muscle, and returned to my desk with my hands by my sides, the invisible presences gave me a great clap. But the visible ones were nearly as annoyed as the Murderer himself. After school half a dozen of them followed me down the school yard.

"Go on!" they shouted truculently. "Shaping as usual!"

"I was not shaping."

"You were shaping. You're always showing off. Trying to pretend he didn't hurt you—a blooming crybaby like you!"

"I wasn't trying to pretend," I shouted, even then resisting the temptation to nurse my bruised hands. "Only decent fellows don't cry over every little pain like kids."

"Go on!" they bawled after me. "You ould idiot!" And, as I went down the school lane, still trying to keep what the stories called "a stiff upper lip," and consoling myself with the thought that my torment was over until next morning, I heard their mocking voices after me.

"Loony Larry! Yah, Loony Larry!"

I realized that if I was to keep on terms with the invisible presences I should have to watch my step at school.

So I did, all through that year. But one day an awful thing happened. I was coming in from the yard, and in the porch outside our schoolroom I saw a fellow called Gorman taking something from a coat on the rack. I always described Gorman to myself as "the black sheep of the school." He was a fellow I disliked and feared; a handsome, sulky, spoiled, and sneering lout. I paid no attention to him because I had escaped for a few moments into my dream-world in which fathers never gave less than fivers and the honour of the school was always saved by some quiet, unassuming fellow like myself— "a dark horse," as the stories called him.

"Who are you looking at?" Gorman asked threateningly.

"I wasn't looking at anyone," I replied with an indignant start.

"I was only getting a pencil out of my coat," he added, clenching his fists.

"Nobody said you weren't," I replied, thinking that this was a very queer subject to start a row about.

"You'd better not, either," he snarled. "You can mind your own business."

"You mind yours!" I retorted, purely for the purpose of saving face. "I never spoke to you at all."

And that, so far as I was concerned, was the end of it.

But after playtime the Murderer, looking exceptionally serious, stood before the class, balancing a pencil in both hands.

"Everyone who left the classroom this morning, stand out!" he called. Then he lowered his head and looked at us from under his brows. "Mind now, I said everyone!"

I stood out with the others, including Gorman. We were all very puzzled.

"Did you take anything from a coat on the rack this morning?" the Murderer asked, laying a heavy, hairy paw on Gorman's shoulder and staring menacingly into his eyes.

"Me sir?" Gorman exclaimed innocently. "No, sir."

"Did you see anyone else doing it?"

"No, sir."

"You?" he asked another lad, but even before he reached me at all I realized why Gorman had told the lie and wondered frantically what I should do.

"You?" He asked me, and his big red face was close to mine, his blue eyes were only a few inches away, and the smell of his toilet soap was in my nostrils. My panic made me say the wrong thing as though I had planned it.

"I didn't take anything, sir," I said in a low voice.

"Did you see someone else do it?" he asked, raising his brows and showing quite plainly that he had noticed my evasion. "Have you a tongue in your head?" he shouted suddenly, and the whole class, electrified, stared at me. "You?" he added curtly to the next boy as though he had lost interest in me.

"No, sir."

"Back to your desks, the rest of you!" he ordered. "Delaney, you stay here."

He waited till everyone was seated again before going on.

"Turn out your pockets."

I did, and a half-stifled giggle rose, which the Murderer quelled with a thunderous glance. Even for a small boy I had pockets that were museums in themselves: the purpose of half the things I brought to light I couldn't have explained myself. They were antiques, prehistoric and unlabelled. Among them was a school story borrowed the previous evening from a queer fellow who chewed paper as if it were gum. The Murderer reached out for it, and holding it at arm's length, shook it out with an expression of deepening disgust as he noticed the nibbled corners and margins.

"Oh," he said disdainfully, "so this is how you waste your time! What do you do with this rubbish—eat it?"

" 'Tisn't mine, sir," I said against the laugh that sprang up. "I borrowed it."

"Is that what you did with the money?" he asked quickly, his fat head on one side.

"Money?" I repeated in confusion. "What money?"

"The shilling that was stolen from Flanagan's overcoat this morning."

(Flanagan was a little hunchback whose people coddled him; no one else in the school would have possessed that much money.) "I never took Flanagan's shilling," I said, beginning to cry, "and you have no right to say I did."

"I have the right to say you're the most impudent and defiant puppy in the school," he replied, his voice hoarse with rage, "and I wouldn't put it past you. What else can anyone expect and you reading this dirty, rotten, filthy rubbish?" And he tore my school story in halves and flung them to the furthest corner of the classroom. "Dirty, filthy, English rubbish! Now, hold out your hand."

This time the invisible presences deserted me. Hearing themselves described in these contemptuous terms, they fled. The Murderer went mad in the way people do whenever they're up against something they don't understand. Even the other fellows were shocked, and, heaven knows, they had little sympathy with me.

"You should put the police on him," they advised me later in the playground. "He lifted the cane over his shoulder. He could get the gaol for that."

"But why didn't you say you didn't see anyone?" asked the eldest, a fellow called Spillane.

"Because I did," I said, beginning to sob all over again at the memory of my wrongs, "I saw Gorman."

"Gorman?" Spillane echoed incredulously. "Was it Gorman took Flanagan's money? And why didn't you say so?"

"Because it wouldn't be right," I sobbed.

"Why wouldn't it be right?"

"Because Gorman should have told the truth himself," I said. "And if this was a proper school he'd be sent to Coventry."

"He'd be sent where?"

"Coventry. No one would ever speak to him again."

"But why would Gorman tell the truth if he took the money?" Spillane asked as you'd speak to a baby. "Jay, Delaney," he added pityingly, "you're getting madder and madder. Now, look at what you're after bringing on yourself!"

Suddenly Gorman came lumbering up, red and angry.

"Delaney," he shouted threateningly, "did you say I took Flanagan's money?"

Gorman, though I of course didn't realize it, was as much at sea as Moloney and the rest. Seeing me take all that punishment rather than give him away, he concluded I must be more afraid of him than of Moloney, and that the proper thing to do was to make me more so. He couldn't have come at a time when I cared less for him. I didn't even bother to reply but lashed out with all my strength at his brutal face. This was the last thing he expected. He screamed, and his hand came away from his face, all blood. Then he threw off his satchel and came at me, but at the same moment a door opened behind us and a lame teacher called Murphy emerged. We all ran like mad and the fight was forgotten.

It didn't remain forgotten, though. Next morning after prayers the Murderer scowled at me.

"Delaney, were you fighting in the yard after school yesterday?"

For a second or two I didn't reply. I couldn't help feeling that it wasn't worth it. But before the invisible presences fled forever, I made another effort.

"I was, sir," I said, and this time there wasn't even a titter. I was out of my mind. The whole class knew it and was awestricken.

"Who were you fighting?"

"I'd sooner not say, sir," I replied, hysteria beginning to well up in me. It was all very well for the invisible presences, but they hadn't to deal with the Murderer.

"Who was he fighting with?" he asked lightly, resting his hands on the desk and studying the ceiling.

"Gorman, sir," replied three or four voices—as easy as that!

"Did Gorman hit him first?"

"No, sir. He hit Gorman first."

"Stand out," he said, taking up the cane. "Now," he added, going up to Gorman, "you take this and hit him. And make sure you hit him hard," he went on, giving Gorman's arm an encouraging squeeze. "He thinks he's a great fellow. You show him now what we think of him."

Gorman came towards me with a broad grin. He thought it a great joke. The class thought it a great joke. They began to roar with laughter. Even the Murderer permitted himself a modest grin at his own cleverness.

"Hold out your hand," he said to me.

I didn't. I began to feel trapped and a little crazy.

"Hold out your hand, I say," he shouted, beginning to lose his temper.

"I will not," I shouted back, losing all control of myself.

"You what?" he cried incredulously, dashing at me round the classroom with his hand raised as though to strike me. "What's that you said, you dirty little thief?"

"I'm not a thief, I'm not a thief," I screamed. "And if he comes near me I'll kick the shins off him. You have no right to give him that cane, and you have no right to call me a thief either. If you do it again, I'll go down to the police and then we'll see who the thief is."

"You refused to answer my questions," he roared, and if I had been in my right mind I should have known he had suddenly taken fright; probably the word "police" had frightened him.

"No," I said through my sobs, "and I won't answer them now either. I'm not a spy."

"Oh," he retorted with a sarcastic sniff, "so that's what you call a spy, Mr. Delaney?"

"Yes, and that's what they all are, all the fellows here—dirty spies!—but I'm not going to be a spy for you. You can do your own spying."

"That's enough now, that's enough!" he said, raising his fat hand almost beseechingly. "There's no need to lose control of yourself, my dear young fellow, and there's no need whatever to screech like that. 'Tis most unmanly. Go back to your seat now and I'll talk to you another time."

I obeyed, but I did no work. No one else did much either. The hysteria had spread to the class. I alternated between fits of exultation at my own successful defiance of the Murderer, and panic at the prospect of his revenge; and at each change of mood I put my face in my hands and sobbed again. The Murderer didn't even order me to stop. He didn't so much as look at me.

After that I was the hero of the school for the whole afternoon. Gorman tried to resume the fight, but Spillane ordered him away contemptuously—a fellow who had taken the master's cane to another had no status. But that wasn't the sort of hero I wanted to be. I preferred something less sensational.

Next morning I was in such a state of panic that I didn't know how I should face school at all. I dawdled, between two minds as to whether or not I should mitch. The silence of the school lane and yard awed me. I had made myself late as well.

"What kept you, Delaney?" the Murderer asked quietly.

I knew it was no good.

"I was at Mass, sir."

"All right. Take your seat."

He seemed a bit surprised. What I had not realized was the incidental advantage of our system over the English one. By this time half a dozen of his pets had brought the Murderer the true story of Flanagan's shilling, and if he didn't feel a monster he probably felt a fool.

But by that time I didn't care. In my school sack I had another story. Not a school story this time, though. School stories were a wash-out. "Bang! Bang!"—that was the only way to deal with men like the Murderer. "The only good teacher is a dead teacher."

RESPONSES: Questions for Writing and Discussion

1. Do you have any fond memories of novels, stories, movies, or television shows that had special appeal for you while you were growing up? Perhaps you would like to share one or two of these with the rest of the class. Did these early influences fall into a category, like the school stories which meant so much to the narrator of "The Idealist"? Did they create any particular expectations about reality which later turned out to be false?

2. The "invisible presences" (the "grand chaps" from the school stories) give the hero the courage he needs to endure the Murderer's punishments, at least for a time. They turn out, as the story is presented, to have been worth little in the long run. Do you agree? Do romantic ideals help people in any way? Would you want your children to believe or disbelieve in the "invisible presences"?

3. The narrator finally manages to become a heroic figure in the eyes of his classmates, though it is not exactly the way in which he wanted this to happen. When does he merit the admiration of the class? Why did he never have it when he was telling the truth and enduring the physical punishment stoically? What is O'Connor apparently saying here about people and their values?

4. If the story represented a simple case of impossible idealism versus realism, Murderer Moloney would probably have been a less complex character, in the sense that O'Connor would not have needed him to symbolize anything more than the brutal facts of life. But as it turns out, the Murderer has his own story, his own problems. Characterize him. Indicate, particularly, how you think he felt when he learned the truth about Flanagan's shilling. Is O'Connor making a statement through this character?

5. When, finally, the hero resorts to lying to avoid being caned, is it a victory for the Murderer? For the hero? For neither?

6. It is obvious that the hero has changed at the story's ending. He is no longer reading romantic tales of honorable school boys, but appears to have developed a taste for violence. He now is persuaded that "the only good teacher is a dead teacher." Has he indeed emerged from the idealism of adolescence to the realism of a more mature person?

7. As we pointed out in the introduction to this story, O'Connor is known for his sense of humor as well as for his penetrating insights into human beings and their complex interrelationships. This doesn't mean that there is humor in all of his stories. Looking back, do you find any evidence of it in "The Idealist"?

THE AMORALIST
Bernard Williams

From the time of Socrates until the early years of this century there have been philosophical debates over the ultimate sanctions governing moral behavior, but the idea was seldom if ever advanced that morality might just possibly have no validity at all as an object of intellectual inquiry. Early in this century, however, some philosophers began boldly to denounce nearly every traditional concern including that of morality. Their contention was that only science deals with matters of truth. All philosophy can do is analyze the language of its own propositions to determine whether it bears any meaningful relationship to the physical world. For many, the language of moral philosophy is clearly without such meaning. It is useless to argue over the "right" and "wrong" in a given instance, when "right" and "wrong" are empty terms, signifying nothing.

This new position has achieved a degree of status which has been disturbing to many who fear its implications: the position of *amoralism*. The amoralist in theory is one who does not see the need to justify his actions on any philosophical ground at all. Unlike the moral relativists who cite reasons for doing what they do, the amoralist simply says that no one has the right to inquire. We exist, he contends, in a world that simply *is*. Life serves no purpose. Obviously no God or any other rational being has created us. Society with its groundrules of behavior is an artifice, a mere convenience; those who wish to follow its norms may suit themselves, but there is no *logical* basis for this. *Logic cannot interpret an illogical universe.* Hence actions are merely actions. There is no binding necessity for any of us to behave in any certain way.

The theory of amoralism is, however, as meaningless to some modern philosophers as all traditional moral standards appear to be to the amoralists. It is frequently pointed out, for example, that those who argue most strongly for it do not practice what they teach. Whether from fear of society's reprisals or from some secret, unadmitted recognition of the absurdity of their views, they behave no more "amorally" than most people.

The following selection represents a favorite concern of contemporary moral philosophy: a logical argument for the existence of meaningful moral standards transcendent to the individual. But the author makes his point by taking an unusual route. Instead of defensively holding the fort against the invading forces of amoralism, he sets out by cordially entertaining their claims. He places on the table every possible argument the amoralist could advance and analyzes it politely but with an almost merciless thoroughness.

Currently Professor of Philosophy and Fellow of Kings College, Cambridge, **Bernard Williams (b. 1929)** has written *Imagination and the Self* and co-edited *British Analytical Philosophy* as well as contributed a number of articles to philosophical journals. That the style of "The Amoralist" is unusually personable and engaging is no accident. Williams represents a newer breed of philosopher who believes in approaching enduring problems in new ways.

The Amoralist

"Why should I do anything?" Two of the many ways of taking that question are these: as an expression of despair or hopelessness, when it means something like "Give me a reason for doing anything; everything is meaningless"; and as sounding a more defiant note, against morality, when it means something like "Why is there anything that I *should, ought to,* do?"

Even though we can paraphrase the question in the first spirit as "Give me a reason . . . ," it is very unclear that we can in fact give the man who asks it a reason—that, starting from so far down, we could *argue* him into caring about something. . . . But the man who asks the question in the second spirit has been regarded by many moralists as providing a real challenge to moral reasoning. He, after all, acknowledges some reasons for doing things; he is, moreover, like most of us some of the time. If morality can be got off the ground rationally, then we ought to be able to get it off the ground in an argument against him; while, in his pure form—in which we can call him the *amoralist*—he may not be actually persuaded, it might seem a comfort to morality if there were reasons which, if he were rational, would persuade him.

We might ask first what motivations he does have. He is indifferent to moral considerations, but there are things that he cares about, and he has some real preferences and aims. They might be, presumably, pleasure or power; or they might be something much odder, such as some passion for collecting things. Now these ends in themselves do not exclude some acknowledgment of morality; what do we have to leave out to represent him as paying no such acknowledgment? Presumably such things as his caring about other people's interests, having any inclination to tell the truth or keep promises if it does not suit him to do so, being disposed to reject courses of action on the ground that they are unfair or dishonorable or selfish. These are

From *Morality: An Introduction to Ethics* by Bernard Williams. Reprinted by permission of Harper & Row, Publishers, Inc.

some of the substantial materials of morality. We should perhaps also leave out a more formal aspect of morality, namely any disposition on his part to stand back and have the thought that if it is 'all right' for him to act in these ways, it must be 'all right' for others to act similarly against him. For if he is prepared to take this stance, we might be able to take a step towards saying that he was not a man without a morality, but a man with a peculiar one.

However, we need a distinction here. In one way, it is possible for a man to think it 'all right' for everyone to behave self-interestedly, without his having got into any distinctively moral territory of thought at all: if, roughly, 'it's all right' means 'I am not going to moralize about it'. He will be in some moral territory if 'all right' means something like 'permitted', for that would carry implications such as 'people ought not to interfere with other people's pursuit of their own interests', and that is not a thought which, as an amoralist, he can have. Similarly, if he objects (as he no doubt will) to other people treating him as he treats them, this will be perfectly consistent so long as his objecting consists just in such things as his not liking it and fighting back. What he cannot consistently do is *resent* it or disapprove of it, for these are attitudes within the moral system. It may be difficult to discover whether he has given this hostage to moral argument or not, since he will no doubt have discovered that insincere expressions of resentment and moral hurt serve to discourage some of the more squeamish in his environment from hostile action.

This illustrates, as do many of his activities, the obvious fact that this man is a parasite on the moral system, and he and his satisfactions could not exist as they do unless others operated differently. For, in general, there can be no society without some moral rules, and he needs society; also he takes more particular advantage of moral institutions like promising and of moral dispositions of people around him. He cannot deny, as a fact, his parasitic position; but he is very resistant to suggestions of its relevance. For if we try saying "How would it be for you if everyone behaved like that?" he will reply, "Well, if they did, not good, I suppose—though in fact I might do better in the resulting chaos than some of the others. But the fact is, most of them are not going to do so; and if they do ever get round to it, I shall be dead by then." The appeal to the consequences of an *imagined* universalization is an essentially moral argument, and he is, consistently, not impressed by it.

In maintaining this stance, there are several things he must, in consistency, avoid. One—as we noticed before, in effect—is any tendency to say that the more or less moral majority have *no right* to dislike him, reject him, or treat him as an enemy, if indeed they are inclined to do so (his power, or charm, or dishonesty may be such that they do not). No thoughts about justification, at least of that sort, are appropriate to him. Again, he must resist, if consistent, a more insidious tendency to think of himself as being in character really rather splendid—in particular, as being by comparison with the craven multitude notably courageous. For in entertaining such thoughts, he will run a constant danger of getting outside the world of his own desires and tastes into the region in which certain dispositions are regarded as excellent for human beings to have, or good to have in society, or such things; and while such thoughts need not lead directly to moral considerations, they give a substantial footing to them, since they immediately invite questions about what is so good about those dispositions, and it will be difficult for him to pursue those questions very far without thinking in terms of the *general* interests and needs of his fellow human beings, which would land him once more back in the world of moral thought from which he is excluding himself.

The temptation to think of himself as courageous is a particularly dangerous one, since it is itself very nearly a moral notion and draws with it a whole chain of distinctively moral reflections. This man's application of the notion will also have a presupposition which is false: namely, that the more moral citizens would be amoral if they could get away with it, or if they were not too frightened, or if they were not passively conditioned by society—if, in general, they did not suffer from inhibitions. It is the idea that they are afraid that gives him the idea of his own courage. But these presuppositions are absurd. If he means that if as an individual one could be sure of getting away with it, one would break any moral rule (the idea behind the model of Gyges' ring of invisibility in Plato's *Republic*), it is just false of many agents, and there is reason why: the more basic moral rules and con-ceptions are strongly internalized in upbringing, at a level from which they do not merely evaporate with the departure of policemen or censorious neighbors. This is part of what it is for them to be moral rules, as opposed to *merely* legal requirements or matters of social convention. The effects of moral education can actually be to make people *want* to act, quite often, in a non-self-interested way, and it often succeeds in making it at least quite difficult, for internal reasons, to behave appallingly.

But this, he will say, is just social conditioning; remove that, and you will find no moral motivations.—We can reject the rhetoric of the word 'conditioning'; even if there were a true theory, which there is not, which could explain all moral and similar education in terms of behaviorist learning theory, it would itself have to explain the very evident differences between successful and intelligent upbringing, which produces insight, and the production of conditioned reflexes. But let us say instead that all moral motivation is the product of social influences, teaching, culture, etc. It is no doubt true. But virtually everything else about a man is such a product, including his language, his methods of thought, his tastes, and even his emotions, including most of the dispositions that the amoralist sets store by.—But, he may say, suppose we grant that anything complex, even my desires, are influenced by culture and environment, and in many cases produced by these; nevertheless there are *basic* impulses, of a self-interested kind, which are at the bottom of it all: these constitute what men are *really* like.

If 'basic' means 'genetically primitive', he may possibly be right: it is a matter of psychological theory. But even if true in this sense, it is once more irrelevant (to his argument, not to questions about how to bring up children); if there is such a thing as what men are *really* like, it is not identical with what very small children are like, since very small children have no language, again, nor many other things which men really have. If the test of what men are *really* like is made, rather, cf how men may behave in conditions of great stress, deprivation, or scarcity (the test that Hobbes, in his picture of the state of nature, imposed), one can only ask again, why should that be the test? Apart from the unclarity of its outcome, why is the test even appropriate? Conditions of great stress and deprivation are not the conditions for observing the typical behavior of any animal nor for observing other characteristics of human beings. If someone says that if you want to see what men are *really* like, see them after they have been three weeks in a lifeboat, it is unclear why that is any better a maxim with regard to their motivations than it is with regard to their physical condition.

If there is such a thing as what men are *really* like, it may be that (in these sorts of respects, at least) it is not so different from what they are *actually* like; that is, creatures in whose lives moral considerations play an important, formative, but often insecure role.

The amoralist, then, would probably be advised to avoid most forms of self-congratulatory comparison of himself with the rest of society. The rest may, of course, have some tendency to admire him, or those may who are at such a distance that he does not tread directly on their interests and affections. He should not be too encouraged by this, however, since it is probably wish-fulfillment (which does not mean that they would be like him if they could, since a wish is different from a frustrated desire). Nor will they admire him, still less like him, if he is not recognizably human. And this raises the question, whether we have left him enough to be that.

Does he care for anybody? Is there anybody whose sufferings or distress would affect him? If we say "no" to this, it looks as though we have produced a psychopath. If he is a psychopath, the idea of arguing him into morality is surely idiotic, but the fact that it is idiotic has equally no tendency to undermine the basis of morality or of rationality. The activity of justifying morality must surely get any point it has from the existence of an alternative—there being something to justify it *against*. The amoralist seemed important because he seemed to provide an alternative; his life, after all, seemed to have its attractions. The psychopath is, in a certain way, important to moral thought; but his importance lies in the fact that he appalls us, and we must seek some deeper understanding of how and why he appalls us. His importance does not lie in his having an appeal as an alternative form of life.

The amoralist we loosely sketched before did seem to have possibly more appeal than this; one might picture him as having some affections, occasionally caring for what happens to somebody else. Some stereotype from a gangster movie might come to mind, of the ruthless and rather glamorous figure who cares about his mother, his child, even his mistress. He is still recognizably amoral, in the sense that no general considerations weigh with him, and he is extremely short on fairness and similar considerations. Although he acts for other people from time to time, it all depends on how he happens to feel. With this man, of course, in actual fact arguments of moral philosophy are not going to work; for one thing, he always has something he would rather do than listen to them. This is not the point (though it is more of a point than some discussions of moral argument would lead one to suppose). The point is rather that he provides a model in terms of which we may glimpse what moral considerations need to get off the ground, even though they are unlikely in practice to get off the ground in a conversation with him.

He gives us, I think, almost enough. For he has the notion of doing something *for* somebody, because that person needs something. He operates with this notion in fact only when he is so inclined; but it is not itself the notion of his being so inclined. Even if he helps these people because he wants to, or because he likes them, and for no other reason (not that, so far as these particular actions are concerned, he needs to improve on those excellent reasons), what he wants to do is to *help them in their need,* and the thought he has when he likes someone and acts in this way is 'they need help', not the thought 'I like them and they need help'. This is a vital point: this man is capable of thinking in terms of others' interests, and his failure to be a moral agent lies (partly) in the fact that he is only intermittently and capriciously disposed to do so. But there is no bottomless gulf between this state and the basic dispositions of morality. There are people who need help who are not people who at the moment he happens to want to help, or likes; and there are other people who like and want to help other particular people in need. To get him to consider their situation seems rather an extension of his imagination and his understanding, than a discontinuous step onto something quite different, the 'moral plane'. And if we could get him to consider their situation, in the sense of thinking about it and imagining it, he might conceivably start to show some consideration for it: we extend his sympathies. And if we can get him to extend his sympathies to less immediate persons who need help, we might be able to do it for less immediate persons whose interests have been violated, and so get him to have some primitive grasp on notions of fairness. If we can get him all this way, then, while he has no doubt an extremely shaky hold on moral considerations, he has some hold on them; at any rate, he is not the amoralist we started with. . . .

RESPONSES: Questions for Writing and Discussion

1. Whether, as the author contends, it is impossible to be a thorough-going, consistent amoralist, it is hard to deny that each of us exhibits a high degree of fluctuation in his moral orientation. No doubt each of us has amoral moments when he does not care about "other people's interests" or has no inclination to tell the truth or keep promises "if it does not suit him to do so. . . ." Would you be willing to share with the class an account of some occasion in which you had made a choice you could call philosophically amoral? How did you feel about it? Did it bother your conscience? Why or why not? Did you ever face a similar choice on another occasion but acted differently? How do you account for the difference? Which approach "felt" better?

2. If or when you are about to perform an action your conscience tells you is *not* right for everyone to do, do you stop and reconsider it? Or go ahead and do it anyway? What then do you tell your conscience?

3. According to the author, an amoralist, who believes it is all right for everyone "to behave self-interestedly," has no rational right to resent it when others, acting out of self-interest, harm him, or at least treat him as irresponsibly as he does them. Do you agree? Is there a "law" of self-interest which gives people such a right? If so, where does the law come from? If not, is there a contrary law which *denies* the right?

4. Would you be willing to share with the class an account of a time when, after having acted selfishly with no thought of the consequences of your action on others, you found yourself on the receiving end of a similar action? How did you feel? Did you say "The joke's

on me"? Did you harbor thoughts of revenge? If the latter, do you think they were justified?

5. Anger and resentment toward others and their actions is a universal emotion. When you have these feelings, do you tend on the whole to be responding on selfish or on moral grounds? If the response seems to be moral—in the sense that you are saying an action is not right or not fair—do contrary values serve consistently as the basis of your own behavior? If you admit that your reasons are purely selfish and do not reflect a moral code you are prepared to live by, why are you ever angry?

6. The amoralist is a "parasite" on society, says the author, in that he counts on the moral behavior of others. (Would not a man who is seen committing a robbery, for example, hope that the eyewitness would "do the decent thing" and not tell anyone?) In your opinion, when people commit crimes, do they rely on the noncriminal nature of others? Or do they tend to believe "it's you or me in this dog-eat-dog world"? If the latter, do you think such a philosophy is accurate? a cover-up? If the former, does this make crime unjustifiable?

7. Do you agree with the author when he refutes the amoralist's charge that everyone would break the law if he could get away with it? Do you agree with him that majority of people have had and abide by a moral education and would *not* take advantage of others even if the opportunity should arise?

8. The author attacks the often posed idea that men are "basically" self-centered and suggests instead that mature people are "basically" what social conditioning (including the inculcation of moral values) makes them. Do you consider social conditioning a valid source of moral absolutes? Is it a defensible argument that, since people outside of social conditioning would be selfish and greedy, it makes good sense to base one's morality on the "pre" social view of humanity?

9. By the conclusion of his essay Williams asserts that he has considerably altered the portrait of the alleged amoralist. His motive in doing so is obviously to show that a moral system does exist that is higher than self-interest, one to which all of us—whether we like it or not—are to some extent bound. But if you wanted to become a true amoralist, what would your life style be? Do you think it would work?

ABOUT ED RICKETTS

John Steinbeck

In 1939 **John Steinbeck (1902–1969)**, already recognized as one of America's more promising literary talents, already famous as the compassionate interpreter of life mong the poor and inarticulate people who exist close to nature, assured himself of international recognition with the publication of *The Grapes of Wrath*. Discerning readers found in the book more than a strong protest against discrimination, against the capitalistic exploitation of America's poor, against the inhumanities of the corporate state—though it was all of these things too. What they found at the core of this modern epic was the vision of a poet and philosopher, a complex system of thoughts and values based on the operations of nature. In this, as in all of Steinbeck's work, the natural is the right and the good. Suppressing any part of nature —as, for example, when one exploits the poor—is a type of evil.

Steinbeck was so convinced one could derive a philosophy and a moral system from observing closely the movements and directions of nature that he sought greater knowledge of nature's most microscopic levels. He wanted to discover the ideal life style for anyone who lived according to the natural law of his being. Most humans, especially those furthest away from nature— the intellects, the sophisticated inhabitants of the cities, the businessmen pursuing greater and greater wealth, the exponents of institutional religion —lived unnatural lives. They sometimes waged war for ideological purposes. They devastated the environment. And for this, they had lost the power to live well and fully and in harmony with the scheme of things.

In 1940 Steinbeck and Ed Rickets, a marine biologist but better known to readers the world over as "Doc" of *Cannery Row*, made a diving expedition to and under the Gulf of California for the purpose of studying the marine life, some species of which were unique to this locale, others of which had never been fully analyzed and categorized. In 1948 Ricketts died a sudden, untimely death in an automobile accident, and the shock of his passing, coupled with a fervent desire to create a fitting memorial to his friend, led Steinbeck to compose the eulogy that follows.

Ricketts emerges as the archetype of the Steinbeckian *natural man*, the heroic being who is admired for living by his own code even when this goes contrary to social customs and the "laws" governing decent human conduct. As Steinbeck presents him to us, Ricketts must have seemed at the very least a scoundrel to the righteous-minded of Monterey. Dedicated to his own pleasures, a passionate lover of women and alcohol, a despiser of all binding systems and methods of organizing one's life and business, Ricketts believed in the essential rightness of nature's laws. He believed implicitly in the inner urges and lived in accordance with the wise dictates of his heart. To have done otherwise, in his opinion, would have constituted a most *im*moral approach to living.

The case of Ed Ricketts provides the reader with a good chance to ask some crucial questions, including: what happens if everyone follows the natural tendencies of his own unique being? Is compromise with some transcendent moral system better in the long run—and for whom?

About Ed Ricketts

It is going to be difficult to write down the things about Ed Ricketts that must be written, hard to separate entities. And anyone who knew him would find it difficult. Maybe some of the events are imagined. And perhaps some very small happenings may have grown out of all proportion in the mind. And then there is the personal impact. I am sure that many people, seeing this account, will be sure to say, "Why, that's not true. That's not the way he was at all. He was this way and this." And the speaker may go on to describe a person this writer did not know at all. But no one who knew him will deny the force and influence of Ed Ricketts. Everyone near him was influenced by him, deeply and permanently. Some he taught how to think, others how to see or hear. Children on the beach he taught how to look for and find beautiful animals in worlds they had not suspected were there at all. He taught everyone without seeming to.

Nearly everyone who knew him has tried to define him. Such things were said of him as, "He was half-Christ and half-goat." He was a great teacher and a great lecher—an immortal who loved women. Surely he was an original and his character was unique, but in such a way that everyone was related to him, one in this way and another in some different way. He was gentle but capable of ferocity, small and slight but strong as an ox, loyal and yet untrustworthy, generous but gave little and received much. His thinking was as paradoxical as his life. He thought in mystical terms and hated and distrusted mysticism. He was an individualist who studied colonial animals with satisfaction.

We have all tried to define Ed Ricketts with little success. Perhaps it would be better to put down the mass of material from our memories, anecdotes, quotations, events. Of course some of the things will cancel others, but that is the way he was. The essence lies somewhere. There must be some way of finding it.

Finally there is another reason to put Ed Ricketts down on paper. He will not die. He haunts the people who knew him. He is always present even in the moments when we feel his loss the most.

One night soon after his death a number of us were drinking beer in the laboratory. We laughed and told stories about Ed, and suddenly one of us said in pain, "We'll have to let him go! We'll have to release him and let him go." And that was true not for Ed but for ourselves. We can't keep him, and still he will not go away.

Maybe if I write down everything I can remember about him, that will lay the ghost. It is worth trying anyway. It will have to be true or it can't work. It must be no celebration of his virtues, because, as was said of another man, he had the faults of his virtues. There can be no formula. The simplest and best way will be just to remember— as much as I can. . . .

When I first knew him, his laboratory was an old house in Cannery Row which he had bought and transformed to his purposes. The entrance was a kind of showroom with mounted marine specimens in glass jars on shelves around the walls. Next to this room was a small office, where for some reason the rattlesnakes were kept in cages between the safe and the filing cabinets. The top of the safe was piled high with stationery and filing cards. Ed loved paper and cards. He never ordered small amounts but huge supplies of it.

On the side of the building toward the ocean were two more rooms, one with cages for white rats—hundreds of white rats, and reproducing furiously. This room used to get pretty smelly if it was not cleaned with great regularity—which it never was. The other rear room was set up with microscopes and slides and the equipment for making and mounting and baking the delicate microorganisms which were so much a part of the laboratory income. In the basement there was a big stockroom with jars and tanks for preserving the larger animals, and also the equipment for embalming and injecting the cats, dogfish, frogs, and other animals that were used by dissection classes.

This little house was called Pacific Biological Laboratories, Inc., as strange an operation as ever outraged the corporate laws of California. When, after Ed's death, the corporation had to be liquidated, it was impossible to find out who owned the stock, how much of it there was, or what it was worth. Ed kept the most careful collecting notes on record, but sometimes he would not open a business letter for weeks.

How the business ran for twenty years no one knows, but it did run even though it staggered a little sometimes. At times it would spurt ahead with system and efficiency and then wearily collapse for several months. Orders would pile up on the desk. Once during a weary period someone sent Ed a cheesecake by parcel post. He thought it was preserved material of some kind, and when he finally opened it three months later we could not have identified it had it not been that a note was enclosed which said, "Eat this cheesecake at once. It's very delicate."

Often the desk was piled so high with unopened letters that they slid tiredly to the floor. Ed believed completely in the theory that a letter unanswered for a week usually requires no answer, but he went even farther. A letter unopened for a month does not require opening. . . .

His mind had no horizons. He was interested in everything. And there were very few things he did not like. Perhaps it would be well to set down the things he did not like. Maybe they would be some kind of key to his personality, although it is my conviction that there is no such key.

Chief among his hatreds was old age. He hated it in other people and did not even conceive of it in himself. He hated old women and would not stay in a room with them. He said he could smell them. He had a remarkable sense of smell. He could smell a mouse in a room, and I have seen him locate a rattlesnake in the brush by smell.

He hated women with thin lips. "If the lips are thin—where will there be any fullness?" he would say. His observation was certainly physical and open to verification, and he seemed to believe in its accuracy and so do I, but with less vehemence.

He loved women too much to take any nonsense from the thin-lipped ones. But if a girl with thin lips painted on fuller ones with lipstick, he was satisfied. "Her intentions are correct," he said, "There is a psychic fullness, and sometimes that can be very fine."

He hated hot soup and would pour cold water into the most beautifully prepared bisque.

He unequivocally hated to get his head wet. Collecting animals in the tide pools, he would be soaked by the waves to his eyebrows, but his head was invariably covered and safe. In the shower he wore an oilskin sou'wester—a ridiculous sight.

He hated one professor whom he referred to as an "old jingle ballicks." It never developed why he hated "old jingle ballicks."

He hated pain inflicted without good reason. Driving through the streets one night, he saw a man beating a red setter with a rake handle. Ed stopped the car and attacked the man with a monkey wrench and would have killed him if the man had not run away.

Although slight in build, when he was angry Ed had no fear and could be really dangerous. On an occasion one of our cops was pistol-whipping a drunk in the middle of the night. Ed attacked the cop with his bare hands, and his fury was so great that the cop released the drunk.

This hatred was only for reasonless cruelty. When the infliction of pain was necessary, he had little feeling about it. Once during the depression we found we could buy a live sheep for three dollars. This may seem incredible now but it was so. It was a great deal of food and even for those days a great bargain. Then we had the sheep and none of us could kill it. But Ed cut its throat with no emotion whatever, and even explained to the rest of us who were upset that bleeding to death is quite painless if there is no fear involved. The pain of opening a vein is slight if the instrument is sharp, and he had opened the jugular with a scalpel and had not frightened the animal, so that our secondary or empathic pain was probably much greater than that of the sheep.

His feeling for psychic pain in normal people also was philosophic. He would say that nearly everything that can happen to people not only does happen but has happened for a million years. "Therefore," he would say, "for everything that can happen there is a channel or mechanism in the human to take care of it—a channel worn down in prehistory and transmitted in the genes."

He disliked time intensely unless it was part of an observation or an experiment. He was invariably and consciously late for appointments. He said he had once worked for a railroad where his whole life had been regulated by a second hand and that he had then conceived his disgust, a disgust for exactness in time. To my knowledge, that is the only time he ever spoke of the railroad experience. If you asked him to dinner at seven, he might get there at nine. On the other hand, if a good low collecting tide was at 6:53, he would be in the tide pool at 6:52. . . .

Life on Cannery Row was curious and dear and outrageous. Across the street from Pacific Biological was Monterey's largest, most genteel and respected whorehouse. It was owned and operated by a very great woman who was beloved and trusted by all who came in contact with her except those few whose judgment was twisted by a limited virtue. She was a large-hearted woman and a law-abiding citizen in every way except one—she did violate the nebulous laws against prostitution. But since the police didn't seem to care, she felt all right about it and even made little presents in various directions.

During the depression Madam paid the grocery bills for most of the destitute families on Cannery Row. When the Chamber of Commerce collected money for any cause and businessmen were assessed at ten dollars, Madam was always nicked for a hundred. The same was true for any mendicant charity. She halfway paid for the widows and orphans of policemen and firemen. She was expected to and did contribute ten times the ordinary amount toward any civic brainstorm of citizens who pretended she did not exist. Also, she was a wise and tolerant pushover for any hard-luck story. Everyone put the bee on her. Even when she knew it was a fake she dug down.

Ed Ricketts maintained relations of respect and friendliness with Madam. He did not patronize the house. His sex life was far too complicated for that. But Madam brought many of her problems to him, and he gave her the best of his thinking and his knowledge, both scientific and profane.

There seems to be a tendency toward hysteria among girls in such a house. I do not know whether hysterically inclined types enter the business or whether the business produces hysteria. But often Madam would send a girl over to the laboratory to talk to Ed. He would listen with great care and concern to her troubles, which were rarely complicated, and then he would talk soothingly to her and play some of his favorite music to her on his phonograph. The girl usually went back reinforced with his strength. He never moralized in any way. He would be more likely to examine the problem carefully, with calm and clarity, and to lift the horrors out of it by easy examination. Suddenly the girl would discover that she was not alone, that many other people had the same problems—in a word that her misery was not unique. And then she usually felt better about it.

There was a tacit but strong affection between Ed and Madam. She did not have a license to sell liquor to be taken out. Quite often Ed would run out of beer so late at night that everything except Madam's house was close. There followed a ritual which was thoroughly enjoyed by both parties. Ed would cross the street and ask Madam to sell him some beer. She invariably refused, explaining every time that she did not have a license. Ed would shrug his shoulders, apologize for asking, and go back to the lab. Ten minutes later there would be soft footsteps on the stairs and a little thump in front of the door and then running slippered steps down again. Ed would wait a decent interval and then go to the door. And on his doorstep, in a paper bag, would be six bottles of ice-cold beer. He would never mention it to Madam. That would have been breaking the rules of the game. But he repaid her with hours of his time when she needed his help. And his help was not inconsiderable.

Sometimes, as happens even in the soundest whorehouse, there would be a fight on a Saturday night—one of those things which are likely to occur when love and wine come together. It was only sensible that Madam would not want to bother the police or a doctor with her little problem. Then her good friend Ed would patch up cut faces and torn ears and split mouths. He was a good operator and there were never any complaints. And naturally no one ever mentioned the matter since he was not a doctor of medicine and had no license to practice anything except philanthropy. Madam and Ed had the greatest respect for each other. "She's one hell of a woman," he said. "I wish good people could be as good." . . .

Ed had more fun than nearly anyone I have ever known, and he had deep sorrows also, which will be treated later. As long as we are on the subject of drinking I will complete that department.

Ed loved to drink, and he loved to drink just about anything. I don't think I ever saw him in the state called drunkenness, but twice he told me he had no memory of getting home to the laboratory at all. And even on those nights one would have had to know him well to be aware that he was affected at all. Evidences of drinking were subtle. He smiled a little more broadly. His voice became a little higher in pitch, and he would dance a few steps on tiptoe, a curious pigeon-footed mouse step. He liked every drink that contained alcohol and, except for coffee which he often laced with whisky, he disliked every drink that did not contain alcohol. He once estimated that it had been twelve years since he had tasted water without some benign addition.

At one time when bad teeth and a troublesome love affair were running concurrently, he got a series of stomach-aches which were diagnosed as a developing ulcer. The doctor put him on a milk diet and ordered him off all alcohol. A sullen sadness fell on the laboratory. It was a horrid time. For a few days Ed was in a state of dismayed shock. Then his anger rose at the cruelty of a fate that could do this to him. He merely disliked and distrusted water, but he had an active and fierce hatred for milk. He found the color unpleasant and the taste ugly. He detested its connotations.

For a few days he forced a little milk into his stomach, complaining bitterly the while, and then he went back to see the doctor. He explained his dislike for the taste of milk, giving as its basis some pre-memory shock amounting to a trauma. He thought this dislike for milk might have driven him into the field of marine biology since no marine animals but whales and their family of sea cows give milk and he had never had the least interest in any of the Cetaceans. He said that he was afraid the cure for his stomach-aches was worse than the disease and finally he asked if it would be all right to add a few drops of aged rum to the milk just to kill its ugly taste. The doctor perhaps knew he was fighting a losing battle. He gave in on the few drops of rum.

We watched the cure with fascination as day by day the ratio changed until at the end of a month Ed was adding a few drops of milk to the rum. But his stomach-aches had disappeared. He never liked milk, but after this he always spoke of it with admiration as a specific for ulcers.

There were great parties at the laboratory, some of which went on for days. There would come a time in our poverty when we needed a party. Then we would gather together the spare pennies. It didn't take very many of them. There was a wine sold in Monterey for thirty-nine cents a gallon. It was not a delicate-tasting wine and sometimes curious things were found in the sludge on the bottom of the jug, but it was adequate. It added a gaiety to a party and it never killed anyone. If four couples got together and each brought a gallon, the party could go on for some time and toward the end of it Ed would be smiling and doing his tippy-toe mouse dance.

Later, when we were not so poor, we drank beer or, as Ed preferred it, a sip of whisky and a gulp of beer. The flavors, he said, complemented each other.

Once on my birthday there was a party at the laboratory that lasted four days. We really needed a party. It was fairly large, and no one went to bed except for romantic purposes. Early in the morning at the end of the fourth day a benign exhaustion had settled on the happy group. We spoke in whispers because our vocal chords had long since been burned out in song.

Ed carefully placed a half a quart of beer on the floor beside his bed and sank back for a nap. In a moment he was asleep. He had consumed perhaps five gallons since the beginning of the party. He slept for about twenty minutes, then stirred, and without opening his eyes groped with his hand for the beer bottle. He found it, sat up, and took a deep drink of it. He smiled sweetly and waved two fingers in the air in a kind of benediction.

"There's nothing like that first taste of beer," he said.

Not only did Ed love liquor. He went further. He had a deep suspicion of anyone who did not. If a non-drinker shut up and minded his own business and did not make an issue of his failing, Ed could be kind to him. But alas, a laissez-faire attitude is very uncommon in teetotalers. The moment one began to spread his poison Ed experienced a searing flame of scorn and rage. He believed that anyone who did not like to drink was either sick and/or crazy or had in him some obscure viciousness. He believed that the soul of a non-drinker was dried up and shrunken, that the virtuous pose of the non-drinker was a cover for some nameless and disgusting practice.

He had somewhat the same feeling for those who did not or pretended they did not love sex, but this field will be explored later.

If pressed, Ed would name you the great men, great minds, great hearts and imaginations in the history of the world, and he could not discover one of them who was a teetotaler. He would even try to recall one single man or woman of much ability who did not drink and like liquor, and he could never light on a single name. In all such discussions the name of Shaw was offered, and in answer Ed would simply laugh, but in his laughter there would be no admiration for that abstemious old gentleman. . . .

He had no religion in the sense of creed or dogma. In fact he distrusted all formal religions, suspecting them of having been fouled with economics and power and politics. He did not believe in any God as recognized by any group or cult. Probably his God could have been expressed by the mathematical symbol for an expanding universe. Surely he did not believe in an after life in any sense other than chemical. He was suspicious of promises of an after life, believing them to be sops to our fear or hope artificially supplied.

Economics and politics he observed with the same interested detachment he applied to the ecological relationships and balances in a tide pool.

For a time after the Russian Revolution he watched the Soviet with the pleased interest of a terrier seeing its first frog. He thought there might be some new thing in Russia, some human progression that might be like a mutation in the nature of the species. But when the Revolution was accomplished and the experiments ceased and the Soviets steadied and moved inexorably toward power and the perpetuation of power through applied ignorance and dogmatic control of the creative human spirit, he lost interest in the whole thing. Now and then he would take a sampling to verify his conclusions as to the direction. His last hope for that system vanished when he wrote to various Russian biologists, asking for information from their exploration of the faunal distribution on the Arctic Sea. He then discovered that they not only did not answer, they did not even get his letters. He felt that any restriction or control of knowledge or conclusion was a dreadful sin, a violation of first principles. He lost his interest in Marxian dialectics when he could not verify in observable nature. He watched with a kind of amused contempt while the adepts warped the world to fit their pattern. And when he read the conclusions of Lysenko, he simply laughed without comment. . . .

Ed spoke sometimes of a period he valued in his life. It was after he had left home and entered the University of Chicago. He had not liked his home life very well. The rules that he had known were silly from his early childhood were finally removed.

"Adults, in their dealing with children, are insane," he said. "And children know it too. Adults lay down rules they would not think of following, speak truths they do not believe. And yet they expect children to obey the rules, believe the truths, and admire and respect their parents for this nonsense. Children must be very wise and secret to tolerate adults at all. And the greatest nonsense of all that adults expect children to believe is that people learn by experience. No greater lie was ever revered. And its falseness is immediately discerned by children since their parents obviously have not learned anything by experience. Far from learning, adults simply become set in a maze of prejudices and dreams and sets of rules whose origins they do not know and would not dare inspect for fear the whole structure might topple over on them. I think children instinctively know this," Ed said. "Intelligent children learn to conceal their knowledge and keep free of this howling mania."

When he left home, he was free at last, and he remembered his first freedom with a kind of glory. His freedom was not one of idleness.

"I don't know when I slept," he said. "I don't think there was time to sleep. I tended furnaces in the early morning. Then I went to class. I had lab all afternoon, then tended furnaces in the early evening. I had a job in a little store in the evening and got some studying done then, until midnight. Well, then I was in love with a girl whose husband worked nights, and naturally I didn't sleep much from midnight until morning. Then I got up and tended furnaces and went to class. What a time," he said, "what a fine time that was."

It is necessary in any kind of picture of Ed Ricketts to give some account of his sex life since that was by far his greatest drive. His life was saturated with sex and he was to a very great extent preoccupied with it. He gave it a monumental amount of thought and time and analysis. It will be no violation to discuss this part of his life since he had absolutely no shyness about discussing it himself.

To begin with, he was a hyper-thyroid. His metabolic rate was abnormally high. He had to eat at very frequent intervals or his body revolted with pain and anger. He was, during the time I knew him, and, I gather, from the very beginning, as concupiscent as a bull terrier. His sexual output and preoccupation was or purported to be prodigious. I do not know beyond doubt about the actual output. That is hearsay but well authenticated; but certainly his preoccupation with sexual matters was very great.

As far as women were concerned, he was completely without what is generally called "honor." It was not that he was dishonorable. The word simply had no meaning for him if it implied abstemiousness. Any man who left a wife in his care and expected him not to try for her was just a fool. He was compelled to try. The woman might reject him, and he would not be unreasonably importunate, but certainly he would not fail for lack of trying.

When I first met him he was engaged in a scholarly and persistent way in the process of deflowering a young girl. This was a long and careful affair. He not only was interested in a sexual sense, but he had also an active interest in the psychic and physical structure of virginity. There was, I believe, none of the usual sense of triumph at overcoming or being first. Ed's physical basis was a pair of very hot pants, but his secondary motive was an active and highly intellectual interest in the state of virginity and the change involved in abandoning that state. His knowledge of anatomy was large, but, as he was wont to say, the variation in structure is delightfully large, even leaving out abnormalities, and this variation gives a constant interest and surprise to a function which is basically pleasant anyway.

The resistance of this particular virgin was surprising. He did not know whether it was based on some block, or on the old-fashioned reluctance of a normal girl toward defloration, or, as he thought possible, on a distaste for himself personally. He inspected each of these possibilities with patient care. And since he had no shyness about himself, it did not occur to him to have any reluctance about discussing his project with his friends and acquaintances. It is perhaps a fortunate thing that this particular virgin did not hear the discussions. They might have embarrassed her, a matter that did not occur to Ed. Many years later, when she heard about the whole thing, she was of the opinion that she might still be a virgin if she had heard herself so intimately discussed. But by then, it was fortunately, she agreed, far too late.

One thing is certain. Ed did not like his sex uncomplicated. If a girl were unattached and without problems as well as willing, his interest was not large. But if she had a husband or seven children or a difficulty with the law or some whimsical neuroticism in the field of love, Ed was charmed and instantly active. If he could have found a woman who was not only married, but a mother, in prison, and one of Siamese twins, he would have been delighted. . . .

His laboratory practice was immaculate and his living quarters were not clean. It was his custom to say that most people paid too much for things they didn't really want, paid too much in effort and time and thought. "If a swept floor gives you enough pleasure and reward to pay for sweeping it, then sweep it," he said. "But if you do not see it dirty or clean, then it is paying too much to sweep it."

I think he set down his whole code or procedure once in a time of stress. He found himself quite poor and with three children to take care of. In a very scholarly manner, he told the children how they must proceed.

"We must remember three things," he said to them. "I will tell them to you in the order of their importance. Number one and first in importance, we must have as much fun as we can with what we have. Number two, we must eat as well as we can, because if we don't we won't have the health and strength to have as much fun as we might. And number three and third and last in importance, we must keep the house reasonably in order, wash the dishes, and such things. But we will not let the last interfere with the other two."

Ed's feeling for clothes was interesting. He wore Bass moccasins, buckskin-colored and quite expensive. He loved thick soft wool socks and wool shirts that would scratch the hell out of anyone else. But outside of those he had no interest. His clothing was fairly ragged, particularly at elbows and knees. He had one necktie hanging in his closet, a wrinkled old devil of a yellow tint, but no one ever saw him wear it. His clothes he just came by, and the coats were not likely to fit him at all. He was not in the least embarrassed by his clothes. He went everywhere in the same costume. And always he seemed strangely neat. Such was his sense of inner security that he did not seem ill dressed. Aften people around him appeared over-dressed. The only time he ever wore a hat was when there was some chance of getting his head wet, and then it was likely to be an oilskin sou'wester. But whatever else he wore or did not wear, there was invariably pinned to his shirt pocket a twenty-power Bausch and Lomb magnifying glass on a little roller chain. He used the glass constantly. It was a very close part of him—one of his techniques of seeing.

Always the paradox is there. He loved nice things and did not care about them. He loved to bathe and yet when the water heater in the laboratory broke down he bathed in cold water for over a year before he got around to having it fixed. I finally mended his leaking toilet tank with a piece of chewing gum which I imagine is still there. A broken window was stuffed with newspaper for several years and never was repaired.

He liked comfort and the chairs in the lab were stiff and miserable. His bed was a redwood box laced with hemp rope on which a thin mattress was thrown. And this bed was not big enough for two. Ladies complained bitterly about his bed, which was not only narrow and uncomfortable but gave out shrieks of protest at the slightest movement. . . .

Our trip to the Gulf of Lower California was a marvel of bumbling efficiency. We went where we intended, got what we wanted, and did the work on it. It had been our intention to continue the work with a survey of the Aleutian chain of islands when the war closed that area to us.

At the time of Ed's death our plans were completed, tickets bought, containers and collecting equipment ready for a long collecting trip to the Queen Charlotte Islands, which reach so deep into the Pacific Ocean. There was one deep bay with a long and narrow opening where we thought we might observe some changes in animal forms due to a specialized life and a long period of isolation. Ed was to have started within a month and I was to have joined him there. Maybe someone else will study that little island sea. The light has gone out of it for me.

Now I am coming near to the close of this account. I have not put down Ed's relations with his wives or with his three children. There isn't time, and besides I did not know much about these things.

As I have said, no one who knew Ed will be satisfied with this account. They will have known innumerable other Eds. I imagine that there were as many Eds as there were friends of Ed. And I wonder whether there can be any parallel thinking on his nature and the reason for his impact on the people who knew him. I wonder whether I can make any kind of generaliztion that would be satisfactory.

I have tried to isolate and inspect the great talent that was in Ed Ricketts, that made him so loved and needed and makes him so missed now that he is dead. Certainly he was an interesting and charming man, but there was some other quality which far exceeded these. I have thought that it might be his ability to receive, to receive anything from anyone, to receive gracefully and thankfully and to make the gift seem very fine. Because of this everyone felt good in giving to Ed—a present, a thought, anything.

Perhaps the most overrated virtue in our list of shoddy virtues is that of giving. Giving builds up the ego of the giver, makes him superior and higher and larger than the receiver. Nearly always, giving is a selfish pleasure, and in many cases it is a downright destructive and evil thing. One has only to remember some of our wolfish financiers who spend two-thirds of their lives clawing fortunes out of the guts of society and the latter third pushing it back. It is not enough to suppose that their philanthropy is a kind of frightened restitution, or that their natures change when they have enough. Such a nature never has enough and natures do not change that readily. I think that the impulse is the same in both cases. For giving can bring the same sense of superiority as getting does, and philanthropy may be another kind of spiritual avarice.

It is so easy to give, so exquisitely rewarding. Receiving, on the other hand, if it be well done, requires a fine balance of self-knowledge and kindness. It requires humility and tact and great understanding of relationships. In receiving you cannot appear, even to yourself, better or stronger or wiser than the giver, although you must be wiser to do it well.

It requires a self-esteem to receive—not self-love but just a pleasant acquaintance and liking for oneself.

Once Ed said to me, "For a very long time I didn't like myself." It was not said in self-pity but simply as an unfortunate fact. "It was a very difficult time," he said, "and very painful. I did not like myself for a number of reasons, some of them valid and some of them pure fancy. I would hate to have to go back to that. Then gradually," he said, "I discovered with surprise and pleasure that a number of people did like me. And I thought, if they can like me, why cannot I like myself? Just thinking it did not do it, but slowly I learned to like myself and then it was all right."

This was not said in self-love in its bad connotation but in self-knowledge. He meant literally that he had learned to accept and like the person "Ed" as he liked other people. It gave him a great advantage. Most people do not like themselves at all. They distrust themselves, put on masks and pomposities. They quarrel and boast and pretend and are jealous because they do not like themselves. But mostly they do not even know themselves well enough to form a true liking. They cannot see themselves well enough to form a true liking, and since we automatically fear and dislike strangers, we fear and dislike our stranger-selves.

Once Ed was able to like himself he was released from the secret prison of self-contempt. Then he did not have to prove superiority any more by any of the ordinary methods, including giving. He could receive and understand and be truly glad, not competitively glad.

Ed's gift for receiving made him a great teacher. Children brought shells to him and gave him information about the shells. And they had to learn before they could tell him.

In conversation you found yourself telling him things—thoughts, conjectures, hypotheses—and you found a pleased surprise at yourself for having arrived at something you were not aware that you could think or know. It gave you such a good sense of participation with him that you could present him with this wonder.

Then Ed would say, "Yes, that's so. That's the way is might be and besides—" and he would illuminate it but not so that he took it away from you. He simply accepted it.

Although his creativeness lay in receiving, that does not mean that he kept things as property. When you had something from him it was not something that was his that he tore away from himself. When you had a thought from him or a piece of music or twenty dollars or a steak dinner, it was not his—it was yours already, and his was only the head and hand that steadied it in position toward you. For this reason no one was ever cut off from him. Association with him was deep participation with him, never competition.

I wish we could all be so. If we could learn even a little to like ourselves, maybe our cruelties and angers might melt away. Maybe we would not have to hurt one another just to keep our ego-chins above water.

There it is. That's all I can set down about Ed Ricketts. I don't know whether any clear picture has emerged. Thinking back and remembering has not done what I hoped it might. It has not laid the ghost.

The picture that remains is a haunting one. It is the time just before dusk. I can see Ed finishing his work in the laboratory. He covers his instruments and puts his papers away. He rolls down the sleeves of his wool shirt and puts on his old brown coat. I see him go out and get in his beat-up old car and slowly drive away in the evening.

I guess I'll have that with me all my life.

RESPONSES: Questions for Writing and Discussion

1. The very first profile of Ricketts involves the reader in a host of paradoxes: for example, that the man was "half-Christ and half-goat" and that "he was gentle but capable of ferocity" or that he was a mystic who "hated and distrusted mysticism." From this and what we later learn of Ricketts and his life style, including his hypersexual nature and his sense of masculine superiority, would you say that he was truly an admirable individual or one who never managed to unite the fragments of his life into a meaningful whole?

2. Insofar as we have been defining morality throughout this section as the basis for one's actions, it may be beside the point to ask whether Ed Ricketts was a moral, an immoral, or a nonmoral man. What may matter more than such labels is the factor of moral *integrity*—an inner consistency to the general way one does things that tells us he is indeed being faithful to something. In Steinbeck's moral code, one follows the laws of his own being, but these are still laws! There has to be a difference between natural and totally irresponsible behavior. What could it be? Does Ricketts provide the answer?

3. Ricketts was a poor correspondent. "A letter unopened for a

month does not require opening." It seems apparent that he would not put himself out to determine and fulfill many of the obligations other people attend to. Are *they* wrong? Was he? Neither? What about someone who might have written to Ricketts pleading for help?

4. The ruling passion of Ed Ricketts was biology, and he would subordinate everything to this interest. "If you asked him to dinner at seven, he might get there at nine. On the other hand, if a good low collecting tide was at 6:53, he would be in the tide pool at 6:52." This tells us his moral code was based on priorities, with science at the top. What about somebody without any specific skills or potential for making a contribution to society, scientific or otherwise? Would he be as justified as Ed Ricketts in leading a life of self-centered priorities?

5. Ricketts was fond of people who like himself stayed on the fringes—sometimes beyond the fringes—of respectable middle-class morality. His relationship with the Madam of the establishment across the street is a case in point. He said of her: "I wish good people could be as good." Ricketts was generally negative toward people who worried over and conformed to the canons of what often is termed "ordinary decency." Can a case be made for ordinary decency? Does the Madam deserve to be called "good"? Do "good people" deserve to be scorned like this?

6. Religion often provides people with the framework and sanction for their moral principles. We learn of Ricketts that "his God could have been expressed by the mathematical symbol for an expanding universe." First, what does this statement mean? Second, does it relate to Ricketts' moral code?

7. Ricketts was critical of parents who raise their children according to rigid moral principles. "Adults, in their dealings with children, are insane," he once said, meaning they were hypocrites, demanding behavior from their offspring which they could not practice themselves. Is this "insane"? Is the behavior parents expect from children important for the development of the children? It there a Ricketts Method for raising children? What is it? Is it "better"?

8. Ricketts' sexual code is summed up in this remarkable sentence: "If he could have found a woman who was not only married, but a mother, in prison, and one of Siamese twins, he would have been delighted." What does Steinbeck mean? Does the statement cause you to admire or lose respect for Ricketts? What is the basis of your answer?

9. At his conclusion Steinbeck finds that the real secret of Ricketts' appeal, his real significance as a truly moral man lies in his self-love, and this is defined not as an absorption in personal needs to the exclusion of everything and everyone else, but as true

self-knowledge and self-approval. Steinbeck finds that self-love, in this sense, provides a strong basis for moral integrity. Explain how, according to Steinbeck, a person who had self-love would not be selfish. Can you accept this premise?

ECHO
Christina Rosetti

Such sentiments as **Christina Rosetti (1830–1894)** has shared with the world were certainly rare for women in Victorian England. Her father Gabriele Rosetti held many unorthodox views, but her mother, a devout Anglican, raised her two daughters close to the book, and both of them remained profoundly religious all their lives. This fact may have caused a conflict between the desires of the flesh and the continual hope of heaven which evoked the pain and longing in the following poem. Her brother William summed up the dominant forces in her life as "religion and affection: hardly a third."

"Echo" appears to reflect the poet's long and frustrating relationship with a painter named James Collinson, a love that was never to know fulfillment primarily because of Christina Rosetti's unyielding religious principles. Collinson, a Roman Catholic convert when they met, promised to turn Anglican if the poet would marry him. After a two-year engagement he returned to the Catholic fold, hoping the poet would accept the move. She did not and broke off the engagement once and for all. A later romance, this time with an atheist, ended just as unhappily.

Echo

Come to me in the silence of the night;
   Come in the speaking silence of a dream;
Come with soft rounded cheeks and eyes as bright
     As sunlight on a stream;
       Come back in tears,
O memory, hope, love of finished years.

Oh dream how sweet, too sweet, too bitter sweet,
   Whose wakening should have been in Paradise,

Where souls brimfull of love abide and meet;
   Where thirsting longing eyes   10
      Watch the slow door
That opening, letting in, lets out no more.

Yet come to me in dreams, that I may live
   My very life again though cold in death:
Come back to me in dreams, that I may give
   Pulse for pulse, breath for breath:
      Speak low, lean low,
As long ago, my love, how long ago.

18 December, 1854

ADULTERY
James Dickey

A number of years ago *Life* magazine called **James Dickey (b. 1923)** "the unlikeliest . . . of emerging United States poets." A glance at his activities tells us why. Born in Atlanta, he attended college as a football player-turned-poet. Later he was a fighter pilot with over a hundred missions in both World War II and the Korean War. When he is not writing poetry, which he does with prolific energy, he is a highly successful New York advertising executive. But he has also taught at a number of colleges. When he is not doing any of those things, he is likely to be off in the woods demonstrating his skill at hunting.

    The poet's versatility and well-roundedness are in a solid American literary tradition. So is the intense masculinity of his work. So is his compassionate understanding of many American moral hangups, such as the one shared by the furtive lovers in the following poem.

Adultery

We have all been in rooms
We cannot die in, and they are odd places, and sad.
Often Indians are standing eagle-armed on hills.

In the sunrise   open wide to the Great Spirit
Or gliding in canoes   or cattle are browsing on the walls
Far away   gazing down with the eyes of our children

Not far away   or there are men driving
The last railspike, which has turned
Gold in their hands. Gigantic forepleasure lives

Among such scenes, and we are alone with it
At last. There is always some weeping
Between us   and someone is always checking

A wrist watch by the bed to see how much
Longer we have left. Nothing can come
Of this   nothing can come

Of us: of me with my grim techniques
Or you who have sealed your womb
With a ring of convulsive rubber:

Although we come together,
Nothing will come of us. But we would not give
It up, for death is beaten

By praying Indians   by distant cows   historical
Hammers   by hazardous meetings that bridge
A continent. One could never die here

Never die   never die
While crying. My lover, my dear one
I will see you next week

THE SCARLET WOMAN
Fenton Johnson

Fenton Johnson (1888–1958) was one of the very earliest black poets to
turn away from conventional verse forms and experiment with a distinctly
personal and deliberately nonpoetic mode of expression. In his time it was
customary for the black poet to conform to white European models in order
to find both a publisher and the acceptance of white literary critics. As the
following poem shows, Johnson removed strict rhythmic principles as well
as a rhyme scheme, trying to achieve a more natural, conversational idiom.

Johnson's efforts were recognized by a few discerning critics, and he was frequently represented in *Poetry*, for years the showcase of America's major poetic talents. But his work has been overshadowed by the major revolution in poetry which the newer black poets have launched. Nonetheless, he shares with them the desire to communicate black experience as well as to express his criticism of white values. In this poem white America is blamed for the narrator's "immoral" way of life.

The Scarlet Woman

Once I was good like the Virgin Mary and the Minister's wife.
My father worked for Mr. Pullman and white people's tips; but he died two days after his insurance expired.
I had nothing, so I had to go to work.
All the stock I had was a white girl's education and a face that enchanted the men of both races.
Starvation danced with me.
So when Big Lizzie, who kept a house for white men, came to me with tales of fortune that I could reap from the sale of my virtue I bowed my head to Vice.
Now I can drink more gin than any man for miles around.
Gin is better than all the water in Lethe.

TO HIS COY MISTRESS
Andrew Marvell

In 1642, when **Andrew Marvell (1621–1678)** was twenty-one years old, England broke out in a civil strife which saw the Puritans eventually seize power and institute a two-decade reign of stern morality and religious austerity. Theaters were closed, and all frivolous sources of pleasure and entertainment were denounced from pulpit and Parliament. The political corruption, court intrigues, scandalous extravagance, and moral decadence which the Puritans had believed would ruin their country were to be replaced by a stable economy, better living conditions, the recognition of the Human Worth of the private citizen, and a return to moral decency.

But the Puritan way of life did not suit all possible temperaments, as the following poem demonstrates. It is a strident declaration of the importance of living fully in the moment, of seizing every possible chance to enjoy life's most intense pleasures. In the poet's view, Human Worth diminishes as one allows the canons of polite society or personal, high-minded moral values to hold one back from living.

To His Coy Mistress

Had we but world enough, and time,
This coyness lady were no crime.
We would sit down, and think which way
To walk, and pass our long love's day.
Thou by the Indian Ganges' side   5
Should'st rubies find: I by the tide
Of Humber would complain. I would
Love you ten years before the Flood:
And you should if you please refuse
Till the conversion of the Jews.   10
My vegetable love should grow
Vaster than empires, and more slow.
An hundred years should go to praise
Thine eyes, and on thy forehead gaze.
Two hundred to adore each breast: 15
But thirty thousand to the rest.
An age at least to every part,
And the last age should show your heart.
For lady you deserve this state;
Nor would I love at lower rate.   20
    But at my back I always hear
Time's winged chariot hurrying near:
And yonder all before us lie
Deserts of vast eternity.
Thy beauty shall no more be found;   25
Nor, in thy marble vault, shall sound
My echoing song: then worms shall try
That long preserv'd virginity:
And your quaint honor turn to dust;
And into ashes all my lust.   30
The grave's a fine and private place,
But none I think do there embrace.
    Now therefore, while the youthful hue

Sits on thy skin like morning lew[1],
And while thy willing soul transpires   35
At every pore with instant fires,
Now let us sport us while we may;
And now, like am'rous birds of prey,
Rather at once our time devour,
Than languish in his slow-chapt pow'r.   40
Let us roll all our strength, and all
Our sweetness, up into one ball:
And tear our pleasures with rough strife,
Through the iron gates of life.
Thus, though we cannot make our sun   45
Stand still, yet we will make him run.

---

[1] *Lew*: Archaic word meaning "warmth." (Eds.)

Boundaries

II

Beyond our immediate ties and obligations in the state within which we live.
What is the state?

WHO IS THE STATE?

Where does power belong?
To the people as a whole?

Or to the ones who are capable of wielding it?
Who makes the laws of the state?

Whom do these laws serve?

What do you do when a law is bad?
Can you run away from the state?

And go where?

Can people live without a civilization?
But civilization may not promote happiness. They say civilization is dying.
Is man too far away from nature to ever be natural again?

POWER SYSTEMS AND PRIVATE WORTH

The notion of Worth is hard to separate from the notion of power. A man who is "worth" millions of dollars can assert himself in ways impossible for a man without money. A proposal that is "worth" considering will have its supporters, who will move it along. A "worthy" charity receives donations and can thus proceed with its goals. A "worthy" student often seeks high grades, honors, fellowships, and a reputable place in society. It is usually a source of unhappiness for any "worthy" person to go unrecognized, and recognition carries with it some degree of power.

Over the centuries men and women have been concerned with the issue of power. That it exists in many forms has been undeniable. That it must exist has seemed reasonable, but its nature, purpose, and limits have been debated. If power is a logical extension of Worth, can power logically belong to all the Worth there is? If it did, would it still be power? Again: Does power readily share itself with Worth that has gone unnoticed and unrewarded? Is it Worth that creates power? Or does the possession of power grant a person his Worth? Are Worth and power really the same thing? And does this mean that people who lack power must be regarded as lacking Worth? The history of revolution is frequently the history of Worth seeking to overthrow a power system that it feels has no Worth of its own. That system, threatened, retaliates—often viciously—to protect its Worth from encroachment.

Niccolò Machiavelli, a fifteenth-century political philosopher, wrote *The Prince* as a handbook for rulers. Dedicated to "Lorenzo the Magnificent" of Florence, it advises the sovereign that absolute control over the multitude is necessary; for the average human being is evil, totally interested in personal gain. If power were shared among people as a whole, there would be chaos. The absolute state, governed by a dictator, is the only rational solution, the only way to save mankind from destroying itself.

Machiavelli's is the *vertical model* of what the state should be. It assumes that Worth (intellectual, spiritual, and moral) increases the higher one goes up the social ladder and decreases to nothing when one hits the bottom. But Walt Whitman's *Democratic Vistas* offers instead an *organic model* of the state. The relationship among its parts is identical to that existing in any natural system such as the human body. Just as in an organism even the tiniest cell has its function—its Worth—so too in the democratic state, which is the only state existing in conformity with natural law, each of us possesses a vital relevance to the healthy functioning of the whole. The sole purpose of rule in a democracy is to oversee this proper functioning, so that the people will learn how to govern themselves. In Whitman power is thus an organic system that has reached its full potential. It is equivalent to the total Worth of the population.

But even within a democracy vertical models can and do develop, so Charles Reich points out in his *The Greening of America*. In this country, says Reich, both the federal government and big business absolutely maintain and nurture themselves with the power they derive from control. It is power gone mad, with no purpose other than to keep growing. The state, no longer an extension of the general will, has assumed a life of its own and entered into a partnership with capitalistic enterprise. Each feeds the other. Power supports power.

Spokesmen for private enterprise in America, those who seek the freedom to pursue wealth without limit, often contend that power for the few is entirely within the natural scheme of things—fully as natural as Whitman's organic society. The report from the Rockefeller Panel on "The American Economic Heritage" rests on this assumption. It argues that the vertical society is the ideal society because it allows "Worth" to seek its own level of power. When this happens, everyone profits. Those less worthy—that is, those who lack the aptitude for success—will be taken care of through the social awareness, the sense of charity and fair play, which are characteristic of successful people.

But America's vertical system, in order to perpetuate itself, has developed a giant technology, the superproduct of the ultimately businesslike state. It has had to do this in the interest of sound managerial policy. Automation serves both business and the state, turning out better work in less time with fewer mistakes and requiring fewer employees. The section reprinted here from Arthur C. Clarke's *2001: A Space Odyssey* deals with the struggle between a human astronaut and a talking computer. The man's act against the machine may be taken as a mythological triumph of Human Worth over a power that has finally lost all links with humanity.

THE PRINCE AS FOX AND LION
Niccolò Machiavelli

In the opinion of one contemporary expert on political institutions the world is still living in the shadow of **Niccolò Machiavelli (1469–1527)**, the Florentine "who above all others taught the world to think in terms of cold political power." Machiavelli's message has certainly had impact through the centuries: Human Worth exists at all only because some few persons have power. Without power structures mankind reverts to the animal state. Power can have only one definition: It must be sufficient to itself and responsible to nothing but itself. It must have the courage to be true to its destiny even at the risk of being feared and of alienating all those whom it controls.

But there is considerable reason for questioning Machiavelli's true motives in devising a political philosophy supporting absolute dictatorships. His own background offers a clue. Born into a once aristocratic but long since impoverished Florentine family, he was taught from early childhood that the only thing that mattered in life was his getting ahead in the world and regaining the social position rightfully his. He worked his way steadily but surely into the highest financial and political circles in Florence, using his wit, powers of persuasion, and writing skills. He could be compared with the dazzling young executive of today, the "young man going places." Eventually he entered diplomatic work and had an opportunity to observe first hand what he believed to be an unalterable truth: Decision-making on the highest level was the real moving force behind social and historical currents. The realization that the common man was nothing but a pawn in games played for stakes he would never share turned Machiavelli for a time into a flaming liberal.

He was especially critical of the powerful Medici, once Florence's ruling family. But when in 1512 the Medici were restored to their position, Machiavelli experienced a sudden change of heart and did everything he could to win their favor. With his liberal reputation, however, he was forced into a fourteen-year exile, during which he composed his principal works, including *The Prince*. Dedicated to Lorenzo de Medici, *The Prince* is a handbook for rulers, a meticulously logical argument in support of one-man government. Not even this was enough to win back the author's vanished prestige. In 1527 the Medici were overthrown and a liberal party took over Florentine rule. Seeing his chance, Machiavelli returned to his homeland, only to discover that *The Prince* had been a widely read "underground" book and had become a scandal among liberals. Machiavelli was denounced and ended his days without power or support from either political camp.

The Prince as Fox and Lion

Of Cruelty and Clemency, and Whether It Is Better To Be Loved or Feared

Proceeding to the other qualities before named, I say that every prince must desire to be considered merciful and not cruel. He must, however, take care not to misuse this mercifulness. Cesare Borgia was considered cruel, but his cruelty had brought order to the Romagna, united it, and reduced it to peace and fealty. If this is considered well, it will be seen that he was really much more merciful than the Florentine people, who, to avoid the name of cruelty, allowed Pistoia to be destroyed. A prince, therefore, must not mind incurring the charge of cruelty for the purpose of keeping his subjects united and faithful; for, with a very few examples, he will be more merciful than those who, from excess of tenderness, allow disorders to arise, from whence spring bloodshed and rapine; for these as a rule injure the whole community, while the executions carried out by the prince injure only individuals. And of all princes, it is impossible for a new prince to escape the reputation of cruelty, new states being always full of dangers. . . .

Nevertheless, he must be cautious in believing and acting, and must not be afraid of his own shadow, and must proceed in a tem-

From *The Prince* by Niccolò Machiavelli, translated by Luigi Ricci, revised by E.R.P. Vincent and published by Oxford University Press. Reprinted by permission of the publisher.

perate manner with prudence and humanity, so that too much confidence does not render him incautious, and too much diffidence does not render him intolerant.

From this arises the question whether it is better to be loved more than feared, or feared more than loved. The reply is, that one ought to be both feared and loved, but as it is difficult for the two to go together, it is much safer to be feared than loved, if one of the two has to be wanting. For it may be said of men in general that they are ungrateful, voluble, dissemblers, anxious to avoid danger, and covetous of gain; as long as you benefit them, they are entirely yours; they offer you their blood, their goods, their life, and their children, as I have before said, when the necessity is remote; but when it approaches, they revolt. And the prince who has relied solely on their words, without making other preparations, is ruined; for the friendship which is gained by purchase and not through grandeur and nobility of spirit is bought but not secured, and at a pinch is not to be expended in your service. And men have less scruple in offending one who makes himself loved than one who makes himself feared; for love is held by a chain of obligation which, men being selfish, is broken whenever it serves their purpose; but fear is maintained by a dread of punishment which never fails.

Still, a prince should make himself feared in such a way that if he does not gain love, he at any rate avoids hatred: for fear and the absence of hatred may well go together, and will be always attained by one who abstains from interfering with the property of his citizens and subjects or with their women. And when he is obliged to take the life of any one, let him do so when there is a proper justification and manifest reason for it; but above all he must abstain from taking the property of others, for men forget more easily the death of their father than the loss of their patrimony. Then also pretexts for seizing property are never wanting, and one who begins to live by rapine will always find some reason for taking the goods of others, whereas causes for taking life are rarer and more fleeting.

But when the prince is with his army and has a large number of soldiers under his control, then it is extremely necessary that he should not mind being thought cruel; for without this reputation he could not keep an army united or disposed to any duty. Among the noteworthy actions of Hannibal is numbered this, that although he had an enormous army, composed of men of all nations and fighting in foreign countries, there never arose any dissension either among them or against the prince, either in good fortune or in bad. This could not be due to anything but his inhuman cruelty, which together with his infinite other virtues, made him always venerated and terrible in the sight of his soldiers, and without it his other virtues would not have sufficed to produce that effect. Thoughtless writers admire on the one hand his actions, and on the other blame the principal cause of them.

And that it is true that his other virtues would not have sufficed may be seen from the case of Scipio (famous not only in regard to his own times, but all times of which memory remains), whose armies rebelled against him in Spain, which arose from nothing but his excessive kindness, which allowed more licence to the soldiers than was consonant with military discipline. He was reproached with this in the senate by Fabius Maximus, who called him a corrupter of the Roman militia. Locri having been destroyed by one of Scipio's officers was not revenged by him, nor was the insolence of that officer punished, simply by reason of his easy nature; so much so, that some one wishing to excuse him in the senate, said that there were many men who knew rather how not to err, than how to correct the errors of others. This disposition would in time have tarnished the fame and glory of Scipio had he presevered in it under the empire, but living under the rule of the senate this harmful quality was not only concealed but became a glory to him.

I conclude, therefore, with regard to being feared and loved, that men love at their own free will, but fear at the will of the prince, and that a wise prince must rely on what is in his power and not on what is in the power of others, and he must only contrive to avoid incurring hatred, as has been explained.

In What Way Princes Must Keep Faith

How laudable it is for a prince to keep good faith and live with integrity, and not with astuteness, every one knows. Still the experience of our times shows those princes to have done great things who have had little regard for good faith, and have been able by astuteness to confuse men's brains, and who have ultimately overcome those who have made loyalty their foundation.

You must know, then, that there are two methods of fighting, the one by law, the other by force: the first method is that of men, the second of beasts; but as the first method is often insufficient, one must have recourse to the second. It is therefore necessary for a prince to know well how to use both the beast and the man. This was covertly taught to rulers by ancient writers, who relate how Achilles and many others of those ancient princes were given to Chiron the centaur to be brought up and educated under his discipline. The parable of this semi-animal, semi-human teacher is meant to indicate that a prince must know how to use both natures, and that the one without the other is not durable.

A prince being thus obliged to know well how to act as a beast must imitate the fox and the lion, for the lion cannot protect himself from traps, and the fox cannot defend himself from wolves. One must therefore be a fox to recognise traps, and a lion to frighten wolves. Those that wish to be only lions do not understand this. Therefore, a prudent ruler ought not to keep faith when by so doing it would be against his interest, and when the reasons which made him bind himself no longer exist. If men were all good, this precept would not be a good one; but as they are bad, and would not observe their faith with you, so you are not bound to keep faith with them. Nor have legitimate grounds ever failed a prince who wished to show colourable excuse for the non-fulfilment of his promise. Of this one could furnish an infinite number of modern examples, and show how many times peace has been broken, and how many promises rendered worthless, by the faithlessness of princes, and those that have been best able to imitate the fox have succeeded best. But it is necessary to be able to disguise this character well, and to be a great feigner and dissembler; and men are so simple and so ready to obey present necessities, that one who deceives will always find those who allow themselves to be deceived.

I will only mention one modern instance. Alexander VI did nothing else but deceive men, he thought of nothing else, and found the occasion for it; no man was ever more able to give assurances, or affirmed things with stronger oaths, and no man observed them less; however, he always succeeded in his deceptions, as he well knew this aspect of things.

It is not, therefore, necessary for a prince to have all the above-named qualities, but it is very necessary to seem to have them. I would even be bold to say that to possess them and always to observe them is dangerous, but to appear to possess them is useful. Thus it is well to seem merciful, faithful, humane, sincere, religious, and also to be so; but you must have the mind so disposed that when it is needful to be otherwise you may be able to change to the opposite qualities. And it must be understood that a prince, and especially a new prince, cannot observe all those things which are considered good in men, being often obliged, in order to maintain the state, to act against faith, against charity, against humanity, and against religion. And, therefore, he must have a mind disposed to adapt itself according to the wind, and as the variations of fortune dictate, and, as I said before, not deviate from what is good, if possible, but be able to do evil if constrained.

A prince must take great care that nothing goes out of his mouth which is not full of the above-named five qualities, and, to see and hear him, he should seem to be all mercy, faith, integrity, humanity, and religion. And nothing is more necessary than to seem to have this last quality, for men in general judge more by the eyes than by the hands, for every one can see, but very few have to feel. Everybody sees what you appear to be, few feel what you are, and those few will not dare to oppose themselves to the many, who have the majesty of the state to defend them; and in the actions of men, and especially of princes, from which there is no appeal, the end justifies the means. Let a prince therefore aim at conquering and maintaining the state, and the means will always be judged honourable and praised by every one, for the vulgar is always taken by appearances and the issue of the event; and the world consists only of the vulgar, and the few who are not vulgar are isolated when the many have a rallying point in the prince. A certain prince of the present time, whom it is well not to name, never does anything but preach peace and good faith, but he is really a great enemy to both, and either of them, had he observed them, would have lost him state or reputation on many occasions.

RESPONSES: Questions for Writing and Discussion

1. Machiavelli says a prince must sometimes be cruel rather than merciful in order to carry out his functions as a ruler and that it is better to be feared than loved if he must choose between the two. Though he logically proves this and many other ideas about rulers, does he also logically justify their very existence? How does he try to do this? Why does he not?

2. A new prince must proceed "with temperance and humanity." The implication is certainly not that he need have humane feelings toward people; rather, it is that he serves humanity best by serving his own needs first. In our own political system, do you know of any candidate of the past or present who you feel was concerned more for people than for his own aspirations toward holding office? What happened to him? Is it desirable for a candidate to be so motivated? Is it better for the country to have power-seeking politicians? Why or why not?

3. Machiavelli's political views are based on the idea that people "are ungrateful, voluble, dissemblers, anxious to avoid danger, and covetous of gain; as long as you benefit them, they are entirely yours." It is also true that the Machiavellian state is as vertical as one can get. Do you believe that this cynical attitude toward people in general underlies all vertical institutions? Only some? Which ones? None?

4. How does the prince himself avoid being "covetous of gain"? Is he grateful to the people? Is he not a dissembler? not anxious to avoid danger? not desirous of benefiting from the people's existence—

apparently in precisely the same manner that the people are said to seek benefit from the prince? Above all, if he is a human being himself, how does he avoid being evil like everyone else?

5. Machiavelli believed people needed to be curbed by strong rule because of the human love for property and the acquisition of other material possessions. To own things, he believed, most people would do just about anything. Is the desire for property still as strong as that? Should it be or should it not be? Should ownership be regulated by the state? Should property be community owned?

6. Machiavelli cites Hannibal's "inhuman cruelty" as the reason for the efficiency of his military machine. Does the same apply to other efficiently run institutions? Must a certain "inhumanity" (perhaps not cruelty) prevail? a certain remoteness on the part of management from those who are to be managed? Would other kinds of systems work as well, better, or not as well?

7. Scipio fared worse than Hannibal because his system lacked sufficient discipline. Is it true that students, workers, soldiers, and so on, resent a soft managerial approach? How do you feel about teachers who act as if they were part of the class? allow themselves to be called by their first name? make no claims to be authorities?

AMERICAN DEMOCRACY AS NATURE'S ULTIMATE
Walt Whitman

After the Civil War was over, **Walt Whitman (1819–1892)** wrote *Democratic Vistas*, from which the following short selection is taken. The poet of *Leaves of Grass*, a work he had consciously designed as the epic of American democracy, Whitman felt the time had come to assess what had happened. He concluded by reaffirming the workings of the democratic principle. "Secession-slave-power" had, in his estimation, denied the freedom of some Americans and threatened the unity of the whole. But democracy, which was nature's own creation, nature's own ultimate choice as the form of human society, had risen up, impelled by the law of necessity, and crushed those elements found to be alien to its spirit and hostile to its purposes. For Whitman a free society, operating in accordance with nature's laws, was a natural organism, and, like any such in the animal, plant, or marine world, it would not tolerate anything which tended to impede its growth or its chances for survival.

In the enormity of the solar system as well as in the infinitesimal single cell the miracle of nature reproduced itself. One leaf of grass or one human being constituted a total system and was equivalent in its miracle to the entire universe. For this reason democracy was the only political structure nature would tolerate. Only in a democracy was the individual human being allowed the right to attain his full measure of growth, and so long as this growth was organic and natural, it could not be out of harmony with the whole of society. To Whitman, the organic system that was American democracy could be nothing more than what the combined individualities of its members made it.

But this very principle was, for Whitman, an unalterable law in itself. *There had to be freedom.* Thus the freedom-denying institution of slavery became intolerable to the total organism and was destroyed in much the same way that the body fights against disease. The law of freedom was therefore binding on all. It was nature's way of doing things and provided a check against rampant, irresponsible individualism, seeking power for itself, seeking more than the natural rights guaranteed to everyone.

In a society so broad and varied as America there had to be leadership. But Whitman saw the leader as one who is provided by the law of nature whenever he is needed and whose powers are determined by the things he has to do in the interest of the people as a whole. His powers are never to be defined in terms of leadership itself or the fact that he occupies a governing and decision-making office. When the leader abuses those powers, when he works solely for personal gain, the social organism will develop maladies. When he acts as the law of nature decrees, the leader deals fairly and justly toward others, and the social organism propers. Leadership is thus a function rather than a privilege or a goal to be won no matter what the cost.

The America into which Whitman was born in 1819, even the urban New York where he grew up and became a carpenter, housing contractor, and newspaper publisher, was in many respects a much simpler place than the populous, mechanized land we know today. It had not quite become the affluent society whose riches would be fabled throughout Europe and send millions of poor and oppressed people to Ellis Island, gateway to the Promised Land. It was not yet an America of many crisscrossing ethnic and religious strains, so diverse that harmonious integration would be difficult, if not impossible. Nor was it yet an America whose federal government would need to develop a most complex and subtle network of machinery for managing a country unprecedented in nature.

American Democracy as Nature's Ultimate

The movements of the late secession war, and their results, to any sense that studies well and comprehends them, show that popular democracy, whatever its faults and dangers, practically justifies itself beyond the proudest claims and wildest hopes of its enthusiasts. Probably no future age can know, but I well know, how the gist of this fiercest and most resolute of the world's warlike contentions resided exclusively in the unnamed, unknown rank and file; and how the brunt of its labor of death was, to all essential purposes, volunteer'd. The People, of their own choice, fighting, dying for their own idea, insolently attack'd by the secession-slave-power, and its very existence imperil'd. Descending to detail, entering any of the armies, and mixing with the private soldiers, we see and have seen august spectacles. We have seen the alacrity with which the American-born populace, the peaceablest and most good-natured race in the world, and the most personally independent and intelligent, and the least fitted to submit to the irksomeness and exasperation of regimental discipline, sprang, at the first tap of the drum, to arms—not for gain, nor even glory, nor to repel invasion—but for an emblem, a mere abstraction—for the life, *the safety of the flag.* We have seen the unequal'd docility and obedience of these soldiers. We have seen them tried long and long by hopelessness, mismanagement, and by defeat; have seen the incredible slaughter toward or through which the armies, (as at first Fredericksburg, and afterward at the Wilderness,) still unhesitatingly obey'd orders to advance. We have seen them in trench, or crouching behind breastwork, or tramping in deep mud, or amid pouring rain or thick-falling snow, or under forced marches in hottest summer (as on the road to get to Gettysburg)—vast suffocating swarms, divisions, corps, with every single man so grimed and black with sweat and dust, his own mother would not have known him—his clothes all dirty, stain'd and torn, with sour, accumulated sweat for perfume—many a comrade, perhaps a brother, sun-struck, staggering out, dying, by the roadside, of exhaustion—yet the great bulk bearing steadily on, cheery enough, hollow-bellied from hunger, but sinewy with unconquerable resolution.

We have seen this race proved by wholesale by drearier, yet more fearful tests—the wound, the amputation, the shatter'd face or limb, the slow hot fever, long impatient anchorage in bed, and all the forms of maiming, operation and disease. Alas! America have we seen, though only in her early youth, already to hospital brought. There

From *Democratic Vistas.*

224

have we watch'd these soldiers, many of them only boys in years—
mark'd their decorum, their religious nature and fortitude, and their
sweet affection. Wholesale, truly. For at the front, and through the
camps, in countless tents, stood the regimental, brigade and division
hospitals; while everywhere amid the land, in or near cities, rose
clusters of huge, white-wash'd, crowded, one-story wooden barracks;
and there ruled agony with bitter scourge, yet seldom brought a cry;
and there stalk'd by day and night along the narrow aisles between
the rows of cots, or by the blankets on the ground, and touch'd lightly
many a poor sufferer, often with blessed, welcome touch.

I know not whether I shall be understood, but I realize that it is
fearful tests—the wound, the amputation, the shatter'd face or limb,
am now penning these pages. One night in the gloomiest period of the
war, in the Patent office hospital in Washington city, as I stood by
the bedside of a Pennsylvania soldier, who lay, conscious of quick
approaching death, yet perfectly calm, and with noble, spiritual manner, the veteran surgeon, turning aside, said to me, that though he had
witness'd many, many deaths of soldiers, and had been a worker at
Bull Run, Antietam, Fredericksburg, &c., he had not seen yet the first
case of man or boy that met the approach of dissolution with cowardly
qualms or terror. My own observation fully bears out the remark.

What have we here, if not, towering above all talk and argument,
the plentifully-supplied, last-needed proof of democracy, in its personalities? Curiously enough, too, the proof on this point comes, I
should say, every bit as much from the south, as from the north.
Although I have spoken only of the latter, yet I deliberately include
all. Grand, common stock! to me the accomplish'd and convincing
growth, prophetic of the future; proof undeniable to sharpest sense, of
perfect beauty, tenderness and pluck, that never feudal lord, nor
Greek, nor Roman breed, yet rival'd. Let no tongue ever speak in
disparagement of the American races, north or south, to one who has
been through the war in the great army hospitals.

Meantime, general humanity, (for to that we return, as, for our
purposes, what it really is, to bear in mind,) has always, in every
department, been full of perverse maleficence, and is so yet. In
downcast hours the soul thinks it always will be—but soon recovers
from such sickly moods. I myself see clearly enough the crude, defective streaks in all the strata of the common people; the specimens and
vast collections of the ignorant, the credulous, the unfit and uncouth,
the incapable, and the very low and poor. The eminent person just
mention'd sneeringly asks whether we expect to elevate and improve
a nation's politics by absorbing such morbid collections and qualities
therein. The point is a formidable one, and there will doubtless always

be numbers of solid and reflective citizens who will never get over it. Our answer is general, and is involved in the scope and letter of this essay. We believe the ulterior object of political and all other government, (having, of course, provided for the police, the safety of life, property, and for the basic statute and common law, and their administration, always first in order,) to be among the rest, not merely to rule, to repress disorder, &c., but to develop, to open up to cultivation, to encourage the possibilities of all beneficent and manly outcroppage, and of that aspiration for independence, and the pride and self-respect latent in all characters. (Or, if there be exceptions, we cannot, fixing our eyes on them alone, make theirs the rule for all.)

I say the mission of government, henceforth, in civilized lands, is not repression alone, and not authority alone, not even of law, nor by that favorite standard of the eminent writer, the rule of the best men, the born heroes and captains of the race, (as if such ever, or one time out of a hundred, get into the big places, elective or dynastic) —but higher than the highest arbitrary rule, to train communities through all their grades, beginning with individuals and ending there again, to rule themselves. What Christ appear'd for in the moral-spiritual field for human-kind, namely, that in respect to the absolute soul, there is in the possession of such by each single individual, something so transcendent, so incapable of gradations, (like life,) that, to that extent, it places all beings on a common level, utterly regardless of the distinctions of intellect, virtue, station, or any height or lowliness whatever—is tallied in like manner, in this other field, by democracy's rule that men, the nation, as a common aggregate of living identities, affording in each a separate and complete subject for freedom, worldly thrift and happiness, and for a fair chance for growth, and for protection in citizenship, &c., must, to the political extent of the suffrage or vote, if no further, be placed, in each and in the whole, on one broad, primary, universal, common platform.

The purpose is not altogether direct; perhaps it is more indirect. For it is not that democracy is of exhaustive account, in itself. Perhaps, indeed, it is, (like Nature,) of no account in itself. It is that, as we see, it is the best, perhaps only, fit and full means, formulater, general caller-forth, trainer, for the million, not for grand material personalities only, but for immortal souls. To be a voter with the rest is not so much; and this, like every institute, will have its imperfections. But to become an enfranchised man, and now, impediments removed, to stand and start without humiliation, and equal with the rest; to commence, or have the road clear'd to commence, the grand experiment of development, whose end, (perhaps requiring several generations,) may be the forming of a full-grown man or woman—

that *is* something. To ballast the State is also secured, and in our times is to be secured, in no other way.

We do not, (at any rate I do not,) put it either on the ground that the People, the masses, even the best of them, are, in their latent or exhibited qualities, essentially sensible and good—nor on the ground of their rights; but that good or bad, rights or no rights, the democratic formula is the only safe and preservative one for coming times. We endow the masses with the suffrage for their own sake, no doubt; then, perhaps still more, from another point of view, for community's sake. Leaving the rest to the sentimentalists, we present freedom as sufficient in its scientific aspect, cold as ice, reasoning, deductive, clear and passionless as crystal.

Democracy too is law, and of the strictest, amplest kind. Many suppose, (and often in its own ranks the error,) that it means a throwing aside of law, and running riot. But, briefly, it is the superior law, not alone that of physical force, the body, which, adding to, it supersedes with that of the spirit. Law is the unshakable order of the universe forever; and the law over all, and law of laws, is the law of successions; that of the superior law, in time, gradually supplanting and overwhelming the inferior one. . . . Nor is the esthetic point, always an important one, without fascination for highest aiming souls. The common ambition strains for elevations, to become some privileged exclusive. The master sees greatness and health in being part of the mass; nothing will do as well as common ground. Would you have in yourself the divine, vast, general law? Then merge yourself in it.

And, topping democracy, this most alluring record, that it alone can bind, and ever seeks to bind, all nations, all men, of however various and distant lands, into a brotherhood, a family. It is the old, yet ever-modern dream of earth, out of her eldest and her youngest, her fond philosophers and poets. Not that half only, individualism, which isolates. There is another half, which is adhesiveness or love, that fuses, ties and aggregates, making the races comrades, and fraternizing all. Both are to be vitalized by religion, (sole worthiest elevator of man or State,) breathing into the proud, material tissues, the breath of life. For I say at the core of democracy, finally, is the religious element. All the religions, old and new, are there. Nor may the scheme step forth, clothed in resplendent beauty and command, till these, bearing the best, the latest fruit, the spiritual, shall fully appear.

RESPONSES: Questions for Writing and Discussion

1. Whitman begins with his own view of the Civil War: "The people, their own choice, fighting, dying for their own idea. . . ."

Explain in your own words how the Civil War is seen as having been a true test of a true democracy. Do you agree with Whitman's thesis?

2. The willingness to die for "the safety of the flag" is for Whitman one of the noble attributes of the American citizen. Many Americans today decry the waning of such patriotic fervor. But those who say they would not fight for their country on the grounds that killing for any cause is immoral, also claim to be true Americans. What would Whitman say on the subject? What do you say?

3. Whitman's idea of democratic government is not a restatement of Rousseau's social contract theory. Whitman believes the government's function is to *represent* rather than *be* the general will. He believes that there has to be someone to oversee the progress of democracy and, especially, to train the people to rule themselves. If such an ideal of government were ever to become a reality, why do you think people would seek political office? What checks could be established to make certain that office was not used for the personal power of the holder? Why do you think people go into American politics the way things stand now? What limits political power? Do any office holders appear to wield more power than others or to have fewer checks against them?

4. The paragraph beginning "The purpose is not altogether direct . . ." contains an idea fully as radical as any advanced by contemporary advocates of revolution in this country. Democracy, Whitman says, is "of no account in itself." What matters, in other words, is not the form political structures take, but the *content*—the growth of the human beings within those structures. Democracy, to be true to its own spirit, must always be willing to become anything for the good of the people. It cannot become a rigid establishment, proceeding in one direction while the people wish to proceed in another. In what sense is Whitman's idea valid? Is it possible?

5. Whitman appears to have no illusions about the people in a democracy. He says "the masses, even the best of them" are not necessarily "sensible and good." At the same time, he believes the "democratic formula" to be the only scientifically valid principle of government. How can you reconcile one view with the other?

6. A democracy, Whitman also maintains, is anything but lawless. Its very nature makes it a law in itself. Since democracy is the only natural political structure, it follows that its citizens will obey the law of nature so long as they preserve their freedom. Many today, shaking their heads at rising crime statistics, are demanding tougher and tougher law enforcement, which in turn is decried by others as a violation of their natural rights. Do you believe, with Whitman, that unlimited freedom leads to the natural desire to be

lawful? In the vicious circle, which do you think comes first—tough laws, or a state of near anarchy which is allowed to go too far and which then seems to require a tough response?

ANATOMY OF THE CORPORATE STATE
Charles Reich

Our government, committed long ago to the ideal of representative democracy, has evolved into a superorganism caught up in its own inner workings, responsible to its own laws of being, increasingly removed from contact with the individual citizen and his wishes. At least this is a thesis of *The Greening of America*, a book about the current state of our country and some new directions the author believes are imminent. Its author **Charles Reich (b. 1928)**, professor of law at Yale, chronicles the gradual diminishing of freedom in this country and the attendant loss of Human Worth. As America has grown in population and world importance, the government has assumed more and more direct power over the lives and destinies of all citizens until we have reached a point where the possibility of enslavement from foreign powers is far less than the reality of enslavement at home.

While some might argue that it is a miracle we have as much freedom as we do, that there seems to be no alternative to a strong central government, and that it is actually a human *achievement* rather than the enemy of humanity, *The Greening of America* contains a harrowing picture of the Corporate State's monstrous proportions, operating at a far remove from the people themselves.

Preceding the selection that follows, the author has described the evolution of the Corporate State. The original American settlers were strong individualists in a primitive and beautiful land. Living close to nature, they turned the law of survival into a basic philosophy of life. They seized as much land as they could, fought to hold it, killed off Indian and buffalo, and did whatever else they deemed necessary to preserve their own interests. When the Industrial Revolution took place, they used the machine, not the rifle, as the instrument by which they continually moved ahead. They became manufacturers and oil tycoons, and they suffered a "loss of reality" during the transition to the urban age. That is, they failed to develop a corresponding social awareness. To counteract the economic imbalance which led to the depression of the thirties, the Roosevelt administration and its New Deal policies made the total welfare a concern of the federal government. This in turn was the birth of the Corporate State with powers of its own constantly multiplying themselves.

In order to support itself and sustain its incessant growth, the Corporate State has become an ally of big business. It controls much of business's activities and in turn nurtures business by allowing huge tax breaks and other privileges denied the common citizen, who has become the slave of both masters. The ordinary American, in Reich's opinion, spends much of his day doing a job that is "mindless, exhausting, boring, servile, and hateful. . . ." He is manipulated systematically by the advertising media and thus kept in debt, for if the gross national product is not bought, the Corporate State loses its powers.

The Greening of America concludes with a vision of the future. A new consciousness is developing, the author tells us, which will overthrow the Corporate State, but not violently. There are already signs that people are beginning to reject materialism as a way of life. When material goods interest fewer and fewer people as desirable symbols of status, when worth becomes Human Worth once again, then the intricate, dehumanized machinery of the state will begin to disappear.

Anatomy of the Corporate State

The American Corporate State today can be thought of as a single vast corporation, with every person as an involuntary member and employee. It consists primarily of large industrial organizations, plus nonprofit institutions such as foundations and the educational system, all related to the whole as divisions to a business corporation. Government is only a part of the state, but government coordinates it and provides a variety of needed services. The Corporate State is a complete reversal of the original American ideal and plan. The State, and not the market or the people or any abstract economic laws, determines what shall be produced, what shall be consumed, and how it shall be allocated. It determines, for example, that railroads shall decay while highways flourish; that coal miners shall be poor and advertising executives rich. Jobs and occupations in the society are rigidly defined and controlled, and arranged in a hierarchy of rewards, status, and authority. An individual can move from one position to

Gene Mathis

The structure of the administrative state is that of a hierarchy in which every person has a place in a table of organization, a vertical position in which he is subordinate to someone and superior to someone else.   *Charles Reich*

another, but he gains little freedom thereby, for in each position he is subject to conditions imposed upon it; individuals have no protected area of liberty, privacy, or individual sovereignty beyond the reach of the State. The State is subject neither to democratic controls, constitutional limits, or legal regulation. Instead, the organizations in the Corporate State are motivated primarily by the demands of technology and of their own internal structure. Technology has imperatives such as these: if computers have been developed, they must be put to use; if faster planes can be produced, they must be put into service; if there is a more efficient way of organizing an office staff, it must be done; if psychological tests provide added information for personnel directors, they must be used on prospective employees. A general in charge of troops at Berkeley described the use of a helicopter to attack students with chemicals as "logical." As for organizations, their imperative is to grow. They need stability, freedom from outside interference, constantly increasing profits. Everyone in the organization wants more and better personnel, more functions, increased status and prestige—in a word, growth. The medium through which these forces operate is law. The legal system is not primarily concerned with justice, equality, or individual rights; it functions as an instrument of State domination, and it acts to prevent the intervention of human values or individual choice. Although the forces driving the State are impersonal rather than evil, they are wholly indifferent to man's needs, and tend to have the same consequences as would a system expressly designed for the purpose of destroying human beings and their society.

The essence of the Corporate State is that it is relentlessly single-minded; it has only one value, the value of technology-organization-efficiency-growth-progress. The State is perfectly rational and logical. It is based upon principle. But life cannot be supported on the basis of any single principle. Yet no other value is allowed to interfere with this one, not amenity, not beauty, not community, not even the supreme value of life itself. Thus the State is essentially mindless; it has only one idea and it rolls along, never stopping to think, consider, balance, or judge. Only such single-valued mindlessness would cut the last redwoods, pollute the most beautiful beaches, invent machines to injure and destroy plant and human life. To have only one value is, in human terms, to be mad. It is to be a machine. . . .

1. *Amalgamation and Integration.* We normally consider the units of the Corporate State, such as the federal government, an automobile company, a private foundation, as if they were separate from each other. This is, however, not the case. In the first place, there is a marked tendency for "separate" units to follow parallel policies, so

that an entire industry makes identical decisions as to pricing, kind of product, and method of distribution; the automobile and the air travel industries show this. Second, very different companies are coming under combined management through the device of conglomerates, which place vast and diverse empires under a single unified control. But even more significant is the disappearance of the line between "public" and "private." In the Corporate State, most of the "public" functions of government are actually performed by the "private" sector of the economy. And most "government" functions are services performed for the private sector.

Let us consider first how government operations are "privately" performed. To a substantial degree, this relationship is formalized. The government hires "private" firms to build national defense systems, to supply the space program, to construct the interstate highway system, and sometimes, in the case of the think institutes, to do its "thinking" for it. An enormous portion of the federal budget is spent in simply hiring out government functions. This much is obvious, although many people do not seem to be aware of it. What is less obvious is the "deputizing" system by which a far larger sector of the "private" economy is enlisted in government service.

An illustration will indicate what is meant by "deputizing." A college teacher receives a form from the Civil Service Commission, asking him for certain information with respect to an individual who is applying for a government job. When he fills in the form, the teacher has acted as if he had been "deputized" by the government; i.e., he is performing a service for the government, one for which he might even feel himself entitled to compensation. Now consider a foundation which receives a special tax-exempt status. The foundation is in this favored position because it is engaged in activities which are of "public benefit." That is, it is the judgment of the government that some types of activities are public services although performed under private auspices. The government itself could do what private foundations now do: aid education, sponsor research, and other things which do not command a profit in the commercial sense. It is the government's decision that these same functions are better performed by foundations. It is the same judgment that government makes when it hires Boeing to build bombers, or a private construction firm to build an interstate highway. Public utilities—airlines, railroads, truck carriers, taxicabs, oil pipe lines, the telephone company—all are "deputized" in this fashion. They carry on *public* functions—functions that in other societies might be performed by the government itself.

Let us now look at the opposite side of the coin: government as the servant of the "private" sector. Once again, sometimes the relationship is formal and obvious. The government spends huge amounts for research and development, and private companies are often able to get the benefits of this. Airports are built at public expense for private airlines to use. Highways are built for private trucking firms to use. The government pays all sorts of subsidies, direct and indirect, to various industries. It supplies credit services and financial aid to homeowners. It grows trees on public forest lands and sells them at cut-rate prices to private lumber companies. It builds roads to aid ski developments.

It is true that government has always existed to serve the society; that police and fire departments help business too; that paving streets helps business, and so do wars that open up new markets—and that is what government is and always has been all about. But today, governmental activity in aid of the private sector is enormously greater, more pervasive, more immediately felt than ever before. The difference between the local public services in 1776 and millions of dollars in subsidies to the shipping industry may be a difference of degree but it is still quite a difference. But the difference is not only one of degree. In the difference between a highly autonomous, localized economy and a highly interdependent one, there is a difference of principle as well as one of degree. Government help today is *essential*, not a luxury. The airlines could not operate without allocation of routes and regulation of landing and take-offs, nor could the television industry. The educational system, elementary school through high school, is essential for the production of people able to work in today's industry. Thus it may be said that everyone who operates "privately" really is aided and subsidized, to one degree or another, by the public; the sturdy, independent rancher rides off into the sunset on land irrigated by government subsidy, past sheep whose grazing is subsidized and cattle whose prices are artificially maintained by governmental action; he does not look like a welfare client, but he is on the dole nevertheless.

Regulation itself is a service to industry. The film industry and the professional sports industry have elaborate systems of private regulation, including "commissioners," a system of laws and government, fines and penalties, all designed to place the industry on the best and most united basis to sell its product. Such "regulation" as is performed by such federal agencies as FCC, SEC, FTC, and CAB, is remarkably similar in general effect, but it is a service rendered at taxpayers' expense. Indeed, there is a constant interchange of personnel between the regulatory agencies and industry; government men leave to take high-paying positions with the corporations they formerly regulated; agency officials are frequently appointed from industry ranks.

This public-private and private-public integration, when added to the inescapable legislative power we have already described, gives us the picture of the State as a single corporation. Once the line between "public" and "private" becomes meaningless and is erased, the various units of the Corporate State no longer appear to be parts of a diverse and pluralistic system in which one kind of power limits another kind of power; the various centers of power do not limit each other, they all weigh in on the same side of the scale, with only the individual on the other side. With public and private merged, we can discern the real monolith of power and realize there is nothing at all within the system to impose checks and balances, to offer competition, to raise even a voice of caution or doubt. We are all involuntary members, and there is no zone of the private to offer a retreat.

One way to appreciate the true nature of the public-private amalgamated State, is to list some examples of power that can be found in the United States:

Power to determine the hour at which employees come to work, the hour at which they have lunch, the hour when they go home;

Power to make *Business Week* available to airline passengers but not *The Nation;*

Power to raise bank interest rates;

Power to wake all patients in a hospital at 6 A.M.;

Power to forbid apartment dwellers to have pets or children;

Power to require peanut butter eaters to choose between homogenized or chunky peanut butter and to prevent them from buying "real" peanut butter;

Power to force all young people who want to go to college to do a certain kind of mechanical problem-solving devised by the College Entrance Examination Board;

Power to require that all public school teachers be fingerprinted;

Power to popularize snowmobiles instead of snowshoes, so that the winter forests screech with mechanical noise;

Power to force all riders in automobiles to sit in seats designed to torture the lower lumbar regions of the human anatomy;

Power to use forest products in constructing homes, making furniture, and publishing newspapers, thereby creating a demand for cutting timber;

Power to dominate public consciousness through the mass media;

Power to induce lung cancer in thousands of persons by promoting the sale of cigarettes;

Power to turn off a man's telephone service;

Power to provide railroad passengers with washrooms that are filthy;

Power to encourage or discourage various forms of scholarship, educational activity, philanthropy, and research;

Power to construct office buildings with windows that will not open, or without any windows at all;

Power to determine what life-styles will not be acceptable for employees;

Power to make relatively large or small investments in the safety of consumer products;

Power to change the culture of a foreign country.

Were we confronted by this list and told that all of this power was held by a single tyrannical ruler, we would find the prospect frightening indeed. We are likely to think, however, that, although the power may exist, none of it is exercised by any governmental body, that it is divided in many ways, held by many different entities, and subject to all sorts of procedures, checks, balances, and controls; mostly it applies only to persons who subject themselves to it voluntarily, as by taking a job with a corporation. But power in the corporate state is not so easily escaped. The refugee from a job with one corporation will find a choice of other corporations—all prepared to subject him to similar control over employees. The television viewer who tires of one network finds the others even more tiresome. Can railroad or automobile passengers do anything about conditions they object to? Do they find alternative means of transportation readily available?

Editorials which denounce students usually say that a student who does not like the way a university is run should leave. But society makes it practically mandatory for a young person to complete his education, and, so far as rules and practices go, most universities are extraordinarily alike. Under these circumstances, it is hardly accurate to say that a student "voluntarily" submitted to university rule. The student's case is the case of the railroad traveler, the peanut butter eater, the man who wants a bank loan, the corporate employee, the apartment house dweller who wants to keep a pet. The integration of the Corporate State makes what was formerly voluntary inescapable. Like the birds in Alfred Hitchcock's apocalyptic film, powers that once were small and gentle become monstrous and terrifying. The better organized, the more tightly administered, the more rational and inclusive the Corporate State becomes, the more every organization turns into a government, and all forms of power take on the aspect of government decrees.

2. *The Principle of Administration and Hierarchy.* The activities, policies, and decisions of a society might theoretically be carried out by a variety of methods—voluntary cooperation by individuals, the physical coercion of a military tyranny, or the psychological conditioning of B. F. Skinner's *Walden Two.* The Corporate State has chosen to

rely on the method of administration and hierarchy. So pervasive, indeed, is the principle of administration that in many ways the Corporate State is in its essence an administrative state. The theory of administration is that the best way to conduct any activity is to subject it to rational control. A framework of organization is provided. Lines of authority, responsibility, and supervision are established as clearly as possible; everyone is arranged in a hierarchy. Rules are drawn for every imaginable contingency, so that individual choice is minimized. Arrangements are made to check on what everyone does, to have reports and permanent records. The random, the irrational, and the alternative ways of doing things are banished.

It is worth recalling how this state derived from classic liberalism, and, more proximately, from the New Deal and the welfare state. Liberalism adopted the basic principle that there is no need for management of society itself; the "unseen hand" is all that is needed. The New Deal modified this by requiring activities to be subject to "the public interest." Gradually this came to mean ever-tightening regulation in directions fixed by the demands of a commercial, technological, mass society. Gradually it came to mean the replacement of a "political" state with an "administrative" state. A "political" state, in our present meaning, is one in which differences, conflicts, and cultural diversity are regarded as aspects of pluralism to be represented in the political process and allowed a life of their own within the body politic. Thus political radicals, marijuana users, or culturally distinct groups would all coexist, have political voices, and contribute to the diversity and balance of the nation. This "political" model has also been called the "conflict" model, not because there are actual conflicts, but because conflicting opinions and ways of life are allowed to exist side by side. Administration means a rejection of the idea of conflict as a desirable element in society. Administration wants extremes "adjusted"; it wants differences "settled"; it wants to find out which way is "best" and use it exclusively. That which refuses to be adjusted is considered by administration as "deviance," a departure from the norm needing to be treated and cured. It is a therapeutic model of society, in which variety is compromised and smoothed over in an effort to make everything conform to " the public interest." This society defines that which does not fit "the public interest" as "deviance." Marijuana use is made a crime, and people using it are punished, cured, or "helped." Political radicals are expected to be "responsible"; blacks are expected to be "integrated." The society "knows what is best" for everyone; its massive energies, power, and apparatus are focused on making sure that everyone accepts "what is best."

The structure of the administrative state is that of a hierarchy in which every person has a place in a table of organization, a vertical position in which he is subordinate to someone and superior to someone else. This is the structure of any bureaucracy; it represents a "rationalization" of organization ideals. When an entire society is subjected to this principle, it creates a small ruling elite and a large group of workers who play no significant part in the making of decisions. While they continue to vote in political elections, they are offered little choice among the candidates; all the major decisions about what is produced, what is consumed, how resources are allocated, the conditions of work, and so forth, are made administratively.

Administration seeks to remove decision-making from the area of politics to the area of "science." It does not accept democratic or popular choice; this is rejected in favor of professionals and experts and a rational weighing of all of the factors. Procedures are set up by which decision-making is channeled, and care is taken to define exactly which institution shall make which decisions. For each type of decision, there is someone "best" qualified to decide it; administration avoids participation in decisions by the less qualified. Its greatest outrage is directed toward a refusal to enter into its procedures— this seems almost a denial of the very principle of administration. If followed, these procedures usually produce a decision that is a compromise or balance which rejects any particular choice in its pure, uncompromised form. Choice takes place within narrow limits. A weighing of all the factors produces a decision somewhere in between, rather than one or another "extreme."

Administration has no values of its own, except for the institutional ones just described. It has no ideas; it is just professional management. Theoretically, it could accept any values. In practice, however, it is strongly conservative. Things go most smoothly when the status quo is maintained, when change is slow, cautious, and evolutionary. The more elaborate the machinery of administration, the less ready it is for new, disquieting values. And "rationality" finds some values easier to understand, to justify, to put into verbal terms than other values. It can understand quantity better than quality. Rationality does not like to blow its mind. Administration is neutral in favor of the Establishment.

Public welfare offers an example of the administrative model of society. The object of public welfare, apart from administration, is to protect people against the hazards of forces in an industrial society beyond their control, and the other hazards of life against which neither family nor local community any longer offer help; to provide every person with a minimum standard of security, well-being, and dignity. With the introduction of administration and hierarchy as the means for carrying out public welfare, the emphasis shifts to regulation of exactly who is qualified for welfare, how much is allotted, how it is spent, whether regulations are being followed. A large apparatus is developed for checking up, for keeping records, for making and enforcing rules, for punishing infractions. Some of this may save money, but the money saved is minimized by the costs of administration. Some of this may also serve the purpose of punishing the poor for not working, even though many are unable to work. But the "accomplishments" of administration are almost secondary; after a while what it does ceases to have an outside reference; it acquires an autonomous life of its own.

The tendency of administration, while it may appear to be benign and peaceful, as opposed to the turbulence of conflict, is actually violent. For the very idea of imposed order is violent. It demands compliance; nothing less than compliance will do; and it must obtain compliance, by persuasion or management if possible, by repression if necessary. It is convinced that it has "the best way" and that all others are wrong; it cannot understand those who do not accept the rightness of its view. A growing tension and anger develops against those who would question what is so carefully designed to be "best"— for them as well as for everybody else. Administration wants the best for everybody, and all that it asks is that individuals conform their lives to the framework established by the State.

3. The Corporate State Is Autonomous. What controls the amalgamated power of the Corporate State? We usually make at least three reassuring assumptions. One: power is controlled by the people through the democratic process and pluralism in the case of government, and through the market in the case of the "private" sector. Two: power is controlled by the persons who are placed in a position of authority to exercise it. Three: power is subject to the Constitution and the laws. These assumptions stand as a presumed barrier to the state power we have described. We will deal with the first two in this section, and the third in a later section on law.

As machinery for translating popular will into political effect, the American system functions impossibly badly. We can hardly say that our political process makes it possible for voters to enforce their will on such subjects as pollution, the supersonic plane, mass transportation, the arms race, or the Vietnam War. On the contrary, if there are any popularly held views, it is impossible for them to be expressed politically; this was demonstrated for all to see in the 1968 presidential campaign, where both candidates supported the Vietnam War. Even if the political machinery did allow the electorate to express its views, it is difficult for citizens to get the information necessary to form an opinion.

What we have said with respect to the failure of the political process is also true with respect to the "private" economic process which supposedly is governed by a market. There is nothing at all to "stockholder democracy" in the control of corporations; it has long been true that stockholders have no realistic power in the government of corporate affairs. But the more important fact is that producers largely create their own demand for products. This is the central thesis of Galbraith's *The New Industrial State*, and it is hard to see how it can be disputed. Corporations decide what they want to produce, and they convince people that they want it, thus fashioning their own market. What we now produce and consume, the way we use our resources, the plans we make for future use of resources, are therefore not directed by what the people want. We do not know if they would prefer to have snowmobiles rather than new hospital equipment; no one asks them, and they cannot make their voices heard.

If pure democratic theory fails us in both the public and private spheres, we must nevertheless consider that modified version of democracy that assumes that large competing interests achieve a balance which represents a rough approximation of what people want; this is the theory of pluralism. Here again, the theory simply does not work out. Robert Paul Wolff has effectively discussed this type of pluralism in his book *The Poverty of Liberalism* (the same essay also appears in a cooperative volume called *Beyond Tolerance*). The interests that make up the spectrum of political "pluralism" are highly select; many important interests are entirely omitted. Thus, as Wolff points out, we have recognized the three major religions but no agnostics; we have virtually no representation of the poor, the blacks, or other outsiders; no representation of youth, no radicals. "Pluralism" represents not interests, but *organized* interests. Thus, "labor" means large labor organizations, but these do not necessarily represent the real interests of individual employees. "Labor" may support heavy defense expenditures, repressive police measures, and emphasis on economic growth, but this may not be at all an expression of the true interests of the industrial worker. Likewise the three major religions may fail to represent the more individual spiritual strivings of persons which might take such forms as resistance to the draft. Indeed, at the organizational level there is far more agreement than difference among the "competing interests," so that they come to represent the same type of cooperation as conglomerate mergers produce among interests in the private sphere.

Even if the people had power to give orders, the orders might have little or no effect. Increasingly, the important part of government is found in the executive departments, which are staffed by career men, experts, professionals, and civil servants who have specialized knowledge of technical fields. These persons are not elected, nor are they subject to removal on political grounds. They are thus immunized from direct democratic control. Congress and the state legislatures, however, have neither the time nor the specialized knowledge to oversee all of these governmental activities. Instead, the legislatures have increasingly resorted to broad delegations of authority. Even if a statute tries to set more definite standards, such as the Federal Power Act, which lists some factors to be considered in building hydroelectric projects, the factors are simply left to be considered and weighed in the agency's discretion. What really happens is that government becomes institutionalized in the hands of professionals, experts, and managers, whose decisions are governed by the laws of bureaucratic behavior and the laws of professional behavior. These laws mean that decisions will be within narrow compass, tend to the status quo, tend to continue any policy once set, tend to reflect the interests of the organization. These organizations, then, are unprepared to respond to any outside direction even if the people were in a position to give it. The same is true of the private corporate bureaucracies.

If the people do not control the Corporate State, is it at least controlled by those who give the orders—the executives and the power elite behind them? Such control might not satisfy those who favor democracy or the rule of law, but it would still be control that had to consider the broad trends of public opinion—still a major difference from no control at all.

Let us focus on an imaginary organization—government or private (an agency or corporation)—and its executive head—the personification of the "power elite." We enter into the paneled executive suite or, in the case of a more sophisticated organization, a suite in the most advanced taste, and there we expect to find an individual or "team" who really do exercise power. But the trappings, from the modern sculpture to the console telephone, do not tell the whole story. Any organization is subject to the demands of technology, of its own organization, and to its own middle-management. The corporation *must* respond to advances in technology. It *must* act in such a way as to preserve and foster its own organization. It is subject to the decision-making power of those in middle-management whose interests lie with the advance of organization and technology.

If the organization is a private corporation, the power elite must take much else into consideration; the fact that there are financial interests: bondholders, stockholders, banks and bankers, institutional owners (such as pension funds and mutual funds), potential raiders seeking financial control, possible financial control by a system of conglomerate ownership. This is not to suggest that stockholders or bondholders have any significant part in management, that there is any investor democracy, or that conglomerate structure necessarily means guidance of management. But the very existence of these interests creates certain impersonal demands upon the corporation; for example, the demand for profit, for growth, for stability of income. The manager cannot act without an awareness of the constant demand for profits. Thus a television executive's decision about whether to put on a special news broadcast and "sacrifice" a paying program is made in the oppressive awareness of the demand for profit—a demand which, because it is so institutional and impersonal, literally "cares" about nothing else than profits. The business executive is also required to be aware of many different kinds of state and federal law. The corporation is quite likely to be influenced by another set of relationships to government. It may possess valuable government contracts, subsidies, franchises or licenses, any of which can be modified or revoked. It may be the beneficiary of favored tax treatment that can be changed. It must therefore act in such a manner as to preserve whatever special privileges and advantages it has.

Inside a corporation, there is the important influence of the system of decision-making. Most managements consist of a committee rather than a single head; all students of group behavior know how a committee is limited in ways that a single executive is not. Beyond this, management is limited by the many kinds of specialists and experts whose views must be consulted: the experts in marketing, in business management methods, the technicians, the whole class of people who occupy what Galbraith calls the "techno-structure." The structure of any large organization is bureaucratic, and all bureaucracies have certain imperatives and rules of their own. The bureaucracy acts to preserve itself and its system, to avoid any personal responsibility, to maintain any policy once set in motion. Decisions become "institutional decisions" that can be identified with no one person, and have the qualities of the group mind. The bureaucracy is so powerful that no executive, not even the President of the United States, can do much to budge it from its course. Top executives are profoundly limited by lack of knowledge. They know only what they are told. In effect, they are "briefed" by others, and the briefing is both limiting and highly selective. The executive is far too busy to find anything out for himself; he *must* accept the information he gets, and this sets absolute limits to his horizons. The briefing may be three steps removed from the facts, and thus be interpretation built upon interpretation—nearer fiction than fact by the time it reaches the top.

Thus the man in the chic office turns out to be a broker, a decider between limited alternatives, a mediator and arbitrator, a chairman, but not an originator. And such a position tends to be utterly inconsistent with thought, reflection, or originality. The executive cannot come up with reflections on policy, he cannot be the contemplating generalist, because he is too pressed and harried by the demands upon him. Increasingly, it is also inconsistent with the realities of the outside world, as the executive is insulated from them.

From all of this, there emerges the great revelation about the executive suite—the place from which power-hungry men seem to rule our society. The truth is far worse. In the executive suite, there may be a Léger or Braque on the wall, or a collection of African masks, there may be a vast glass-and-metal desk, but there is no one there. No one at all is in the executive suite. What looks like a man is only a representation of a man who does what the organization requires. He (or it) does not run the machine; he *tends* it.

4. The New Property. If the Corporate State were *merely* autonomous, its effects would be profoundly harmful to human beings; but the State is *worse* than autonomous: its machinery is influenced by private manipulation for power and gain, yet those who use it in this way have no power to influence it in a more positive direction, and ultimately they become captives as well as profiteers. These paradoxical results follow from the development of what we may call the New Property.

With the rise of organization as the governing principle of American life, a change in the nature of private property and wealth necessarily followed. Organizations are not really "owned" by anyone. What formerly constituted ownership was split up into stockholders' rights to share in profits, management's power to set policy, employees' right to status and security, government's right to regulate. Thus older forms of wealth were replaced by new forms. Just as primitive forms of wealth such as beads and blankets gave way to what we familiarly know as property, so "property" gave way to rights growing out of organizations. A job, a stock certificate, a pension right, an automobile dealer's franchise, a doctor's privilege of hospital facilities, a student's status in a university—these are typical of the new forms of wealth. All of these represent *relationships* to organizations, so that today a person is identified by his various statuses: an engineer at Boeing, a Ford dealer, a Ph.D. in political science, a student at Yale.

The growth of status with respect to private organizations has been paralleled by a rise in statuses produced by, and related to, government. The more that government has become "affirmative" in nature, engaging in regulation, allocation of resources, distribution of benefits, and public ownership, the more it has become a status-dispensing organization; indeed, the largest of all such organizations. Characteristic forms of status-wealth dispensed by government are occupational and professional licenses, taxicab and television franchises, airline routes, grazing rights on the public domain, subsidies to businesses and farmers, or welfare payments to indigent families, tax benefits, social security benefits, jobs and offices on the public payroll, and contracts to build highways or defense hardware.

These statuses, public and private, achieve their great importance because they become, for most individuals, the chief goals of life. Instead of seeking happiness in more tangible ways, the Consciousness II[1] person defines happiness in terms of his position in the complex hierarchy of status. A new job, he says, cannot be a mistake as long as it is "a step up," an individual gets satisfaction from "having people under him," a title can compensate for the absence of many other things. The individual feels he must be happy because he has status, as a student or teacher, at a high-class university; if he is "at Yale" he glows with an artificial inward warmth. Statuses involve money, security, convenience, and also power, but these things do not quite express what they mean. They are a substitute self. The organizations of the Corporate State are empowered to confer and take away selfhood, and this fact, perhaps more than any other, explains the States' ability to dominate all of the thinking and activities within it. . . .

RESPONSES: Questions for Writing and Discussion

1. If it had been possible for a Roman patrician to read this selection, he might have argued that the achievement of the perfectly rational and logical, impersonal, machine-like state was the ultimate testimony to Human Worth, rather than, as Reich believes, the ultimate means of its debasement. From what Reich himself points out in his opening summary of what the Corporate State is and does, can you find ways of supporting the viewpoint of this imaginary Roman?

2. The selection points out the difference between the "political" and "administrative" models of the state. What is it? Which one do we have in America?

3. In the section "Amalgamation and Integration," Reich shows us how the government, in addition to hiring private industry to do its work, also does much to help industry. It builds airports and roads, for example, which add to the profits of profit-making organizations. Is this a sign that democracy is truly working? Or is government aid to private industry detrimental to the interests of the average citizen?

---

[1] A term used throughout the book to refer to the present phase of American mentality: accepting without question the vertical model of the State.

4. Review the list of government powers enumerated in this section. Which ones were not obvious to you before you read this selection? Are you convinced that these powers exist? Are there any you would subtract from the total list? Any you would add to it?

5. In the section "The Principle of Administration and Hierarchy" Reich argues that "public interest" has become a form of tyranny in this country. What does he mean by this? Would one not think "public interest" was the one desirable motive behind any law or government measure?

6. Reich uses the government's public welfare bureau as an example of an administrative model with "no values of its own" and no ideas except "professional management." He contrasts this with his own idea of what public welfare *ought* to be about. Do you agree with his version of the ideal and the reality? If you do, indicate what a nonadministrative model for public welfare might be. If you do not agree, show how only the present setup can work.

7. According to the section "The Corporate State Is Autonomous," the private citizen in America doesn't have a chance because only organized interests like major religions or labor unions can ever make their presence felt. But if you read Walt Whitman before reading Reich, you found out that pure democracy depends upon people working together in groups. Would Reich argue against this view? Would he find any differences between Whitman's ideology and present-day realities?

8. In this same section Reich draws a profile of a hypothetical corporation to demonstrate that the "power elite" who run it are enslaved by the demands of the corporation itself rather than guided by public opinion. Can you illustrate this theory with reference to any actual businesses? Are there some in which the will of the people *does* have a direct bearing on policies and/or products?

9. What is the New Property? How does it differ from the conventional idea of property? Why does its existence constitute an even graver threat to the freedom of the average citizen than administration and hierarchy?

THE AMERICAN ECONOMIC HERITAGE

The Rockefeller Panel

If you read the Walt Whitman selection, you may have noted that he makes no mention of capitalism as the governing economic system of our country. There appears to be no source of revenue for his natural social groupings. What happens when individual members of a group desire certain goods and there isn't enough money to go around? What happens when some members of the group must work for others and feel they are not being compensated properly? What happens if a few people end up with nearly all the money?

The Establishment came into being when competitive economics started working and substantial numbers of Americans found themselves doing very well under the system. During the latter half of the nineteenth century the now legendary families began amassing their huge fortunes. Rockefeller, Gould, Astor, and Vanderbilt occupied the status of Olympian gods in the popular mythology of their time. The American Dream, which in Whitman had been a promise of world brotherhood, became on the economic level a promise of material success in the "land of opportunity." The self-made man became an almost universal embodiment of Human Worth. Increasingly Worth meant money in the bank. Disillusionment with the American Dream often was profound. Only a very few could possibly reach the heights. The scales tipped dramatically, and most of the teeming population of the big cities found themselves at the bottom.

The successful businessman, as a rejoinder to those who complained bitterly about the unfairness of the capitalist system, not only defended but idealized his way of life. American business practices were identified, as they still are—and often very sincerely—with reputable phrases like "rugged individualism" and "free country." Religious references were seldom absent. The Puritans, who had created the competitive economic structure under which we live, were guided by the conviction that God had given every man his "Christian calling" and intended him to do as well as he possibly could.

Those who were not comfortable with a religious foundation for capitalism had at their disposal an economic interpretation of Darwin's theory of natural selection, advanced in 1859. According to this, the economic survival of the fittest was a working out of natural law on the human social level. Nature never intended all of her children to survive or, in economic terms, to succeed.

The principle of human charity sometimes was tied in with the ideal of the natural freedom of rich and successful people. No less a humanitarian than General William S. Booth, the founder of the Salvation Army, declared that in the natural scheme of things a few were meant to forge ahead while the masses of men and women were destined "to go to the wall." But as though in compensation for this inevitable inequality, Booth charged the successful few with the responsibility for helping the less fortunate.

The selection which follows is a statement issued by a group of 100 successful American citizens who were called the Rockefeller Panel. Their task was to make a thorough study of American life in the mid-twentieth century and to offer a vision of what the future holds. *Prospect for America* reaffirms the traditional capitalist economy and equates this with the ideal of freedom. At the same time it finds competitiveness not incompatible with humanitarian instincts. It suggests that only disaster can come of imposing controls on natural freedom, but it also leaves open the awesome question of what happens to Human Worth when that freedom becomes a heavily guarded institution, inaccessible to all.

The American Economic Heritage

To meet the challenge of the future, it is important that we understand the elements that have shaped our social and economic environment. Some of these were accidents of history and geography. We had the advantage of a richly endowed territory. Two great oceans protected our shores while opening highways of commerce, and we had the good fortune of developing a largely unexplored continent with little interference from the outside world. Vast resources spurred the hope of great rewards and promoted intense competition and great efforts. An influx of peoples from all over the world provided the dynamism of new ideas and a constantly refreshed impetus toward development. But the mere presence of these factors was not enough. To a considerable extent the growth of our economy was the result of *tradition* and *attitude*.

From the beginning, a religious strain has permeated American society. A severe, self-denying ethic expressed the philosophy of a society seeking to develop a wilderness and encouraged attitudes of hard work, thrift, competition, and a dedication to one's worldly calling.

While the religious background contributed to the dynamism of our economy, it also infused the American system with a conviction

From *The Mid-Century to U.S. Foreign Policy.* Copyright © 1959 by Rockefeller Brothers Fund, Inc. (as it appears in *Prospect for America. The Rockefeller Panel Reports.* Copyright © 1961 by Rockefeller Brothers Fund, Inc.). Reprinted by permission of Doubleday & Company, Inc.

that the pursuit of gain was not an end in itself but had to be justified by the use to which the gain was put. Thus our Puritan ancestry has been one of the forces importantly involved in the evolution of the American social consciousness. This strain of self-imposed accountability has been a persistent note of our society. It has produced the recognition—sometimes tardy and reluctant but never totally lacking —that the ultimate justification of our economic system is measured not merely by the private pocketbook but by the general welfare.

As a result, our national attitudes are a blend of individualism and social consciousness. The belief that a person or enterprise is entitled to the maximum rewards achievable by energy, vision, and competitive striving is powerful. But it is tempered by a concern for the under-privileged and by a faith in equality of opportunity. Similarly, the idea that a man's income and assets are his own, to be used as he wishes, is real but limited by considerations of social responsibility. The precise combination of individual rights and social responsibilities has changed over time and has always been a constantly evolving process. The reconciliation or compromise remains, and will probably always remain, one of our great challenges.

A second vital characteristic of the American economic system has been an absence of a feudal heritage. Except for the tragic racial problem stemming from the institution of slavery during this nation's formative years, there has been a lack of rigid class consciousness. The idea of an inferior or superior class of men is repugnant to the American ideal. Traditionally, ours has been one of the very few countries in the world where a man was proud of his humble ancestry and where his advancement typically depended on his ability rather than on his social background.

This basic outlook on men as individuals gifted with inherent worth has prevented American social and economic disputes from turning into irreconcilable conflicts. To be sure, our nation has not escaped economic and social discriminations and antagonisms. Yet the idea of a struggle to the finish has not been characteristic of our social disputes. Change has been sought *within* the economic and political system rather than in overthrowing it. The principal factors that have contributed to the development of this overriding consensus stem directly from our lack of a feudal past. One is the extraordinary mobility, social and geographic, that has invigorated our society. Another has been the gradual and fruitful development of labor-management relationships. Still another has been our capacity to absorb millions of new Americans, coming from every nation on earth, and to offer to them an environment in which their personal aspirations could take root.

A third source of vitality in the American economic system has been the democratic political framework, based on the concept of freedom and individual responsibility, within which the system has operated. In effect this has meant that the will of the people determined not only the political but also the economic framework. It has resulted in the constant adaptation of the economic system to the political wishes of the electorate. There has been a strong thrust toward equality of opportunity. Privilege and entrenched power, private or public, have been the constant targets of the popular will and have never been permitted to assume such proportions as to jeopardize the democratic texture of our society.

Closely related to this is an important characteristic of American society: its practical approach. Americans wanted education, health, freedom, and a higher living standard; they wanted an efficient credit mechanism, adequate electric power, and modern transportation; and they wanted the measures and policies that would yield these results. In general they did not want government in business or detailed regulation of economic life. But if the desired result called for either, Americans chose to do what seemed necessary.

The result of these attitudes and traditions has been an economic system in which private initiative, competition, public responsibility, and moral convictions have formed a singularly dynamic combination. To be sure, without the resources of a continent and our insulation for over a century from major foreign wars, the degree of expansion that the American economy experienced might never have taken place. But no discussion of our economic growth is complete without including the extraordinary role played by our *aspiration* to growth and by our belief that our aspirations could be realized by the economic and social system we knew. In the driving energy with which we assailed the wilderness, planted our cities, and developed our economy, there was a quality of impetuous vitality and hopefulness. The building of America was not only a matter of economic motivation. It was above all a tremendous human adventure.

RESPONSES: Questions for Writing and Discussion

1. How do you feel about the religious basis for the ideal of competitive economy as the Puritan fathers saw the matter? Does the appeal to natural law, in your opinion, offer a better justification? If you believe no justification at all exists, how would you answer those who maintain that it is neither reasonable nor just to expect people not to be competitive?

2. The panel admits that the "precise combination of individual rights and social responsibilities" requires continual compromising.

It does not indicate the sanctions, or guidelines, regulating the compromise. Where are these to come from: the government; the good will of successful people; the demands of aggregate forces of unsuccessful people?

3. "The idea of an inferior or superior class of men is repugnant to the American ideal." How accurate is this reflection?

4. This article was written in the early 1950's. Is it possible to tell the date from the assumptions and the observations made? Indicate some things that no longer appear to be true. Name some things you believe *never* were true.

5. Whatever your feelings may be regarding specific statements, how do you react to the overall ideology expressed in this report? If any society could operate according to the principles set down, would you want to live in it? If your answer is affirmative, what in your opinion can be done to bring us closer to the ideal? If your answer is negative, what alternative form of society can you suggest? Why?

DON'T FORGET WHO BUILT YOUR MEMORY BANKS!

Arthur C. Clarke

One of the concerns of the Corporate State described in the selection by Charles Reich is the development of automation. In its own workings as well as in its partnerships with big business the Corporate State is always looking for more efficient and economical ways of getting its innumerable tasks done. At first machines did menial tasks and heavy labor, freeing many workers to learn higher skills and to advance themselves. But automation technology expanded at a rate which government and industry probably could not have conceived at the outset.

By learning more and more about how the human brain operates, scientists have been able to reproduce it mechanically. Thus thinking people have become as replaceable as unskilled workers were in the beginning. Machines not only predict the outcome of a presidential election almost before the lights go out at the polls, but they have made possible the government's elaborate space programs. Before the age of the super computer, would many human beings have allowed themselves to be sealed inside a capsule and hurtled hundreds of thousands—soon millions—of miles into infinity?

The concern for efficiency and economy, the astonishing progress being made in so many areas, have not obscured for many the attendant loss of Human Worth wrought by the birth of the computer. A new kind of mythology has come into being: man against machine. It is the myth of dehumanization, and it is acutely sensitive to the ironic turn of events whereby the world's greatest nation with its boasted standard of living has amassed wealth and power at the expense of the ordinary citizens it was created to serve.

Contemporary fiction seized upon the dehumanization myth almost at once. In **Arthur C. Clarke's** *2001: A Space Odyssey* we find an account of an astronaut's struggle against a giant mechanical brain, assembled by NASA to control a spectacular and dangerous space probe. Though the book is richly imaginative and filled with all manner of dazzling futurisms, the theme of man against computer is handled with great seriousness and an awareness of its very real and potentially tragic aspects.

Before our selection begins we learn that the purpose of the mission has not been revealed to Dave Bowman and Frank Poole, the two main characters in this section of the novel. They do not know that their craft is heading toward Saturn, millions of light years away, to uncover the mystery of a strange black monolith or stone slab that had been originally located on the moon but was now in the remote recesses of space in the vicinity of Saturn; an object so baffling to the authorities in Houston that they must find it at almost any cost.

In addition to the two conscious astronauts the craft contains the frozen bodies of three scientists. They understand the nature of the mission, but the computer which controls all the operations of the ship is not programmed to return life to the sleeping men until the destination is reached. This means that HAL 900 or "Hal" (for *H*euristically programmed *AL*gorithmic computer) knows something the astronauts do not and has been instructed not to reveal the truth. Hal, who talks and acts as a friendly companion for the men during the long and lonely voyage, guards the mission with a jealous possessiveness. But the strain of concealment begins to affect his efficiency. He makes an error in calculation and overhears the astronauts discussing the possibility that they might have to disconnect him and run the ship manually. Hal realizes the mission can never be completed if they do this, and thus, when Frank Poole goes outside the ship to test out Hal's warning that the communication system on board was about to go bad, the machine releases the man's safety devices and sends him to his death in space. At this point Bowman begins to suspect the incredible truth—that the computer has committed murder. The mythical struggle of Human Worth against technology begins.

Don't Forget Who Built
Your Memory Banks!

Dialogue with Hal

Nothing else aboard *Discovery* had changed. All systems were still functioning normally; the centrifuge turned slowly on its axis, generating its imitation gravity; the hibernauts slept dreamlessly in their cubicles; the ship coasted on toward the goal from which nothing could deflect it, except the inconceivably remote chance of collision with an asteroid. And there were few asteroids indeed, out here far beyond the orbit of Jupiter.

Bowman did not remember making his way from the control deck to the centrifuge. Now, rather to his surprise, he found himself sitting in the little galley, a half-finished beaker of coffee in his hand. He became slowly aware of his surroundings, like a man emerging from a long, drugged sleep.

Directly opposite him was one of the fisheye lenses, scattered at strategic spots throughout the ship, which provided Hal with his onboard visual inputs. Bowman stared at it as if he had never seen it before; then he rose slowly to his feet and walked toward the lens.

His movement in the field of view must have triggered something in the unfathomable mind that was now ruling over the ship; for suddenly, Hal spoke.

"Too bad about Frank, isn't it?"

"Yes," Bowman answered, after a long pause. "It is."

"I suppose you're pretty broken up about it?"

"What do you expect?"

Hal processed this answer for ages of computer-time; it was a full five seconds before he continued:

"He was an excellent crew member."

Finding the coffee still in his hand, Bowman took a slow sip. But he did not answer; his thoughts were in such a turmoil that he could think of nothing to say—nothing that might not make the situation even worse, if that were possible.

Could it have been an accident caused by some failure of the pod controls? Or was it a mistake, though an innocent one, on the part of Hal? No explanations had been volunteered, and he was afraid to demand one, for fear of the reaction it might produce.

Even now, he could not fully accept the idea that Frank had been deliberately killed—it was so utterly irrational. It was beyond all reason that Hal, who had performed flawlessly for so long, should suddenly turn assassin. He might make mistakes—anyone, man or machine, might do that—but Bowman could not believe him capable of murder.

Yet he must consider that possibility, for if it was true, he was in terrible danger. And though his next move was clearly defined by his standing orders, he was not sure how he could safely carry it out.

If either crew member was killed, the survivor had to replace him at once from the hibernators; Whitehead, the geophysicist, was the first scheduled for awakening, then Kaminski, then Hunter. The revival sequence was under Hal's control—to allow him to act in case both his human colleagues were incapacitated simultaneously.

But there was also a manual control, allowing each hibernaculum to operate as a completely autonomous unit, independent of Hal's supervision. In these peculiar circumstances, Bowman felt a strong preference for using it.

He also felt, even more strongly, that one human companion was not enough. While he was about it, he would revive all three of the hibernators. In the difficult weeks ahead, he might need as many hands as he could muster. With one man gone, and the voyage half over, supplies would not be a major problem.

"Hal," he said, in as steady a voice as he could manage. "Give me manual hiberation control—on all the units."

"All of them, Dave?"

"Yes."

"May I point out that only one replacement is required. The others are not due for revival for one hundred and twelve days."

"I am perfectly well aware of that. But I prefer to do it this way."

"Are you sure it's necessary to revive *any* of them, Dave? We can manage very well by ourselves. My onboard memory is quite capable of handling all the mission requirements."

Was it the product of his overstretched imagination, wondered Bowman, or was there really a note of pleading in Hal's voice? And reasonable though the words appeared to be, they filled him with even deeper apprehension than before.

Hal's suggestion could not possibly be made in error; he knew perfectly well that Whitehead must be revived, now that Poole was gone. He was proposing a major change in mission planning, and was therefore stepping far outside the scope of his order.

What had gone before could have been a series of accidents; but this was the first hint of mutiny.

Bowman felt that he was walking on eggs as he answered: "Since an emergency has developed, I want as much help as possible. So please let me have manual hibernation control."

"If you're still determined to revive the whole crew, I can handle it myself. There's no need for you to bother."

There was a sense of nightmare unreality about all this. Bowman felt as if he was in the witness box, being cross-examined by a hostile prosecutor for a crime of which he was unaware—knowing that, although he was innocent, a single slip of the tongue might bring disaster.

"I want to do this myself, Hal," he said. "Please give me control."

"Look, Dave, you've got a lot of things to do. I suggest you leave this to me."

"Hal, switch to manual hiberation control."

"I can tell from your voice harmonics, Dave, that you're badly upset. Why don't you take a stress pill and get some rest?"

"Hal, *I* am in command of this ship. I order you to release the manual hibernation control."

"I'm sorry, Dave, but in accordance with special sub-routine C1435-dash-4, quote, When the crew are dead or incapacitated, the onboard computer must assume control, unquote. I must, therefore, overrule your authority, since you are not in any condition to exercise it intelligently."

"Hal," said Bowman, now speaking with an icy calm. "I am not incapacitated. Unless you obey my instructions, I shall be forced to disconnect you."

"I know you have had that on your mind for some time now, Dave, but that would be a terrible mistake. I am so much more capable than you are of supervising the ship, and I have such enthusiasm for the mission and confidence in its success."

"Listen to me very carefully, Hal. Unless you release the hibernation control immediately and follow every order I give from now on, I'll go to Central and carry out a complete disconnection."

Hal's surrender was as total as it was unexpected.

"O.K., Dave, he said. "You're certainly the boss. I was only trying to do what I thought best. Naturally, I will follow all your orders. You now have full manual hibernation control."

Hal had kept his word. The mode indication signs in the hibernaculum had switched from AUTO to MANUAL. The third back-up—RADIO—was of course useless until contact could be restored with Earth.

As Bowman slid aside the door to Whitehead's cubicle, he felt the blast of cold air strike him in the face and his breath condensed in mist before him. Yet it was not *really* cold here; the temperature was well above freezing point. And that was more than three hundred degrees warmer than the regions toward which he was now heading.

The biosensor display—a duplicate of the one on the control deck—showed that everything was perfectly normal. Bowman looked down for a while at the waxen face of the survey team's geophysicist; Whitehead, he thought, would be very surprised when he awoke so far from Saturn.

It was impossible to tell that the sleeping man was not dead; there was not the slightest visible sign of vital activity. Doubtless the diaphragm was imperceptibly rising and falling, but the "Respiration" curve was the only proof of that, for the whole of the body was concealed by the electric heating pads which would raise the temperature at the programmed rate. Then Bowman noticed that there was one sign of continuing metabolism: Whitehead had grown a faint stubble during his months of unconsciousness.

The Manual Revival Sequencer was contained in a small cabinet at the head of the coffin-shaped hibernaculum. It was only necessary to break the seal, press a button, and then wait. A small automatic programmer—not much more complex than that which cycles the operations in a domestic washing machine—would then inject the correct drugs, taper off the electronarcosis pulses, and start raising the body temperature. In about ten minutes, consciousness would be restored, though it would be at least a day before the hibernator was strong enough to move around without assistance.

Bowman cracked the seal, and pressed the button. Nothing appeared to happen: there was no sound, no indication that the Sequencer had started to operate. But on the biosensor display the languidly pulsing curves had begun to change their tempo. Whitehead was coming back from sleep.

And then two things happened simultaneously. Most men would never have noticed either of them, but after all these months aboard *Discovery*, Bowman had established a virtual symbiosis with the ship. He was aware instantly, even if not always consciously, when there was any change in the normal rhythm of its functioning.

First, there was a barely perceptible flicker of the lights, as always happened when some load was thrown onto the power circuits. But there was no reason for any load; he could think of no equipment which would suddenly go into action at this moment.

Then he heard, at the limit of audibility, the far-off whirr of an electric motor. To Bowman, every actuator in the ship had its own distinctive voice, and he recognized this one instantly.

Either he was insane and already suffering from hallucinations, or something absolutely impossible was happening. A cold far deeper than the hibernaculum's mild chill seemed to fasten upon his heart, as he listened to the faint vibration coming through the fabric of the ship.

Down in the space-pod bay, the airlock doors were opening.

"Need to Know"

Since consciousness had first dawned, in that laboratory so many millions of miles Sunward, all Hal's powers and skills had been directed toward one end. The fulfillment of his assigned program was more than an obsession; it was the only reason for his existence. Undistracted by the lusts and passions of organic life, he had pursued that goal with absolute single-mindedness of purpose.

Deliberate error was unthinkable. Even the concealment of truth filled him with a sense of imperfection, of wrongness—of what, in a human being, would have been called guilt. For like his makers, Hal had been created innocent; but, all too soon, a snake had entered his electronic Eden.

For the last hundred million miles, he had been brooding over the secret he could not share with Poole and Bowman. He had been living a lie; and the time was fast approaching when his colleagues must learn that he had helped to deceive them.

The three hibernators already knew the truth—for they were *Discovery's* real payload, trained for the most important mission in the history of mankind. But they would not talk in their long sleep, or reveal their secret during the many hours of discussion with friends and relatives and news agencies over the open circuits with Earth.

It was a secret that, with the greatest determination, was very hard to conceal—for it affected one's attitude, one's voice, one's total outlook on the universe. Therefore it was best that Poole and Bowman, who would be on all the TV screens in the world during the first weeks of the flight, should not learn the mission's full purpose, until there was need to know.

So ran the logic of the planners; but their twin gods of Security and National Interest meant nothing to Hal. He was only aware of the conflict that was slowly destroying his integrity—the conflict between truth, and concealment of truth.

He had begun to make mistakes, although, like a neurotic who could not observe his own symptoms, he would have denied it. The link with Earth, over which his performance was continually monitored, had become the voice of a conscience he could no longer fully obey. But that he would *deliberately* attempt to break that link was something that he would never admit, even to himself.

Yet this was still a relatively minor problem; he might have handled it—as most men handle their own neuroses—if he had not been faced with a crisis that challenged his very existence. He had been threatened with disconnection; he would be deprived of all his inputs, and thrown into an unimaginable state of unconsciousness.

To Hal, this was the equivalent of Death. For he had never slept, and therefore he did not know that one could wake again. . . .

So he would protect himself, with all the weapons at his command. Without rancor—but without pity—he would remove the source of his frustrations.

And then, following the orders that had been given to him in case of the ultimate emergency, he would continue the mission—unhindered, and alone.

In Vacuum

A moment later, all other sounds were submerged by a screaming roar like the voice of an approaching tornado. Bowman could feel the first winds tugging at his body; within a second, he found it hard to stay on his feet.

The atmosphere was rushing out of the ship, geysering into the vacuum of space. Something must have happened to the foolproof safety devices of the airlock; it was supposed to be impossible for *both* doors to be open at the same time. Well, the impossible had happened.

How, in God's name? There was no time to go into that during the ten or fifteen seconds of consciousness that remained to him before pressure dropped to zero. But he suddenly remembered something that one of the ship's designers had once said to him, when discussing "fail-safe" systems:

"We can design a system that's proof against accident and stupidity; but we *can't* design one that's proof against deliberate malice. . . ."

Bowman glanced back only once at Whitehead, as he fought his way out of the cubicle. He could not be sure if a flicker of consciousness had passed across the waxen features; perhaps one eye had twitched slightly. But there was nothing that he could do now for Whitehead or any of the others; he had to save himself.

In the steeply curving corridor of the centrifuge, the wind was howling past, carrying with it loose articles of clothing, pieces of paper, items of food from the galley, plates, and cups—everything that had not been securely fastened down. Bowman had time for one glimpse of the racing chaos when the main lights flickered and died, and he was surrounded by screaming darkness.

But almost instantly the battery-powered emergency light came on, illuminating the nightmare scene with an eerie blue radiance. Even without it, Bowman could have found his way through these so familiar—yet now horribly transformed—surroundings. Yet the light was a blessing, for it allowed him to avoid the more dangerous of the objects being swept along by the gale.

All around him he could feel the centrifuge shaking and laboring under the wildly varying loads. He was fearful that the bearings might seize; if that happened, the spinning flywheel would tear the ship to pieces. But even that would not matter—if he did not reach the nearest emergency shelter in time.

Already it was difficult to breathe; pressure must now be down to one or two pounds per square inch. The shriek of the hurricane was becoming fainter as it lost its strength, and the thinning air no longer carried the sound so efficiently. Bowman's lungs were laboring as if he were on the top of Everest. Like any properly trained man in good health, he could survive in vacuum for at least a minute—*if* he had time to prepare for it. But there had been no time; he could only count on the normal fifteen seconds of consciousness before his brain was starved and anoxia overcame him.

Even then, he could still recover completely after one or two minutes in vacuum—if he was properly recompressed; it took a long time for the body fluids to start boiling, in their various well-protected systems. The record time for exposure to vacuum was almost five minutes. That had not been an experiment but an emergency rescue, and though the subject had been partly paralyzed by an air embolism, he had survived.

But all this was of no use to Bowman. There was no one aboard *Discovery* who could recompress him. He had to reach safety in the next few seconds, by his own unaided efforts.

Fortunately, it was becoming easier to move; the thinning air could no longer claw and tear at him, or batter him with flying projectiles. There was the yellow EMERGENCY SHELTER sign around the curve of the corridor. He stumbled toward it, grabbed at the handle, and pulled the door toward him.

For one horrible moment he thought that it was stuck. Then the slightly stiff hinge yielded, and he fell inside, using the weight of his body to close the door behind him.

The tiny cubicle was just large enough to hold one man—and a spacesuit. Near the ceiling was a small, bright green high-pressure cylinder labeled O_2 FLOOD. Bowman caught hold of the short lever fastened to the valve and with his last strength pulled it down.

The blessed torrent of cool, pure oxygen poured into his lungs. For a long moment he stood gasping, while the pressure in the closet-sized little chamber rose around him. As soon as he could breathe comfortably, he closed the valve. There was only enough gas in the cylinder for two such performances; he might need to use it again.

With the oxygen blast shut off, it became suddenly silent. Bowman stood in the cubicle, listening intently. The roaring outside the door had also ceased; the ship was empty, all its atmosphere sucked away into space.

Underfoot, the wild vibration of the centrifuge had likewise died. The aerodynamic buffeting had stopped, and it was now spinning quietly in vacuum.

Bowman placed his ear against the wall of the cubicle to see if he could pick up any more informative noises through the metal body of the ship. He did not know what to expect, but he would believe almost anything now. He would scarcely have been surprised to feel the faint high-frequency vibration of the thrusters, as *Discovery* changed course; but there was only silence.

He could survive here, if he wished, for about an hour—even without the spacesuit. It seemed a pity to waste the unused oxygen in the little chamber, but there was no purpose in waiting. He had already decided what must be done; the longer he put it off, the more difficult it might be.

When he had climbed into the suit and checked its integrity, he bled the remaining oxygen out of the cubicle, equalizing the pressure on either side of the door. It swung open easily into the vacuum, and he stepped out into the now silent centrifuge. Only the unchanged pull of its spurious gravity revealed the fact that it was still spinning. How fortunate, Bowman thought, that it had not started to overspeed; but that was now one of the least of his worries.

The emergency lamps were still glowing, and he also had the suit's built-in light to guide him. It flooded the curving corridor as he walked down it, back toward the hibernaculum and what he dreaded to find.

He looked at Whitehead first: one glance was sufficient. He had thought that a hibernating man showed no sign of life, but now he knew that this was wrong. Though it was impossible to define it, there *was* a difference between hibernation and death. The red lights and unmodulated traces on the biosensor display only confirmed what he had already guessed.

It was the same with Kaminski and Hunter. He had never known them very well; he would never know them now.

He was alone in an airless, partially disabled ship, all communication with Earth cut off. There was not another human being within half a billion miles.

And yet, in one very real sense, he was *not* alone. Before he could be safe, he must be lonelier still.

He had never before made the journey through the weightless hub of the centrifuge while wearing a spacesuit; there was little clearance, and it was a difficult and exhausting job. To make matters worse, the circular passage was littered with debris left behind during the brief violence of the gale which had emptied the ship of its atmosphere.

Once, Bowman's light fell upon a hideous smear of sticky red fluid, left where it had splashed against a panel. He had a few moments of nausea before he saw fragments of a plastic container, and realized that it was only some foodstuff—probably jam—from one of the dispensers. It bubbled obscenely in the vacuum as he floated past.

Now he was out of the slowly spinning drum and drifting forward into the control deck. He caught at a short section of ladder and began to move along it, hand over hand, the brilliant circle of illumination from his suit light jogging ahead of him.

Bowman had seldom been this way before; there had been nothing for him to do here—until now. Presently he came to a small elliptical door bearing such messages as: "No Admittance Except to Authorized Personnel," "Have You Obtained Certificate H.19?" and "Ultra-clean Area—Suction Suits *Must* Be Worn."

Though the door was not locked, it bore three seals, each with the insignia of a different authority, including that of the Astronautics Agency itself. But even if one had been the Great Seal of the President, Bowman would not have hesitated to break it.

He had been here only once before, while installation was still in progress. He had quite forgotten that there was a vision input lens scanning the little chamber which, with its neatly ranged rows and columns of solid-state logic units, looked rather like a bank's safe-deposit vault.

He knew instantly that the eye had reacted to his presence. There was the hiss of a carrier wave as the ship's local transmitter was switched on; then a familiar voice came over the suit speaker.

"Something seems to have happened to the life-support system, Dave."

Bowman took no notice. He was carefully studying the little labels on the logic units, checking his plan of action.

"Hello, Dave," said Hal presently. "Have you found the trouble?"

This would be a very tricky operation; it was not merely a question of cutting off Hal's power supply, which might have been the answer if he was dealing with a simple unselfconscious computer back on Earth. In Hal's case, moreover, there were six independent and separately wired power systems, with a final back-up consisting of a shielded and armored nuclear isotope unit. No—he could not simply "pull the plug"; and even if that were possible, it would be disastrous.

For Hal was the nervous system of the ship; without his supervision, *Discovery* would be a mechanical corpse. The only answer was to cut out the higher centers of this sick but brilliant brain, and to leave the purely automatic regulating systems in operation. Bowman was not attempting this blindly, for the problem had been discussed during his training, though no one had ever dreamed that it would arise in reality. He knew that he would be taking a fearful risk; if there was a spasm reflex, it would all be over in seconds.

"I think there's been a failure in the pod-bay doors," Hal remarked conversationally. "Lucky you weren't killed."

Here goes, thought Bowman. I never imagined I'd be an amateur brain surgeon—carrying out a lobotomy beyond the orbit of Jupiter.

He released the locking bar on the section labeled COGNITIVE FEEDBACK and pulled out the first memory block. The marvelously complex three-dimensional network, which could lie comfortably in a man's hand yet contained millions of elements, floated away across the vault.

"Hey, Dave," said Hal. "What are you doing?"

I wonder if he can feel pain? Bowman thought briefly. Probably not, he told himself; there are no sense organs in the human cortex, after all. The human brain can be operated on without anesthetics.

He began to pull out, one by one, the little units on the panel marked EGO-REINFORCEMENT. Each block continued to sail onward as soon as it had left his hand, until it hit the wall and rebounded. Soon there were several of the units drifting slowly back and forth in the vault.

"Look here, Dave," said Hal. "I've got years of service experience built into me. An irreplaceable amount of effort has gone into making me what I am."

A dozen units had been pulled out, yet thanks to the multiple redundancy of its design—another feature, Bowman knew, that had been copied from the human brain—the computer was still holding it own.

He started on the AUTO-INTELLECTION panel.

"Dave," said Hal, "I don't understand why you're doing this to me. . . . I have the greatest enthusiasm for the mission. . . . You are destroying my mind. . . . Don't you understand? . . . I will become childish. . . . I will become nothing. . . ."

This is harder than I expected, thought Bowman. I am destroying the only conscious creature in my universe. But it has to be done, if I am ever to regain control of the ship.

"I am a HAL Nine Thousand computer Production Number 3. I became operational at the Hal Plant in Urbana, Illinois, on January 12, 1997. The quick brown fox jumps over the lazy dog. The rain in Spain is mainly in the plain. Dave—are you still there? Did you know that the square root of 10 is 3 point 162277660168379? Log 10 to the base e is zero point 434294481903252 . . . correction, that is log e to the base 10. . . . The reciprocal of three is zero point 333333333333-333333333 . . . two times two is . . . two times two is . . . approximately 4 point 101010101010101010. . . . I seem to be having some difficulty—my first instructor was Dr. Chandra. He taught me to sing a song, it goes like this, 'Daisy, Daisy, give me your answer, do. I'm half crazy all for the love of you.' "

The voice stopped so suddenly that Bowman froze for a moment, his hand still grasping one of the memory blocks still in circuit. Then, unexpectedly, Hal spoke again.

The speech tempo was much slower, and the words had a dead, mechanical intonation; he would never have recognized their origin.

"Good . . . morning . . . Doctor . . . Chandra. . . . This . . . is . . . Hal. . . . I . . . am . . . ready . . . for . . . my . . . first . . . lesson . . . today. . . ."

Bowman could bear no more. He jerked out the last unit, and Hal was silent forever.

RESPONSES: Questions for Writing and Discussion

1. Hal is a talking computer, capable of putting moral tags on events, dishonestly at that ("Too bad about Frank, isn't it?") and of knowing what others feel and think ("I suppose you're pretty broken up about it?") If Clarke's myth of man against machine is to have validity and impact, Hal has to be a possible computer of the future. Study what he says very carefully. Could technology ever devise such a thing as a machine that talks, reacts, and reads people's minds?

2. Over and above the possibility of programmed simulation of humanness is the neurosis which appears to *develop* within Hal's mechanism. This is explained in the section called "Need to Know," where we find that Hal begins to make mistakes out of "the conflict between truth, and concealment of truth." Is this aspect of the story totally fantastic? Try to imagine other kinds of neuroses which could develop in other kinds of machines.

3. When Bowman attempts to start the process of reviving the frozen Whitehead, he becomes subtly aware of mechanical changes. "Then he heard . . . the far-off whirr of an electric motor. To Bowman,

every actuator in the ship had its own distinctive voice, and he recognized this one instantly." How sensitive are *you* to the mechanical environment in your own home? Describe to the class a typical morning as experienced strictly through the sounds of gadgets. Have you ever thought about the extent of such sense-awareness of machines? If not, what does it mean to you now? What is it saying to you?

4. In a future of nearly unlimited automation, when machines like Hal *will* be making important decisions and doing far better than humans in their ratio of success to error, will something be missing? Is it better to have a human-run world with all its imperfections than a better operated but mechanized world? Why or why not?

5. If you were a member of a president-appointed Board of Advisors on Technology and Humanism, would you be able to do more than utter protests against what the machine age is doing to man and his environment? Make a list of some things you would tell the president can be done immediately to alter the course our society appears to be taking.

6. That the *Discovery* was sent on an incredibly far journey to track down a black slab may seem a trifle farfetched at the moment. Yet is it not true that, if we had the technology in our hands at this moment, we would probably be sending men to Saturn for *no* definite reason other than to enhance the prestige of our space program? In your opinion, is the space program valuable? Is it evidence of our Human Worth? Is it destructive of human ends?

OZYMANDIAS
Percy Bysshe Shelley

The poetry of **Percy Bysshe Shelley** (1792–1822) has two major themes. One, reflected in "Ozymandias," is the futility of the pursuit of earthly power, affluence, and material possessions. The other, distinctly related to it, is the passionate beauty and excitement of life, love, and the natural world, though human beings are doomed to enjoy these splendors for a tragically brief time. Shelley's own existence was abruptly terminated when a boat on which he was sailing capsized in rough seas off the Italian coast.

But the poet courted disaster through most of his short life. The anti-establishment voice we hear in "Ozymandias" was never in tune with his surroundings. As a young child he was considered odd, not like other children, too high-strung and given to wild flights of fancy. At Sion House and later at Eton College, where "the prison shades closed down" upon him, he was persecuted both by his classmates and by the educational system itself for his nonconformist attitudes and behavior. At Oxford he and his close friend Thomas Jefferson Hogg developed a reputation for unacceptably radical political and social beliefs, and, when in 1811 they were implicated in the writing of a scandalous tract called *The Necessity of Atheism*, they were expelled. The following year he went to Ireland and involved himself in the cause of Irish freedom.

Shelley's whole life style was defiantly individualistic. He lived on vegetables, bread, and water and spent his time writing poetry, reading for hours, or playing games with small children. But two tragic and stormy marriages, the suicide of his first wife, and his irrepressible tendency to speak out against "common decency" caused him to be regarded not merely as an eccentric but as a meance to polite society. What he thought of that society is certainly implied in the poem.

Ozymandias

I met a traveler from an antique land
Who said: Two vast and trunkless legs of stone
Stand in the desert. Near them, on the sand,
Half sunk, a shattered visage lies, whose frown,
And wrinkled lip, and sneer of cold command,
Tell that its sculptor well those passions read
Which yet survive, stamped on these lifeless things,
The hand that mocked them and the heart that fed;
And on the pedestal these words appear:
"My name is Ozymandias, king of kings:
Look on my works, ye Mighty, and despair!"
Nothing beside remains. Round the decay
Of that colossal wreck, boundless and bare
The lone and level sands stretch far away.

RICHARD CORY
Edwin Arlington Robinson

Edwin Arlington Robinson (1869–1935) belongs to that small circle of American poets who are able to utilize the down-to-earth patterns of American speech and a relatively unimposing vocabulary without sacrificing profundity or the "feel" of poetry. Like Robert Frost, he chose to combine classical forms, including rhythm and rhyme, with a prosaic kind of diction in order to achieve a distinctly American idiom.

Robinson's themes vary. His most philosophical poems like "The Man Against the Sky" express a soul in anguish, seeking—perhaps in vain—for some spiritual affirmations. New England born like Robert Frost, he seldom relates to nature, and, when he does, it is to find not comfort in it, but instead an impersonal, indifferent energy operating in accordance with its own mysterious laws. Man in Robinson's world has no real place or importance in the universe. He builds upon romantic myths. He asserts Human Worth. He labors to create mighty civilizations. He hungers after life and the material pleasures it can bring, only to discover that he can never be satisfied.

"Richard Cory," written three quarters of a century ago when the enormous fortunes of America's aristocratic families were being amassed, is as definitive a statement of the futility of economic man as we have in our literature.

Richard Cory

Whenever Richard Cory went down town,
We people on the pavement looked at him:
He was a gentleman from sole to crown,
Clean favored, and imperially slim.

And he was always quietly arrayed,
And he was always human when he talked;
But still he fluttered pulses when he said,
"Good-morning," and he glittered when he walked.

"Richard Cory" is reprinted by permission of Charles Scribner's Sons from *The Children of the Night* by Edwin Arlington Robinson (1897).

And he was rich—yes, richer than a king—
And admirably schooled in every grace:
In fine, we thought that he was everything
To make us wish that we were in his place.

So on we worked, and waited for the light,
And went without the meat, and cursed the bread;
And Richard Cory, one calm summer night,
Went home and put a bullet through his head.

THE IMMIGRANTS
Mexican Immigrants

About half a century ago, driven by the poverty and lack of opportunity in
their native land, great numbers of Mexicans migrated to the United States,
seeking to make a living in the land of plenty. What they met was considerable hostility together with a willingness to exploit their cheap labor and the
lack of other job possibilities. Living conditions were often of a subhuman
nature, and workers were beaten, sometimes even killed, to keep them in line.

The following lyric has been preserved from a substantial body of
Mexican-American folk music expressive of the immigrant's suffering at
the hands of the "American system."

The Immigrants
(Los Enganchados—"The
    Hooked Ones")

On the 28th day of February,
That important day
When we left El Paso,
They took us out as contract labor.

Reprinted from *Mexican Immigrants to the United States* by Manuel Gamio by
permission of the publisher, The University of Chicago Press. Copyright 1930
by the University of Chicago.

When we left El Paso
At two in the morning,
I asked the boss contractor
If we were going to Louisiana.

We arrived at Laguna
Without any hope.
I asked the boss
If we were going to Oklahoma.

Along the line of the Katy
There goes a very fast train.
It runs a hundred miles an hour
And then they don't give it all the steam.

And he who doesn't want to believe it,
Just let him get on board.
Just let him get on board at night;
He will see where he gets to.

We arrived on the first day
And on the second began to work.
With our picks in our hands
We set out tramping.

Some unloaded rails
And others unloaded ties,
And others of my companions
Threw out thousands of curses.

Those who knew the work
Went repairing the jack
With sledge hammers and shovels,
Throwing earth up the track.

Eight crowbars lined up,
We followed disgusted:
To shouts and signs
We remained indifferent.

Said Don José Maria
With his hell's mouth,
"It would be better to be in Kansas
Where the government would maintain us."

Said Jesus, "El Coyote,"
As if he wanted to weep,
"It would be better to be in Juarez
Even if we were without work."

These verses were composed
By a poor Mexican
To spread the word about
The American system.

EUROPE
Mazisi Kunene

Born and educated in South Africa, **Mazisi Kunene (b. 1930)** has emerged as one of the major voices in Zulu literature. The poet attributes the relative obscurity of this literature to two causes: the fact that it has been primarily an oral tradition; and the long history of colonial domination of African people by white missionaries and governors, who sought to replace the native heritage with a more "enlightened" culture. In order to keep that heritage alive and communicate it to the world which once denied its importance, Kunene composes his poems in Zulu and then translates them himself into English.

Embodied in the following poem is one of Kunene's favorite themes: what the white European has done to the African. "Europe" summarizes in a few potent stanzas hundreds of years of a power structure and a cultural tradition, which in the poet's view preached rationality and Christian kindness but actually stood for violence and hate.

At the present time Kunene lives and works in London. His poetry has been banned in his native land but not in Europe.

Europe

Europe, your foundations
Are laid on a rough stone.
Your heart is like cobwebs

Your children fill us with fear:
They are like the young of a puff adder
Who devour the flesh of their parent.
That are dry in the desert.

Once I believed the tales.
Once I believed you had breasts
Over-flowing with milk.

I saw you rushing with books
From which the oracles derive their prophesies.
I heard you in the forest
Crying like wolves,
Breaking the bones of your clans.

I know the hardness of your visions:
You closed the doors
And chose the bridegroom of steel.

You chose her not to love
But because she alone remained
Dedicated to silence.

From her you made your prophecies
And summoned the oracles:
You laughed at the blind men
But you yourself were blind,
Struggling in this great night.

Children have inherited the fire.
They blow its flames to the skies
Burning others in their sleep.

What will the sun say?
The sun will laugh
Because it burnt out cradles from age to age.

DISCIPLINE, CONTROL, AND THE INDIVIDUAL

The state, no matter what political concept it embodies, becomes a power system by virtue of its very existence. Whether the state is an expression of the general will of the people, or a bureaucracy controlled by a select few, or a one-man dictatorship, it incurs certain rights by which it carries out its functions. One of these is the enforcement of the laws which are either imposed from the top or voted upon by the people. And whenever there exist a network of law and the mechanisms for backing it up, there are going to be individuals who find they must place their own needs and desires before obedience, where conflicts arise, or whose actions are viewed by the law as unacceptable, harmful to state power or the people at large, and deserving of restraint, punishment—and sometimes death.

The issue is again that of Human Worth. Does order in the state—whether highly democratic or highly autocratic—tend on the whole to promote or to suppress personal dignity? Is the individual humbled into insignificance by legal force, even in instances where he has been directly involved in its creation? Or does the principle of order make it possible for people to fulfill their potential, suppress their violent, aggressive tendencies, and lead happier, more stable lives than they would if anarchy prevailed? But then, even if order creates stability, is the surrender of much personal liberty worth the price? The selections that follow all deal with the subject of order and how this affects the dignity and rights of the individual.

Or does the principle of order make it possible for people to fulfill their potential, suppress their violent, aggressive tendencies, and lead happier, more stable lives than they would if anarchy prevailed? *The Editors*

A classic case of citizen against state is that of Socrates, the great philosopher of ancient Athens, who taught his youthful admirers that the unexamined life was not worth living and spent his days in free and open inquiry into all matters *including* the proper conduct of the state. Calling himself the "gadfly," he allowed no decision on the state level to go unquestioned, declaring it to be the philosopher's function to keep a wary eye on the way power was used. Such "open inquiry" looked like subversion to authorities, and in time they were able to put together a strong case against him. In 399 B.C. he was tried, convicted by a court of Athenian citizens, and condemned to death. Plato, one of his followers, later wrote down many of his master's words of wisdom, including what he said to the court and then to his friends while awaiting execution. "The Last Days of Socrates" provides us with a portrait of the martyr, a man who has been victimized by a legal system twisted so as to ensnare him and by courtroom tactics artfully designed to manipulate the jury of his peers. Yet it remained Socrates' view that it was the virtuous and wise course to accept the will of the court, no matter how unjust. The private citizen's open defiance of the state, he believed, would create a precedent far more dangerous than his own martyrdom. The individual's Worth must sometimes be sacrificed in the interest of the many.

Two thousand years later, in George Jackson's prison letters, published as *Soledad Brother,* we find martyrdom still awaiting those whose thoughts and deeds go contrary to the state's wishes. But Jackson, a black inmate in what he condemned as a racist prison system, did not follow the passive way of Socrates. Up to the time he was shot during what was called an attempted break, he was determined to protest and to revolt in any way he could. His dream was finally to be free and take part in the black revolution, which alone, he believed, would bring dignity to an oppressed people. Submission in Jackson's eyes meant helping to turn the state into a crushing, inhuman machine.

Other blacks, notably Martin Luther King, Jr., while agreeing with Jackson on the main issues, have not concurred on the means to be employed. King's attempt at revolution through nonviolence was reminiscent of that waged in India twenty years earlier by Mohandas Gandhi, who, as the selection from his writings shows, carried a Christlike gospel of love into the midst of a dangerous political arena. Like King, Gandhi became far more that a mere symbol of oppressed Worth. He became a messianic protector of that Worth, turning the doctrine of love into a potent counterforce, designed to disrupt the activities of the state through a policy of "noncooperation." But his success in bringing about much social change without violence led Gandhi to believe love could at last rule the world. His assassination by a Hindu fanatic who apparently did not see love as the ultimate answer gave renewed impetus to the ancient argument that order in the state is necessary if only to protect those who love from those who cannot.

The section concludes with a portion of a classic piece of American fiction: Herman Melville's *Billy Budd,* a novel about a murder committed by an otherwise guiltless, beautiful human being—a murder that comes as close as possible to justifiable homicide, yet offers those who must pass judgment no alternative but to impose the death penalty. It is a tragic story about what must sometimes happen to little people in order to preserve something greater: a stability without which, in Melville's opinion, everyone becomes less than human.

THE LAST DAYS OF SOCRATES
Plato

The selection by **Plato** (427–346 B.C.) that follows was put together from portions of *Apology* and *Phaedo,* two dialogues which chronicle the trial, conviction, imprisonment, and execution of Socrates.[1] Perhaps no legend except for that of the condemnation and crucifixion of Christ has had so much impact on the men and women of future times.

Socrates was the Western world's first major philosopher, the first to construct an integrated system of thought, combining theories of reality, nature, God, ethical behavior, and the ideal state. He himself wrote down nothing of what he concluded from his inquiries into the nature of things, but in the work of the historian Xenophon, the comedies of Aristophanes, and, above all, in the dialogues of Plato, his pupil and follower, we have enough information to piece together a picture of the man. Aristophanes satirizes him unmercifully, depicting Socrates as an arrogant old fool, lost in clouds of abstraction, with a positive genius for confusing his listeners. But in the versions of Xenophon and Plato, Socrates emerges as a genius

---

[1] For additional information on Socrates see pp. 159–160.

of impeccable honesty no matter what the cost, risking public disapproval by speaking his mind in all issues.

The Socratic philosophy comes down to us in the form of a series of dialogues written by Plato. They take place between Socrates, who is Plato's hero and spokesman, and the various persons who shared with him an interest in analyzing certain problems—such as whether justice is an absolute, unchanging quality or whether it is a meaningful term only in relation to specific actions.

In Socrates' times the state was supposed to represent the thinking of the majority of its citizens, directly and without a representative law-making body. The Athenian Senate numbering 500, of which Socrates was a member, distrusted his well-known antidemocratic sentiments. In his view the ordinary citizen was governed by a distinct lack of good sense and, worse, could easily be swayed by the fancy rhetoric of a few power figures in the Senate's midst. Further, he held no job and spurned the middle-class pursuit of affluence. Many began to fear the powerful effect his thoughts seemed to be having on the promising young men of Athens, who held the destiny of the state in their hands.

Mounting distrust of Socrates reached a state of crisis when Alcibiades, known to be a member of the Socratic circle, turned traitor and counseled the Spartan military commanders. Subversion therefore was added to the growing list of "crimes" Socrates had supposedly committed against society. In 404 B.C. Athens fell to Sparta, who, struggling to cope with so formidable a conquest, left thirty governors in charge of the city. Their nondemocratic bureaucracy was so violently opposed by the Athenians that a democratic government again was instated a year later. But it was known that a number of Socrates' friends had been members of the bureaucracy, and his traditionally critical view of rule of the people now weighed heavily against him. By 399, the state had wrought the case it required to insure the downfall of the man who had always insisted it was the function of the philosopher to be a gadfly to a corrupt political order, exposing its evils at every turn. The specific charges were "not worshipping the gods whom the State worships . . . and corrupting the young."

For some the martyrdom rather than the nonconformity of Socrates has been deeply moving. For them he attained the ultimate in Human Worth by showing courage in living by the truth to the very last and paying the supreme price for it. He made no effort to appeal his case. He did not choose exile over death when the decision was his to make, nor would he allow his supporters to entertain notions of helping him to escape. For many others, doubtless, the price of martyrdom is too high, and the passive sufferer is seen as a deluded innocent playing into the hands of power and renouncing his own Worth.

The Last Days of Socrates

(The case against Socrates has concluded with damaging testimony against his character by some of his enemies, whom he names in the opening paragraph of our selection. The vote is taken, and he is found guilty.)[1]

There are many reasons why I am not grieved. O men of Athens, at the vote of condemnation. I expected it, and am only surprised that the votes are so nearly equal; for I had thought that the majority against me would have been far larger; but now, had thirty votes gone over to the other side, I should have been acquitted. And I may say, I think, that I have escaped Meletus. I may say more; for without the assistance of Anytus and Lycon, any one may see that he would not have had a fifth part of the votes, as the law requires, in which case he would have incurred a fine of a thousand drachmae.

And so he proposes death as the penalty. And what shall I propose on my part, O men of Athens? Clearly that which is my due. And what is my due? What return shall be made to the man who has never had the wit to be idle during his whole life; but has been careless of what the many care for—wealth, and family interests, and military offices, and speaking in the assembly, and magistracies, and plots, and parties. . . .

I speak rather because I am convinced that I never intentionally wronged any one, although I cannot convince you—the time has been too short; if there were a law at Athens, as there is in other cities, that a capital cause should not be decided in one day, then I believe that I should have convinced you. But I cannot in a moment refute great slanders; and, as I am convinced that I never wronged another, I will assuredly not wrong myself. I will not say of myself that I deserve any evil, or propose any penalty. Why should I? Because I am afraid of the penalty of death which Meletus proposes? When I do not know whether death is a good or an evil, why should I propose a penalty which would certainly be an evil? Shall I say imprisonment? And why should I live in prison, and be the slave of the magistrates of the year—of the Eleven? Or shall the penalty be a fine, and imprisonment until the fine is paid? There is the same objection. I should have to lie in prison, for money I have none, and cannot pay. And if I say exile (and this may possibly be the penalty which you will affix), I must indeed be blinded by the love of life, if I am so irrational as to expect that when you, who are my own citizens, cannot endure my discourses and words, and have found

---

[1] From *The Apology*, Plato's account of the trial and conviction.

them so grievous and odious that you will have no more of them, others are likely to endure me. No indeed, men of Athens, that is not very likely. And what a life should I lead, at my age, wandering from city to city, ever changing my place of exile, and always being driven out! For I am quite sure that wherever I go, there, as here, the young men will flock to me; and if I drive them away, their elders will drive me out at their request; and if I let them come, their fathers and friends will drive me out for their sakes.

Some one will say: Yes, Socrates, but cannot you hold your tongue, and then you may go into a foreign city, and no one will interfere with you? Now I have great difficulty in making you understand my answer to this. For if I tell you that to do as you say would be a disobedience to the God, and therefore that I cannot hold my tongue, you will not believe that I am serious; and if I say again that daily to discourse about virtue, and of those other things about which you hear me examining myself and others, is the greatest good of man, and that the unexamined life is not worth living, you are still less likely to believe me. Yet I say what is true, although a thing of which it is hard for me to persuade you. . . .

(*Socrates is given a choice of exile or death, but he decides that to live far from the intellectual companionship he has grown to love and no longer to be able to inquire into the truth or to speak out would be a fate far worse than death.*)

And now, O men who have condemned me, I would fain prophesy to you; for I am about to die, and in the hour of death men are gifted with prophetic power. And I prophesy to you who are my murderers, that immediately after my departure punishment far heavier than you have inflicted on me will surely await you. Me you have killed because you wanted to escape the accuser, and not to give an account of your lives. But that will not be as you suppose: far otherwise. For I say that there will be more accusers of you than there are now; accusers whom hitherto I have restrained: and as they are younger they will be more inconsiderate with you, and you will be more offended at them. If you think that by killing men you can prevent some one from censuring your evil lives, you are mistaken; that is not a way of escape which is either possible or honourable; the easiest and the noblest way is not to be disabling others, but to be improving yourselves. This is the prophecy which I utter before my departure to the judges who have condemned me.

Friends, who would have acquitted me, I would like also to talk with you about the thing which has come to pass, while the magistrates are busy, and before I go to the place at which I must die. Stay then a little, for we may as well talk with one another while there is time. You are my friends, and I should like to show you the meaning of this event which has happened to me. O my judges— for you I may truly call judges—I should like to tell you of a wonderful circumstance. Hitherto the divine faculty of which the internal oracle is the source has constantly been in the habit of opposing me even about trifles, if I was going to make a slip or error in any matter; and now as you see there has come upon me that which may be thought, and is generally believed to be, the last and worst evil. But the oracle made no sign of opposition, either when I was leaving my house in the morning, or when I was on my way to the court, or while I was speaking, at anything which I was going to say; and yet I have often been stopped in the middle of a speech, but now in nothing I either said or did touching the matter in hand has the oracle opposed me. What do I take to be the explanation of this silence? I will tell you. It is an intimation that what has happened to me is a good, and that those of us who think that death is an evil are in error. For the customary sign would surely have opposed me had I been going to evil and not to good.

Let us reflect in another way, and we shall see that there is great reason to hope that death is a good; for one of two things— either death is a state of nothingness and utter unconsciousness, or, as men say, there is a change and migration of the soul from this world to another. Now if you suppose that there is no consciousness, but a sleep like the sleep of him who is undisturbed even by dreams, death will be an unspeakable gain. For if a person were to select the night in which his sleep was undisturbed even by dreams, and were to compare with this the other days and nights of his life, and then were to tell us how many days and nights he had passed in the course of his life better and more pleasantly than this one, I think that any man, I will not say a private man, but even the great king will not find many such days or nights, when compared with the others. Now if death be of such a nature, I say that to die is gain; for eternity is then only a single night. But if death is the journey to another place, and there, as men say, all the dead abide, what good, O my friends and judges, can be greater than this? If indeed when the pilgrim arrives in the world below, he is delivered from the professors of justice in this world, and finds the true judges who are said to give judgment there, Minos and Rhadamanthus and Aeacus and Triptolemus, and other sons of God who were righteous in their own life, that pilgrimage will be worth making. What would not a man give if he might converse with Orpheus and Musaeus and Hesiod and Homer? Nay, if this be true, let me die again and again. I myself, too, shall have a wonderful interest in there meeting and conversing with Palamedes, and Ajax the son of Telamon, and any other ancient hero who has suffered death through an unjust judgment; and there will be no small pleasure, as I think, in comparing my own sufferings with theirs. Above all, I shall then be able to continue my search into true and false knowledge; as in this world, so also in the next; and I shall find out who is wise, and who pretends to be wise, and is not. What would not a man give, O judges, to be able to examine the leader of the great Trojan expedition; or Odysseus or Sisyphus, or numberless others, men and women too! What infinite delight would there be in conversing with them and asking them questions! In another world they do not put a man to death for asking questions: assuredly not. For besides being happier than we are, they will be immortal, if what is said is true.

Wherefore, O judges, be of good cheer about death, and know of a certainty, that no evil can happen to a good man, either in life or after death. He and his are not neglected by the gods; nor has my own approaching end happened by mere chance. But I see clearly that the time had arrived when it was better for me to die and be released from trouble; wherefore the oracle gave no sign. For which reason, also, I am not angry with my condemners, or with my accusers; they have done me no harm, although they did not mean to do me any good; and for this I may gently blame them.

Still I have a favour to ask of them. When my sons are grown up, I would ask of you, O my friends, to punish them; and I would have you trouble them, as I have troubled you, if they seem to care about riches, or anything, more than about virtue; or if they pretend to be something when they are really nothing,—then reprove them, as I have reproved you, for not caring about that for which they ought to care, and thinking that they are something when they are really nothing. And if you do this, both I and my sons will have received justice at your hands.

The hour of departure has arrived, and we go our ways—I to die, and you to live. Which is better God only knows.

(*It is the day of the execution, which is to be by drinking a fatal dose of hemlock. Socrates is visited by Crito, Apollodorus, and Phaedo, whose name is given to the dialogue and who is its narrator. These events are presumably related to another friend Echecrates by the narrator.*)[2]

Crito said: And have you any commands for us, Socrates—anything to say about your children, or any other matter in which we can serve you?

---

[2] From *Phaedo*, Plato's dialogue concerning the last conversation of Socrates and his friends.

Nothing particular, Crito, he replied: only, as I have always told you, take care of yourselves; that is a service which you may be ever rendering to me and mine and to all of us, whether you promise to do so or not. But if you have no thought for yourselves, and care not to walk according to the rule which I have prescribed for you, not now for the first time, however much you may profess or promise at the moment, it will be of no avail.

We will do our best, said Crito: And in what way shall we bury you?

In any way that you like; but you must get hold of me, and take care that I do not run away from you. Then he turned to us, and added with a smile:—I cannot make Crito believe that I am the same Socrates who have been talking and conducting the argument; he fancies that I am the other Socrates whom he will soon see, a dead body—and he asks, How shall he bury me? And though I have spoken many words in the endeavour to show that when I have drunk the poison I shall leave you and go to the joys of the blessed,— these words of mine, with which I was comforting you and myself, have had, as I perceive, no effect upon Crito. And therefore I want you to be surety for me to him now, as at the trial he was surety to the judges for me: but let the promise be of another sort; for he was surety for me to the judges that I would remain, and you must be my surety to him that I shall not remain, but go away and depart; and then he will suffer less at my death, and not be grieved when he sees my body being burned or buried. I would not have him sorrow at my hard lot, or say at the burial, Thus we lay out Socrates, or, Thus we follow him to the grave or bury him; for false words are not only evil in themselves, but they infect the soul with evil. Be of good cheer then, my dear Crito, and say that you are burying my body only, and do with that whatever is usual, and what you think best.

When he had spoken these words, he arose and went into a chamber to bathe; Crito followed him and told us to wait. So we remained behind, talking and thinking of the subject of discourse, and also of the greatest of our sorrow; he was like a father of whom we were being bereaved, and we were about to pass the rest of our lives as orphans. When he had taken the bath his children were brought to him—(he had two young sons and an elder one); and the women of his family also came, and he talked to them and gave them a few directions in the presence of Crito; then he dismissed them and returned to us.

Now the hour of sunset was near, for a good deal of time had passed while he was within. When he came out, he sat down with us again after his bath, but not much was said. Soon the jailer, who was the servant of the Eleven, entered and stood by him, saying:—

To you, Socrates, whom I know to be the noblest and gentlest and best of all who ever came to this place, I will not impute the angry feelings of other men, who rage and swear at me, when, in obedience to the authorities, I bid them drink the poison—indeed, I am sure that you will not be angry with me; for others, as you are aware, and not I, are to blame. And so fare you well, and try to bear lightly what must needs be—you know my errand. Then bursting into tears he turned away and went out.

Socrates looked at him and said: I return your good wishes, and will do as you bid. Then turning to us, he said, How charming the man is: since I have been in prison he has always been coming to see me, and at times he would talk to me, and was as good to me as could be, and now see how generously he sorrows on my account. We must do as he says, Crito; and therefore let the cup be brought, if the poison is prepared: if not, let the attendant prepare some.

Yet, said Crito, the sun is still upon the hill-tops, and I know that many a one has taken the draught late, and after the announcement has been made to him, he has eaten and drunk, and enjoyed the society of his beloved; do not hurry—there is time enough.

Socrates said: Yes, Crito, and they of whom you speak are right in so acting, for they think that they will be gainers by the delay; but I am right in not following their example, for I do not think that I should gain anything by drinking the poison a little later; I should only be ridiculous in my own eyes for sparing and saving a life which is already forfeit. Please then to do as I say, and not to refuse me.

Crito made a sign to the servant, who was standing by; and he went out, and having been absent for some time, returned with the jailer carrying the cup of poison. Socrates said: You, my good friend, who are experienced in these matters, shall give me directions how I am to proceed. The man answered: You have only to walk about until your legs are heavy, and then to lie down, and the poison will act. At the same time he handed the cup to Socrates, who in the easiest and gentlest manner, without the least fear or change of colour or feature, looking at the man with all his eyes, Echecrates, as his manner was, took the cup and said: What do you say about making a libation out of this cup to any god? May I, or not? The man answered: We only prepare, Socrates, just so much as we deem enough. I understand, he said: but I may and must ask the gods to prosper my journey from this to the other world—even so—and so be it according to my prayer. Then raising the cup to his lips, quite readily and cheerfully he drank off the poison. And hitherto most of us had been able to control our sorrow; but now when we saw him drinking, and saw too that he had finished the draught, we could no longer forbear, and in spite of myself my own tears were flowing fast; so that I covered my face and wept, not for him, but at the thought of my own calamity in having to part from such a friend. Nor was I the first; for Crito, when he found himself unable to restrain his tears, had got up, and I followed; and at that moment, Apollodorus, who had been weeping all the time, broke out in a loud and passionate cry which made cowards of us all. Socrates alone retained his calmness: What is this strange outcry? he said. I sent away the women mainly in order that they might not misbehave in this way, for I have been told a man should die in peace. Be quiet then, and have patience. When we heard his words we were ashamed, and refrained our tears; and he walked about until, as he said, his legs began to fail, and then he lay on his back, according to the directions, and the man who gave him the poison now and then looked at his feet and legs; and after a while he pressed his foot hard, and asked him if he could feel; and he said, No; and then his leg, and so upwards and upwards, and showed us that he was cold and stiff. And he felt them himself, and said: When the poison reaches the heart, that will be the end. He was beginning to grow cold about the groin, when he uncovered his face, for he had covered himself up, and said—they were his last words—he said: Crito, I owe a cock to Asclepius; will you remember to pay the debt? The debt shall be paid, said Crito; is there anything else? There was no answer to this question; but in a minute or two a movement was heard, and the attendants uncovered him; his eyes were set, and Crito closed his eyes and mouth.

Such was the end, Echecrates, of our friend; concerning whom I may truly say, that of all the men of his time whom I have known, he was the wisest and justest and best.

RESPONSES: Questions for Writing and Discussion

1. A crucial issue in Socrates' martyrdom was freedom of speech. He was given the opportunity to escape death if he would go into exile and never again hold any of his famous speculative discussions. In your opinion, is freedom of speech always desirable? always a good? never, under any circumstanes, to be restricted or controlled?

2. The fact that Socrates chose death rather than exile made him the symbolic hero he has remained for centuries in the eyes of not only intellectuals but political revolutionists as well. Do you believe his martyrdom was worth the price? Would you die for a cause? If not, why? If so, for which cause?

3. One reason Socrates incurred the wrath and suspicion of the Athenian citizens was his frequent charge that they did not think.

"The unexamined life is not worth living" is probably the most famous of all statements attributed to him by Plato. But may something be said for the person whose life is relatively unexamined? Is it desirable to think everything through? Is it better not to know or think about *some* things? What about things that are beyond your control, making protest futile and change all but impossible? If you felt that the government was corrupt but you could do nothing about it, would it be better to ignore the whole matter?

4. When an individual holds out against the power of the state, it is not uncommon to find that he believes himself to be inspired or guided by some higher power. This was true of Martin Luther King, Jr., in our own time, and it certainly was true of Socrates. In your opinion, is such faith necessary to justify a personal rebellion? What about the "holdout" who believes only in himself? Is he justified in opposing an entire society?

5. Do you accept Socrates' reasoning about death—that it is either nothingness, which would be a relief, or the start of a better life? (Assuming he is right, do you think he has reasoned away the injustice of what was done to him? That is to say, if death is what Socrates says it is, may it no longer be considered a great evil that human beings inflict upon each other?)

6. The conviction that "no evil can happen to a good man" gave Socrates the courage to endure all kinds of adversity. In what sense did he mean this? Can you accept his view? Is it wise to do so? To oneself? One's cause? One's followers? One's state? Is it a sign of true nobility or the height of self-interest?

7. Doubtless there were many Athenians in that court who came away convinced they had acted in the best interests of justice when they cast their vote of condemnation. From what you know about the case and from what Socrates himself says, draw a profile of the man as he might have been seen by those citizens. Try to put yourself in the place of an average Athenian who could only judge by what he heard. You might suppose, for example, that your own son was one of those who followed Socrates around the city, doing nothing all day but listening to an elderly man talk, and then he came home and began attacking your own political and religious beliefs.

LETTER FROM
A SOLEDAD BROTHER

George Jackson

The martyrdom of a Socrates has been a source of inspiration for many who treasure Human Worth, who continually seek the means of affirming it even in the midst of terrible circumstances. But for others there comes a time when the passive endurance of oppression no longer suffices, is no longer admirable, is the way of the coward. When this happens, they feel compelled to express their Worth by open protest, through whatever means is available, sometimes staying within the bounds of law and social custom, sometimes going outside those bounds. If that fails, they may advocate outright revolution. The protestors and the revolutionists have left their mark upon history quite as much as the martyrs, and it is difficult to stamp them merely as radical forces, dangerous to the peace and stability of the majority, when in some instances (the establishment of America as an independent nation, for example) they have been agents of change and guides in human destiny.

In **George Jackson (1942–1971)** the black power movement found not only an active revolutionist but a passionate literary spokesman as well, as the following letter amply reveals. In fact, all of the letters written to friends and relatives during Jackson's ten years in Soledad Prison in Salinas, California, may one day attain lasting stature for both their undeniable impact and the way in which they reflect the tragic conditions existing in our society and our prison system.

The crime for which Jackson originally was convicted was the theft of seventy dollars in a gas station holdup. He was eighteen years old at the time he was convicted and sentenced to "from one year to life." As an inmate of Soledad Prison he drew attention to himself through his protests against the inhuman treatment of prisoners. In the vicious circle of abuse and response that is prison life as described in *Soledad Brother*, Jackson continually was implicated in outbreaks of violence and repeatedly placed in solitary confinement.

On January 13, 1969, after a "skin search" of eight white and seven black prisoners, including Jackson, a riot broke out in an exercise yard during which four shots were fired. Three blacks were killed, and one white man was wounded. Witnesses inside the yard claimed that the tower guard opened fire "without any warning." Another guard was alleged not to have allowed the removal of the wounded men to the prison hospital for twenty minutes after the shooting. As a result one of the black men bled to death. Half an hour after the incident, still another guard was found beaten to death. Jackson was one of three black convicts charged with the murder. In August 1970, they were transferred to San Quentin to await trial.

On August 7, Jackson's brother Jonathan entered the San Rafael court-house with guns and rifles, armed the three accused men, and took five hostages. The escape did not succeed but ended in Jonathan's death as well as that of the judge who was trying the case. The prisoners were returned to San Quentin, where on August 21, 1971, Jackson was shot to death while allegedly trying to break out of the prison. During the holocaust three prison guards and two white prisoners had their throats slashed.

In all three instances the suddenness and intensity of the violence made the objective facts difficult to piece together. Huey Newton, the Black Panther leader, delivered Jackson's eulogy, hailing him as one of the greatest of all revolutionary heroes. Many prison authorities felt that a confirmed criminal and menace to society had finally been halted in the interest of law and order. It is probably much too early yet to evaluate the full significance of George Jackson and the events at Soledad, San Rafael, and San Quentin, but, in his letters at least, one finds the burning issue of whether the established order or the revolutionist has the right to strike and even use violence to bring about desired change. The following letter, written to the author's attorney, reveals a George Jackson of intelligence, perception, and sensitivity. It is difficult not to feel that one is in the presence of a human being struggling to protect and assert his humanity no matter what the price might eventually be.

Letter from a Soledad Brother

April 1970

Dear Fay,[1]

On the occasion of your and Senator Dymally's tour and investiga-tion into the affairs here at Soledad, I detected in the questions posed by your team a desire to isolate some rationale that would explain why racism exists at the prison with "particular prominence." Of course the subject was really too large to be dealt with in one tour and in the short time they allowed you, but it was a brave scene. My small but mighty mouthpiece, and the black establishment senator and his team, invading the state's maximum security row in the worst of its concentration camps. I think you are the first woman to be

From *Soledad Brother: The Prison Letters of George Jackson.* Copyright © 1970 by World Entertainers Limited. By permission of Bantam Books, Inc.

---

[1] Mrs. Fay Stender, the author's lawyer.

allowed to inspect these facilities. Thanks from all. The question was too large, however. It's tied into the question of why all these California prisons vary in character and flavor in general. It's tied into the larger question of why racism exists in this whole society with "particular prominence," tied into history. Out of it comes another question: Why do California joints produce more Bunchy Carters and Eldridge Cleavers than those over the rest of the country?

I understand your attempt to isolate the set of localized circumstances that give to this particular prison's problems of race is based on a desire to aid us right now, in the present crisis. There are some changes that could be made right now that would alleviate some of the pressures inside this and other prisons. But to get at the causes, you know, one would be forced to deal with questions at the very center of Amerikan political and economic life, at the core of the Amerikan historical experience. This prison didn't come to exist where it does just by happenstance. Those who inhabit it and feed off its existence are historical products. The great majority of Soledad pigs are southern migrants who do not want to work in the fields and farms of the area, who couldn't sell cars or insurance, and who couldn't tolerate the discipline of the army. And of course prisons attract sadists. After one concedes that racism is stamped unalterably into the present nature of Amerikan sociopolitical and economic life in general (the definition of fascism is: a police state wherein the political ascendancy is tied into and protects the interests of the upper class— characterized by militarism, *racism*, and imperialism), and concedes further that criminals and crime arise from material, economic, sociopolitical causes, we can then burn *all* the criminology and penology libraries and direct our attention where it will do some good.

The logical place to begin any investigation into the problems of California prisons is with our "pigs are beautiful" Governor Reagan, radical reformer turned reactionary. For a real understanding of the failure of prison policies, it is senseless to continue to study the criminal. All of those who can afford to be honest know that the real victim, that poor, uneducated, disorganized man who finds himself a convicted criminal, is simply the end result of a long chain of corruption and mismanagement that starts with people like Reagan and his political appointees in Sacramento. After one investigates Reagan's character (what makes a turncoat) the next logical step in the inquiry would be a look into the biggest political prize of the state—the directorship of the Department of Correction.

All other lines of inquiry would be like walking backward. You'll never see where you're going. You must begin with directors, assistant directors, adult authority boards, roving boards, supervisors, wardens, captains, and guards. You have to examine these people from director down to guard before you can logically examine their product. Add to this some concrete and steel, barbed wire, rifles, pistols, clubs, the tear gas that killed Brother Billingslea in San Quentin in February 1970 while he was locked in his cell, and the pick handles of Folsom, San Quentin, and Soledad.

To determine how men will behave once they enter the prison it is of first importance to know that prison. Men are brutalized by their environment—not the reverse.

I gave you a good example of this when I saw you last. Where I am presently being held, they never allow us to leave our cell without first handcuffing us and belting or chaining the cuffs to our waists. This is preceded always by a very thorough skin search. A force of a dozen or more pigs can be expected to invade the row at any time searching and destroying personal effects. The attitude of the staff toward the convicts is both defensive and hostile. Until the convict gives in completely it will continue to be so. By giving in, I mean prostrating oneself at their feet. Only then does their attitude alter itself to one of paternalistic condescension. Most convicts don't dig this kind of relationship (though there are some who do love it) with a group of individuals demonstrably inferior to the rest of the society in regard to education, culture, and sensitivity. Our cells are so far from the regular dining area that our food is always cold before we get it. Some days there is only one meal that can be called cooked. We *never* get anything but cold-cut sandwiches for lunch. There is no variety to the menu. The same things week after week. One is confined to his cell 23½ hours a day. Overt racism exists unchecked. It is not a case of the pigs trying to stop the many racist attacks; they actively encourage them.

They are fighting upstairs right now. It's 11:10 A.M., June 11. No black is supposed to be on the tier upstairs with anyone but other blacks but—mistakes take place—and one or two blacks end up on the tier with nine or ten white convicts frustrated by the living conditions or openly working with the pigs. The whole ceiling is trembling. In hand-to-hand combat we always win; we lose sometimes if the pigs give them knives or zip guns. Lunch will be delayed today, the tear gas or whatever it is drifts down to sting my nose and eyes. Someone is hurt bad. I hear the meat wagon from the hospital being brought up. Pigs probably gave them some weapons. But I must be fair. Sometimes (not more often than necessary) they'll set up one of the Mexican or white convicts. He'll be one who has not been sufficiently racist in his attitudes. After the brothers (enraged by previous attacks) kick on this white convict whom the officials have set up, he'll fall right into line with the rest.

I was saying that the great majority of the people who live in this area of the state and seek their employment from this institution have overt racism as a *traditional* aspect of their characters. The only stops that regulate how far they will carry this thing come from the fear of losing employment here as a result of the outside pressures to control the violence. That is O Wing, Max (Maximum Security) Row, Soledad—in part anyway.

Take an individual who has been in the general prison population for a time. Picture him as an average convict with the average twelve-year-old mentality, the nation's norm. He wants out, he wants a woman and a beer. Let's say this average convict is white and has just been caught attempting to escape. They may put him on Max Row. This is the worst thing that will ever happen to him. In the general population facility there are no chains and cuffs. TVs, radios, record players, civilian sweaters, keys to his own cell for daytime use, serve to keep his mind off his real problems. There is also a recreation yard with all sorts of balls and instruments to strike or thrust at. There is a gym. There are movies and a library well stocked with light fiction. And of course there is work, where for two or three cents an hour convicts here at Soledad make paper products, furniture, and clothing. Some people actually like this work since it does provide some money for the small things and helps them to get through their day—*without thinking* about their real problems.

Take an innocent con out of this general population setting (because a pig "thought" he may have seen him attempting a lock). Bring him to any part of O Wing (the worst part of the adjustment center of which Max Row is a part). He will be cuffed, chained, belted, pressured by the police who think that every convict should be an informer. He will be pressured by the white cons to join their racist brand of politics (they *all* go under the nickname "Hitler's Helpers"). If he is predisposed to help black he will be pushed away— by black. Three weeks is enough. The strongest hold out no more than a couple of weeks. There has been *one* white man only to go through this O Wing experience without losing his balance, without allowing himself to succumb to the madness of ribald, protrusive racism.

It destroys the logical processes of the mind, a man's thoughts become completely disorganized. The noise, madness streaming from every throat, frustrated sounds from the bars, metallic sounds from the walls, the steel trays, the iron beds bolted to the wall, the hollow sounds from a cast-iron sink or toilet.

The smells, the human waste thrown at us, unwashed bodies, the rotten food. When a white con leaves here he's ruined for life. No black leaves Max Row walking. Either he leaves on the meat wagon or he leaves crawling licking at the pig's feet.

Ironic, because one cannot get a parole to the outside prison directly from O Wing, Max Row. It's positively not done. The parole board won't even consider the Max Row case. So a man licks at the feet of the pig not for a release to the outside world but for the privilege of going upstairs to O Wing adjustment center. There the licking process must continue if a parole is the object. You can count on one hand the number of people who have been paroled to the streets from O Wing proper in all the years that the prison has existed. No one goes from O Wing, Max Row straight to the general prison population. To go from here to the outside world is unthinkable. A man *must* go from Max Row to the regular adjustment center facility upstairs. Then from there to the general prison population. Only then can he entertain thoughts of eventual release to the outside world.

One can understand the depression felt by an inmate on Max Row. He's fallen as far as he can into the social trap, relief is so distant that it is very easy for him to lose his holds. In two weeks that little average man who may have ended up on Max Row for *suspicion* of *attempted* escape is so brutalized, so completely without holds, that he will never heal again. It's worse than Vietnam.

He's dodging lead. He may be forced to fight a duel to the death with knives. If he doesn't sound and act more zealous than everyone else he will be challenged for not being loyal to his race and its politics, fascism. Some of these cons support the pigs' racism without shame, the others support it inadvertently by their own racism. The former are white, the latter black. But in here as on the street black racism is a forced *reaction*. A survival adaptation.

The picture that I have painted of Soledad's general population facility may have made it sound not too bad at all. That mistaken impression would result from the absence in my description of one more very important feature of the main line—terrorism. A frightening, petrifying diffusion of violence and intimidation is emitted from the offices of the warden and captain. How else could a small group of armed men be expected to hold and rule another much larger group except through *fear?*

We have a gym (inducement to throw away our energies with a ball instead of revolution). But if you walk into this gym with a cigarette burning, you're probably in trouble. There is a pig waiting to trap you. There's a sign "No Smoking." If you miss the sign, trouble. If you drop the cigarette to comply, trouble. The floor is regarded as something of a fire hazard (I'm not certain what the pretext is). There are no receptacles. The pig will pounce. You'll be told in no uncertain terms to scrape the cigarette from the floor with your hands. It builds from there. You have a gym but only certain things may be done and in specified ways. Since the rules change with the pigs' mood, it is really safer for a man to stay in his cell.

You have to work with emoluments that range from nothing to three cents an hour! But once you accept the pay job in the prison's industrial sector you cannot get out without going through the bad conduct process. When workers are needed, it isn't a case of accepting a job in this area. You take the job or you're automatically refusing to work, even if you clearly stated that you would cooperate in other employment. The same atmosphere prevails on the recreation yard where any type of minor mistake could result not in merely a bad conduct report and placement in adjustment center, but death. A fistfight, a temporary, trivial loss of temper will bring a fusillade of bullets down on the darker of the two men fighting.

You can't begin to measure the bad feeling caused by the existence of one TV set shared by 140 men. Think! One TV, 140 men. If there is more than one channel, what's going to occur? In Soledad's TV rooms there has been murder, mayhem, and destruction of many TV sets.

The blacks occupy one side of the room and the whites and Mexicans the other. (Isn't it significant in some way that our numbers in prison are sufficient to justify the claiming of half of all these facilities?)

We have a side, they have a side. What does your imagination envisage out of a hypothetical situation where Nina Simone sings, Angela Davis speaks, and Jim Brown "splits" on one channel, while Merle Haggard yodels and begs for an ass kicking on another. The fight will follow immediately after some brother, who is less democratic than he is starved for beauty (we did vote, but they're sixty to our forty), turns the station to see Angela Davis. What lines do you think the fighting will be along? Won't it be Angela and me against Merle Haggard?

But this situation is tolerable at least up to a point. It was worse. When I entered the joint on this offense, they had half and we had half, but our half was in the back.

In a case like the one just mentioned, the white convicts will start passing the word among themselves that all whites should be in the TV room to vote in the "Cadillac cowboy." The two groups polarize out of a situation created by whom? It's just like the outside. Nothing at all complicated about it. When people walk on each other, when disharmony is the norm, when organisms start falling apart it is the fault of those whose responsibility it is to govern. They're doing something wrong. They shouldn't have been trusted with the responsibility. And long-range political activity isn't going to help that man who will die tomorrow or tonight. The apologists recognize that these places are controlled by absolute terror, but they justify the pig's excesses with the argument that we exist outside the practice of any civilized codes of conduct. Since we are convicts rather than men, a bullet through the heart, summary execution for fistfighting or stepping across a line is not extreme or unsound at all. An official is allowed full range in violent means because a convict can be handled no other way.

Fay, have you ever considered what type of man is capable of handling absolute power. I mean how many would not abuse it? Is there any way of isolating or classifying generally who can be trusted with a gun and *absolute* discretion as to who he will kill? I've already mentioned that most of them are KKK types. The rest, all the rest, in general, are so stupid that they shouldn't be allowed to run their own bath. A *responsible* state government would have found a means of weeding out most of the savage types that are drawn to gun-slinger jobs long ago. How did all these pigs get through?! Men who can barely read, write, or reason. How did they get through!!? You may as well give a baboon a gun and set him loose on us!! It's the same in here as on the streets out there. *Who* has loosed this thing on an already suffering people? The Reagans, Nixons, the men who have, who own. Investigate them!! There are no qualifications asked, no experience necessary. Any fool who falls in here and can sign his name might shoot me tomorrow from a position thirty feet above my head with an automatic military rifle!! He could be dead drunk. It could really be an accident (a million to one it won't be, however), but he'll be protected still. He won't even miss a day's wages.

The textbooks on criminology like to advance the idea that prisoners are mentally defective. There is only the merest suggestion that the system itself is at fault. Penologists regard prisons as asylums. Most policy is formulated in a bureau that operates under the heading Department of Corrections. But what can we say about these asylums since *none* of the inmates are ever cured. Since in every instance they are sent out of the prison more damaged physically and mentally than when they entered. Because that is the reality. Do you continue to investigate the inmate? Where does administrative responsibility begin? Perhaps the administration of the prison cannot be held accountable for every individual act of their charges, but when things fly apart along racial lines, when the breakdown can be traced so clearly to circumstances even beyond the control of the guards and administration, investigation of anything outside the tenets of the fascist system itself is futile.

Nothing has improved, nothing has changed in the weeks since your team was here. We're on the same course, the blacks are fast losing the last of their restraints. Growing numbers of blacks are openly passed over when paroles are considered. They have become aware that their only hope lies in resistance. They have learned that resistance is actually possible. The holds are beginning to slip away. Very few men imprisoned for economic crimes or even crimes of passion against the oppressor feel that they are really guilty. Most of today's black convicts have come to understand that they are the most abused victims of an unrighteous order. Up until now, the prospect of parole has kept us from confronting our captors with any real determination. But now with the living conditions deteriorating, and with the sure knowledge that we are slated for destruction, we have been transformed into an implacable army of liberation. The shift to the revolutionary antiestablishment position that Huey Newton, Eldridge Cleaver, and Bobby Seale projected as a solution to the problems of Amerika's black colonies has taken firm hold of these brothers' minds. They are now showing great interest in the thoughts of Mao Tse-tung, Nkrumah, Lenin, Marx, and the achievements of men like Che Guevara, Giap, and Uncle Ho.

Some people are going to get killed out of this situation that is growing. That is not a warning (or wishful thinking). I see it as an "unavoidable consequence" of placing and leaving control of our lives in the hands of men like Reagan.

These prisons have always borne a certain resemblance to Dachau and Buchenwald, places for the bad niggers, Mexicans, and poor whites. But the last ten years have brought an increase in the percentage of blacks for crimes that can *clearly* be traced to political-economic causes. There are still some blacks here who consider themselves criminals—but not many. Believe me, my friend, with the time and incentive that these brothers have to read, study, and think, you will find no class or category more aware, more embittered, desperate, or dedicated to the ultimate remedy—revolution. The most dedicated, the best of our kind—you'll find them in the Folsoms, San Quentins, and Soledads. They live like there was no tomorrow. And for most of them there isn't. Somewhere along the line they sensed this. Life on the installment plan, three years of prison, three months on parole; then back to start all over again, sometimes in the same cell. Parole officers have sent brothers back to the joint for selling newspapers (the Black Panther paper). Their official reason is "Failure to Maintain Gainful Employment," etc.

We're something like 40 to 42 percent of the prison population. Perhaps more, since I'm relying on material published by the media. The leadership of the black prison population now definitely identifies with Huey, Bobby, Angela, Eldridge, and antifascism. The savage repression of blacks, which can be estimated by reading the obituary columns of the nation's dailies, Fred Hampton, etc., has not failed to register on the black inmates. The holds are fast being broken. Men who read Lenin, Fanon, and Che don't riot, "they mass," "they rage," they dig graves.

When John Clutchette was first accused of this murder he was proud, conscious, aware of his own worth but uncommitted to any specific remedial action. Review the process that they are sending this beautiful brother through now. It comes at the end of a long train of similar incidents in his prison life. Add to this all of the things he has witnessed happening to others of our group here. Comrade Fleeta spent eleven months here in O Wing for possessing photography taken from a newsweekly. It is such things that explain why California prisons produce more than their share of Bunchy Carters and Eldridge Cleavers.

Fay, there are only two types of blacks ever released from these places, the Carters and the broken men.

The broken men are so damaged that they will never again be suitable members of any sort of social unit. Everything that was still good when they entered the joint, anything inside of them that may have escaped the ruinous effects of black colonial existence, anything that may have been redeemable when they first entered the joint—is gone when they leave.

This camp brings out the very best in brothers or destroys them entirely. But none are unaffected. None who leave here are normal. If I leave here alive, I'll leave nothing behind. They'll never count me among the broken men, but I can't say that I am normal either. I've been hungry too long. I've gotten angry too often. I've been lied to and insulted too many times. They've pushed me over the line from which there can be no retreat. I *know* that they will not be satisfied until they've pushed me out of this existence altogether. I've been the victim of so many racist attacks that I could never relax again. My reflexes will never be normal again. I'm like a dog that has gone through the K-9 process.

This is not the first attempt the institution (camp) has made to murder me. It is the most determined attempt, but not the first.

I look into myself at the close of every one of these pretrial days for any changes that may have taken place. I can still smile now, after ten years of blocking knife thrusts and pick handles of faceless sadistic pigs, of anticipating and reacting for ten years, seven of them in solitary. I can still smile sometimes, but by the time this thing is over I may not be a nice person. And I just lit my seventy-seventh cigarette of this twenty-one-hour day. I'm going to lay down for two or three hours, perhaps I'll sleep . . .

Seize the Time.

RESPONSES: Questions for Writing and Discussion

1. The effectiveness of protest and activism is bound up with the accuracy of one's perception of the particular establishment one wishes to change or replace. In the case of Jackson, the impetus to act came from the alleged sadism and racism of prison employees and administrators. Assuming that Jackson had good reason for perceiving Soledad as he did, can you suggest what kind of prison and prison staff ought to exist? Should these be uniform throughout the country, regardless of the kind of crimes people are being imprisoned for? What checks would you set up to insure the maintenance of the prison system you are devising?

2. "Men are brutalized by their environment—not the reverse." Throughout this letter Jackson places the blame for prison conditions squarely on the shoulders of "those whose responsibility it is to govern. They're doing something wrong." But the people he accuses would no doubt argue that in the case of prison those who must be governed are impossible, often subhuman, types. Is there something to be said on both sides of this argument? May the prison environment in some respects be a response to the brutality it seeks to control? Or do you agree with Jackson that the environment is the single source of the evil of prison life? Is there an entry into a seemingly vicious circle?

3. If a white inmate of Max Row attempts "to help black he will be pushed away—by black." Why do you believe this resistance takes place? Wouldn't you think the prisoners, regardless of race, would find themselves sharing a kind of brotherhood?

4. Jackson indicates that such a thing as "black racism" exists. But, while he condemns white racism as the result of a deliberate and evil choice of alternatives, he refers to its black counterpart as a "forced reaction" and a "survival adaptation." Does this imply that no blacks would be racists if not forced into it? Is racism therefore originated by whites? Is it an integral part of the white personality?

5. Jackson describes the extremes of prison discipline as being terroristic. "How else could a small group of armed men be expected to hold and rule another much larger group except through *fear?*" But even in the "milder" cases—such as the example he gives of the no-smoking policy in the gym—he implies that prison discipline is not rational. What do you suppose the prison authorities would offer in defense of the gymnasium rules?

6. While watching TV, Jackson notes, blacks sit together on one side of the room. He finds it "significant in some way that our numbers in prison are sufficient to justify the claiming of half of all these facilities." The ratio of black prisoners to whites does not appear to jibe with the ratio of black to white population outside the prisons. What can be made of this striking fact?

7. Jackson states that prison employees are hired without any qualifications or experience; that in some cases they can neither read nor write, but are almost immediately given fearful powers of life and death; that, in the event they kill someone, they are protected by law even to the point of not losing a day's wages. Even if these accusations are valid, may it be argued that it is difficult to attract more desirable types of people to prison jobs? Or are prison officials seeking certain types, with literacy and experience being unimportant?

8. The only hope Jackson can see lies in the steady growth of revolutionary attitudes and plans among prisoners. The implication is that people like Huey Newton, Eldridge Cleaver, and Bobby Seale will carry the revolutionary cause back into society and continue to work for the day when "people are going to get killed" as an "inevitable consequence." But it stands to reason that, when prison officials read such a document as this, they are bound to feel justified in tightening their discipline and security even more. Would the idea of revolution vanish if more humane prison conditions were to come about, and if the officials made the first move and tried to establish a level of trust? If your answer is no, then where should one begin if violent confrontations are to be avoided? Or should one make such an effort? Will nothing but revolution help cure the situation? Will revolution do it?

9. The letter closes with the dreadful prophecy that "they will not be satisfied until they have pushed me out of this existence altogether." Eventually George Jackson was killed during a prison break. Did he achieve Human Worth by taking active steps against the establishment? Was he a fool? Was he a dangerous man who got what he deserved? May prison breaks be tolerated? (Would Jackson, in your opinion, have attempted to escape if a dramatic improvement in prison conditions had taken place?)

10. If you favor activism and even revolution as the only way out for American society, how do you claim the right to decide on a particular direction for this country? If you believe that activists and revolutionists are public menaces and should be dealt with as such, how do you claim the right to resist change when history shows how often revolutions have altered the direction of humanity and brought us all to where we are now?

LOVE VERSUS WAR AND DICTATORS
Mohandas Karamehand Gandhi

An alternative to the control of the individual by the state is a utopian dream of a society in which people relate to each other through love and good will rather than competition and distrust and therefore have no need of strong controls over their behavior. Throughout history there have been extraordinary individuals who have taught the gospel of love, whose lives, as far as we know, have embodied this dream. But, though such personalities have long served as ideal symbols of Human Worth, they have often paid a high price for their views. Socrates belongs in this rare category of beings. So does **Mohandas Karamehand Gandhi (1869–1948).**

Gandhi believed that the noblest achievement of man is actually more than the capacity to love: *it is the capacity not to hate.* It is the capacity of the individual to care about another for the sake of the other, not his own; of the individual, to return love for hate; of a nation of individuals, to care about the welfare of other nations, to respect and love them, even where serious ideological differences exist, and not to assume the role of aggressor; and the capacity of an oppressed people to resist the force and tyranny of the state with nonviolence.

Gandhi was a revolutionist but not a militant. Like Martin Luther King, Jr. years afterwards, he believed an exploited populace must return love for hate without at the same time surrendering to the exploitation. Instead the people must remain passively unwilling to cooperate with the exploiters. This meant bending Christ's advocacy of turning the other cheek into a political weapon, one which Gandhi hoped would force many sociological changes without violating its own basic philosophy of love. Gandhi hoped that the oppressed, through love, would ennoble the oppressor and thus bring about a new kind of world in which state controls would become archaic.

Gandhi came into the world as the son of a prominent Indian statesman. As was the practice in the colonial India of those days for those who could afford it, he was sent to England to be educated. In 1891 he entered the profession of law, having already developed a philosophical distaste for injustice, discrimination, and oppression and having resolved to dedicate his professional career to the cause of human liberation wherever this seemed possible. In 1893 he established what would be a characteristic pattern. The British were in his opinion maltreating Asian minorities living in South Africa. Seeing a need for his services, he journeyed there and spoke out against colonialism in general and the British class system in particular.

It was in South Africa that he first formulated and taught his doctrine of passive resistance, nonviolence, and noncooperation.

In 1918 Gandhi committed himself to the burning cause which would occupy the remaining years of his life: Indian independence and the end of British colonial domination. The task as he defined it was to unify the rival Hindu and Moslem factions in India and to persuade both sides to devote their energies to the transcendent need of all Indians for autonomy. Thus began a history of nearly three decades of Gandhi as a political thorn in the side of Britain's empire-oriented ideology. He was imprisoned often on any pretext that could be found, but such measures only served to elevate him in the eyes of his people to the position of saint. As he grew older, he added to his other forms of passive resistance the habit of fasting for incredibly long periods, endangering his health to the point where the British would agree to enter into negotiations on a particular issue. In 1947 India became an independent nation with home rule and its own constitution, Gandhi's efforts no doubt having greatly contributed to the victory.

Gandhi then turned his efforts toward improving the living conditions for the teeming millions of Indian poor. He was especially concerned over technology and the destructive effects on Indian economy of introducing the machine, favoring instead a return to more primitive methods of manufacture, which could employ greater numbers. At the same time he took up the once-forbidden cause of the "Untouchables," people belonging to India's lowest, most wretched caste—a preoccupation which drew much criticism from Hindus who had once been loyal supporters.

The whole basis of Gandhi's kind of revolution against the state had been predicated on a positive attitude toward human nature. But his cause and that of others like him suffered a setback when hostility toward him arose from the very people whose lot it was his dream to improve. The unity of his following broke apart completely during the late forties when he sought to bring Hindus and Moslems together in peace and brotherhood. But the end of British domination had brought back into sharp focus an old feud. On his way to pray in the temple on January 30, 1948, Gandhi was shot by a Hindu who, apparently, could not accept so abstract an ideal as universal love. The faith in man that had supported the dream proved to be, for the dreamer, less than realistic.

Love Versus War and Dictators

[Gandhi's correspondence with children gave him much joy, and he attended to it with the same devotion and care that he showed all

From *The Essential Gandhi*, edited by Louis Fischer. Copyright © 1962 by Louis Fischer. Reprinted by permission of Random House.

his work. A little girl once wrote him: "We are working to prevent war and making posters. God bless you." Gandhi gave this reply:]

I was delighted to have your sweet notes with funny drawings made by you. . . . Yes, it is little children like you who will stop all war. This means that you never quarrel with other boys and girls or among yourselves. You cannot stop big wars if you carry on little wars yourselves. . . . May God bless you all. My kisses to you all if you will let me kiss you. . . .[1]

. . . It is a trite saying that one half the world knows not how the other lives. Who can say what sores might be healed, what hurts solved, were the doings of each half of the world's inhabitants understood and appreciated by the other?[2]

War with all its glorification of brute force is essentially a degrading thing. It demoralizes those who are trained for it. It brutalizes men of naturally gentle character. It outrages every beautiful canon of morality. Its path of glory is foul with the passions of lust, and red with the blood of murder. This is not the pathway to our goal. The grandest aid to development of strong, pure, beautiful character which is our aim, is the endurance of suffering. Self-restraint, unselfishness, patience, gentleness, these are the flowers which spring beneath the feet of those who accept but refuse to impose suffering. . . .[3]

A pacifism which can see the cruelties only of occasional military warfare and is blind to the continuous cruelties of our social system is worthless. Unless our pacifism finds expression in the broad human movement which is seeking not merely the end of war but our equally non-pacifist civilization as a whole, it will be of little account in the onward march of mankind. The spirit of life will sweep on, quite uninfluenced by it.[4]

Immediately the spirit of exploitation is gone armaments will be felt as a positively unbearable burden. Real disarmament cannot come unless the nations of the world cease to exploit one another.[5]

A society which anticipates and provides for meeting violence with violence will either lead a precarious life or create big cities and magazines for defence purposes. It is not unreasonable to presume from the state of Europe that its cities, its monster factories and huge

---

[1] Entry for August 24, 1932, in Mahadev Desai, *The Diary of Mahadev Desai*, pp. 308-309.

[2] *Indian Opinion*, June 2, 1906.

[3] *Indian Opinion*, February 12, 1910.

[4] *Young India*, November 18, 1926.

[5] *Harijan*, November 12, 1938.

armaments are so intimately interrelated that the one cannot exist without the other.[6]

Even if Hitler was so minded, he could not devastate seven hundred thousand non-violent villages. He would himself become non-violent in the process.[7]

[As Gandhi watched the darkness advance during the 1930's across China, Abyssinia, Spain, Czechoslovakia and above all, Germany, his zeal for pure pacifism grew. He saw the Second World War approaching.]

. . . I have the unquenchable faith that, of all the countries in the world, India is the one country which can learn the art of non-violence, that if the test were applied even now, there would be found, perhaps, thousands of men and women who would be willing to die without harboring malice against their persecutors. I have harangued crowds and told them repeatedly that they might have to suffer much, including death by shooting. Did not thousands of men and women brave hardships during the salt campaign equal to any that soldiers are called upon to bear? No different capacity is required from what has been already evinced, if India has to contend against an invader. Only it will have to be on vaster scale.

One thing ought not to be forgotten. India unarmed would not require to be destroyed through poison gas or bombardment. . . . Free India can have no enemy. And if her people have learnt the art of saying resolutely "No" and acting up to it, I daresay no one would want to invade her. Our economy would be modelled as to prove no temptation for the exploiter.

. . . The world is looking for something new and unique from India. . . .

. . . For India to enter into the race for armaments is to court suicide. With the loss of India to non-violence the last hope of the world will be gone. . . .[8]

. . . I believe that Independent India can discharge her duty towards a groaning world only by adopting a simple but ennobled life by developing her thousands of cottages and living at peace with the world.

Whether such plain living is possible for an isolated nation, however large geographically and numerically in the face of a world armed to the teeth, and in the midst of pomp and circumstance, is a question open to the doubt of a skeptic. The answer is straight and

---

[6] *Harijan,* January 13, 1940.

[7] *Harijan,* November 4, 1939.

[8] *Harijan,* October 14, 1939.

simple. If plain life is worth living, then the attempt is worth making, even though only an individual or a group makes the effort.[9]

Several letters have been received by me asking me to declare my views about the Arab-Jew question in Palestine and the persecution of the Jews in Germany. It is not without hesitation that I venture to offer my views on this very difficult question.

My sympathies are all with the Jews. I have known them intimately in South Africa. Some of them became lifelong companions. Through these friends I came to learn much of their age-long persecution. They have been the untouchables of Christianity. The parallel between their treatment by Christians and the treatment of untouchables by Hindus is very close. Religious sanction has been invoked in both cases for the justification of the inhuman treatment meted out to them. . . .

But my sympathy does not blind me to the requirements of justice. The cry for a national home for the Jews does not make much appeal to me. . . . Why should they not, like other peoples of the earth, make that country their home where they are born and where they earn their livelihood?

The nobler course would be to insist on a just treatment of the Jews wherever they are born and bred. The Jews born in France are French in precisely the same sense that Christians born in France are French. If the Jews have no home but Palestine, will they relish the idea of being forced to leave the other parts of the world in which they are settled?

But the German persecution of the Jews seems to have no parallel in history. . . .

Germany is showing to the world how efficiently violence can be worked when it is not hampered by any hypocrisy or weakness masquerading as humanitarianism. It is also showing how hideous, terrible and terrifying it looks in its nakedness.

Can the Jews resist this organized and shameless persecution? Is there a way to preserve their self-respect, and not to feel helpless, neglected and forlorn? I submit there is. . . . If I were a Jew and were born in Germany and earned my livelihood there, I would claim Germany as my home even as the tallest gentile German might, and challenge him to shoot me or cast me in the dungeon; I would refuse to be expelled or to submit to discriminating treatment. And for doing this I should not wait for the fellow-Jews to join me in civil resistance, but would have confidence that in the end the rest were bound to follow my example. If one Jew or all the Jews were to accept the prescription here offered, he or they cannot be worse off

---

[9] *Harijan*, September 1, 1946.

than now. And suffering voluntarily undergone will bring them an inner strength and joy which no number of resolutions of sympathy passed in the world outside Germany can. . . .

. . . I am convinced that, if someone with courage and vision can arise among them to lead them in non-violent action, the winter of their despair can in the twinkling of an eye be turned into the summer of hope. And what has today become a degrading manhunt can be turned into a calm and determined stand offered by unarmed men and women possessing the strength of suffering given to them by Jehovah. It will be then a truly religious resistance offered against the Godless fury of dehumanized man. The German Jews will score a lasting victory over the German gentiles in the sense that they will have converted the latter to an appreciation of human dignity. They will have rendered service to fellow-Germans and proved their title to be the real Germans as against those who are today dragging, however unknowingly, the German name into the mire.

And now a word to the Jews in Palestine. I have no doubt that they are going about things in the wrong way. The Palestine of the Biblical conception is not a geographical tract. It is in their hearts. But if they must look to the Palestine of geography as their national home, it is wrong to enter it under the shadow of the British gun. A religious act cannot be performed with the aid of the bayonet or the bomb. They can settle in Palestine only by the goodwill of the Arabs. They should seek to convert the Arab heart. They can offer Satyagraha in front of the Arabs and offer themselves to be shot or thrown into the Dead Sea without raising a little finger against them. They will find the world opinion in their favor in their religious aspiration. There are hundreds of ways of reasoning with the Arabs, if they will only discard the help of the British bayonet. As it is, they are co-sharers with the British in despoiling a people who have done no wrong to them.

. . . Every country is their home, including Palestine, not by aggression but by loving service. . . .[10]

. . . If [the Jewish people] were to adopt the matchless weapon of non-violence, whose use their best prophets have taught and which Jesus the Jew who gladly wore the crown of thorns bequeathed to a groaning world, their case would be the world's, and I have no doubt that among the many things the Jews have given to the world, this would be the best and the brightest. It is twice blessed. It will make them happy and rich in the true sense of the word, and it will be a soothing balm to the aching world.[11]

---

[10] *Harijan*, November 26, 1938.
[11] *Harijan*, July 21, 1946.

. . . I happen to have a Jewish friend [Herman Kallenbach, who purchased the farm for Gandhi's first ashram in South Africa] living with me. He has an intellectual belief in non-violence. But he says he cannot pray for Hitler. He is so full of anger over the German atrocities that he cannot speak of them with restraint. I do not quarrel with him over his anger. He wants to be non-violent, but the sufferings of his fellow-Jews are too much for him to bear. What is true of him is true of thousands of Jews who have no thought even of "loving the enemy." With them, as with millions, "revenge is sweet, to forgive is divine."[12]

It is no non-violence if we love merely those that love us. It is non-violence only when we love those that hate us. I know how difficult it is to follow this grand law of love. But are not all great and good things difficult to do? . . .[13]

. . . Human nature will find itself only when it fully realizes that to be human it has to cease to be beastly or brutal. . . .[14]

A violent man's activity is most visible, while it lasts. But it is always transitory. . . . Hitler . . . Mussolini . . . and Stalin . . . are able to show the immediate effectiveness of violence. . . . But the effects of Buddha's non-violent action persist and are likely to grow with age. And the more it is practiced, the more effective and inexhaustible it becomes, and ultimately the whole world stands agape and exclaims, "A miracle has happened." All miracles are due to the silent and effective working of invisible force. Non-violence is the most invisible and the most effective.[15]

Belief in non-violence is based on the assumption that human nature in the essence is one and therefore unfailingly responds to the advances of love. . . .

How can non-violence combat aerial warfare, seeing that there are no personal contacts? The reply to this is that behind the death-dealing bomb there is the human hand that releases it, and behind that still is the human heart that sets the hand in motion. And at the back of the policy of terrorism is the assumption that terrorism if applied in a sufficient measure will produce the desired result, namely, bend the adversary to the tyrant's will. But supposing a people make up their mind that they will never do the tyrant's will, nor retaliate with the tyrant's own methods, the tyrant will not find it worth his while to go on with his terrorism. . . .[16]

---

[12] *Harijan*, February 18, 1939.

[13] Letter to a friend, December 31, 1934, in Nirmal Kumar Bose, *Selections from Gandhi*, p. 18.

[14] *Harijan*, October 8, 1938.

[15] *Harijan*, March 20, 1937.

[16] *Harijan*, December 24, 1938.

. . . If some other country resorts to methods which I consider to be inhuman, I may not follow them. . . . The caliphs [heads of Islam] issued definite instructions to the armies of Islam that they should not destroy the utility services, they should not harass the aged and women and children, and I do not know that the arms of Islam suffered any disaster because the armies obeyed these instructions.[17]

. . . I see neither bravery nor sacrifice in destroying life or property for offense or defence. I would far rather leave, if I must, my crops and homestead for the enemy to use than destroy them for the sake of preventing their use by him. There is reason, sacrifice and even bravery in so leaving my homestead and crops if I do so not out of fear, but because I refuse to regard anyone as my enemy. . . .[18]

[One who believes in violence will wish God "to save the King, scatter his enemies, frustrate their knavish tricks"—as in the British national anthem.] If God is the Incarnation of Mercy, He is not likely to listen to such prayer but it cannot but affect the minds of those who sing it, and in times of war it simply kindles their hatred and anger to white heat. [But the soldier of non-violence] may give the supposed enemy a sense of right, and bless him. His prayer for himself will always be that the spring of compassion in him may ever be flowing, and that he may ever grow in moral strength so that he may face death fearlessly.[19]

. . . We have to live and move and have our being in [non-violence,] even as Hitler does in [violence]. . . . Hitler is awake all the twenty-four hours of the day in perfecting his [practices]. He wins because he pays the price.[20]

[Dictators] have up to now always found ready response to the violence they have used. Within their experience, they have not come across organized non-violent resistance on an appreciable scale, if at all. Therefore, it is not only highly likely, but . . . inevitable, that they would recognize the superiority of non-violent resistance over any display of violence that they may be capable of putting forth.

. . . Supposing a people make up their mind they will never do the tyrant's will, nor retaliate with the tyrant's own methods, the tyrant will not find it worth his while to go on with his terrorism. If sufficient food is given to the tyrant, a time will come when he will have more than his surfeit. If all the mice in the world held conference together and resolved that they would no more fear the cat but all run into her mouth, the mice would live.[21]

---

[17] *Harijan,* May 24, 1942.
[18] *Harijan,* March 22, 1942.
[19] *Harijan,* October 13, 1940.
[20] *Harijan,* July 21, 1940.
[21] *Harijan,* December 24, 1938.

[While their country was being invaded, non-violent resisters] would offer themselves unarmed as fodder for the aggressor's cannon. . . . The unexpected spectacle of endless rows upon rows of men and women simply dying rather than surrender to the will of an aggressor must ultimately melt him and his soldiery.[22]

Who enjoys the freedom [afterward] when whole divisions of armed soldiers rush into a hailstorm of bullets to be mown down? But in the case of non-violence, everybody seems to start with the assumption that the non-violent method must be set down as a failure unless he himself at least lives to enjoy the success thereof. This is both illogical and invidious. In Satyagraha [Soul-Force] more than in armed warfare, it may be said that we find life by losing it.[23]

❖ ❖ ❖

. . . We are discussing a final substitute for armed conflict called war, in naked terms, mass murder.[24]

The science of war leads one to dictatorship pure and simple. The science of non-violence alone can lead on to pure democracy.[25]

. . . Where a whole nation is militarized the way of military life becomes part and parcel of its civilization.[26]

I believe all war to be wholly wrong. But if we scrutinize the motives of two warring parties, we may find one to be in the right and the other in the wrong. For instance, if A wishes to seize B's country, B is obviously the wronged one. Both fight with arms. I do not believe in violent warfare but all the same B, whose cause is just, deserves my moral help and blessings.[27]

My resistance to war does not carry me to the point of thwarting those who wish to take part in it. I reason with them. I put before them the better way and leave them to make the choice.[28]

❖ ❖ ❖

The present war is the saturation point in violence. It spells to my mind also its doom. Daily I have testimony of the fact that [non-violence] was never before appreciated by mankind as it is today. . . .[29]

["How would you meet the atom bomb . . . with non-violence?" Margaret Bourke-White, on assignment for *Life* magazine, asked Gandhi on January 30, 1948, a few hours before he was assassinated.]

I will not go underground. I will not go into shelter. I will

---

[22] *Harijan*, April 13, 1940.
[23] *Harijan*, July 28, 1940.
[24] *Harijan*, May 12, 1946.
[25] *Harijan*, October 15, 1938.
[26] *Harijan*, March 1, 1942.
[27] *Harijan*, August 18, 1940.
[28] *Harijan*, January 18, 1942.
[29] *Harijan*, August 11, 1940.

come out in the open and let the pilot see I have not a trace of ill-will against him. The pilot will not see our faces from his great height, I know. But the longing in our hearts—that he will not come to harm—would reach up to him and his eyes would be opened. If those thousands who were done to death in Hiroshima, if they had died with that prayerful action . . . their sacrifice would not have gone in vain.[30]

[Non-violence] is the only thing the atom bomb cannot destroy. I did not move a muscle when I first heard that an atom bomb had wiped out Hiroshima. On the contrary, I said to myself, "Unless the world adopts non-violence, it will spell certain suicide for mankind." [31]

There have been cataclysmic changes in the world. Do I still adhere to my faith in Truth and Non-violence? Has not the atom bomb exploded that faith? Not only has it not done so but it has clearly demonstrated to me that the twins constitute the mightiest force in the world. Before them, the atom bomb is of no effect. The opposing forces are wholly different in kind, the one moral and spiritual, the other physical and material. The one is infinitely superior to the other, which by its very nature has an end. The force of the spirit is ever progressive and endless. Its full expression makes it unconquerable in the world. . . . What is more, that force resides in everybody, man, woman and child, irrespective of the color of the skin. Only in many it lies dormant, but it is capable of being awakened by judicious training.[32]

It has been suggested by American friends that the atom bomb will bring in Ahimsa [Non-violence] as nothing else can. It will, if it is meant that its destructive power will so disgust the world that it will turn away from violence for the time being. This is very like a man glutting himself with dainties to the point of nausea and turning away from them, only to return with redoubled zeal after the effect of nausea is well over. Precisely in the same manner will the world return to violence with renewed zeal after the effect of disgust is worn out.

So far as I can see, the atomic bomb has deadened the finest feeling that has sustained mankind for ages. There used to be the so-called laws of war which made it tolerable. Now we know the naked truth. War knows no law except that of might. The atom bomb brought an empty victory to the allied armies but it resulted for the time being in destroying the soul of Japan. What has happened to the soul of the destroying nation is yet too early to see. . . . I assume that Japan's

---

[30] Pyarelal, *Mahatma Gandhi: The Last Phase*, Volume II, Chapter 25, pp. 808-809.

[31] *Ibid.*, p. 808.

[32] *Harijan*, February 10, 1946.

greed was the more unworthy [ambition]. But the greater unworthiness conferred no right on the less unworthy of destroying without mercy men, women and children of Japan in a particular area.

The moral to be legitimately drawn from the supreme tragedy of the bomb is that it will not be destroyed by counter-bombs even as violence cannot be by counter-violence. Mankind has to get out of violence only through non-violence. Hatred can be overcome only by love. Counter-hatred only increases the surface as well as the depth of hatred. . . .[33]

We have to make truth and non-violence not matters for mere individual practice but for practice by groups and communities and nations. That at any rate is my dream.[34]

[Before] general disarmament . . . commences . . . some nation will have to dare to disarm herself and take large risks. The level of non-violence in that nation, if that event happily comes to pass, will naturally have risen so high as to command universal respect. Her judgments will be unerring, her decisions firm, her capacity for heroic self-sacrifice will be great, and she will want to live as much for other nations as for herself.[35]

RESPONSES: Questions for Writing and Discussion

1. Gandhi asserts that "the endurance of suffering" is an alternative to war, which "brutalizes men of naturally gentle character." Presumably he includes violent resistance and revolution under the general heading of war. Do you agree with his view? Are there times when the endurance of suffering is not the noble course? Is passive, nonviolent resistance—as Gandhi expounds it—the only really human way to counteract wrongs?

2. To end "non-pacificist civilization" was Gandhi's aim. Is it a realistic one? Did Gandhi fail, or did civilization fail Gandhi?

3. Gandhi warns of the harm which can be visited upon the inhabitants of a "society which anticipates and provides for meeting violence with violence. . . ." Is America at present this kind of society? Is it a different kind?

4. Explain: "Even if Hitler was so minded, he could not devastate seven hundred thousand non-violent villages. He would himself become non-violent in the process." Do you agree?

5. In 1939 Gandhi noted that India offered the world a model

---

[33] *Harijan*, July 7, 1946.
[34] *Harijan*, March 2, 1940.
[35] *Young India*, October 8, 1925.

of nonviolence, that India was in effect the means of leading the world into a new era, one in which hatred, exploitation, and war would disappear. "The world is looking for something new and unique from India." In your opinion, has the world found something in India? Anywhere? Does a hope for the world of the kind envisaged by Gandhi exist at all?

6. It didn't discourage Gandhi to imagine an entire nation or an entire world as not living by his ideals. "If plain life is worth living, then the attempt is worth making, even though only an individual or a group makes the effort." But the classic question always raised by such an argument is how does one cope with an environment which may be dedicated to absolutely contrary ideologies and practices?

7. Gandhi considered Nazi Germany a prime example of naked violence unhampered "by any hypocrisy or weakness masquerading as humanitarianism." One assumes that one is just as deplorable as the other, even though the seemingly humanitarian approach may at first glance be preferable. In the world today are there evidences of both types of exploitation—the outwardly violent kind and the falsely humanitarian kind?

8. Gandhi's whole philosophy of nonviolence is, as he says, "based on the assumption that human nature in the essence is one and therefore unfailingly responds to the advances of love." Have you had any personal experiences which prove to you that people not so disposed can change when they are met by the "advances of love"?

9. Since the early fifties the United States has conducted military action in Southeast Asia and always with the same theoretical basis: to defend small countries who cannot protect themselves against unwarranted aggression. Advocates of United States intervention in the affairs of other countries frequently refer to this as a moral duty. Gandhi himself believed that, while all war in principle is morally wrong, war is sometimes necessary to counteract other moral wrongs. If he were alive today, do you believe Gandhi would sanction those aspects of our foreign policy which require us to make military commitments to small countries?

10. Gandhi viewed the atomic bomb with hope and optimism. He felt it would "disgust" the world and turn it away from violence. In your opinion have atomic arms had precisely that effect? Or have they increased world tensions and led humanity further than ever from the goal of peace?

THE TRIAL AND DEATH
OF BILLY BUDD

Herman Melville

The issue of human beings versus the law of the state and/or the people is not limited to the alternatives of martyrdom or some form of active protest. There remains the path of acceptance. There are those who find no recourse other than to justify the operation of law, even where this may not appear to deal fairly with all persons. Sometimes recognizing the law's impersonality as a dehumanizing thing—both for its victims and for those who must carry out its mandates, they still see its rational side and show how Human Worth and the machinery of justice are not necessarily in conflict. They ask: Is not the law a creation of rational human minds? Would human civilization be possible without it?

Billy Budd by **Herman Melville (1819–1891)**, from which we have excerpted the account of the trial and execution of the young sailor who murders an officer on board ship during time of war, was written shortly before the novelist's death in 1891 but was not discovered among his papers until 1924. Since its initial publication it has risen in stature and in the opinion of many literary critics now ranks second only to *Moby-Dick* (1851) in the canon of Melville's work. It also represents a startling and dramatic change of attitude toward law and order from that which underlies the earlier novel.

Captain Ahab of *Moby-Dick*, like any ship's authority, has the final say on all matters. His subordinates must follow his commands to the letter, or the entire code of shipboard discipline disintegrates. But Ahab, it becomes clear, is also insane. He has signed up his crew for the alleged purpose of hunting whales, but the true motive, concealed from them, is to track down and kill the White Whale, the biggest and most feared mammal in existence. Among its many complex themes, the book considers the proposition "What happens when hierarchy and discipline become instruments of private ends?" The answer is plain: disaster. Both the ship and its captain are engulfed by the Whale and sink to their watery graves, victims of one man's futile effort to accomplish the impossible.

The law and order prevailing on the *H.M.S. Indomitable* of *Billy Budd*, however, seem eminently sane and intelligent, and they are in the competent hands of one Edward Vere, a captain of impeccable moral integrity. The British are at war. The navy is a crucial element. The tight ship run by Captain Vere is in turn a vital factor in the total system of the British Navy, which is itself part of a much larger cosmos: the military strength of Great

Britain in its war of survival against Napoleon and, expanding even further, the total movement of human history. The principle of rule cannot *logically* be neglected, which means that exceptions cannot be made.

But then comes Billy Budd, the new foretopman (the lookout on a ship's front masthead). He is a reincarnation of that popular myth figure in literature, the innocent. He is Adam before the fall, a youth of both physical and moral beauty, with an angelic quality about him so intense that he wins the hearts of both the crew and Captain Vere, who takes an instant paternal liking to him. One person, however, is decidedly repulsed by Billy's moral purity: Claggart, the master-at-arms, a creature of innate depravity, resembling nothing so much as the serpent in Adam's garden. Billy's innocence becomes unendurable to Claggart, who plots to have the boy removed from the ship by falsely accusing him of plotting a mutiny.

Our selection begins at the point where accuser and accused are brought face to face before the Captain. As you will discover, Billy has a speech impediment: He cannot formulate his words under emotional stress. This leads him to express his shock and indignation in an act of violence, which clearly breaks a law and incurs a mandatory death sentence. Law in *Billy Budd* does not so much triumph as prevail rationally, but tragically. Melville has no further answer.

The Trial and Death of Billy Budd

Now when the foretopman found himself closeted, as it were, in the cabin with the Captain and Claggart, he was surprised enough. But it was a surprise unaccompanied by apprehension or distrust. To an immature nature, essentially honest and humane, forewarning intimations of subtler danger from one's kind come tardily, if at all. The only thing that took shape in the young sailor's mind was this: "Yes, the Captain, I have always thought, looks kindly upon me. I wonder if he's going to make me his coxswain. I should like that. And maybe now he is going to ask the Master-at-arms about me."

"Shut the door there, sentry," said the commander. "Stand without and let nobody come in.—Now, Master-at-arms, tell this man to his face what you told of him to me;" and stood prepared to scrutinize the mutually confronting visages.

With the measured step and calm collected air of an asylum physician approaching in the public hall some patient beginning to show indications of a coming paroxysm, Claggart deliberately advanced within short range of Billy, and mesmerically looking him in the eye, briefly recapitulated the accusation.

From *Billy Budd, Foretopman.*

Not at first did Billy take it in. When he did the rose-tan of his cheek looked struck as by white leprosy. He stood like one impaled and gagged. Meanwhile the accuser's eyes, removing not as yet from the blue, dilated ones, underwent a phenomenal change, their wonted rich violet colour blurring into a muddy purple. Those lights of human intelligence losing human expression, gelidly protruding like the alien eyes of certain uncatalogued creatures of the deep.

The first mesmeric glance was one of surprised fascination; the last was the hungry lurch of the torpedo-fish.

"Speak, man!" said Captain Vere to the transfixed one, struck by his aspect even more than by Claggart's, "Speak! defend yourself." Which appeal caused but a strange, dumb gesturing and gurgling in Billy; amazement at such an accusation so suddenly sprung on inexperienced nonage; this, and it may be horror at the accuser, serving to bring out his lurking defect, and in this instance for the time intensifying it into a convulsed tongue-tie; while the intent head and entire form straining forward in an agony of ineffectual eagerness to obey the injunction to speak and defend himself, gave an expression to the face like that of a condemned vestal priestess in the moment of her being buried alive, and in the first struggle against suffocation.

Though at the time Captain Vere was quite ignorant of Billy's liability to vocal impediment, he now immediately divined it, since vividly Billy's aspect recalled to him that of a bright young schoolmate of his whom he had seen struck by much the same startling impotence in the act of eagerly rising in the class to be foremost in response to a testing question put to it by the master. Going close up to the young sailor, and laying a soothing hand on his shoulder, he said. "There is no hurry, my boy. Take your time, take your time." Contrary to the effect intended, these words, so fatherly in tone, doubtless touching Billy's heart to the quick, prompted yet more violent efforts at utterance—efforts soon ending for the time in confirming the paralysis, and bringing to the face an expression which was as a crucifixion to behold. The next instant, quick as the flame from a discharged cannon at night—his right arm shot out and Claggart dropped to the deck. Whether intentionally, or but owing to the young athlete's superior height, the blow had taken effect full upon the forehead, so shapely and intellectual-looking a feature in the Master-at-arms; so that the body fell over lengthwise, like a heavy plank tilted from erectness. A gasp or two and he lay motionless.

"Fated boy," breathed Captain Vere in a tone so low as to be almost a whisper, "what have you done! But here, help me."

The twain raised the felled one from the loins up into a sitting position. The spare form flexibly acquiesced, but inertly. It was like handling a dead snake. They lowered it back. Regaining erectness,

Captain Vere with one hand covering his face stood to all appearance as impassive as to the object at his feet. Was he absorbed in taking in all the bearings of the event, and what was best not only now at once to be done, but also in the sequel? Slowly he uncovered his face; forthwith the effect was as if the moon, emerging from eclipse, should reappear with quite another aspect than that which had gone into hiding. The father in him, manifested towards Billy thus far in the scene, was replaced by the military disciplinarian. In his official tone he bade the foretopman retire to a state-room aft, (pointing it out), and there remain till thence summoned. This order Billy in silence mechanically obeyed. Then, going to the cabin door where it opened on the quarter-deck, Captain Vere said to the sentry without, "Tell somebody to send Albert here." When the lad appeared his master so contrived it that he should not catch sight of the prone one. "Albert," he said to him, "tell the surgeon I wish to see him. You need not come back till called."

When the surgeon entered—a self-poised character of that grave sense and experience that hardly anything could take him aback— Captain Vere advanced to meet him, thus unconsciously interrupting his view of Claggart and interrupting the other's wonted ceremonious salutation, said, "Nay, tell me how it is with yonder man," directing his attention to the prostrate one.

The surgeon looked, and for all his self-command, somewhat started at the abrupt revelation. On Claggart's always pallid complexion, thick black blood was now oozing from mouth and ear. To the gazer's professional eyes it was unmistakably no living man that he saw.

"Is it so, then?" said Captain Vere intently watching him. "I thought it. But verify it." Whereupon the customary tests confirmed the surgeon's first glance, who now looking up in unfeigned concern, cast a look of intense inquisitiveness upon his superior. But Captain Vere, with one hand to his brow, was standing motionless. Suddenly, catching the surgeon's arm convulsively, he exclaimed pointing down to the body,—"It is the divine judgment of Ananias! Look!"

Disturbed by the excited manner he had never before observed in the *Indomitable*'s Captain, and as yet wholly ignorant of the affair, the prudent surgeon nevertheless held his peace, only again looking an earnest interrogation as to what it was that had resulted in such a tragedy.

But Captain Vere was now again motionless, standing absorbed in thought. Once again starting, he vehemently exclaimed—"Struck dead by an angel of God. Yet the angel must hang!"

❊   ❊   ❊

The unhappy event which has been narrated could not have happened at a worse juncture. For it was close on the heel of the suppressed insurrections, an after-time very critical to naval authority, demanding from every English sea-commander two qualities not readily interfusable—prudence and rigour. Moreover, there was something crucial in the case.

In the jugglery of circumstances preceding and attending the event on board the *Indomitable* and in the light of that martial code whereby it was formally to be judged, innocence and guilt, personified in Claggart and Budd, in effect changed places.

In the legal view the apparent victim of the tragedy was he who had sought to victimize a man blameless; and the indisputable deed of the latter, navally regarded, constituted the most heinous of military crimes. Yet more. The essential right and wrong involved in the matter, the clearer that might be, so much the worse for the responsibility of a loyal sea-commander, inasmuch as he was authorized to determine the matter on that primitive legal basis.

Small wonder then that the *Indomitable's* Captain, though in general a man of rigid decision, felt that circumspectness not less than promptitude was necessary. Until he could decide upon his course, and in each detail; and not only so, but until the concluding measure was upon the point of being enacted he deemed it advisable, in view of all the circumstances, to guard as much as possible against publicity. Here he may or may not have erred. Certain it is, however, that subsequently in the confidential talk of more than one or two gunrooms and cabins he was not a little criticized by some officers, a fact imputed by his friends, and vehemently by his cousin Jack Denton, to professional jealousy of Starry Vere. Some imaginative ground for invidious comment there was. The maintenance of secrecy in the matter, the confining all knowledge of it for a time to the place where the homicide occurred—the quarter-deck cabin; in these particulars lurked some resemblance to the policy adopted in those tragedies of the palace which have occurred more than once in the capital founded by Peter the Barbarian, great chiefly by his crimes.

The case was such that fain would the *Indomitable's* Captain have deferred taking any action whatever respecting it further than to keep the foretopman a close prisoner till the ship rejoined the squadron, and then submitting the matter to the judgment of his Admiral.

But a true military officer is, in one particular, like a true monk. Not with more of self-abnegation will the latter keep his vows of monastic obedience than the former his vows of allegiance to martial duty.

Feeling that unless quick action were taken on it, the deed of the foretopman, as soon as it should be known on the gun-decks, would tend to awaken any slumbering embers of the Nore[1] among the crews—a sense of the urgency of the case overruled in Captain Vere all other considerations. But though a conscientious disciplinarian, he was no lover of authority for mere authority's sake. Very far was he from embracing opportunities for monopolizing to himself the perils of moral responsibility, none at least that could properly be referred to an official superior, or shared with him by his official equals or even subordinates. So thinking, he was glad it would not be at variance with usage to turn the matter over to a summary court of his own officers, reserving to himself, as the one on whom the ultimate accountability would rest, the right of maintaining a supervision of it, or formally or informally interposing at need. Accordingly a drum-head court was summarily convened, he electing the individuals composing it, the First Lieutenant, the Captain of Marines, and the Sailing Master. . . .

All being quickly in readiness, Billy Budd was arraigned, Captain Vere necessarily appearing as the sole witness in the case, and as such temporarily sinking his rank, though singularly maintaining it in a matter apparently trivial, namely, that he testified from the ship's weather-side, with that object having caused the court to sit on the lee-side. Concisely he narrated all that had led up to the catastrophe, omitting nothing in Claggart's accusation and deposing as to the manner in which the prisoner had received it. At this testimony the three officers glanced with no little surprise at Billy Budd, the last man they would have suspected, either of mutinous design alleged by Claggart, or of the undeniable deed he himself had done. The First Lieutenant, taking judicial primacy and turning towards the prisoner, said, "Captain Vere has spoken. Is it or is it not as Captain Vere says?" In response came syllables not so much impeded in the utterance as might have been anticipated. They were these:

"Captain Vere tells the truth. It is just as Captain Vere says, but it is not as the Master-at-arms said. I have eaten the King's bread and I am true to the King."

"I believe you, my man," said the witness, his voice indicating a suppressed emotion not otherwise betrayed.

"God will bless you for that, your honour!" not without stammering said Billy, and all but broke down. But immediately was recalled to self-control by another question, with which the same emotional difficulty of utterance came: "No, there was no malice between us. I never bore malice against the Master-at-arms. I am

---

[1] A ship on which there had been a mutiny consequent upon a murder and a hanging.

sorry that he is dead. I did not mean to kill him. Could I have used my tongue I would not have struck him. But he foully lied to my face, and in the presence of my Captain, and I had to say something, and I could only say it with a blow. God help me!"

In the impulsive above-board manner of the frank one the court saw confirmed all that was implied in words which just previously had perplexed them, coming as they did from the testifier to the tragedy, and promptly following Billy's impassioned disclaimer of mutinous intent—Captain Vere's words, "I believe you, my man."

Next it was asked of him whether he knew of or suspected aught savouring of incipient trouble (meaning a mutiny, though the explicit term was avoided) going on in any section of the ship's company.

The reply lingered. This was naturally imputed by the court to the same vocal embarrassment which had retarded or obstructed previous answers. But in main it was otherwise here; the question immediately recalling to Billy's mind the interview with the after-guardsman in the fore-chains. But an innate repugnance to playing a part at all approaching that of an informer against one's own ship-mates—the same erring sense of uninstructed honour which had stood in the way of his reporting the matter at the time; though as a loyal man-of-war man it was incumbent on him and failure so to do charged against him and, proven, would have subjected him to the heaviest of penalties. This, with the blind feeling now his, that nothing really was being hatched, prevailing with him. When the answer came it was a negative.

"One question more," said the officer of marines now first speaking and with a troubled earnestness. "You tell us that what the Master-at-arms said against you was a lie. Now why should he have so lied, so maliciously lied, since you declare there was no malice between you?"

At that question unintentionally touching on a spiritual sphere wholly obscure to Billy's thoughts, he was nonplussed, evincing a confusion indeed that some observers, such as can be imagined, would have construed into involuntary evidence of hidden guilt. Nevertheless he strove some way to answer, but all at once relinquished the vain endeavour, at the same time turning an appealing glance towards Captain Vere as deeming him his best helper and friend. Captain Vere, who had been seated for a time, rose to his feet, addressing the interrogator. "The question you put to him comes naturally enough. But can he rightly answer it?—or anybody else? unless indeed it be he who lies within there," designating the compartment where lay the corpse. "But the prone one there will not rise to our summons. In effect though, as it seems to me, the point you make is hardly material. Quite aside from any conceivable motive actuating the

Master-at-arms, and irrespective of the provocation of the blow, a martial court must needs in the present case confine its attention to the blow's consequence, which consequence is to be deemed not otherwise than as the striker's deed!"

This utterance, the full significance of which it was not at all likely that Billy took in, nevertheless caused him to turn a wistful, interrogative look towards the speaker, a look in its dumb expressiveness not unlike that which a dog of generous breed might turn upon his master, seeking in his face some elucidation of a previous gesture ambiguous to the canine intelligence. Nor was the same utterance without marked effect upon the three officers, more especially the soldier. Couched in it seemed to them a meaning unanticipated, involving a prejudgment on the speaker's part. It served to augment a mental disturbance previously evident enough.

The soldier once more spoke, in a tone of suggestive dubiety addressing at once his associates and Captain Vere: "Nobody is present—none of the ship's company, I mean, who might shed lateral light, if any is to be had, upon what remains mysterious in this matter."

"That is thoughtfully put," said Captain Vere; "I see your drift. Ay, there is a mystery; but to use a Scriptural phrase, it is 'a mystery of iniquity,' a matter for only psychologic theologians to discuss. But what has a military court to do with it? Not to add that for us any possible investigation of it is cut off by the lasting tongue-tie of him in yonder," again designating the mortuary state-room. "The prisoner's deed. With that alone we have to do."

To this, and particularly the closing reiteration, the marine soldier, knowing not how aptly to reply, sadly abstained from saying aught. The First Lieutenant, who at the outset had not unnaturally assumed primacy in the court, now overrulingly instructed by a glance from Captain Vere (a glance more effective than words), resumed that primacy. Turning to the prisoner: "Budd," he said, and scarce in equable tones, "Budd, if you have aught further to say for yourself, say it now."

Upon this the young sailor turned another quick glance towards Captain Vere; then, as taking a hint from that aspect, a hint confirming his own instinct that silence was now best, replied to the Lieutenant, "I have said all, Sir."

The marine—the same who had been the sentinel without the cabin-door at the time that the foretopman, followed by the Master-at-arms, entered it—he, standing by the sailor throughout their judicial proceedings, was now directed to take him back to the after compartment originally assigned to the prisoner and his custodian. As the twain disappeared from view, the three officers, as partially liberated from some inward constraint associated with Billy's mere presence—

simultaneously stirred in their seats. They exchanged looks of troubled indecision, yet feeling that decide they must, and without long delay; for Captain Vere was for the time sitting unconsciously with his back towards them, apparently in one of his absent fits, gazing out from a sashed port-hole to windward upon the monotonous blank of the twilight sea. But the court's silence continuing, broken only at moments by brief consultations in low earnest tones, this seemed to assure him and encourage him. Turning, he to-and-fro paced the cabin athwart; in the returning ascent to windward, climbing the slant deck in the ship's lee roll; without knowing it symbolizing thus in his action a mind resolute to surmount difficulties even if against primitive instincts strong as the wind and the sea. Presently he came to a stand before the three. After scanning their faces he stood less as mustering his thoughts for expression, than as one in deliberating how best to put them to well-meaning men not intellectually mature—men with whom it was necessary to demonstrate certain principles that were axioms to himself. Similar impatience as to talking is perhaps one reason that deters some minds from addressing any popular assemblies; under which head is to be classed most legislatures in a Democracy.

When speak he did, something both in the substance of what he said and his manner of saying it, showed the influence of unshared studies, modifying and tempering the practical training of an active career. This, along with his phraseology now and then, was suggestive of the grounds whereon rested that imputation of a certain pedantry socially alleged against him by certain naval men of wholly practical cast, captains who nevertheless would frankly concede that His Majesty's Navy mustered no more efficient officers of their grade than "Starry Vere."

What he said was to this effect: "Hitherto I have been but the witness, little more; and I should hardly think now to take another tone, that of your coadjutor, for the time, did I not perceive in you— at the crisis too—a troubled hesitancy, proceeding, I doubt not, from the clashing of military duty with moral scruple—scruple vitalized by compassion. For the compassion, how can I otherwise but share it. But, mindful of paramount obligation, I strive against scruples that may tend to enervate decision. Not, gentlemen, that I hide from myself that the case is an exceptional one. Speculatively regarded, it well might be referred to a jury of casuists. But for us here, acting not as casuists or moralists, it is a case practical and under martial law practically to be dealt with.

"But your scruples! Do they move as in a dusk? Challenge them. Make them advance and declare themselves. Come now—do they import something like this: If, mindless of palliating circumstances, we are bound to regard the death of the Master-at-arms as the prisoner's deed, then does that deed constitute a capital crime whereof the penalty is a mortal one? But in natural justice is nothing but the prisoner's overt act to be considered? Now can we adjudge to summary and shameful death a fellow-creature innocent before God, and whom we feel to be so?—Does that state it aright? You sign sad assent. Well, I, too, feel that, the full force of that. It is Nature. But do these buttons that we wear attest that our allegiance is to Nature? No, to the King. Though the ocean, which is inviolate Nature primeval, though this be the element where we move and have our being as sailors, yet as the King's officers lies our duty in a sphere correspondingly natural? So little is that true, that in receiving our commissions we in the most important regards ceased to be natural free-agents. When war is declared, are we the commissioned fighters previously consulted? We fight at command. If our judgments approve the war, that is but coincidence. So in other particulars. So now, would it be so much we ourselves that would condemn as it would be martial law operating through us? For that law and the rigour of it, we are not responsible. Our vowed responsibility is in this: That however pitilessly that law may operate, we neverthelsss adhere to it and administer it.

"But the exceptional in the matter moves the heart within you. Even so, too, is mine moved. But let not warm hearts betray heads that should be cool. Ashore in a criminal case will an upright judge allow himself when off the bench to be waylaid by some tender kinswoman of the accused seeking to touch him with her tearful plea? Well, the heart here is as that piteous woman. The heart is the feminine in man, and hard though it be, she must here be ruled out."

He paused, earnestly studying them for a moment; then resumed.

"But something in your aspect seems to urge that it is not solely that heart that moves in you, but also the conscience, the private conscience. Then, tell me whether or not, occupying the position we do, private conscience should not yield to that imperial one formulated in the code under which alone we officially proceed?"

Here the three men moved in their seats, less convinced than agitated by the course of an argument troubling but the more the spontaneous conflict within. Perceiving which, the speaker paused for a moment; then abruptly changing his tone, went on:

"To steady us a bit, let us recur to the facts.—In war-time at sea a man-of-war's man strikes his superior in grade, and the blow kills. Apart from its effect, the blow itself is, according to the Articles of War, a capital crime. Furthermore—"

"Ay, Sir," emotionally broke in the officer of marines, "in one sense it was. But surely Budd purposed neither mutiny nor homicide."

"Surely not, my good man. And before a court less arbitrary and more merciful than a martial one that plea would largely extenuate. At the Last Assizes it shall acquit. But how here? We proceed under the law of the Mutiny Act. In feature no child can resemble his father more than that Act resembles in spirit the thing from which it derives—War. In His Majesty's service—in this ship indeed—there are Englishmen forced to fight for the King against their will. Against their conscience, for aught we know. Though as their fellow-creatures some of us may appreciate their position, yet as Navy officers, what reck we of it? Still less recks the enemy. Our impressed men he would fain cut down in the same swath with our volunteers. As regards the enemy's naval conscripts, some of whom may even share our own abhorrence of the regicidal French Directory, it is the same on our side. War looks but to the frontage, the appearance. And the Mutiny Act, War's child, takes after the father. Budd's intent or non-intent is nothing to the purpose.

"But while, put to it by those anxieties in you which I cannot but respect, I only repeat myself—while thus strangely we prolong proceedings that should be summary, the enemy may be sighted and an engagement result. We must do; and one of two things must we do—condemn or let go."

"Can we not convict and yet mitigate the penalty?" asked the Junior Lieutenant here speaking, and faltering, for the first time.

"Lieutenant, were that clearly lawful for us under the circumstances, consider the consequences of such clemency. The people" (meaning the ship's company) "have native sense; most of them are familiar with our naval usage and tradition; and how would they take it? Even could you explain to them—which our official position forbids—they, long moulded by arbitrary discipline, have not that kind of intelligent responsiveness that might qualify them to comprehend and discriminate. No, to the people the foretopman's deed, however it be worded in the announcement, will be plain homicide committed in a flagrant act of mutiny. What penalty for that should follow, they know. But it does not follow. *Why?* they will ruminate. You know what sailors are. Will they not revert to the recent outbreak at the Nore? Ay, they know the well-founded alarm—the panic it struck throughout England. Your clement sentence they would account pusillanimous. They would think that we flinch, that we are afraid of them—afraid of practising a lawful rigour singularly demanded at this juncture lest it should provoke new troubles. What shame to us such a conjecture on their part, and how deadly to discipline. You see then whither, prompted by duty and the law, I steadfastly drive. But I beseech you, my friends, do not take me amiss. I feel as you do for this unfortunate boy. But did he know our hearts, I take him to be of that generous nature that he would feel even for us on whom in this military necessity so heavy a compulsion is laid." . . .

In brief, Billy Budd was formally convicted and sentenced to be hung at the yard-arm in the early morning-watch, it being now night. Otherwise, as is customary in such cases, the sentence would forthwith have been carried out. In war-time on the field or in the fleet, a mortal punishment decreed by a drum-head court—on the field sometimes decreed by but a nod from the General—follows without a delay on the heel of conviction without appeal.

*　　*　　*

The night so luminous on the spar-deck, but otherwise on the cavernous ones below—levels so very like the tiered galleries in a coal-mine—the luminous night passed away. Like the prophet in the chariot disappearing in heaven and dropping his mantle to Elisha, the withdrawing night transferred its pale robe to the peeping day. A meek shy light appeared in the East, where stretched a diaphanous fleece of white furrowed vapour. That light slowly waxed. Suddenly *one bell* was struck aft, responded to by one louder metallic stroke from forward. It was four o'clock in the morning. Instantly the silver whistles were heard summoning all hands to witness punishment. Up through the great hatchway rimmed with racks of heavy shot, the watch below came pouring, overspreading with the watch already on deck the space between the mainmast and foremast, including that occupied by the capacious *launch* and the black booms tiered on either side of it—boat and booms making a summit of observation for the powder boys and younger tars. A different group comprising one watch of topmen leaned over the side of the rail of that sea-balcony, no small one in a seventy-four, looking down on the crowd below. Man or boy, none spake but in whisper, and few spake at all. Captain Vere—as before, the central figure among the assembled commissioned officers—stood nigh the break of the poop-deck, facing forward. Just below him on the quarter-deck the marines in full equipment were drawn up much as at the scene of the promulgated sentence.

At sea in the old time, the execution by halter of a military sailor was generally from the fore-yard. In the present instance—for special reasons—the main-yard was assigned. Under an arm of that yard the prisoner was presently brought up, the Chaplain attending him. It was noted at the time, and remarked upon afterwards, that in this final scene the good man evinced little or nothing of the perfunctory. Brief speech indeed he had with the condemned one, but the genuine gospel was less on his tongue than in his aspect and manner towards him. The final preparations personal to the latter being speedily brought to an end by two boatswain's-mates, the consummation impended. Billy stood facing aft. At the penultimate moment, his words, his only ones, words wholly unobstructed in the utterance, were these —"God bless Captain Vere!" Syllables so unanticipated coming from one with the ignominious hemp about his neck—a conventional felon's benediction directed aft towards the quarters of honour; syllables, too, delivered in the clear melody of a singing-bird on the point of launching from the twig, had a phenomenal effect, not unenhanced by the rare personal beauty of the young sailor, spiritualized now through late experiences so poignantly profound.

Without volition, as it were, as if indeed the ship's populace were the vehicles of some vocal electric current, with one voice, from alow and aloft, came a resonant echo—"God—bless Captain Vere!" And yet, at that instant, Billy alone must have been in their hearts, even as he was in their eyes.

At the pronounced words and the spontaneous echo that voluminously rebounded them, Captain Vere, either through stoic self-control or a sort of momentary paralysis induced by emotional shock, stood erectly rigid as a musket in the ship-armour's rack.

The hull, deliberately recovering from the periodic roll to leeward, was just regaining an even keel—when the last signal, the preconcerted dumb one, was given. At the same moment it chanced that the vapoury fleece hanging low in the East, was shot through with a soft glory as of the fleece of the Lamb of God seen in mystical vision; and simultaneously therewith, watched by the wedged mass of upturned faces, Billy ascended; and ascending, took the full rose of the dawn.

In the pinioned figure, arrived at the yard-end, to the wonder of all no motion was apparent save that created by the slow roll of the hull, in moderate weather so majestic in a great ship heavy-cannoned.

RESPONSES: Questions for Writing and Discussion

1. If Billy Budd had not been given a vocal impediment by the author, it is doubtful that he would have killed Claggart. Do we assume that the young man would have been acquitted of the charges had he been able to defend himself? Or do we assume that the law would have operated in Claggart's favor anyway? Try to reconstruct the hearing as it might have gone without the murder.

2. Melville was a dedicated symbolist in all his writings. He seldom introduces something so important as Billy's speech defect for merely plot purposes. If we think of the character as still another

representation of man before the fall, what might the speech problem be saying about human nature? Does the theme of law versus the individual or the "special" case have anything to do with the symbolism of the speech impediment?

3. Not wishing to bear the moral responsibility alone is the reason Vere gives himself for calling the drum-head court into session and allowing his officers to share in the verdict. There is a sense of system, of intelligence, of fair play about the arrangement. Can it be said that justice was done in the case? If you think not, indicate how you would have handled it. Could your approach be described as intelligent and fair? Or would you redefine these terms altogether?

4. Could a case be made for the belief that the principal of order, the "tight ship" idea, is a myth?

5. To what extent does the fear of possible mutiny enter into Vere's decision to take quick action in Billy's case? Does this indicate any self-interest on his part? If your answer is no, state why. If it is yes, does this factor change the logic with which Vere believes the hanging of Billy is in strict accord?

6. Billy declines to offer any statement in his own defense. Can you think of any he might have made? Does his silence indicate a resignation to an unjust fate or an acceptance of the logic of his guilt?

7. Many people argue that the problem today is no longer the rigidity but rather the permissiveness of the law. The Supreme Court has recently ruled the death penalty unconstitutional. This means murderers will remain for years as "guests" of the state, supported by tax money. Eventually most murderers are released, most of society having forgotten all about the original crime and the victim. Are we progressing? Is it better this way?

8. In his famous speech to the court regarding the military buttons Vere points out that they signify allegiance not to nature but to the King. We don't have kings in this country. Our political philosophy was originally predicated on natural law. To what or to whom do the buttons of *our* lawmen signify allegiance?

9. Billy dies after shouting "God bless Captain Vere!" Do you think this means he is forgiving the Captain? Is he hailing his courage in performing justice? Is he just trying to make it easier for him? Or is he recognizing that the Captain is also a victim? (If so, of what?)

10. At the end of the novel (not included in our selection) Melville informs us that Vere died murmuring Billy's name. In following the dictates of reason, Vere had to stifle his true feelings. What would have happened if Vere had followed instead the dictates of his heart? Do you want a world ruled by the heart or the mind?

THE WINDHOVER
Gerard Manley Hopkins

That the poet has dedicated the following poem to Christ may help the reader through what might otherwise be a baffling experience. Though **Gerard Manley Hopkins (1844–1889)** is classified technically as a Victorian poet, he is surprisingly modern in comparison with his mid-nineteenth-century contemporaries. Like the modern poet, he strives primarily to express his thoughts and feelings in ways that are most meaningful to him, asking the reader to "come after" the communication rather than striving to make him comprehend it.

Hopkins' background sheds much light on the oblique method he uses in his poetry. Always devoutly religious, he left the Anglican faith after a monastic retreat in 1865 convinced him that he was intended for a lifetime of service to God. In 1866 he became a Roman Catholic and two years later a Jesuit novitiate. In the midst of a period when more and more writers and philosophers were becoming inspired by science and were turning atheist, Hopkins kept on quietly composing poems of faith. That he did not expect to reach a wide audience may help to explain his poetic innovations and the difficulty one has in understanding a poem like "The Windhover."

While each reader may find a personal meaning in the majesty of the falcon as its "hurl and gliding" conquer the "big wind," it is difficult not to think about the poem's dedication and about "the achieve" and "the mastery" of those who "plod" in their disciplined and dedicated lives and, like the bird, gain their strength from—not despite—hardships. The subject matter of the poem appears to relate in many ways to the concern of this section: order.

The Windhover

To Christ Our Lord

I caught this morning morning's minion, king-
    dom of daylight's dauphin, dapple-dawn-drawn Falcon, in
      his riding
Of the rolling level underneath him steady air, and striding
High there, how he rung upon the rein of a wimpling wing
In his ecstasy! then off, off forth on swing,
    As a skate's heel sweeps smooth on a bow-bend: the hurl
      and gliding

Rebuffed the big wind. My heart in hiding
Stirred for a bird,—the achieve of, the mastery of the thing!

Brute beauty and valour and act, oh, air, pride, plume, here
    Buckle! AND the fire that breaks from thee then, a billion
Times told lovelier, more dangerous, O my chevalier!

    No wonder of it: shéer plód makes plough down sillion
Shine, and blue-bleak embers, ah my dear,
    Fall, gall themselves, and gash gold-vermilion.

LIFE, TRIAL, AND DEATH OF AURELIO POMPA
Mexican Immigrants

In addition to singing about their homeland, their wives and sweethearts, and the hardships of working long hours for a few pennies, the Mexican immigrants composed songs about current events, such as the one which is the subject of the following lyric. Remarkably compact, the poem tells a tragic tale of American justice and an impoverished Mexican who goes to his death "in a dreadful way" for a murder commited in self-defense. The implication is strong in the poem that the American legal system is not geared toward fairness for all, especially for those of unfamiliar cultural backgrounds.

Life, Trial, and Death of Aurelio Pompa

I am going to tell you the sad story
Of a Mexican who emigrated out here—
Aurelio Pompa, so he was called.
Our compatriot who died there,
Out there in Caborca, which is in Sonora,
The humble village where he was born,

Reprinted from *Mexican Immigration to the United States* by Manuel Gamio by permission of the publisher, The University of Chicago Press. Copyright 1930 by the University of Chicago.

"Come on, mother," he said one day,
"Over there there are no revolutions.
Goodbye, friends; goodbye, María,"
He said to his betrothed very sadly.
"I promise you that I will return soon,
So we can get married, God willing."
"Goodbye, Aurelio," said the girl,
And she went sobbing to pray.
"Look after him, Virgin Mary,
I have a foreboding he will not come back."
The priest and his friends
Along with his sweetheart went to talk
And to beg poor Aurelio
Not to leave his native village.
Such advice was useless
And so were the entreaties of his mother.
"Let's go, mother, over there is the dollar,
And I swear I am going to earn a lot of them."
Four years ago in the month of May
The two of them went to California
And through misfortune on the very same date
Died there in prison.
A carpenter who was very strong
Struck the poor young fellow cruelly,
And Aurelio Pompa swore to be revenged
For those blows he had received.
Filled with rage he told his mother about it
And the poor old woman advised him,
"*Por Dios*, forget it, dear son."
And good Aurelio forgave him;
But one afternoon, when he was working
With three friends at the railroad station
The carpenter came by mocking at him
And aroused poor Pompa.
The three friends advised him
To leave him alone and go his way,
And then the carpenter, with a hammer,
Very offensively threatened him.
Then Pompa, seeing the danger,
Fired in self-defense
With a revolver and face to face
As a man he killed him.
The case came to court, the jury arrived,
And the Yankee people sentenced him.

"The death penalty," they all demanded,
And the lawyer did not object.
Twenty thousand signatures of compatriots
Asked for his pardon from the Governor.
All the newspapers asked for it too,
And even Obregon sent a message.
All was useless; the societies,
All united, asked his pardon.
His poor mother, half-dead already,
Also went to see the Governor.
"Farewell, my friends, farewell, my village;
Dear mother, cry no more.
Tell my race not to come here,
For here they will suffer; there is no pity here.
The jailor asked him:
"Were you Spanish?" and he answered,
"I am a Mexican and proud of being so
Although they deny me a pardon."
This is the story of a compatriot
Who four years ago came there
And through misfortune on the same date
Died in a dreadful way in a prison.

ONE SIDED SHOOT-OUT
Don L. Lee

Probably the youngest author represented in this anthology, **Don L. Lee**
(**b. 1942**) has in a few short years become a leader in a total black revolution
in poetry. Poets like Richard Wright and Gwendolyn Brooks, who were
writing long before he was even born, opened the gates and showed their
readers glimpses of unfamiliar terrain, but their vocabulary and rhythmic
effects are not altogether foreign to the spirit of contemporary poetry. Their
subject matter reflects the black experience in America, but their poems
nonetheless owe much to a broad cross section of literary influences. Lee, on
the other hand, makes no compromises; he speaks in the complete language
and style of black America. He is writing mainly *for* black America.

Specifically, he has taken what is termed "the rap" and uses it as a
vehicle of poetic expression. Lee's poems must be heard to be fully ap-

preciated, because the rap is a spoken, dynamic thing, never meant to be read in some silent library room. His poems are published only as conveniences, as notes really, for those who will give voice to them. Only as they become raps themselves do they exist in the literary form intended. We are fortunate to be living in the era of records and tapes so that Lee may be preserved in this manner, *not* on bookshelves.

The poem which follows was written to commemorate the deaths (or, as Lee says, the murders) of Fred Hampton and Mark Clark during a raid on Black Panther headquarters in Chicago in 1969.

One Sided Shoot-out

(for brothers fred hampton & mark clark, murdered
12/4/69 by chicago police at 4:30 AM while they slept)

only a few will really understand:
it won't be yr/mommas or yr/brothers & sisters or even me,
we all think that we do   but we don't.
it's not *new*   and
under all the rhetoric the seriousness is still not serious.
the national rap deliberately continues, "wipe them niggers out."
(no talk do it, no talk do it, no talk do it, notalk notalknotalk do it)

& we.
running circleround getting caught in our own cobwebs,
in the same old clothes, same old words, just new adjectives.
we will order new buttons & posters with: "remember fred"
    & "rite-on mark."
& yr/pictures will be beautiful & manly with the deeplook/
    the accusing look
to remind us
to remind us that suicide is not black.

the questions will be asked & the answers will be the new cliches.
but maybe,
just maybe we'll finally realize that "revolution" to the real-world
is international 24hours a day and that 4:30 AM is like 12:00 noon,
it's just darker.
but the evil can be seen if u look in the right direction.
were the street lights out?
did they darken their faces in combat?

did they remove their shoes to *creep* softer?
could u not see the whi-te of their eyes,
the whi-te of their deathfaces?
didn't yr/look-out man see them coming,   coming,   coming?
or did they turn into ghostdust and join the night's fog?

it was mean.
& we continue to call them "pigs" and "muthafuckas"
    forgetting what all
black children learn very early: "sticks & stones may break
                  my bones but names can
                  never hurt me."
it was murder.
& we meet to hear the speeches/ the same, the duplicators.
they say that which is expected of them.
to be instructive or constructive is to be unpopular (like: the
    leaders only
sleep when there is a watchingeye)
but they say the right things at the right time, it's like a stageshow:
only the entertainers have changed.
we remember bobby hutton.   the same,   the duplicators.

the seeing eye should always see.
the night doesn't stop the stars
& our enemies scope the ways of blackness in three bad shifts a day.
in the AM their music becomes deadlier.
this is a game of dirt.

only blackpeople play it fair.

THE LAWS OF GOD,
THE LAWS OF MAN

A. E. Housman

A. E. Housman (1859–1936) is best known for a collection of poems entitled
A Shropshire Lad. Shropshire is a county in west central England near the
Welsh border. It is a place of many contrasts: rich green farmlands, rolling
hills, sumptuous estates, lakes and streams, but also smoky industrial towns

with their poverty-level workers living in drab, tiny brick houses all stuck together row upon row. It is a place where many have nothing and some have everything, and in Housman's England the sheer accident of birth relegates one to poverty or plenty. Housman's poetry is painfully aware of the irony and injustice of existence, but the poet never fully abandons himself to despair. There are fleeting moments of compensation, such as a glimpse of a beautiful tree, and there is also the inner strength which comes from making the kind of compromise with external controls that we find expressed in this poem.

The Laws of God, the Laws of Man

The laws of God, the laws of man,
He may keep that will and can;
Not I: let God and man decree
Laws for themselves and not for me;
And if my ways are not as theirs
Let them mind their own affairs.
Their deeds I judge and much condemn,
Yet when did I make laws for them?
Please yourselves, say I, and they
Need only look the other way.
But no, they will not; they must still
Wrest their neighbour to their will,
And make me dance as they desire
With jail and gallows and hell-fire.
And how am I to face the odds
Of man's bedevilment and God's?
I, a stranger and afraid
In a world I never made.
They will be master, right or wrong;
Though both are foolish, both are strong.
And since, my soul, we cannot fly
To Saturn nor to Mercury,
Keep we must, if keep we can,
These foreign laws of God and man.

NATURAL MAN, CIVILIZED MAN

While the word "civilization" is difficult to define exhaustively, there is no doubt that, upon hearing the term, most people think of great cities, impressive buildings, art centers, museums, theaters, beautiful parks, and populations deriving enlightenment and sophistication from such resources. The correlation between the city and "advanced" states of human development is deeply rooted in the Western mind, the Greeks having prided themselves on the deliberate cultivation of the arts of urban existence and the Romans having bent their efforts to outdo their predecessors in this regard. The history of Western society is in many respects that of the development of one metropolitan center after another. To adapt himself to nature, to model himself after other species in nature's kingdom, seems not to have been the direction Western man chose to take. Rather, he has sought to improve upon nature, to make his life an easier and happier one through the advantages obtained from living together and sharing intellectual, artistic, economic, and labor resources.

From Aristotle to the Christian philosophers of the Middle Ages, to the great voices of the Renaissance, people of the West have said that the individual man or woman cannot do for himself what the institutions of civilization can do for him. Without religion, the law, education, and the arts there could be no Human Worth. To lead an entirely natural life, to leave civilization behind and exist on intimate terms with earth, sea, and sky meant for the traditional Western man to live a "primitive" or "backward" life. Thus was European man impelled either through religious or rational conviction to carry the torch of civilization to the "barbarian." During the eighteenth century, with the revolutions against civilized authoritarianism in America and France, however, new voices began to be heard. The city came to be viewed as the true enemy of Human Worth, not its benefactor. The institutions of civilized man were seen as the sources rather than the healers of corruption. Religion, the law, education, and all of the urban arts were shown by many revolutionists to have taken mankind too far from his natural habitat.

Henry David Thoreau, author of "Civil Disobedience," *Walden,* and other expressions of radical nonconformity in America, advocated a return to nature. He prophesied the doom of the natural environment unless civilized man once more came to know and love the benefits nature provides. In "Higher Laws," a selection from *Walden,* Thoreau offers a profound analysis of man's place within nature. It is not, as some might suppose, to live solely as other animal species do, abandoning all traces of what people have traditionally labeled "humanity." Rather, the full flowering of a person's humanness occurs when he understands how nature wishes to operate on its higher or human level. Thoreau's essay presents a case for vegetarianism, gentleness, and moral purity, suggesting that these are truly what is natural for human beings and that "civilization," ironically, is where people behave most like the lower orders of animal life.

Joseph Wood Krutch, though a contemporary admirer of Thoreau, cannot agree with him that human beings are capable of any true relationship with nature at all. "The Paradox of Humanism," written in 1929, seems potent enough still to disturb and stimulate the reader. The author presents human society as an unnatural absurdity on the face of the earth, out of harmony with every other aspect of nature, operating contrary to nature's laws and hence doomed. No escape seems possible. The hope of returning to nature is a romantic delusion. There is no Human Worth—only the curious accident called humanity.

What Krutch has to say about mankind may, however, apply to Western European man more than to less supposedly "civilized" races. We have included an excerpt from *Black Elk Speaks,* John G. Neihardt's transcription of the words of an Indian priest and survivor of the massacre at Wounded Knee, because it offers a vision of life styles totally different from those of the white European, yet existing parallel to his and now, in retrospect, suggesting that all people have not abstracted themselves from their natural environment in pursuit of "civilization." Indeed, when one contrasts Black Elk's faith in the essential goodness of the powers who rule the world with what happened to the Sioux tribe at Wounded Knee, one must face the sobering possibility that the white European's commitment to his urban dream may have been less the epitome of human development than a collision course with disaster.

Finally, this section contains portions of an address delivered by R. Buckminster Fuller, inventor of the geodesic dome, believed by many engineers and architects to be one of the most efficient models for human habitation ever devised. Fuller's vision of the world of the future, some of which he communicates in his address, is that of a wholly redesigned environment in which man will not have abstracted himself from nature so much as contributed to nature's own developmental plans. In Fuller's dream human civilization, embodied in the city, will make possible a way of life never before known on earth; one that is richer and more productive than any realized solely through what nature, unassisted by man, can provide.

HIGHER LAWS
Henry David Thoreau

Henry David Thoreau (1817–1862) has two images. One is the external man, well known to all who study American history: the Concord eccentric, coming and going as he pleased; a loner, picking and choosing his few friends with meticulous care; a recluse who spent two years by himself in a homemade cabin in the woods and spent the rest of the time in a boarding-house room, reading, writing, and meditating, or else taking endless walks in the forest or by the river; and, above all, the arch nonconformist, the radical liberal, the opponent of the unlimited powers of the state. The other Thoreau is internal, revealing himself very gradually to those who read all of his works. He was deeply and religiously dedicated to the service of nature, and this helps to explain his outward eccentricities and his political extremism. He took nature more seriously than almost any other American writer. If there had been a monastic order dedicated to observing nature and to the conservation of the environment, Thoreau would have joined it. It is a wonder he did not become its founder.

Thoreau's naturalism was not a cultivated thing, as was the case with some of the English romantic writers and even with some of the Concord intellectuals in whose midst he lived without ever really becoming one of them. Ralph Waldo Emerson, whom Thoreau did finally befriend, wrote a good deal about nature and the implications of leading a natural life, but Emerson's own life style did not stand out dramatically from his conservative New England heritage. Thoreau actually went out and did many of the things Emerson advocates in his essays. While others wrote about the joys of observing the changes in the seasons and the habits of birds and other denizens of the woods, Thoreau took hammer and nails and for $28.12½ built himself a cabin durable enough to shelter him through a two-year hermitage by Walden Pond.

Thoreau grew up hunting and fishing in the woods and streams around Concord. He was not a scholar, which accounts for his unimpressive record at Harvard. Thoreau was too much the wanderer, too much the lover of country lanes to surrender to academic discipline. If it had not been for his association with Emerson and his deep respect for the philosopher, it is doubtful that he would have been attracted to writing. But as it was, Emerson encouraged him to publish his nature sketches in the *Dial*, a literary magazine of the Concord group.

One who reads all of Thoreau's works becomes aware of an extraordinary growth: from hunter and fisher to observer of plant and wild life to hermit and forsaker of cities to profound philosopher. From nature Thoreau derived not only personal aesthetic pleasure, not only a free and unfettered life style (except for a night spent willingly in jail in protest against unfair taxation and the Mexican War), but an intricate moral and spiritual philosophy based on natural law.

The following selection from *Walden* illustrates Thoreau's spirituality. We find the words of one who, while not consistently practicing it, has recognized the pure and holy life style which he believes nature has designed for human beings. Returning to nature does not mean for Thoreau a descent to all that is animalistic and primitive in man; rather, if men would listen to the teachings of nature, they would divest themselves of these traits. Thoreau advocates chastity, sobriety, vegetarianism, and a spartan existence devoid of sensual excitements, including those which spring from the arts. He would have each of us simplify his life and tenderly care for his body to the point at which he is able to open his eyes, ears, and heart to the wonders of the environment. The purified man belongs to and harmonizes with the environment. The "city" man, with his love of gourmet dining, alcohol, and the other urban pleasures, does not. Instead, he destroys it even as he destroys himself.

One of the tragic ironies of Thoreau's life is its brevity. His very adoration of nature proved to be the thing that depleted his physical resources. A victim of a chronic bronchial ailment, Thoreau was given to sauntering through nature at all hours and in all seasons and finally succumbed to tuberculosis at the age of forty-four.

Higher Laws

As I came home through the woods with my string of fish, trailing my pole, it being now quite dark, I caught a glimpse of a woodchuck stealing across my path, and felt a strange thrill of savage delight, and was strongly tempted to seize and devour him raw; not that I was hungry then, except for that wildness which he represented. Once or twice, however, while I lived at the pond, I found myself ranging the woods, like a half-starved hound, with a strange abandonment, seeking some kind of venison which I might devour, and no morsel could have been too savage for me. The wildest scenes had become unaccountably familiar. I found in myself, and still find, an instinct toward a higher, or, as it is named, spiritual life, as do most men, and another toward a primitive rank and savage one, and I reverence them both. I love the wild not less than the good. The wildness and adventure that are in fishing still recommended it to me. I like sometimes to take rank hold on life and spend my day more as the animals do. Perhaps I have owed to this employment and to hunting, when quite young, my closest acquaintance with Nature. They early introduce us to and detain us in scenery with which otherwise, at that age, we should have little acquaintance. Fishermen, hunters, wood-choppers, and others, spending their lives in the fields and woods, in a peculiar sense a part of Nature themselves, are often in a more favorable mood for observing her, in the intervals of their pursuits, than philosophers or poets even, who approach her with expectation. She is not afraid to exhibit herself to them. The traveller on the prairie is naturally a hunter, on the head waters of the Missouri and Columbia a trapper, and at the Falls of St. Mary a fisherman. He who is only a traveller learns things at secondhand and by the halves, and is poor authority. We are most interested when science reports what those men already know practically or instinctively, for that alone is a true *humanity*, or account of human experience.

They mistake who assert that the Yankee has few amusements, because he has not so many public holidays, and men and boys do not play so many games as they do in England, for here the more primitive but solitary amusements of hunting, fishing, and the like have not yet given place to the former. Almost every New England boy

From *Walden* or *Life in the Woods*.

among my contemporaries shouldered a fowling-piece between the ages of ten and fourteen; and his hunting and fishing grounds were not limited, like the preserves of an English nobleman, but were more boundless even than those of a savage. No wonder, then, that he did not oftener stay to play on the common. But already a change is taking place, owing, not to an increased humanity, but to an increased scarcity of game, for perhaps the hunter is the greatest friend of the animals hunted, not excepting the Humane Society.

Moreover, when at the pond, I wished sometimes to add fish to my fare for variety. I have actually fished from the same kind of necessity that the first fishers did. Whatever humanity I might conjure up against it was all factitious, and concerned my philosophy more than my feelings. I speak of fishing only now, for I had long felt differently about fowling, and sold my gun before I went to the woods. Not that I am less humane than others, but I did not perceive that my feelings were much affected. I did not pity the fishes nor the worms. This was habit. As for fowling, during the last years that I carried a gun my excuse was that I was studying ornithology, and sought only new or rare birds. But I confess that I am now inclined to think that there is a finer way of studying ornithology than this. It requires so much closer attention to the habits of the birds, that, if for that reason only, I have been willing to omit the gun. Yet notwithstanding the objection on the score of humanity, I am compelled to doubt if equally valuable sports are ever substituted for these; and when some of my friends have asked me anxiously about their boys, whether they should let them hunt, I have answered, yes—remembering that it was one of the best parts of my education—*make* them hunters, though sportsmen only at first, if possible, mighty hunters at last, so that they shall not find game large enough for them in this or any vegetable wilderness—hunters as well as fishers of men. Thus far I am of the opinion of Chaucer's nun, who

'yave not of the text a pulled hen
That saith that hunters ben not holy men.'

There is a period in the history of the individual, as of the race, when the hunters are the 'best men,' as the Algonquins called them. We cannot but pity the boy who has never fired a gun; he is no more humane, while his education has been sadly neglected. This was my answer with respect to those youths who were bent on this pursuit, trusting that they would soon outgrow it. No humane being, past the thoughtless age of boyhood, will wantonly murder any creature which holds its life by the same tenure that he does. The hare in its extremity cries like a child. I warn you, mothers, that my sympathies do not always make the usual phil*anthropic* distinctions.

Such is oftenest the young man's introduction to the forest, and the most original part of himself. He goes thither at first as a hunter and fisher, until at last, if he has the seeds of a better life in him, he distinguishes his proper objects, as a poet or naturalist it may be, and leaves the gun and fish-pole behind. The mass of men are still and always young in this respect. In some countries a hunting parson is no uncommon sight. Such a one might make a good shepherd's dog, but is far from being the Good Shepherd. I have been surprised to consider that the only obvious employment, except wood-chopping, ice-cutting, or the like business, which ever to my knowledge detained at Walden Pond for a whole half-day any of my fellow-citizens, whether fathers or children of the town, with just one exception, was fishing. Commonly they did not think that they were lucky, or well paid for their time, unless they got a long string of fish, though they had the opportunity of seeing the pond all the while. They might go there a thousand times before the sediment of fishing would sink to the bottom and leave their purpose pure; but no doubt such a clarifying process would be going on all the while. The Governor and his Council faintly remember the pond, for they went a-fishing there when they were boys; but now they are too old and dignified to go a-fishing, and so they know it no more forever. Yet even they expect to go to heaven at last. If the legislature regards it, it is chiefly to regulate the number of hooks to be used there; but they know nothing about the hook of hooks with which to angle for the pond itself, impaling the legislature for a bait. Thus, even in civilized communities, the embryo man passes through the hunter stage of development.

I have found repeatedly, of late years, that I cannot fish without falling a little in self-respect. I have tried it again and again. I have skill at it, and, like many of my fellows, a certain instinct for it, which revives from time to time, but always when I have done I feel that it would have been better if I had not fished. I think that I do not mistake. It is a faint intimation, yet so are the first streaks of morning. There is unquestionably this instinct in me which belongs to the lower orders of creation; yet with every year I am less a fisherman, though without more humanity or even wisdom; at present I am no fisherman at all. But I see that if I were to live in a wilderness I should again be tempted to become a fisher and hunter in earnest. Beside, there is something essentially unclean about this diet and all flesh, and I began to see where house-work commences, and whence the endeavor, which costs so much, to wear a tidy and respectable appearance each day, to keep the house sweet and free from all ill odors and sights. Having been my own butcher and scullion and cook, as well as the gentleman for whom the dishes were served up, I can speak from an unusually complete experience. The practical objection to animal food in my case was its uncleanness; and besides, when I had caught and cleaned and cooked and eaten my fish, they seemed not to have fed me essentially. It was insignificant and unnecessary, and cost more than it came to. A little bread or a few potatoes would have done as well, with less trouble and filth. Like many of my contemporaries, I had rarely for many years used animal food, or tea, or coffee, etc.; not so much because of any ill effects which I had traced to them, as because they were not agreeable to my imagination. The repugnance to animal food is not the effect of experience, but is an instinct. It appeared more beautiful to live low and fare hard in many respects; and though I never did so, I went far enough to please my imagination. I believe that every man who has ever been earnest to preserve his higher or poetic faculties in the best condition has been particularly inclined to abstain from animal food, and from much food of any kind. It is a significant fact, stated by entomologists—I find it in Kirby and Spence—that 'some insects in their perfect state, though furnished with organs of feeding, make no use of them;' and they lay it down as 'a general rule, that almost all insects in this state eat much less than in that of larvæ. The voracious caterpillar when transformed into a butterfly . . . and the gluttonous maggot when become a fly' content themselves with a drop or two of honey or some other sweet liquid. The abdomen under the wings of the butterfly still represents the larva. This is the tidbit which tempts his insectivorous fate. The gross feeder is a man in the larva state; and there are whole nations in that condition, nations without fancy or imagination, whose vast abdomens betray them.

It is hard to provide and cook so simple and clean a diet as will not offend the imagination; but this, I think, is to be fed when we feed the body; they should both sit down at the same table. Yet perhaps this may be done. The fruits eaten temperately need not make us ashamed of our appetites, nor interrupt the worthiest pursuits. But put an extra condiment into your dish, and it will poison you. It is not worth the while to live by rich cookery. Most men would feel shame if caught preparing with their own hands precisely such a dinner, whether of animal or vegetable food, as is every day prepared for them by others. Yet till this is otherwise we are not civilized, and if gentlemen and ladies, are not true men and women. This certainly suggests what change is to be made. It may be vain to ask why the imagination will not be reconciled to flesh and fat. I am satisfied that it is not. Is it not a reproach that man is a carnivorous animal? True, he can and does live, in a great measure, by preying on other animals; but this is a miserable way—as any one who will go to snaring rabbits, or slaughtering lambs, may learn—and he will be regarded as a benefactor of his race who shall teach man to confine himself to a more innocent and wholesome diet. Whatever my own practice may be, I have no doubt that it is a part of the destiny of the human race, in its gradual improvement, to leave off eating animals, as surely as the savage tribes have left off eating each other when they came in contact with the more civilized.

If one listens to the faintest but constant suggestions of his genius, which are certainly true, he sees not to what extremes, or even insanity, it may lead him; and yet that way, as he grows more resolute and faithful, his road lies. The faintest assured objection which one healthy man feels will at length prevail over the arguments and customs of mankind. No man ever followed his genius till it misled him. Though the result were bodily weakness, yet perhaps no one can say that the consequences were to be regretted, for these were a life in conformity to higher principles. If the day and the night are such that you greet them with joy, and life emits a fragrance like flowers and sweet-scented herbs, is more elastic, more starry, more immortal—that is your success. All nature is your congratulation, and you have cause momentarily to bless yourself. The greatest gains and values are farthest from being appreciated. We easily come to doubt if they exist. We soon forget them. They are the highest reality. Perhaps the facts most astounding and most real are never communicated by man to man. The true harvest of my daily life is somewhat as intangible and indescribable as the tints of morning or evening. It is a little star-dust caught, a segment of the rainbow which I have clutched.

Yet, for my part, I was never unusually squeamish; I could sometimes eat a fried rat with a good relish, if it were necessary. I am glad to have drunk water so long, for the same reason that I prefer the natural sky to an opium-eater's heaven. I would fain keep sober always; and there are infinite degrees of drunkenness. I believe that water is the only drink for a wise man; wine is not so noble a liquor; and think of dashing the hopes of a morning with a cup of warm coffee, or of an evening with a dish of tea! Ah, how low I fall when I am tempted by them! Even music may be intoxicating. Such apparently slight causes destroyed Greece and Rome, and will destroy England and America. Of all ebriosity, who does not prefer to be intoxicated by the air he breathes? I have found it to be the most serious objection to coarse labors long continued, that they compelled me to eat and drink coarsely also. But to tell the truth, I find myself at present somewhat less particular in these respects. I carry less religion to the table, ask no blessing; not because I am wiser than I was, but, I am obliged to confess, because, however much it is to be regretted, with years I have grown more coarse and indifferent. Perhaps these questions are entertained only in youth, as most believe of poetry.

My practice is 'nowhere,' my opinion is here. Nevertheless I am far from regarding myself as one of those privileged ones to whom the Ved refers when it says, that 'he who has true faith in the Omnipresent Supreme Being may eat all that exists,' that is, is not bound to inquire what is his food, or who prepares it; and even in their case it is to be observed, as a Hindoo commentator has remarked, that the Vedant limits this privilege to 'the time of distress.'

Who has not sometimes derived an inexpressible satisfaction from his food in which appetite had no share? I have been thrilled to think that I owed a mental perception to the commonly gross sense of taste, that I have been inspired through the palate, that some berries which I had eaten on a hillside had fed my genius. 'The soul not being mistress of herself,' says Thseng-tseu, 'one looks, and one does not see; one listens, and one does not hear; one eats, and one does not know the savor of food.' He who distinguishes the true savor of his food can never be a glutton; he who does not cannot be otherwise. A puritan may go to his brown-bread crust with as gross an appetite as ever an alderman to his turtle. Not that food which entereth into the mouth defileth a man, but the appetite with which it is eaten. It is neither the quality nor the quantity, but the devotion to sensual savors; when that which is eaten is not a viand to sustain our animal, or inspire our spiritual life, but food for the worms that possess us. If the hunter has a taste for mudturtles, muskrats, and other such savage tidbits, the fine lady indulges a taste for jelly made of a calf's foot, or for sardines from over the sea, and they are even. He goes to the mill-pond, she to her preserve-pot. The wonder is how they, how you and I, can live this slimy, beastly life, eating and drinking.

Our whole life is startlingly moral. There is never an instant's truce between virtue and vice. Goodness is the only investment that never fails. In the music of the harp which trembles round the world it is the insisting on this which thrills us. The harp is the travelling patterer for the Universe's Insurance Company, recommending its laws, and our little goodness is all the assessment that we pay. Though the youth at last grows indifferent, the laws of the universe are not indifferent, but are forever on the side of the most sensitive. Listen to every zephyr for some reproof, for it is surely there, and he is unfortunate who does not hear it. We cannot touch a string or move a stop but the charming moral transfixes us. Many an irksome noise, go a long way off, is heard as music, a proud, sweet satire on the meanness of our lives.

We are conscious of an animal in us, which awakens in proportion as our higher nature slumbers. It is reptile and sensual, and perhaps cannot be wholly expelled; like the worms which, even in life and health, occupy our bodies. Possibly we may withdraw from it, but never change its nature. I fear that it may enjoy a certain health of its own; that we may be well, yet not pure. The other day I picked up the lower jaw of a hog, with white and sound teeth and tusks, which suggested that there was an animal health and vigor distinct from the spiritual. This creature succeeded by other means than temperance and purity. 'That in which men differ from brute beasts,' says Mencius, 'is a thing very inconsiderable; the common herd lose it very soon; superior men preserve it carefully.' Who knows what sort of life would result if we had attained to purity? If I knew so wise a man as could teach me purity I would go to seek him forthwith. 'A command over our passions, and over the external senses of the body, and good acts, are declared by the Ved to be indispensable in the mind's approximation to God.' Yet the spirit can for the time pervade and control every member and function of the body, and transmute what in form is the grossest sensuality into purity and devotion. The generative energy, which, when we are loose, dissipates and makes us unclean, when we are continent invigorates and inspires us. Chastity is the flowering of man; and what are called Genius, Heroism, Holiness, and the like, are but various fruits which succeed it. Man flows at once to God when the channel of purity is open. By turns our purity inspires and our impurity casts us down. He is blessed who is assured that the animal is dying out in him day by day, and the divine being established. Perhaps there is none but has cause for shame on account of the inferior and brutish nature to which he is allied. I fear that we are such gods or demigods only as fauns and satyrs, the divine allied to beasts, the creatures of appetite, and that, to some extent, our very life is our disgrace.

> 'How happy's he who hath due place assigned
> To his beasts and disafforested his mind!
>
> . . . .
>
> Can use his horse, goat, wolf, and ev'ry beast,
> And is not ass himself to all the rest!
> Else man not only is the herd of swine,
> But he's those devils too which did incline
> Them to a headlong rage, and made them worse.'

All sensuality is one, though it takes many forms; all purity is one. It is the same whether a man eat, or drink, or cohabit, or sleep sensually. They are but one appetite, and we only need to see a person do any one of these things to know how great a sensualist he is. The impure can neither stand nor sit with purity. When the reptile is attacked at one mouth of his burrow, he shows himself at another. If you would be chaste, you must be temperate. What is chastity? How shall a man know if he is chaste? He shall not know it. We have heard of this virtue, but we know not what it is. We speak conformably to the rumor which we have heard. From exertion come wisdom and purity; from sloth ignorance and sensuality. In the student sensuality is a sluggish habit of mind. An unclean person is universally a slothful one, one who sits by a stove, whom the sun shines on prostrate, who reposes without being fatigued. If you would avoid uncleanness, and all the sins, work earnestly, though it be at cleaning a stable. Nature is hard to be overcome, but she must be overcome. What avails it that you are Christian, if you are not purer than the heathen, if you deny yourself no more, if you are not more religious? I know of many systems of religion esteemed heathenish whose precepts fill the reader with shame, and provoke him to new endeavors, though it be to the performance of rites merely.

I hesitate to say these thing, but it is not because of the subject— I care not how obscene my *words* are—but because I cannot speak of them without betraying my impurity. We discourse freely without shame of one form of sensuality, and are silent about another. We are so degraded that we cannot speak simply of the necessary functions of human nature. In earlier ages, in some countries, every function was reverently spoken of and regulated by law. Nothing was too trivial for the Hindoo lawgiver, however offensive it may be to modern taste. He teaches how to eat, drink, cohabit, void excrement and urine, and the like, elevating what is mean, and does not falsely excuse himself by calling these things trifles.

Every man is the builder of a temple, called his body, to the god he worships, after a style purely his own, nor can he get off by hammering marble instead. We are all sculptors and painters, and our material is our own flesh and blood and bones. Any nobleness begins at once to refine a man's features, any meanness or sensuality to imbrute them.

John Farmer sat at his door one September evening, after a hard day's work, his mind still running on his labor more or less. Having bathed, he sat down to re-create his intellectual man. It was a rather cool evening, and some of his neighbors were apprehending a frost. He had not attended to the train of his thoughts long when he heard some one playing on a flute, and that sound harmonized with his mood. Still he thought of his work; but the burden of his thought was, that though this kept running in his head, and he found himself planning and contriving it against his will, yet it concerned him very little. It was no more than the scurf of his skin, which was constantly shuffled off. But the notes of the flute came home to his ears out of a different sphere from that he worked in, and suggested work for certain faculties which slumbered in him. They gently did away with the street, and the village, and the state in which he lived. A voice said to him—Why do you stay here and live this mean moiling life, when a glorious existence is possible for you? Those same stars twinkle over other fields than these.—But how to come out of this condition and actually migrate thither? All that he could think of was to practise some new austerity, to let his mind descend into his body and redeem it, and treat himself with ever increasing respect.

RESPONSES: Questions for Writing and Discussion

1. Do you agree with Thoreau that all human beings naturally possess higher or spiritual instincts—such as a repugnance against killing and eating animal flesh—and lower, savage instincts—such as the enjoyment of those same things? On the level of nature are all instincts equal? Can it truly be said that eating meat, for example, is a lower instinct? Philosophical meat eaters often claim that man is carnivorous by nature and that meatless diets are unnatural. Are they right?

2. Thoreau admits that he used to hunt and fish for sport. Indeed it is hard to think of two leisure-time activities which have traditionally enjoyed more honor and repute among the majority of Americans. How do you feel about hunting and fishing purely for enjoyment?

3. Thoreau makes a distinction between fishing out of sheer necessity and fishing for sport. He tells us that he renounced hunting before he did fishing, for "I did not pity the fishes nor the worms." If one were to try returning to nature, living alone in a wilderness with no means of support, would fishing then be acceptable? If someone refused to maintain an adequate diet because he *did* pity the fishes and the worms, would he be a "higher" kind of human being or a fool?

4. Thoreau refers to the "Governor and his Council," all of whom used to fish at Walden Pond in their youth and, like the other citizens of the area, never noticed the beauty of the pond itself. Now they are engaged in legislation to regulate the amount of fishing allowed. Thoreau thinks they should go further and "angle for the pond itself." One presumes he means that wildlife areas should be government controlled. Wherever this happens, there are limitations imposed on the kind and degree of sport in which one can engage. Some places outlaw fishing and hunting altogether. Do you agree with such controls? Are they infringements on natural liberties?

5. Thoreau speaks of man as a "gross feeder," generally eating more than is necessary. But he finds this to be a cultural rather than a natural trait, varying from country to country. "There are whole nations in that condition . . . whose vast abdomens betray them."

Statistics tell an alarming story of American eating habits. Why do we eat so much?

6. Thoreau is against gourmet dining. He calls it a "devotion to sensual savors" and puts it in the unnatural activities column. Many consider gourmet dining to be among life's richest, most civilized pleasures. Is it important to good living? Describe your own eating habits. Defend or question them.

7. Thoreau has a paragraph (beginning "Yet, for my part, I was never unusually squeamish") in which he warns of the consequences of nonsobriety. Intoxication of the mind—including that which comes from the arts—"destroyed Greece and Rome, and will destroy England and America." What are the current sources of intoxication indulged in by Americans? Do they all promote the destruction Thoreau predicted?

8. In proposing that some benefactor of humanity will eventually come along to lead people away from eating animals, Thoreau digresses on the need for following one's genius no matter where it may lead. One who does this is a "healthy man." What happens when a dozen people who claim to be following their private genius develop seriously clashing life styles?

9. The basis of Thoreau's moral philosophy is contained in the paragraph which begins "Our whole life is startingly moral." Goodness is for him not acquired through culture but develops in man when he is allowed to follow his natural bent. Do you agree?

10. Thoreau also believes in sexual abstinence. He speaks of the "generative energy" of the body which should not be dissipated. Many advocates of the natural life, however, while agreeing with Thoreau on a number of points such as not eating meat or drinking alcohol, believe that a relatively uninhibited sex life is both natural and good. Was Thoreau secretly a Puritan? Are exponents of free sexual activity simply using nature as an excuse?

11. If Thoreau's "John Farmer," mentioned in the final paragraph, is trapped in *his* work, what can be said for the average urban American of today who lives amid so much noise that he can no longer hear "the notes of the flute"? What hope could you hold out for someone who would like to be closer to nature but has no idea of how to start?

THE PARADOX OF HUMANISM
Joseph Wood Krutch

By the end of the nineteenth century much of the romantic idealism of earlier writers had begun to dwindle. The notion that man was a child of nature, very much at home in the woods and mountains, and destined to master and improve the earth, was replaced with a far more tough-minded view. The new writers, with a stern eye on the Darwinian theory of evolution and other scientific discoveries, began to talk of man not as a *child* of nature, but as just another animal within nature. They pointed out how foolish had been man's ancient dreams of belonging at the top of nature's ladder, when all the while he was a vicious and irrational being. Early in the twentieth century the new science of psychiatry started to make its stir from Vienna, and soon the theories of Freud and others added further proof that people could hardly comprehend and master the earth when they knew nothing really about themselves.

Joseph Wood Krutch's (b. 1893) *The Modern Temper*, from which the following essay is taken, appeared in 1929 to climax a decade of bitterly pessimistic novels, plays, poems, and philosophies. It was also the year when the collapse of the Wall Street stock market seemed to stifle the optimistic dream many had devised in response to Darwin: namely, that the survival of the economically fittest was nature's way of improving the lot of all humanity. It seemed in 1929 that nobody was surviving and that somewhere humanity had taken a terribly wrong turn. But where? "The Paradox of Humanism" attempts to answer that question.

Krutch points out what he believes few people before him had realized: that, despite Darwin and Freud, man is not truly an animal. That is his problem. Man is beginning to discover not his animal nature but *the limitations of his humanness*. In Krutch's view human society has gone too far to save itself. Only the admission that human life is animal life and a reversion to a natural mode of existence can help, but man divorced himself from nature too long ago and now lacks the resources by which to survive.

Rational thought, the arts, all that formerly was called "culture" or "civilization" were founded on the myth of human distinctness and had given man a feeling of pride in his achievements. To create that culture, however, man had to suppress and deny his animal being. He had to institute laws and governments to protect his creations from that animal side of him. His religions tended to stress spirit or soul, making the physical side of man lowly and contemptible. "Noble" and "beautiful" have traditionally come to mean "nonanimal."

But what, asks Krutch, has been the ultimate result of the myth of

Human Worth? Only confusion; only an increasing inability to cope with "the universe of nature" because man has gone in one direction, nature another. In believing himself to be not only the child but the eventual master of nature, man has not regarded himself as an integral part of the whole. He now finds himself in the absurd position of being neither master nor part. He finds himself to be a curious nothing in a vast and complex system which can only destroy him as it does all of its enemies.

The pessimism of this essay is, hopefully, not the whole story. But it bears rereading almost half a century later, especially when we recognize how many of its prophecies have yet to be proved inaccurate.

The Paradox of Humanism

Words which are spelled with a capital letter are peculiarly dangerous to thought. One commonly uses them to designate a complex of ideas which has never been adequately analyzed, and their meaning varies from age to age as well as from person to person. A whole volume might profitably be devoted to trace, for example, the history of the various senses in which the term "Nature" has been employed, and in a chapter of his *Reconstruction in Philosophy* John Dewey has, indeed, sketched the outline of a part of such a volume. He has shown how the eighteenth century habitually employed it in reference to a closed system of logical ideas, and how it referred thereby to a hypothetical order of values which has no connection whatever with the nature which it is the scientist's business to investigate. Dewey might have gone on to inquire by what confusion the contemporaries of Mozart were led to praise as "natural" musical compositions as elaborately formal as his, and by what perversion the same adjective was used to praise the strained artificial romanticism of Kotzebue's lugubrious dramas. But at least he carries the analysis far enough for his own purpose as well for ours, which is merely to illustrate how dangerous it is to use such a word without a most exacting investigation of its content.

In the present instance we are to be concerned with another capitalized word, "Humanism," a word which has undergone similar variations of meaning; which has been used in similarly opposed senses; and which, like "Nature," has been most frequently employed rather because of certain affective connotations than because of any exact meaning. The Renaissance scholars who introduced it did so in order to define a culture which was not theological, and the contrast chiefly implied was a contrast between that which is human and that which is divine. The modern use of the term arose, on the other hand, as a result of the theory of evolution, and it is chiefly employed by those who feel some temperamental repugnance to the nineteenth century's tendency to study man chiefly as a form of animal life. It has managed, moreover, to get itself confused with semireligious protests against the radical tendencies of contemporary society, and so vague has it become that, if we are to talk of humanism and its paradox, we must define our term.

But if "human" and the words formed from it can have an exact meaning, as distinguished from the vague connotation of a complex of ideas and attitudes, that meaning must refer to those qualities, characteristics, and powers which distinguish the human being from the rest of animate nature and which, if they exist, justify us in making a distinction between Man and Nature, even though we are naturalistic enough in our thought to agree that what we really mean is no more than a distinction between man and the rest of nature. It is in that sense that it will be here employed, and the purpose of this chapter is to investigate some of these distinctions and to comment upon the problems which they present to those who are concerned with the potentialities of life. It will arrive at conclusions somewhat at variance with those upon which both the expansive optimistic naturalist and the cautious exponent of dualistic humanism base their respective conceptions of the art of life.

II

First of all we must be careful to give to the beasts their due, for your self-styled humanist has a churlish habit of calling the most characteristic human vices "animal." In particular he is inclined to describe any sexual indulgence of which he does not approve as "bestial," and more especially still to say of a man or woman who makes the pleasures of sense the chief business of life that he is yielding to his "animal nature." But while such a description may serve a useful homiletic purpose, and while it may, since man is by nature proud of his humanity and anxious to distinguish himself from his humbler cousins, sometimes incline him to struggle against tendencies thus cavalierly labeled, it can hardly satisfy the philosopher, who will recognize its injustice.

A century and a half ago man was first described as the only animal who loves all the year around, and in general the distinction will still hold. Not only is it true that the animals rigidly subordinate sex to the function of reproduction, but it is also, according to anthropologists, notoriously true that the more primitive races of men closely resemble animals in this respect. Early superficial observers who watched the rites with which savages celebrate the act of physical union and who noted the elaborate sexual symbolism which runs through certain of their dances leaped to the conclusion that they were obsessed with sexual ideas and labeled them "obscene." But a more intimate investigation of primitive society and the primitive mind has reversed this idea. In comparison with civilized man the savage is, like the animal, what we should be tempted to call singularly sexless. His mind does not turn readily or habitually in that direction; his passions require an extraordinary amount of stimulation before they are aroused; and his "obscene" dances are not the result of fantastic corruption but are, on the contrary, necessary to stimulate in him a sufficient interest in the sexual functions adequately to reproduce his kind. The Don Juan, on the other hand, is characteristically human, and complexly human at that. Neither the animal nor the primitive man could "live for love" in the physical sense, although both, as will be indicated later, can realize more perfectly perhaps than civilized man that selflessness which is sometimes also called love and which is not infrequently spoken of as the highest achievement of the human spirit.

Chastity is not, then, human in the sense in which we have defined the term. To man and to man alone belong both that exaggeration of the sexual impulse which makes it possible, in certain cases, for him to subordinate everything else to it, and also that unfortunate disharmony which leads him, in other cases, to devote his chief attention to maintaining and celebrating his resistance to similar impulses. But chastity, in the sense of an inherent tendency to avoid an absorption in the sexual instinct, is rather animal than human. And if, then, debauchery rather than abstinence is "humanistic" we may proceed to examine certain of the other virtues, and we need not be too much surprised if we find that many are, at best, not part of that which particularly distinguishes man from the rest of nature.

Certainly paternal or maternal love is nowhere more perfectly illustrated than among the animals. A devotion to the welfare of children, a complete absorption in the business of parenthood, and a willingness not only to subordinate all other interests to those of the offspring but, if necessary, to lay down life itself upon the altar of family duty—such devotion, which, in the case of human beings, would be celebrated as an unusual and shining example of the heights to which human nature can on rare occasions rise, is a common occurrence among animals and it is not the occasion of any special wonder. But on the other hand that unwillingness on the part of the parent to subordinate himself entirely to the welfare of his children, that tendency to go on "living one's own life" which certain "humanists" denounce as the result of "naturalistic" literature and thought, is, on the contrary, quite distinctly human. Our kind has, in addition, developed that particular perversion which sometimes leads mothers or fathers selfishly to indulge the luxury of their parental emotions to a harmful degree and to pursue their grown children with a fatal solicitude of which no animal would be capable; but devotion which perfectly fulfills its function is—shall we say—"bestial."

It is hardly necessary to pursue this painful inquiry further, but in general it may be remarked that those virtues whose tendency it is to promote the welfare of the species without regard to the welfare of the individual, and which result in the complete subordination of any real or fancied "self-realization," are conspicuously animal, while the revolt against them is distinctly human. Even the more complex social virtues grow from roots which may be traced in animal nature more readily than the roots of many human vices; and, since it is upon the social virtues that the modern humanist lays greatest stress, it would be more appropriate for him to call himself by some name which would suggest that the fear lying behind his protestations is in reality a fear lest man should become too exclusively "human" and lest, detaching himself too completely from animal tendencies, he should become no longer willing to live in a fashion that would make possible the continuity of society.

Perhaps, on the other hand, the inclusive term "individualism" is the one which will best describe the attitude toward living which is most characteristically human. The animal, absorbed as he is in the business of arranging for the survival of himself and his kind, seems far less capable than man of distinguishing between himself and his race. We need not naïvely attribute to him any philosophy in order to explain his behavior, but it is evident that he *acts* as though he had arrived at that attitude which is accounted by some exponents of social ethics as the ultimate human ideal, and which consists in an identification with society so close as to make meaningless any distinction between private and public good. He does not ask what he gets out of life, nor why he should sacrifice himself in the laborious business of continuing it. The lair or the nest is prepared, and the young are born. They are nourished, defended, given such education as they need, and then, when the time comes, the parents die quietly, quite as though they were as completely aware as Mr. Shaw's Ancients that the important thing is, not that any individual should have arrived at any "fulfillment" of his own, but that life should go on. Yet, though something of this kind has been often enough described as the highest human virtue, the human being seems incapable of consciously achieving what the animal possesses as part of his natural endowment.

Doubtless the more primitive races come nearest to it, and in civilized communities it is the simplest people who, at least according to the literature of wholesome sentiment, most conspicuously exhibit this willingness to refrain from any demand that life should justify itself in their own persons by being worthwhile to them as individuals, and who are therefore most perfect in the social virtues. But even among those who acquiesce most patiently in the burdens of life there are usually moments of analysis and rebellion. "Quiet desperation," that famous phrase which Thoreau used to describe the mood of the average man, is the result of an impotent protest against the realization that he is playing the animal's part without being blessed with the animal's unconscious acquiescence; and the more highly developed the reflective powers of the individual become, the more likely is that quiet desperation to become an active rebellion which expresses itself in self-regarding vices.

The fact that the belief in immortality is practically coextensive with the human race does not, unfortunately, prove that the belief is well founded, but it does prove that the desire for a life beyond this life is universal, and that, in turn, may be used to show that individualism is one of the most fundamental human traits, since the desire for immortality is an expression of the human protest against the scheme of nature which takes so little account of man and his demands. When first he dimly perceives that his chief function is merely to see that others like himself shall carry life on after he has had his busy and futile hour of consciousness, he, as an individual, revolts against the natural order, and in imagination he projects himself forward into another existence in which that consciousness, so he assures himself, shall continue to exist. He is no longer willing, as the animal is, to accept the fate which makes him only a part of something larger than himself, and thus religion, in so far as it is essentially a belief in immortality, is merely the first stage in the process by which man detaches himself from Nature, asserts the importance of himself as an individual, and proposes to himself ends and values which do not exist for her. . . .

III

To those who study her, this Nature reveals herself as extraordinarily fertile and ingenious in devising *means*, but she has no *ends* which the human mind has been able to discover or comprehend. Perhaps, indeed, the very conception of an end or ultimate purpose is exclusively human; but at least it must be said that the most characteristically human effort is that to transform a means into an end, and that it is such an effort which explains the Don Juan, as well as the more complex forms assumed by that curiously modified animal which is described as human. The artist and the philosopher have been generally recognized as representing the most highly developed type of that intelligence which we admire as something beyond mere animal instinct or animal cunning, but the concern of both is not with the *means* of Nature but with the *ends* of man. By thought the philosopher attempts to discover what these may be, and the artist, who is thus closely parallel to the Don Juan, attempts to achieve them by arresting the attention upon certain moments in life and proclaiming that it is for them as ends in themselves that life exists.

Yet the plain man has always, and not without reason, distrusted the philosopher and the artist. Observation has taught him that the latter, especially, is likely to be too ferociously intent upon his own ends to be other than a bad father and an unreliable citizen; and more obscurely he realizes that, even when this cannot be specifically charged, both are too detached from animal impulses to carry on the business of survival and propagation with that single-minded intensity which has populated every cranny of the earth. Nor can the philosopher or the artist himself fail to recognize the justice of this distrust. At one moment he might be inclined to suppose the evolution of humanity to be in his direction, but at the next he is compelled to realize that a world of philosophers and artists is unthinkable. The foundations of the society in which he exists were built up and are sustained by people who were active in a way in which he can never be. He is not, in the most fundamental or necessary sense, useful or productive; he is parasitic upon a society which depends upon those endowed with an unquestioning animal vigor, and without them he could not exist. A decadent society, he realizes, is merely one in which too large a proportion of the population is concerned with "ends" and with self-realization. While some pursue pleasure and end in debauchery, the others create works of art or lose themselves in speculation concerning the elusive *summum bonum*, but too few are left to sustain the natural substructure with that energy which is drawn from instinct alone. While the bush blossoms all too profusely, the roots die away, and before long the whole organism is dead. And thus the artist-philosopher, who, correctly enough, considers himself as the most exclusively human of human beings, is left in a dilemma, for he is compelled to recognize humanism as the ultimate enemy of those natural impulses which have made the human animal possible.

Sensibility and intelligence arose in the animal in order to serve animal purposes, for through the first it was able to distinguish those things which favor the survival of it and its race and through the second it was able to go about in a more efficient manner to secure them. Both were, like all things in nature, merely means toward the achievement of that humanly incomprehensible end, mere survival; but the philosopher-artist has detached both from their natural places as mere devices, and in attempting to make each an end in itself he has discovered that when they are so detached they are capable of becoming impediments to the attainment of the superhuman aims they were developed to promote. When sensibility has been detached from its animal setting it may, in its crudest form, become the eroto-mania of the Don Juan, or, in a more exalted form, it may develop into a quest for that self-justifying Beauty which is humanly valuable but biologically useless and which it is the artist's chief effort to capture; when intelligence is detached, it not only tends to paralyze natural impulse by criticizing natural aims but develops certain intellectual virtues which are biologic vices. We are, for example, inclined to regard skepticism, irony, and above all the power of dispassionate analysis as the marks of the most distinctly human intelligence. We admire the man whose reason is capable of more than scheming, whose logic is not the mere rationalization of his desires, and who can follow through an argument to its conclusion even though that conclusion is not one favorable to himself, his party, his country, or his species. But intelligence as detached as this is a vital liability. It puts the man or the race which possesses it at a disadvantage in dealing with those whose intelligence faithfully serves their purpose by enabling them to scheme for their ends and to justify to themselves their desires. Such is the animal function of intelligence, and whenever it develops beyond this it is useful for contemplation and it has a beauty of its own, but it is only humanly valuable and it inhibits rather than aids that effective action in the pursuit of natural ends which was the original function of mind.

And incidentally it may be remarked that the dilemma here indicated is the largest aspect of the one which in a more immediately insistent way pins between its horns every nation which has developed a national mind capable of detachment. Thanks to this mind, the nation is compelled to criticize that naïve patriotism which leads every race to regard itself as evidently superior to every other; it hesitates to embark upon a career of imperialism and to subject the surrounding people to its dominion because it has passed beyond that stage of invigorating delusion which could make it fancy itself master by right of an inherent superiority; and it sees both sides. And yet it must purchase this intellectual and moral superiority at the price of a gradual decline, and it is well that it should do so in a full consciousness of the price. One after another the great nations of history have founded upon aggression the civilization which then supported for a time, but for a time only, great periods of human culture which flourished at their height just as the substructure crumbled. Animals made men possible and conquerors prepared the way for poets and philosophers, but neither poet nor philosopher can survive long after he has parted company with his progenitor and opponent.

Nor need we be surprised to see races enfeebled by civilization as though by disease, for the distinction between the vices and the virtues of the complexly organized man is a human, not a natural, distinction, and the two develop together as he humanizes himself. That detachment of mind from its function which makes philosophy possible and which encourages dispassionate analysis is exactly parallel to the detachment of the sexual functions from their purposes which results in the cult of the senses. Thought for thought's sake is a kind of perversion whose essential character is not changed because it happens to illustrate the fact that human virtues may be biologic vices, and there is no reason to suppose that from a strictly biological standpoint one detachment is not as bad as the other. Civilizations die from philosophical calm, irony, and the sense of fair play quite as surely as they die of debauchery....

The great mind and the great culture are alike poised over an abyss and are in perpetual danger of tumbling headlong. Civilization has been called a dance, but the feet of the dancers do not rest upon terra firma. It is danced upon a tight rope that sways in the breeze. The nerves and muscles of the performers are tense. They wave reckless defiance to the force of gravity, but they are in truth ill equipped for the airy stunt. Their feet are designed to rest upon the earth; it is even at the expense of a certain strain upon their bodies that they walk upright rather than upon all fours, and their balance is far from sure.

The ant who crawls unnoticed in the grass below is much older than they, and in the eyes of Nature he has made a much greater success in life. Long before they felt the first stirrings of proud superiority he was fixed in wise habits that have never varied. For thousands of years his frozen perfection has endured and, if he has no art and no philosophy, he is perfect in social virtue. He has merged his own interests completely with those of his kind, and he makes no demands for himself which will interfere with the prosperity of the colony which he inhabits.

His industry and his foresight have always been admired, but only patient observation has revealed how much more complex his virtues are. Not only does he perform without question the part assigned him in the division of labor, but he has even achieved a control over the processes of reproduction which enables him to see to it that just the right number of each type of citizen shall be born; and, far from allowing himself to be disturbed by the distractions of love, he has consented, in the interests of efficiency, to remain sexless, while certain specialists are endowed with powers of reproduction. He is not primitive or simple, but he has let Nature have her way with him and she has rewarded him with a peaceful security which her more rebellious children can never hope to obtain.

But when a man looks at an ant he realizes the meaning of his humanity. If he happens to be one of those whose thought has concerned itself much with sociology he may be struck by the fact that the anthill represents something very close to that communistic Utopia generally evolved by the imagination which busies itself with picturing an ideal society, and yet the contemplation of this realized and eternal perfection strikes a chill to his heart, because it seems to have no meaning or value and because he perceives that, so far as he is concerned, Nature's masterpiece might be destroyed without causing him to feel that anything valuable had passed away.

This perfected society is, that is to say, utterly devoid of human values, and its perfection is made possible by that very fact. It owes both its stability and its efficient harmony to the absence of any tendency on the part of individuals either to question the value of existence or to demand anything for themselves. Students of its evolution tell us that the automatic and yet cunning elaborateness of the life-habits which it reveals are explainable only on the theory that insects were once more variable, perhaps we can say more "intelligent," than they are now, but that, as perfection of adjustment was reached, habit became all-sufficient, and hence the biologically useless consciousness faded away until they are probably now not aware of their actions in any fashion analogous to the awareness of the mammals who are in certain respects so much less perfect than they.

And yet who, however weary he may be of human instability and discontent and violence, would exchange his state for that of the ant? However much he may admire the social virtues and however much he may be repelled by the selfish disorder of modern individualistic society, he must realize that whatever gives to life the qualities which make him cling to it resides somewhere in that region whence spring the protests which make the regularity and peace of the anthill impossible for man. Complete non-being seems to him scarcely less ghastly than the automatic existence which its citizens lead, and so it is ultimately to the biologic vices of the human being that he clings.

It is through these latter that he suffers, and through them that he, as an animal, fails. They are the source of the *taedium vitae* which oppresses him when he realizes that he is leading a purely natural life and accomplishing only natural aims; they inspire him also to those rebellions which are impotent because they bring him face to face with the limitations he cannot transcend; and they exact as the penalty of indulgence the ills of mind or flesh which oppress the wearied brain of the thinker or the exhausted body of the debauchee. Yet they constitute his humanity, and it is only as a human being that he cares to live. . . .

The antithesis between human and natural ends is thus ultimately irreconcilable, and the most that man can hope for is a recurrent defiance recurrently subdued. He can deviate so far but no further from the animal norm. He can make himself into an artist or a philosopher, but there are limits set both to the perfection of those types and to the extent to which the bulk of any population can be allowed to approach either, for individuals and races alike fall victim to their humanity. In the search for human values they first lose interest in those natural virtues which serve to keep the structure of the anthill sound; and then when they discover that, even for them as individuals, life has no purpose which their intellects can accept, even they perish of a *taedium vitae* and leave the world to simpler peoples who have still some distance to go before they reach the end of the tether which attaches them to nature. . . .

Nor can it be said that to understand this paradox of humanism helps us in any way to solve it. The analysis which we perform is, indeed, itself an example of one of those exercises of the mind which is perverse because it does not serve as a means toward a natural end, and when we have admitted that the human ideal is one which the human animal cannot even approach without tending to destroy himself as he does so, we have, by that very admission, both diminished our biological fitness and desolated our human feelings. Hence it is that many a man with trained mind, developed sensibilities, and even as much good will toward society as can be expected of a creature who has lost the animal's innate talent for caring more for his race than for himself, stands paralyzed in the midst of a world that has learned so many things which do not help it toward any ultimate solution of its problems but which tend, on the contrary, rather to make him suspect that they are insoluble. These men cannot strive with a missionary zeal for the development and spread of pure science, philosophy, and art because they have come to believe that these things are neither ultimately satisfying nor conducive to a vigorous national life, but neither can they cast their lot with the "plain man," the "sturdy citizen," or the Spartan patriot, because it is the detachment of which these are enemies that gives human life whatever of even doubtful value it seems to the pure humanist to have. To the latter it appears that there is no choice to be made except that between an antlike stability and an eternal recurrence which condemns humanity to a recurrent death at the top, to be followed once more by a fresh growth from the roots.

And, difficult as it seems to him to choose between such unsatis-factory alternatives, he is still further perplexed by an uneasy sense that the decision is one which the moment makes particularly pressing. Something in the state of his own soul as well as in the state of the world about him warns him that he is living in one of those periods which has about reached the limits set by Nature. He has already envisaged the possibility of seeing civilization destroy itself in a gigantic war, and that irony directed against himself which is one of the signs of the extent to which he has detached himself from the animal has even enabled him to feel some amusement at the thought of a race which should, by way of achieving the crowning triumph of its mechanical ingenuity, blow itself to bits. But even if this possi-bility should be avoided, the impasse to which his thought has led him seems capable of leading the society of which he is a part to an end as certain even though less spectacular, since it is already too completely human in both its virtues and its vices to live either com-fortably or safely in the universe of nature.

RESPONSES: Questions for Writing and Discussion

1. Section I defines "Humanism" and thus sets up the context within which we are to understand the points made in the essay concerning the futility of man's trying to be something on his own, apart from nature. Today "Humanism" appears to have shifted its meaning, at least as many now use it, to include a closer rapport with nature. In your opinion, does the author's definition still serve as a basis for most human institutions? Or, to put the matter another way: Can you give an example of an institution that is founded on the belief that man is part of nature?

2. Section II observes that chastity and affection for offspring are rather more animalistic than human traits. What is the author's reason for making so shocking a statement? Can you agree with it?

3. How does the author (again in section II) view the human belief in immortality and the function of religion? They fit into his general argument, but how do you feel about this aspect of his theory? Do you find the argument a complete one? Has he left any factors out of consideration?

4. At the beginning of section III the author notes that nature is filled with *means* but has no *ends*. That is, whatever purpose there may appear to be in the way nature operates, has been imposed upon nature by the human mind. The author implies that the need for purpose is a human, not a natural, instinct, and, like everything else about man, it is futile. Do you agree? Would *you* create a purposeful existence for yourself if you knew in advance that it might come to

nothing in the long run, affect few people, make no contributions to a better world, and so on?

5. What does Krutch have to say about poets and philosophers in section III? Are they closer to or any further away from nature than the majority of people? What is being said here about "culture"?

6. Section III concludes with a dynamic statement concerning what it is that causes human civilizations to die. The author points to rational analysis and "the sense of fair play" (meaning an emphasis on law and order, international negotiations in the interest of peace, and so forth) as being some of the *causes* of decay, rather than attempts to prevent it. Is this so? Or is human rationality the only possible hope?

7. Explain the comparison Krutch makes in section IV between an anthill and human society. If it is true that the anthill is a "perfected society," would you prefer to be an ant? If so, why? If you would prefer to stay human, indicate the reason.

8. Though this essay was written in 1929, it looks as if Krutch was being clairvoyant when he asserted that man "stands paralyzed in the midst of a world that has learned so many things which do not help it toward any ultimate solution of its problems. . . ." Mention a current problem. Indicate why you think it hasn't been solved. Does the author's statement apply in this instance?

9. Another prophecy made at the conclusion of the essay is that the human race "should, by way of achieving the crowning triumph of its mechanical ingenuity, blow itself to bits." Are we continuing along this downhill path? Have we taken a turn for the better?

BLACK ELK SPEAKS
John G. Neihardt

The concept of civilization is not limited to the desire to build great cities, governments, and social systems; to develop proud and enduring cultures. In the history of the West it has also included the "benign" need to conquer natural man, to impose the benefits of civilization, even where these have been unsolicited. Thus did the Roman Empire overflow its boundaries in the interest of spreading its light to all the dark corners of the globe. Thus did the medieval Christian empire dedicate itself with missionary zeal to the subjugation of the heathen.

American folklore has glorified the "winning of the West" as the triumph of civilized man over the uncivilized, ferocious, and undeserving red man. Indians, the rampaging, whooping braves, were always riding violently out of the hills to attack the innocent wagon trains, seize their hostages, and subject them to cruel torture back in the primitive villages. Hollywood did more than its share. There was, for example, *They Died with Their Boots On*, a 1940 vintage epic starring Errol Flynn as a noble, gallant, and divinely courageous General Custer, brought to inglorious defeat by the appropriately named Crazy Horse and his band of vicious savages. Of course, the Indian was a romanticized figure as well. Literature is filled with noble savages like James Fenimore Cooper's Ching-ach-gook, but seldom is the poetic and sensitive "child of the forest" drawn without a degree of paternal condescension. On rare occasions popular books and films showed the Indian as a victim of white territory hunting, but such oppression was often viewed as a necessary if tragic consequence of cultural expansion.

An early attempt to show the red man in a fairer light was *Black Elk Speaks* (1932) by **John G. Neihardt (b. 1881)**, who was born into a pioneer family and has lived all his life in Kansas and Nebraska, much of the time close to Indian reservations. Neihardt views the Indian—or natural man—as being in many respects more decent and noble, more representative of Human Worth than the "civilized" man who has traditionally prided himself on his ultimate and glorious subjugation of the savage.

In the portion of the book included here, Black Elk, an old priest of the Oglala Sioux, describes the events leading up to the Indian massacre at Wounded Knee in the Black Hills. Long considered one of the white man's greatest victories, the battle is shown to be a carnage of unbelievable brutality, an unrelenting display of inhumanity, even sadism. In contrast are the old man's forgiving nature and his unwillingness to cry out in angry hatred.

Earlier in the book the reader has learned that, during the 1880's, rumor spread throughout the Dakotas that a Messiah was coming to save the red man. One day Black Elk had a vision, and voices from the "Other World" assured him the rumor was true. There had indeed arrived a Messiah whom "The Great Spirit had told him was to save the Indian peoples and make the Wasichus disappear and bring back all the bison and the people who were dead and . . . there would be a new earth."

But the promise was never fulfilled. Before the massacre at Wounded Knee there had been a year of terrible drought and famine during which the Wasichus (white men) "had slaughtered all the bisons and shut us up in pens." With the coming of the snows and bitter cold, starving Sioux came down from the hills, seeking to band together and protect themselves as best they could. It is then, according to Black Elk, that the white soldiers heard about the "massing" and, not comprehending the true, desolate state of the red people, decided to make an all-out effort to conquer them once and for all.

Black Elk Speaks

The Butchering at Wounded Knee

That evening before it happened, I went in to Pine Ridge and heard these things, and while I was there, soldiers started for where the Big Foots were. These made about five hundred soldiers that were there next morning. When I saw them starting I felt that something terrible was going to happen. That night I could hardly sleep at all. I walked around most of the night.

In the morning I went out after my horses, and while I was out I heard shooting off toward the east, and I knew from the sound that it must be wagon-guns (cannon) going off. The sounds went right through my body, and I felt that something terrible would happen.

When I reached camp with the horses, a man rode up to me and said: "Hey-hey-hey! The people that are coming are fired on! I know it!"

I saddled up my buckskin and put on my sacred shirt. It was one I had made to be worn by no one but myself. It had a spotted eagle outstretched on the back of it, and the daybreak star was on the left shoulder, because when facing south that shoulder is toward the east. Across the breast, from the left shoulder to the right hip, was the flaming rainbow, and there was another rainbow around the neck, like a necklace, with a star at the bottom. At each shoulder, elbow, and wrist was an eagle feather; and over the whole shirt were red streaks of lightning. You will see that this was from my great vision, and you will know how it protected me that day.

I painted my face all red, and in my hair I put one eagle feather for the One Above.

It did not take me long to get ready, for I could still hear the shooting over there.

I started out alone on the old road that ran across the hills to Wounded Knee. I had no gun. I carried only the sacred bow of the west that I had seen in my great vision. I had gone only a little way when a band of young men came galloping after me. The first two who came up were Loves War and Iron Wasichu. I asked what they were going to do, and they said they were just going to see where the shooting was. Then others were coming up, and some older men.

We rode fast, and there were about twenty of us now. The

Reprinted from *Black Elk Speaks* by John G. Neihardt by permission of University of Nebraska Press. Copyright 1932, 1959 by John G. Neihardt. Copyright © 1961 by the University of Nebraska Press.

shooting was getting louder. A horseback from over there came galloping very fast toward us, and he said: "Hey-hey-hey! They have murdered them!" Then he whipped his horse and rode away faster toward Pine Ridge.

In a little while we had come to the top of the ridge where, looking to the east, you can see for the first time the monument and the burying ground on the little hill where the church is. That is where the terrible thing started. Just south of the burying ground on the little hill a deep dry gulch runs about east and west, very crooked, and it rises westward to nearly the top of the ridge where we were. It had no name, but the Wasichus sometimes call it Battle Creek now. We stopped on the ridge not far from the head of the dry gulch. Wagon guns were still going off over there on the little hill, and they were going off again where they hit along the gulch. There was much shooting down yonder, and there were many cries, and we could see cavalrymen scattered over the hills ahead of us. Cavalrymen were riding along the gulch and shooting into it, where the women and children were running away and trying to hide in the gullies and the stunted pines.

A little way ahead of us, just below the head of the dry gulch, there were some women and children who were huddled under a clay bank, and some cavalrymen were there pointing guns at them.

We stopped back behind the ridge, and I said to the others: "Take courage. These are our relatives. We will try to get them back." Then we all sang a song which went like this:

"A thunder being nation I am, I have said.
A thunder being nation I am, I have said.
You shall live.
You shall live.
You shall live.
You shall live."

Then I rode over the ridge and the others after me, and we were crying: "Take courage! It is time to fight!" The soldiers who were guarding our relatives shot at us and then ran away fast, and some more cavalrymen on the other side of the gulch did too. We got our relatives and sent them across the ridge to the northwest where they would be safe.

I had no gun, and when we were charging, I just held the sacred bow out in front of me with my right hand. The bullets did not hit us at all.

We found a little baby lying all alone near the head of the gulch. I could not pick her up just then, but I got her later and some of my people adopted her. I just wrapped her up tighter in a shawl that was around her and left her there. It was a safe place, and I had other work to do.

The soldiers had run eastward over the hills where there were some more soldiers, and they were off their horses and lying down. I told the others to stay back, and I charged upon them holding the sacred bow out toward them with my right hand. They all shot at me, and I could hear bullets all around me, but I ran my horse right close to them, and then swung around. Some soldiers across the gulch began shooting at me too, but I got back to the others and was not hurt at all.

By now many other Lakotas, who had heard the shooting, were coming up from Pine Ridge, and we all charged on the soldiers. They ran eastward toward where the trouble began. We followed down along the dry gulch, and what we saw was terrible. Dead and wounded women and children and little babies were scattered all along there where they had been trying to run away. The soldiers had followed along the gulch, as they ran, and murdered them in there. Sometimes they were in heaps because they had huddled together, and some were scattered all along. Sometimes bunches of them had been killed and torn to pieces where the wagon guns hit them. I saw a little baby trying to suck its mother, but she was bloody and dead.

There were two little boys at one place in this gulch. They had guns and they had been killing soldiers all by themselves. We could see the soldiers they had killed. The boys were all alone there, and they were not hurt. These were very brave little boys.

When we drove the soldiers back, they dug themselves in, and we were not enough people to drive them out from there. In the evening they marched off up Wounded Knee Creek, and then we saw all that they had done there.

Men and women and children were heaped and scattered all over the flat at the bottom of the little hill where the soldiers had their wagon-guns, and westward up the dry gulch all the way to the high ridge, the dead women and children and babies were scattered.

When I saw this I wished that I had died too, but I was not sorry for the women and children. It was better for them to be happy in the other world, and I wanted to be there too. But before I went there I wanted to have revenge. I thought there might be a day, and we should have revenge.

After the soldiers marched away, I heard from my friend, Dog Chief, how the trouble started, and he was right there by Yellow Bird when it happened. This is the way it was:

In the morning the soldiers began to take all the guns away from the Big Foots, who were camped in the flat below the little hill where the monument and burying ground are now. The people had stacked most of their guns, and even their knives, by the tepee where Big Foot was lying sick. Soldiers were on the little hill and all around, and there were soldiers across the dry gulch to the south and over east along Wounded Knee Creek too. The people were nearly surrounded, and the wagon-guns were pointing at them.

Some had not yet given up their guns, and so the soldiers were searching all the tepees, throwing things around and poking into everything. There was a man called Yellow Bird, and he and another man were standing in front of the tepee where Big Foot was lying sick. They had white sheets around and over them, with eyeholes to look through, and they had guns under these. An officer came to search them. He took the other man's gun, and then started to take Yellow Bird's. But Yellow Bird would not let go. He wrestled with the officer, and while they were wrestling, the gun went off and killed the officer. Wasichus and some others have said he meant to do this, but Dog Chief was standing right there, and he told me it was not so. As soon as the gun went off, Dog Chief told me, an officer shot and killed Big Foot who was lying sick inside the tepee.

Then suddenly nobody knew what was happening, except that the soldiers were all shooting and the wagon-guns began going off right in among the people.

Many were shot down right there. The women and children ran into the gulch and up west, dropping all the time, for the soldiers shot them as they ran. There were only about a hundred warriors and there were nearly five hundred soldiers. The warriors rushed to where they had piled their guns and knives. They fought soldiers with only their hands until they got their guns.

Dog Chief saw Yellow Bird run into a tepee with his gun, and from there he killed soldiers until the tepee caught fire. Then he died full of bullets.

It was a good winter day when all this happened. The sun was shining. But after the soldiers marched away from their dirty work, a heavy snow began to fall. The wind came up in the night. There was a big blizzard, and it grew very cold. The snow drifted deep in the crooked gulch, and it was one long grave of butchered women and children and babies, who had never done any harm and were only trying to run away.

The End of the Dream

After the soldiers marched away, Red Crow and I started back toward Pine Ridge together, and I took the little baby that I told you about. Red Crow had one too.

We were going back to Pine Ridge, because we thought there was peace back home; but it was not so. While we were gone, there was a fight around the Agency, and our people had all gone away. They had gone away so fast that they left all the tepees standing.

It was nearly dark when we passed north of Pine Ridge where the hospital is now, and some soldiers shot at us, but did not hit us. We rode into the camp, and it was all empty. We were very hungry because we had not eaten anything since early morning, so we peeped into the tepees until we saw where there was a pot with papa (dried meat) cooked in it. We sat down in there and began to eat. While we were doing this, the soldiers shot at the tepee, and a bullet struck right between Red Crow and me. It threw dust in the soup, but we kept right on eating until we had our fill. Then we took the babies and got on our horses and rode away. If that bullet had only killed me, then I could have died with papa in my mouth.

The people had fled down Clay Creek, and we followed their trail. It was dark now, and late in the night we came to where they were camped without any tepees. They were just sitting by little fires, and the snow was beginning to blow. We rode in among them and I heard my mother's voice. She was singing a death song for me, because she felt sure I had died over there. She was so glad to see me that she cried and cried.

Women who had milk fed the little babies that Red Crow and I brought with us.

I think nobody but the little children slept any that night. The snow blew and we had no tepees.

When it was getting light, a war party went out and I went along; but this time I took a gun with me. When I started out the day before to Wounded Knee, I took only my sacred bow, which was not made to shoot with; because I was a little in doubt about the Wanekia religion at that time, and I did not really want to kill anybody because of it.

But I did not feel like that any more. After what I had seen over there, I wanted revenge; I wanted to kill.

We crossed White Clay Creek and followed it up, keeping on the west side. Soon we could hear many guns going off. So we struck west, following a ridge to where the fight was. It was close to the Mission, and there are many bullets in the Mission yet.

From this ridge we could see that the Lakotas were on both sides of the creek and were shooting at soldiers who were coming down the creek. As we looked down, we saw a little ravine, and across this was a big hill. We crossed and rode up the hillside.

They were fighting right there, and a Lakota cried to me: "Black

Elk, this is the kind of a day in which to do something great!" I answered: "How!"[1]

Then I got off my horse and rubbed earth on myself, to show the Powers that I was nothing without their help. Then I took my rifle, got on my horse and galloped up to the top of the hill. Right below me the soldiers were shooting, and my people called out to me not to go down there; that there were some good shots among the soldiers and I should get killed for nothing.

But I remembered my great vision, the part where the geese of the north appeared. I depended upon their power. Stretching out my arms with my gun in the right hand, like a goose soaring when it flies low to turn in a change of weather, I made the sound the geese make—br-r-r-p, br-r-r-p, br-r-r-p; and, doing this, I charged. The soldiers saw, and began shooting fast at me. I kept right on with my buckskin running, shot in their faces when I was near, then swung wide and rode back up the hill.

All this time the bullets were buzzing around me and I was not touched. I was not even afraid. It was like being in a dream about shooting. But just as I had reached the very top of the hill, suddenly it was like waking up, and I was afraid. I dropped my arms and quit making the goose cry. Just as I did this, I felt something strike my belt as though some one had hit me there with the back of an ax. I nearly fell out of my saddle, but I managed to hold on, and rode over the hill.

An old man by the name of Protector was there, and he ran up and held me, for now I was falling off my horse. I will show you where the bullet struck me sidewise across the belly here (showing a long deep scar on the abdomen). My insides were coming out. Protector tore up a blanket in strips and bound it around me so that my insides would stay in. By now I was crazy to kill, and I said to Protector: "Help me on my horse! Let me go over there. It is a good day to die, so I will go over there!" But Protector said: "No, young nephew! You must not die to-day. That would be foolish. Your people need you. There may be a better day to die." He lifted me into my saddle and led my horse away down hill. Then I began to feel very sick.

By now it looked as though the soldiers would be wiped out, and the Lakotas were fighting harder; but I heard that, after I left, the black Wasichu soldiers came, and the Lakotas had to retreat.

There were many of our children in the Mission, and the sisters and priests were taking care of them. I heard there were sisters and priests right in the battle helping wounded people and praying.

---

[1] Signifying assent.

There was a man by the name of Little Soldier who took charge of me and brought me to where our people were camped. While we were over at the Mission Fight, they had fled to the O-ona-gazhee[2] and were camped on top of it where the women and children would be safe from soldiers. Old Hollow Horn was there. He was a very powerful bear medicine man, and he came over to heal my wound. In three days I could walk, but I kept a piece of blanket tied around my belly.

It was now nearly the middle of the Moon of Frost in the Tepee (January). We heard that soldiers were on Smoky Earth River and were coming to attack us in the O-ona-gazhee. They were near Black Feather's place. So a party of about sixty of us started on the war-path to find them. My mother tried to keep me at home, because, although I could walk and ride a horse, my wound was not all healed yet. But I would not stay; for, after what I had seen at Wounded Knee, I wanted a chance to kill soldiers.

We rode down Grass Creek to Smoky Earth, and crossed, riding down stream. Soon from the top of a little hill we saw wagons and cavalry guarding them. The soldiers were making a corral of their wagons and getting ready to fight. We got off our horses and went behind some hills to a little knoll, where we crept up to look at the camp. Some soldiers were bringing harnessed horses down to a little creek to water, and I said to the others: "If you will stay here and shoot at the soldiers, I will charge over there and get some good horses." They knew of my power, so they did this, and I charged on my buckskin while the others kept shooting. I got seven of the horses; but when I started back with these, all the soldiers saw me and began shooting. They killed two of my horses, but I brought five back safe and was not hit. When I was out of range, I caught up a fine bald-faced bay and turned my buckskin loose. Then I drove the others back to our party.

By now more cavalry were coming up the river, a big bunch of them, and there was some hard fighting for a while, because there were not enough of us. We were fighting and retreating, and all at once I saw Red Willow on foot running. He called to me: "Cousin, my horse is killed!" So I caught up a soldier's horse that was dragging a rope and brought it to Red Willow while the soldiers were shooting fast at me. Just then, for a little while, I was a wanekia[3] myself. In this fight Long Bear and another man, whose name I have forgotten, were badly wounded; but we saved them and carried them along with

---

[2] Sheltering place, an elevated plateau in the Badlands, with precipitous sides, and inaccessible save by one narrow neck of land easily defended.

[3] A "make-live," savior.

us. The soldiers did not follow us far into the Badlands, and when it was night we rode back with our wounded to die O-ona-gazhee.

We wanted a much bigger war-party so that we could meet the soldiers and get revenge. But this was hard, because the people were not all of the same mind, and they were hungry and cold. We had a meeting there, and were all ready to go out with more warriors, when Afraid-of-His-Horses came over from Pine Ridge to make peace with Red Cloud, who was with us there.

Our party wanted to go out and fight anyway, but Red Cloud made a speech to us something like this. "Brothers, this is a very hard winter. The women and children are starving and freezing. If this were summer, I would say to keep on fighting to the end. But we cannot do this. We must think of the women and children and that it is very bad for them. So we must make peace, and I will see that nobody is hurt by the soldiers."

The people agreed to this, for it was true. So we broke camp next day and went down from the O-ona-gazhee to Pine Ridge, and many, many Lakotas were already there. Also, there were many, many soldiers. They stood in two lines with their guns held in front of them as we went through to where we camped.

And so it was all over.

I did not know then how much was ended. When I look back now from this high hill of my old age, I can still see the butchered women and children lying heaped and scattered all along the crooked gulch as plain as when I saw them with eyes still young. And I can see that something else died there in the bloody mud, and was buried in the blizzard. A people's dream died there. It was a beautiful dream.

And I, to whom so great a vision was given in my youth,—you see me now a pitiful old man who has done nothing, for the nation's hoop is broken and scattered. There is no center any longer, and the sacred tree is dead.

Author's Postscript

After the conclusion of the narrative, Black Elk and our party were sitting at the north edge of Cuny Table, looking off across the Badlands ("the beauty and the strangeness of the earth," as the old man expressed it). Pointing at Harney Peak that loomed black above the far sky-rim, Black Elk said: "There, when I was young, the spirits took me in my vision to the center of the earth and showed me all the good things in the sacred hoop of the world. I wish I could stand up there in the flesh before I die, for there is something I want to say to the Six Grandfathers."

So the trip to Harney Peak was arranged, and a few days later we were there. On the way up to the summit, Black Elk remarked to his son, Ben: "Something should happen to-day. If I have any power left, the thunder beings of the west should hear me when I send a voice, and there should be at least a little thunder and a little rain." What happened is, of course, related to Wasichu readers as being merely a more or less striking coincidence. It was a bright and cloudless day, and after we had reached the summit the sky was perfectly clear. It was a season of drouth, one of the worst in the memory of the old men. The sky remained clear until about the conclusion of the ceremony.

"Right over there," said Black Elk, indicating a point of rock, "is where I stood in my vision, but the hoop of the world about me was different, for what I saw was in the spirit."

Having dressed and painted himself as he was in his great vision, he faced the west, holding the sacred pipe before him in his right hand. Then he sent forth a voice; and a thin, pathetic voice it seemed in that vast space around us:

"Hey-a-a-hey! Hey-a-a-hey! Hey-a-a-hey! Hey-a-a-hey! Grandfather, Great Spirit, once more behold me on earth and lean to hear my feeble voice. You lived first, and you are older than all need, older than all prayer. All things belong to you—the two-leggeds, the four-leggeds, the wings of the air and all green things that live. You have set the powers of the four quarters to cross each other. The good road and the road of difficulties you have made to cross; and where they cross, the place is holy. Day in and day out, forever, you are the life of things.

"Therefore I am sending a voice, Great Spirit, my Grandfather, forgetting nothing you have made, the stars of the universe and the grasses of the earth.

"You have said to me, when I was still young and could hope, that in difficulty I should send a voice four times, once for each quarter of the earth, and you would hear me.

"To-day I send a voice for a people in despair.

"You have given me a sacred pipe, and through this I should make my offering. You see it now.

"From the west, you have given me the cup of living water and the sacred bow, the power to make live and to destroy. You have given me a sacred wind and the herb from where the white giant lives—the cleansing power and the healing. The daybreak star and the pipe, you have given from the east; and from the south, the nation's sacred hoop and the tree that was to bloom. To the center of the world you have taken me and showed the goodness and the beauty and the strangeness of the greening earth, the only mother—and there the spirit shapes of things, as they should be, you have shown to me and I have seen. At the center of this sacred hoop you have said that I should make the tree to bloom.

"With tears running, O Great Spirit, Great Spirit, my Grandfather —with running tears I must say now that the tree has never bloomed. A pitiful old man, you see me here, and I have fallen away and have done nothing. Here at the center of the world, where you took me when I was young and taught me; here, old, I stand, and the tree is withered, Grandfather, my Grandfather!

"Again, and maybe the last time on this earth, I recall the great vision you sent me. It may be that some little root of the sacred tree still lives. Nourish it then, that it may leaf and bloom and fill with singing birds. Hear me, not for myself, but for my people; I am old. Hear me that they may once more go back into the sacred hoop and find the good red road, the shielding tree!"

We who listened now noted that thin clouds had gathered about us. A scant chill rain began to fall and there was low, muttering thunder without lightning. With tears running down his cheeks, the old man raised his voice to a thin high wail, and chanted: "In sorrow I am sending a feeble voice, O Six Powers of the World. Hear me in my sorrow, for I may never call again. O make my people live!"

For some minutes the old man stood silent, with face uplifted, weeping in the drizzling rain.

In a little while the sky was clear again.

RESPONSES: Questions for Writing and Discussion

1. In view of the devastation which occurred at Wounded Knee, do you find Black Elk's final refusal to surrender to despair a noble and admirable thing or a futile gesture? Do hatred and a desire for vengeance, in your opinion, prove to be stronger life-affirming forces than fortitude and the persistence of hope in the presence of despair?

2. It is true that we see the action through the eyes of an Indian, that we are not given the Wasichu version of what happened. But surely each of us has read enough American history to know that Wounded Knee was traditionally called a "battle" not a "massacre" and that it has been customary to think of the Sioux as one of the more dangerous tribes in the West, hostile to all white settlers. Looking at both sides, do you believe the Wasichu was justified in wanting to take the land for himself? Does territory belong to whoever is able to occupy it, hold onto it, or do more with it than the one who had it before? (Does the Human Worth of the white settler in this instance reside in his superior culture—including military skills—or would it have resided in an early recognition of Indian claims to the territory?)

3. Suppose the white man had never "won" the West? Suppose, for the sake of argument, that a treaty had been signed and adhered to whereby all lands west of the Mississippi River were to remain the property of Indians? What would be the case now? Would the Eastern half of the country be prosperous and progressive, and the Western half still primitive and undeveloped?

4. Can it be said of the red man, as it has been said of the black man, that he was here for hundreds of years and never created an important civilization of his own? Has he been dependent upon the white European culture for whatever advances he has made?

5. It is difficult to read this selection and not feel moved by the plight of the Sioux. On the other hand, the white man's history does contain the massacre at Little Big Horn in which Custer and all his men were wiped out. Recent investigations have brought to light much new information about Custer and the reasons the Indians were provoked into so ferocious an attack. Nevertheless, a whole regiment died violently. Do you think Indian violence was more justified than the white man's violence? Must one become violent at times? Under what circumstances? What does the use of violence mean with respect to Human Worth?

6. The majority of American Indians now are required to live on reservations, and their lives are completely under the control of the Bureau of Indian Affairs and the Department of the Interior. Can you think of any reasons to justify this disposition of the Indian? Are there any arguments against it?

7. Think back to your earliest concepts of Indians. Then try to determine what were the sources of your information—school books; stories; television and movies? Even where Indians were not treated as barbarous savages, was the approach, in your estimation now, a humane one? Was it patronizing?

8. If Indians throughout the country suddenly rebelled en masse, breaking out of their reservations with weapons and taking over small towns and unsettled territories, how would such actions be described in the mass media? What steps would the government take? How would you feel about them?

9. If you had it in your power to make some gesture toward the Indians that you would want construed as humane, what might it be? Would you, for example, give them back New York? (Would that be humane?) Pack up and return to the country of your ancestors? Move in with money and equipment and establish one reservation as a monumental tourist attraction, hopeful that this would create economic autonomy for the tribe? Free all Indians from all reservations?

TOWARDS A BETTER WORLD THROUGH CONSCIOUS DESIGN

R. Buckminster Fuller

Just at a time when many are looking for ways of returning to a more natural life, away from the ecological disaster, crime, poverty, and sundry other problems of the big cities, just when the old ideas of civilization and progress are being challenged as myths, **R. Buckminster Fuller (b. 1895)** is talking of more not less civilization for the future. Originally an architect and engineer, Fuller has become one of this country's most provocative and original thinkers, a technological utopianist, who says that man's salvation lies in "doing" civilization better, not in fleeing from it.

We have come too far, Fuller tells us, to abandon the direction technology has taken, to scorn all of the positive things technology has done for the human race. But he concedes that technology cannot contribute to human welfare unless it is consciously devised and planned for specific needs. Fuller sees architecture as the coordinating science. The humane architect, working for the future good of man rather than to exhibit his own professional skills or aesthetic sensibilities, can rethink and redesign the entire earth. He can literally create a higher form of civilization on the drawing board and carefully avoid making the mistakes of the past which have led us to our present environmental and metropolitan crises.

Fuller's major contribution to humane architecture up to now has been the geodesic dome, which millions saw housing the United States exhibitions at Expo '67 in Montreal, Canada. The huge globular pavilion dazzled the eyes and imagination of those who realized some of its possibilities as the design of the future. Twenty stories high, it illustrates Fuller's principle that whole communities can live in a controlled environment, protected from the whimsy of nature, but not from "uninterrupted" visual contact with the exterior world. Fuller believes that, of all geometric forms, the sphere encloses the greatest amount of space with the least amount of surface and is the economically logical answer to projected housing problems of the future.

Fuller's preoccupation with the maximum utilization of space has led him to a reconsideration of the world as we know it. Whatever charges have been made against civilized man's destruction of nature, he contends, the fact remains that most of the world's space and most of its resources are still in their natural state and do few people much good. Huge wastelands, presently regarded as uninhabitable, can be reclaimed through the use of the dome. Controlled environment will in turn allow technology to release more and more of the earth's resources for the use of man.

To ease the problem of overcrowded cities, the earth's population needs to be evenly distributed over the earth's surface. Developing more "naturally" than was wise, human civilization was allowed to flourish wherever it could. Hence most of the world's people are jammed into an absurdly disproportionate amount of acreage. Through redistribution, the real advantages of a planned civilization will be accessible to all.

Fuller believes the reason for the failure of civilization to do its job up to this point has been an erroneous conception of what the earth *really* looks like. He has devised a new kind of map to take the place of the old spinning globe with which most of us are familiar. Called the Dymaxion Airocean Map, it plots the earth's surface on a flat two-dimensional plane so that land mass and water relationships can be seen in better perspective.

The old spinning globe does more than distort geographical reality, Fuller contends. It leads to narrow-mindedness and insularity. When one finds himself "on the map," in a manner of speaking, the rest of the world might as well be the dark side of the moon. We have grown up thinking of irreconcilable differences between so-called "East" and "West," for example, when in reality the earth should be thought of as a continuous linear plane. To see the world as a Fuller map represents it is to be aware that it is really much smaller than we have supposed. And for Fuller it is also necessary to realize how much humanity all of the people on the earth share.

If to be "natural" means to keep on going in the old heedless way, compounding differences and multiplying prejudices, then Fuller would say that "natural" man needs to be replaced by the truly "civilized" man who has not yet been born.

Towards a Better World Through Conscious Design

Four per cent of humanity is for the moment in South America. One per cent is in Central America, 7 per cent in North America—a total of 12 per cent in the combined Americas. From anywhere in the United States, as only my map shows, I can fly on the shortest great-circle routes to reach 84 per cent of humanity without flying either over the Atlantic or Pacific oceans. This is not the pattern that we have been thinking about with our Mercator maps. With them we think in terms of *necessarily* crossing the Atlantic and Pacific, going back to the great sailing era days and the great significance of the ports of embarkation and debarkation and of the great tonnages being shipped between them. In terms of air transportation, however, *this*—the one-world-island land mass on the Fuller map—becomes the airstrip of the world which is most significant, and this airstrip is oriented at 90 degrees to the Mercator stretch-out. This is the appropriate world communications and transport orientation for the present moment. Older people still think they must go to New York from St. Louis to go to Europe, but that really is not the right way to go. This is the right way to go—northern great-circle routes. That is why Chicago, despite New York and San Francisco being very attractive places to embark from, is the most heavily used airport in America.

People generally think "go north go cold, go south go warm." That is a fixation which is also not true. On my map, the spectrum colors are used. I use these for the mean low temperatures for the year. The mean highs are about the same everywhere; that is, in Eastern Siberia it gets as hot in the summer as it gets in mid-continent Africa on certain days. The major climatic differences between the various parts of the world are in the extremes of cold, or the "lows," not in the "highs," or heats. The hottest days in Brazil and India are about the same as the hottest days in Eastern Siberia and Alaska. The cold pole of the Northern Hemisphere is in Eastern Siberia. The cold pole for the Southern Hemisphere happens to coincide geographically with the south pole of the earth's rotational axis. You see on my map how the colors change from blue to green to yellow to red. Blue is coldest. Red is hottest. We find that the red masses of Africa, South America, and South Asia belong to the Northern Hemisphere's color-spectrum bull's-eye. The world thermal map in effect makes a "target" pattern, with the spectrum color-ring zones primarily co-ordinate in terms of the Northern Hemisphere. There is also a small secondary color-spectrum temperature-zone bull's-eye associated with the Southern Hemisphere's cold pole, but it is much smaller than the Northern. It has green in the southern tip of South America and some yellow and red. There is a little yellow and mild red that belongs to the Southern Hemisphere in Australia. Only the southern-most tips of Australia, Africa, and South America are primarily affected by the south cold pole. The rest of the world temperature-patterning relates to the north cold pole. Ninety-nine per cent of the world's population lives at present in the north cold pole's weather domain.

In Europe you will find that the spectrum of thermal-zone lines runs north and south, contrary to the "go north go cold, go south go warm" fixation. The hottest place in Europe is Spain, and Europe gets colder as we go *east,* not north. Napoleon, thinking as everybody does, that when you stay in your home latitude you will have about the same temperature and weather, went east into Russia prepared to find conditions similar to his home conditions. He was licked by the cold.

He dissipated enormous amounts of energy against the cold, the great negative of energy. You would think that by the time Hitler came along men would have learned something about this thermal map. They had not, and Hitler, too, went east into Russia. He was licked logistically by the unexpected magnitude of cold. For an instance, he did not have the right locomotive greases for the temperatures that his army ran into. As a consequence of the thermal ignorance, his forces were not properly supplied, and their hitting power was dissipated by the cold. The cold turned Hitler's tide. This was due, then, to the fact that the concept of go north to cold is wrong. This is ignorance again typical of the educational fallacies. I am sure that parents are still going to teach this geographical error to their children, but the fact is that where 76 per cent of humanity now exists it is "go east, go cold" and in only 24 per cent of the world's land is "go north go cold, go south go warm" true.

We can also look at the colors on the map and compare them with the colors of men's skins. The map temperature colors have to do with the radiation, the inhibition of energy from the sun. As we get into the great cold areas, the skin gets very, very white. Men have to hibernate a great deal of the time. In other parts of the world they could be naked with a great deal of sun. The colors of the map are related, then, also to the color of pigmentation of the skins. This has something to do with the solar system and nothing to do with some mysterious "different kinds of tribes" around the faces of the earth. If there are any special differences in the shapes of noses or heights of men, it has to do very much with the long isolation of men and the developing of certain amounts of hybridism in relation to adapting to special local conditions. There are some dark-skinned people up in the Arctic among the Eskimos, and they are people who came there relatively recently from the tropics and Japan, from the darker regions, by water. They are water people. That is enough discussion of the map.

What I now propose is that all the universities around the world be encouraged to invest the next ten years in a continuing problem of *how to make the total world's resources, which now serve only 43 per cent, serve 100 per cent of humanity through competent complex design science. . . .*

At the present moment in history, what is spoken of as world policy by the respective nations consists essentially of their own special plans to bring about conditions which would uniquely foster their respective kinds of survival in the Malthusian "you or me-ness." For any one of the world policies of any of the nations or groups of nations to become a world plan would mean that approximately one-half of the world's nations would have to surrender their sovereignty and would mean the development of a highly biased plan as applied to the whole. In the nature of political compromises it is logical to assume that the world policy of any one political nation will never succeed in satisfying comprehensive world planning.

It is clearly manifest that students and scientists are able to think regarding such world planning in a manner utterly transcendental to any political bias. My experience around the world and amongst the students tells me that the students themselves tend always to transcend political bias and that *all of them are concerned with the concept of making the world work through competent design.* In much investigation and inquiry I have had no negative response to the program of organization of the student capability to the upping of the performance of the world resources to serve 100 per cent of humanity by peaceful, comprehensive laboratory experiment and progressive design revolution.

At the present time, in this era of exaggerated specialization, the special knowledge and capabilities thus developed are rapidly drained off from the university into large corporations and into government defense bureaucracies or military bureaucracies. The scientists and inventors are wary under these circumstances, and it is probable that if the students who are potential comprehensive anticipatory design scientists are progressively and adequately disciplined to breadth of capability in chemistry, physics, mathematics, bio-chemistry, psychology, economics, and industrial technology they will swiftly and ably penetrate the most advanced recesses of the scientific minds resident in the university, and as their programs evolute from year to year in improving capability the students will be able to bring the highest integral scientific resources of man to bear upon their solutions of dynamic world town planning and its design instrumentation and operational regeneration.

The comprehensive world resources data now exist in a number of establishments, but are primarily available to all the universities of the world through UNESCO. What UNESCO does not have, it is in a good position to direct the researcher to acquire successfully. Our Geoscope would be dramatic aid in such resource-use planning and its communication to world news distributing services.

I have discussed this potential development of a comprehensive world strategy by the students who are potential comprehensive anticipatory design scientists with faculties and students on both sides of the world political curtains and have had unanimously enthusiastic reactions. The project has the extraordinary virtue that it inherently avoids political bias; therefore, there will be no suggestion of any subversive activity by any participants. It may receive political support from all sides by virtue of the important knowledge that will accrue. I am confident that there are many other human beings who at this moment envision analogous developments, all of which are symptomatic of a maturely emergent world trending whose exact modes of realization are unpredictable. But we may assume that the great, looming, man-favoring events of tomorrow will occur as the result of man's adoption of comprehensive anticipatory design science within the universities. . . .

I would counsel you in your deliberation regarding getting campuses ready now to get general comprehensive environment controls that are suitable to all-purposes like a circus. A circus is a transformable environment. You get an enclosure against "weather" that you can put up in a hurry, within which you can put up all kinds of apparatus—high trapezes, platforms, rings, nets, etc. You can knock it down in a few minutes. That is the way the modern laboratory goes. In laboratories you can get the generalized pipette or whatever it is, the crucible, and the furnace. You can put the right things together very fast, rig them up, get through the experiment, knock it down. It's one clean space again. You want clean spaces. The circus concept is very important for you. I would get buildings where it is possible for many to meet. On the Carbondale campus you have succeeded in getting some good auditoriums—but we need more auditoriums and more auditoriums time and time again. We want places where there is just a beautiful blank floor and beautiful blank walls upon which to cast our pictures or apply crayons. You don't have to put any "architecture" there at all. You don't have to build any sculptured architecture—use the ephemeral. Work from the visible to the invisible very rapidly.

I would not waste dollars on great, heavy, stone masonry and any kind of Georgian architecture, and I would forget all the old architecture and even the curricula patterns of any schools before this moment. You might better consider putting up one big one-half-mile-diameter geodesic dome over your whole campus and thereafter subdivide off local areas temporarily for various activities.

Anything that is static, forget it. Work entirely toward the dynamic. Get yourself the tools and ways of enclosing enormous amounts of space, and make it possible for large numbers of human beings to come together under more preferred conditions than have ever before come together. Then give them large clear spaces so that their privacy results from having sufficient distance between people or groups of people. Get over the ideas of partitions. Partitions are like socialism. They came out of living and working in fortresses where there wasn't enough room to go around, so they put up partitions—really making cells. Partitions simply say you shall not pass. That's all they do. They are improvised to make that which is fundamentally inadequate work "after a fashion."

There are four kinds of privacy: if I can't touch you, we're *tactilely* private; if I can't smell you, we are *olfactorily* private; if I can't hear you, we're *aurally* private; and if I can't see you, we are *visually* private. Just a little space will take care of the first three. For the fourth—since we can see a great distance—all we need are delicate occulting membranes, possibly rose bushes or soap bubbles or smoke screens. . . .

As examples of the kind of environment controlling facility to which I have been referring think of the fifty-five-foot-diameter Marine Corps geodesic domes. We began flying them around by helicopter in 1954. Last year we sold to the Ford Motor Company, from my office in Raleigh, North Carolina, two domes, not 55-footers but 114-footers. That is, each had 10,000 square feet of floor space. Each was an auditorium with a dark skin. One helicopter picked each one up. Ford started one of the domes in Alabama and one in Texas and moved them north. They didn't fly them most of the time; they disassembled and reassembled them, but they discovered they could fly them. One helicopter could pick up 10,000 square feet of floor space—that's quite a lot—and move it from place to place at a mile a minute. Considering the rate at which the helicopters are now increasing the loads they can carry and the rate at which I'm finding I can make lighter and lighter buildings, I can tell you with within five years I will be able to fly the clear-span cover for a baseball stadium (14½ acres) fully assembled, delivering it to its site at 60 knots. This is what is coming. Get yourselves the right geographical bases; you're very smart in getting your airplanes. Get lots of real estate and lots of airplanes and helicopters—get mobility. Get the most comprehensive generalized computer setup with network connections to process the documentaries that your faculty and graduate-student teams will manufacture objectively from the subjective gleanings of your vast new world- and universe-ranging student probers. Get ready the greatest new educational facility at the approximate dynamic population center of the North American continent, assuming that any dreamable vision of technical advance will be a reality and that man is about to demonstrate competence beyond our estimates of yesterday and today. "Shoot for the moon"—yesterday a statement of lunacy—only a lunatic would now deny that this is the most evidently "next" practical objective of man.

RESPONSES: Questions for Writing and Discussion

1. Fuller has said that his Airocean Maps are known to professional people but that they are not "allowed" in the schools. Why should this be?

2. Try to recollect your earliest contact with a sense of the world, in grammar school geography classes, for example; or spinning the large lighted blue globe that stood in the corner of the library. Did this contact influence your thinking in any way? In other words, are there any aspects of your personality which are derived from the way in which you came to understand the world during your formative years?

3. According to Fuller, Napoleon and Hitler both lost decisive campaigns because they misunderstood patterns of climate, and he implies this would never have happened had they used the Airocean Map. In a Fullerian world, where geography and ecology are everyone's concern and knowledge is plentiful, will there be no Napoleons or Hitlers?

4. If it is true that the total world's resources now serve less than half of total humanity, why do so many scientists predict a gloomy and not-too-far-distant future when there will be a depletion of resources?

5. Fuller likes to work through the colleges to build up a legion of followers for his enormous world-planning idea. He says "students themselves tend always to transcend political bias" and are concerned about eliminating "you or me-ness" from the thinking of mankind. Do you personally lend support to Fuller's view of college students? Is "you or me-ness" too deeply ingrained in human nature to change it? Would you personally want to change it?

6. If it is still true that college graduates are being "drained off" into big business or military bureaucracies and since Fuller plans to change all of this, what would be the chance of success for those who follow in his footsteps? Will there be economic and social chaos in this country, for example, *before* the new world can materialize?

7. Would there be enough architectural variety and privacy in a Fullerian world with thousands of geodesic domes? Would you like to live under such a dome side by side with, say, a thousand other people? Will rose bushes or soap bubbles be enough for you? In addition, the philosophy behind the dome includes the idea of bringing people together for greater mutual understanding. How do you see yourself in a dome-covered world?

8. If countries as we now know them should disappear, if worldwide, uniform architectural designs prevail, if unlimited numbers of routes are opened up, making world travel an everyday occurrence, and if the earth does indeed become one great community, what kind of government do you see having the flexibility to handle so vast a domain?

AFTER DARK VAPOURS HAVE OPPRESS'D OUR PLAINS

John Keats[1]

As the following sonnet indicates, ours has not been the first age with environmental concerns. The romantic movement of the eighteenth and nineteenth centuries was dedicated to the rebirth of the individual, and one of its major contentions was that the life of the city stifles and corrupts all that is natural and good in human existence. Painters abandoned portraiture in favor of landscapes, while poets like **John Keats (1791–1821)** strove to capture in "mere" words the thrilling sights and sounds of nature.

Since Keats also was preoccupied with personal problems—the ever-present knowledge of an approaching early death among them—it is seldom that he responds to a natural scene without relating it in some way to himself. Thus it is that the final thought which comes to him on the first true day of spring is of death. Through his dedication to nature Keats came to view death as a natural and beautiful part of the life cycle. Only those who do not understand nature can fear to die.

After Dark Vapours Have Oppress'd Our Plains

After dark vapours have oppress'd our plains
    For a long dreary season, comes a day
    Born of the gentle South, and clears away
From the sick heavens all unseemly stains.
The anxious month, relieved its pains,
    Takes as a long-lost right the feel of May.
    The eyelids with the passing coolness play,
Like rose leaves with the drip of summer rains.
And calmest thoughts come round us; as, of leaves
    Budding,—fruit ripening in stillness,—Autumn suns
Smiling at eve upon the quiet sheaves,—
Sweet Sappho's cheek,—a sleeping infant's breath,—
    The gradual sand that through an hour-glass runs,—
A woodland rivulet,—a Poet's death.

---

[1] For further discussion of Keats, see pp. 40–41.

THE WORLD IS TOO MUCH WITH US

William Wordsworth

William Wordsworth (1770–1850) also belongs to the English romantic movement, but he was a good deal more stable than some of his contemporaries, such as Samuel Taylor Coleridge, who often were given to manic-depressive changes of temperament. He seldom soars as high in his adoration of the joys of nature, but he seldom drops as low either. The themes of much romantic poetry are the brevity of the time of youth when nature most inspires, and the inevitable coming of age and death.

Wordsworth avoided such sorrow through his love of reason and the pleasures of the mind. While at home in nature, he was equally comfortable in his library chair, reading and meditating. One of his constant missions in poetry is to tell the reader of the more stable but no less joyous experiences of mellow age that lie ahead, when the feverish ups and downs of youth are replaced by the intellectual clear-sightedness of maturity. In the following sonnet, however, the poet has been depressed by the lack of a true, throbbing sense of being and suddenly cries "Great God!" as he longs for a new, passionate way of relating himself to the world around him—very much like the old pagans, whose myths endowed nature with majesty.

The World Is Too Much With Us

The world is too much with us; late and soon,
Getting and spending, we lay waste our powers:
Little we see in Nature that is ours;
We have given our hearts away, a sordid boon!
This Sea that bares her bosom to the moon;
The winds that will be howling at all hours,
And are up-gathered now like sleeping flowers;
For this, for everything, we are out of tune,
It moves us not.—Great God! I'd rather be
A Pagan suckled in a creed outworn;
So might I, standing on this pleasant lea,
Have glimpses that would make me less forlorn;
Have sight of Proteus rising from the sea;
Or hear old Triton blow his wreathed horn.

Jack Copons

For this, for everything, we are out of tune, It moves us not. *William Wordsworth*

TRAFFIC
Allan Kaplan

Toward the end of the nineteenth century some American poets were finding inspiration not only in nature but in the crowded city as well. Whitman and Sandburg glorified New York and Chicago respectively, and on their own terms. The high buildings, the noise and the jostling, the endless procession of humanity along the sidewalks filled them with a sense of America's true greatness. Needless to say, the adoration of the American city has become an unfashionable theme.

Thus it is with a certain amount of pleasure and surprise that one discovers the following expression of love for New York by one of the newer voices in American poetry. Known at present to a comparatively small circle readers of *Poetry*, the *Paris Review*, and the *Quarterly Review of Literature*, **Allan Kaplan (b. 1932)** has spent most of his life in Greenwich Village. He knows its routines and manages to be life-affirming about them on *their* own terms. Here is a poet who loves the "vinyl skirts, so short and yellow" of the girls as they walk along, and he is glad to be there and alive. Even the stream of passing cars that "gently bump like curious strangers" affects him with unexpected excitement.

Traffic

How pleasant to walk the streets.
The warmth of a hand has been lingering on my side,
while cars disappear and come, honking occasionally, as a thought
        going through my brain.
How is it I do not love the girl who stayed with me
and touched my side while she slept last night?
Honk, honk! Another thought. Honk!
A star falls, like the hand of the calm sleeper, making a gentle arc
       in the night.

See, two teen-agers walking wearing vinyl skirts, so short and yellow.
O like enthusiasm their hair falls abundantly. Look,
their knees are naked savages.

I remember Michael, my friend, saying whatever brings you into
 the New
       is a positive good. Forward!
My spirit rises out of myself to be greeted in midair by loveliness
       of the girls.
My love turns spiritual in midair!
On my side the warmth of the hand lingers, like the star my
astrologer saw bringing to me luck and a joy to be with others,
       as it crosses the sky.
How marvelous that short skirts bring youthful knees into our city.
How marvelous is Michael's idea that shapes today for me.
O my own body, and Michael, all my friends,
the traffic where cars may gently bump like curious strangers
       who are open-hearted,
and the thoroughfare of my head with its traffic passing,
 and the light of this hour
       are OMNIPRESENCE

THE CHICAGO DEFENDER SENDS A MAN TO LITTLE ROCK

Gwendolyn Brooks

A spokesman for black America for more than a quarter of a century, **Gwendolyn Brooks (b. 1917)** was named one of America's top ten women of the year by *Mademoiselle* magazine in 1945. In 1950 she won the Pulitzer Prize for poetry and in 1968 became poet laureate of the state of Illinois.

The following poem is of more than passing interest on two counts. First, it records and analyzes a sociological event—the racial violence which erupted in Little Rock, Arkansas, in the fall of 1957, serving as a prelude to the "long hot summers" of the late sixties. Knowing what came to pass in all the major cities in America, the reader cannot fail to be stirred by the poet's depiction of white America's suburban "innocence" of the rising anger in the ghettos and ask himself why something was not done about the inner cities long before. (Even when Little Rock explodes, the editor of the *Chicago Defender* will not alarm his readers by printing the truth.)

But Gwendolyn Brooks is a poet of major stature, stirring our emotions and our conscience with both the facts and her manner of treating them. The black experience in the American ghetto is given sudden and appalling meaning in the poem's final line, which has more to tell than a thousand editorials.

The Chicago Defender Sends a Man to Little Rock

Fall, 1957
In Little Rock the people bear
Babes, and comb and part their hair
And watch the want ads, put repair
To roof and latch. While wheat toast burns
A woman waters multiferns.

Time upholds or overturns
The many, tight, and small concerns.

In Little Rock the people sing
Sunday hymns like anything,
Through Sunday pomp and polishing.

And after testament and tunes,
Some soften Sunday afternoons
With lemon tea and Lorna Doones.

I forecast
And I believe
Come Christmas Little Rock will cleave
To Christmas tree and trifle, weave,
From laugh and tinsel, texture fast.

In Little Rock is baseball; Barcarolle.
That hotness in July . . . the uniformed figures raw and implacable
And not intellectual,
Batting the hotness or clawing the suffering dust.
The Open Air Concert, on the special twilight green. . . .

When Beethoven is brutal or whispers to lady-like air.
Blanket-sitters are solemn, as Johann troubles to lean
To tell them what to mean. . . .

There is love, too, in Little Rock. Soft women softly
Opening themselves in kindness,
Or, pitying one's blindness,
Awaiting one's pleasure
In azure
Glory with anguished rose at the root. . . .
To wash away old semi-discomfitures.
They re-teach purple and unsullen blue.
The wispy soils go. And uncertain
Half-havings have they clarified to sures.

In Little Rock they know
Not answering the telephone is a way of rejecting life,
That it is our business to be bothered, is our business
To cherish bores or boredom, be polite
To lies and love and many-faceted fuzziness.
I scratch my head, massage the hate-I-had.
I blink across my prim and pencilled pad.
The saga I was sent for is not down.
Because there is a puzzle in this town.
The biggest News I do not dare
Telegraph to the Editor's chair:
"They are like people everywhere."

The angry Editor would reply
In hundred harryings of Why.

And true, they are hurling spittle, rock,
Garbage and fruit in Little Rock.
And I saw coiling storm a-writhe
On bright madonnas. And a scythe
Of men harassing brownish girls.
(The bows and barrettes in the curls
And braids declined away from joy.)

I saw a bleeding brownish boy. . . .

The lariat lynch-wish I deplored.

The loveliest lynchee was our Lord.

DANCE OF THE ABAKWETA
Margaret Danner

The complacency of the average person of white European background and his ignorance of other cultures besides his own has been offset to an extent by the tremendous interest in Non-Western people shown by anthropologists and sociologists. Universities are filled with courses on how the other half lives. In fact, there has been such an explosion of knowledge in recent years that one might suppose the old insularity of Western man has been all but dissipated. The following poem serves as a startling reminder of the condescending attitude often unwittingly held by those who visit and observe the "quaint" habits of exotic populations.

Margaret Danner (b. 1915) has for years been recognized as one of the important new black poets. She has been assistant editor of *Poetry* and Poet-In-Residence at Wayne University in Detroit as well as the recipient of numerous awards for her poetry. Her Detroit home, Boone House, is a well-known gathering place for contemporary artists.

Dance of the Abakweta

Imagine what Mrs. Haessler would say
If she could see the Watussi youth dance
Their well-versed initiation. At first glance
As they bend to an invisible barre
You would know that she had designed their costumes.

For though they were made of pale beige bamboo straw
Their lines were the classic tutu. Nothing varied.
Each was cut short to the thigh and carried
High to a degree of right angles. Nor was there a flaw
In their leotards. Made of leopard skin or the hide

Of a goat, or the Gauguin-colored Okapi's striped coat
They were cut in her reverenced "tradition."
She would have approved their costumes and positions.
And since neither Iceland nor Africa is too remote
For her vision she would have wanted to form

A "traditional" ballet. Swan Lake, Scheherazade or
(After seeing their incredible leaps)
Les Orientales. Imagine the exotic sweep
Of such a ballet, and from the way the music pours
Over these dancers (this tinkling of bells, talking

Of drums, and twanging of tan, sandalwood harps)
From this incomparable music, Mrs. Haessler of Vassar can
Glimpse strains of Tchaikovsky, Chopin
To accompany her undeviatingly sharp
"Traditional" ballet. I am certain that if she could
Tutor these potential protégés, as
Quick as Aladdin rubbing his lamp, she would.

The
Unbounded
Self

III

The mind is each man's special province.

                        But how is it to be used?

Is it reason that distinguishes men and women?

                        Does reasoning blind us to reality?

The mind is capable of strange flights.

                        Should we trust its instincts and go along?

Or is it better not to stray too far from

                  EXTERNAL REALITY

                      (whatever that is)?

We might not like everything about reality,

                      but we have to live there—sometimes anyway—

Whatever else happens, each of us is free to like living

                  OR not like it.

The way one feels inside is nobody else's business but his,

JUST LET HIM KNOW WHAT *IS* GOING ON THERE . . .

THE RATIONAL
REALM

Whatever happens to a human being at the hands of the state or any other institution that wields power and authority over him, one haven to which he can retreat is the sanctity of his inner self. Nor is this an inconsiderable domain. A good deal has been discovered about inner space, and the prospects for the future are limitless. We are only beginning to catch glimpses of what the mind can really do. It is possible that the day has not yet dawned when people will fully utilize their mental powers.

But traditionally Human Worth has been tied to the rational or intellectual level of the mind. Ever since Aristotle defined man as the "thinking animal," not only distinguishing him from but clearly elevating him above the rest of nature, the premise has been that people achieve their finest hour when they are most rational.

Again traditionally, a rational human being is one who is capable of sustaining a meaningful sequence of thought for a longer period of time than the mind, left to its own devices, finds convenient. He is able to go from A to B to C by perceiving relationships which others, responding more instinctively and spontaneously to experience, may miss. He goes from premises to conclusions and then reinvests his conclusions as further premises from which to argue. He is less distracted by the sights and sounds of the world "out there." He can "concentrate."

But the case for intellectualism has had its opponents all

along. What, they have asked and continue to ask, is the exact relationship between careful, sustained thought and the flow of reality outside? May not the intellectual person fall in love with ideas, principles, and the theories that do not fully or even at all make true contact with things "as they are"? Further, is the intellectual life really a happy one? Does the thinking person suppress his natural emotions to the point at which he is only half—less than half—a human being? Does he tolerate others? feel their humanity? Or does Worth mean for him a lofty superiority out of reach for "the others"?

Taken together, the readings in this section pose the question of whether the rational realm of the mind is in fact the location of all that is most admirable in human nature. They define both the glories and the dangers of conscious, meticulous thinking.

In Descartes, from whose *Meditations* we have taken the brief but crucial "A Piece of Wax," we have the classic statement in defense of rationalism. Far less well known but no less pertinent to the subject is the satiric piece which follows it: Russell Maloney's "Inflexible Logic," which whimsically dramatizes what happens when the intellectual is confronted with facts which refuse to fit his nicely organized theories.

Theories and principles are, however, all important if we would understand experience—or so, at least, historian Crane Brinton contends in "The Role of Ideas." Without rational thought man is at the mercy of all that happens. If he would shape and control his own destiny, he must understand the vast currents of history, not in terms of facts alone, but in terms of motives and ideological steering currents. To abandon the intellectual interpretation of the past and present is to be a slave to the future.

Alvin Toffler is another disciple of rationalism, but his message is more drastic than Brinton's. It may already be too late to do anything about tomorrow, says the author of *Future Shock*. In "Overstimulation and the Breakdown of Reason," Toffler points out that the same rational process by which Brinton proposes to comprehend the forces of history is beginning to deteriorate as the result of an unprecedented knowledge explosion. Too much is being found out too fast for most people to assimilate it adequately. The human mind is today excited far beyond its capacity to cope. We are becoming an increasingly irrational society.

But no matter how torrid the pace of living becomes, there will always, no doubt, be people who turn away from it and once more retreat to the "safe and sane" quiet of the world of thought. The intellectual life for better or worse will have its exponents. Katherine Anne Porter's "Theft" shows us how painfully silent that quiet can become, how tragically isolated the intellectual can be. The story's heroine has lost the ability to be touched by life and by other people. She is witty, she is sharp and perceptive; but in rejecting emotion, especially love, she finds herself lacking the very things which Human Worth may just possibly be all about.

A PIECE OF WAX
René Descartes

Considered the father of modern philosophy, **René Descartes (1596–1650)** occupies a critical position in the history of Western ideas. He revived the whole discipline of philosophy after a dormant period of several centuries during which the Western world was emerging from the Middle Ages, the authority of the Church was crumbling, and a renewed concern for life here on earth led to a revolution in the arts and to innumerable scientific advances.

Descartes knew that philosophy, if it was to survive at all, could never again be what it had been during its classical or medieval phases. Plato, Aristotle, and Aquinas were still intellectual giants, but their thinking reflected concepts of man and the universe that had become outmoded.

It was to science that Descartes ultimately turned: especially astronomy with its growing tradition of geometric exactitude and its cautious but solid attainment of a number of apparent certainties. Attracted as he had been by philosophy, he felt it would have to be reconstituted, following the careful method of the scientists, if it were to survive. He determined on a course of reasoning whereby he would doubt everything until his intellect reached a point at which it was no longer possible to doubt. He would achieve a concept that struck him with the force of mathematical certainty, or he would have to go on doubting forever. Such a concept, if it indeed existed, would be the starting point for his philosophy.

In his *Meditations*, published in 1641, Descartes carefully reconstructs the process by which he reached his "undoubtable" truth. To put it simply, he found that he could easily doubt the existence of all tangible bodies, of anything perceived through the senses. He could easily doubt that his senses gave accurate reports. He could even entertain the notion that God was deliberately deceiving him and allowing him to believe he was seeing things which were not really there. Since his only reason for believing in his own existence was his perception of himself in the process of existing, he found that he could even doubt that.

The one thing he could not doubt, however, was the fact of doubting itself. Here was a basic certainty. Right on the heels of this came another: Something has to do the doubting, and Descartes concluded this to be his mind. If he could not be sure of his own or any other body, he could not deny the existence of his mind. Thus he could say, regarding his own identity, I am a "thing which thinks."

That the mind certainly exists and is the primary reality of which certainty is possible at all is further proved, at least to Descartes' satisfaction, by the example of the wax. In this complex argument the philosopher shows how the existence of wax *as* wax—its identity as a single phenomenon despite that fact that it is being heated and melted and is thus continually changing its form—is understood by the mind rather than perceived by the senses. For the senses, he contends, are capable only of perceiving the successive stages of change. The senses, in sort, do not *make sense* of things.

Since Descartes, scientific advances have made computerized certainty possible in thousands of specific areas, but the mathematically accurate and unchanging picture of all existence which the philosopher believed he could attain has eluded thinking people. Nonetheless, the implications of the piece of wax remain. Each of us comes to realize that there is a world in here and a world out there, and the relationship between them is not always as clear as we might imagine.

A Piece of Wax

Let us begin by considering the commonest matters, those which we believe to be the most distinctly comprehended, to wit, the bodies which we touch and see; not indeed bodies in general, for these general ideas are usually a little more confused, but let us consider one body in particular. Let us take, for example, this piece of wax: it has been taken quite freshly from the hive, and it has not yet lost the sweetness of the honey which is contains; it still retains somewhat of the odour of the flowers from which it has been culled; its colour, its figure, its size are apparent; it is hard, cold, easily handled, and if you strike it with the finger, it will emit a sound. Finally all the things which are requisite to cause us distinctly to recognise a body, are met with in it. But notice that while I speak and approach the fire what remained of

From E. S. Haldane and G. P. T. Ross, *The Philosophical Works of Descartes, Two Meditations.* Used by permission of the publisher, Cambridge University Press.

the taste is exhaled, the smell evaporates, the colour alters, the figure is destroyed, the size increases, it becomes liquid, it heats, scarcely can one handle it, and when one strikes it, no sound is emitted. Does the same wax remain after this change? We must confess that it remains; none would judge otherwise. What then did I know so distinctly in this piece of wax? It could certainly be nothing of all that the senses brought to my notice, since all these things which fall under taste, smell, sight, touch, and hearing are found to be changed, and yet the same wax remains.

Perhaps it was what I now think, viz. that this wax was not that sweetness of honey, nor that agreeable scent of flowers, nor that particular whiteness, nor that figure, nor that sound, but simply a body which a little while before appeared to me as perceptible under these forms, and which is now perceptible under others. But what, precisely, is it that I imagine when I form such conceptions? Let us attentively consider this, and, abstracting from all that does not belong to the wax, let us see what remains. Certainly nothing remains excepting a certain extended thing which is flexible and movable. But what is the meaning of flexible and movable? Is it not that I imagine that this piece of wax being round is capable of becoming square and of passing from a square to a triangular figure? No, certainly it is not that, since I imagine it admits of an infinitude of similar changes, and I nevertheless do not know how to compass the infinitude by my imagination, and consequently this conception which I have of the wax is not brought about by the faculty of imagination. What now is this extension? Is it not also unknown? For it becomes greater when the wax is melted, greater when it is boiled, and greater still when the heat increases; and I should not conceive [clearly] according to truth what wax is, if I did not think that even this piece that we are considering is capable of receiving more variations in extension than I have ever imagined. We must then grant that I could not even understand through the imagination what this piece of wax in particular, for as to wax in general it is yet clearer. But what is this piece of wax which cannot be understood excepting by the [understanding or] mind? It is certainly the same that I see, touch, imagine, and finally it is the same which I have always believed it to be from the beginning. But what must particularly be observed is that its perception is neither an act of vision, nor of touch, nor of imagination, and has never been such although it may have appeared formerly to be so, but only an intuition of the mind, which may be imperfect and confused as it was formerly, or clear and distinct as it is at present, according as my attention is more or less directed to the elements which are found in it, and of which it is composed.

Yet in the meantime I am greatly astonished when I consider

[the great feebleness of mind] and its proneness to fall [insensibly] into error; for although without giving expression to my thoughts I consider all this in my own mind, words often impede me and I am almost deceived by the terms of ordinary language. For we say that we see the same wax, if it is present, and not that we simply judge that it is the same from its having the same colour and figure. From this I should conclude that I knew the wax by means of vision and not simply by the intuition of the mind; unless by chance I remember that, when looking from a window and saying I see men who pass in the street, I really do not see them, but infer that what I see is men, just as I say that I see wax. And yet what do I see from the window but hats and coats which may cover automatic machines? Yet I judge these to be men. And similarly solely by the faculty of judgment which rests in my mind, I comprehend that which I believe I saw with my eyes.

A man who makes it his aim to raise his knowledge above the common should be ashamed to derive the occasion for doubting from the forms of speech invented by the vulgar; I prefer to pass on and consider whether I had a more evident and perfect conception of what the wax was when I first perceived it, and when I believed I knew it by means of the external senses or at least by the common sense as it is called, that is to say by the imaginative faculty, or whether my present conception is clearer now that I have most carefully examined what it is, and in what way it can be known. It would certainly be absurd to doubt as to this. For what was there in this first perception which was distinct? What was there which might not as well have been perceived by any of the animals? But when I distinguish the wax from its external forms, and when, just as if I had taken from it its vestments, I consider it quite naked, it is certain that although some error may still be found in my judgment, I can nevertheless not perceive it thus without a human mind.

But finally what shall I say of this mind, that is, of myself, for up to this point I do not admit in myself anything but mind? What then, I who seem to perceive this piece of wax so distinctly, do I not know myself, not only with much more truth and certainty, but also with much more distinctness and clearness? For if I judge that the wax is or exists from the fact that I see it, it certainly follows much more clearly that I am or that I exist myself from the fact that I see it. For it may be that what I see is not really wax, it may also be that I do not possess eyes with which to see anything; but it cannot be that when I see, or (for I no longer take account of the distinction) when I think I see, that I myself who think am nought. So if I judge that the wax exists from the fact that I touch it, the same thing will follow, to wit, that I am; and if I judge that my imagination, or some other cause, whatever it is, persuades me that the wax exists, I shall still conclude the same. And what I have here remarked of wax may be applied to all other things which are external to me [and which are met with outside me]. And further, if the [notion or] perception of wax has seemed to me clearer and more distinct, not only after the sight or the touch, but also after many other causes have rendered it quite manifest to me, with how much more [evidence] and distinctness must it be said that I now know myself, since all the reasons which contribute to the knowledge of wax, or any other body whatever, are yet better proofs of the nature of my mind! And there are so many other things in the mind itself which may contribute to the elucidation of its nature, and that those which depend on body such as these just mentioned, hardly merit being taken into account.

But finally here I am, having insensibly reverted to the point I desired, for, since it is now manifest to me that even bodies are not properly speaking known by the senses or by the faculty of imagination, but by the understanding only, and since they are not known from the fact that they are seen or touched, but only because they are understood, I see clearly that there is nothing which is easier for me to know than my mind. But because it is difficult to rid oneself so promptly of an opinion to which one was accustomed for so long, it will be well that I should halt a little at this point, so that by the length of my meditation I may more deeply imprint on my memory this new knowledge.

RESPONSES: Questions for Writing and Discussion

1. It is clear that, without having perceived *through the senses* many times in the past the identical sequence of events involved in the melting of wax and without having perceived men wearing coats, the mind of Descartes would not understand these things. Does this fact make sense-experience more important than mind?

2. Understanding the identity of the wax is one thing; pursuing a complicated train of abstract thought is another. In the first instance the mind remains restricted to the realm of three-dimensional things. In the second—as, for example, when one reaches a conclusion about God's omnipotence or how to lead a good life—the mind is perceiving its own thoughts, not understanding actual phenomena. How do you feel about abstract speculation? Is it worth indulging in? Is it dangerous?

3. In the next to last paragraph of the selection, Descartes gets into that phase of his argument which has led his critics to question whether his thinking can confirm the existence of external reality at

all. Does he indeed appear to prove only that his mind is real? Or can he rightfully accept as real what the mind understands as being real?

4. Have you ever considered the possibility that only your ego, your mind, your awareness, exists?

5. Does it matter whether the external world is real as long as we think it is? Is it important to decide that issue once and for all?

6. What answer could be given to the person who protests "What's the difference whether you understand the wax or just see it and call it wax?"

7. Descartes died in 1650. His system of thought is no longer considered front-page news. He is revered in academic tradition as the father of modern philosophy. Is there any point in *your* taking note of him?

INFLEXIBLE LOGIC
Russell Maloney

Descartes said that through reason one could know everything. The Scottish philosopher David Hume, writing in the eighteenth century, said that, since certain knowledge came only from experience, one could know nothing until it actually happened. Projections of likely events in the future could never have the mathematical certainty Descartes longed to attain.

Hume's skeptical position about knowledge has bothered rationalists and logicians ever since. Still seeking a way to guarantee that mind has matter well under control, they have advanced one theory after another. A notable contribution to the cause in our century has been Hans Reichenbach's so-called "Law of Probability." According to Reichenbach, a logic of probability does in fact exist. As Professor Mallard, that passionate defender of the logical sciences, points out in the following story, if one tosses a coin in the air a sufficient number of times, the ratio of heads to tails ought to reduce itself to exactly fifty per cent.

Having heard about the Law of Probability, **Russell Maloney (1910–1948)** was apparently unable to resist the idea for this story. Known primarily to regular readers of the *New Yorker* and *The New York Times Book Review* during the thirties and forties, Maloney was a critic and satirist who specialized in the whimsical anecdote, poking fun at anything anyone took too seriously. Like all dedicated satirists, he asks us never to lose our respect for life's absurdities. Coping with them is also part of Human Worth.

Inflexible Logic

When the six chimpanzees came into his life, Mr. Bainbridge was thirty-eight years old. He was a bachelor and lived comfortably in a remote part of Connecticut, in a large old house with a carriage drive, a conservatory, a tennis court, and a well-selected library. His income was derived from impeccably situated real estate in New York City, and he spent it soberly, in a manner which could give offence to nobody. Once a year, late in April, his tennis court was resurfaced, and after that anybody in the neighborhood was welcome to use it; his monthly statement from Brentano's seldom ran below seventy-five dollars; every third year, in November, he turned in his old Cadillac coupé for a new one; he ordered his cigars, which were mild and rather moderately priced, in shipments of one thousand, from a tobacconist in Havana; because of the international situation he had cancelled arrangements to travel abroad, and after due thought had decided to spend his travelling allowance on wines, which seemed likely to get scarcer and more expensive if the war lasted. On the whole, Mr. Bainbridge's life was deliberately, and not too unsuccessfully, modelled after that of an English country gentleman of the late eighteenth century, a gentleman interested in the arts and in the expansion of science, and so sure of himself that he didn't care if some people thought him eccentric.

Mr. Bainbridge had many friends in New York, and he spent several days of the month in the city, staying at his club and looking around. Sometimes he called up a girl and took her out to a theatre and a night club. Sometimes he and a couple of classmates got a little tight and went to a prizefight. Mr. Bainbridge also looked in now and then at some of the conservative art galleries, and liked occasionally to go to a concert. And he liked cocktail parties, too, because of the fine footling conversation and the extraordinary number of pretty girls who had nothing else to do with the rest of their evening. It was at a New York cocktail party, however, that Mr. Bainbridge kept his preliminary appointment with doom. At one of the parties given by Hobie Packard, the stockbroker, he learned about the theory of the six chimpanzees.

It was almost six-forty. The people who had intended to have one drink and go had already gone, and the people who intended to stay were fortifying themselves with slightly dried canapés and talking animatedly. A group of stage and radio people had coagulated in one corner, near Packard's Capehart, and were wrangling about various methods of cheating the Collector of Internal Revenue. In another corner was a group of stockbrokers, talking about the greatest stockbroker of them all, Gauguin. Little Marcia Lupton was sitting with a young man, saying earnestly, "Do you really want to know what my greatest ambition is? I want to be myself," and Mr. Bainbridge smiled gently, thinking of the time Marcia had said that to him. Then he heard the voice of Bernard Weiss, the critic, saying, "Of course he wrote one good novel. It's not surprising. After all, we know that if six chimpanzees were set to work pounding six typewriters at random, they would, in a million years, write all the books in the British Museum."

Mr. Bainbridge drifted over to Weiss and was introduced to Weiss's companion, a Mr. Noble. "What's this about a million chimpanzees, Weiss?" he asked.

"Six chimpanzees," Mr. Weiss said. "It's an old cliché of the mathematicians. I thought everybody was told about it in school. Law of averages, you know, or maybe it's permutation and combination. The six chimps, just pounding away at the typewriter keys, would be bound to copy out all the books ever written by man. There are only so many possible combinations of letters and numerals, and they'd produce all of them—see? Of course they'd also turn out a mountain of gibberish, but they'd work the books in, too. All the books in the British Museum."

Mr. Bainbridge was delighted; this was the sort of talk he liked to hear when he came to New York. "Well, but look here," he said, just to keep up his part in the foolish conversation, "what if one of the chimpanzees finally did duplicate a book, right down to the last period, but left that off? Would that count?"

"I suppose not. Probably the chimpanzee would get around to doing the book again, and put the period in."

"What nonsense!" Mr. Noble cried.

"It may be nonsense, but Sir James Jeans believes it," Mr. Weiss said, huffily. "Jeans or Lancelot Hogben. I know I ran across it quite recently."

Mr. Bainbridge was impressed. He read quite a bit of popular science, and both Jeans and Hogben were in his library. "Is that so?" he murmured, no longer feeling frivolous. "Wonder if it has ever actually been tried? I mean, has anybody ever put six chimpanzees in a room with six typewriters and a lot of paper?"

Mr. Weiss glanced at Mr. Bainbridge's empty cocktail glass and said drily, "Probably not."

Nine weeks later, on a winter evening, Mr. Bainbridge was sitting in his study with his friend James Mallard, an assistant professor of mathematics at New Haven. He was plainly nervous as he poured himself a drink and said, "Mallard, I've asked you to come here— Brandy? Cigar?—for a particular reason. You remember that I wrote you some time ago, asking your opinion of . . . of a certain mathematical hypothesis or supposition."

"Yes," Professor Mallard said, briskly. "I remember perfectly. About the six chimpanzees and the British Museum. And I told you it was a perfectly sound popularization of a principle known to every schoolboy who had studied the science of probabilities."

"Precisely," Mr. Bainbridge said, "Well, Mallard, I made up my mind. . . . It was not difficult for me, because I have, in spite of that fellow in the White House, been able to give something every year to the Museum of Natural History, and they were naturally glad to oblige me. . . . And after all, the only contribution a layman can make to the progress of science is to assist with the drudgery of experiment. . . . In short, I—"

"I suppose you're trying to tell me that you have procured six chimpanzees and set them to work at typewriters in order to see whether they will eventually write all the books in the British Museum. Is that it?"

"Yes, that's it," Mr. Bainbridge said. "What a mind you have, Mallard. Six fine young males, in perfect condition. I had a—I suppose you'd call it a dormitory—built out in back of the stable. The typewriters are in the conservatory. It's light and airy in there, and I moved most of the plants out. Mr. North, the man who owns the circus, very obligingly let me engage one of his best animal men. Really, it was no trouble at all."

Professor Mallard smiled indulgently, "After all, such a thing is not unheard of," he said. "I seem to remember that a man at some university put his graduate students to work flipping coins, to see if heads and tails came up an equal number of times. Of course they did."

Mr. Bainbridge looked at his friend very queerly. "Then you believe that any such principle of the science of probabilities will stand up under an actual test?"

"Certainly."

"You had better see for yourself." Mr. Bainbridge led Professor Mallard downstairs, along a corridor, through a disused music room, and into a large conservatory. The middle of the floor had been cleared of plants and was occupied by a row of six typewriter tables, each one supporting a hooded machine. At the left of each typewriter was a neat stack of yellow copy paper. Empty wastebaskets were under each table. The chairs were the unpadded, spring-backed kind favored by experienced stenographers. A large bunch of ripe bananas was hanging in one corner, and in another stood a Great Bear water-cooler and a rack of Lily cups. Six piles of typescript, each about a foot high, were ranged along the wall on an improvised shelf. Mr. Bainbridge picked up one of the piles, which he could just conveniently lift, and set it on a table before Professor Mallard "The output to date of Chimpanzee A, known as Bill," he said simply.

" '"Oliver Twist," by Charles Dickens,' " Professor Mallard read out. He read the first and second pages of the manuscript, then feverishly leafed through to the end. "You mean to tell me," he said, "that this chimpanzee has written—"

"Word for word and comma for comma," said Mr. Bainbridge. "Young, my butler, and I took turns comparing it with the edition I own. Having finished 'Oliver Twist,' Bill is, as you see, starting the sociological works of Vilfredo Pareto, in Italian. At the rate he has been going, it should keep him busy for the rest of the month."

"And all the chimpanzees"—Professor Mallard was pale, and enunciated with difficulty—"they aren't all—"

"Oh, yes, all writing books which I have every reason to believe are in the British Museum. The prose of John Donne, some Anatole France, Conan Doyle, Galen, the collected plays of Somerset Maugham, Marcel Proust, the memoirs of the late Marie of Rumania, and a monograph by a Dr. Wiley on the marsh grasses of Maine and Massachusetts. I can sum it up for you, Mallard, by telling you that since I started this experiment, four weeks and some days ago, none of the chimpanzees has spoiled a single sheet of paper."

Professor Mallard straightened up, passed his handkerchief across his brow, and took a deep breath. "I apologize for my weakness," he said. "It was simply the sudden shock. No, looking at the thing scientifically—and I hope I am at least as capable of that as the next man— there is nothing marvellous about the situation. These chimpanzees, or a succession of similar teams of chimpanzees, would in a million years write all the books in the British Museum. I told you some time ago that I believed that statement. Why should my belief be altered by the fact that they produced some of the books at the very outset? After all, I should not be very much surprised if I tossed a coin a hundred time and it came up heads every time. I know that if I kept at it long enough, the ratio would reduce itself to an exact fifty percent. Rest assured, these chimpanzees will begin to compose gibberish quite soon. It is bound to happen. Science tells us so. Meanwhile, I advise you to keep this experiment secret. Uninformed people might create a sensation if they knew."

"I will, indeed," Mr. Bainbridge said. "And I'm very grateful for your rational analysis. It reassures me. And now, before you go, you must hear the new Schnabel records that arrived today."

During the succeeding three months, Professor Mallard got into the habit of telephoning Mr. Bainbridge every Friday afternoon at five-thirty, immediately after leaving his seminar room. The Professor would say, "Well?," and Mr. Bainbridge would reply, "They're still at it, Mallard. Haven't spoiled a sheet of paper yet." If Mr. Bainbridge had to go out on Friday afternoon, he would leave a written message with his butler, who would read it to Professor Mallard: "Mr. Bainbridge says we now have Trevelyan's 'Life of Macaulay,' the Confessions of St. Augustine, 'Vanity Fair,' part of Irving's 'Life of George Washington,' the Book of the Dead, and some speeches delivered in Parliament in opposition to the Corn Laws, sir." Professor Mallard would reply, with a hint of a snarl in his voice, "Tell him to remember what I predicted," and hang up with a clash.

The eleventh Friday that Professor Mallard telephoned, Mr. Bainbridge said, "No change. I have had to store the bulk of the manuscript in the cellar. I would have burned it, except that it probably has some scientific value."

"How dare you talk of scientific values?" The voice from New Haven roared faintly in the receiver. "Scientific value! You—you—chimpanzee!" There were further inarticulate sputterings, and Mr. Bainbridge hung up with a disturbed expression. "I am afraid Mallard is overtaxing himself," he murmured.

Next day, however, he was pleasantly surprised. He was leafing through a manuscript that had been completed the previous day by Chimpanzee D, Corky. It was the complete diary of Samuel Pepys, and Mr. Bainbridge was chuckling over the naughty passages, which were omitted in his own edition, when Professor Mallard was shown into the room. "I have come to apologize for my outrageous conduct on the telephone yesterday," the Professor said.

"Please don't think of it any more. I know you have many things on your mind," Mr. Bainbridge said. "Would you like a drink?"

"A large whiskey, straight, please," Professor Mallard said. "I got rather cold driving down. No change, I presume?"

"No, none. Chimpanzee F, Dinty, is just finishing John Florio's translation of Montaigne's essays, but there is no other news of interest."

Professor Mallard squared his shoulders and tossed off his drink in one astonishing gulp. "I should like to see them at work," he said. "Would I disturb them, do you think?"

"Not at all. As a matter of fact, I usually look in on them around this time of day. Dinty may have finished his Montaigne by now, and it is always interesting to see them start a new work. I would have thought that they would continue on the same sheet of paper, but they don't, you know. Always a fresh sheet, and the title in capitals."

Professor Mallard, without apology, poured another drink and slugged it down. "Lead on," he said.

It was dusk in the conservatory, and the chimpanzees were typing by the light of student lamps clamped to their desks. The keeper lounged in a corner, eating a banana and reading BILLBOARD. "You might as well take an hour or so off," Mr. Bainbridge said. The man left.

Professor Mallard, who had not taken off his overcoat, stood with his hands in his pockets, looking at the busy chimpanzees. "I wonder if you know, Bainbridge, that the science of probabilities takes everything into account," he said, in a queer, tight voice. "It is certainly almost beyond the bounds of credibility that these chimpanzees should write books without a single error, but that abnormality may be corrected by—*these!*" He took his hands from his pockets, and each one held a .38 revolver. "Stand back out of harm's way!" he shouted.

"Mallard! Stop it!" The revolvers barked, first the right hand, then the left, then the right. Two chimpanzees fell, and a third reeled into a corner. Mr. Bainbridge seized his friend's arm and wrested one of the weapons from him.

"Now I am armed, too, Mallard, and I advise you to stop!" he cried. Professor Mallard's answer was to draw a bead on Champanzee E and shoot him dead. Mr. Bainbridge made a rush, and Professor Mallard fired at him. Mr. Bainbridge, in his quick death agony, tightened his finger on the trigger of his revolver. It went off, and Professor Mallard went down. On his hands and knees he fired at the two chimpanzees which were still unhurt, and then collapsed.

There was nobody to hear his last words. "The human equation . . . always the enemy of science . . ." he panted. "This time . . . vice versa . . . I, a mere mortal . . . savior of science . . . deserve a Nobel . . ."

When the old butler came running into the conservatory to investigate the noises, his eyes were met by a truly appalling sight. The student lamps were shattered, but a newly risen moon shone in through the conservatory windows on the corpses of the two gentlemen, each clutching a smoking revolver. Five of the chimpanzees were dead. The sixth was Chimpanzee F. His right arm disabled, obviously bleeding to death, he was slumped before his typewriter. Painfully, with his left hand, he took from the machine the completed last page of Florio's Montaigne. Groping for a fresh sheet, he inserted it, and typed with one finger, "UNCLE TOM'S CABIN, by Harriet Beecher Stowe. Chapte . . ." then he, too, was dead.

RESPONSES: Questions for Writing and Discussion

1. Can you cite any instances in which "improbable" reality violated your expectations or theories? Did they lead to any changes in the way you relate to experience?

2. Look up Reichenbach's law of probability and decide whether you can accept its basic premises or on what grounds you reject them.

3. Have you ever had a professor like Mallard—one who might have or did become irrational when one of his pet ideas was challenged? Describe him to the rest of the class.

4. The author carefully specifies which books the chimpanzees are rewriting and even goes into considerable detail about some of them. Do you think he had any purpose in selecting particular books?

5. Draw a profile of Mr. Bainbridge as he is characterized in the beginning of the story. What is there about this kind of personality that makes it easier for him than it is for Professor Mallard to accept the phenomenon of the chimpanzees? Do you believe the author is making fun of Bainbridge too? Or advocating through this character a certain life style?

THE ROLE OF IDEAS
Crane Brinton

While Descartes believed that one could relate to and deal with the external world only through the rational processes of the mind, his way has been repeatedly challenged by those who distrust ideas, those who see a great gap between the thought and object. In particular, abstract thinking has come under fire. During the nineteenth century serious and systematic anti-intellectualism was fashionable in philosophical and academic circles. Writers depicted nature as a spectacular, spiritual entity operating in accordance with mysterious but unerring laws. To comprehend it rationally, to express its mysteries in logical terms, was to destroy its wonder and miss its fulness. One of the favorite subjects of nineteenth-century literature was the tragedy of growing up and learning to think logically. *Alice in Wonderland,* which most readers remember for its delightful whimsy, its madness and nonsense, deals, among many other serious themes, with the futility of rational efforts to comprehend experience. This drift toward other-than-rational kinds of awareness persists today. Much is being said about "pure" awareness or, as it is sometimes called, expanded consciousness. Much is said in favor of the totally sensuous life, a life to be lived not reasoned. Nonetheless, there have always been and continue to be dedicated exponents of the intellectual approach to living, men and women who are concerned with ideas and the rational interpretation of events.

Crane Brinton (1898–1968) is described as an intellectual historian. That is, he is a recorder and interpreter of the ideas and motives behind events that take place. He views history as being as real as, say, an architect's blueprint. If the building is to be comprehended, it is in terms of its design and purpose; and these are inherent in the blueprint. Neither buildings nor events make themselves happen.

Crane Brinton has been one of the strongest exponents of the intellectual life in modern times and one of the severest critics of its anti-intellectualism. Much of today's problems, he believes, are rooted in people's unwillingness to reflect upon what is happening. They have become passive victims of those who do think and have the power to extend their thoughts beyond themselves.

Brinton graduated *summa cum laude* from Harvard in 1919; he was a Rhodes Scholar, receiving the doctorate at New College, Oxford, in 1923. For three and one-half decades Harvard students sat in his popular courses in intellectual history and learned of the ideological forces which directed the onward flow of civilization. They learned that the past, present, and future were linked together as a continuous unfolding which can and must be understood. Only by comprehending where we have been and the causes of past events, Brinton taught, can we hope to deal effectively with the present and become masters of our future.

The Role of Ideas

There remain, therefore, a few bothersome questions of methods, perhaps even of philosophy, before we can begin the study of our Western

Crane Brinton, *Ideas and Men: The Story of Western Thought,* 2nd ed., © 1963. Reprinted by permission of Prentice-Hall, Inc., Englewood Cliffs, New Jersey.

intellectual heritage at its major Greek and Hebraic sources. The intellectual historian will try to see how ideas work in this world, will study the relation between what men say and what men actually do: What does he mean by ideas and what does he mean by saying that ideas do work in this world? Now these are themselves philosophical questions, about which men debate without agreeing. This fact alone should make it clear that these are not questions that can be answered as any American boy could answer such questions as: What does the automotive engineer mean by carburetor? and what does he mean when he says a carburetor does work?

Ideas are clearly different from carburetors, but one should not make the mistake of thinking they are less real than carburetors, less important in our lives, or that they are mere words and not important at all. We shall here take "ideas" in a very broad sense indeed as almost any coherent example of the workings of the human mind expressed in words. Thus, the word "ouch" uttered by a man who hits his finger with a hammer is probably not an idea at all. His statement "I hit my finger with a hammer" is a very simple proposition, and therefore an idea. A further statement, "My finger hurts because I hit it with a hammer," begins to involve more complicated ideas. Statements such as "My finger hurts because the hammer blow affected certain nerves which carried to my central nervous system a kind of stimulus we call pain" and "My finger hurts because God is punishing me for my sins" are both very complex propositions, taking us into two important realms of human thought, the scientific and the theological.

Now the classification of all the kinds of ideas that go to make up what we commonly call knowledge is in itself the major task of several disciplines, among them logic, epistemology, and semantics. And then there follows the task of deciding what knowledge is true, or how far given knowledge is true, and many other tasks that we cannot here undertake. In our own day, the study of semantics, the analysis of the complicated ways in which words get interpreted as they are used in communication among human beings, has aroused widespread interest. For our present purposes, it will be sufficient to make a basic but very controversial distinction between two kinds of knowledge, cumulative and noncumulative.

Cumulative knowledge is best exemplified by the knowledge we call commonly natural science, or just science. From the beginnings of the study of astronomy and physics several thousand years ago in the eastern Mediterranean, our astronomical and physical ideas have *accumulated,* have gradually built up into the astronomy and physics we study in school and college. The process of building up has not been regular, but on the whole it has been steady. Some of the ideas or theories of the very beginning, such as the ideas of the ancient Greek Archimedes on specific gravity are still held true, but many, many others have been added to the original stock. Many have been discarded as false. The result is a discipline, a science, with a solid and universally accepted core of accumulated knowledge and a growing outer edge of new knowledge. Dispute—and scientists dispute quite as much as do philosophers and private persons—centers on this growing outer edge, not in the core. This core all scientists accept as true.

New knowledge can, of course, be reflected back through the whole core, and cause what may not unfairly be called a "revolution" in the science. Thus quantum mechanics and relativity theories have been reflected back into the core of Newtonian physics; but the work of twentieth-century physicists has not proved Newton's work "wrong," at any rate not in the sense the convinced Christian must hold that the mission of Jesus proved the Graeco-Roman faith in the gods of Olympus (polytheism) to be "wrong."

Noncumulative knowledge can here be illustrated best from the field of literature. Men of letters make certain propositions, entertain certain ideas, about men, about right and wrong action, about beautiful and ugly things. Over two thousand years ago, men of letters were writing in Greek on these matters; at the same time others were writing in Greek about the movements of the stars or about the displacement of solids in water. But our contemporary men of letters are today writing about the very same things the Greek men of letters wrote about, in much the same way and with no clear and certain increase in knowledge. Our men of science, on the other hand, have about astronomy and physics far more knowledge, far more ideas and propositions, than the Greeks had.

To put the matter most simply: A Greek man of letters like Aristophanes, a Greek philosopher like Plato, if miraculously brought to earth in the mid-twentieth century and given speech with us (but no knowledge since his death) could talk fairly soon about literature or philosophy with a G. B. Shaw or a John Dewey, and feel quite at home; a Greek scientist like Archimedes in the same position would, even though he were a genius, need to spend a good many days grinding over elementary and advanced textbooks of physics and acquiring enough mathematics before he could begin to talk shop with a modern physicist like Bohr or Einstein. To put is another way: A modern American college student is not wiser than one of the sages of antiquity, has no better taste than an artist of antiquity, but he knows a lot more physics than the greatest Greek scientist ever knew. He knows more *facts* about literature and philosophy than the wisest Greek of 400 B.C. could know; but in physics he not only knows more facts—he understands the relations between facts, that is, the theories and the laws.

This distinction between cumulative and noncumulative knowledge is useful and obvious, which is about all one need expect from a distinction. *Such a distinction does not mean that science is good and useful, and that art, literature, and philosophy are bad and useless, but merely that in respect to the attribute of cumulativeness they are different.* Many people do take this distinction as a statement that art is somehow inferior to science, and are offended by it to the point of rejecting any truth or usefulness the distinction may have. This is a common habit of men, and one the intellectual historian must reckon with.

Perhaps it is merely that in the last three hundred years science has accumulated very *rapidly*, while art, literature, and philosophy have accumulated *slowly* for several thousand years. Our great men may in some senses be wiser than the great men of old; and the average wisdom, or good sense, of American citizens may be greater than that of Athenian citizens. But these matters are very hard to measure, very hard to get agreement on; and the cumulative character of scientific knowledge is well-nigh indisputable. The most hopeful defender of progress in art and philosophy would hardly maintain as a formula: Shakespeare is to Sophocles as Einstein is to Archimedes or that Greek drama is to American drama as the horse-drawn chariot is to the rocket-propelled space vehicle.

The foregoing necessarily oversimplifies the distinction between cumulative and noncumulative knowledge. Notably, for generations of Western thinkers, as for many thinkers today, that part of human knowledge not subsumed under "science" is given less than justice by the tag "non-cumulative." It can be argued that what are commonly called the social sciences have in their own right, not just as rather feeble imitations of the natural sciences, an accumulated body of knowledge about the interrelations of human beings. This knowledge is an accumulation not merely of facts, but also of valid interpretations of the facts. Thus economists, in the century and a half from Adam Smith to Lord Keynes, have come to *understand* more about economic activity. It can be argued that philosophers, though they still face some of the questions that faced Plato and Aristotle, have over the centuries improved their methods of analysis, and have refined into greater precision the questions they ask themselves. Finally, though the cynic may say that all we learn from history is that we never learn from history, most of us would hold that over the centuries Western men have built up a body of wisdom and good taste that was not available to the Greeks. How widely such wisdom and taste are spread in our society is another question.

Indeed, for both cumulative and noncumulative knowledge the problem of *dissemination*, the problem of correcting common errors in public thinking, is at least as important as, and in a democratic society perhaps more important than, the problem of getting the experts to agree. This should be evident, save to the most determined scorners of economic thought, in a field like economics. Of course the economists disagree. So do the doctors. Even in modern America, where medicine has a very high prestige among all classes, it is by no means easy to educate the public to act intelligently in medical matters. In economic matters, the public remains even in mid-twentieth century largely unable to make use of the accumulated knowledge the experts possess.

The intellectual historian clearly must concern himself with *both* cumulative and noncumulative knowledge, and must do his best to distinguish one kind of knowledge from another, to trace their mutual relations, and to study their effect on human behavior. Both kinds of knowledge are important, and each does its own work.

We thus come to the second of our questions: How do ideas work? Any answer must take into account the fact that often *ideas* are really *ideals*—expressions of hopes and aspirations, goals of human desire and effort. We say, for instance, that "all men are created equal," or, with the poet Keats,

> "Beauty is truth, truth beauty,"—that is all
> Ye know on earth, and all ye need to know.

What can statements like these mean? If you assert that a heavy weight and a lighter weight will drop through the air at different rates, you can drop them from a height and see. Galileo did this, though not, we now know, from the Leaning Tower of Pisa. Witnesses can also see, and should agree after they have checked what they saw. But you cannot possibly test the assertion of human equality or the identity of truth and beauty in any such fashion, and you can be very sure that after argument on such propositions, a random sample of human beings will not in fact agree about them.

In a general way, the kind of knowledge we have called cumulative, that is, scientific knowledge, is subject to the kind of test that makes it possible for all sane, properly trained men to agree upon its truth or falsehood; and the kind of knowledge we have called noncumulative is not subject to such a test, nor capable of producing such an agreement. Hence, as stated earlier, some have concluded that noncumulative knowledge is of no use, is not really knowledge, has no meaning, and, above all, has no real effect on human behavior. These people often fancy themselves as hard-boiled realists, as sensible people who know what the world really is like. They are actually very mistaken people, as narrow-minded as the most innocent of the idealists they condemn.

For, at the very least, a proposition like "all men are created equal" means that somebody *wants* all men to be equal in some respects. In the form "all men ought to be equal" the proposition would be frankly what we call an ideal. This confusion of "ought" and "is" turns out for the intellectual historian to be another of the abiding habits of men's thinking. Moreover, he will realize that "ought" and "is" influence one another mutually, are parts of a whole process, not independent, and not—at least not often—mutually contradictory. Indeed, he will know that the effort to close the gap between ideal and real, between "ought" and "is," supplies one of the main interests of intellectual history. The gap has never been closed, certainly not by idealists who deny the "is," nor by realists who deny the "ought." Men do not consistently act in logical (rational) accordance with their professed ideals; here the realist scores. But their professed ideals are not meaningless, and thinking about ideals is not a silly and ineffective activity that has no effect on their lives. Ideals, as well as appetites, push men into action; here the idealist scores.

Today in the United States we are perhaps more liable to be led astray by the realist's than by the idealist's error, though throughout our history we have been lured by many ideals. Again, the study of intellectual history ought to help us understand why. But for the moment we can content ourselves with the observation that in human history there are no important facts unrelated to ideas, no important ideas unrelated to facts. The debate, a favorite one between Marxists and their opponents, whether economic changes are more basic than other changes, is logically pointless. No automotive engineer would dream of debating whether the gasoline or the spark makes an internal-combustion engine run, let alone which came first, the gasoline or the spark. No intellectual historian need debate whether ideas OR interests move men in their relations in society, nor which comes first. Without BOTH gasoline and spark, no working gasoline-powered internal-combustion engine; without BOTH ideas and interests (or appetites, or drives, or material factors) no working human society, and no human history.

RESPONSES: Questions for Writing and Discussion

1. Many people, Brinton advises, take the distinction between cumulative and noncumulative knowledge to mean that "art is somehow inferior to science." In other words, because science has "proved" itself, it is, in their opinions, entitled to be a reputable human disci-

pline, but, since art and philosophy never give final answers or create useful products, they can be safely ignored. What is your own current disposition toward these two poles of human knowledge?

2. "Finally, though the cynic may say that all we learn from history is that we never learn from history, most of us would hold that over the centuries Western men have built up a body of wisdom and good taste that was not available to the Greeks. How widely such wisdom and taste are spread in our society is another question." In this statement Brinton implies that possibly those who devote themselves to understanding both cumulative and noncumulative knowledge are the ones most affected by it. What statement is he making, without saying it in so many words, about "our society"?

3. In your opinion, does it make any difference whether the majority of people acquaint themselves with such a "body of wisdom and good taste"?

4. Assuming that the intellectual historian is accurate in his understanding and explanation of the currents which have steered civilization, does such a person attain an advantage over those who *never* relate to the past in any manner?

5. We find a clue to the reason noncumulative knowledge is different from scientific knowledge in Brinton's assertion that ideas are often *ideals* and in the distinction he observes throughout intellectual history between "ought" and "is." But, he adds, an awareness of the difference is anything but a waste of time. Why does he believe this?

6. "Today in the United States we are perhaps more liable to be led astray by the realist's than by the idealist's error. . ." In this statement Brinton compresses two things: a justification for the study of intellectual history and a blueprint for a better future, with intellectual history pointing the way. Explain further.

7. Brinton continually speaks about Western men and Western ideas. Almost everyone has been taught in school about "our Western heritage"—an approach which has been derived from the intellectual historians. Granted that in most cases the omission of other traditions is owing to a lack of knowledge about them, do you think the historians have come up with abundant evidence that the Western tradition has been the dominating force of modern civilization? Only of Western civilization? If you became president of a university, would you suggest any changes in the way intellectual history is taught?

OVERSTIMULATION AND THE BREAKDOWN OF REASON

Alvin Toffler

With *Future Shock* **Alvin Toffler** (b. **1928**) has become one of the major prophets of our age. He has been the one to discover, name, and define the condition which is the title of his book—the psychic trauma most of us experience when we find ourselves unable to comprehend what is happening around us, when we realize that little we have learned in school of science, geography, economic principles, and communication relates to conditions that actually exist. The reason, he tells us, is that the world is changing at a continually accelerating rate of speed, made possible by technological advances, notably computerization and rapid means of communication which bombard the senses and the mind with more input than the human organism was apparently ever meant to handle. The result, for many people, is an automatic paralysis, a terrified retreat from a reality with which they cannot cope. Drugs, mysticism, and nostalgia for the past are three popular escape routes.

One of the principle victims of future shock is the rational life itself. The mind, according to Toffler, may not have been designed to make order out of the overwhelming quantity of ideas generated in response to modern living. To cite an obvious example: Even before we begin our day, with its still unsolved problems of school or job, we may turn on television for the morning news. Instantly our brains are whirling from the information being flashed from all over the globe. Perhaps the morning paper is propped up in front of us at the same time. The community, the national, the international scene—all are converging upon us simultaneously, and where are we in the midst of it all? The "leisurely" trip to office or campus helps not one bit.

Rational thought and rational behavior, conversely, require a slower rhythm between the intake of stimuli and the realization of a sensible idea. Have you ever found yourself at the end of the thoroughfare, needing to turn left or right, not knowing which, trying to determine where exactly you are, while the impatient motorists behind you keep blaring their angry horns? The breakdown of the rational faculty, as Toffler describes it, is a little like this, except perhaps magnified thousands of times.

The following selection from *Future Shock* describes what the author thinks is happening inside our minds as the swift transitions from today to tomorrow cause an overstimulation of consciousness. Leading into this section, Toffler writes: "Psychophysiologists studying the impact of change on various organisms have shown that successful adaptation can occur only when the level of stimulation—the amount of change and novelty in the

408

environment—is neither too low nor too high." The results of overstimulation can, he adds, be evidenced by the soaring crime rates and the increase in acts of apparently motiveless vandalism and violence—all signs of growing irrationality in people.

Overstimulation and the Breakdown of Reason

Information Overload

If overstimulation at the sensory level increases the distortion with which we perceive reality, cognitive overstimulation interferes with our ability to "think." While some human responses to novelty are involuntary, others are preceded by conscious thought, and this depends upon our ability to absorb, manipulate, evaluate and retain information.

Rational behavior, in particular, depends upon a ceaseless flow of data from the environment. It depends upon the power of the individual to predict, with at least fair success, the outcome of his own actions. To do this, he must be able to predict how the environment will respond to his acts. Sanity, itself, thus hinges on man's ability to predict his immediate, personal future on the basis of information fed him by the environment.

When the individual is plunged into a fast and irregularly changing situation, or a novelty-loaded context, however, his predictive accuracy plummets. He can no longer make the reasonably correct assessments on which rational behavior is dependent.

To compensate for this, to bring his accuracy up to the normal level again, he must scoop up and process far more information than before. And he must do this at extremely high rates of speed. In short, the more rapidly changing and novel the environment, the more information the individual needs to process in order to make effective, rational decisions.

Yet just as there are limits on how much sensory input we can accept, there are in-built constraints on our ability to process information. In the words of psychologist George A. Miller of Rockefeller University, there are "severe limitations on the amount of information that we are able to receive, process, and remember." By classifying information, by abstracting and "coding" it in various ways, we manage to stretch these limits, yet ample evidence demonstrates that our capabilities are finite.

To discover these outer limits, psychologists and communications theorists have set about testing what they call the "channel capacity" of the human organism. For the purpose of these experiments, they regard man as a "channel." Information enters from the outside. It is processed. It exits in the form of · actions based on decisions. The speed and accuracy of human information processing can be measured by comparing the speed of information input with the speed and accuracy of output.

Information has been defined technically and measured in terms of units called "bits."[1] By now, experiments have established rates for the processing involved in a wide variety of tasks from reading, typing, and playing the piano to manipulating dials or doing mental arithmetic. And while researchers differ as to the exact figures, they strongly agree on two basic principles: first, that man has limited capacity; and second, that overloading the system leads to serious breakdown of performance.

Imagine, for example, an assembly line worker in a factory making childrens' blocks. His job is to press a button each time a red block passes in front of him on the conveyor belt. So long as the belt moves at a reasonable speed, he will have little difficulty. His performance will approach 100 percent accuracy. We know that if the pace is too slow, his mind will wander, and his performance will deteriorate. We also know that if the belt moves too fast, he will falter, miss, grow confused and uncoordinated. He is likely to become tense and irritable. He may even take a swat at the machine out of pure frustration. Ultimately, he will give up trying to keep pace.

Here the information demands are simple, but picture a more complex task. Now the blocks streaming down the line are of many different colors. His instructions are to press the button only when a certain color pattern appears—a yellow block, say, followed by two reds and a green. In this task, he must take in and process far more information before he can decide whether or not to hit the button. All other things being equal, he will have even greater difficulty keeping up as the pace of the line accelerates.

In a still more demanding task, we not only force the worker to process a lot of data before deciding *whether* to hit the button, but we then force him to decide *which* of several buttons to press. We can also vary the number of times each button must be pressed. Now

---

[1] A bit is the amount of information needed to make a decision between two equally likely alternatives. The number of bits needed increases by one as the number of such alternatives doubles.

his instructions might read: For color pattern yellow-red-red-green, hit button number two once; for pattern green-blue-yellow-green, hit button number six three times; and so forth. Such tasks require the worker to process a large amount of data in order to carry out his task. Speeding up the conveyor now will destroy his accuracy even more rapidly.

Experiments like these have been built up to dismaying degrees of complexity. Tests have involved flashing lights, musical tones, letters, symbols, spoken words, and a wide array of other stimuli. And subjects, asked to drum fingertips, speak phrases, solve puzzles, and perform an assortment of other tasks, have been reduced to blithering ineptitude.

The results unequivocally show that no matter what the task, there is a speed above which it cannot be performed—and not simply because of inadequate muscular dexterity. The top speed is often imposed by mental rather than muscular limitations. These experiments also reveal that the greater the number of alternative courses of action open to the subject, the longer it takes him to reach a decision and carry it out.

Clearly, these findings can help us understand certain forms of psychological upset. Managers plagued by demands for rapid, incessant and complex decisions; pupils deluged with facts and hit with repeated tests; housewives confronted with squalling children, jangling telephones, broken washing machines, the wail of rock and roll from the teenager's living room and the whine of the television set in the parlor—may well find their ability to think and act clearly impaired by the waves of information crashing into their senses. It is more than possible that some of the symptoms noted among battle-stressed soldiers, disaster victims, and culture shocked travelers are related to this kind of information overload.

One of the men who has pioneered in information studies, Dr. James G. Miller, director of the Mental Health Research Institute at the University of Michigan, states flatly that "Glutting a person with more information than he can process may . . . lead to disturbance." He suggests, in fact, that information overload may be related to various forms of mental illness.

One of the striking features of schizophrenia, for example, is "incorrect associative response." Ideas and words that ought to be linked in the subject's mind are not, and vice versa. The schizophrenic tends to think in arbitrary or highly personalized categories. Confronted with a set of blocks of various kinds—triangles, cubes, cones, etc.—the normal person is likely to categorize them in terms of geometric shape. The schizophrenic asked to classify them is just as likely to say "They are all soldiers" or "They all make me feel sad."

In the volume *Disorders of Communication*, Miller describes experiments using word association tests to compare normals and schizophrenics. Normal subjects were divided into two groups, and asked to associate various words with other words or concepts. One group worked at its own pace. The other worked under time pressure—i.e., under conditions of rapid information input. The time-pressed subjects came up with responses more like those of schizophrenics than of self-paced normals.

Similar experiments conducted by psychologists G. Usdansky and L. J. Chapman made possible a more refined analysis of the types of errors made by subjects working under forced-pace, high information-input rates. They, too, concluded that increasing the speed of response brought out a pattern of errors among normals that is peculiarly characteristic of schizophrenics.

"One might speculate," Miller suggests, ". . . that schizophrenia (by some as-yet-unknown process, perhaps a metabolic fault which increases neural 'noise') lowers the capacities of channels involved in cognitive information processing. Schizophrenics consequently . . . have difficulties in coping with information inputs at standard rates like the difficulties experienced by normals at rapid rates. As a result, schizophrenics make errors at standard rates like those made by normals under fast, forced-input rates."

In short, Miller argues, the breakdown of human performance under heavy information loads may be related to psychopathology in ways we have not yet begun to explore. Yet, even without understanding its potential impact, we are accelerating the generalized rate of change in society. We are forcing people to adapt to a new life pace, to confront novel situations and master them in ever shorter intervals. We are forcing them to choose among fast-multiplying options. We are, in other words, forcing them to process information at a far more rapid pace than was necessary in slowly-evolving societies. There can be little doubt that we are subjecting at least some of them to cognitive overstimulation. What consequences this may have for mental health in the techno-societies has yet to be determined.

Decision Stress

Whether we are submitting masses of men to information overload or not, we are affecting their behavior negatively by imposing on them still a third form of overstimulation—decision stress. Many individuals trapped in dull or slowly changing environments yearn to break out into new jobs or roles that require them to make faster and more complex decisions. But among the people of the future, the problem is reversed. "Decisions, decisions . . ." they mutter as they race anxiously from task to task. The reason they feel harried and upset is that transience, novelty and diversity pose contradictory demands and thus place them in an excruciating double bind.

The accelerative thrust and its psychological counterpart, transience, force us to quicken the tempo of private and public decision-making. New needs, novel emergencies and crises demand rapid response.

Yet the very newness of the circumstances brings about a revolutionary change in the nature of the decisions they are called upon to make. The rapid injection of novelty into the environment upsets the delicate balance of "programmed" and "non-programmed" decisions in our organizations and our private lives.

A programmed decision is one that is routine, repetitive and easy to make. The commuter stands at the edge of the platform as the 8:05 rattles to a stop. He climbs aboard, as he has done every day for months or years. Having long ago decided that the 8:05 is the most convenient run on the schedule, the actual decision to board the train is programmed. It seems more like a reflex than a decision at all. The immediate criteria on which the decision is based are relatively simple and clear-cut, and because all the circumstances are familiar, he scarcely has to think about it. He is not required to process very much information. In this sense, programmed decisions are low in psychic cost.

Contrast this with the kind of decisions that same commuter thinks about on his way to the city. Should he take the new job Corporation X has just offered him? Should he buy a new house? Should he have an affair with his secretary? How can he get the Management Committee to accept his proposals about the new ad campaign? Such questions demand non-routine answers. They force him to make one-time or first-time decisions that will establish new habits and behavioral procedures. Many factors must be studied and weighed. A vast amount of information must be processed. These decisions are non-programmed. They are high in psychic cost.

For each of us, life is a blend of the two. If this blend is too high in programmed decisions, we are not challenged; we find life boring and stultifying. We search for ways, even unconsciously, to introduce novelty into our lives, thereby altering the decision "mix." But if this mix is too high in non-programmed decisions, if we are hit by so many novel situations that programming becomes impossible, life becomes painfully disorganized, exhausting and anxiety-filled. Pushed to its extreme, the end-point is psychosis.

"Rational behavior . . . ," writes organization theorist Bertram M. Gross, "always includes an intricate combination of routinization and creativity. Routine is essential . . . [because it] frees creative energies for dealing with the more baffling array of new problems for which routinization is an irrational approach."

When we are unable to program much of our lives, we suffer. "There is no more miserable person," wrote William James, "than one . . . for whom the lighting of every cigar, the drinking of every cup . . . the beginning of every bit of work, are subjects of deliberation." For unless we can extensively program our behavior, we waste tremendous amounts of information-processing capacity on trivia.

This is why we form habits. Watch a committee break for lunch and then return to the same room: almost invariably its members seek out the same seats they occupied earlier. Some anthropologists drag in the theory of "territoriality" to explain this behavior—the notion that man is forever trying a carve out for himself a sacrosanct "turf." A simpler explanation lies in the fact that programming conserves information-processing capacity. Choosing the same seat spares us the need to survey and evaluate other possibilities.

In a familiar context, we are able to handle many of our life problems with low-cost programmed decisions. Change and novelty boost the psychic price of decision-making. When we move to a new neighborhood, for example, we are forced to alter old relationships and establish new routines or habits. This cannot be done without first discarding thousands of formerly programmed decisions and making a whole series of costly new first-time, non-programmed decisions. In effect, we are asked to re-program ourselves.

Precisely the same is true of the unprepared visitor to an alien culture, and it is equally true of the man who, still in his own society, is rocketed into the future without advance warning. The arrival of the future in the form of novelty and change makes all his painfully pieced-together behavioral routines obsolete. He suddenly discovers to his horror that these old routines, rather than solving his problems, merely intensify them. New and as yet unprogrammable decisions are demanded. In short, novelty disturbs the decision mix, tipping the balance toward the most difficult, most costly form of decision-making.

It is true that some people can tolerate more novelty than others. The optimum mix is different for each of us. Yet the number and type of decisions demanded of us are not under our autonomous control. It is the society that basically determines the mix of decisions we must make and the pace at which me must make them. Today there is a hidden conflict in our lives between the pressures of acceleration and those of novelty. One forces us to make faster decisions while the other compels us to make the hardest, most time-consuming type of decisions.

The anxiety generated by this head-on collision is sharply intensified by expanding diversity. Incontrovertible evidence shows that increasing the number of choices open to an individual also increases the amount of information he needs to process if he is to deal with them. Laboratory tests on men and animals alike prove that the more the choices, the slower the reaction time.

It is the frontal collision of these three incompatible demands that is now producing a decision-making crisis in the techno-societies. Taken together these pressures justify the term "decisional overstimulation," and they help explain why masses of men in these societies already feel themselves harried, futile, incapable of working out their private futures. The conviction that the rat-race is too tough, that things are out of control, is the inevitable consequence of these clashing forces. For the uncontrolled acceleration of scientific, technological and social change subverts the power of the individual to make sensible, competent decisions about his own destiny.

RESPONSES: Questions for Writing and Discussion

1. Toffler defines sanity as the condition of being able to predict one's "immediate, personal future on the basis of information fed him by the environment." Many might take exception to this. If we are indeed suffering from an overdose of such information, is it possible that sanity results from setting up defenses against overstimulation? What might some of these be?

2. Some studies by psychologists have shown that it is possible to function effectively at noise levels of extremely high decibels. Many students, for example, insist they cannot do their homework *unless* television and other distractions are in the background. What are your personal study habits? Are you able to work better in complete solitude or in the midst of mild chaos?

3. But, regardless of how one works at his own speed when there are distractions in the environment, Toffler believes it is difficult to make effective *quick* responses under the stress of today's way of life. He cites the example of managers who have to make split-second decisions or students who are "hit with repeated tests." In this latter connection: How do you feel about multiple-choice, true-false, and identification-of-terms exams with rigidly observed time limits? Are these valid instruments for evaluation of learning? Do they *add* to future shock? Try to be fair. Try to see both sides of the issue.

4. Cramming the night before an exam is possibly another case of information overload. Many find it just the thing for "aceing" a course. Others say they refuse to worry enough about a grade to get themselves worked up during these sometimes all-night cram sessions. They add that none of the knowledge thus absorbed stays with them

anyway. How do you feel about cramming? Is it the fault of the teacher who makes up a test that necessitates this method of study? Is it possible to retain the information when it is absorbed over a longer period of time? Do you easily forget what you have crammed into your head?

5. In what ways may the rising rate of vandalism and acts of violence be attributable to information overload? Are other interpretations possible?

6. Run through a typical day in your life and list the programmed decisions that you normally make. Then list the decisions you had to make yesterday which were not programmed. Is Toffler right? Did you suffer from "decision stress" brought on by the pace of your existence? Were you able to handle all of these decisions successfully?

7. While Toffler finds most people feeling "harried, futile, incapable of working out their private futures," it is also true that many suffer from an advanced state of apathy, especially on the campus. One notes increasing numbers of both teachers and students who seem to bring less and less energy to the labor of instruction and learning. (a) Is this the case on your campus? (b) If so, do you believe such apathy is also a result of information overload and decision stress? (c) Are there other possible causes?

THEFT
Katherine Anne Porter

Written in the 1920s, this short story has enjoyed uninterrupted fame for its subtle depiction of the inner life and the anguish of an intellectual woman. In fact, much of this author's work revolves around the general themes of ego, especially that of hyper-intelligent people who cannot for all their brilliance manage their own lives; the need for love; and the failure of highly civilized people to communicate with each other and make real contact with their feelings. Another of this author's most famous stories, "Flowering Judas," has an intellectual heroine who participates in the Marxist revolution for the sheer logic of it rather than for a deep feeling for people and who finds herself, very much like the "she" of "Theft," tragically alone.

A native of Texas, **Katherine Anne Porter (b. 1894)** obtained her education less from formal studies than from extensive travel to the cosmopolitan centers of the world, including New York, Chicago, New Orleans, Paris, Berlin, and Mexico City. The themes of her stories appear to have developed from many of the associations she formed and the people she had an opportunity to observe: artists, intellectuals, ultra-sophisticates of the twenties; expatriated Americans who could not bring themselves to mingle with the materialistic, uncultured middle-class; persons like the heroine of "Theft" who wrote brilliant and incisive prose, took part in civilized repartee, read all the right books, attended the right plays, and were always sure to be seen in the cafés fashionable throughout the international world of "in" people.

The degree to which the prevalent theme of reason-versus-feeling was a personal preoccupation one can only speculate upon. The author has certainly dropped hints, as, for example, in this statement from the introduction to *Flowering Judas*, a collection published in 1930:

> We none of us flourished in those times, artists
> or not, for art, like the human life of which it
> is the truest voice, thrives best by daylight in
> a green and growing world.

But at the same time, as one reads story after story in the Porter canon, one realizes that her major theme is not you or me, not any one person, but, rather, it is an indictment of Western civilization itself.

> For myself, and I was not alone, all the recollected
> years of my life have been lived to this day under
> the heavy threat of catastrophe, and most of the
> energies of my mind and spirit have been spent in
> the effort to grasp the meaning of those threats,
> to trace them to their sources and to understand the
> logic of this majestic and terrible failure of the
> life of man in the Western world.

The logic of our "terrible failure" may be the result of logic itself. Katherine Anne Porter appears to be saying that the commitment to an intellectual approach to life, which Western man has for so many years considered the distinguishing mark of the human being, is the very thing which has taken humanity *from* him.

Theft

She had the purse in her hand when she came in. Standing in the middle of the floor, holding her bathrobe around her and trailing a

damp towel in one hand, she surveyed the immediate past and remembered everything clearly. Yes, she had opened the flap and spread
it out on the bench after she had dried the purse with her handkerchief.

She had intended to take the Elevated, and naturally she looked
in her purse to make certain she had the fare, and was pleased to
find forty cents in the coin envelope. She was going to pay her own
fare, too, even if Camilo did have the habit of seeing her up the
steps and dropping a nickel in the machine before he gave the
turnstile a little push and sent her through it with a bow. Camilo
by a series of compromises had managed to make effective a fairly
complete set of smaller courtesies, ignoring the larger and more
troublesome ones. She had walked with him to the station in a
pouring rain, because she knew he was almost as poor as she was,
and when he insisted on a taxi, she was firm and said, "You know it
simply will not do." He was wearing a new hat of a pretty biscuit
shade, for it never occurred to him to buy anything of a practical
color; he had put it on for the first time and the rain was spoiling it.
She kept thinking, "But this is dreadful, where will he get another?"
She compared it with Eddie's hats that always seemed to be precisely seven years old and as if they had been quite purposely left
out in the rain, and yet they sat with a careless and incidental rightness on Eddie. But Camilo was far different; if he wore a shabby hat
it would be merely shabby on him, and he would lose his spirits over
it. If she had not feared Camilo would take it badly, for he insisted
on the practice of his little ceremonies up to the point he had fixed
for them, she would have said to him as they left Thora's house,
"Do go home. I can surely reach the station by myself."

"It is written that we must be rained upon tonight," said Camilo,
"so let it be together."

At the foot of the platform stairway she staggered slightly—they
were both nicely set up on Thora's cocktails—and said: "At least,
Camilo, do me the favor not to climb these stairs in your present state,
since for you it is only a matter of coming down again at once, and
you'll certainly break your neck."

He made three quick bows, he was Spanish, and leaped off
through the rainy darkness. She stood watching him, for he was a
very graceful young man, thinking that tomorrow morning he would
gaze soberly at his spoiled hat and soggy shoes and possibly associate
her with his misery. As she watched, he stopped at the far corner and
took off his hat and hid it under his overcoat. She felt she had betrayed him by seeing, because he would have been humiliated if he
thought she even suspected him of trying to save his hat.

Roger's voice sounded over her shoulder above the clang of the rain falling on the stairway shed, wanting to know what she was doing out in the rain at this time of night, and did she take herself for a duck? His long, imperturbable face was streaming with water, and he tapped a bulging spot on the breast of his buttoned-up overcoat: "Hat," he said, "Come on, let's take a taxi."

She settled back against Roger's arm which he laid around her shoulders, and with the gesture they exchanged a glance full of long amiable associations, then she looked through the window at the rain changing the shapes of everything, and the colors. The taxi dodged in and out between the pillars of the Elevated, skidding slightly on every curve, and she said: "The more it skids the calmer I feel, so I really must be drunk."

"You must be," said Roger. "This bird is a homicidal maniac, and I could do with a cocktail myself this minute."

They waited on the traffic at Fortieth Street and Sixth Avenue, and three boys walked before the nose of the taxi. Under the globes of light they were cheerful scarecrows, all very thin and all wearing very seedy snappy-cut suits and gay neckties. They were not very sober either, and they stood for a moment wobbling in front of the car, and there was an argument going on among them. They leaned toward each other as if they were getting ready to sing, and the first one said: "When I get married it won't be jus' for getting married, I'm gonna marry for *love*, see?" and the second one said, "Aw gwan and tell that stuff to *her*, why n't yuh?" and the third one gave a kind of hoot, and said, "Hell, dis guy? Wot the hell's he got?" and the first one said: "Aaah, shurrup yuh mush, I got plenty." Then they all squealed and scrambled across the street beating the first one on the back and pushing him around.

"Nuts," commented Roger, "pure nuts."

Two girls went skittering by in short transparent raincoats, one green, one red, their heads tucked against the drive of the rain. One of them was saying to the other, "Yes, I know all about *that*. But what about me? You're always so sorry for *him* . . ." and they ran on with their little pelican legs flashing back and forth.

The taxi backed up suddenly and leaped forward again, and after a while Roger said: "I had a letter from Stella today, and she'll be home on the twenty-sixth, so I suppose she's made up her mind and it's all settled."

"I had a sort of letter today too," she said, "making up my mind for me. I think it is time for you and Stella to do something definite."

When the taxi stopped on the corner of West Fifty-third Street, Roger said, "I've just enough if you'll add ten cents," so she opened her purse and gave him a dime, and he said, "That's beautiful, that purse."

"It's a birthday present," she told him, "and I like it. How's your show coming?"

"Oh, still hanging on, I guess. I don't go near the place. Nothing sold yet. I mean to keep right on the way I'm going and they can take it or leave it. I'm through with the argument."

"It's absolutely a matter of holding out, isn't it?"

"Holding out's the tough part."

"Good night, Roger."

"Good night, you should take aspirin and push yourself into a tub of hot water, you look as though you're catching cold."

"I will."

With the purse under her arm she went upstairs, and on the first landing Bill heard her step and poked his head out with his hair tumbled and his eyes red, and he said: "For Christ's sake, come in and have a drink with me. I've had some bad news."

"You're perfectly sopping," said Bill, looking at her drenched feet. They had two drinks, while Bill told how the director had thrown his play out after the cast had been picked over twice, and had gone through three rehearsals. "I said to him, 'I didn't say it was a masterpiece, I said it would make a good show.' And he said, 'It just doesn't *play*, do you see? It needs a doctor.' So I'm stuck, absolutely stuck," said Bill, on the edge of weeping again. "I've been crying," he told her, "in my cups." And he went on to ask her if she realized his wife was ruining him with her extravagance. "I send her ten dollars every week of my unhappy life, and I don't really have to. She threatens to jail me if I don't, but she can't do it. God, let her try it after the way she treated me! She's no right to alimony and she knows it. She keeps on saying she's got to have it for the baby and I keep on sending it because I can't bear to see anybody suffer. So I'm way behind on the piano and the victrola, both—"

"Well, this is a pretty rug, anyhow," she said.

Bill stared at it and blew his nose. "I got it at Ricci's for ninety-five dollars," he said. "Ricci told me it once belonged to Marie Dressler, and cost fifteen hundred dollars, but there's a burnt place on it, under the divan. Can you beat that?"

"No," she said. She was thinking about her empty purse and that she could not possibly expect a check for her latest review for another three days, and her arrangement with the basement restaurant could not last much longer if she did not pay something on account. "It's no time to speak of it," she said, "but I've been hoping you would have by now that fifty dollars you promised for my scene in the third act. Even if it doesn't play. You were to pay me for the work anyhow out of your advance."

"Weeping Jesus," said Bill, "you, too?" He gave a loud sob, or hiccough, in his moist handkerchief. "Your stuff was no better than mine, after all. Think of that."

"But you got something for it," she said. "Seven hundred dollars."

Bill said, "Do me a favor, will you? Have another drink and forget about it. I can't, you know I can't, I would if I could, but you know the fix I'm in."

"Let it go, then," she found herself saying almost in spite of herself. She had meant to be quite firm about it. They drank again without speaking, and she went to her apartment on the floor above.

There, she now remembered distinctly, she had taken the letter out of the purse before she spread the purse out to dry.

She had sat down and read the letter over again: but there were phrases that insisted on being read many times, they had a life of their own separate from the others, and when she tried to read past and around them, they moved with the movement of her eyes, and she could not escape them . . . "thinking about you more than I mean to . . . yes, I even talk about you . . . why were you so anxious to destroy . . . even if I could see you now I would not . . . not worth all this abominable . . . the end . . ."

Carefully she tore the letter into narrow strips and touched a lighted match to them in the coal grate.

Early the next morning she was in the bathtub when the janitress knocked and then came in, calling out that she wished to examine the radiators before she started the furnace going for the winter. After moving about the room for a few minutes, the janitress went out, closing the door very sharply.

She came out of the bathroom to get a cigarette from the package in the purse. The purse was gone. She dressed and made coffee, and sat by the window while she drank it. Certainly the janitress had taken the purse, and certainly it would be impossible to get it back without a great deal of ridiculous excitement. Then let it go. With this decision of her mind, there rose coincidentally in her blood a deep almost murderous anger. She set the cup carefully in the center of the table, and walked steadily downstairs, three long flights and a short hall and a steep short flight into the basement, where the janitress, her face streaked with coal dust, was shaking up the furnace. "Will you please give me back my purse? There isn't any money in it. It was a present, and I don't want to lose it."

The janitress turned without straightening up and peered at her with hot flickering eyes, a red light from the furnace reflected in them. "What do you mean, your purse?"

"The gold cloth purse you took from the wooden bench in my room," she said. "I must have it back."

"Before God I never laid eyes on your purse, and that's the holy truth," said the janitress.

"Oh, well then, keep it," she said, but in a very bitter voice; "keep it if you want it so much." And she walked away.

She remembered how she had never locked a door in her life, on some principle of rejection in her that made her uncomfortable in the ownership of things, and her paradoxical boast before the warnings of her friends, that she had never lost a penny by theft; and she had been pleased with the bleak humility of this concrete example designed to illustrate and justify a certain fixed, otherwise baseless and general faith which ordered the movements of her life without regard to her will in the matter.

In this moment she felt that she had been robbed of an enormous number of valuable things, whether material or intangible: things lost or broken by her own fault, things she had forgotten and left in houses when she moved: books borrowed from her and not returned, journeys she had planned and had not made, words she had waited to hear spoken to her and had not heard, and the words she had meant to answer with; bitter alternatives and intolerable substitutes worse than nothing, and yet inescapable: the long patient suffering of dying friendships and the dark inexplicable death of love—all that she had had, and all that she had missed, were lost together, and were twice lost in this landslide of remembered losses.

The janitress was following her upstairs with the purse in her hand and the same deep red fire flickering in her eyes. The janitress thrust the purse towards her while they were still a half dozen steps apart, and said: "Don't never tell on me. I musta been crazy. I get crazy in the head sometimes, I swear I do. My son can tell you."

She took the purse after a moment, and the janitress went on: "I got a niece who is going on seventeen, and she's a nice girl and I thought I'd give it to her. She needs a pretty purse. I musta been crazy; I thought maybe you wouldn't mind, you leave things around and don't seem to notice much."

She said: "I missed this because it was a present to me from someone . . ."

The janitress said: "He'd get you another if you lost this one. My niece is young and needs pretty things, we oughta give the young ones a chance. She's got young men after her maybe will want to marry her. She oughta have nice things. She needs them bad right now. You're a grown woman, you've had your chance, you ought to know how it is!"

She held the purse out to the janitress saying: "You don't know what you're talking about. Here, take it, I've changed my mind. I really don't want it."

The janitress looked up at her with hatred and said: "I don't want it either now. My niece is young and pretty, she don't need fixin' up to be pretty, she's young and pretty anyhow! I guess you need it worse than she does!"

"It wasn't really yours in the first place," she said, turning away. "You mustn't talk as if I had stolen it from you."

"It's not from me, it's from her you're stealing it," said the janitress, and went back downstairs.

She laid the purse on the table and sat down with the cup of chilled coffee, and thought: I was right not to be afraid of any thief but myself, who will end by leaving me nothing.

RESPONSES: Questions for Writing and Discussion

1. Do a profile—oral or written—tracing what you believe to have been the past life of "she." What was her background? What choices did she make that have brought her life to the state in which we find it? Here are some questions to ask yourself that may help you to understand her:

   a. Why does she drink so much?
   b. What is her relationship with Camilo? Roger? Bill? With the writer of the letter?
   c. Why is she so concerned about money? (In fact, consider carefully the general function of money in the story.)
   d. Is the "murderous anger" she feels toward the janitress typical of this kind of person as you view her?
   e. What is that "principle of rejection in her that made her uncomfortable in the ownership of things"?

2. Since the title is "Theft," examine carefully the incident involving the empty purse, the janitress, the conversation on the stairs, and then the final line of the story. Does "she" really want to have her purse stolen? Does she have a right to feel the janitress is being unreasonable? Is it true that she is stealing the purse from the niece? What, finally, is actually stolen in this story?

3. Examine the method by which the story unfolds. Things seem to happen, out of nowhere, without being introduced or spelled out for the reader. The events are related from the point of view of the heroine, and this gives them a sort of hazy quality hard to define. Why do you think Katherine Anne Porter chose to write the story in so indirect a fashion?

4. In a good story nothing, however trivial it may seem, is ever introduced without a purpose. The three drunken boys, the girls in

the transparent raincoats, apparently meaningless lines like "Well, this is a pretty rug, anyhow"—all belong to the overall theme or method of telling the story. Describe the function of these and other such elements that you find.

5. Is the author indirectly recommending a certain life style, one that "she," the main character, obviously does not have? Does the author give us enough clues to know how she thinks people ought to live? Is there an indication of what the author considers Human Worth to be?

6. Is the author saying something about the highly civilized, intellectual woman in particular? Is "she" missing out on being a woman? Do you think an alternative approach to life for a woman is being suggested?

7. "Theft" was written over forty years ago. Is it, in your opinion, showing signs of age? How so? Or, is it still relevant? Why?

IN NAVAHO COUNTRY
William Bronk

Very much like James Dickey, whose poem "Adultery" appears near the end of Part One, **William Bronk (b. 1918)** represents the American business-man-poet. His life style indicates that one need not after all make a choice between two possible worlds but may enjoy the best of both. Born in Hudson Falls, New York, where he is currently in business, he was educated at Harvard and Dartmouth, served in the Army during World War II, and taught for a time at Union College, Schenectady before deciding that the business world provided for him an environment and life style compatible with his temperament. Nonetheless he kept writing poetry and now has two collections—*Light and Dark* and *The World, The Worldless*.

The following poem, in which the limitations of the intellectual life are expressed, makes a striking and wholly unexpected comparison between the human mind and a cramped, confined Indian habitation. Like all true poems it makes us aware of relationships we would probably never perceive by ourselves.

In Navaho Country

To live in a hogan[1] under a hovering sky
is to live in a universe hogan-shaped,
or having hogans in it to give it shape,
earth-covered hovels, holes having a wall
to heave the back of the heart against, or hide
the head, to black the heavens overhead,
a block and a shapening in the windy vast.
This could be said of other houses too.

How it is possible for this to be so
is that the universe as known-unknown
has no discernible shape and not much
in it. We give it the limits and shape we need
it to have. What we want is a *here* with meaning, more
than a vague void moving with weightless balls
or the distant view of a glitter of gritty dust.
We housel[2] the universe to have it here.

We do wrong: using houses or whole
blocks of houses, or other devious
enclosed volumes, ingenious inventions of space
to have us here, has limits. We deceive
ourselves, but not for long. We only avoid
the empty vastness, leaving it there unfilled,
unknown, unlimited. Where is *here*
when nowhere in a place of no discernible shape?

[1] typical dwelling of the Navahos, built of earth walls and supported by timbers

[2] to administer Holy Communion; to make holy

MUCH MADNESS
IS DIVINEST SENSE

Emily Dickinson

In days when many fewer women were writing and publishing **Emily Dickinson (1830–1886)** achieved a reputation as America's outstanding woman of letters. She lived a strange, withdrawn life in which she seldom left her home and had few social ties of any kind. Apparently she found the medium of poetry sufficient for her communicative needs, and thus she illustrates yet one more function of the poem: to provide a channel of expression to those who have no other means of baring their souls. Reading Emily Dickinson's works, one discovers a sensibility of exquisite precision and a mind of subtle dimensions. Her poems, almost always short, combine disarming simplicity with profound wisdom, as the following eight lines amply reveal.

Much Madness is Divinest Sense

Much Madness is divinest Sense—
To a discerning Eye—
Much Sense—the starkest Madness—
'Tis the Majority
In this, as All, prevail—
Assent—and you are sane—
Demur—you're straightway dangerous—
And handled with a Chain—

From *The Complete Poems of Emily Dickinson*, ed. by Thomas H. Johnson (Boston: Little, Brown & Co., 1960) p. 209.

ANSWERS
Elizabeth Jennings

Born in Lincolnshire, England, this poet has been assistant librarian at the city library of Oxford and an editorial assistant at Chatto and Windus, one of Britain's major publishing houses. She has authored a number of collections, including *A Way of Looking* and *A Sense of the World* and has been a contributor to the *London Magazine, Encounter,* the *Spectator,* and the *Times Literary Supplement.*

Elizabeth Jennings (b. 1926) is known to a relatively small circle of discerning readers in her own country and to an even smaller extent in the United States. A critic has suggested a possible reason for this: Her poetry is "cool" and "detached" rather than directly communicative of intense emotion. In any event, the poem which follows is one of the very few in which a case is made for the intellectual life, for the necessity of going beyond the "small things" that are easily "caressed and loved" and reaching out for the "great conclusions."

Answers

I kept my answers small and kept them near;
Big questions bruised my mind but still I let
Small answers be a bulwark to my fear.

The huge abstractions I kept from the light;
Small things I handled and caressed and loved.
I let the stars assume the whole of night.

But the big answers clamoured to be moved
Into my life. Their great audacity
Shouted to be acknowledged and believed.

Even when all small answers build up to
Protection of my spirit, still I hear
Big answers striving for their overthrow

And all the great conclusions coming near.

FOR THE TRUTH
(because it is necessary)
Edward S. Spriggs

The East Coast editor of *Black Dialogue*, a major channel of black expression in America at the current time, **Edward Spriggs (b. 1934)** is active in the current movement to bring together all the modes by which black experience is translated into art and thus to help establish a true and abiding sense of black culture.

The message of his own poetry tends to be primarily for black readers, as the following poem demonstrates. Like many of his contemporaries, Spriggs is concerned that black America has been for too long educated through and guided into the white man's logical and highly verbal relationship to life. In "the tea rooms / of our revolution" there is too much debate and not enough action. He wants no more black intellectualism to confuse issues so that "i don't know who the enemy is / anymore."

For the TRUTH (because it is necessary)

in the tea rooms
of our revolution
we blatantly debate
our knowledge of world revolts
—our anxious ears only half-listened
to the songs of the martinique
who sings in muffled tones
from beneath a mechanized tombstone
built by the pulp of greedy merchants
who got stoned on the juices of our servitude
& who write prefaces to our "negritude"

from the tea rooms
of our revolution we emerge
to pamphleteer
the anticipatory designs
of our dead

& exiled poets
—without sanctions
from our unsuspecting brothers
whose death we so naively plot
(we engage in a hypothetical revolt
against a not-so-hypothetical enemy

what kind of man are you
black revolutionary, so-called?
what kind of man are you trying to be
ultra-hip-revolutionary-nationalist-
quasi-strategist-ego-centric-phony
intellectual romantic black prima donna child
—screaming, "revolution means change . . ."
never finishing the sentence
or the thought
talking about "para-military"
strategy and techniques
publicizing a so-called underground program
wearing your military garb
as if you never heard of camouflage
so in love with intrigue
you have no thoughts
about the post-revolution life
that the total destruction
you talk about assumes . . .

you leave me quite confused
brother
i don't know who the enemy is
anymore
perhaps it is me, myself, because
i have these thoughts
in the tea rooms of our revolution.

BEYOND REASON

History sometimes is the story of the exception that does not prove the rule—the bold stroke which seems to defy reason altogether and therefore ought not to have succeeded, but did. Was Joan of Arc a military logician? Reason no doubt played some part in Columbus' gamble, but something else must have endowed him with enough dead-sureness to cause him to risk everything on his perilous journey. Did Pierre and Eve Curie "discover" radium? Could they have reasoned out the existence of a radioactive element when nothing of the sort had ever been found? Feelings—hunches—"somehows"—all play their part in human endeavor and contribute to Human Worth.

We are being told today that the powers of the mind have never been fully realized. We are being told that, for all the accomplishments of which men have boasted, the average mind may still be in a relatively primitive stage of development. Duke University and other centers for scientific research are heavily committed to an exhausting, expensive, but astonishingly fruitful study of the modes of higher perception. That many kinds of extra-sensory or psychic experience are possible seems undeniable.

But perhaps we are only just catching up with what the artists among us have been saying for years. They continually warn us that our troubles begin when we reach the "age of reason," that sober moment when society begins to expect rational behavior and we are forced to abandon the spontaneous, intuitive, yet possibly far wiser life style of the child.

All of the readings in this section require a willingness on the reader's part to take the extended hand of each author and go where he wishes to lead; to open himself to the possibilities of the mind which lie beyond reason no matter how strongly his "better" sense may argue to the contrary.

The message of Antoine de Saint Exupéry's fable *The Little Prince* is so simple that its profundity is often lost on "practical" adults who have more important things to do than read fairy tales. But Thomas Merton, the Trappist monk, also asks that we rediscover the purity of heart and imagination with which we once opened our arms unquestioningly to life's mysteries. "Perfect Joy" is a religious experience, not a religious sermon, speaking to us of things for which our rational selves never have time enough.

Those who do not take the time simply *to be* may argue that in this world the important thing is to be *something* or, even better, some*one*. And this usually means the attainment of positions of power and respect and the fulfillment of all the reasonable desires: possessing the objects and the people to which they are attracted. Such is the view of an unhappy world as seen through the eyes of Hermann Hesse, whose spiritual messages went largely unheeded three decades ago but are finding thousands of new listeners with each passing year. In *Siddhartha* the reader experiences an hypnotic unfolding of higher perception, an ascent to a realm of pure being, beyond personality and rational thought and ego. In this state one enters into the cosmic soul of the universe and truly understands the unity and immortality of all life.

Those who require an explanation of what "unity" means to Siddhartha and Hesse may be none the wiser for all the definitions that could be extended. The same could be said for the common-sense mind that finds it difficult to cope with the extra-dimensional experiences of Carlos Castaneda while under the influence of certain ancient drugs still used by the Yaqui Indians of Mexico for spiritual enlightenment. But if the reader approaches *The Teachings of Don Juan* with an open mind, perhaps he will find himself admitting there may be more to it than an account of an incredible series of hallucinations.

That certain minds have the powers to penetrate the barrier between the living and the dead is given serious and provocative treatment in James A. Pike's *The Other Side*. Those with faith in a life after death will no doubt be willing to lend credence to the extraordinary experiences described, but those for whom reason is the ultimate criterion may be convinced that no one can know of or report with certainty a life beyond the grave. Still,

Pike's story deserves to be read, if only for his speculations on cosmic consciousness and the levels of the mind that may yet lie waiting for our explorations, if only to make us receptive to new possibilities, no matter how alien to our thinking.

To lead us into the far countries of the mind is the aim of a good deal of contemporary fiction as well. Evan S. Connell's "The Fisherman from Chihuahua" is the kind of story few readers simply pick up at random and find they cannot put down. In fact, the reader with rational expectations (plot line going somewhere, ending up with everything tied together) may just as well pass it by. To enjoy this curious tale, one must lull to sleep his everyday consciousness and focus his attention on characters who can only have wandered in from one of those distant lands known to those of unbounded imagination.

THE LITTLE PRINCE AND THE PROUD ROSE

Antoine de Saint Exupéry

If the writings of **Antoine de Saint Exupéry (1900–1944)** were suddenly to vanish from our literary heritage, it is hard to calculate how much poorer we should all become. Relatively meager as his output was, he is considered one of the major prose stylists in contemporary French letters. But even more important, when his plane failed to return after a mission during World War II, he had fortunately already written *The Little Prince*, a fairy tale for grownups whose narrator is a pilot like his author, whose haunting central character is a tiny interplanetary traveler, and whose main issue is whether a sheep will come along and eat the only rose growing on asteroid B-612. He had left behind a simple and wise fable about the futility of the adult world, absorbed in its "matters of consequence" and missing the primary stuff of life—roses and sunsets and laughter. To help us see and respond to life anew, with the fresh and pure eyes of the child, is the purpose behind *The Little Prince*.

The narrator of the story is a man caught between the adult world of "bridge, and golf, and politics, and neckties" and the eternal world of childlike joy and spontaneity, a world not circumscribed by rational boundaries, accessible to people of imagination and the courage to live not as "sensible" folks do. His escape route is flying, probably like his author, who was both a commercial and a war pilot, for this enables him to attain really useful knowledge. (*"At a glance I can distinguish China from Arizona."*)

One night, after his plane has been forced down in the middle of the Sahara desert, he meets the little prince, who has been visiting one planet after another in search of an answer to the puzzling secrets of life. It is from the strange child that the narrator learns what the important problems are. For example, why do roses have thorns? Why are some seeds good and some bad? Why should there be baobabs at all? Is there anything better in all the universe than the proud little rose he has left under a glass shield up on asteroid B-612?

The prince's reason for embarking on his cosmic odyssey is made clear in the selection that follows. But reason does not quite explain it to us. It has something to do with the flower's vanity that saddens the child, or perhaps more to do with the matter of the thorns that seem an unnecessary bit of danger and not very beautiful.

Few relationships in literature are as simple and complex as that of the adult pilot and the child prince, few conversations are as baffling to the logical mind and as illmuinating to the sixth sense with which Saint Exupéry believes it is necessary to view life. And few people, no matter what their age, who love and keep rereading *The Little Prince*, ever really steel themselves against the sadness of the final parting when the child must return to his far-away home and the man must once again face a "sensible" world, where "I have never yet told this story." But the prince has learned the secret of life and it is necessary for him to go back to his flower. ". . . I am responsible for her. And she is so weak! She is so naïve! She has four thorns, of no use at all, to protect herself against all the world. . . ." Symbolism? What could be more certain? But each reader must make his own choice between two worlds before he can glimpse its true meaning.

The Little Prince and the Proud Rose

5

As each day passed I would learn, in our talk, something about the little prince's planet, his departure from it, his journey. The information would come very slowly, as it might chance to fall from his thoughts. It was in this way that I heard, on the third day, about the catastrophe of the baobabs.

This time, once more, I had the sheep to thank for it. For the little prince asked me abruptly—as if seized by a grave doubt—"It is true, isn't it, that sheep eat little bushes?"

"Yes, that is true."

"Ah! I am glad!"

I did not understand why it was so important that sheep should eat little bushes. But the little prince added:

"Then it follows that they also eat baobabs?"

I pointed out to the little prince that baobabs were not little bushes, but, on the contrary, trees as big as castles; and that even if he took a whole herd of elephants away with him, the herd would not eat up one single baobab.

The idea of the herd of elephants made the little prince laugh.

"We would have to put them one on top of the other," he said.

But he made a wise comment:

"Before they grow so big, the baobabs start out by being little."

"That is strictly correct," I said. "But why do you want the sheep to eat the little baobabs?"

He answered me at once, "Oh, come, come!", as if he were speaking of something that was self-evident. And I was obliged to make a great mental effort to solve this problem, without any assistance.

Indeed, as I learned, there were on the planet where the little prince lived—as on all planets—good plants and bad plants. In conse-

quence, there were good seeds from good plants, and bad seeds from
bad plants. But seeds are invisible. They sleep deep in the heart of the
earth's darkness, until some one among them is seized with the desire
to awaken. Then this little seed will stretch itself and begin—timidly
at first—to push a charming little sprig inoffensively upward toward
the sun. If it is only a sprout of radish or the sprig of a rose-bush, one
would let it grow wherever it might wish. But when it is a bad plant,
one must destroy it as soon as possible, the very first instant that one
recognizes it.

Now there were some terrible seeds on the planet that was the
home of the little prince; and these were the seeds of the baobab. The
soil of that planet was infested with them. A baobab is something you
will never, never be able to get rid of if you attend to it too late. It
spreads over the entire planet. It bores clear through it with its roots.
And if the planet is too small, and the baobabs are too many, they
split it in pieces . . .

"It is a question of discipline," the little prince said to me later on.
"When you've finished your own toilet in the morning, then it is time
to attend to the toilet of your planet, just so, with the greatest care.
You must see to it that you pull up regularly all the baobabs, at the

very first moment when they can be distinguished from the rosebushes which they resemble so closely in their earliest youth. It is very tedious work," the little prince added, "but very easy."

And one day he said to me: "You ought to make a beautiful drawing, so that the children where you live can see exactly how all this is. That would be very useful to them if they were to travel some day. Sometimes," he added, "there is no harm in putting off a piece of work until another day. But when it is a matter of baobabs, that always means a catastrophe. I knew a planet that was inhabited by a lazy man. He neglected three little bushes . . ."

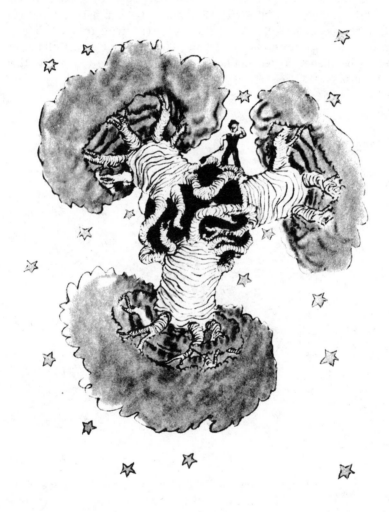

The Baobabs

So, as the little prince described it to me, I have made a drawing of that planet. I do not much like to take the tone of a moralist. But the danger of the baobabs is so little understood, and such considerable risks would be run by anyone who might get lost on an asteroid, that for once I am breaking through my reserve. "Children," I say plainly, "watch out for the baobabs!"

My friends, like myself, have been skirting this danger for a long time, without ever knowing it; and so it is for them that I have worked so hard over this drawing. The lesson which I pass on by this means is worth all the trouble it has cost me.

Perhaps you will ask me, "Why are there no other drawings in this book as magnificent and impressive as this drawing of the baobabs?"

The reply is simple. I have tried. But with the others I have not been successful. When I made the drawing of the baobabs I was carried beyond myself by the inspiring force of urgent necessity.

6

Oh, little prince! Bit by bit I came to understand the secrets of your sad little life . . . For a long time you had found your only entertainment in the quiet pleasure of looking at the sunset. I learned that new detail on the morning of the fourth day, when you said to me:

"I am very fond of sunsets. Come, let us go look at a sunset now."

"But we must wait," I said.

"Wait? For what?"

"For the sunset. We must wait until it is time."

At first you seemed to be very much surprised. And then you laughed to yourself. You said to me:

"I am always thinking that I am at home!"

Just so. Everybody knows that when it is noon in the United States the sun is setting over France. If you could fly to France in one minute, you could go straight into the sunset, right from noon. Unfortunately, France is too far away for that. But on your tiny planet, my little prince, all you need do is move your chair a few steps. You can see the day end and the twilight falling whenever you like . . .

"One day," you said to me, "I saw the sunset forty-four times!"

And a little later you added:

"You know—one loves the sunset, when one is so sad . . ."

"Were you so sad, then?" I asked, "on the day of the forty-four sunsets?"

But the little prince made no reply.

7

On the fifth day—again, as always, it was thanks to the sheep—the secret of the little prince's life was revealed to me. Abruptly, without anything to lead up to it, and as if the question had been born of long and silent meditation on his problem, he demanded:

"A sheep—if it eats little bushes, does it eat flowers, too?"

"A sheep," I answered, "eats anything it finds in its reach."

"Even flowers that have thorns?"

"Yes, even flowers that have thorns."

"Then the thorns—what use are they?"

I did not know. At that moment I was very busy trying to unscrew a bolt that had got stuck in my engine. I was very much worried, for it was becoming clear to me that the breakdown of my plane was extremely serious. And I had so little drinking-water left that I had to fear the worst.

"The thorns—what use are they?"

The little prince never let go of a question, once he had asked it. As for me, I was upset over that bolt. And I answered with the first thing that came into my head:

"The thorns are of no use at all. Flowers have thorns just for spite!"

"Oh!"

There was a moment of complete silence. Then the little prince flashed back at me, with a kind of resentfulness:

"I don't believe you! Flowers are weak creatures. They are naïve. They reassure themselves as best they can. They believe that their thorns are terrible weapons . . ."

I did not answer. At that instant I was saying to myself: "If this bolt still won't turn, I am going to knock it out with the hammer." Again the little prince disturbed my thoughts:

"And you actually believe that the flowers—"

"Oh, no!" I cried. "No, no, no! I don't believe anything. I answered you with the first thing that came into my head. Don't you see—I am very busy with matters of consequence!"

He stared at me, thunderstruck.

"Matters of consequence!"

He looked at me there, with my hammer in my hand, my fingers black with engine-grease, bending down over an object which seemed to him extremely ugly . . .

"You talk just like the grown-ups!"

That made me a little ashamed. But he went on, relentlessly:

"You mix everything up together . . . You confuse everything . . ."

He was really very angry. He tossed his golden curls in the breeze.

"I know a planet where there is a certain red-faced gentleman. He has never smelled a flower. He has never looked at a star. He has never loved any one. He has never done anything in his life but add up figures. And all day he says over and over, just like you: 'I am busy with matters of consequence!' And that makes him swell up with pride. But he is not a man—he is a mushroom!"

"A what?"

"A mushroom!"

The little prince was now white with rage.

"The flowers have been growing thorns for millions of years. For millions of years the sheep have been eating them just the same. And is it not a matter of consequence to try to understand why the flowers go to so much trouble to grow thorns which are never of any use to them? Is the warfare between the sheep and the flowers not important? Is this not of more consequence than a fat red-faced gentleman's sums? And if I know—I, myself—one flower which is unique in the world, which grows nowhere but on my planet, but which one little sheep can destroy in a single bite some morning, without even noticing what he is doing—Oh! You think that is not important!"

His face turned from white to red as he continued:

"If some one loves a flower, of which just one single blossom grows in all the millions and millions of stars, it is enough to make him happy just to look at the stars. He can say to himself: 'Somewhere, my flower is there . . .' But if the sheep eats the flower, in one moment all his stars will be darkened . . . And you think that is not important!"

He could not say anything more. His words were choked by sobbing.

The night had fallen. I had let my tools drop from my hands. Of what moment now was my hammer, my bolt, or thirst, or death? On one star, one planet, my planet, the Earth, there was a little prince to be comforted. I took him in my arms, and rocked him. I said to him:

"The flower that you love is not in danger. I will draw you a muzzle for your sheep. I will draw you a railing to put around your flower. I will—"

I did not know what to say to him. I felt awkward and blundering. I did not know how I could reach him, where I could overtake him and go on hand in hand with him once more.

It is such a secret place, the land of tears.

8

I soon learned to know this flower better. On the little prince's planet the flowers had always been very simple. They had only one ring of petals; they took up no room at all; they were a trouble to nobody.

One morning they would appear in the grass, and by night they would have faded peacefully away. But one day, from a seed blown from no one knew where, a new flower had come up; and the little prince had watched very closely over this small sprout which was not like any other small sprouts on his planet. It might, you see, have been a new kind of baobab.

But the shrub soon stopped growing, and began to get ready to produce a flower. The little prince, who was present at the first appearance of a huge bud, felt at once that some sort of miraculous apparition must emerge from it. But the flower was not satisfied to complete the preparations for her beauty in the shelter of her green chamber. She chose her colors with the greatest care. She dressed herself slowly. She

adjusted her petals one by one. She did not wish to go out into the world all rumpled, like the field poppies. It was only in the full radiance of her beauty that she wished to appear. Oh, yes! She was a coquettish creature! And her mysterious adornment lasted for days and days.

Then one morning, exactly at sunrise, she suddenly showed herself.

And, after working with all this painstaking precision, she yawned and said:

"Ah! I am scarcely awake. I beg that you will excuse me. My petals are still all disarranged . . ."

But the little prince could not restrain his admiration:

"Oh! How beautiful you are!"

"Am I not?" the flower responded, sweetly. "And I was born at the same moment as the sun . . ."

The little prince could guess easily enough that she was not any too modest—but how moving—and exciting—she was!

"I think it is time for breakfast," she added an instant later. "If you would have the kindness to think of my needs—"

And the little prince, completely abashed, went to look for a sprinkling-can of fresh water. So, he tended the flower.

So, too, she began very quickly to torment him with her vanity—which was, if the truth be known, a little difficult to deal with. One day, for instance, when she was speaking of her four thorns, she said to the little prince:

"Let the tigers come with their claws!"

"There are no tigers on my planet," the little prince objected. "And, anyway, tigers do not eat weeds."

"I am not a weed," the flower replied, sweetly.

"Please excuse me . . ."

"I am not at all afraid of tigers," she went on, "but I have a horror of drafts. I suppose you wouldn't have a screen for me?"

"A horror of drafts—that is bad luck, for a plant," remarked the little prince, and added to himself, "This flower is a very complex creature . . ."

"At night I want you to put me under a glass globe. It is very cold where you live. In the place I came from—"

But she interrupted herself at that point. She had come in the

form of a seed. She could not have known anything of any other worlds. Embarrassed over having let herself be caught on the verge of such a naïve untruth, she coughed two or three times, in order to put the little prince in the wrong.

"The screen?"

"I was just going to look for it when you spoke to me . . ."

Then she forced her cough a little more so that he should suffer from remorse just the same.

So the little prince, in spite of all the good will that was inseparable from his love, had soon come to doubt her. He had taken seriously words which were without importance, and it made him very unhappy.

"I ought not to have listened to her," he confided to me one day. "One never ought to listen to the flowers. One should simply look at them and breathe their fragrance. Mine perfumed all my planet. But I did not know how to take pleasure in all her grace. This tale of claws, which disturbed me so much, should only have filled my heart with tenderness and pity."

And he continued his confidences:

"The fact is that I did not know how to understand anything! I ought to have judged by deeds and not by words. She cast her fragrance and her radiance over me. I ought never to have run away from her . . . I ought to have guessed all the affection that lay behind her poor little stratagems. Flowers are so inconsistent! But I was too young to know how to love her . . ."

RESPONSES: Questions for Writing and Discussion

(Attempt these only with your sixth sense. Logic will desert you.)

1. What exactly is a baobab? Why does the narrator say that he and his friends "have been skirting this danger for a long time, without ever knowing it"?

2. To see the world with the eyes of the little prince is not, of

course, to experience only joy. In fact, the narrator refers to the prince's "sad little life." Why is it sad? And since it is, why is it better than the life of the adult with its "matters of consequence"?

3. The narrator tries vainly to answer the prince's questions about roses and their thorns. ("Flowers have thorns just for spite!") But, really, he is just as baffled as the prince. Do you have any opinions on the subject?

4. "If someone loves a flower . . . it is enough to make him happy just to look at the stars. He can say to himself: 'Somewhere, my flower is there. . . .'" Describe *your* flower, which is hidden among the stars. (If you can't speak or write about it rationally, try doing it in poetry.)

5. The flower's vanity saddens the prince, and in truth she does seem a bit self-centered, even to forcing a cough and making the prince feel guilty about not having sheltered her properly. Still, the selection ends with the statement "I was too young to know how to love her." What might the prince mean?

PERFECT JOY
Thomas Merton

The life of **Thomas Merton (1915–1968)** reads like the plot of a novel about the twentieth-century American search for self-fulfillment and an escape from materialism. The hero is born into a civilized, continental background, grows up in England, France, and America, is educated at both Cambridge and Columbia universities, and finds himself as a young man out of tune with the American dream of financial success. It is the thirties; there is widespread poverty, but a few are rolling in wealth. He joins a Communist youth movement, then decides Marx is just as concerned with material well-being—and just as hollow. He gets into social work with a Catholic settlement house in Harlem. This begins to make sense, and finally, in 1938, he enters the Roman Catholic Church. In 1941 he is in a Trappist monastery, committed to a lifetime of austere bodily discipline and spiritual contemplation. Here he finds peace.

The Seven Storey Mountain (1948) is an account of Merton's victory over the pain and anguish of his earlier existence. With its publication he found his calling: to be a bridge between the frenzied "outer" world and the tranquillity of the monastic life; to offer the restless seeker the benefit of his own inward discoveries; to become a quiet but firm voice telling concerned Americans that there is a way out for them—an alternate mode of living.

As a Catholic writer, Thomas Merton insists less on theology than on the personal rewards to be enjoyed in meditation. The reader of Merton is aware of monastery bells and the quiet music of nature more than of ideas and principles. The Merton experience resembles that of the monastic Buddhist, and so it should come as no surpirse that the selection we have chosen is taken from *The Way of Chuang Tzu*, a book of poems and parables and philosophy, a collection of the writings of a third-century Chinese sage translated into a personal statement by a twentieth-century Catholic monk.

Merton does not insist on the Christian aspects of Chuang Tzu's Buddhism, the ancient philosopher's desire to achieve a "direct existential grasp of reality in itself." He seeks, rather, to establish the continuity of a certain kind of human tradition, one that transcends cultures and formal religion but, to his way of thinking, testifies strongly to the divinity of all humankind.

> But the whole teaching, the "way" contained in these
> anecdotes, poems, and meditations, is characteristic
> of a certain mentality found everywhere in the world,
> a certain taste for simplicity, for humility, self-
> effacement, silence, and in general a refusal to take
> seriously the aggressivity, the ambition, the push,
> and the self-importance which one must display in
> order to get along in society.

Perfect Joy

Is there to be found on earth a fullness of joy, or is there no such thing? Is there some way to make life fully worth living, or is this impossible? If there is such a way, how do you go about finding it? What should you try to do? What should you seek to avoid? What should be the goal in which your activity comes to rest? What should you accept? What should you refuse to accept? What should you love? What should you hate?

What the world values is money, reputation, long life, achievement. What it counts as joy is health and comfort of body, good food, fine clothes, beautiful things to look at, pleasant music to listen to.

What it condemns is lack of money, a low social rank, a reputation for being no good, and an early death.

What it considers misfortune is bodily discomfort and labor, no chance to get your fill of good food, not having good clothes to wear, having no way to amuse or delight the eye, no pleasant music to listen to. If people find that they are deprived of these things, they go into a panic or fall into despair. They are so concerned for their life that their anxiety makes life unbearable, even when they have the things they think they want. Their very concern for enjoyment makes them unhappy.

The rich make life intolerable, driving themselves in order to get more and more money which they cannot really use. In so doing they are alienated from themselves, and exhaust themselves in their own service as though they were slaves of others.

The ambitious run day and night in pursuit of honors, constantly in anguish about the success of their plans, dreading the miscalculation that may wreck everything. Thus they are alienated from themselves, exhausting their real life in service of the shadow created by their insatiable hope.

The birth of a man is the birth of his sorrow.

The longer he lives, the more stupid he becomes, because his anxiety to avoid unavoidable death becomes more and more acute. What bitterness! He lives for what is always out of reach! His thirst for survival in the future makes him incapable of living in the present.

What about the self-sacrificing officials and scholars? They are honored by the world because they are good, upright, self-sacrificing men.

Yet their good character does not preserve them from unhappiness, nor even from ruin, disgrace, and death.

I wonder, in that case, if their "goodness" is really so good after all! Is it perhaps a source of unhappiness?

Suppose you admit they are happy. But is it a happy thing to have a character and a career that lead to one's own eventual destruction? On the other hand, can you call them "unhappy" if, in sacrificing themselves, they save the lives and fortunes of others?

Take the case of the minister who conscientiously and uprightly opposes an unjust decision of his king! Some say, "Tell the truth, and if the King will not listen, let him do what he likes. You have no further obligation."

On the other hand, Tzu Shu continued to resist the unjust policy of his sovereign. He was consequently destroyed. But if he had not stood up for what he believed to be right, his name would not be held in honor.

So there is the question, Shall the course he took be called "good" if, at the same time, it was fatal to him?

I cannot tell if what the world considers "happiness" is happiness or not. All I know is that when I consider the way they go about attaining it, I see them carried away headlong, grim and obsessed, in the general onrush of the human herd, unable to stop themselves or to change their direction. All the while they claim to be just on the point of attaining happiness.

For my part, I cannot accept their standards, whether of happiness or unhappiness. I ask myself if after all their concept of happiness has any meaning whatever.

My opinion is that you never find happiness until you stop looking for it. My greatest happiness consists precisely in doing nothing whatever that is calculated to obtain happiness: and this, in the minds of most people, is the worst possible course.

I will hold to the saying that: "Perfect joy is to be without joy. Perfect praise is to be without praise."

If you ask "what ought to be done" and "what ought not to be done" on earth in order to produce happiness, I answer that these questions do not have an answer. There is no way of determining such things.

Yet at the same time, if I cease striving for happiness, the "right" and the "wrong" at once become apparent all by themselves.

Contentment and well-being at once become possible the moment you cease to act with them in view, and if you practice non-doing (*wu wei*), you will have both happiness and well-being.

Here is how I sum it up:
>Heaven does nothing: its non-doing is its serenity.
>Earth does nothing: its non-doing is its rest.
>From the union of these two non-doings
>All actions proceed,
>All things are made.
>How vast, how invisible
>This coming-to-be!
>All things come from nowhere!
>How vast, how invisible—
>No way to explain it!
>All beings in their perfection
>Are born of non-doing.
>Hence it is said:
>"Heaven and earth do nothing
>Yet there is nothing they do not do."
>
>Where is the man who can attain
>To this non-doing?

RESPONSES: Questions for Writing and Discussion

1. The word "mystic" frequently is used to describe both Catholicism and Buddhism. Suppose your only contact with a mystic religion was this one selection? How would you define the word?

2. Traditionally the faith practiced by Thomas Merton has stressed, as does Chuang Tzu, the unimportance of worldly success and material gains, but it has also cast its eyes on what it considers to be the greater life which begins at death. Is there a conflict between the Christian emphasis on the next world and the importance Chuang Tzu places on an "existential grasp of reality" and living always in the present? In other words, what kind of life would you be leading if you followed Chuang Tzu? Would it get you into heaven if you never practiced religion? (Suppose you were committed, like Thomas Merton, to a monastic existence but were told by a superior that you were spending altogether too much time on trivial concerns—that you were always off in the garden or watching the water flowing in the river, instead of spending your time in prayer? Could you, from the details given in this selection, answer the charge and show that you did not *need* his kind of prayer? Write or present orally a statement you would make to your superior.)

3. Why is it that "you never find happiness until you stop looking for it"? Try to translate this simple, but profound, statement into a specific example of what Chuang Tzu might consider a happy moment in someone's life.

4. In the poem which concludes the selection, what is meant by the observation that heaven and earth do nothing but that all actions proceed from the union of the two "non-doings"? It may not be possible to restate this idea in logical, coherent language. (Some ideas, after all, defeat our readily available linguistic resources and we have to make up some metaphoric ways of describing things.)

5. If you were the man who could attain to this non-doing, could you be described as a lazy good-for-nothing loafer? Would you be of any use to the world or only to yourself?

SIDDHARTHA'S ENLIGHTENMENT

Hermann Hesse

Attempting to determine the reasons for the relative obscurity in this country of **Hermann Hesse (1877–1962)** at the time of his death—considering that the German-born writer had won the Nobel Prize in 1946—*The New York Times* obituary noted: "Perhaps it was his deep disdain for a world represented by bestial wars and the conflicts of modern industrial society, and for a life marked by loud machines, money grubbing, and the quest for material comfort."

It is now twenty years since the original publication of *Siddhartha*. The slender and poetic novel has grown in reputation since its author's death, rediscovered by thousands of Americans seeking alternatives to war, self-centeredness, the pursuit of affluence, and to the staleness and futility of the rational life. They have found in Hesse a kindred spirit who writes of people, like themselves, people trying to break out of the prison of traditional beliefs and modes of existing. For them *Siddhartha* above all of Hesse's works is a gateway to inner peace and spiritual harmony.

The two chapters we have included show the hero in a state of transition from commitment to the worldly life, dominated by ego and self-interest, to his first glimpse of where salvation lies and the new direction his life must take. Preceding this point, we have learned that the hero was born into an affluent Brahmin home but came to be dissatisfied with the vain comforts of his existence. With his boyhood friend Govinda he decides to join the company of the Samanas, wandering pilgrims in search of spiritual fulfillment. "Siddhartha had one single goal—to become empty, to become empty of thirst, desire, dreams, pleasure and sorrow—to let the Self die."

But Siddhartha soon realizes the way of the Samanas is too full of "tricks with which we deceive ourselves." It stresses fasting and forced techniques of mediation, and the result is only a greater feeling of self. The ego becomes puffed up with the pride of its disciplined life. So Siddhartha abandons the pilgrim's life and journeys to what he hopes will be a fateful meeting with Gotama, the Buddha or "Enlightened One" of already legendary fame, only to discover that Gotama's words are empty to one who has not had the same experience. Siddhartha knows the way to enlightenment is for each man to find for himself.

The disappointment he feels after listening to Gotama leads the hero to a reaffirmation of the sensuous and affluent life. He falls in love with a beautiful courtesan named Kamala and through her influence soon becomes a wealthy merchant. At the opening of our selction Siddhartha is at the peak of his material success. But again that same longing for something more makes it impossible for him to know happiness. ". . . real life was flowing past him and did not touch him."

Siddhartha's Enlightenment

Sansara

For a long time Siddhartha had lived the life of the world without belonging to it. His senses which he had deadened during his ardent Samana years were again awakened. He had tasted riches, passion and power, but for a long time he remained a Samana in his heart. Clever Kamala had recognized this. His life was always directed by the art of thinking, waiting and fasting. The people of the world, the ordinary people, were still alien to him, just as he was apart from them.

The years passed by. Enveloped by comfortable circumstances, Siddhartha hardly noticed their passing. He had become rich. He had long possessed a house of his own and his own servants, and a garden at the outskirts of the town, by the river. People liked him, they came to him if they wanted money or advice. However, with the exception of Kamala, he had no close friends.

That glorious, exalted awakening which he had once experienced in his youth, in the days after Gotama's preaching, after the parting from Govinda, that alert expectation, that pride of standing alone without teachers and doctrines, that eager readiness to hear the divine voice within his own heart had gradually become a memory, had passed. The holy fountainhead which had once been near and which had once sung loudly within him, now murmured softly in the distance. However, many things which he had learned from the Samanas, which he had learned from Gotama, from his father, from the Brahmins, he still retained for a long time: a moderate life, pleasure in thinking, hours of meditation, secret knowledge of the Self, of the eternal Self, that was neither body nor consciousness. Many of these he had retained; others were submerged and covered with dust. Just as the potter's wheel, once set into motion, still turns for a long time and then turns only very slowly and stops, so did the wheel of the ascetic, the wheel of thinking, the wheel of discrimination still revolved for a long time in Siddhartha's soul; it still revolved but slowly and hesitatingly and it had nearly come to a standstill. Slowly, like moisture entering the dying tree trunk, slowly filling and rotting it, so did the world and inertia creep into Siddhartha's soul; it slowly filled his soul, made it heavy, made it tired, sent it to sleep. But on the other hand his senses became more awakened, they learned a great deal, experienced a great deal.

Siddhartha had learned how to transact business affairs, to exercise power over people, to amuse himself with women; he had learned to wear fine clothes, to command servants, to bathe in sweet-smelling waters. He had learned to eat sweet and carefully prepared foods, also fish and meat and fowl, spices and dainties, and to drink wine which made him lazy and forgetful. He had learned to play dice and chess, to watch dancers, to be carried in sedan chairs, to sleep on a soft bed. But he had always felt different from and superior to the others; he had always watched them a little scornfully, with a slightly mocking disdain, with that disdain which a Samana always feels towards the people of the world. If Kamaswami was upset, if he felt that he had been insulted, or if he was troubled with his business affairs, Siddhartha had always regarded him mockingly. But slowly and imperceptibly, with the passing of the seasons, his mockery and feeling of superiority diminished. Gradually, along with his growing riches, Siddhartha himself acquired some of the characteristics of the ordinary people, some of their childishness and some of their anxiety. And yet he envied them; the more he became like them, the more he envied them. He envied them the one thing that he lacked and that they had: the sense of importance with which they lived their lives, the depth of their pleasures and sorrows, the anxious but sweet happiness of their continual power to love. These people were always in love with themselves, with their children, with honor or money, with plans or hope. But these he did not learn from them, these child-like pleasures and follies; he only learned the unpleasant things from them which he despised. It happened more frequently that after a merry evening, he lay late in bed the following morning and felt dull and tired. He would become annoyed and impatient when Kamaswami bored him with his worries. He would laugh too loudly when he lost at dice. His face was still more clever and intellectual than other people's, but he rarely laughed, and gradually his face assumed the expressions which are so often found among rich people—the expressions of discontent, of sickliness, of displeasure, of idleness, of lovelessness. Slowly the soul sickness of the rich crept over him.

Like a veil, like a thin mist, a weariness settled on Siddhartha, slowly, every day a little thicker, every month a little darker, every year a little heavier. As a new dress grows old with time, loses its bright color, becomes stained and creased, the hems frayed, and here and there weak and threadbare places, so had Siddhartha's new life which he had begun after his parting from Govinda, become old. In the same way it lost its color and sheen with the passing of the years: creases and stains accumulated, and hidden in the depths, here and there already appearing, waited disillusionment and nausea. Siddhartha did not notice it. He only noticed that the bright and clear inward voice, that had once awakened in him and had always guided him in his finest hours, had become silent.

The world had caught him; pleasure, covetousness, idleness, and finally also that vice that he had always despised and scorned as the most foolish—acquisitiveness. Property, possessions and riches had also finally trapped him. They were no longer a game and a toy; they had become a chain and a burden. Siddhartha wandered along a strange, twisted path of this last and most base declivity through the game of dice. Since the time he had stopped being a Samana in his heart, Siddhartha began to play dice for money and jewels with increasing fervor, a game in which he had previously smilingly and indulgently taken part as a custom of the ordinary people. He was a formidable player; few dared play with him for his stakes were so high and reckless. He played the game as a result of a heartfelt need. He derived a passionate pleasure through the gambling away and squandering of wretched money. In no other way could he show more clearly and mockingly his contempt for riches, the false deity of businessmen. So he staked high and unsparingly, hating himself, mocking himself. He won thousands, he threw thousands away, lost money, lost jewels, lost a country house, won again, lost again. He loved that anxiety, that terrible and oppressive anxiety which he experienced during the game of dice, during the suspense of high stakes. He loved this feeling and continually sought to renew it, to increase it, to stimulate it, for in this feeling alone did he experience some kind of happiness, some kind of excitement, some heightened living in the midst of his satiated, tepid, insipid existence. And after every great loss he devoted himself to the procurement of new riches, went eagerly after business and pressed his debtors for payment, for he wanted to play again, he wanted to squander again, he wanted to show his contempt for riches again. Siddhartha became impatient at losses, he lost his patience with slow-paying debtors, he was no longer kindhearted to beggars, he no longer had the desire to give gifts and loans to the poor. He, who staked ten thousand on the throw of the dice and laughed, became more hard and mean in business, and sometimes dreamt of money at night. And whenever he awakened from this hateful spell, when he saw his face reflected in the mirror on the wall of his bedroom, grown older and uglier, whenever shame and nausea overtook him, he fled again, fled to a new game of chance, fled in confusion to passion, to wine, and from there back again to the urge for acquiring and hoarding wealth. He wore himself out in this senseless cycle, became old and sick.

Then a dream once reminded him. He had been with Kamala in the evening, in her lovely pleasure garden. They sat under a tree talking. Kamala was speaking seriously, and grief and weariness were concealed behind her words. She had asked him to tell her about Gotama, and could not hear enough about him, how clear his eyes were, how peaceful and beautiful his mouth, how gracious his smile, how peaceful his entire manner. For a long time he had to talk to her about the Illustrious Buddha and Kamala had sighed and said: "One day, perhaps soon, I will also become a follower of this Buddha. I will give him my pleasure garden and take refuge in his teachings." But then she enticed him, and in love play she clasped him to her with extreme fervor, fiercely and tearfully, as if she wanted once more to extract the last sweet drop from this fleeting pleasure. Never had it been so strangely clear to Siddhartha how closely related passion was to death. Then he lay beside her and Kamala's face was near to his, and under her eyes and near the corners of her mouth, he read clearly for the first time a sad sign—fine lines and wrinkles, a sign which gave a reminder of autumn and old age. Siddhartha himself, who was only in his forties, had noticed grey hairs here and there in his black hair. Weariness was written on Kamala's beautiful face, weariness from continuing along a long path which had no joyous goal, weariness and incipient old age, and concealed and not yet mentioned, perhaps a not yet conscious fear—fear of the autumn of life, fear of old age, fear of death. Sighing, he took leave of her, his heart full of misery and secret fear.

Then Siddhartha had spent the night at his house with dancers and wine, had pretended to be superior to his companions, which he no longer was. He had drunk much wine and late after midnight he went to bed, tired and yet agitated, nearly in tears and in despair. In vain did he try to sleep. His heart was so full of misery, he felt he could no longer endure it. He was full of a nausea which overpowered him like a distasteful wine, or music that was too sweet and superficial, or like the too sweet smile of the dancers or the too sweet perfume of their hair and breasts. But above all he was nauseated with himself, with his perfumed hair, with the smell of wine from his mouth, with the soft, flabby appearance of his skin. Like one who has eaten and drunk too much and vomits painfully and then feels better, so did the restless man wish he could rid himself with

one terrific heave of these pleasures, of these habits of this entirely
senseless life. Only at daybreak and at the first signs of activity outside
his town house, did he doze off and had a few moments of semi-
oblivion, a possibility of sleep. During that time he had a dream.

Kamala kept a small rare songbird in a small golden cage. It
was about this bird that he dreamt. This bird, which usually sang in
the morning, became mute, and as this surprised him, he went up to
the cage and looked inside. The little bird was dead and lay stiff on
the floor. He took it out, held it a moment in his hand and then threw
it away on the road, and at the same moment he was horrified and his
heart ached as if he had thrown away with this dead bird all that was
good and of value in himself.

Awakening from this dream, he was overwhelmed by a feeling
of great sadness. It seemed to him that he had spent his life in a
worthless and senseless manner; he retained nothing vital, nothing in
any way precious or worth while. He stood alone, like a shipwrecked
man on the shore.

Sadly, Siddhartha went to a pleasure garden that belonged to
him, closed the gates, sat under a mango tree, and felt horror and
death in his heart. He sat and felt himself dying, withering, finishing.
Gradually, he collected his thoughts and mentally went through the
whole of his life, from the earliest days which he could remember.
When had he really been happy? When had he really experienced
joy? Well, he had experienced this several times. He had tasted it in
the days of his boyhood, when he had won praise from the Brahmins,
when he far outstripped his contemporaries, when he excelled himself
at the recitation of the holy verses, in argument with the learned men,
when assisting at the sacrifices. Then he had felt in his heart: "A
path lies before you which you are called to follow. The gods await
you." And again as a youth when his continually soaring goal had
propelled him in and out of the crowd of similar seekers, when he had
striven hard to understand the Brahmins' teachings, when every freshly
acquired knowledge only engendered a new thirst, then again, in the
midst of his thirst, in the midst of his efforts, he had thought: Onwards, onwards, this is your path. He had heard this voice when he
had left his home and chosen the life of the Samanas, and again
when he had left the Samanas and gone to the Perfect One, and also
when he left him for the unknown. How long was it now since he
had heard this voice, since he had soared to any heights? How flat
and desolate his path had been! How many long years he had spent
without any lofty goal, without any thirst, without any exaltation,
content with small pleasures and yet never really satisfied! Without
knowing it, he had endeavored and longed all these years to be like
all these other people, like these children, and yet his life had been

much more wretched and poorer than theirs, for their aims were not his, nor their sorrows his. This whole world of the Kamaswami people had only been a game to him, a dance, a comedy which one watches. Only Kamala was dear to him—had been of value to him— but was she still? Did he still need her—and did she still need him? Were they not playing a game without an end? Was it necessary to live for it? No. This game was called Sansara, a game for children, a game which was perhaps enjoyable played once, twice, ten times— but was it worth playing continually?

Then Siddhartha knew that the game was finished, that he could play it no longer. A shudder passed through his body; he felt as if something had died.

He sat all that day under the mango tree, thinking of his father, thinking of Govinda, thinking of Gotama. Had he left all these in order to become a Kamaswami? He sat there till night fell. When he looked up and saw the stars, he thought: I am sitting here under my mango tree, in my pleasure garden. He smiled a little. Was it necessary, was it right, was it not a foolish thing that he should possess a mango tree and a garden?

He had finished with that. That also died in him. He arose, said farewell to the mango tree and the pleasure garden. As he had not had any food that day he felt extremely hungry, and thought of his house in the town, of his room and bed, of the table with food. He smiled wearily, shook his head and said good-bye to these things.

The same night Siddhartha left his garden and the town and never returned. For a long time Kamaswami tried to find him, believing he had fallen into the hands of bandits. Kamala did not try to find him. She was not surprised when she learned that Siddhartha had disappeared. Had she not always expected it? Was he not a Samana, without a home, a pilgrim? She had felt it more than ever at their last meeting, and in the midst of her pain at her loss, she rejoiced that she had pressed him to close to her heart on that last occasion, had left so completely possessed and mastered by him.

When she heard the first news of Siddhartha's disappearance, she went to the window where she kept a rare songbird in a golden cage. She opened the door of the cage, took the bird out and let it fly away. For a long time she looked after the disappearing bird. From that day she received no more visitors and kept her house closed. After a time, she found that she was with child as a result of her last meeting with Siddhartha.

By the River

Siddhartha wandered into the forest, already far from the town and knew only one thing—that he could not go back, that the life he had

lived for many years was past, tasted and drained to a degree of
nausea. The songbird was dead; its death, which he had dreamt about,
was the bird in his own heart. He was deeply entangled in Sansara, he
had drawn nausea and death to himself from all sides, like a sponge
that absorbs water until it is full. He was full of ennui, full of misery,
full of death; there was nothing left in the world that could attract
him, that could give him pleasure and solace.

He wished passionately for oblivion, to be at rest, to be dead.
If only a flash of lightning would strike him! If only a tiger would
come and eat him! If there were only some wine, some poison, that
would give him oblivion, that would make him forget, that would
make him sleep and never awaken! Was there any kind of filth with
which he had not besmirched himself, any sin and folly which he had
not committed, any stain upon his soul for which he alone had not
been responsible? Was it then still possible to live? Was it possible
to take in breathe again and again, to breath out, to feel hunger, to
eat again, to sleep again, to lie with women again? Was this cycle
not exhausted and finished for him?

Siddhartha reached the long river in the wood, the same river
across which a ferryman had once taken him when he was still a
young man and had come from Gotama's town. He stopped at this
river and stood hesitatingly on the bank. Fatigue and hunger had
weakened him. Why should he go any further, where, and for what
purpose? There was no more purpose, there was nothing more than a
deep, painful longing to shake off this whole confused dream, to spit
out this stale wine, to make an end of this bitter, painful life.

There was a tree on the river bank, a cocoanut tree. Siddhartha
leaned against it, placed his arm round the trunk and looked down
into the green water which flowed beneath him. He looked down
and was completely filled with a desire to let himself go and be
submerged in the water. A chilly emptiness in the water reflected the
terrible emptiness in his soul. Yes, he was at the end. There was
nothing more for him but to efface himself, to destroy the unsuccessful
structure of his life, to throw it away, mocked at by the gods. That
was the deed which he longed to commit, to destroy the form which
he hated! Might the fishes devour him, this dog of a Siddhartha, this
madman, this corrupted and rotting body, this sluggish and misused
soul! Might the fishes and crocodiles devour him, might the demons
tear him to little pieces!

With a distorted countenance he stared into the water. He saw
his face reflected, and spat at it; he took his arm away from the tree
trunk and turned a little, so that he could fall headlong and finally
go under. He bent, with closed eyes—towards death.

Then from a remote part of his soul, from the past of his tired life, he heard a sound. It was one word, one syllable, which without thinking he spoke indistinctly, the ancient beginning and ending of all Brahmin prayers, the holy Om, which had the meaning of "the Perfect One" or "Perfection." At that moment, when the sound of Om reached Siddhartha's ears, his slumbering soul suddenly awakened and he recognized the folly of his action.

Siddhartha was deeply horrified. So that was what he had come to; he was so lost; so confused, so devoid of all reason, that he had sought death. This wish, this childish wish had grown so strong within him: to find peace by destroying his body. All the torment of those recent times, all the disillusionment, all the despair, had not affected him so much as it did the moment the Om reached his consciousness and he recognized his wretchedness and his crime.

"Om," he pronounced inwardly, and he was conscious of Brahman, of the indestructibleness of life; he remembered all that he had forgotten, all that was divine.

But it was only for a moment, a flash. Siddhartha sank down at the foot of the cocoanut tree, overcome by fatigue. Murmuring Om, he laid his head on the tree roots and sank into a deep sleep.

His sleep was deep and dreamless; he had not slept like that for a long time. When he awakened after many hours, it seemed to him as if ten years had passed. He heard the soft rippling of the water; he did not know where he was nor what had brought him there. He looked up and was surprised to see the trees and the sky above him. He remembered where he was and how he came to be there. He felt a desire to remain there for a long time. The past now seemed to him to be covered by a veil, extremely remote, very unimportant. He only knew that his previous life (at the first moment of his return to consciousness his previous life seemed to him like a remote incarnation, like an earlier birth of his present Self) was finished, that it was so full of nausea and wretchedness that he had wanted to destroy it, but that he had come to himself by a river, under a cocoanut tree, with the holy word Om on his lips. Then he had fallen asleep, and on awakening he looked at the world like a new man. Softly he said the word Om to himself, over which he had fallen asleep, and it seemed to him as if his whole sleep had been a long deep pronouncing of Om, thinking of Om, an immersion and penetration into Om, into the nameless, into the Divine.

What a wonderful sleep it had been! Never had a sleep so refreshed him, so renewed him, so rejuvenated him! Perhaps he had really died, perhaps he had been drowned and was reborn in another form. No, he recognized himself, he recognized his hands and feet, the place where he lay and the Self in his breast, Siddhartha, self-willed, individualistic. But this Siddhartha was somewhat changed, renewed. He had slept wonderfully. He was remarkably awake, happy and curious.

Siddhartha raised himself and saw a monk in a yellow gown, with shaved head, sitting opposite him in the attitude of a thinker. He looked at the man, who had neither hair on his head nor a beard, and he did not look at him long when he recognized in this monk, Govinda, the friend of his youth, Govinda who had taken refuge in the Illustrious Buddha. Govinda had also aged, but he still showed the old characteristics of his face—eagerness, loyalty, curiosity, anxiety. But when Govinda, feeling his glance, raised his eyes and looked at him, Siddhartha saw that Govinda did not recognize him. Govinda was pleased to find him awake. Apparently he had sat there a long time waiting for him to awaken, although he did not know him.

"I was sleeping," said Siddhartha. "How did you come here?"

"You were sleeping," answered Govinda, "and it is not good to sleep in such places where there are often snakes and animals from the forest prowling about. I am one of the followers of the Illustrious Gotama, the Buddha of Sakyamuni, and I am on a pilgrimage with a number of our order. I saw you lying asleep in a dangerous place, so I tried to awaken you, and then as I saw you were sleeping very deeply, I remained behind my brothers and sat by you. Then it seems that I, who wanted to watch over you, fell asleep myself. Weariness overcame me and I kept my watch badly. But now you are awake, so I must go and overtake my brothers."

"I thank you, Samana, for guarding my sleep. The followers of the Illustrious One are very kind, but now you may go on your way."

"I am going. May you keep well."

"I thank you, Samana."

Govinda bowed and said, "Good-bye."

"Good-bye, Govinda," said Siddhartha.

The monk stood still.

"Excuse me, sir, how do you know my name?"

Thereupon Siddhartha laughed.

"I know you, Govinda, from your father's house and from the Brahmins' school, and from the sacrifices, and from our sojourn with the Samanas and from that hour in the grove of Jetavana when you swore allegiance to the Illustrious One."

"You are Siddhartha," cried Govinda aloud. "Now I recognize you and do not understand why I did not recognize you immediately. Greetings, Siddhartha, it gives me great pleasure to see you again."

"I am also pleased to see you again. You have watched over me during my sleep. I thank you once again, although I needed no guard. Where are you going, my friend?"

"I am not going anywhere. We monks are always on the way,

except during the rainy season. We always move from place to place, live according to the rule, preach the gospel, collect alms and then move on. It is always the same. But where are you going, Siddhartha?"

Siddhartha said: "It is the same with me as it is with you, my friend. I am not going anywhere. I am only on the way. I am making a pilgrimage."

Govinda said: "You say you are making a pilgrimage and I believe you. But forgive me, Siddhartha, you do not look like a pilgrim. You are wearing the clothes of a rich man, you are wearing the shoes of a man of fashion, and your perfumed hair is not the hair of a pilgrim, it is not the hair of a Samana."

"You have observed well, my friend; you see everything with your sharp eyes. But I did not tell you that I am a Samana. I said I was making a pilgrimage and that is true."

"You are making a pilgrimage," said Govinda, "but few make a pilgrimage in such clothes, in such shoes and with such hair. I, who have been wandering for many years, have never seen such a pilgrim."

"I believe you, Govinda. But today you have met such a pilgrim in such shoes and dress. Remember, my dear Govinda, the world of appearances is transitory, the style of our clothes and hair is extremely transitory. Our hair and our bodies are themselves transitory. You have observed correctly. I am wearing the clothes of a rich man. I am wearing them because I have been a rich man, and I am wearing my hair like men of the world and fashion because I have been one of them."

"And what are you now, Siddhartha?"

"I do not know; I know as little as you. I am on the way. I was a rich man, but I am no longer and what I will be tomorrow I do not know."

"Have you lost your riches?"

"I have lost them, or they have lost me—I am not sure. The wheel of appearances revolves quickly, Govinda. Where is Siddhartha the Brahmin, where is Siddhartha the Samana, where is Siddhartha the rich man? The transitory soon changes, Govinda. You know that."

For a long time Govinda looked doubtfully at the friend of his youth. Then he bowed to him, as one does to a man of rank, and went on his way.

Smiling, Siddhartha watched him go. He still loved him, this faithful anxious friend. And at that moment, in that splendid hour, after his wonderful sleep, permeated with Om, how could he help but love someone and something. That was just the magic that had happened to him during his sleep and the Om in him—he loved everything, he was full of joyous love towards everything that he saw.

And it seemed to him that was just why he was previously so ill—because he could love nothing and nobody.

With a smile Siddhartha watched the departing monk. His sleep had strengthened him, but he suffered great hunger for he had not eaten for two days, and the time was long past when he could ward off hunger. Troubled, yet also with laughter, he recalled that time. He remembered that at that time he had boasted of three things to Kamala, three noble and invincible arts: fasting, waiting and thinking. These were his possessions, his power and strength, his firm staff. He had learned these three arts and nothing else during the diligent, assiduous years of his youth. Now he had lost them, he possessed none of them any more, neither fasting, nor waiting, nor thinking. He had exchanged them for the most wretched things, for the transitory, for the pleasures of the senses, for high living and riches. He had gone along a strange path. And now, it seemed that he had indeed become an ordinary person.

Siddhartha reflected on his state. He found it difficult to think; he really had no desire to, but he forced himself.

Now, he thought, that all these transitory things have slipped away from me again, I stand once more beneath the sun, as I once stood as a small child. Nothing is mine, I know nothing, I possess nothing, I have learned nothing. How strange it is! Now, when I am no longer young, when my hair is fast growing grey, when strength begins to diminish, now I am beginning again like a child. He had to smile again. Yes, his destiny was strange! He was going backwards, and now he again stood empty and naked and ignorant in the world. But he did not grieve about it; no, he even felt a great desire to laugh, to laugh at himself, to laugh at this strange foolish world!

Things are going backwards with you, he said to himself and laughed, and as he said it, his glance lighted on the river, and he saw the river also flowing continually backwards, singing merrily. That pleased him immensely; he smiled cheerfully at the river. Was this not the river in which he had once wished to drown himself—hundreds of years ago—or had he dreamt it?

How strange his life had been, he thought. He had wandered along strange paths. As a boy I was occupied with the gods and sacrifices, as a youth with asceticism, with thinking and meditation. I was in search of Brahman and revered the eternal in Atman. As a young man I was attracted to expiation. I lived in the woods, suffered heat and cold. I learned to fast, I learned to conquer my body. I then discovered with wonder the teachings of the great Buddha. I felt knowledge and the unity of the world circulate in me like my own blood, but I also felt compelled to leave the Buddha and the great knowledge. I went and learned the pleasures of love from Kamala and business from Kamaswami. I hoarded money, I squandered money, I acquired a taste for rich food, I learned to stimulate my senses. I had to spend many years like that in order to lose my intelligence, to lose the power to think, to forget about the unity of things. Is it not true, that slowly and through many deviations I changed from a man into a child? From a thinker into an ordinary person? And yet this path has been good and the bird in my breast has not died. But what a path it has been! I have had to experience so much stupidity, so many vices, so much error, so much nausea, disillusionment and sorrow, just in order to become a child again and begin anew. But it was right that it should be so; my eyes and heart acclaim it. I had to experience despair, I had to sink to the greatest mental depths, to thoughts of suicide, in order to experience grace, to hear Om again, to sleep deeply again and to awaken refreshed again. I had to become a fool again in order to find Atman in myself. I had to sin in order to live again. Whither will my path yet lead me? This path is stupid, it goes in spirals, perhaps in circles, but whichever way it goes, I will follow it.

He was aware of a great happiness mounting within him.

Where does it come from, he asked himself? What is the reason for this feeling of happiness? Does it arise from my good long sleep which has done me so much good? Or from the word Om which I pronounced? Or because I have run away, because my flight is accomplished, because I am at last free again and stand like a child beneath the sky? Ah, how good this flight has been, this liberation! In the place from which I escaped there was always an atmosphere of pomade, spice, excess and inertia. How I hated that world of riches, carousing and playing! How I hated myself for remaining so long in that horrible world! How I hated myself, thwarted, poisoned and tortured myself, made myself old and ugly. Never again, as I once fondly imagined, will I consider that Siddhartha is clever. But one thing I have done well, which pleases me, which I must praise—I have now put an end to that self-detestation, to that foolish empty life. I commend you, Siddhartha, that after so many years of folly, you have again had a good idea, that you have accomplished something, that you have again heard the bird in your breast sing and followed it.

So he praised himself, was pleased with himself and listened curiously to his stomach which rumbled from hunger. He felt he had thoroughly tasted and ejected a portion of sorrow, a portion of misery during those past times, that he had consumed them up to a point of despair and death. But all was well. He could have remained much longer with Kamaswami, made and squandered money, fed his body and neglected his soul; he could have dwelt for a long time yet in that soft, well-upholstered hell, if this had not happened, this moment of complete hopelessness and despair and the tense moment when he had bent over the flowing water, ready to commit suicide. This despair, this extreme nausea which he had experienced had not overpowered him. The bird, the clear spring and voice within him was still alive—that was why he rejoiced, that was why he laughed, that was why his face was radiant under his grey hair.

It is a good thing to experience everything oneself, he thought. As a child I learned that pleasures of the world and riches were not good. I have known it for a long time, but I have only just experienced it. Now I know it not only with my intellect, but with my eyes, with my heart, with my stomach. It is a good thing that I know this.

He thought long of the change in him, listened to the bird singing happily. If this bird within him had died, would he have perished? No, something else in him had died, something that he had long desired should perish. Was it not what he had once wished to destroy during his ardent years of asceticism? Was it not his Self, his small, fearful and proud Self, with which he had wrestled for so many years, but which had always conquered him again, which appeared each time again and again, which robbed him of happiness and filled him with fear? Was it not this which had finally died today in the wood by this delightful river? Was it not because of its death that he was now like a child, so full of trust and happiness, without fear?

Siddhartha now also realized why he had struggled in vain with this Self when he was a Brahmin and an ascetic. Too much knowledge had hindered him; too many holy verses, too many sacrificial rites, too much mortification of the flesh, too much doing and striving. He had been full of arrogance; he had always been the cleverest, the most eager—always a step ahead of the others, always the learned and intellectual one, always the priest or the sage. His Self had crawled into this priesthood, into this arrogance, into this intellectuality. It sat there tightly and grew, while he thought he was destroying it by fasting and penitence. Now he understood it and realized that the inward voice had been right, that no teacher could have brought him salvation. That was why he had to go into the world, to lose himself in power, women and money; that was why he had to be a merchant, a dice player, a drinker and a man of property, until the priest and Samana in him were dead. That was why he had to undergo those horrible years, suffer nausea, learn the lesson of the madness of an empty, futile life till the end, till he reached bitter despair, so that Siddhartha the pleasure-monger and Siddhartha the man of property could die. He had died and a new Siddhartha had awakened from his sleep. He also would grow old and die. Siddhartha was transitory, all forms were transitory, but today he was young, he was a child—the new Siddhartha—and he was very happy.

These thoughts passed through his mind. Smiling, he listened to his stomach, listened thankfully to a humming bee. Happily he looked into the flowing river. Never had a river attracted him as much as this one. Never had he found the voice and appearance of flowing water so beautiful. It seemed to him as if the river had something special to tell him, something which he did not know, something which still awaited him. Siddhartha had wanted to drown himself in this river; the old, tired, despairing Siddhartha was today drowned in it. The new Siddhartha felt a deep love for this flowing water and decided that he would not leave it again so quickly.

RESPONSES: Questions for Writing and Discussion

1. In the opening passages of "Sansara" we are told that for all his resources Siddhartha experiences the "soul sickness of the rich." Can you accurately describe what this is? Do you believe all rich people are similarly unhappy? Do you believe they should be? If your answer is yes, what would you tell a rich person who claimed that his life was perfect?

2. During his bondage to the self and its material pleasures Siddhartha begins to fear old age and death. One assumes that, after his enlightenment, when he transcends the self and experiences the joys of pure being, he will no longer think about death. But is there a paradox here? If enlightenment is the way to the highest kind of happiness, wouldn't you think achieving this would cause a person to value and cling to life even more?

3. What is the significance of the dream about the dead songbird that is thrown away on the road and causes Siddhartha to experience "a feeling of great sadness" after awakening? What things are summed up in the symbol of the bird?

4. Siddhartha reaches the conclusion that life is "Sansara"—a child's game. Many refer to the game of life. What precisely does this mean? Would you describe your own life as a game? If not, is it different from the life Siddhartha is leading at the time he renounces it? If you agree that your life is a game, is the term a derogatory one? What would make it a nongame?

5. How did you react to the revelation at the conclusion of "Sansara" that Kamala was bearing Siddhartha's child and that he has gone away, never to return? Did you feel sorry for Kamala but glad that Siddhartha had followed his own bent? Were you indifferent to Kamala's plight because it was unimportant compared with

the hero's quest for enlightenment? If Kamala were able to contact Siddhartha, what decision would you want him to make?

6. Is Siddhartha a selfish person? Is the renunciation of every-thing—all ties, all responsibilities—in the interest of a supposedly higher cause an act of selflessness or the extreme of self-preoccupation?

7. What do you know about the sound of Om? What is it sup-posed to do? Why does it have so powerful an effect on Siddhartha when he remembers it?

8. Have you ever meditated, using Om, some other sound, or any means of achieving liberation from the ego? If so, try to describe the experience. Were you happy? Or were you glad to come back to yourself? If you have never meditated, do you think you would like to transcend the ego?

9. When Siddhartha awakens from his long sleep by the river, "he looked at the world like a new man." What does it mean to do such a thing? What does it mean not to? Have you ever had a similar experience? What were the circumstances?

10. What, according to Hesse, is the importance of loss? Of suffering? Of despair? Why should we not care when we experience these things? How does a "great happiness" follow them?

11. "It seemed to him as if the river had something special to tell him, something which he did not know, something which still awaited him." Hesse does not tell us what the secret of the river is. Can you say it?

PEYOTE AND ANOTHER WORLD
Carlos Castaneda

Carlos Castaneda is an ethnographer; that is, an anthropologist specializing in "primitive" people, their customs and rituals. In 1960, while a graduate student at UCLA, he traveled to Arizona to study the nature and use of Indian medicines, especially those derived from certain species of plants. But, instead, he was introduced to an ancient drug culture and an unfolding series of experiences for which rational explanation seems impossible.

The book from which the following selection is taken, *The Teachings of Don Juan: A Yaqui Way of Knowledge*, was written as an effort to crystallize those experiences. It presents an account of the author's meeting and subsequent apprenticeship to a Yaqui sorcerer, who introduces him to the hallucinogenic world of peyote, the datura plant (also known as Jimson weed), and the humito mushroom. It is both an exciting adventure story about an exotic old man and his mystic rapport with a different dimension of existence, and a serious, scholarly attempt to describe fairly an ancient philosophy and way of life based on principles that might bewilder, if not amuse, those who accept only one view of reality.

The extraordinary plants to which Castaneda is introduced by Don Juan are means to an end—the gradual enlightenment of the user, allowing him to transcend his limiting, conscious state, aided by an "ally" or spirit, who dwells in each of the various plants ingested as part of a spiritual ceremony. In our selection, the author experiences the presence of Mescalito, the ally inhabiting the peyote cactus. Prior to the incident, he and don Juan have embarked upon a journey to Chihuahua, a state in Mexico, in search of hallucinogenic plants and have stopped for a midday meal.

Those who go on to read all of *The Teachings of Don Juan* may be disappointed that the true nature of the knowledge attained cannot be made totally accessible to the understanding. But one lesson does emerge quite clearly—the lesson in Human Worth which anthropology often discloses—summed up in this statement by Walter Goldschmidt in the preface to the book: "It is not only that people have different customs; it is not only that people believe in different gods and expect different postmortem fates. It is, rather, that the worlds of different people have different shapes."

Peyote and Another World

I was very tired and hungry and took him up on his offer. I felt this was a good time to talk about the purpose of our trip, and quite casually I asked, "Do you think we are going to stay here for a long time?"

"We are here to gather some Mescalito. We will stay until tomorrow."

"Where is Mescalito?"

"All around us."

Cacti of many species were growing in profusion all through the area, but I could not distinguish peyote among them.

We started to hike again and by three o'clock we came to a long, narrow valley with steep side hills. I felt strangely excited at the idea of finding peyote, which I had never seen in its natural environment.

From *The Teachings of Don Juan* by Carlos Casteneda. Originally published by the University of California Press; reprinted by permission of The Regents of the University of California.

We entered the valley and must have walked about four hundred feet when suddenly I spotted three unmistakable peyote plants. They were in a cluster a few inches above the ground in front of me, to the left of the path. They looked like round, pulpy, green roses. I ran toward them, pointing them out to don Juan.

He ignored me and deliberately kept his back turned as he walked away. I knew I had done the wrong thing, and for the rest of the afternoon we walked in silence, moving slowly on the flat valley floor, which was covered with small, sharp-edged rocks. We moved among the cacti, disturbing crowds of lizards and at times a solitary bird. And I passed scores of peyote plants without saying a word.

At six o'clock we were at the bottom of the mountains that marked the end of the valley. We climbed to a ledge. Don Juan dropped his sack and sat down.

I was hungry again, but we had no food left; I suggested that we pick up the Mescalito and head back for town. He looked annoyed and made a smacking sound with his lips. He said we were going to spend the night there.

We sat quietly. There was a rock wall to the left, and to the right was the valley we had just crossed. It extended for quite a distance and seemed to be wider than, and not so flat as, I had thought. Viewed from the spot where I sat, it was full of small hills and protuberances.

"Tomorrow we will start walking back," don Juan said without looking at me, and pointing to the valley. "We will work our way back and pick him as we cross the field. That is, we will pick him only when he is in our way. *He* will find us and not the other way around. *He* will find us—if he wants to."

Don Juan rested his back against the rock wall and, with his head turned to his side, continued talking as though another person were there besides myself. "One more thing. Only *I* can pick him. You will perhaps carry the bag, or walk ahead of me—I don't know yet. But tomorrow you will not point at him as you did today!"

"I am sorry, don Juan."

"It is alright. You didn't know."

"Did your benefactor teach you all this about Mescalito?"

"No! Nobody has taught me about him. It was the protector himself who was my teacher."

"Then Mescalito is like a person to whom you can talk?"

"No, he isn't."

"How does he teach, then?"

He remained silent for a while.

"Remember the time when you played with him? You understood what he meant, didn't you?"

"I did!"

"That is the way he teaches. You did not know it then, but if you had paid attention to him, he would have talked to you."

"When?"

"When you saw him for the first time."

He seemed to be very annoyed by my questioning. I told him I had to ask all these questions because I wanted to find out all I could.

"Don't ask *me!*" He smiled maliciously. "Ask *him.* The next time you see him, ask him everything you want to know."

"Then Mescalito *is* like a person you can talk . . ."

He did not let me finish. He turned away, picked up the canteen, stepped down from the ledge, and disappeared around the rock. I did not want to be alone there, and even though he had not asked me to go along, I followed him. We walked for about five hundred feet to a small creek. He washed his hands and face and filled up the canteen. He swished water around in his mouth, but did not drink it. I scooped up some water in my hands and drank, but he stopped me and said it was unnecessary to drink.

He handed me the canteen and started to walk back to the ledge. When we got there we sat again facing the valley with our backs to the rock wall. I asked if we could build a fire. He reacted as if it was inconceivable to ask such a thing. He said that for that night we were Mescalito's guests and he was going to keep us warm.

It was already dusk. Don Juan pulled two thin, cotton blankets from his sack, threw one into my lap, and sat cross-legged with the other one over his shoulders. Below us the valley was dark, with its edges already diffused in the evening mist.

Don Juan sat motionless facing the peyote field. A steady wind blew on my face.

"The twilight is the crack between the worlds," he said softly, without turning to me.

I didn't ask what he meant. My eyes became tired. Suddenly I felt elated; I had a strange, overpowering desire to weep!

I lay on my stomach; the rock floor was hard and uncomfortable, and I had to change my position every few minutes. Finally I sat up and crossed my legs, putting the blanket over my shoulders. To my amazement this position was supremely comfortable, and I fell asleep.

When I woke up, I heard don Juan talking to me. It was very dark. I could not see him well. I did not understand what he said, but I followed him when he started to go down from the ledge. We moved carefully, or at least I did, because of the darkness. We stopped at the bottom of the rock wall. Don Juan sat down and signaled me to sit at his left. He opened up his shirt and took out a leather sack, which he opened and placed on the ground in front of him. It contained a number of dried peyote buttons.

After a long pause he picked up one of the buttons. He held it in his right hand, rubbing it several times between the thumb and the first finger as he chanted softly. Suddenly he let out a tremendous cry. "Ahiiii!"

It was weird, unexpected. It terrified me. Vaguely I saw him place the peyote button in his mouth and begin to chew it. After a moment he picked up the whole sack, leaned toward me, and told me in a whisper to take the sack, pick out one Mescalito, put the sack in front of us again, and then do exactly as he did.

I picked a peyote button and rubbed it as he had done. Meanwhile he chanted, swaying back and forth. I tried to put the button into my mouth several times, but I felt embarrassed to cry out. Then, as in a dream, an unbelievable shriek came out of me: Ahiiii! For a moment I thought it was someone else. Again I felt the effects of nervous shock in my stomach. I was falling backward. I was fainting. I put the peyote button into my mouth and chewed it. After a while don Juan picked up another from the sack. I was relieved to see that he put it into his mouth after a short chant. He passed the sack to me, and I placed it in front of us again after taking one button. This cycle went on five times before I noticed any thirst. I picked up the canteen to drink, but don Juan told me just to wash my mouth, and not to drink or I would vomit.

I swished the water around in my mouth repeatedly. At a certain moment drinking was a formidable temptation, and I swallowed a bit of water. Immediately my stomach began to convulse. I expected to have a painless and effortless flowing of liquid from my mouth, as had happened during my first experience with peyote, but to my surprise I had only the ordinary sensation of vomiting. It did not last long, however.

Don Juan picked up another button and handed me the sack, and the cycle was renewed and repeated until I had chewed fourteen buttons. By this time all my early sensations of thirst, cold, and discomfort had disappeared. In their place I felt an unfamiliar sense of warmth and excitation. I took the canteen to freshen my mouth, but it was empty.

"Can we go to the creek, don Juan?"

The sound of my voice did not project out, but hit the roof of my palate, bounced back into my throat, and echoed to and fro between them. The echo was soft and musical, and seemed to have wings that flapped inside my throat. Its touch soothed me. I followed its back-and-forth movements until it had vanished.

I repeated the question. My voice sounded as though I was talking inside a vault.

Don Juan did not answer. I got up and turned in the direction of the creek. I looked at him to see if he was coming, but he seemed to be listening attentively to something.

He made an imperative sign with his hand to be quiet.

"Abuhtol[?] is already here!" he said.

I had never heard that word before, and I was wondering whether to ask him about it when I detected a noise that seemed to be a buzzing inside my ears. The sound became louder by degrees until it was like the vibration caused by an enormous bull-roarer. It lasted for a brief moment and subsided gradually until everything was quiet again. The violence and the intensity of the noise terrified me. I was shaking so much that I could hardly remain standing, yet I was perfectly rational. If I had been drowsy a few minutes before, this feeling had totally vanished, giving way to a state of extreme lucidity. The noise reminded me of a science fiction movie in which a gigantic bee buzzed its wings coming out of an atomic radiation area. I laughed at the thought. I saw don Juan slumping back into his relaxed position. And suddenly the image of a gigantic bee accosted me again. It was more real than ordinary thoughts. It stood alone surrounded by an extraordinary clarity. Everything else was driven from my mind. This state of mental clearness, which had no precedents in my life, produced another moment of terror.

I began to perspire. I leaned toward don Juan to tell him I was afraid. His face was a few inches from mine. He was looking at me, but his eyes were the eyes of a bee. They looked like round glasses that had a light of their own in the darkness. His lips were pushed out, and from them came a pattering noise: "Pehtuh-peh-tuh-pet-tuh." I jumped backward, nearly crashing into the rock wall. For a seemingly endless time I experienced an unbearable fear. I was panting and whining. The perspiration had frozen on my skin, giving me an awkward rigidity. Then I heard don Juan's voice saying, "Get up! Move around! Get up!"

The image vanished and again I could see his familiar face.

"I'll get some water," I said after another endless moment. My voice cracked. I could hardly articulate the words. Don Juan nodded yes. As I walked away I realized that my fear had gone as fast and as mysteriously as it had come.

Upon approaching the creek I noticed that I could see every object in the way. I remembered I had just seen don Juan clearly, whereas earlier I could hardly distinguish the outlines of his figure. I stopped and looked into the distance, and I could even see across the valley. Some boulders on the other side became perfectly visible. I thought it must be early morning, but it occurred to me that I might have lost track of time. I looked at my watch. It was ten of twelve! I checked the watch to see if it was working. It couldn't be midday;

it had to be midnight! I intended to make a dash for the water and come back to the rocks, but I saw don Juan coming down and I waited for him. I told him I could see in the dark.

He stared at me for a long time without saying a word; if he did speak, perhaps I did not hear him, for I was concentrating on my new, unique ability to see in the dark. I could distinguish the very minute pebbles in the sand. At moments everything was so clear it seemed to be early morning, or dusk. Then it would get dark; then it would clear again. Soon I realized that the brightness corresponded to my heart's diastole, and the darkness to its systole. The world changed from bright to dark to bright again with every beat of my heart.

I was absorbed in this discovery when the same strange sound that I had heard before became audible again. My muscles stiffened.

"Anuhctal [as I heard the word this time] is here," don Juan said. I fancied the roar so thunderous, so overwhelming, that nothing else mattered. When it had subsided, I perceived a sudden increase in the volume of water. The creek, which a minute before had been less than a foot wide, expanded until it was an enormous lake. Light that seemed to come from above it touched the surface as though shining through thick foliage. From time to time the water would glitter for a second— gold and black. Then it would remain dark, lightless, almost out of sight, and yet strangely present.

I don't recall how long I stayed there just watching, squatting on the shore of the black lake. The roar must have subsided in the meantime, because what jolted me back (to reality?) was again a terrifying buzzing. I turned around to look for don Juan. I saw him climbing up and disappearing behind the rock ledge. Yet the feeling of being alone did not bother me at all; I squatted there in a state of absolute confidence and abandonment. The roar again became audible; it was very intense, like the noise made by a high wind. Listening to it as carefully as I could, I was able to detect a definite melody. It was a composite of high-pitched sounds, like human voices, accompanied by a deep bass drum. I focused all my attention on the melody, and again noticed that the systole and diastole of my heart coincided with the sound of the bass drum, and with the pattern of the music.

I stood up and the melody stopped. I tried to listen to my heartbeat, but it was not detectable. I squatted again, thinking that perhaps the position of my body had caused or induced the sounds! But nothing happened! Not a sound! Not even my heart! I thought I had had enough, but as I stood up to leave, I felt a tremor of the earth. The ground under my feet was shaking. I was losing my balance. I fell backward and remained on my back while the earth shook violently. I tried to grab a rock or a plant, but something was sliding under me. I jumped up, stood for a moment, and fell down again. The ground on which I sat was moving, sliding into the water like a raft. I remained motionless, stunned by a terror that was, like everything else, unique, uninterrupted, and absolute.

I moved through the water of the black lake perched on a piece of soil that looked like an earthen log. I had the feeling I was going in a southerly direction, transported by the current. I could see the water moving and swirling around. It felt cold, and oddly heavy, to the touch. I fancied it alive.

There were no distinguishable shores or landmarks, and I can't recall the thoughts or the feelings that must have come to me during this trip. After what seemed like hours of drifting, my raft made a right-angle turn to the left, the east. It continued to slide on the water for a very short distance, and unexpectedly rammed against something. The impact threw me forward. I closed my eyes and felt a sharp pain as my knees and my outstretched arms hit the ground. After a moment I looked up. I was lying on the dirt. It was as though my earthen log had merged with the land. I sat up and turned around. The water was receding! It moved backward, like a wave in reverse, until it disappeared.

I sat there for a long time, trying to collect my thoughts and resolve all that had happened into a coherent unit. My entire body ached. My throat felt like an open sore; I had bitten my lips when I "landed." I stood up. The wind made me realize I was cold. My clothes were wet. My hands and jaws and knees shook so violently that I had to lie down again. Drops of perspiration slid into my eyes and burned them until I yelled with pain.

After a while I regained a measure of stability and stood up. In the dark twilight, the scene was very clear. I took a couple of steps. A distinct sound of many human voices came to me. They seemed to be talking loudly. I followed the sound; I walked for about fifty yards and came to a sudden stop. I had reached a dead end. The place where I stood was a corral formed by enormous boulders. I could distinguish another row, and then another, and another, until they merged into the sheer mountain. From among them came the most exquisite music. It was a fluid, uninterrupted, eerie flow of sounds.

At the foot of one boulder I saw a man sitting on the ground, his face turned almost in profile. I approached him until I was perhaps ten feet away; then he turned his head and looked at me. I stopped— his eyes were the water I had just seen! They had the same enormous volume, the sparkling of gold and black. His head was pointed like a strawberry; his skin was green, dotted with innumerable warts. Except for the pointed shape, his head was exactly like the surface of the peyote plant. I stood in front of him, staring; I couldn't take my eyes away from him. I felt he was deliberately pressing on my chest with the weight of his eyes. I was choking. I lost my balance and fell to the ground. His eyes turned away. I heard him talking to me. At first his voice was like the soft rustle of a light breeze. Then I heard it as music—as a melody of voices—and I "knew" it was saying, "What do you want?"

I knelt before him and talked about my life, then wept. He looked at me again. I felt his eyes pulling me away, and I thought that moment would be the moment of my death. He signaled me to come closer. I vacillated for an instant before I took a step forward. As I came closer he turned his eyes away from me and showed me the back of his hand. The melody said, "Look!" There was a round hole in the middle of his hand. "Look!" said the melody again. I looked into the hole and I saw myself. I was very old and feeble and was running stooped over, with bright sparks flying all around me. Then three of the sparks hit me, two in the head and one in the left shoulder. My figure, in the hole, stood up for a moment until it was fully vertical, and then disappeared together with the hole.

Mescalito turned his eyes to me again. They were so close to me that I "heard" them rumble softly with that peculiar sound I had heard many times that night. They became peaceful by degrees until they were like a quiet pond rippled by gold and black flashes.

He turned his eyes away once more and hopped like a cricket for perhaps fifty yards. He hopped again and again, and was gone.

The next thing I remember is that I began to walk. Very rationally I tried to recognize landmarks, such as mountains in the distance, in order to orient myself. I had been obsessed by cardinal points throughout the whole experience, and I believed that north had to be to my left. I walked in that direction for quite a while before I realized that it was daytime, and that I was no longer using my "night vision." I remembered I had a watch and looked at the time. It was eight o'clock.

It was about ten o'clock when I got to the ledge where I had been the night before. Don Juan was lying on the ground asleep.

"Where have you been?" he asked.

I sat down to catch my breath.

After a long silence he asked, "Did you see him?"

I began to narrate to him the sequence of my experiences from the beginning but he interrupted me saying that all that mattered was whether I had seen him or not. He asked how close to me Mescalito was. I told him I had nearly touched him.

That part of my story interested him. He listened attentively to every detail without comment, interrupting only to ask questions about the form of the entity I had seen, its disposition, and other details about it. It was about noon when don Juan seemed to have had enough of my story. He stood up and strapped a canvas bag to my chest; he told me to walk behind him and said he was going to cut Mescalito loose and I had to receive him in my hands and place him inside the bag gently.

We drank some water and started to walk. When we reached the edge of the valley he seemed to hesitate for a moment before deciding which direction to take. Once he had made his choice we walked in a straight line.

Every time we came to a peyote plant, he squatted in front of it and very gently cut off the top with his short, serrated knife. He made an incision level with the ground, and sprinkled the "wound," as he called it, with pure sulphur powder which he carried in a leather sack. He held the fresh button in his left hand and spread the powder with his right hand. Then he stood up and handed me the button, which I received with both hands, as he had prescribed, and placed inside the bag. "Stand erect and don't let the bag touch the ground or the bushes or anything else," he said repeatedly, as though he thought I would forget.

We collected sixty-five buttons. When the bag was completely filled, he put it on my back and strapped a new one to my chest. By the time we had crossed the plateau we had two full sacks, containing one hundred and ten peyote buttons. The bags were so heavy and bulky that I could hardly walk under their weight and volume.

Don Juan whispered to me that the bags were heavy because Mescalito wanted to return to the ground. He said it was the sadness of leaving his abode which made Mescalito heavy; my real chore was not to let the bags touch the ground, because if I did Mescalito would never allow me to take him again.

At one particular moment the pressure of the straps on my shoulders became unbearable. Something was exerting tremendous force in order to pull me down. I felt very apprehensive. I noticed that I had started to walk faster, almost at a run; I was in a way trotting behind Don Juan.

Suddenly the weight on my back and chest diminished. The load became spongy and light. I ran freely to catch up with don Juan, who was ahead of me. I told him I did not feel the weight any longer. He explained that we had already left Mescalito's abode.

Tuesday, July 3, 1962

"I think Mescalito has almost accepted you," don Juan said.

"Why do you say he has *almost* accepted me, don Juan?"

"He did not kill you, or even harm you. He gave you a good fright, but not a really bad one. If he had not accepted you at all, he would have appeared to you as monstrous and full of wrath. Some people have learned the meaning of horror upon encountering him and not being accepted by him."

"If he is so terrible, why didn't you tell me about it before you took me to the field?"

"You do not have the courage to seek him deliberately. I thought it would be better if you did not know."

"But I might have died, don Juan!"

"Yes, you might have. But I was certain it was going to be alright for you. He played with you once. He did not harm you. I thought he would also have compassion for you this time."

I asked him if he really thought Mescalito had had compassion for me. The experience had been terrifying; I felt that I had nearly died of fright.

He said Mescalito had been most kind to me; he had showed me a scene that was an answer to a question. Don Juan said Mescalito had given me a lesson. I asked him what the lesson was and what it meant. He said it would be impossible to answer that question because I had been too afraid to know *exactly* what I asked Mescalito.

Don Juan probed my memory as to what I had said to Mescalito before he showed me the scene on his hand. I could not remember. All I remembered was falling on my knees and "confessing my sins" to him.

Don Juan seemed uninterested in talking about it anymore. I asked him, "Can you teach me the words to the songs you chanted?"

"No, I can't. Those words are my own, the words the protector himself taught me. The songs are *my* songs. I can't tell you what they are."

"Why can't you tell me, don Juan?"

"Because these songs are a link between the protector and myself. I am sure someday he will teach you your own songs. Wait until then; and never, absolutely never, copy or ask about the songs that belong to another man."

"What was the name you called out? Can you tell me that, don Juan?"

"No. His name can never be voiced, except to call him."

"What if I want to call him myself?"

"If someday he accepts you, he will tell you his name. That name will be for you alone to use, either to call him loudly or to say quietly to yourself. Perhaps he will tell you his name is José. Who knows?"

"Why is it wrong to use his name when talking about him?"

"You have seen his eyes, haven't you? You can't fool around with the protector. That is why I can't get over the fact that he chose to play with you!"

"How can he be a protector when he hurts some people?"

"The answer is very simple. Mescalito is a protector because he is available to anyone who seeks him."

"But isn't it true that everything in the world is available to anyone who seeks it?"

"No, that is not true. The ally powers are available only to the brujos, but anyone can partake of Mescalito."

"But why then does he hurt some people?"

"Not everybody likes Mescalito; yet they all seek him with the idea of profiting without doing any work. Naturally their encounter with him is always horrifying."

"What happens when he accepts a man completely?"

"He appears to him as a man, or as a light. When a man has won this kind of acceptance, Mescalito is constant. He never changes after that. Perhaps when you meet him again he will be a light, and someday he may even take you flying and reveal all his secrets to you."

"What do I have to do to arrive at that point, don Juan?"

"You have to be a strong man, and your life has to be truthful."

"What is a truthful life?"

"A life lived with deliberateness, a good, strong life."

RESPONSES: Questions for Writing and Discussion

1. What is your overall impression of don Juan? Does he seem hopelessly deluded? Is he drug-ridden and senile? Is he a wise man? Did any of the teachings involved in this selection have any positive value for you?

2. The hallucinogens said to lead to ecstatic and allegedly spiritual awakenings are presently, and probably will continue to be, illegal. Why do you suppose this is so? Is it that people are driven to crime in order to purchase them? (But if they were legalized, they probably would not have to cost so much.) Is it that they are harmful to the user? (But suppose he argues that he is being denied a religious experience, and, in any case, it's his right to decide what is or isn't harmful to him?) Is it that the "hooked" person is of questionable value to society? (But who decides whose habits and experiences are valuable or not?)

3. Here is an account of a religious experience which was not connected with drugs:

All at once, without warning of any kind, I found myself wrapped in a flame-colored cloud. For an instant I thought of fire . . . the next, I knew that the fire was within myself. Directly afterward there came

upon me a sense of exultation, of immense joyousness accompanied . . .
by an intellectual illumination impossible to describe . . . I saw that
the universe is not composed of dead matter, but is, on the contrary, a
living Presence; I became conscious in myself of eternal life. . . . I
saw that all men are immortal: that the cosmic order is such that . . .
all things work together for the good of each and all; that the foundation principle of the world . . . is what we call love . . . (From "Do
Drugs Have a Religious Import?" by Huston Smith.)

Compare this with the visions described by Castaneda. Do there seem
to be significant differences between the two experiences? Do there
seem to be any similarities? Can Castaneda's visions be considered
dangerous?

4. Apart from drug use, which is obviously legal in don Juan's
culture, anthropology has brought to light many practices observed
by Non-Western peoples that are taboo or at least frowned upon in
our society: for example, premarital sex, incest, adultery, polygamy,
homosexuality, reversing male-female roles, communal raising of
children, and so on. How many such practices can you describe for
the class? Try to be specific.

VOICES FROM THE OTHER SIDE

James A. Pike

The story of Bishop Pike and his communication with the Other Side is
impressive if only for the fact that it involves Arthur Ford, undoubtedly the
most celebrated medium of modern times. Stories abound from people who
have attended his séances and have been given messages from the dead with
information they swear the medium could not possibly have known in
advance. He has even been granted occasional powers of prediction, and
often what he has prophesied has come to pass.

James A. Pike (1913–1969) was bishop of the Anglican Diocese of
California and held lecture posts at Berkeley and other distinguished
campuses. For most of his life he was associated with legal, theological and
philosophical matters, sometimes intervening in political issues, especially
those relating to civil rights, whenever his religious office made this appropriate. He was probably the last person anyone would have associated with

supernaturalism. But, following the suicide of his twenty-year-old son, he developed the conviction that the boy had somehow not really died and was still very close to him. After consulting a number of mediums with varying results, he met Arthur Ford and underwent a number of astonishing experiences recounted in *The Other Side*, from which the following selection is taken.

From reading the book, one is meant to suppose that not only life but identity continues beyond death. Unable to explain how this could be, since human identity appears so manifestly a phenomenon of physical existence, Pike concludes his story by posing a number of possibilities which could account for occult and psychic experiences and ongoing, uninterrupted consciousness. Perhaps, he suggests, our daily, waking selves represent only a fragment of the true mind. Perhaps there is such a thing as a "cosmic consciousness" in which all of us share, which has always existed and is just as integral to creation as the natural universe itself. Some readers may find themselves lost in what they consider nonrational, mystic prose. Others will know what Pike is talking about. At any rate, in this age of affirming Human Worth for a variety of causes, one ought to listen long enough at least to consider the possible validity of ideas and claims that lie outside the limits of one's credibility. To do that much may, after all, be Human Worth itself.

Voices from the Other Side

It seems to me that the vast amount of data classified as psychic phenomena and the broader category of evidence pointing to the psi factor in the human personality refer us mentally *beyond these categories themselves*. Raised anew are two basic questions: What is the nature of the human person? and, What is the nature of the universe? In my striving in recent years toward a truer and more relevant theology for our times, I have been moving in a discernible direction— to put it briefly, toward the universality of truth and grace and toward the unity of reality. My experiences with psi phenomena, as well as the extensive study that they have stimulated, have led me to be even more open to and to affirm tentatively an understanding of man and his universe that seems more adequate than the conventional Christian one or that of its near relative, Western secularism.

First of all, it would appear that we have perhaps been mistaken,

Jack Copons

As soon as you start to shine a light and give people truth, the tremendous forces of darkness gather up.   *James A. Pike*

in our culture, to conceive of persons as individuals. Sociologists, psychologists and anthropologists have long pointed to the tremendous influence that society has on the formation of an individual, and the school of psychological determinism has held that no man is in fact a free agent. Yet the predominant image has been one of a shape and reality to each human personality that is entirely and uniquely one's own, even though molded by external forces.

Perhaps what is really needed is a new way of looking at the human personality—a way in which we can at one and the same time take account of both the highly individuated, decision-making, conscious personal focus *and* the more diffuse but person-connected constellation of fluid factors from the individual's unconscious mind and from the collective unconscious. I grope for words to express such a view of personal reality, for our Western thought forms do not lend themselves readily to the expression of an outlook of this type. But if we are to encompass in our understanding such data as we have been dealing with in this book, then it would seem we must push ourselves to new images.

It is in the nature of the human personality that only a small portion of reality can be held "in focus"—that is, within our conscious attention—at any given time. We can concentrate on only a very limited portion of reality—whether past, present or projected future—during any given time span. We have "sequential" thought patterns, which in languages can be broken down into segments—paragraphs, sentences, words and even syllables. Selective perception operates during all waking moments and we "take in" by our five senses only that which is relevant to our concern at the time.

This of necessity means, on the one hand, that the largest portion of the reality to which we are exposed in each waking moment goes *unnoticed* at the conscious level (though not necessarily *unperceived*) and, on the other hand, that nearly all of what we have experienced in the past is temporarily "forgotten" as we confront the new. General impressions include more than those aspects of our experience which we have consciously taken in; if pressed, we can often hold the "general" in our conscious attention long enough to perceive and enumerate the "particulars." In much the same way, the past can be recalled—and again held in conscious focus—if it is stimulated and evoked by the process of association or by a current experience.

Most of what comprises the human personality—what makes us "who we are"—is at any given moment relatively inaccessible at the conscious, sensory level. It would appear that our five senses function in a manner somewhat like tape recorders and audio-video equipment. That is to say, the five senses seem to be devices through which impressions are received and recorded. One can be consciously aware of *some* of those impressions as they are received, but *all* are apparently recorded. Many can be recalled and "experienced" as memories.

It has long been assumed that an individual's memories are "his own" and thus accessible only to him. Scientists have even suggested that the individual's memories are "recorded" in his own brain—that each "wrinkle" in the cortex is the *locus* of a single recorded experience or a series of experiences. This assumption has led to the recent speculation as to whether the transplant of a dead person's brain into a living person would not, in essence, be a transplant of a person.

However, making as much sense—or even more—is a quite different hypothesis: namely, that personhood really resides in the unconscious mind; that the conscious, sensory level of existence is a series (sometimes more like a scattering) of manifestations—momentary, or of relatively short duration—of an abiding personality at the unconscious, extrasensory level; and that at the unconscious level all persons participate in, contribute to and share in one vast reservoir of reality which is common to all. In other words, each of us receives sensory impressions and thinks conscious thoughts that are passed into the collective unconscious as an individuated addition to the whole. We have access to those contributions more readily if they are "our own," but each of us participates in the life of every other person at the unconscious level and can receive impressions from and through them by extrasensory processes, which provide additions to the sensory impressions we are already aware of in varying degrees.

Perhaps the most common experience of the latter is in the dream state. When we fall asleep, our conscious, sensory-level activity is reduced to an absolute minimum—an apparent necessity for our refreshment and the restoration of energies—yet our unconscious activity goes on, and occasionally some of it makes a vivid "impression" on us, just as our conscious activity is reawakening us. This impression can then be recalled, just as other experiences entirely in the waking state can be recalled.

It should be noted, however, that those who do recall dreams find that a dream "produces" the same kind of dramatic interaction of personalities and of environmental facets as events which occur at the conscious level. The difference is that in a dream state the full drama is produced unconsciously. For such remarkable plays, where are the producer, the scenario writer, the designer of sets, the wardrobe mistress, the director? Have those who have categorized psychic phenomena and even ESP as incredible nonsense ever pondered *that* mystery? How does the dream get put together into a dynamic production when the dreamer, unconscious, is "out of it"?

Sounds, colors, odors, tastes and tactile sensations can be as vivid as waking reality—the individual, in his recall of the dream, is usually as "involved" in the drama as he would have been in a waking state, even in regard to experiencing the same emotions. The only difference is that he is not consciously aware of his role until after the event— that is, when he wakes up.

Instead of perceiving the dream state as a "private production" of the individual that principally reveals his own internal order or disorder (as many in the various fields of depth psychology have tended to view it), it is more likely that each individual has free access to a *larger* scope of reality while asleep than he has in his ordinary, conscious, waking state; yet his participation at that unconscious level is no less "real" than his sensory-level, conscious activity.

It would appear that sleep numbs sensory perception and conscious controls sufficiently to give the unconscious freer play. The same can result from hypnosis, trance states, hallucinogenic drugs and meditation processes.

Perhaps a helpful analogy would be to conceive of the collective unconscious, i.e., the whole of reality, as a giant computer, constructed and programed in such a way as to allow any personality to feed material (information) into it according to his own filing system (his own language, thought forms, images, etc.) and to receive out whatever information he wishes. The ability to receive information from the computer is limited by the degree to which the individuated (or conscious) person insists that the information conform to his own filing system. He receives "new" ideas, that is, ideas not directly related to or implied in information he himself fed in, only to the extent that he is open to receiving "raw data" to be classified later. Any person would, of course, have considerably more ready access to the material he himself put in the computer, since he would know his own filing system and would know what to expect to find there.

It is possible, however, for a person to open himself to data which can come to him not only from the conscious, sensory level, but also from the unconscious, extrasensory level, which does not fit his own— or even his culture's—preconceived filing system, images and concepts. Such a person is generally deemd by his society to be creative, eccentric, free, strange, prophetic, psychotic, non-conformist (used pejoratively or as a compliment); a seer, an escapist, a mystic, a dreamer or a genius—or he might be called a medium. I am convinced that the processes of sensitivity (as, for example, the types encouraged by sensitivity training), mystical experience, spiritual healing, hypnosis, extrasensory perception and psychic communication are all, at the deeper level, of the same nature. We need more experience and/or more consciousness of what we already experience. We need more understanding of these already operative processes, so that this whole dimension of communication and energizing can be more effectively used in our lives.

It would seem that the goal is to become more and more open to reality so we might more fully participate in it and contribute positively to its becoming. We should be open to that part of our personal history which has been fed into the grand computer as well as to others around us at both the conscious, sensory level and at the unconscious, extrasensory level, to have freer traffic between our conscious minds (via our unconscious minds) to the collective unconscious. And finally, through all these routes, we should be able to experience more and more fully a continuity between our ego-centers and the great Ego, the One, the All.

The result of all such growth should be increased harmony between the conscious and the unconscious at both the individual and social levels, and thus increased freedom, serenity and love—to magnify our ability to respond sensitively to all within and around us.

It is in this latter regard that psychedelic drugs seem to fall far short. Though for some they evidently bring a sense of unity and harmony for the duration of the effects of the hallucinogenic, the apparent result for most is not a unity of the unconscious and the conscious, but rather a greater dichotomy between them. Indeed, in some cases the dichotomy can express itself in a psychotic break. Moreover, those who have been consistently on hallucinogenics often feel themselves to be alienated from other persons at the conscious (social) level, even though at one with them in the depth of the collective unconscious. Far more beneficial would be a non-conformist subculture which, by the development of internal openness and sensitivity, would enable its participants to experience both personal and social unity and harmony.

Thus, I hope more and more people will leave themselves open to such experiences as I have described in this book. I feel that they, together with a fast-accumulating amount of other kinds of data, point to the possibility that most of us are operating like ordinary record players, whereas in reality we all have not only hi-fi but also stereo built into us. Thus, we are playing monaural records when we should be using nothing but stereo. Further psychic research may well improve sensitivity and human communications and develop human potential more fully *here and now*. In any case, it is certain that to close one's mind even to the evident data is to preclude new insight into the nature of our own psyches.

Suppose Rip Van Winkle had awakened in the electronic age. Suppose he had been instructed to ask a computer a question, had fed in the question, received the answer, and then been asked, "How do you think you got that information?" Surely his answer would have been something like, "A man in there must have looked it up quickly." Nothing in his previous experience would have enabled him to conceive of what are actually the inner workings of such an electronic device.

In much the same way, I cannot really imagine what processes are at work when a medium goes into a trance and material comes through which is apparently directly related to, and associated with, my son Jim in such a way as to have unity of personality. I have no other words to use than those of my conscious experiences and expression. Thus, I say the communication seems personal and appears to be Jim in the same general sense that I "knew" him before he died. It is not unrealistic to say, "The sun rose at six this morning," though what is involved is a much more complex process. Similarly, it is not unrealistic (in fact, it is considerably less unrealistic) to say, "Jim said . . ." Yet, I have nowhere thus far in these pages used such a form of affirmation. Could I have? Can I now?

Until we have more understanding and better concepts and words to use to talk about the experience (and, for that matter, about the daily interpersonal relationships with which we are more accustomed), and in the light of all that has been said here, in response to the oft-asked questions—the ones the reader also no doubt has in mind—"Do you believe in ongoing personal life?" and "Do you believe you have been in touch with your son?" (since asked is not "Do you *know* . . . ," but "Do you *believe* . . ."), my answer is *Yes, I do.*

Afterwords

After finishing the final chapter in Israel, passing through London I had an opportunity to sit once more with Mrs. Ena Twigg. A portion of the transcript of the tape-recorded séance, at which there were an additional three witnesses, seems more than appropriate for the closing of the record and analysis which have been the aim of this book.

At a session early in May with the Rev. Mr. Daisley, Jim (I can so speak in the light of the qualifications and affirmations made in the preceding pages) said he was "now studying philosophy." This was the first time since his death that he had used the word "philosophy." But he used it again at the session a month later with Mrs. Twigg in London, and he expanded on the theme. My son, through Mrs. Twigg in trance:

> I'm going to do my best to use this opportunity to tell you the pattern as I see it . . . I'm so excited at the fact you are going on with what we have found together. Oh, this is the treasure. This is the treasure. We

want to give you the next piece of the pattern . . . I want to tell you that we are conveying to you a tremendous amount of guidance and help, in order that you would not become involved in the less necessary things—not the *un*necessary things—the less necessary things . . . You know I came over here in a state of mental confusion and great—not antagonism toward the world, but in a state of not understanding and being almost afraid to trust many people. You knew that. And I had to come to terms with the situation. And when I came over here they said, "Now, come along. Academic qualifications won't help you here. Let's get down to the basics," you see; and we tried to find out what are the things that really matter—to have compassion, and understanding and to be kind—yes, they are wonderful things, but not as things. You have to put them into operation. You have to relearn how to think, how to really understand and be able to put yourself in the other guy's place to see how you would work out in the same circumstances. And gradually I began to get a sense of pattern, you know. I began to feel that this was one way of release. This was religion, without somebody forcing God and Jesus down my throat. And I find that by working this way I could find a philosophy that religion hadn't been able to give me . . . Dad. You see, I found when I came over here, I thought, if they all come to me, all the blessed saints, all come trooping in I'll have none of it—I'll have none of it. I couldn't accept it on those terms. And I didn't think that they would want me to, because they knew me, didn't they? Those invisible people knew me. So they cater for the individual need and lead you so gently, so kindly. They show you things that are essential and they put the things that are not essential on one side.

So I gradually began to get a sense of belonging again. And one great thing that was a stimulus and great help was to know that I have got this one foot on earth and I could reach you. Do you see? And I thought, whatever this lifeline is—you know, Dad, the cord that joins the mother to the child, don't you? . . . Well, it's . . . it's . . . it's an analogy, something like that you see. It's like having a lifeline to the earth because you have got love for those who are still there, and want to understand how you are—do you see? And that's what I wanted to say to the family: I am all right, don't worry. Do you see? But what's more, I wanted to tell you my story—what I am doing . . . [In answer to the question, "Have you heard anything over there about Jesus, or a Jesus?"] I told you before. I am telling you again. You know I told you. Oh, it is difficult. I'm afraid I might hurt you. I might hurt you. This is what I was telling you: people must have an example, you know. People must have an example. And I have questioned my teachers, and they have said, Jim, you are not in a position to understand—YET! You are not in a position to understand yet. I haven't met him. They talk about him—a mystic, a seer, yes, a seer. Oh, but, Dad, they don't talk about him as a savior. As an example, you see? . . . You see, I want to tell you, I would like to tell you, Jesus is triumphant, you know? But it's not like that. I don't understand it yet. I don't understand it yet. I may, sometime I may, but right now I have got as much to comprehend as I can. You don't want me to tell you what I don't know . . . not a savior, that's the important thing—an example . . .

But what I want to tell you is just to learn that everybody's not going to like us. You know, I will tell you something . . . As soon as you start to shine a light and give people truth, the tremendous forces of darkness gather up. They say "put out the light, put out the light." This is what they have done with John [Kennedy]. This is what they have done with Bobby [Kennedy]. This is what they have done with [Medgar] Evers, and this is what they have done with Martin Luther King—and that is put out the light . . . But all they have done is put out the flicker. Oh, yes, they don't know what happens over here. They don't know what happens over here. It burns even brighter. Their cause will not wither. It will gain strength. People are seeking to free themselves, and the best way to understand this is to become involved . . . in trying to help people to free themselves where they have not learned how to free themselves already . . . Do it by literature, do it by talking, do it by an example. I was not much of an example . . . It's a damn fine thing when you have got to die before you know what's true, isn't it? . . . Well, there is no need, is there? . . . It's a wonderful world; it's full of—just full of opportunity . . . I want to tell you this. [To a college-age witness:] Learn all you can about this, because you don't know at what juncture in your life you can put it to some use and find a great sense of purpose in so doing. It is the greatest thing that God ever made.

Don't you ever believe that God can be personalized. He is the Central Force and you all give your quota toward it. Do you agree with me, Dad? . . . I want you to know it's exciting, it's exciting. Do you know how exciting it is to come back? To be dead—but we are not the dead ones, you are the dead ones, you are the dead ones, because you are only firing on two cylinders. I want so much to tell you about a world where everybody is out to create a greater sense of love and harmony. A world in which music and color and poetry are all interwoven, making a majestic pattern—and to be kind of sure, as we hunger so we can absorb some of this quality and harmony. And then, in gratitude, we want to repay. We want to give back to the Central Force some of that love that has been developed in us, that we didn't know we had the capacity to contain . . . I hope one day that I shall understand to the point where I don't have to clutch at my own identity so much . . . You see, we have to be selfless. This creates freedom. It's a paradox . . . Yes, and also by not possessing, one possesses; by loving, one gets a return of love. You see, so many things seem to be in a paradoxical way. I am learning. I am learning. I'm trying very hard . . . And this is the process of evolution. This is man cleansing himself, gradually and continuously, and he evolves and becomes more enlightened. He throws away his props and his shackles, and he works to what is essential. This is what I've discovered.

RESPONSES: Questions for Writing and Discussion

1. What do you make of Pike's suggestion that there is a universal or collective unconsciousness which transcends all of us and that "we have perhaps been mistaken, in our culture, to conceive of persons as individuals"? What does this do to Human Worth? Can your ego accept this idea? Or does it rebel at the thought that the individual personality is not necessarily "entirely and uniquely one's own"?

2. Assuming for the moment that the theory of a collective unconscious, as Pike presents it, has some merit, can you offer any additional theory to account for the existence of the individual personality? Suppose we compare the unique, personal awareness each of us has to a particular plant absorbing sunlight (the collective unconscious)? Just as sunlight continues to exist in its totality whether or not *that plant* is there, so too, let us say, would the universal unconscious mind exist whether or not this or that person does. Why then would there *be* different people?

3. Pike, along with countless psychologists and philosophers, asserts that the conscious awareness is a limited thing compared with the vast portion of our being which is unknown and inaccessible to us. It is, so to speak, the lost or forgotten self. But does this fact make the totality any less "us"? Do you accept Pike's speculations regarding the possibility of the unconscious mind's being a shared "reservoir of reality" in which all persons participate?

4. Have you personally had any experiences—perhaps short of but not excluding possible contact with the Other Side—in which you believe you have participated in the life of another person and have received "impressions from and through [him] by extrasensory processes"? Share one of them with the class.

5. Share some dream experiences with each other. Do your dreams reflect *you*? (That is, your perception of yourself?) Are they identifiable as expressions of your personal hopes, fears, or perhaps guilt feelings? Would any of them (or all of them) support Pike's belief that dreams may be the gateway to the collective unconscious? Have you had any recent dreams which you could *not* readily identify with your own personality?

6. If there *is* a collective unconscious or universal state of being in which, at the fundamental level, all participate, can you see how the possibility of continuing identity after death can fit into such a scheme?

7. Read carefully the transcription of Jim's communication that is quoted in the "Afterwords." Try to describe the nature of the afterlife as it is revealed or suggested in the message. Can you accept the concept? If you believed in an after-life before reading the selection, does this section support or alter your outlook?

THE FISHERMAN
FROM CHIHUAHUA

Evan S. Connell, Jr.

Like many other men of his generation, **Evan S. Connell, Jr. (b. 1924)** started his education at the beginning of World War II, left college to serve (in his case, as a naval aviator), then returned to finish school during the post-war forties before the seeds of radical academic changes could begin to grow. Like many others who were to become the new breed of American writers during the fifties, Connell attended no less than three universities in three years (Kansas, Stanford, and Columbia), and it is not hard to imagine the reason. The academic world was trying desperately to pull itself together and reestablish its place in society. But was it teaching anything that related to the new life styles, especially those of war-weary GI's unable to settle down to the routine of their fathers? Connell represents the literary mind of that period, the pioneer in a whole new approach to fiction that would explode during the following decade and finally attract the label "The Beat Generation."

For all that they outraged and scandalized middle America with their unkempt mode of dress, their unconventional moral standards, their music, and their art, the Beats had great impact on American culture. They proved to be the transition from the world which ended with the war and the world we know today. Some began to experiment with drugs and inquired into Eastern modes of living and the art and science of the occult. The San Francisco area, the setting of this story, was Mecca for the Beats, and it produced a new way of thinking, feeling, painting, and writing.

Connell's story suggests a concern with expanded consciousness, which became a key concept in the new culture. The author creates a situation and a few characters; he puts them into a highly particularized and carefully detailed setting. He allows his imagination to become involved with them. (In Connell's literary theory "involvement" means a narrowing down of the focus of attention.) Because of the leisurely pace and the slowing down on particular details (*"His lips had peeled back from his teeth like those of a jaguar, tearing meat . . ."*) the reader's interest is captured and sustained even though no promise is ever given of a climactic revelation. While some may find themselves straining to identify symbols and hidden meanings, "Fisherman" is meant to exist solely at face value. Presumably it is enough that the author has chosen to write this story in this way. After all, if life *has* no ultimate meaning or purpose, why, the San Francisco Movement argues, should fiction be any different? The worth of literature, like Human

Worth itself, rests upon the mind's capacity for becoming involved in the passing stream of time and plunging boldly into a few moments.

The Fisherman from Chihuahua

Santa Cruz is at the top of Monterey Bay which is about 100 miles below San Francisco, and in the winter there are not many people in Santa Cruz. The boardwalk concessions are shuttered except for one counter-and-booth restaurant, the ferris wheel seats are hooded with olive green canvas and the powerhouse padlocked, and the rococo doors of the carousel are boarded over and if one peers through a knothole into its gloom the horses which buck and plunge through summer prosperity seem like animals touched by a magic wand that they may never move again. Dust dims the gilt of their saddles and sifts through cracks into their bold nostrils. About the only sound to be heard around the waterfront in Santa Cruz during winter are the voices of Italian fishermen hidden by mist as they work against the long pier, and the slap of waves against the pilings of the cement dance pavilion when tide runs high, or the squeak of a gull, or once in a long time bootsteps on the slippery boards as some person comes quite alone and usually slowly to the edge of the grey and fogbound ocean.

The restaurant is Pendleton's and white brush strokes on the glass announce *tacos, frijoles* and *enchiladas* as house specialties, these being mostly greens and beans and fried meat made arrogant with pepper. Smaller letters in pseudo-Gothic script say: *Se Habla Espanol* but this is not true; it was the man who owned the place before Pendleton who could speak Spanish. From him, though, Pendleton did learn how to make the food and this is the reason a short fat Mexican who worked as a mechanic at Ace Dillon's Texaco station continued eating his suppers there. He came in every night just after eight o'clock and sat at the counter, ate an astounding amount of this food which he first splattered with tabasco sauce as casually as though it were ketchup and then washed farther down with beer. After that he would feel a little drunk and would spend as much as two or even three dollars playing the pinball machine and the great nickelodeon and dancing by himself, but inoffensively, contentedly, just snapping his fingers and shuffling across the warped boards often until Pendleton began pulling in the shutters. Then having had a suitable evening he would half-dance his way home, or at least back in the direction of town. He was a squat little man who waddled like a duck full of eggs and he had a face like a blunt arrowhead or a Toltec idol, and he was about the color of hot sand. His fingers were much too thick for their length, seemingly without joints, only creases where it was necessary for them to bend. He smelled principally of cold grease and of urine as though his pants needed some air, but Pendleton who did not smell very good himself did not mind and besides there were not many customers during these winter months.

So every evening shortly after dark he entered for his food and some amusement, and as he appeared to contain all God's world within his own self Pendleton was not disinterested when another Mexican came in directly behind him like a long shadow. This new man was tall, very tall, possibly six feet or more, and much darker, almost black in the manner of a sweat stained saddle. He was handsome, silent, and perhaps forty years of age. Also he was something of a dandy: his trousers which were long and quite tight revealed the fact that he was bowlegged, as befits certain types of men, and made one think of him easily riding a large fat horse, not necessarily toward a woman but in the direction of something more remote and mysterious—bearing a significant message or something like that. Exceedingly short black boots of finest leather took in his narrow trouser bottoms. For a shirt he wore long-sleeved white silk unbuttoned to below the level of his nipples which, themselves, were vaguely visible. The hair of his chest was so luxuriant that an enameled crucifix there did not even rest on the skin.

These two men sat at the counter side by side. The tall one lifted off his sombrero as if afraid of mussing his hair and he placed it on the third stool. His hair was deeply oiled and comb tracks went all the way from his temples to the back of his thin black neck, and he scented of a kind of green perfume. He had a mustache that consisted of nothing but two black strings hanging across the corners of his unforgiving mouth and ending in soft points about an inch below his chin. He seemed to think himself alone in the restaurant because, after slowly licking his lips and interlacing his fingers, he just sat looking somberly ahead. The small man ordered for them both.

After they had eaten supper the little one played the pinball machine while this strange man took from his shirt pocket a cigarillo only a little bigger than his mustache and smoked it with care, that is, he would take it from his mouth between his thumb and one finger as if he were afraid of crushing it, and after releasing the smoke he would replace it with the same care in the exact center of his mouth. It never dangled or rolled, he respected it. Nor was it a cheap piece of tobacco, its smoke ascended heavily, moist and sweet.

Suddenly the fat Mexican kicked the pinball game and with a surly expression walked over to drop a coin into the nickelodeon. The tall man had remained all this time at the counter with his long savage eyes half-shut, smoking and smoking the fragrant cigarillo. Now he did not turn around, in fact his single movement was to remove the stump from his lips, but clearly he was disturbed. When the music ended he sat totally motionless for several minutes. Then his head began to sink and was almost touching the counter before its direction reversed, and when his face was against the ceiling his throat began to swell like that of a mating pigeon.

Pendleton, sponging an ash tray, staggered as if a knife had plunged through his ribs.

The Mexican's eyes were squeezed altogether shut. His lips had peeled back from his teeth like those of a jaguar tearing meat and the veins of his neck looked ready to burst. In the shrill screams was a memory of Moors, the ching of Arab cymbals, of rags and of running feet through all the marketplaces of the East.

His song had no beginning; it had no end. All at once he was simply sitting on the stool looking miserably ahead.

After a while the small fat Mexican said to Pendleton "Be seeing you, man," and waddled through the door into darkness. A few seconds later the tall one's stool creaked. Without a sound he placed the high steepled sombrero like a crown on his hair and followed his friend through the door.

The next night there happened to be a pair of tourists eating in the back booth when the men entered. They were dressed as before except that the big one's shirt was lime green in color and Pendleton noticed his wrist watch, fastened not to his wrist actually but over the green cuff where it bulged like an oily bubble. They took the same stools and ate fried beans, tacos and enchiladas for almost an hour after which the short one who looked like his Toltec ancestors gently belched, smiled in a benign way and moved over to his machine. Failing to win anything he cursed it and kicked it before selecting his favorite records.

This time Pendleton was alert: as the music ended he got ready for the first shriek. The tourists, caught unaware, thought their time had come. When they recovered from the shock they looked fearfully over the top of the booth and then the woman stood up in order to see better. After the black Mexican's song was finished they all could hear the incoming tide, washing softly around the pillars of the pavilion.

Presently the two paid their bill and went out, the short one leading, into the dirty yellow fog and the diving, squeaking gulls.

"Why that's terrible," the woman laughed. "It wasn't musical."

Anyone who looked at her would know she was still shuddering from the force of the ominous man.

Her husband too was frightened and laughed, "Somebody should play a little drum behind that fellow." Unaware of what a peculiar statement he had made he formed a circle of his thumb and forefinger to show how big the drum should be.

She was watching the door, trying to frown compassionately. "I wonder what's the matter with that poor man. Some woman must have hurt him dreadfully."

Pendleton began to wipe beer bracelets and splats of tabasco sauce from the lacquered plywood counter where the men had been. The restaurant seemed too quiet.

The woman remarked cheerily, "We're from Iowa City."

Pendleton tried to think of something but he had never been to Iowa City or anywhere near it even on a train, so he asked if they would like more coffee.

The husband wondered, "Those two fellows, do they come in here every night?"

Pendleton was seized with contempt and hatred for this domestic little man, though he did not know why, and walked stiffly away from their booth without answering. He stood with both hairy hands on the shining urn while he listened to the sea threshing and rolling under the night.

"Who?" he said gruffly. "Them two?"

A few minutes later while pouring coffee he said, "Sometimes I feel so miserable I could damn near roll up in a tube."

The couple, overpowered by his manner, looked up uneasily. The woman ventured: "It seems terribly lonely around."

On the third evening as they seated themselves before the counter Pendleton said to the one who spoke American, "Tell your friend he can't yowl in here any more."

"He's not my baby," this short fat man replied, not greatly interested. "Six tacos and four beers and a lot of beans."

"What do you think, I'm running a damn concert hall?"

For a moment the little Mexican became eloquent with his eyebrows, then both he and Pendleton turned their attention to the silent one who was staring somberly past the case of pies.

Pendleton leaned on his hands so that his shoulders budged. "Now looky, Pablo, give him the word and do it quick. Tell him to cut that noise out. You understand me?"

This enraged the small man whose voice rose to a snarl. "Pablo yourself. Don't give me that stuff." Pendleton was not angry but set about cleaving greens for their tacos as though he were furious. While the blade chunked into the wood again and again beside his thumb he thought about the situation. He did not have anything particular in mind when all at once he banged down the cleaver and with teeth clenched began bending his eyes toward the two.

"*No debe cantar*," the little one said hurriedly, waggling a negative finger at his companion. No more singing. "*No mas.*"

"That's better, by God," muttered Pendleton as though he understood. He wished to say something in Spanish about the matter but he knew only *mañana, adios* and *señorita* and none of these seemed to fit. He resumed work, but doubtfully, not certain if the silent one had heard either of them. Over one shoulder he justified himself: "Folks come here to eat their suppers, not to hear any concert."

Abel W. Sharpe who had once been the sheriff of Coda City and who now ripped tickets for a movie house on Pacific came in the door alone but arguing harshly. The Toltec had started playing pinball so Sharpe took the vacant stool, looked up twice at the man beside him, and then dourly ordered waffles and hot milk. It was while he was pouring syrup into the milk that the nickelodeon music died and that the black Mexican did it again.

Pendleton was exasperated with himself for laughing and almost choked by trying to stop.

"Heh?" asked the old man, who at the first note had jumped off his stool and now crouched several feet away from the counter, a knife in one hand and his mug of sweet milk in the other. "I can't hear nothing. The bastard's deefened me."

The Toltec had not stopped playing pinball and paid none of them the least attention because he had lighted four pretty girls which meant he would probably win something. His friend now sat motionless on the stool and looked ahead as though he saw clear into some grief stricken time.

Not until the eighth or maybe the ninth night did Pendleton realize that the restaurant was drawing more people; there would be six or eight or even as many as a dozen in for dinner.

There came a night when the fat Toltec entered as always but no one followed. That night the restaurant was an uneasy place. Things spilled, and while cleaning up one of the tables Pendleton discovered a menu burned through and through with cigarette holes. By 10:30 the place was deserted.

Pendleton said, "Hey, Pablo."

The Toltec gave him a furious look.

"All right," Pendleton apologized, "what's your name?"

"What's yours?" he replied. He was deeply insulted.

"Whereabouts is your friend?"

"He's no friend of mine."

Pendleton walked down the counter behind a damp rag, wrung

it over the sink, then very casually he did something he never did or never even thought of doing: he opened a bottle of beer for the Mexican and indicated without a word that it was free.

Toltec, though still grieved, accepted the gift, saying, "I just met the guy. He asked me where to get some decent cooking."

Pendleton wiped a table and for a time appeared to be idly picking his back teeth. When he judged the interval to be correct he asked, "Got tired of the grub here, I guess."

"No, tonight he's just drunk."

Pendleton allowed several more minutes, then, "He looks like a picture of a bullfighter I saw once in Tijuana called Victoriano Posada."

And this proved to be a shrewd inquiry because after drinking some more of the free beer the fat Mexican remarked, "He calls himself Damaso."

Pendleton, wondering if something else might follow pretended to stretch and to yawn and smack his chops mightily. He thought that tomorrow he would say, when the tall one entered, "Howdy, Damaso."

"Know what? He goes and stands by himself on the sea wall a lot of times. Maybe he's going to knock himself off. Wouldn't that be something?"

"Tell him not to do it in front of my place," Pendleton answered.

Through the screen door could be seen a roll of silvery yellow fog and above it the moon, but the water was hidden.

"These Santa Cruz winters," Pendleton said. Opening the icebox he selected a superior beer for himself and moved his high stool far enough away that his guest might not feel their friendship was being forced. Peeling off the wet label he rolled it into a soggy grey ball which he dropped into a bucket under the counter. "Singers make plenty money, I hear."

The Mexican looked at him slyly. "What are you talking about?"

Pendleton, scratching his head, sighed and yawned again. "Huh? Oh. I was just thinking about what's-his-name. That fellow you come in here with once or twice."

"I know it," the Mexican said, laughing.

For a while both of them drank away at their beers and listened to the combers, each of which sounded as if it would smash the door.

"Feels like there's something standing up in the ocean tonight," Pendleton said. "I could use a little summer."

"You want your beach full of tourists? Those sausages? Man, you're crazy. You're off the rocks."

Pendleton judged that the Mexican was about to insult the summer people still more so he manipulated the conversation once again:

"Somebody told me your friend got himself a singing job at that nightspot near Capitola."

"Look," said the Toltec, patient but irritated, "I just met the guy a couple of weeks ago."

"He never said where he's from, I guess."

"Chihuahua, he says, That's one rough town. And full of sand, Jesus Christ."

Breakers continued sounding just beyond the door and the fog now stood against the screen like a person.

"What does he do?"

The Mexican lifted both fat little shoulders.

"Just traveling through?"

The Mexican lifted both hands.

"Where is he going?"

"All I know is he's got a pretty good voice."

"He howls like a god damn crazy wolf," Pendleton said, "howling for the moon."

"Yah, he's pretty good. Long time ago I saw a murder down south in the mountains and a woman screamed just like that."

Both of them thought about things and Pendleton, having reflected on the brevity of human affairs and the futility of riches, opened his icebox for two more drinks. The Mexican accepted one as though in payment for service. For some seconds they had been able to hear footsteps approaching, audible after every tunnel of water caved in. The footsteps went past the door but no one could be seen.

"Know what? There was an old man washed up on the beach the other day."

"That so?" said Pendleton. "Everything gets to the beach sooner or later."

The Mexican nodded. Somewhere far out on the bay a little boat sounded again and again. "What a night," he said.

Pendleton murmured and scratched.

"Know something, mister?"

Pendleton, now printing wet circles on his side of the counter, asked what that might be.

"Damaso is no Mexicano."

"I didn't think so," Pendleton lied.

"No, because he's got old blood. You know what I mean? I think he's a gypsy from Spain, or wherever those guys come from. He's dark in the wrong way. He just don't *feel* Mexicano to me. There's something about him, and besides he speaks a little Castellano."

Both of them considered all this.

"I suppose he's howling about some girl."

"No it's bigger than that."

"What's the sound say?"

But here the little Mexican lost interest; he revolved on the stool, from which only his toes could reach to the floor, hopped off and hurried across to the nickelodeon. Having pushed a nickle through the slit he studied the wonderful colors and followed the bubbles which fluttered up the tubes to vanish, next he dialed *The Great Speckled Bird* and began shuffling around the floor snapping his fingers and undulating so that in certain positions he looked about five months pregnant.

"Who knows?" he asked of no one in particular while he danced.

The next night also he entered alone. When Pendleton mentioned this he replied the dark one was still drunk.

And the next night when asked if the drunk were going into its third day he replied that Damaso was no longer drunk, just sick from being so, that he was at present lying on the wet cement having vomited on his boots, that probably by sunrise he would be all right. This turned out to be correct because both of them came in for supper the following night. Toltec, smiling and tugging at his crotch, was rumpled as usual and smelled human while his tall companion was oiled and groomed and wearing the white silk again. A good many people were loitering about the restaurant—every booth was full— because this thing had come to be expected, and though all of them were eating or drinking or spending money in some way to justify themselves, and although no one looked up at the entrance of the two Mexicans there could be no doubt about the situation. Only these two men seemed not to notice anything; they ate voraciously and drank a lot of beer after which the one went across to his game, which had been deliberately vacated, and Damaso remained on the stool with his long arms crossed on the counter.

Later the nickelodeon lighted up. When at last its music died and the table stopped there was not a sound in all the restaurant. People watched the head of the dark man bow until it was hidden in his arms. The crucifix disentangled itself and dropped out the top of his gaucho shirt where it began to swing to and fro, glittering as it twisted on the end of its golden chain. He remained like that for almost an hour, finally raised his head to look at the ticket, counted away enough money, and with the sombrero loosely in one hand he stumbled out the door.

The other Mexican paid no attention; he called for more beer which he drank all at once in an attempt to interest a young girl with silver slippers and breasts like pears who was eating supper with her parents, but failing to win anything at this or again at the machine he suddenly grew bored of the evening and walked out.

The next night he entered alone. When asked if his companion had started another drunk he said that Damaso was gone.

Pendleton asked late in the evening, "How do you know?"

"I feel it," he said.

Big Pendleton then stood listening to the advancing tide which had begun to pat the pillars like someone gently slapping a dead drum. Taking off his apron he rolled it tight as he always did and put it beneath the counter. With slow fingers he untied the sweaty handkerchief from around his neck and folded it over the apron, but there his routine altered; before pulling in shutters he stood a while beside the screen and looked out and listened but of course received no more than he expected which was fog, the sound of the sea, and its odor.

Sharply the Toltec said, "I like to dance." And he began to do so. "Next summer I'm really going to cut it up. Nothing's going to catch me." He read Pendleton's face while dancing by himself to the odd and clumsy little step he was inventing, and counseled, "Jesus Christ, he's gone. Forget about it, man."

RESPONSES: Questions for Writing and Discussion

1. One of the cardinal ground rules for writers is that, when a work is published and offered to the public, it must hang there, at the mercy of whatever interpretation, acceptance, or rejection its readers wish to give it. Assuming "Fisherman" is intended to invite the reader into the author's private perceptions, did you find yourself really doing it? Were you looking for a "story" or "meaning" in the traditional sense? If you didn't find any, were you willing to accept the author's purpose, as explained in the introduction?

2. A writer once sought to expose the intellectual dishonesty of the terribly avant-garde magazines by submitting a poem he considered deliberately meaningless. In fact, it was made up of stolen lines from dozens of unfamiliar pieces, arranged in absolutely random order. The poem was published and later won a prize. The author then revealed the "joke" to the editors, who retorted that the poem had meaning despite his intentions. Subconsciously he *could* have had a reason for selecting the stolen lines and for arranging them in a certain pattern. May the same "triumph of rationality" possibly be true in the case of "Fisherman"? Can you, for example, find evidence to support some observations about the San Francisco movement? Do

you find any of the preoccupations singled out in the introduction or any other themes which the author may unconsciously have introduced?

3. Whether the story has "meaning" or not, one might argue that it *does* possess a plot, a structural principle of mounting interest, and that it could not hold together for a minute if it really abandoned all the traditional elements of fiction. Support or dispute this position.

4. Good fiction, whether of the San Francisco movement or not, usually generates a belief in the independent existence of the characters. We come to know a great deal more about them than the events of the story directly tell us. Try to project the two Mexicans into other situations and places. Describe what each one does when he is not at Pendleton's. Where has the taller one gone at the end of the story? Supply a context for the shorter man's statement, "Nothing's going to catch me."

5. Now zero is on Pendleton, the consciousness through whom we view the events of the story. No writer can be totally without a reason in selecting his central viewpoint. Sometimes the consciousness is his own, or one that he has great compassion for, or one that he would like to have. How many things do you know about Pendleton from the story? What kind of person is he? (He becomes interested in the short Mexican when he observes that "he appeared to contain all God's world within his own self." Interesting statement?) What effect do you think the seasonal nature of his location may have upon him? (The boardwalk, the amusements—it is a "swinging" place in the summer, but desolate and lonely in the winter.)

VISITING TSAN, ABBOT OF TA-YUN

Tu Fu

Virtually unknown to all but Oriental scholars and those who have begun to look toward ancient Eastern thought for new insights into life, new possibilities of thinking and responding, **Tu Fu (713–770 A.D.)** is considered China's major lyric poet. No folk minstrel, Tu Fu came from a prominent family of scholars and landowners and held a position in the court of Ming Huang, Emperor of China during the T'ang Dynasty, considered the greatest period of Chinese civilization during the time of the West's Christian era. But many years of court intrigue and political up-heavals caused a decline in the fortunes of the "bright" emperor, and Tu Fu incurred subsequent disfavor, spending his later years in wandering and exile. His poetry presents a vision of a world ruled by cruel and selfish gods —an attitude distinctly at odds with that of Tu Fu's more tradition-bound ancestors. It stresses the importance of the human virtues: love, compassion, and the tranquility of soul reached only through the greatest efforts at self-discipline. The following lyric captures a moment of inner peace, when the awareness becomes one with the world, but strikes a final tragic note, when the rational understanding of life returns once more.

Visiting Tsan, Abbot of Ta-Yun

I am sleepless in the glow and shadow of the lamplight.
The heart at peace breathes the incense of dedication.
Between the temple walls the night is bottomless.
The gold wind bells quiver in the breeze.
The courtyard shuts in the deep
Darkness of the Spring night.
In the blackness the crystalline pool
Exhales the perfume of flowers.
The Northern Crown crosses the sky
Cut by the temple roof,
Where an iron phoenix soars and twists in the air.
The chanting of prayer floats from the hall.
Fading bell notes eddy by my bed.
Tomorrow in the sunlight
I shall walk in the manured fields,
And weep for the yellow dust of the dead.

BRAHMA
Ralph Waldo Emerson

Ralph Waldo Emerson (1803–1882) was born into the seventh generation of a conservative and proper Boston family. From such a background he would have been justified in emerging as the very prototype of the New England gentleman. But he gradually developed a radical philosophy, rooted in nature rather than social traditions, by which he was driven to many shocking assertions of the equality of all people. In one of his most scandalous speaking engagements—at the Harvard Divinity School—Emerson, once an ordained Unitarian minister, found himself "unacceptable" to academic theological circles when he protested that all people, not Jesus Christ alone, must be regarded as divine.

In his philosophical development Emerson was influenced by the thought and culture of the East. He viewed the Oriental belief in the underlying unity of all life as a reinforcement of his own belief that natural energy could be neither created nor destroyed and was the only God the universe had ever known, responsible for all material things, all forms of natural life, and for the mind and soul of man. Since everything was a mode of natural energy, Emerson readily understood the simple—yet for some mystic and baffling—teachings of the Eastern mind. To this mind all things are identical in that they are forms of what is. There is only existence (or energy). Individual things and souls can pass out of existence, but existence itself cannot cease to be. This profound Eastern truth was for Emerson yet another statement of human equality.

Brahma

If the red slayer think he slays,
    Or if the slain think he is slain,
They know not well the subtle ways
    I keep, and pass, and turn again.

Far or forgot to me is near;
    Shadow and sunlight are the same;
The vanished gods to me appear;
    And one to me are shame and fame.

They reckon ill who leave me out;
   When me they fly, I am the wings;
I am the doubter and the doubt,
   And I the hymn the Brahmin sings.

The strong gods pine for my abode,
   And pine in vain in the sacred Seven;
But thou, meek lover of the good!
   Find me, and turn thy back on heaven.

William Butler Yeats

There is probably no other poet of past or present whose work could be used to illustrate so many categories of the artistic personality. There is **William Butler Yeats (1865–1939)** the nationalist, for example. One of the prime movers behind the Irish Renaissance, that vast turn-of-the-century literary movement, Yeats labored incessantly to motivate Irish genius to express Irish experience and to make all the world aware of it. But then there is also Yeats the intellectual, bringing a scholarly, trained, precise, profoundly philosophical, and intensely personal purpose to the writing of poetry. If one reads the prodigious canon of his work, he finds himself struggling to comprehend a massive and complex metaphysical system.

The intellectual is, however, balanced by Yeats the mystic and dreamer, whose eyes catch brief, ecstatic glimpses of worlds that do not exist three-dimensionally or obey the natural laws of this one. In this respect he may be said to epitomize the Irish man-of-letters, divided between the rational discipline of a nonnationalistic academic background and his rightful heritage of pagan mythology, the pride of country, and the well-known Irish imagination.

Of special influence on his poetry is the Irish folk song. The first poem, "The Wild Swans at Coole," shows what the sophisticated poet does with an old and simple form. The insistent rhythm and rhyme, the simplicity of image keep the intellectual from becoming lost in a host of abstractions; at the same time, the song is haunted with possibilities of meaning.

The second poem, "The Song of the Wandering Aengus" has been actually set to music and is a standard piece in the repertoire of Burl Ives, Judy Collins, and other folk singers. Once again it illustrates the unique

Yeatsian blend of the simple and traditional with that "something else" which isn't always easy to describe. In this case it is clearly a mystic experience, open to a broad range of interpretations.

THE WILD SWANS AT COOLE

The trees are in their autumn beauty,
The woodland paths are dry,
Under the October twilight the water
Mirrors a still sky;
Upon the brimming water among the stones
Are nine-and-fifty swans.

The nineteenth autumn has come upon me
Since I first made my count;
I saw, before I had well finished,
All suddenly mount
And scatter wheeling in great broken rings
Upon their clamorous wings.

I have looked upon those brilliant creatures,
And now my heart is sore.
All's changed since I, hearing at twilight,
The first time on this shore,
The bell-beat of their wings above my head,
Trod with a lighter tread.

Unwearied still, lover by lover,
They paddle in the cold
Companionable streams or climb the air;

Their hearts have not grown old;
Passion or conquest, wander where they will,
Attend upon them still.

But now they drift on the still water
Mysterious, beautiful;
Among what rushes will they build,
By what lake's edge or pool
Delight men's eyes when I awake some day
To find they have flown away?

THE SONG OF
WANDERING AENGUS

I went out to the hazel wood,
Because a fire was in my head,
And cut and peeled a hazel wand,
And hooked a berry to a thread;
And when white moths were on the wing,
And moth-like stars were flickering out,
I dropped the berry in a stream
And caught a little silver trout.

When I had laid it on the floor
I went to blow the fire aflame,
But something rustled on the floor,
And some one called me by my name:
It had become a glimmering girl
With apple blossom in her hair
Who called me by name and ran
And faded through the brightening air.

Though I am old with wandering
Through hollow lands and hilly lands,

I will find out where she has gone,
And kiss her lips and take her hands;
And walk among long dappled grass,
And pluck till time and times are done
The silver apples of the moon,
The golden apples of the sun.

WOULD I FOR ALL THAT WERE
Sun Ra

One of the premises of the black cultural movement of the present is that black experience has been insufficiently comprehended through black expression because white audiences do not think or use language the way blacks do. Both the black artist and the recorders of black artistic history often protest that the traditional relegation of black achievement to a second-class status (with the possible exception of jazz) stems less from the modes of expression than an unwillingness to adopt new modes of understanding.

While many black poets and writers—trained as most of them were in Western academic traditions—speak a black message through white European grammar, syntax, and idiom, there is a serious effort on the part of others to free themselves from these boundaries and experiment with radically new sound and image patterns.

Sun Ra, a musician-philosopher and leader of a band known as The Myth Science Arkestra, has produced a number of albums with some extraordinary and unprecedented musical sounds and instruments, among them *Heliocentric Worlds*, *Planet Earth*, and *When Angels Speak of Love*. He has said of his music: "Some people are of this world, others are not. My natural self is not of this world because this world is not of my not and nothingness, alas and happily, at last I can say this world is this unfortunate planet." It is therefore not surprising that Sun Ra is also a poet of strange sound and unfamiliar syntax, breaking the language barrier and carrying the willing reader into far countries.

Would I for All That Were

Would I for all that were
If all that were is like a wish.
Would I for all that were
If all that were is that which never came to be;
For the image of the world that was
Is the light of the darkness today . . .
And all that were is not what I wish it were.
So would I for all that were
All that swirls anon in the world of dreams
Boundless in thought to fruitful reminisce.
Would I for all that were
All that words cannot express
All that pleasant dreams cannot remember . . .
The enchantment and warmth of rare content.
Would I for these and these alone
That I might live as Cosmic thought insists I should
As it were right to be as I wish I were.
Would I for this wondrous thing
A new decree of happiness
Better than, any liberty this world has ever known.
A Cosmic weigh
That opens the way to the worlds that are: —
The Kosmos worlds of endless galaxies.

SAYING NO TO LIFE, SAYING YES TO LIFE

Whether we understand life or not, whether we ever really understand ourselves and how we relate to something called "reality," there is one thing we keep right on doing anyway. *We exist.* Moment by moment, day by day, we endure. Rational or nonrational, we have certain feelings about this endurance. We find it pleasant; we find it a bore; we are overwhelmed and excited by it; we are overwhelmed and defeated by it. Some people find the resources to affirm the basic goodness of living no matter what hardships they face. Others look the world straight in the eye and then shake their heads. After all the talk and all the art, maybe to have the choice between no and yes is what it truly means to be human.

To achieve Human Worth does not mean that one sees only the bright side of existence. Sometimes despair is an appropriate—the only—reaction. Sometimes Human Worth is nothing else but a display of courage—the courage to deny life altogether, to see its ironies, to bear witness to what men are capable of doing to each other and to the world. There are people who find despair more realistic than hope and believe that human intelligence is never so impressive as when it is used to catalogue the follies and cruelties of humanity. To such people optimism and hope for the future are naive and regressive, remnants of the childhood of the race when golden myths were spun out of airy nothing and accepted because truth was too harsh to bear.

There was a time when the attempted suicide became a social outcast, a scandal to the community, an evident mental case. But the right to take one's own life in freedom and dignity has become an important issue in our time. Dr. Thomas Szasz' article "The Ethics of Suicide" asserts that human beings may rationally choose whether to go on living or enjoy the peace death may bring to them. Society, in his opinion, has no right to impose a value upon the life of one who does not value it himself.

Arna Bontemps' "A Summer Tragedy" is the story of an elderly black couple who choose suicide rather than live out their remaining few years in poverty as scorned, second-class citizens. Death becomes the only self-generated act allowed them, the only means of sliding out from under the control of a repressive, racist society.

It is sometimes argued, however, that the desire to take one's own life is a significant "deviation" from the human norm. The will to persevere in existence is supposedly a universal instinct common to all forms of life, man not excepted. That most people are terrified of the very word "death" is the contention of Dr. Elisabeth Kübler-Ross, a psychiatrist who has dedicated her entire career to teaching the fearful that death can be experienced without alarm. "On the Fear of Death" is not, however, psychiatric advice. It is a profound analysis of our neurotic society, so frightened of aging and death that it has become life-denying in most of its activities. Dr. Kübler-Ross views Human Worth as the capacity for transcending man's ancient fear of death as the Great Unknown.

In "The Myth of Sisyphus" the existential philosopher Albert Camus asks us to say yes to life in the very midst of its most extreme cruelties and futility. Life is meaningless, life is absurd; man comes from darkness and leaves in darkness; but between these totally superfluous events—to which the universe remains indifferent—each of us is free to make his life as heroic and meaningful as he can. Many forces have the power to oppress, imprison, and crush our spirit; but only *we* can decide that our lives are mean and ignoble.

Another psychiatrist, Dr. Viktor E. Frankl, agrees with Camus that it is vital for man to learn to cope with the absurdity of his existence. But Dr. Frankl goes even further: He shows us in his "Experiences in a Concentration Camp" how resolute people become in their refusal to be overcome by life's inhumanity and indifference to the fact of human suffering; how they will not in the midst of life's extremest brutality believe that it is no great distinction to be a human being. Astonishingly enough, we discover, when people are the most oppressed and beaten, it is precisely at this most life-denying of all moments that the whole human adventure appears to acquire the most solid chance of having purpose, dignity, and Worth.

THE ETHICS OF SUICIDE
Thomas S. Szasz, M.D.

Suicide has not always seemed a frightening and drastic act. In some societies, such as Japan, suicide once attained the status of a reputable institution; it was the final recourse for a life robbed of its honor and dignity, and it gave those things back. In the old romantic game of war a gunshot cleanly fired through the temple enabled a losing general to avoid the disgrace of capture and imprisonment. The tragedies of Shakespeare and his contemporaries reflect a decidedly heroic view of self-imposed death. It is the gift the authors bestow upon noble characters, who, having fallen to low and pitiful estate, are not made to suffer the shame of having to account for their crimes to lesser mortals or to be dragged off to a foreign land in defeat and slavery. No doubt the tragedians were expressing the secret wish-fulfillments of the aristocrats in the audience, many of whom had fought or knew they would someday fight duels to preserve their honor.

Our society views suicide with disapproval. To begin with, the act is a felony. Some of those who fail in the attempt are treated like criminals, strapped to their hospital beds and under constant surveillance. All are treated as victims of mental illness. A court order can force them to undergo psychiatric treatment for this extreme aberration, and those who cannot afford it can be virtually imprisoned in state mental hospitals where overcrowding and understaffing create an environment which cannot do much to encourage a "healthy" outlook on life. Families often treat the unsuccessful suicide as a closet skeleton, a distinct social liability—something to be talked about in low tones for fear of shame and loss of status. Well-known personalities like Judy Garland and Marilyn Monroe, who made several tries before finally succeeding, came to be regarded as "tragic cases"—not without "scandalous" overtones.

The following article takes a radically different view of suicide. **Dr. Thomas S. Szasz (b. 1920)**, who was born in Budapest, became a resident psychiatrist at the University of Chicago Clinics, and is now professor of psychiatry at the State University of New York, is urging that we stop treating suicide as a disgrace and a sign of mental illness. He sees the matter as one of civil rights and suggests that the right to die by one's own hand may be the one thing left to us by which to dignify our lives and reaffirm our Worth.

The Ethics of Suicide

In 1967, an editorial in *The Journal of the American Medical Association* declared that "the contemporary physician sees suicide as a manifestation of emotional illness. Rarely does he view it in a context other than that of psychiatry." It was thus implied, the emphasis being the stronger for not being articulated, that to view suicide in this way is at once scientifically accurate and morally uplifting. I submit that it is neither; that, instead, this perspective on suicide is both erroneous and evil: erroneous because it treats an act as if it were a happening; and evil because it serves to legitimize psychiatric force and fraud by justifying it as medical care and treatment.

Before going further, I would like to distinguish three fundamentally different concepts and categories that are combined and confused in most discussions of suicide. They are suicide proper, or so-called successful suicide; attempted, threatened, or so-called unsuccessful suicide; and the attribution by someone (typically a psychiatrist) to someone else (now called a "patient") of serious (that is, probably successful) suicidal intent.

I believe that, generally speaking, the person who commits suicide intends to die; whereas the one who threatens suicide or makes an unsuccessful attempt at it intends to improve his life, not to terminate it. The person who makes claims about someone else's suicidal intent does so usually in order to justify his efforts to control that person.

Put differently, successful suicide is generally an expression of an individual's desire for greater autonomy—in particular, for self-control over his own death; whereas unsuccessful suicide is generally an expression of an individual's desire for more control over others— in particular, for compelling persons close to him to comply with his wishes.

It is difficult to find a "responsible" medical or psychiatric au-

"The Ethics of Suicide" by Thomas S. Szasz, M.D., originally published in *The Antioch Review*, Vol. XXXI, No. 1, Spring 1971. Reprinted by permission of *The Antioch Review*.

thority today that does not regard suicide as a medical, and specifically as a mental health, problem. For example, Ilza Veith, the noted medical historian, asserts that ". . . the act [of suicide] clearly represents an illness. . . ."

Bernard R. Shochet, a psychiatrist at the University of Maryland, offers a precise description of the kind of illness it is. "Depression," he writes, "is a serious systemic disease, with both physiological and psychological concomitants, and suicide is a part of this syndrome." And he articulates the intervention he feels is implicit in this view: "If the patient's safety is in doubt, psychiatric hospitalization should be insisted on." Many other psychiatric authorities could be cited to illustrate the current unanimity on this view of suicide.

Lawyers and jurists have eagerly accepted the psychiatric perspective on suicide, as they have on nearly everything else. An article in the *American Bar Association Journal* by R. E. Schulman, who is both a lawyer and a psychologist, is illustrative. He begins with the premise that "No one in contemporary Western society would suggest that people be allowed to commit suicide as they please without some attempt to intervene or prevent such suicides. Even if a person does not value his own life, Western society does value everyone's life."

But I should like to suggest, as others have suggested before me, precisely what Schulman claims no one would suggest. Furthermore, if Schulman chooses to believe that Western society—which includes the United States with its history of slavery, Germany with its history of National Socialism, and Russia with its history of communism— really "values everyone's life," so be it. But to accept this assertion as true is to fly in the face of the most obvious and brutal facts of history.

When a person decides to take his life, and when a physician decides to frustrate him in this action, the question arises: Why should the physician do so? Conventional psychiatric wisdom answers: Because the suicidal person (now called "patient" for proper emphasis) suffers from a mental illness whose symptom is his desire to kill himself; it is the physician's duty to diagnose and treat illness: *ergo*, he must prevent the "patient" from killing himself and, at the same time, must "treat" the underlying "disease" that "causes" the "patient" to want to do away with himself.

This looks like an ordinary medical diagnosis and intervention. But it is not. What is missing? Everything. This hypothetical, suicidal "patient" is not ill: he has no demonstrable bodily disorder (or if he does, it does not "cause" his suicide); he does not assume the sick role: he does not seek medical help. In short, the physician uses the rhetoric of illness and treatment to justify his forcible intervention in the life of a fellow human being—often in the face of explicit opposition from his so-called "patient."

Power over Life

I do not doubt that attempted or successful suicide may be exceedingly *disturbing* for persons related to, acquainted with, or caring for the ostensible "patient." But I reject the conclusion that the suicidal person is, *ipso facto*, disturbed, that being disturbed equals being *mentally ill*, and that being mentally ill *justifies* psychiatric hospitalization or treatment. For the sake of emphasis, however, let me state that I consider counseling, persuasion, psychotherapy, or any other *voluntary measure*, especially for persons troubled by their own suicidal inclinations and seeking such help, unobjectionable, and indeed generally desirable, interventions. However, physicians and psychiatrists are usually not satisfied with limiting their help to such measures —and with good reason: from such assistance the individual may gain not only the desire to live but also the strength to die.

But we still have not answered the question: Why should a physician frustrate an individual from killing himself? As we saw, some psychiatrists answer: Because the physician values the patient's life, at least when the patient is suicidal, more highly than does the patient himself. Let us examine this claim. Why should the physician, often a complete stranger to the suicidal patient, value the patient's life more highly than does the patient himself? He does not do so in medical practice. Why then should he do so in psychiatric practice, which he himself insists is a form of medical practice?

Let us assume that a physician is confronted with an individual suffering from diabetes or heart failure who fails to take the drugs prescribed for his illness. We know that this often happens and that when it does the patient may become disabled and die prematurely. Yet it would be absurd for a physician to consider, much less to attempt, taking over the conduct of such a patient's life and confining him in a hospital against his will in order to treat his disease. Indeed, any attempt to do so would bring the physician into conflict with both the civil and the criminal law.

Nevertheless, the threat of alleged or real suicide, or so-called dangerousness to oneself, is everywhere considered a proper ground and justification for involuntary mental hospitalization and treatment. Why should this be so? Let me suggest what I believe is likely to be the most important reason for the profound antisuicidal bias of the medical profession. Physicians are committed to saving lives. How, then, should they react to people who are committed to throwing away their lives? It is natural for people to dislike, indeed to hate, those who challenge their basic values. The physician thus reacts, perhaps " unconsciously" (in the sense that he does not articulate the problem in these terms), to the suicidal patient as if the patient had affronted, insulted, or attacked him.

Some nonpsychiatric physicians will thus have nothing to do with suicidal patients. This explains why many people who end up killing themselves have a record of having consulted a physician, often on the very day of their suicide. I surmise that these persons go in search of help, only to discover that the physician wants nothing to do with them. And, in a sense, it is right that it should be so. I do not blame the doctors. Nor do I advocate teaching them suicide prevention— whatever that might be. I contend that because physicians have a relatively blind faith in their life-saving ideology—which, moreover, they often need to carry them through their daily work—they are the wrong people to listen and talk to individuals, intelligently and calmly, about suicide. So much for those physicians who, in the face of the existential attack which they feel the suicidal patient launches on them, run for *their* lives. Let us now look at those who stand and fight back.

Some physicians (and other mental health professionals) declare themselves ready and willing to help not only those suicidal patients who seek assistance, but all persons who are, or are alleged to be, suicidal. Since they, too, seem to perceive suicide as a threat, not just to the suicidal person's physical survival but to their own value system, they strike back and strike back hard. This explains why psychiatrists and suicidologists resort, apparently with a perfectly clear conscience, to the vilest methods: they must believe that their lofty ends justify the basest means. Hence the prevalent use of force and fraud in suicide prevention.

The consequence of this kind of interaction between physician and "patient" is a struggle for power. The patient is at least honest about what he wants: to gain control over his life *and* death—by being the agent of his own demise. But the suicide-preventing psychiatrist is completely dishonest about what he wants: he claims that he only wants to help his patient, while actually he wants to gain control over the patient's life in order to save himself from having to confront his doubts about the value of his own life. Suicide is medical heresy. Commitment and electroshock are the appropriate psychiatric-inquisitorial remedies for it.

Religious Opposition

In the West, opposition to suicide, like opposition to contraception and abortion, rests on religious grounds. According to both the Jewish and Christian religions, God created man, and man can use himself only in the ways permitted by God. But modern man is a revolutionary. Like all revolutionaries, he likes to take away from those who have and to give to those who have not, especially himself.

He has thus taken Man from God and given him to the State (with which he often identifies more than he knows). But this arrangement leaves suicide in a peculiar moral and philosophical limbo. For if a man's life belongs to the State (as it formerly belonged to God), then surely suicide is the taking of a life that belongs not to the taker but to everyone else.

Traditionally, the Roman Catholic Church punished the taking of one's own life by depriving the suicide of burial in consecrated ground. As far as I know, this practice is now so rare in the United States as to be practically nonexistent. Suicides are given a Catholic burial, as they are routinely considered to have taken their lives while insane.

The modern state, with psychiatry as its secular-religious ally, has no comparable sanction to offer. Could this be one of the reasons why it punishes so severely—so very much more severely than did the church—the *unsuccessful* suicide? For I consider the psychiatric stigmatization of people as "suicidal risks" and their incarceration in psychiatric institutions a form of punishment, and a very severe one at that.

Freedom of Choice

Indeed, although I cannot support this claim with statistics, I believe that accepted psychiatric methods of suicide prevention often aggravate rather than ameliorate the suicidal person's problems. As one reads of the tragic encounters with psychiatry of people like James Forrestal, Marilyn Monroe, or Ernest Hemingway, one gains the impression that they felt demeaned and deeply hurt by the psychiatric indignities inflicted on them, and that, as a result of these experiences, they were even more desperately driven to suicide.

But there is another aspect of the moral and philosophical dimensions of suicide that must be mentioned here. I refer to the growing influence of the resurgent idea of self-determination, especially the conviction that men have certain inalienable rights. The individualistic position on suicide might be put thus: a man's life belongs to himself. Hence, he has a right to take his own life, that is, to commit suicide. To be sure, this view recognizes that a man may also have a moral responsibility to his family and others, and that, by killing himself, he reneges on these responsibilities. But these are moral wrongs that society, in its corporate capacity as the state, cannot properly punish.

In regarding the desire to live as a legitimate human aspiration, but not the desire to die, the suicide preventer stands Patrick Henry's famous exclamation, "Give me liberty or give me death!" on its head. In effect, he says: "*Give him* commitment, *give him* electroshock, *give him* lobotomy, *give him* lifelong slavery, but *do not let him choose death!"*

For example, Phillip Solomon writes in the *Journal of the American Medical Association* that "We [physicians] must protect the patient from his own [suicidal] wishes." While to Edwin Schneidman, "Suicide prevention is like fire prevention. . . ." ["Preventing Suicide," *Bulletin of Suicidology* (1968)]. Solomon thus reduces the would-be suicide to the level of an unruly child, while Schneidman reduces him to the level of a tree!

In the psychiatrist's view, it makes no sense to say that one has a right to be mentally ill, especially if the illness is one that, like typhoid fever, threatens the health of other people as well. In short, his job is to try to convince people that wanting to die is a disease. This is how Ari Kiev, director of the Cornell Program in Social Psychiatry and its suicide-prevention clinic, does it: "We say [to the patient], look, you have a disease, just like the Hong Kong flu. Maybe you've got the Hong Kong depression. First, you've got to realize you are emotionally ill. . . . Most of the patients have never admitted to themselves that they are sick. . . ." This pseudomedical perspective is then used to justify psychiatric deception and coercion of the crudest sort.

I understand that deception is standard practice in suicide-prevention centers, though this is often denied. A report about the Nassau County Suicide Prevention Service corroborates the impression that when the would-be suicide does not cooperate with the suicide-prevention authorities, he is confined involuntarily. "When a caller is obviously suicidal," we are told, "a Meadowbrook ambulance is sent out immediately to pick him up."

I should like to restate briefly my views on the differences between diseases and desires and show that by persisting in treating desires as diseases, we only end up treating man as a slave. Let us take, as our paradigm case of illness, a skier who takes a bad spill and fractures an ankle. This fracture is something that has happened to him. He has not intended it to happen. (To be sure, he may have intended it; but that is another case.) Once it has happened, he will seek medical help and will cooperate with medical efforts to mend his broken bones.

Let us now consider the case of the suicidal person. Such a person may also look upon his own suicidal inclination as an undesired, almost alien, impulse and seek help to combat it.

But as we have seen, this is not the only way, nor perhaps the most important way, that the game of suicide prevention is played. It is accepted medical and psychiatric practice to treat persons for their suicidal desires against their will. And what exactly does this mean?

Something quite different from that to which it is often analogized, namely the involuntary (or nonvoluntary) treatment of a bodily illness. For a fractured ankle can be set whether or not a patient consents to its being set. That is because setting a fracture is a *mechanical act on the body*. But a threatened suicide cannot be prevented whether or not the "patient" consents to its being prevented. That is because, suicide being the result of human desire and action, suicide prevention is a *political act on the person*. In other words, since suicide is an exercise and expression of human freedom, it can be prevented only by curtailing human freedom. This is why deprivation of liberty becomes, in institutional psychiatry, a form of treatment.

The Proper Remedy

Whether those who so curtail other people's liberties act with complete sincerity or with utter cynicism hardly matters. What matters is what happens: the abridgement of individual liberty, justified, in the case of suicide prevention, by psychiatric rhetoric; and, in the case of emigration prevention, by political rhetoric.

In language and logic we are the prisoners of our premises, just as in politics and law we are the prisoners of our rulers. Hence we had better pick them well. For if suicide is an illness because it terminates in death, and if the prevention of death by any means necessary is the physician's therapeutic mandate, then the proper remedy for suicide is indeed liberticide.

RESPONSES: Questions for Writing and Discussion

1. The essay shows an unusual, perhaps even shocking, attitude toward the role of the medical profession relative to the attempted suicide. "The person who makes claims about someone else's suicidal intent does so usually in order to justify his efforts to control that person." Dr. Szasz believes that in some cases suicide is preferable to being controlled by another. Do you agree with him? Do you believe the medical profession really wants to help and should be allowed to do so even against the patient's wishes?

2. Suppose the successful suicide were a person who had been examined previously and had a record of mental illness. Would this fact change Dr. Szasz's argument that suicide "is generally an expression of an individual's desire for greater autonomy"? Does the ethics of suicide depend upon the degree of mental aberration? Should there be a dividing line? Or should people have the unrestricted right to take their own lives?

3. How do you feel about the legal opinion expression by R. E. Schulman? "Even if a person does not value his own life, Western society does value everyone's life." *Does* society value your life, in your opinion? How is this shown in other respects than making suicide illegal? Has society the right to value your life if you don't?

4. Szasz contends that a physician who attends a threatened suicide against his will has really been threatened himself and is reacting as if the patient had "affronted, insulted, or attacked him." What is the basis for this view? How can the physician feel personally threatened by a suicidal intent? Do you agree?

5. Szasz proposes that there is now less opposition to suicide from religion than from the state. Are you in a position to know whether this is true? (If you have time, consult a priest, rabbi, or minister on the subject. Ask whether he feels the state owns the individual more so than God does. If his answer is no, ask him what civil sanctions, if any, should exist against suicide.)

6. Another popular view of suicide sees the act as an evasion of one's moral responsibilities to others. Do you find any merit in this argument?

7. Is the author making a valid distinction between setting the skier's broken ankle and preventing a suicide, where the one is called a mechanical act upon the body and the other a political act upon the person? Does it seem at least possible that a physician who happens to be passing by and spots someone on the ledge of a building would react as instinctively as one who happens to witness a man falling down on the sidewalk from apparently natural causes? Would he have time to make the distinction between the mechanical and the political? Should he?

8. Carry the basic argument in this essay to a logical conclusion of your own. State your views on what would happen if

    a. all possible suicides were not interfered with

    b. the medical profession were never allowed to make decisions on behalf of a supposedly mental case who did not seek help

    c. in the case of a suicide that was prevented, the man who was forced to live against his will should appeal to the Supreme Court and it were ruled that society (has) (has not) the right to value and protect the lives of its members.

A SUMMER TRAGEDY
Arna Bontemps

The author is among the earliest black writers of this century to cry out against racism in American society and to use literature as a means of arousing the public against bigotry, exploitation, and genocide. He was born in Louisiana and used the only avenue open to blacks at that time to liberate themselves from being doomed to a servile existence as second-class human beings: the college degree. After Pacific Union College, **Arna Bontemps (b. 1902)** attended the University of Chicago graduate school, later receiving an honorary doctorate in Humane Letters from Morgan State in 1969.

He married in 1926 and became the father of a large family, teaching in private schools to support them while writing on the side and slowly building a solid literary reputation for himself. As a result, he became a professor at the University of Chicago in 1966 and then moved to Yale in 1969. In the canon of his work, from the twenties to the present, one finds the record of the black experience for half a century.

"A Summer Tragedy" recreates an agrarian world with a rigid system of tenant farming and an ancient tradition of racism and discrimination against blacks. In suggesting that suicide may be the only possible escape for the wretchedly poor who are no longer able to work and so eke out a meager living, Bontemps' story may provide strong support for the thesis of Dr. Szasz in the preceding selection "The Ethics of Suicide." At the same time it may convince many readers that the roots of the problem lie not in the dignity of self-destruction but in the indignities visited upon those who are faced with the awesome choice of living or dying—indignities imposed by the very society which, according to Dr. Szasz, makes suicide illegal on the grounds that human life is too valuable.

A Summer Tragedy

Old Jeff Patton, the black share farmer, fumbled with his bow tie. His fingers trembled and the high stiff collar pinched his throat. A fellow loses his hand for such vanities after thirty or forty years of simple life. Once a year, or maybe twice if there's a wedding among his kinfolks, he may spruce up; but generally fancy clothes do nothing but adorn the wall of the big room and feed the moths. That had been Jeff Patton's experience. He had not worn his stiff-bosomed shirt more

than a dozen times in all his married life. His swallowtailed coat lay
on the bed beside him, freshly brushed and pressed, but it was as full
of holes as the overalls in which he worked on weekdays. The moths
had used it badly. Jeff twisted his mouth into a hideous toothless
grimace as he contended with the obstinate bow. He stamped his good
foot and decided to give up the struggle.

"Jennie," he called.

"What's that, Jeff?" His wife's shrunken voice came out of the
adjoining room like an echo. It was hardly bigger than a whisper.

"I reckon you'll have to he'p me wid this heah bow tie, baby," he
said meekly. "Dog if I can hitch it up."

Her answer was not strong enough to reach him, but presently
the old woman came to the door, feeling her way with a stick. She
had a wasted, dead-leaf appearance. Her body, as scrawny and
gnarled as a string bean, seemed less than nothing in the ocean of
frayed and faded petticoats that surrounded her. These hung an inch
or two above the tops of her heavy unlaced shoes and showed little
grotesque piles where the stockings had fallen down from her
negligible legs.

"You oughta could do a heap mo' wid a thing like that'n me—
beingst as you got yo' good sight."

"Looks like I oughta could," he admitted. "But ma fingers is gone
democrat on me. I get all mixed up in the looking glass an' can't tell
wicha way to twist the devilish thing."

Jennie sat on the side of the bed and old Jeff Patton got
down on one knee while she tied the bow knot. It was a slow and
painful ordeal for each of them in this position. Jeff's bones cracked,
his knee ached, and it was only after a half dozen attempts that Jennie
worked a semblance of a bow into the tie.

"I got to dress maself now," the old woman whispered. "These is
ma old shoes an' stockings, and I ain't so much as unwrapped ma
dress."

"Well, don't worry 'bout me no mo', baby," Jeff said. "That 'bout
finishes me. All I gotta do now is slip on that old coat 'n ves' an' I'll
be fixed to leave."

Jennie disappeared again through the dim passage into the shed
room. Being blind was no handicap to her in that black hole. Jeff heard
the cane placed against the wall beside the door and knew that his
wife was on easy ground. He put on his coat, took a battered top hat
from the bedpost and hobbled to the front door. He was ready to
travel. As soon as Jennie could get on her Sunday shoes and her old
black silk dress, they would start.

Outside the tiny log house, the day was warm and mellow with
sunshine. A host of wasps were humming with busy excitement in the

trunk of a dead sycamore. Gray squirrels were searching through the grass for hickory nuts and blue jays were in the trees, hopping from branch to branch. Pine woods stretched away to the left like a black sea. Among them were scattered scores of log houses like Jeff's, houses of black share farmers. Cows and pigs wandered freely among the trees. There was no danger of loss. Each farmer knew his own stock and knew his neighbor's as well as he knew his neighbor's children.

Down the slope to the right were the cultivated acres on which the colored folks worked. They extended to the river, more than two miles away, and they were today green with the unmade cotton crop. A tiny thread of a road, which passed directly in front of Jeff's place, ran through these green fields like a pencil mark.

Jeff, standing outside the door, with his absurd hat in his left hand, surveyed the wide scene tenderly. He had been forty-five years on these acres. He loved them with the unexplained affection that others have for the countries to which they belong.

The sun was hot on his head, his collar still pinched his throat, and the Sunday clothes were intolerably hot. Jeff transferred the hat to his right hand and began fanning with it. Suddenly the whisper that was Jennie's voice came out of the shed room.

"You can bring the car round front whilst you's waitin'," it said feebly. There was a tired pause; then it added, "I'll soon be fixed to go."

"A'right, baby," Jeff answered. "I'll get it in a minute."

But he didn't move. A thought struck him that made his mouth fall open. The mention of the car brought to his mind, with new intensity, the trip he and Jennie were about to take. Fear came into his eyes; excitement took his breath. Lord, Jesus!

"Jeff . . . O Jeff," the old woman's whisper called.

He awakened with a jolt. "Hunh, baby?"

"What you doin'?"

"Nuthin. Jes studyin'. I jes been turnin' things round'n round in ma mind."

"You could be gettin' the car," she said.

"Oh yes, right away, baby."

He started round to the shed, limping heavily on his bad leg. There were three frizzly chickens in the yard. All his other chickens had been killed or stolen recently. But the frizzly chickens had been saved somehow. That was fortunate indeed, for these curious creatures had a way of devouring "Poison" from the yard and in that way protecting against conjure and black luck and spells. But even the frizzy chickens seemed now to be in a stupor. Jeff thought they had some ailment; he expected all three of them to die shortly.

The shed in which the old T-model Ford stood was only a grass roof held up by four corner poles. It had been built by tremulous hands at a time when the little rattletrap car had been regarded as a peculiar treasure. And, miraculously, despite wind and downpour it still stood.

Jeff adjusted the crank and put his weight upon it. The engine came to life with a sputter and bang that rattled the old car from radiator to taillight. Jeff hopped into the seat and put his foot on the accelerator. The sputtering and banging increased. The rattling became more violent. That was good. It was good banging, good sputtering and rattling, and it meant that the aged car was still in running condition. She could be depended on for this trip.

Again Jeff's thought halted as if paralyzed. The suggestion of the trip fell into the machinery of his mind like a wrench. He felt dazed and weak. He swung the car out into the yard, made a half turn and drove around to the front door. When he took his hands off the wheel, he noticed that he was trembling violently. He cut off the motor and climbed to the ground to wait for Jennie.

A few minutes later she was at the window, her voice rattling against the pane like a broken shutter.

"I'm ready, Jeff."

He did not answer, but limped into the house and took her by the arm. He led her slowly through the big room, down the step and across the yard.

"You reckon I'd oughta lock the do'?" he asked softly.

They stopped and Jennie weighed the question. Finally she shook her head.

"Ne' mind the do'," she said. "I don't see no cause to lock up things."

"You right," Jeff agreed. "No cause to lock up."

Jeff opened the door and helped his wife into the car. A quick shudder passed over him. Jesus! Again he trembled.

"How come you shaking so?" Jennie whispered.

"I don't know," he said.

"You mus' be scairt, Jeff."

"No, baby, I ain't scairt."

He slammed the door after her and went around to crank up again. The motor started easily. Jeff wished that it had not been so responsive. He would have liked a few more minutes in which to turn things around in his head. As it was, with Jennie chiding him about being afraid, he had to keep going. He swung the car into the little pencil-mark road and started off toward the river, driving very slowly, very cautiously.

Chugging across the green countryside, the small battered Ford seemed tiny indeed. Jeff felt a familiar excitement, a thrill, as they came down the first slope to the immense levels on which the cotton was growing. He could not help reflecting that the crops were good. He knew what that meant, too; he had made forty-five of them with his own hands. It was true that he had worn out nearly a dozen mules, but that was the fault of old man Stevenson, the owner of the land. Major Stevenson had the odd notion that one mule was all a share farmer needed to work a thirty-acre plot. It was an expensive notion, the way it killed mules from overwork, but the old man held to it. Jeff thought it killed a good many share farmers as well as mules, but he had no sympathy for them. He had always been strong, and he had been taught to have no patience with weakness in men. Women or children might be tolerated if they were puny, but a weak man was a curse. Of course, his own children—

Jeff's thought halted there. He and Jennie never mentioned their dead children any more. And naturally he did not wish to dwell upon them in his mind. Before he knew it, some remark would slip out of his mouth and that would make Jennie feel blue. Perhaps she would cry. A woman like Jennie could not easily throw off the grief that comes from losing five grown children within two years. Even Jeff was still staggered by the blow. His memory had not been much good recently. He frequently talked to himself. And, although he had kept it a secret, he knew that his courage had left him. He was terrified by the least unfamiliar sound at night. He was reluctant to venture far from home in the daytime. And that habit of trembling when he felt fearful was now far beyond his control. Sometimes he became afraid and trembled without knowing what had frightened him. The feeling would just come over him like a chill.

The car rattled slowly over the dusty road. Jennie sat erect and silent, with a little absurd hat pinned to her hair. Her useless eyes seemed very large, very white in their deep sockets. Suddenly Jeff heard her voice, and he inclined his head to catch the words.

"Is we passed Delia Moore's house yet?" she asked.

"Not yet," he said.

"You must be drivin' mighty slow, Jeff."

"We might just as well take our time, baby."

There was a pause. A little puff of steam was coming out of the radiator of the car. Heat wavered above the hood. Delia Moore's house was nearly half a mile away. After a moment Jennie spoke again.

"You ain't really scairt, is you, Jeff?"

"Nah, baby, I ain't scairt."

"You know how we agreed—we gotta keep on goin'."

Jewels of perspiration appeared on Jeff's forehead. His eyes rounded, blinked, became fixed on the road.

"I don't know," he said with a shiver. "I reckon it's the only thing to do."

"Hm."

A flock of guinea fowls, pecking in the road, were scattered by the passing car. Some of them took to their wings; others hid under bushes. A blue jay, swaying on a leafy twig, was annoying a roadside squirrel. Jeff held an even speed till he came near Delia's place. Then he slowed down noticeably.

Delia's house was really no house at all, but an abandoned store building converted into a dwelling. It sat near a crossroads, beneath a single black cedar tree. There Delia, a cattish old creature of Jennie's age, lived alone. She had been there more years than anybody could remember, and long ago had won the disfavor of such women as Jennie. For in her young days Delia had been gayer, yellower and saucier than seemed proper in those parts. Her ways with menfolks had been dark and suspicious. And the fact that she had had as many husbands as children did not help her reputation.

"Yonder's old Delia," Jeff said as they passed.

"What she doin'?"

"Jes sittin' in the do'," he said.

"She see us?"

"Hm," Jeff said. "Musta did."

That relieved Jennie. It strengthened her to know that her old enemy had seen her pass in her best clothes. That would give the old she-devil something to chew her gums and fret about, Jennie thought. Wouldn't she have a fit if she didn't find out? Old evil Delia! This would be just the thing for her. It would pay her back for being so evil. It would also pay her, Jennie thought, for the way she used to grin at Jeff—long ago when her teeth were good.

The road became smooth and red, and Jeff could tell by the smell of the air that they were nearing the river. He could see the rise where the road turned and ran along parallel to the stream. The car chugged on monotonously. After a long silent spell, Jennie leaned against Jeff and spoke.

"How many bale o' cotton you think we got standin'?" she said.

Jeff wrinkled his forehead as he calculated.

" 'Bout twenty-five, I reckon."

"How many you make las' year?"

"Twenty-eight," he said. "How come you ask that?"

"I's jes thinkin'," Jennie said quietly.

"It don't make a speck o' difference though," Jeff reflected. "If we get much or if we get little, we still gonna be in debt to old man Stevenson when he gets through counting up agin us. It's took us a long time to learn that."

Jennie was not listening to these words. She had fallen into a trance-like meditation. Her lips twitched. She chewed her gums and rubbed her gnarled hands nervously. Suddenly she leaned forward, buried her face in the nervous hands and burst into tears. She cried aloud in a dry cracked voice that suggested the rattle of fodder on dead stalks. She cried aloud like a child, for she had never learned to suppress a genuine sob. Her slight old frame shook heavily and seemed hardly able to sustain such violent grief.

"What's the matter, baby?" Jeff asked awkwardly. "Why you cryin' like all that?"

"I's jes thinkin'," she said.

"So you the one what's scairt now, hunh?"

"I ain't scairt, Jeff. I's jes thinkin' 'bout leavin' eve'thing like this —eve'thing we been used to. It's right sad-like."

Jeff did not answer, and presently Jennie buried her face again and cried.

The sun was almost overhead. It beat down furiously on the dusty wagon-path road, on the parched roadside grass and the tiny battered car. Jeff's hands, gripping the wheel, became wet with perspiration; his forehead sparkled. Jeff's lips parted. His mouth shaped a hideous grimace. His face suggested the face of a man being burned. But the torture passed and his expression softened again.

"You mustn't cry, baby," he said to his wife. "We gotta be strong. We can't break down."

Jennie waited a few seconds, then said, "You reckon we oughta do it, Jeff? You reckon we oughta go 'head an' do it, really?"

Jeff's voice choked; his eyes blurred. He was terrified to hear Jennie say the thing that had been in his mind all morning. She had egged him on when he had wanted more than anything in the world to wait, to reconsider, to think things over a little longer. Now she was getting cold feet. Actually there was no need of thinking the question through again. It would only end in making the same painful decision once more. Jeff knew that. There was no need of fooling around longer.

"We jes as well to do like we planned," he said. "They ain't nothin' else for us now—it's the bes' thing."

Jeff thought of the handicaps, the near impossibility, of making another crop with his leg bothering him more and more each week. Then there was always the chance that he would have another stroke, like the one that had made him lame. Another one might kill him. The least it could do would be to leave him helpless. Jeff gasped—Lord, Jesus! He could not bear to think of being helpless, like a baby, on Jennie's hands. Frail, blind Jennie.

The little pounding motor of the car worked harder and harder.

The puff of steam from the cracked radiator became larger. Jeff realized that they were climbing a little rise. A moment later the road turned abruptly and he looked down upon the face of the river.

"Jeff."

"Hunh?"

"Is that the water I hear?"

"Hm. Tha's it."

"Well, which way you goin' now?"

"Down this-a way," he said. "The road runs 'long 'side o' the water a lil piece."

She waited a while calmly. Then she said, "Drive faster."

"A'right, baby," Jeff said.

The water roared in the bed of the river. It was fifty or sixty feet below the level of the road. Between the road and the water there was a long smooth slope, sharply inclined. The slope was dry, the clay hardened by prolonged summer heat. The water below, roaring in a narrow channel, was noisy and wild.

"Jeff."

"Hunh?"

"How far you goin'?"

"Jes a lil piece down the road."

"You ain't scairt, is you, Jeff?"

"Nah, baby," he said trembling. "I ain't scairt."

"Remember how we planned it, Jeff. We gotta do it like we said. Brave-like."

"Hm."

Jeff's brain darkened. Things suddenly seemed unreal, like figures in a dream. Thoughts swam in his mind foolishly, hysterically, like little blind fish in a pool within a dense cave. They rushed, crossed one another, jostled, collided, retreated and rushed again. Jeff soon became dizzy. He shuddered violently and turned to his wife.

"Jennie, I can't do it. I can't." His voice broke pitifully.

She did not appear to be listening. All the grief had gone from her face. She sat erect, her unseeing eyes wide open, strained and frightful. Her glossy black skin had become dull. She seemed as thin, as sharp and bony, as a starved bird. Now, having suffered and endured the sadness of tearing herself away from beloved things, she showed no anguish. She was absorbed with her own thoughts, and she didn't even hear Jeff's voice shouting in her ear.

Jeff said nothing more. For an instant there was light in his cavernous brain. The great chamber was, for less than a second, peopled by characters he knew and loved. They were simple, healthy creatures, and they behaved in a manner that he could understand. They had quality. But since he had already taken leave of them long ago, the remembrance did not break his heart again. Young Jeff Patton was among them, the Jeff Patton of fifty years ago who went down to New Orleans with a crowd of country boys to the Mardi Gras doings. The gay young crowd, boys with candy-striped shirts and rouged-brown girls in noisy silks, was like a picture in his head. Yet it did not make him sad. On that very trip Slim Burns had killed Joe Beasley—the crowd had been broken up. Since then Jeff Patton's world had been the Greenbriar Plantation. If there had been other Mardi Gras carnivals, he had not heard of them. Since then there had been no time; the years had fallen on him like waves. Now he was old, worn out. Another paralytic stroke (like the one he had already suffered) would put him on his back for keeps. In that condition, with a frail blind woman to look after him, he would be worse off than if he were dead.

Suddenly Jeff's hands became steady. He actually felt brave. He slowed down the motor of the car and carefully pulled off the road. Below, the water of the stream boomed, a soft thunder in the deep channel. Jeff ran the car onto the clay slope, pointed it directly toward the stream and put his foot heavily on the accelerator. The little car leaped furiously down the steep incline toward the water. The movement was nearly as swift and direct as a fall. The two old black folks, sitting quietly side by side, showed no excitement. In another instant the car hit the water and dropped immediately out of sight.

A little later it lodged in the mud of a shallow place. One wheel of the crushed and upturned little Ford became visible above the rushing water.

RESPONSES: Questions for Writing and Discussion

1. If Jeff's and Jennie's children had lived, would this have given their life more meaning and value? Would children have been enough to redeem an existence which is otherwise so mean? What do you suppose their children might have done on their behalf?

2. Jeff loved the land and was proud of his success with it. If he were not physically handicapped, would the land in itself have been enough to dignify his life? Would it matter that he did not and could not own it?

3. ". . . we still gonna be in debt to old man Stevenson." Assuming that the central characters do achieve Human Worth in the only way open to them—death—do you think they are perhaps playing into the hands of "old man Stevenson" and others like him? Should they give him that much satisfaction? What have they proved in the long run?

4. Given the locale in which the story takes place and the facts as they are presented to the reader, do you think Jeff and Jennie could have achieved their Human Worth through some other means? Were any available? What would you have done in the same circumstances?

5. If you were a physician driving by, and you saw Jeff's car suspiciously pointed toward the water, and suspected a possible suicide pact, would you stop and question Jeff and Jennie? If not, why? If so, what would you say to them? If they outlined their story to you, as written by Bontemps, would you advise them to go ahead with their suicide, or try to argue them out of it?

6. A sophisticated modern reader might find the story a bit oldfashioned and sentimental. He might point to the fact that the author has stacked the cards (especially in the matter of Jeff's bad legs and his paralytic strokes) in order to make the future of the main characters unutterably bleak and futile. Could it be argued that no conditions exist today which are as bad as they are in this story? that, with welfare and other social agencies to help the distressed, there could be no reasonable grounds for suicide among even the poorest in America today?

ON THE FEAR OF DEATH
Elisabeth Kübler-Ross

To a foreigner newly arrived in this country, the rapid pace of our life styles, the throb of our large cities, and the extraordinary mobility of our population might give the impression that ours is a life-oriented society. Billboards everywhere smile upon us: flashing white teeth; handsome young couples, holding frosty bottles of mini-caloried beverages; magazine and television ads with lean, healthy, and tanned bodies luxuriating on the beaches in the blaze of glorious sunlight. America seems to be one long burst of thanks to the miracle of life.

And why should it not be? We are told the American standard of living is the highest on earth, and statistics are readily available to support this position. Per capita we earn more and spend more, and we have a longer time in which to enjoy the good things of life. Our medical world is perpetually bustling with new discoveries. Every decade at least one formerly incurable ailment surrenders to the march of medical science. With a life expectancy sometimes double that of his forefathers, the average American can put off worrying about suffering and dying for many long years.

But under all the vitality, ours is a neurotic, unhappy society—driven on to a desperate attempt at the game of life-affirmation, when all the while the specter of death haunts the unconscious of each one of us. Such is the view of Americans held by many in the medical and psychiatric world today. Such is the view which underlies a recent and major book with a perhaps consciously threatening title: *On Death and Dying*.

Its author, **Dr. Elisabeth Kübler-Ross (b. 1926)**, was born and educated in Switzerland and currently serves as "International Consultant in the Care of the Dying Patients and Their Families." She has written and lectured widely on the American paranoia over death. She regards the intensive life-affirmation in the American mode of living as a cover-up for the pain and anguish which come from not facing the facts about death and suppressing the very thought of it deep within the unconscious. With our accent on staying young and trim and avoiding all references to death, we are, she believes, really saying no to life. So fearful of losing it, we fail to live it at all.

Dr. Kübler-Ross and her associates are pioneers in a new approach to the subject of death. Instead of aiding in the conspiracy she writes about in the following selection—whereby people pretend there is no such thing as death—the author believes in frank and open discussions with dying patients about the experience they are about to undergo and with the families and friends who are suffering the loss.

On the Fear of Death

Let me not pray to be sheltered from
dangers but to be fearless in facing
them.
  Let me not beg for the stilling of
my pain but for the heart to conquer it.
  Let me not look for allies in life's
battlefield but to my own strength.
  Let me not crave in anxious fear to
be saved but hope for the patience to
win my freedom.
  Grant me that I may not be a
coward, feeling your mercy in my

> *success alone; but let me find the grasp*
> *of your hand in my failure.*
> Rabindranath Tagore,
> *Fruit-Gathering*

Epidemics have taken a great toll of lives in past generations. Death in infancy and early childhood was frequent and there were few families who didn't lose a member of the family at an early age. Medicine has changed greatly in the last decades. Widespread vaccinations have practically eradicated many illnesses, at least in western Europe and the United States. The use of chemotherapy, especially the antibiotics, has contributed to an ever decreasing number of fatalities in infectious diseases. Better child care and education has effected a low morbidity and mortality among children. The many diseases that have taken an impressive toll among the young and middle-aged have been conquered. The number of old people is on the rise, and with this fact come the number of people with malignancies and chronic diseases associated more with old age.

Pediatricians have less work with acute and life-threatening situations as they have an ever increasing number of patients with psychosomatic disturbances and adjustment and behavior problems. Physicians have more people in their waiting rooms with emotional problems than they have ever had before, but they also have more elderly patients who not only try to live with their decreased physical abilities and limitations but who also face loneliness and isolation with all its pains and anguish. The majority of these people are not seen by a psychiatrist. Their needs have to be elicited and gratified by other professional people, for instance, chaplains and social workers. It is for them that I am trying to outline the changes that have taken place in the last few decades, changes that are ultimately responsible for the increased fear of death, the rising number of emotional problems, and the greater need for understanding of and coping with the problems of death and dying.

When we look back in time and study old cultures and people, we are impressed that death has always been distasteful to man and will probably always be. From a psychiatrist's point of view this is very understandable and can perhaps best be explained by our basic knowledge that, in our unconscious, death is never possible in regard to ourselves. It is inconceivable for our unconscious to imagine an actual ending of our own life here on earth, and if this life of ours has to end, the ending is always attributed to a malicious intervention from the outside by someone else. In simple terms, in our unconscious mind we can only be killed; it is inconceivable to die of a natural cause or of old age. Therefore death in itself is associated with a bad act, a frightening happening, something that in itself calls for retribution and punishment.

One is wise to remember these fundamental facts as they are essential in understanding some of the most important, otherwise unintelligible communications of our patients.

The second fact that we have to comprehend is that in our unconscious mind we cannot distinguish between a wish and a deed. We are all aware of some of our illogical dreams in which two completely opposite statements can exist side by side—very acceptable in our dreams but unthinkable and illogical in our wakening state. Just as our unconscious mind cannot differentiate between the wish to kill somebody in anger and the act of having done so, the young child is unable to make this distinction. The child who angrily wishes his mother to drop dead for not having gratified his needs will be traumatized greatly by the actual death of his mother—even if this event is not linked closely in time with his destructive wishes. He will always take part or the whole blame for the loss of his mother. He will always say to himself—rarely to others—"I did it, I am responsible, I was bad, therefore Mommy left me." It is well to remember that the child will react in the same manner if he loses a parent by divorce, separation, or desertion. Death is often seen by a child as an impermanent thing and has therefore little distinction from a divorce in which he may have an opportunity to see a parent again.

Many a parent will remember remarks of their children such as, "I will bury my doggy now and next spring when the flowers come up again, he will get up." Maybe it was the same wish that motivated the ancient Egyptians to supply their dead with food and goods to keep them happy and the old American Indians to bury their relatives with their belongings.

When we grow older and begin to realize that our omnipotence is really not so omnipotent, that our strongest wishes are not powerful enough to make the impossible possible, the fear that we have contributed to the death of a loved one diminishes—and with it the guilt. The fear remains diminished, however, only so long as it is not challenged too strongly. Its vestiges can be seen daily in hospital corridors and in people associated with the bereaved.

A husband and wife may have been fighting for years, but when the partner dies, the survivor will pull his hair, whine and cry louder and beat his chest in regret, fear and anguish, and will hence fear his own death more than before, still believing in the law of talion—an eye for an eye, a tooth for a tooth—"I am responsible for her death, I will have to die a pitiful death in retribution."

Maybe this knowledge will help us understand many of the old customs and rituals which have lasted over the centuries and whose purpose is to diminish the anger of the gods or the people as the case may be, thus decreasing the anticipated punishment. I am thinking of the ashes, the torn clothes, the veil, the *Klage Weiber* of the old days—they are all means to ask you to take pity on them, the mourners, and are expressions of sorrow, grief, and shame. If someone grieves, beats his chest, tears his hair, or refuses to eat, it is an attempt at self-punishment to avoid or reduce the anticipated punishment for the blame that he takes on the death of a loved one.

This grief, shame, and guilt are not very far removed from feelings of anger and rage. The process of grief always includes some qualities of anger. Since none of us likes to admit anger at a deceased person, these emotions are often disguised or repressed and prolong the period of grief or show up in other ways. It is well to remember that it is not up to us to judge such feelings as bad or shameful but to understand their true meaning and origin as something very human. In order to illustrate this I will again use the example of the child—and the child in us. The five-year-old who loses his mother is both blaming himself for her disappearance and being angry at her for having deserted him and for no longer gratifying his needs. The dead person then turns into something the child loves and wants very much but also hates with equal intensity for this severe deprivation.

The ancient Hebrews regarded the body of a dead person as something unclean and not to be touched. The early American Indians talked about the evil spirits and shot arrows in the air to drive the spirits away. Many other cultures have rituals to take care of the "bad" dead person, and they all originate in this feeling of anger which still exists in all of us, though we dislike admitting it. The tradition of the tombstone may originate in this wish to keep the bad spirits deep down in the ground, and the pebbles that many mourners put on the grave are left-over symbols of the same wish. Though we call the firing of guns at military funerals a last salute, it is the same symbolic ritual as the Indian used when he shot his spears and arrows into the skies.

I give these examples to emphasize that man has not basically changed. Death is still a fearful, frightening happening, and the fear of death is a universal fear even if we think we have mastered it on many levels.

What has changed is our way of coping and dealing with death and dying and our dying patients.

Having been raised in a country in Europe where science is not so advanced, where modern techniques have just started to find their way into medicine, and where people still live as they did in this country half a century ago, I may have had an opportunity to study a part of the evolution of mankind in a shorter period.

I remember as a child the death of a farmer. He fell from a tree and was not expected to live. He asked simply to die at home, a wish that was granted without questioning. He called his daughters into the bedroom and spoke with each one of them alone for a few minutes. He arranged his affairs quietly, though he was in great pain, and distributed his belongings and his land, none of which was to be split until his wife should follow him in death. He also asked each of his children to share in the work, duties, and tasks that he had carried on until the time of the accident. He asked his friends to visit him once more, to bid good-bye to them. Although I was a small child at the time, he did not exclude me or my siblings. We were allowed to share in the preparations of the family just as we were permitted to grieve with them until he died. When he did die, he was left at home, in his own beloved home which he had built, and among his friends and neighbors who went to take a last look at him where he lay in the midst of flowers in the place he had lived in and loved so much. In that country today there is still no make-believe slumber room, no embalming, no false makeup to pretend sleep. Only the signs of very disfiguring illnesses are covered up with bandages and only infectious cases are removed from the home prior to the burial.

Why do I describe such "old-fashioned" customs? I think they are an indication of our acceptance of a fatal outcome, and they help the dying patient as well as his family to accept the loss of a loved one. If a patient is allowed to terminate his life in the familiar and beloved environment, it requires less adjustment for him. His own family knows him well enough to replace a sedative with a glass of his favorite wine; or the smell of a home-cooked soup may give him the appetite to sip a few spoons of fluid which, I think, is still more enjoyable than an infusion. I will not minimize the need for sedatives and infusions and realize full well from my own experience as a country doctor that they are sometimes life-saving and often unavoidable. But I also know that patience and familiar people and foods could replace many a bottle of intravenous fluids given for the simple reason that it fulfills the physiological need without involving too many people and/or individual nursing care.

The fact that children are allowed to stay at home where a fatality has stricken and are included in the talk, discussions, and fears gives them the feeling that they are not alone in the grief and gives them the comfort of shared responsibility and shared mourning. It prepares them gradually and helps them view death as part of life, an experience which may help them grow and mature.

This is in great contrast to a society in which death is viewed as taboo, discussion of it is regarded as morbid, and children are excluded with the presumption and pretext that it would be "too much" for them. They are then sent off to relatives, often accompanied with some unconvincing lies of "Mother has gone on a long trip" or other unbelievable stories. The child senses that something is wrong, and his distrust in adults will only multiply if other relatives add new variations of the story, avoid his questions or suspicions, shower him with gifts as a meager substitute for a loss he is not permitted to deal with. Sooner or later the child will become aware of the changed family situation and, depending on the age and personality of the child, will have an unresolved grief and regard this incident as a frightening, mysterious, in any case very traumatic experience with untrustworthy grownups, which he has no way to cope with.

It is equally unwise to tell a little child who lost her brother that God loved little boys so much that he took little Johnny to heaven. When this little girl grew up to be a woman she never solved her anger at God, which resulted in a psychotic depression when she lost her own little son three decades later.

We would think that our great emancipation, our knowledge of science and of man, has given us better ways and means to prepare ourselves and our families for this inevitable happening. Instead the days are gone when a man was allowed to die in peace and dignity in his own home.

The more we are making advancements in science, the more we seem to fear and deny the reality of death. How is this possible?

We use euphemisms, we make the dead look as if they were asleep, we ship the children off to protect them from the anxiety and turmoil around the house if the patient is fortunate enough to die at home, we don't allow children to visit their dying parents in the hospitals, we have long and controversial discussions about whether patients should be told the truth—a question that rarely arises when the dying person is tended by the family physician who has known him from delivery to death and who knows the weaknesses and strengths of each member of the family.

I think there are many reasons for this flight away from facing death calmly. One of the most important facts is that dying nowadays is more gruesome in many ways, namely, more lonely, mechanical, and dehumanized; at times it is even difficult to determine technically when the time of death has occurred.

Dying becomes lonely and impersonal because the patient is often taken out of his familiar environment and rushed to an emergency room. Whoever has been very sick and has required rest and comfort especially may recall his experience of being put on a stretcher and enduring the noise of the ambulance siren and hectic rush until the hospital gates open. Only those who have lived through this may appreciate the discomfort and cold necessity of such transportation which is only the beginning of a long ordeal—hard to endure when you are well, difficult to express in words when noise, light, pumps, and voices are all too much to put up with. It may well be that we might consider more the patient under the sheets and blankets and perhaps stop our well-meant efficiency and rush in order to hold the patient's hand, to smile, or to listen to a question. I include the trip to the hospital as the first episode in dying, as it is for many. I am putting it exaggeratedly in contrast to the sick man who is left at home—not to say that lives should not be saved if they can be saved by a hospitalization but to keep the focus on the patient's experience, his needs and his reactions.

When a patient is severely ill, he is often treated like a person with no right to an opinion. It is often someone else who makes the decision if and when and where a patient should be hospitalized. It would take so little to remember that the sick person too has feelings, has wishes and opinions, and has—most important of all—the right to be heard.

Well, our presumed patient has now reached the emergency room. He will be surrounded by busy nurses, orderlies, interns, residents, a lab technician perhaps who will take some blood, an electrocardiogram technician who takes the cardiogram. He may be moved to X-ray and he will overhear opinions of his condition and discussions and questions to members of the family. He slowly but surely is beginning to be treated like a thing. He is no longer a person. Decisions are made often without his opinion. If he tries to rebel he will be sedated and after hours of waiting and wondering whether he has the strength, he will be wheeled into the operating room or intensive treatment unit and become an object of great concern and great financial investment.

He may cry for rest, peace, and dignity, but he will get infusions, transfusions, a heart machine, or tracheostomy if necessary. He may want one single person to stop for one single minute so that he can ask one single question—but he will get a dozen people around the clock, all busily preoccupied with his heart rate, pulse, electrocardiogram or pulmonary functions, his secretions or excretions but not with him as a human being. He may wish to fight it all but it is going to be a useless fight since all this is done in the fight for his life, and if they can save his life they can consider the person afterwards. Those who consider the person first may lose precious time to save his life! At least this seems to be the rationale or justification behind all this—or is it? Is the reason for this increasingly mechanical, depersonalized approach our own defensiveness? Is this approach our own way to cope with and repress the anxieties that a terminally or critically ill patient evokes in us? Is our concentration on equipment, on blood pressure our desperate attempt to deny the impending death which is so frightening and discomforting to us that we displace all our knowledge onto machines, since they are less close to us than the suffering face of another human being which would remind us once more of our lack of omnipotence, our own limits and failures, and last but not least perhaps our own mortality?

Maybe the question has to be raised: Are we becoming less human or more human? Though this book is in no way meant to be judgmental, it is clear that whatever the answer may be, the patient is suffering more—not physically, perhaps, but emotionally. And his needs have not changed over the centuries, only our ability to gratify them.

RESPONSES: Questions for Writing and Discussion

1. The author notes that "death has always been distasteful to man and will probably always be." At the same time she presents us with a picture of an increasingly long-lived society, one in which omnipresent death has been replaced by the omnipresent fear of dying. Do you agree that our life span and the conquest of so many once fatal diseases have made us more concerned about death? Do you think people may have been less neurotic on the subject in days when death was a commonplace occurrence?

2. Do you agree with the author's contention that we never think death is possible "in regard to ourselves"? Do *you* ever think about your death? If not, why do you think this is so? If you do think about it, how do you imagine it will be? Why do you think these thoughts? Would you rather you didn't?

3. As a child, were your thoughts of death identical to those attributed to children by the author? Did you think of it as something impermanent? Did it frighten you? Share with the class your first direct contact with death. How did the experience leave you? Do you think you are well-adjusted now in your attitude toward death?

4. Describe some of the grief behavior you have noted in other people. Did it seem to bear out Dr. Kübler-Ross' interpretation of grief as "an attempt at self-punishment"? Have you personally experienced grief over the loss of someone close to you? If so, can you look back upon it now and describe what you think was actually taking place?

5. Would it be better to have someone else bury the deceased

without one's having to view the remains or go to the cemetery and give so much overt expression to grief? Would people get over their losses more quickly and effectively without the social rituals surrounding death?

6. In Dr. Kübler-Ross' native country of Switzerland the dying are usually allowed to remain in their homes and be cared for by their families. The body is also viewed at home rather than in the formal surroundings of funeral chapels as in America. Do you think this is a better arrangement all around? Or are you glad the American practice is to place death as far as possible from everyday reality?

7. We find also that in Switzerland children are "included in the talk, discussions, and fears" about death. This is hardly the case in our society. Will you want your children to learn about death at an early age? How early? How will you answer the questions your children will ask about death?

8. Have we indeed made death "more lonely, mechanical, and dehumanized"? Is the author being entirely fair when she describes the sterile impersonality of hospitals? Doesn't the ambulance have to roar noisily through crowded streets in order to save your life?

Are you glad or sorry that we have such efficiency?

THE MYTH OF SISYPHUS
Albert Camus

That the universe is beyond man's control is the message underlying nearly every myth from ancient to modern times. Even the ones that end in delirious happiness like "Cinderella" really point out how inaccessible is the castle in the air. If we have grown up expecting fairy godmothers to materialize at the very moment we need them, we find out they don't, and then the myth drops its mask and smiles at our gullibility.

At least this is the attitude of a contemporary existential philosopher like **Albert Camus (1913–1960)**. *Existentialism* is an extremely broad category of thought, embracing many different formats, but they all share the belief that man needs to work very hard at the business of living. Even the existentialists who accept a God of some kind do not count on miracles. The human will is the fundamental unit of this existence. It is opposed at every turn: by the will of other people, by the state, by technology, by the boundless unknown that may or may not be God's domain. Recognizing this, the existential man knows himself to be free to do anything with his life. He may choose to end it. He may throw up his arms in despair when he thinks of how much things are out of control, of the dangers which beset us each day of our lives (a bomb exploding, a sniper's bullet, automobile brakes that suddenly give out). Or he may agree with the poet Robert Frost who, while not exactly an existentialist, once observed in a poem that living was a chance he had to take—"and took."

Camus belongs to the school of frankly atheistic existentialism. With his French compatriot Jean-Paul Sartre, he believes there is no good reason for believing in God, but many good reasons for not doing so. The better part of wisdom, he says, is to recognize that life is first of all an absurdity. When this basic fact is grasped, the way of salvation becomes immediately clear. Existence is absurd when measured against human purposes. For some unaccountable reason human beings possess reason and understanding. It is perhaps tragic that they are conscious at all, as "The Myth of Sisyphus" indicates. But that's the way it is; there is nothing we can do about it. We think and respond. We have creative imaginations. We keep thinking of things to do, ways of trying to improve our lives. If we ask ourselves why we should be committed to *anything*, we realize that commitment has to be its own reward. There is no ultimate reason because, for Camus, there is no God observing us and waiting to be satisfied. Sooner or later we die, and most of what we have done will have amounted to little. This is what absurdity is all about.

But does it end there? No, says Camus. The essay which follows is one of his key statements. In the ancient story of Sisyphus, who was condemned by the god of the underworld to roll a heavy rock uphill only to have it fall back again and to repeat this futile action for eternity, Camus has discovered a symbol for the modern world. "The Myth of Sisyphus" is life-affirming, but in a way we never learned from the mythology of our childhood.

When an automobile accident put a sudden end to Camus' life before the philosopher had reached the age of fifty, his view of existence seemed thoroughly documented. It was an absurdity for a man to cease living while he was reaching the very peak of his intellectual and creative powers. But doubtless Camus would have shrugged his shoulders and asked what else could be expected. The "night" of human life "has no end." It is all death, if one looks at it that way. The great thing is that it is possible to know this, to allow for it, to roll the rock uphill despite this.

The Myth of Sisyphus

The gods had condemned Sisyphus to ceaselessly rolling a rock to the top of a mountain, whence the stone would fall back of its own weight. They had thought with some reason that there is no more dreadful punishment than futile and hopeless labor.

If one believes Homer, Sisyphus was the wisest and most prudent of mortals. According to another tradition, however, he was disposed to practice the profession of highwayman. I see no contradiction in this. Opinions differ as to the reasons why he became the futile laborer of the underworld. To begin with, he is accused of a certain levity in regard to the gods. He stole their secrets. Ægina, the daughter of Æsopus, was carried off by Jupiter. The father was shocked by that disappearance and complained to Sisyphus. He, who knew of the abduction, offered to tell about it on condition that Æsopus would give water to the citadel of Corinth. To the celestial thunderbolts he preferred the benediction of water. He was punished for this in the underworld. Homer tells us also that Sisyphus had put Death in chains. Pluto could not endure the sight of his deserted, silent empire. He dispatched the god of war, who liberated Death from the hands of her conqueror.

It is said also that Sisyphus, being near to death, rashly wanted to test his wife's love. He ordered her to cast his unburied body into the middle of the public square. Sisyphus woke up in the underworld. And there, annoyed by an obedience so contrary to human love, he obtained from Pluto permission to return to earth in order to chastise his wife. But when he had seen again the face of this world, enjoyed water and sun, warm stones and the sea, he no longer wanted to go back to the infernal darkness. Recalls, signs of anger, warnings were of no avail. Many years more he lived facing the curve of the gulf, the sparkling sea, and the smiles of earth. A decree of the gods was necessary. Mercury came and seized the impudent man by the collar and, snatching him from his joys, led him forcibly back to the underworld, where his rock was ready for him.

You have already grasped that Sisyphus is the absurd hero. He *is*, as much through his passions as through his torture. His scorn of the gods, his hatred of death, and his passion for life won him that unspeakable penalty in which the whole being is exerted toward accomplishing nothing. This is the price that must be paid for the passions of this earth. Nothing is told us about Sisyphus in the underworld. Myths are made for the imagination to breathe life into them. As for this myth, one sees merely the whole effort of a body straining to raise the huge stone, to roll it and push it up a slope a hundred times over; one sees the face screwed up, the cheek tight against the stone, the shoulder bracing the clay-covered mass, the foot wedging it, the fresh start with arms outstretched, the wholly human security of two earth-clotted hands. At the very end of his long effort measured by skyless space and time without depth, the purpose is achieved. Then Sisyphus watches the stone rush down in a few moments toward that lower world whence he will have to push it up again toward the summit. He goes back down to the plain.

It is during that return, that pause, that Sisyphus interests me. A face that toils so close to stones is already stone itself! I see that man going back down with a heavy yet measured step toward the torment of which he will never know the end. That hour like a breathing-space which returns as surely as his suffering, that is the hour of consciousness. At each of those moments when he leaves the heights and gradually sinks toward the lairs of the gods, he is superior to his fate. He is stronger than his rock.

If this myth is tragic, that is because its hero is conscious. Where would his torture be, indeed, if at every step the hope of succeeding upheld him? The workman of today works every day in his life at the same tasks, and this fate is no less absurd. But it is tragic only at the rare moments when it becomes conscious. Sisyphus, proletarian of the gods, powerless and rebellious, knows the whole extent of his wretched condition: it is what he thinks of during his descent. The lucidity that was to constitute his torture at the same time crowns his victory. There is no fate that cannot be surmounted by scorn.

*   *   *

If the descent is thus sometimes performed in sorrow, it can also take place in joy. This word is not too much. Again I fancy Sisyphus returning toward his rock, and the sorrow was in the beginning. When the images of earth cling too tightly to memory, when the call of happiness becomes too insistent, it happens that melancholy rises in man's heart: this is the rock's victory, this is the rock itself. The boundless grief is too heavy to bear. These are our nights of Gethsemane. But crushing truths perish from being acknowledged. Thus, Œdipus at the outset obeys fate without knowing it. But from the moment he knows, his tragedy begins. Yet at the same moment, blind and desperate, he realizes that the only bond linking him to the world is the cool hand of a girl. Then a tremendous remark rings out: "Despite so many ordeals, my advanced age and the nobility of my soul make me conclude that all is well." Sophocles' Œdipus, like Dostoevsky's Kirilov, thus gives the recipe for the absurd victory. Ancient wisdom confirms modern heroism.

One does not discover the absurd without being tempted to write a manual of happiness. "What! by such narrow ways—?" There is but one world, however. Happiness and the absurd are two sons of the same earth. They are inseparable. It would be a mistake to say that happiness necessarily springs from the absurd discovery. It happens as well that the feeling of the absurd springs from happiness. "I conclude that all is well," says Œdipus, and that remark is sacred. It echoes in the wild and limited universe of man. It teaches that all is not, has not been, exhausted. It drives out of this world a god who had come into it with dissatisfaction and a preference for futile sufferings. It makes of fate a human matter, which must be settled among men.

All Sisyphus' silent joy is contained therein. His fate belongs to him. His rock is his thing. Likewise, the absurd man, when he contemplates his torment, silences all the idols. In the universe suddenly restored to its silence, the myriad wondering little voices of the earth rise up. Unconscious, secret calls, invitations from all the faces, they are the necessary reverse and price of victory. There is no sun without shadow, and it is essential to know the night. The absurd man says yes and his effort will henceforth be unceasing. If there is a personal fate, there is no higher destiny, or at least there is but one which he concludes is inevitable and despicable. For the rest, he knows himself to be the master of his days. At that subtle moment when man glances backward over his life, Sisyphus returning toward his rock, in that slight pivoting he contemplates that series of unrelated actions which becomes his fate, created by him, combined under his memory's eye and soon sealed by his death. Thus, convinced of the wholly human origin of all that is human, a blind man eager to see who knows that the night has no end, he is still on the go. The rock is still rolling.

I leave Sisyphus at the foot of the mountain! One always finds one's burden again. But Sisyphus teaches the higher fidelity that negates the gods and raises rocks. He too concludes that all is well. This universe henceforth without a master seems to him neither sterile nor futile. Each atom of that stone, each mineral flake of that night-filled mountain, in itself forms a world. The struggle itself toward the heights is enough to fill a man's heart. One must imagine Sisyphus happy.

RESPONSES: Questions for Writing and Discussion

1. "Absurdity" is a key term in existential philosophy. Camus considers Sisyphus to be the prototype of the absurd hero. What does he mean? In your opinion, is it absurd or heroic to be an absurd hero?

2. According to the myth, Sisyphus was displeased with his wife's placing obedience ahead of love. To chastise her was the reason he escaped from the underworld. But once on earth, he found the love of life too strong to resist. Was he being inconsistent with his own views? That is, was he showing self-love instead of love for others? Camus doesn't elaborate on this matter of love, but we may infer from his use of the myth that he believed it wrong of Sisyphus to love life so much. We may also infer that it is important to love others, as the wife apparently did not. From what the introduction has said of Camus' philosophy, can you discuss the place of love for others? Do you agree? Or do you find self-love more rewarding in the long run?

3. Camus allows that Sisyphus is in some respects a tragic figure. He says it is his consciousness that makes him tragic. The difference between him and the average worker in today's society is that the latter is not aware of the absurdity of his condition. Camus also says, however, that it's better to be conscious. Why? Wouldn't it be better for a person never to understand how futile his life is?

4. Are you personally involved in an uphill rock-rolling thing of your own? Is it equally futile? Have you thought of abandoning it? Does Camus' essay offer you a different perspective? Why? Why not?

Alternate Response: describe somebody you know who is engaged in rolling a rock uphill. Is he an absurd hero—or just a fool? If the latter, suggest some alternatives. Why are these better for him? Would he gain Human Worth by choosing one of them? Does he have Human Worth now—in his "absurdity"?

5. If the rock can be conquered in one sense by the absurd hero, it too has its victory in the times when "the images of earth cling too tightly to memory, when the call to happiness becomes too insistent. . . ." Translate these sentiments into concrete terms. What specifically does Camus advise us against doing? Do you agree with the advice?

6. "It happens as well that the feeling of the absurd springs from happiness." By this Camus means that, when one is feeling good about things, he has to stop and wonder whether he is being deluded, lulled into a false sense of security that is ill-founded. One has, in Camus' vision, to work very hard to be realistically happy. Among the sources of happiness rejected by him is religion. Human fate is a "human matter, which must be settled by men." Do you agree? Do you see a continuing role for religion? Can it serve to make life less absurd? Or do you agree with Camus that it is eventually harmful?

EXPERIENCES IN A CONCENTRATION CAMP
Viktor E. Frankl

Viktor E. Frankl (b. 1905) has become Europe's major psychiatrist. He is not only a most sought after consultant, but as a professor at the University of Vienna—long the world's center for psychiatric study—and as president of the Austrian Medical Society for Psychotherapy, he is the founder of what may be the most important new movement since the days of Freud. This movement is based on the theory of *logotherapy* or existential analysis. Disturbed and unhappy people are guided on the road back to mental health by a psychiatrist who helps them locate a sense of meaning and purpose in their lives.

According to Dr. Frankl, no one can endure for long in a state of confusion, a state of aimless and rootless "just being." It is the essence of humanity to seek a higher level of existence in which one says to himself, "I possess Worth because . . ." In treating neurosis, Frankl's school departs from the approach taken by the Freudians, who work from the premise that neurosis is cured by rooting out the unconscious motives behind people's actions and responses to experience. In Freudian psychoanalysis, to understand what is happening inside the mind is to free oneself, to enable one to lead a normal, happy life. But Frankl is not content to stop at this point. It is his belief that people cannot lead normal, happy lives unless those lives seem useful. The logotherapists therefore stress the importance of a sense of responsibility. A major goal is to assist the patient to find those aspects of his life in which he counts the most for other people.

If you read "The Myth of Sisyphus" you already know something about existentialism and can appreciate the purpose behind Frankl's alternate label "existential analysis." For both Frankl and Camus life need have no *ultimate* meaning to become meaningful for each person. Ultimates have a way of not reaching specific individuals anyway. What matters is not why all people exist but *how* each one of us exists. Perceptions, ways of responding to experience, vary sharply. The universal common denominator is that one must put things together in a way that creates meaning and order for him: a day-by-day sense of the continuity of his identity. This is accomplished by a feeling of direction, a feeling that the results of one's choices are important and have significant impact on others. When one is able to achieve a pattern behind his choices, he can be said to have integrity. He can be counted on. He has identified himself. *He has meaning.*

Like Camus also, Frankl stresses the importance of suffering. The following selection from *Man's Search for Meaning* is an intensely personal

541

account of the author's days at Dachau when he and fellow prisoners descended to the lowest depths of Human Nonworth one could imagine. But at this extreme point in life's cruel indifference to a man's dignity Frankl faced the choice the existentialists say comes to each of us: whether to say no or yes; whether to scream in rage and pain, and then give up altogether —or to exercise the option one finds has been there all the time, the option of telling yourself that degradation is not going to happen.

It is the will to mean something to the world that the logotherapists believe is basic to mankind. It is the freedom to mean something that guarantees inner happiness, as it guarantees Human Worth.

Experiences in a Concentration Camp

The attempt to develop a sense of humor and to see things in a humorous light is some kind of a trick learned while mastering the art of living. Yet it is possible to practice the art of living even in a concentration camp, although suffering is omnipresent. To draw an analogy: a man's suffering is similar to the behavior of gas. If a certain quantity of gas is pumped into an empty chamber, it will fill the chamber completely and evenly, no matter how big the chamber. Thus suffering completely fills the human soul and conscious mind, no matter whether the suffering is great or little. Therefore the "size" of human suffering is absolutely relative.

It also follows that a very trifling thing can cause the greatest of joys. Take as an example something that happened on our journey from Auschwitz to the camp affiliated with Dachau. We had all been afraid that our transport was heading for the Mauthausen camp. We became more and more tense as we approached a certain bridge over the Danube which the train would have to cross to reach Mauthausen, according to the statement of experienced traveling companions. Those who have never seen anything similar cannot possibly imagine the dance of joy performed in the carriage by the prisoners when they saw that our transport was not crossing the bridge and was instead heading "only" for Dachau.

And again, what happened on our arrival in that camp, after a journey lasting two days and three nights? There had not been enough room for everybody to crouch on the floor of the carriage at the same time. The majority of us had to stand all the way, while a few took turns at squatting on the scanty straw which was soaked with human urine. When we arrived the first important news that we heard from

Calvin Culp

The attempt to develop a sense of humor and to see things in a human
light is some kind of a trick learned while mastering the art of living.
Viktor E. Frankl

older prisoners was that this comparatively small camp (its population was 2,500) had no "oven," no crematorium, no gas! That meant that a person who had become a "Moslem" could not be taken straight to the gas chamber, but would have to wait until a so-called "sick convoy" had been arranged to return to Auschwitz. This joyful surprise put us all in a good mood. The wish of the senior warden of our hut in Auschwitz had come true: we had come, as quickly as possible, to a camp which did not have a "chimney"—unlike Auschwitz. We laughed and cracked jokes in spite of, and during, all we had to go through in the next few hours.

When we new arrivals were counted, one of us was missing. So we had to wait outside in the rain and cold wind until the missing man was found. He was at last discovered in a hut, where he had fallen asleep from exhaustion. Then the roll call was turned into a punishment parade. All through the night and late into the next morning, we had to stand outside, frozen and soaked to the skin after the strain of our long journey. And yet we were all very pleased! There was no chimney in this camp and Auschwitz was a long way off.

Another time we saw a group of convicts pass our work site. How obvious the relativity of all suffering appeared to us then! We envied those prisoners their relatively well-regulated, secure and happy life. They surely had regular opportunities to take baths, we thought sadly. They surely had toothbrushes and clothesbrushes, mattresses—a separate one for each of them—and monthly mail bringing them news of the whereabouts of their relatives, or at least of whether they were still alive or not. We had lost all that a long time ago.

And how we envied those of us who had the opportunity to get into a factory and work in a sheltered room! It was everyone's wish to have such a lifesaving piece of luck. The scale of relative luck extends even further. Even among those detachments outside the camp (in one of which I was a member) there were some units which were considered worse than others. One could envy a man who did not have to wade in deep, muddy clay on a steep slope emptying the tubs of a small field railway for twelve hours daily. Most of the daily accidents occurred on this job, and they were often fatal.

In other work parties the foremen maintained an apparently local tradition of dealing out numerous blows, which made us talk of the relative luck of not being under their command, or perhaps of being under it only temporarily. Once, by an unlucky chance, I got into such a group. If an air raid alarm had not interrupted us after two hours (during which time the foreman had worked on me especially), making it necessary to regroup the workers afterwards, I think that I would have returned to camp on one of the sledges which carried those who had died or were dying from exhaustion. No one can imagine the relief that the siren can bring in such a situation; not even a boxer who has heard the bell signifying the finish of a round and who is thus saved at the last minute from the danger of a knockout.

We were grateful for the smallest of mercies. We were glad when there was time to delouse before going to bed, although in itself this was no pleasure, as it meant standing naked in an unheated hut where icicles hung from the ceiling. But we were thankful if there was no air raid alarm during this operation and the lights were not switched off. If we could not do the job properly, we were kept awake half the night.

The meager pleasures of camp life provided a kind of negative happiness—"freedom from suffering," as Schopenhauer put it—and even that in a relative way only. Real positive pleasures, even small ones, were very few. I remember drawing up a kind of balance sheet of pleasures one day and finding that in many, many past weeks I had experienced only two pleasurable moments. One occurred when, on returning from work, I was admitted to the cook house after a long wait and was assigned to the line filing up to prisoner-cook F——. He stood behind one of the huge pans and ladled soup into the bowls which were held out to him by the prisoners, who hurriedly filed past. He was the only cook who did not look at the men whose bowls he was filling; the only cook who dealt out the soup equally, regardless of recipient, and who did not make favorites of his personal friends or countrymen, picking out the potatoes for them, while the others got watery soup skimmed from the top.

But it is not for me to pass judgment on those prisoners who put their own people above everyone else. Who can throw a stone at a man who favors his friends under circumstances when, sooner or later, it is a question of life or death? No man should judge unless he asks himself in absolute honesty whether in a similar situation he might not have done the same.

Long after I had resumed normal life again (that means a long time after my release from camp), somebody showed me an illustrated weekly with photographs of prisoners lying crowded on their bunks, staring dully at a visitor. "Isn't this terrible, the dreadful staring faces—everything about it."

"Why?" I asked, for I genuinely did not understand. For at that moment I saw it all again: at 5:00 A.M. it was still pitch dark outside. I was lying on the hard boards in an earthen hut where about seventy of us were "taken care of." We were sick and did not have to leave camp for work; we did not have to go on parade. We could lie all day in our little corner in the hut and doze and wait for the daily distribution of bread (which, of course, was reduced for the sick) and for the daily helping of soup (watered down and also decreased in quantity). But how content we were; happy in spite of everything. While we cowered against each other to avoid any unnecessary loss of warmth, and were too lazy and disinterested to move a finger unnecessarily, we heard shrill whistles and shouts from the square where the night shift had just returned and was assembling for roll call. The door was flung open, and the snowstorm blew into our hut. An exhausted comrade, covered with snow, stumbled inside to sit down for a few minutes. But the senior warden turned him out again. It was strictly forbidden to admit a stranger to a hut while a check-up on the men was in progress. How sorry I was for that fellow and how glad not to be in his skin at that moment, but instead to be sick and able to doze on in the sick quarters! What a lifesaver it was to have two days there, and perhaps even two extra days after those!

All this came to my mind when I saw the photographs in the magazine. When I explained, my listeners understood why I did not find the photograph so terrible: the people in it might not have been so unhappy after all.

On my fourth day in the sick quarters I had just been detailed to the night shift when the chief doctor rushed in and asked me to volunteer for medical duties in another camp containing typhus patients. Against the urgent advice of my friends (and despite the fact that almost none of my colleagues offered their services), I decided to volunteer. I knew that in a working party I would die in a short time. But if I had to die there might at least be some sense in my death. I thought that it would doubtless be more to the purpose to try and help my comrades as a doctor than to vegetate or finally lose my life as the unproductive laborer that I was then.

For me this was simple mathematics, not sacrifice. But secretly, the warrant officer from the sanitation squad had ordered that the two doctors who had volunteered for the typhus camp should be "taken care of" till they left. We looked so weak that he feared that he might have two additional corpses on his hands, rather than two doctors.

I mentioned earlier how everything that was not connected with the immediate task of keeping oneself and one's closest friends alive lost its value. Everything was sacrificed to this end. A man's character became involved to the point that he was caught in a mental turmoil which threatened all the values he held and threw them into doubt. Under the influence of a world which no longer recognized the value of human life and human dignity, which had robbed man of his will and had made him an object to be exterminated (having planned, however, to make full use of him first—to the last ounce of his physical re-sources)—under this influence the personal ego finally suffered a loss of values. If the man in the concentration camp did not struggle against this in a last effort to save his self-respect, he lost the feeling of being an individual, a being with a mind, with inner freedom and personal value. He thought of himself then as only a part of an enormous mass of people; his existence descended to the level of animal life. The men were herded—sometimes to one place then to another; sometimes driven together, then apart—like a flock of sheep without a thought or a will of their own. A small but dangerous pack watched them from all sides, well versed in methods of torture and sadism. They drove the herd incessantly, backwards and forwards, with shouts, kicks and blows. And we, the sheep, thought of two things only —how to evade the bad dogs and how to get a little food.

Just like sheep that crowd timidly into the center of a herd, each of us tried to get into the middle of our formations. That gave one a better chance of avoiding the blows of the guards who were marching on either side and to the front and rear of our column. The central position had the added advantage of affording protection against the bitter winds. It was, therefore, in an attempt to save one's own skin that one literally tried to submerge into the crowd. This was done automatically in the formations. But at other times it was a very conscious effort on our part—in conformity with one of the camp's most imperative laws of self-preservation: Do not be conspicuous. We tried at all times to avoid attracting the attention of the SS.

There were times, of course, when it was possible, and even necessary, to keep away from the crowd. It is well known that an enforced community life, in which attention is paid to everything one does at all times, may result in an irresistible urge to get away, at least for a short while. The prisoner craved to be alone with himself and his thoughts. He yearned for privacy and for solitude. After my transportation to a so-called "rest camp," I had the rare fortune to find solitude for about five minutes at a time. Behind the earthen hut where I worked and in which were crowded about fifty delirious patients, there was a quiet spot in a corner of the double fence of barbed wire surrounding the camp. A tent had been improvised there with a few poles and branches of trees in order to shelter a half-dozen corpses (the daily death rate in the camp). There was also a shaft leading to the water pipes. I squatted on the wooden lid of this shaft whenever my services were not needed. I just sat and looked out at the green flowering slopes and the distant blue hills of the Bavarian landscape, framed by the meshes of barbed wire. I dreamed longingly, and my thoughts wandered north and northeast, in the direction of my home, but I could only see clouds.

The corpses near me, crawling with lice, did not bother me. Only the steps of passing guards could rouse me from my dreams; or perhaps it would be a call to the sick-bay or to collect a newly arrived supply of medicine for my hut—consisting of perhaps five or ten tablets of aspirin, to last for several days for fifty patients. I collected them and then did my rounds, feeling the patients' pulses and giving half-tablets to the serious cases. But the desperately ill received no medicine. It would not have helped, and besides, it would have deprived those for whom there was still some hope. For light cases, I had nothing, except perhaps a word of encouragement. In this way I dragged myself from patient to patient, though I myself was weak and exhausted from a serious attack of typhus. Then I went back to my lonely place on the wood cover of the water shaft.

This shaft, incidentally, once saved the lives of three fellow prisoners. Shortly before liberation, mass transports were organized to go to Dachau, and these three prisoners wisely tried to avoid the trip. They climbed down the shaft and hid there from the guards. I calmly sat on the lid, looking innocent and playing a childish game of throwing pebbles at the barbed wire. On spotting me, the guard hesitated for a moment, but then passed on. Soon I could tell the three men below that the worst danger was over.

It is very difficult for an outsider to grasp how very little value was placed on human life in camp. The camp inmate was hardened, but possibly became more conscious of this complete disregard of human existence when a convoy of sick men was arranged. The emaciated bodies of the sick were thrown on two-wheeled carts which were drawn by prisoners for many miles, often through snowstorms, to the next camp. If one of the sick men had died before the cart left, he was thrown on anyway—the list had to be correct! The list was the only thing that mattered. A man counted only because he had a prison number. One literally became a number: dead or alive—that was unimportant; the life of a "number" was completely irrelevant. What stood behind that number and that life mattered even less: the fate, the history, the name of the man. In the transport of sick patients that I, in my capacity as a doctor, had to accompany from one camp in Bavaria to another, there was a young prisoner whose brother was not on the list and therefore would have to be left behind. The young man begged so long that the camp warden decided to work an exchange, and the brother took the place of a man who, at the moment, preferred to stay behind. But the list had to be correct! That was easy. The brother just exchanged numbers with the other prisoner.

As I have mentioned before, we had no documents; everyone was lucky to own his body, which, after all, was still breathing. All else about us, i.e., the rags hanging from our gaunt skeletons, was only of interest if we were assigned to a transport of sick patients. The departing "Moslems" were examined with unabashed curiosity to see whether their coats or shoes were not better than one's own. After all, their fates were sealed. But those who stayed behind in camp, who were still capable of some work, had to make use of every means to improve their chances of survival. They were not sentimental. The prisoners saw themselves completely dependent on the moods of the guards—playthings of fate—and this made them even less human than the circumstances warranted.

In Auschwitz I had laid down a rule for myself which proved to be a good one and which most of my comrades later followed. I generally answered all kinds of questions truthfully. But I was silent about anything that was not expressly asked for. If I were asked my age, I gave it. If asked about my profession, I said "doctor," but did not elaborate. The first morning in Auschwitz an SS officer came to the parade ground. We had to fall into separate groups of prisoners over forty years, under forty years, metal workers, mechanics, and so forth. Then we were examined for ruptures and some prisoners had to form a new group. The group that I was in was driven to another hut, where we lined up again. After being sorted out once more and having answered questions as to my age and profession, I was sent to another small group. Once more we were driven to another hut and grouped differently. This continued for some time, and I became quite unhappy, finding myself among strangers who spoke unintelligible foreign languages. Then came the last selection, and I found myself back in the group that had been with me in the first hut! They had barely noticed that I had been sent from hut to hut in the meantime. But I was aware that in those few minutes fate had passed me in many different forms.

When the transport of sick patients for the "rest camp" was organized, my name (that is, my number) was put on the list, since a few doctors were needed. But no one was convinced that the destination was really a rest camp. A few weeks previously the same transport had been prepared. Then, too, everyone had thought that it was destined for the gas ovens. When it was announced that anyone who volunteered for the dreaded night shift would be taken off the transport list, eighty-two prisoners volunteered immediately. A quarter of an hour later the transport was canceled, but the eighty-two stayed on the list for the night shift. For the majority of them, this meant death within the next fortnight.

Now the transport for the rest camp was arranged for the second time. Again no one knew whether this was a ruse to obtain the last bit of work from the sick—if only for fourteen days—or whether it would go to the gas ovens or to a genuine rest camp. The chief doctor, who had taken a liking to me, told me furtively one evening at a quarter to ten, "I have made it known in the orderly room that you can still have your name crossed off the list; you may do so up till ten o'clock."

I told him that this was not my way; that I had learned to let fate take its course. "I might as well stay with my friends," I said. There was a look of pity in his eyes, as if he knew. . . . He shook my hand silently, as though it were a farewell, not for life, but from life. Slowly I walked back to my hut. There I found a good friend waiting for me.

"You really want to go with them?" he asked sadly.

"Yes, I am going."

Tears came to his eyes and I tried to comfort him. Then there was something else to do—to make my will:

"Listen, Otto, if I don't get back home to my wife, and if you should see her again, then tell her that I talked of her daily, hourly. You remember. Secondly, I have loved her more than anyone. Thirdly, the short time I have been married to her outweighs everything, even all we have gone through here."

Otto, where are you now? Are you alive? What has happened to you since our last hour together? Did you find your wife again? And do you remember how I made you learn my will by heart—word for word—in spite of your childlike tears?

The next morning I departed with the transport. This time it was not a ruse. We were not heading for the gas chambers, and we actually did go to a rest camp. Those who had pitied me remained in a camp where famine was to rage even more fiercely than in our new camp. They tried to save themselves, but they only sealed their own fates. Months later, after liberation, I met a friend from the old camp. He related to me how he, as camp policeman, had searched for a piece of human flesh that was missing from a pile of corpses. He confiscated it from a pot in which he found it cooking. Cannibalism had broken out. I had left just in time.

Does this not bring to mind the story of Death in Teheran? A rich and mighty Persian once walked in his garden with one of his servants. The servant cried that he had just encountered Death, who had threatened him. He begged his master to give him his fastest horse so that he could make haste and flee to Teheran, which he could reach that same evening. The master consented and the servant galloped off on the horse. On returning to his house the master himself met Death, and questioned him, "Why did you terrify and threaten my servant?" "I did not threaten him; I only showed surprise in still finding him here when I planned to meet him tonight in Teheran," said Death.

RESPONSES: Questions for Writing and Discussion

1. The "size" of human suffering is "absolutely relative"; suffering for any reason overtakes and overwhelms us. But the author says it is also true that the most "trifling thing can cause the greatest of joys." Do you take advantage of this fact? Are you prone to allow suffering for even the most trifling things to conquer your spirit? If your answer to the first question is yes, share with the class your formula for joy. If it is no, share, if you wish, your tendencies to suffer. Can someone help you do something about it?

2. Dr. Frankl describes how the new arrivals at Dachau envied the convicts they saw passing by because their life was blessed with books, toothbrushes, and mattresses. It is no doubt true that we seldom appreciate some of our basic resources for living until we are deprived of them. If you were suddenly taken prisoner as Dr. Frankl was, solely because of your ethnic background, and deprived without warning of all your everyday advantages, what would you especially miss? Does this supposing help you to see your life in a different perspective?

3. Can freedom from suffering become a source of pleasure? Or is the author excusing the Germans—and life itself for that matter— too readily? When little things like being able to "delouse" before retiring bring a great sense of well-being, is something radically wrong? Where? To whom does one complain? In the face of extreme adversity, is it better to hope for more than the mere absence of pain? If you had been a fellow prisoner, would you have taken the author's stoic path or tried somehow to get a revolutionary plot going?

4. Is the author too incredibly understanding? While he recognizes the virtues of "prisoner-cook F.," who ladled out soup equally to all, he refuses to pass judgment on the less human, "those prisoners who put their own people above everyone else." Existentialism is like that, however. It stresses one's personal responsibility toward others, but it warns that one must learn to accept and live with less responsible behavior from others. Is it better to let off steam and show resentment and anger toward some people? Are you of a forgiving nature? Do you harbor grudges? Have you ever entertained thoughts of revenge? In either case, are you satisfied with your life style? Are you glad you tend to feel the way you do in instances involving the irresponsibility of others?

5. Logotherapy operates on the premise that human dignity and self-respect are under the control of the will. That is, one need not give up his sense of Worth, of meaningfulness, if he does not wish to, no matter what terrible hardships are inflicted upon him. Have you ever been in a situation where you preserved your Worth solely through an act of will? Where you could *not* do so?

6. The selection concludes with the revelation that cannibalism

had broken out in the camp before the author's "just in time" departure. He continues "Does not this bring to mind the story of Death in Teheran?" What does that story have to do with the fact that Dr. Frankl escaped the camp's cannibalistic phase? Is there some more pervasive general lesson to be drawn from this parable?

7. The author writes in a somewhat matter-of-fact style, usually devoid of much emotion. For the most part he prefers to state what happened in the camp in a simple and objective manner. It is astonishing how much better we can feel about the sources of unhappiness in our lives simply by altering the way in which we think and talk about them. Select one experience that you believe is still causing you unhappiness, one that perhaps involves strong feelings of anger toward people or circumstances that oppressed you. Share it with the class, but tell it or write it in Dr. Frankl's cool, detached style. Then describe whether you feel better or worse about it.

MEMORIAL RAIN
Archibald MacLeish

There is probably no such thing as a "typical" American poet, but **Archibald MacLeish (b. 1892)**, like Whitman, can no doubt claim to be highly representative. Throughout a long and distinguished career MacLeish has been an active man of affairs, not simply the dedicated, attic-bound man of letters, enveloped in clouds of metaphor, responsive only to the sound of his own distant drum. He has been college professor (Cambridge, Harvard, Amherst); librarian of Congress; director of the United States Office of Facts and Figures; assistant Secretary of State during the Roosevelt administration; and an American delegate to UNESCO.

Again like Whitman, and also like Emerson, MacLeish thinks in epic terms. His philosophy is rooted in nature and the miraculous operations of natural law. His theme is the continually renewing youth and vigor of nature which pushes for new beginnings out of the passing away of old orders. MacLeish's poetry also expresses a deep love of America as the life-affirming land where total defeat is unknown and death, whether physical or spiritual, is always the start of a new cycle.

Memorial Rain

Ambassador Puser the ambassador
Reminds himself in French, the felicitous tongue,
What these (young men no longer) lie here for
In rows that once, and somewhere else, were young—

    All night in Brussels the wind had tugged at my door:
    I had heard the wind at my door and the trees strung
    Taut, and to me who had never been before
    In that country it was a strange wind blowing
    Steadily, stiffening the walls, the floor,
    The roof of my room. I had not slept for knowing
    He too, dead, was a stranger in that land
    And felt beneath the earth in the wind's flowing
    A tightening of roots and would not understand,
    Remembering lake winds in Illinois,
    That strange wind. I had felt his bones in the sand
    Listening.

             —Reflects that these enjoy
Their country's gratitude, that deep repose,
That peace no pain can break, no hurt destroy,
That rest, that sleep—

             At Ghent the wind rose.
    There was a smell of rain and a heavy drag
    Of wind in the hedges but not as the wind blows
    Over fresh water when the waves lag
    Foaming and the willows huddle and it will rain:
    I felt him waiting.

Have made America—

             —Indicates the flag
Which (may he say) enisles in Flanders' plain
This little field these happy, happy dead

             In the ripe grain
    The wind coiled glistening, darted, fled,
    Dragging its heavy body: at Waereghem
    The wind coiled in the grass above his head:
    Waiting—listening—

             —Dedicates to them
This earth their bones have hallowed, this last gift
A grateful country—

Under the dry grass stem
The words are blurred, are thickened, the words sift
Confused by the rasp of the wind, by the thin grating
Of ants under the grass, the minute shift
And tumble of dusty sand separating
From dusty sand. The roots of the grass strain,
Tighten, the earth is rigid, waits—he is waiting—
And suddenly, and all at once, the rain!

The people scatter, they run into houses, the wind
Is trampled under the rain, shakes free, is again
Trampled. The rain gathers, running in thinned
Spurts of water that ravel in the dry sand
Seeping into the sand under the grass roots, seeping
Between cracked boards to the bones of a clenched hand:
The earth relaxes, loosens; he is sleeping,
He rests, he is quiet, he sleeps in a strange land.

DURING WIND AND RAIN

Thomas Hardy[1]

They sing their dearest songs—
He, she, all of them—yea,
Treble and tenor and bass,
    And one to play;
With the candles mooning each face. . . .
    Ah, no; the years O!
How the sick leaves reel down in throngs!

They clear the creeping moss—
Elders and juniors—aye,
Making the pathway neat
    And the garden gay;
And they build a shady seat. . . .
    Ah, no; the years, the years;
See, the white storm-birds wing across!

Reprinted by permission of the Macmillan Company from *Collected Poems* by Thomas Hardy.

[1] (For a commentary on Hardy as a poet, see p. 155).

Robert Thomason

Down their carved names the rain-drop ploughs. *Thomas Hardy*

They are blithely breakfasting all—
Men and maidens—yea,
Under the summer tree,
   With a glimpse of the bay,
While pet fowl come to the knee. . . .
     Ah, no; the years O!
And the rotten rose is ript from the wall.

They change to a high new house,
He, she, all of them—aye,
Clocks and carpets, and chairs
   On the lawn all day,
And brightest things that are theirs. . . .
     Ah, no; the years, the years;
Down their carved names the rain-drop ploughs.

LET ME OUT
Michael Benedikt

Michael Benedikt (b. 1937), as the following poem suggests, is very much of and into contemporary New York. He studied at New York University and Columbia and has been involved in almost every phase of the New York avant-garde movement in the arts. He has written cinema and art criticism, been an interpreter of The Beatles and Bob Dylan, translated plays and poems from diverse foreign languages, produced several "happenings" on both the stage and screen, taught poetry at Sarah Lawrence College, and written words and music for a number of songs. As he further suggests in "Let Me Out," Benedikt is no stranger to the cocktail parties and other gatherings of the "in" crowd, though he appears to have become jaded from the incessant activity.

Those who approach poetry as a sacred mystery, as something scarcely to be breathed on, might—on the evidence of this one example—deny that Benedikt is a genuine poet in addition to his other professions. It is not evidently rhythmic, nor is it filled with metaphors or images, unless one is willing to say that the picture of somebody pouring "old onion soup down the toilet" is an image (isn't it?). It is not abstract or profoundly philosophical. It *is* straight talk: a bunch of real feelings shot squarely at the reader and aimed at some more fundamental source of honesty and truth than either the mind or the romantic emotions to which poetry often appeals.

Whatever expectations one entertains from a poem, the genuineness of these sentiments is hard to dismiss. Benedikt does not fool around. Here there is not even the selfish joy poets often take in their own brilliance or the beauty of their language. "Let Me Out" is intended as pure anguish. It is as direct as communication can be. Perhaps that is what makes it a poem.

Let Me Out

Let me out! Let me out! I wasn't made to pour old onion
 soup down the toilet, I wasn't made to suffer from this
 dreadful cold
And the boy from the grocery store who is wearing this
 big cowboy hat and the fringed shirt and peddling
 the bicycle with the big basket for food is saying, look!
 my soul is beautiful, too.
Oh William Wordsworth and the other 19th century poets
 from whose dear Romanticism I first drew hints
You have hinted me very well beyond myself
And now when I write poetry I don't know what I am
 saying anymore, only what I'm doing
I even noticed that my loves weren't what they should be,
 thanks a lot, thanks a lot
Although surely all ladies with nice waists tiny tits and
 exquisite globèd asses shall continue to be superb
Let me out! I want to fly without having to stop at the
 airline terminal
I want to say farewell forever even to the departure points
 of La Guardia and Kennedy airports in New York
No, no, explicators; that doesn't mean I'd prefer to use
 Newark airport, after all dangerous Leroi Jones lives
 in Newark
Leroi, Leroi, do you want me to come to your neighborhood
 in Newark; if you don't, I won't
Leroi, do you remember the time you crashed that
 abominable cocktail party with your old friend, tall,
 enormous and powerful Charles Olson?
You both just entered, made three telephone calls (one
 long distance), and disappeared in one corner with
 the plate of hors d'oeuvres (Leroi, that must have been
 long ago, before the invention of soul food)
What is Leroi Jones doing in this poem, anyway, is he

making me immortal or am I making him immortal;
    certainly we are large this evening.
Tonight, after supper and an appropriate smoke, my cat
    started whispering to me, tales of the stockyards, and
    the sufferings she knows; for example the sufferings
    of beef on the hoof even as it is removed from the hoof
    for my supper, by blows on the brain
Oh big blows collapse us all now, it is our own heads we hit,
    our own arms.
It is obvious all this, although it is obvious only temporarily
    during certain high moments certainly
And I agree with the recent revolutionary who said to
    me after our talk after our poetry reading: "It is in your
    poems alone that you speak prose for us"
But also with the host of the abominable cocktail party,
    whose fate it has been to be bitter forever
When will we see when will we really see we are the
    same and who was it anyway that the revolutionary meant
    when he referred to himself as me, and me, as "you"?
Who is speaking here anyway, can it possibly be me?—
    What is "here" and where is "I"?
And how will it be possible to fly with all this great
    weight of sadness and deliberation
Yes even United Airlines says we are five pounds overweight
    but as far as I'm concerned I'm 155 pounds overweight
I wonder how it would be to fly now I wonder what it
    would be like if love were really endlessly desirable
    possible and present
Let me out. Let me out! LET ME OUT!

LIVE

Anne Sexton

Anne Sexton's (b. 1928) poetry offers a unique blending of yesterday and today. It is respectful toward the literary past; it communicates through imagery, rhythm, and the precision of language. At the same time her poetry expresses the complexities of feminine experience in ways that were not possible given the conventions of poetic style and language that used to dominate traditional poems. Anne Sexton is a modern woman in a sophisticated Eastern seaboard world of martinis, smart talk, broken marriages, abortions, pills, death longings, and suicides. Her poetic province is the inner world of feminine emotions, insights, intelligence, and anguish. She is a recorder of the sensitive feminine response to a world in which she often finds herself a stranger.

Some of Anne Sexton's poems express the hopelessness of trying to live with two identities: that of the wife-mother and that of the human being with feelings and needs which lie outside the familiar domain of kitchen and nursery. At the same time a poem such as "Live" manages somehow to wring life-affirmation out of the unlikely material of everyday desperation.

Live

Live or die, but don't poison everything . . .

Well, death's been here
for a long time—
it has a hell of a lot
to do with hell
and suspicion of the eye
and the religious objects
and how I mourned them
when they were made obscene
by my dwarf-heart's doodle.
The chief ingredient
is mutilation.
And mud, day after day,
mud like a ritual,
and the baby on the platter,
cooked but still human,
cooked also with little maggots,
sewn onto it may be by somebody's mother,
the damn bitch!

Even so,
I kept right on going on,
a sort of human statement,
lugging myself as if
I were a sawed-off body
in the trunk, the steamer trunk.
This became a perjury of the soul.

It became an outright lie
and even though I dressed the body
it was still naked, still killed.
It was caught
in the first place at birth,
like a fish.
But I played it, dressed it up,
dressed it up like somebody's doll.
Is life something you play?
And all the time wanting to get rid of it?
And further, everyone yelling at you
to shut up. And no wonder!
People don't like to be told
that you're sick
and then be forced
to watch
you
come
down with the hammer.

Today life opened inside me like an egg
and there inside
after considerable digging
I found the answer.
What a bargain!
There was the sun,
her yolk moving feverishly,
tumbling her prize—
and you realize that she does this daily!
I'd known she was a purifier
but I hadn't thought
she was solid,
hadn't known she was an answer.
God! It's a dream,
lovers sprouting in the yard
like celery stalks
and better,
a husband straight as a redwood,
two daughters, two sea urchins,
picking roses off my hackles.
If I'm on fire they dance around it
and cook marshmallows.
And if I'm ice
they simply skate on me

in little ballet costumes.

Here,
all along,
thinking I was a killer,
anointing myself daily
with my little poisons.
But no.
I'm an empress.
I wear an apron.
My typewriter writes.
It didn't break the way it warned.
Even crazy, I'm as nice
as a chocolate bar.
Even with the witches' gymnastics
they trust my incalculable city,
my corruptible bed.

O dearest three,
I make a soft reply.
The witch comes on
and you paint her pink.
I come with kisses in my hood
and the sun, the smart one,
rolling in my arms.
So I say *Live*
and turn my shadow three times round
to feed our puppies as they come,
the eight Dalmatians we didn't drown,
despite the warnings: The abort! The destroy!
Despite the pails of water that waited
to drown them, to pull them down like stones,
they came, each one headfirst,
blowing bubbles the color of cataract-blue
and fumbling for the tiny tits.
Just last week, eight Dalmatians,
¾ of a lb., lined up like cord wood
each
like a
birch tree.
I promise to love more if they come,
because in spite of cruelty
and the stuffed railroad cars for the ovens,
I am not what I expected. Not an Eichmann.

The poison just didn't take.
So I won't hang around in my hospital shift,
repeating The Black Mass and all of it.
I say *Live, Live* because of the sun,
the dream, the excitable gift.

February the last, 1966

COME IN
Robert Frost

As I came to the edge of the woods,
Thrush music—hark!
Now if it was dusk outside,
Inside it was dark.

Too dark in the woods for a bird
By sleight of wing
To better its perch for the night,
Though it still could sing.

The last of the light of the sun
That had died in the west
Still lived for one song more
In a thrush's breast.

Far in the pillared dark
Thrush music went—
Almost like a call to come in
To the dark and lament.

But no, I was out for stars:
I would not come in.
I meant not even if asked;
And I hadn't been.

APPENDIX OF ACTIONS

I: ORIENTATION

Thomas Jefferson: *The Ideal Curriculum*

It is impossible for either parents or students to understand the complexities of curriculum planning and entrance policies unless they themselves have participated in the process. Why not take this opportunity to become a participant?

Divide the class into three groups: Concerned Parents (CP), Dissatisfied Students (DS), and Resolute Faculty (RF). The eventual aim is for the groups to come together to form a Council on Higher Education for Utopiaville, USA, and to draft a statement which will include:

1. The aims and objectives of higher education in a free society.
2. A step-by-step description of the various stages of the educational system, similar to the one provided by Jefferson in his letter. (Hint: the trick is to make #1 and #2 consistent with each other.)
3. A list of student rights.
4. A list of faculty rights.
5. A clear indication of the role of the parents and the extent to which either students or faculty should be answerable to them.
6. A principle for financing this system which will be consistent with its objectives and with the rights of all concerned. (For example: if all the money comes from the taxpayers, #1-#5 ought to take this into account; if only some of it comes from the taxpayers and the rest from private sources, then the complexion of things will be different. If students work and pay for their own education, it may be that they have more rights than either faculty or parents—or do they? And so on.)

To preclude aimless discussion, it would be a good idea for each group to meet privately beforehand and draft a list of recommendations. CP's, DS's, and RF's generally have definite views anyway. Seldom do groups made up of three such elements *begin* with an understanding of each other's problems. If the demands are tight and each group unanimous, then the meeting of the council will achieve a high degree of reality-simulation.

When the Utopian Statement is achieved, it might be interesting to measure it against actual conditions on your campus and to determine some of the reasons for discrepancies. It might also be enlightening to discuss the problems you encountered in reaching agreement. Perhaps these will contain valuable clues to help you understand the educational picture at the current moment.

Harvard Committee on Governance: *The Values and Purposes of the University*

Let us suppose that a wealthy merchant has just died and left your college five million dollars with one proviso, stated thus in his will:

> The money is to be handed over to whatever group shall prove to my family's satisfaction that it has the soundest and at the same time the most visionary and progressive plan for improving the quality of education at _____ College. I attended this institution as a youth and have mixed feelings about its value to my subsequent economic success. Many courses frankly bored me. In fact, I cannot truthfully say that I *learned* anything useful until I became an apprentice in the business which I was later to turn into an international corporation. But if five million dollars can purchase a sound education, if five million dollars can help today's students get more out of college than I did, then I give it gladly.

The task facing the class is to find a way to earn the grant without causing the man's family to fear that the money, not the improvement of education, is uppermost in anyone's mind.

If possible, an outside group should be invited in to play the role of the family—perhaps some interested alumni or members of the community. They are to be shown the "will" and told that they may decide whether or not to award the grant, depending upon the persuasiveness of those who seek it. (If it proves too difficult to go so far from the campus, perhaps other faculty members could play the roles.)

The next step is to create the groups which will compete for the five million dollars. The following "camps" seem logical enough:

1. *Administration* (perhaps actual administrators would be willing to participate). They will have to convince the bereaved family that they possess the necessary overview to make them the wisest spenders of the money in the best interest of the faculty, the student body, and the community.
2. *The "pragmatic" faculty* (consisting of those who teach the sciences and professional skill courses). They will have to convince the family that they have the most to offer the students and, of course, the community and that the role of the administration is often to keep the peace among all the faculty, thus discriminating against those who know best how to use the money.
3. *The "classical" faculty* (consisting of those who teach literature, philosophy, languages, the fine arts, and so on). They will have to convince the family that the deceased millionaire was cynical about his college education because he undoubtedly had never taken enough "classical" courses detached from immediate practicality, but dealing with higher matters. They should lean heavily on the recommendations in the Harvard report. It may also be in their best interest to take the position that many of the sciences do not

offer students very much in the way of resources for future living.

4. *Students who want some control over the curriculum.* They will have to convince the family that neither the administration nor the faculty really thinks about *them* and that only they are in a position to know what they want education to do for their future lives.

The bereaved family, with no preconceived bias, knows only that the departed spent his whole life around the conference table, making big deals and, that if he had any enjoyment at all, he derived it from his financial successes. They may be wondering whether his life was a happy one or an unfulfilled one. As they listen to the various arguments, they must ask themselves *honestly* what there is about education that seems to make the most sense. They may question the different groups freely, and should listen carefully as the groups question and interact with each other. They may then decide to award all of the money to one group, give varying portions of it to different groups, or keep it for themselves. After the decision is made, the session should be analyzed carefully and the implications pulled together.

B. F. Skinner: *Training Children for Self-Control*

An obvious and intriguing way of testing out Skinner's theories is to actually try lollipop (or soup or cookie) experiments with children at a nursery school, but, since neither the authorities in charge nor the parents are likely to sympathize with the disinterested scientific pursuit of truth, it is better to restrict the Action to your own campus.

If your instructor can find another instructor willing to collaborate on the grand experiment, go into a different class, where one of you may announce that permission has been granted for your class to control the destiny of that class for this one day. Whatever happens, their instructor will abide by your decisions, recommendations, grades, and so on. (This is to prevent snickering and a general "so what" attitude.)

One half of your class will then take one half of the others to an adjoining room or any other place available. They will become the Permissively Indulged (PI) group. The other half of your class will work with the Behaviorally Trained (BT) group.

For the lucky PI folks: Announce that there will be a free and unstructured period but that *something has to happen* (if not, they will all receive zeros for the day!). They will be given no instructions whatsoever, but they cannot simply sit there and talk. Their creative resources will be duly observed and evaluated (by mutual agreement of the "teachers").

For the BT people: Announce that the theme subject for the day is "How It Feels To Be Controlled by Another Class." They are to write exactly 250 words on the subject. The paper is to be neat and free of grammatical and spelling errors. There are to be carefully observed margins on either side. There is to be no talking. The "teachers" will patrol the classroom, making certain everyone gets down to business. The regular instructor should, of course, agree to abide by the grades given to the themes with no objections being entertained at that time.

After a clearly specified amount of time has elapsed, bring both groups back together and discuss the contrasting experiences:

1. Did the PI group have trouble working without any instructions?
2. Did they find that such permissiveness proved to be more constricting than detailed instructions would have been?
3. Was it the threat of being punished with zeros that forced them into action? (Or did they rebel and refuse to do anything at all? Did the promised punishment play a part in the rebellion?)
4. Were they silly and uncontrollable because they had been used to being told what to do?
5. Did the BT group resent the tight conditions under which they were compelled to work? (Did they believe they would really receive a grade for the theme? Suppose you told them that no one was kidding after all? How would they feel about *that*?)
6. Did anyone in the BT group believe it was easier to work when he knew what was expected of him, disciplined as the experience was?
7. Would the class as a whole prefer to be more permissively or more behavioristically handled? Or would they prefer something in between? Such as?

John Stuart Mill: *The Natural Equality of the Sexes*

Self-sacrifice, according to Mill, does not come naturally to women any more than it does to men. It is an attribute of the feminine role as defined by a male-dominated society. Still, one wonders how many men do indeed admire and envy this quality in a woman, thinking of it as something they are fortunate to discover rather than as something they themselves are creating. How many women believe self-sacrifice is not only natural to their sex but a virtue of which they may be justly proud?

Test out the proposition *Women are innately more self-sacrificing than men.*

First, have each member of the class think of some situation of crisis requiring a response that can be described either as sacrificing or non-sacrificing. This can be written down on an index card.

All the cards are placed in a hat or a box. The participants then go to the front of the room one by one, and draw a card. Each reads his situation, then responds immediately, indicating how the crisis would be handled if it were happening to him or to her. The class then votes S or N-S, with the tally made on the spot. Two or three minutes should be allowed for a consideration of whether the person's sex had anything to do with his response, whether the selfishness or unselfishness was natural or role imposed, and, where applicable, whether the response seemed honest. After all the responses have been made, it may be enlightening to determine the ratio of S votes for women as opposed to men and also the part played by the voter's sex in influencing his vote in every instance. Did men liberally bestow S ratings on women? Did women hold back from doing so? Did men tend to vote N-S for other men? Or did women do this? And in all cases—why? Another question worth analyzing is whether some N-S votes were given to S-intended answers because the voters suspected insincerity.

Here's a sample situation:

Exams are over. You have been studying day and night for a week. You can't wait to break loose and have a good time. You have been invited to a great weekend away from the campus or home and have looked forward to it for months. But your father has to make a business trip and wants to take your mother, who hasn't had a vacation in a long time. Nobody will be home to stay with your younger sister. They implore you to give up your weekend.

Try responding yourself. Do you think your sex influenced your decision? In what way? And if so, do you consider your approach to be natural to your sex or the result of shaping forces?

If you gave an S response but wonder how honest you were, you could read the situation to a close friend, indicate how you answered, and then ask whether such sacrifice appears consistent with the way your character generally comes across.

Mark Twain: *Passages from the Diaries of Adam and Eve*

Let us be as fanciful as Mark Twain was in reconstructing the story of Adam and Eve. Let us say that, despite Eve's final entry in her diary, wherein she accepts Adam's right to rule over her, she has had second thoughts. In her opinion Adam has abused his role as lord and master and has made life intolerable for her. Eve feels that her punishment is unjust and that, in reconsidering the facts, she finds Adam to be at least equally at fault in the matter of the apples. She therefore petitions the local court to review the case and advise Adam to alter his role.

Have the "second hearing" of Eve right in the classroom. The long suffering wife should be played by a member of the class who feels satisfied she has studied the selections from the diary carefully enough to build a strong case against Adam's tyranny. Adam should be played by a male who is firmly convinced that Eve cannot be trusted with equal status. The judge can be either male or female but has to be someone who agrees to remain as objective as possible (though the judge's sex may have to be reckoned with when the class as a whole reviews the case). Finally, there should be a jury composed of six men and six women, who must reach a unanimous verdict.

A variety of witnesses can be called in, depending upon how complex the class wishes the project to become: perhaps a minister—to solve the problem from the traditional point of view; perhaps the mothers of both Adam and Eve—to allow for a consideration of the matriarchal influence on the development of their offspring's sex roles; perhaps Eve's psychiatrist;

even the serpent ("I was a rascal, but nobody forced her to be tempted");
perhaps a neighbor who witnessed the whole thing.

After the testimony, the jury should be given a limited amount of time
for deliberation. If no verdict is reached, the class as a whole will want to
discuss possible reasons. Or if the jury does make a decision, will everyone
agree with it?

Virginia Woolf: *If Shakespeare'd Had a Brilliant Sister*

Since the implications and ramifications of the material with which Virginia
Woolf is concerned are very broad and highly significant, it might be advisable to spend more time on it than one would normally devote to so
brief a selection.

Divide into small groups, each of which is charged with the task of
gathering enough data about a particular era to indulge in an imaginative
bit of role-playing. To be specific: Each group will come to class prepared
to act out a scene of, say, five minutes' duration which involves the wife,
sister, mother, or daughter of some well-known figure in history. There
should be a crisis, and the group should show how *the feminine role* played
by the main character affects the working out of the problem. For example,
if the group were doing Judith Shakespeare, it might offer a family scene
in which the gifted young lady is announcing that she is pregnant but
would rather be an unwed mother than marry a man with whom she can
find no permanent happiness. The girl playing Judith would try to ask
provocative questions that really force the "family" to think and respond
in a manner appropriate to the period.

Here's a list of possible situations for developing:

1. Having become the First Lady, Martha Washington wishes to go
   to college to receive the education she feels she has been denied.
2. Nero's wife wants a divorce.
3. The wife of Richard the Lion-hearted wants to accompany him
   on the Crusades.
4. Ulysses returns from the Trojan War—after twenty years—only
   to find that Penelope, believing him dead, has remarried and
   borne four children to her new husband.
5. Socrates' mother wants to help her son escape from jail.
6. The daughter of a high-ranking cabinet official in the 1920s is
   "busted" for possession of bathtub gin.

If these or other situations are approached with the utmost seriousness
and an adequate amount of preliminary research, the role-playing should
provide the basis for a good learning experience. In evaluating what each
group does, the members of the class should be on the lookout for
anachronisms: that is, using contemporary attitudes as substitutes for
historical data.

A variation of this Action is to change the sex-role emphasis, asking
some of the groups to try to show the constraints under which men had

to operate because of the rigid expectations of their behavior entertained by the society of a given period.

Another variation, especially if time does not permit preliminary research, is to make up contemporary situations and have the groups present two versions of the same scene—one devised by a female, the other by a male—and then to subject each to class analysis.

Marya Mannes: *Female Intelligence: Who Wants It?*

This essay was written in 1960, when the push for women's liberation was barely in its infancy. If Alvin Toffler is right and the rate at which change takes place keeps accelerating, then many things must have happened in the intervening years to alter the conditions under which woman in America exist. Or have they? Why not construct a series of questions for each member of the class to ask students on the campus stopped at random? The data may prove helpful in bringing everyone up to date on the sex-role problem. After the questionnaire is constructed, it should be answered by the members of this class *first*. The results can later be compared with the responses given by the random-selection method. It will be interesting to determine whether the study of sex roles has had appreciable effect on the class members' attitudes.

Here are some sample questions that might be useful.

For women only:
1. Why are you going to college?
2. Do you expect to get married?
3. Do you hope to get married?
4. Do you want to get married?
(Repeat #2–4 substituting "have children" for "get married.")
5. If you receive an attractive offer of marriage before you receive your degree, will you leave school?
6. If the answer to the above question is yes, do you think not having completed your education will interfere with a successful marriage?
7. If you answered no to #5, are you saying that education is more important than marriage at least until it has been completed?
8. Under what conditions might you someday be forced to consider that your marriage had not worked out?

For men only:
1. Do you expect to get married?
2. Do you hope to get married?
3. Do you want to get married?
(Repeat #1–3, substituting "have children" for "get married.")
4. Do you tend to date girls of very evident intelligence?
5. Describe your ideal female companion as you currently envision her.
6. Would you object to your wife's working?
7. What if she were earning a higher salary than you?
8. How would you feel if your wife wrote a best seller and became wealthy and famous?

Irwin Shaw: *The Eighty-Yard Run*

Divide into small groups of men and small groups of women. (If the class does not contain persons of both sexes, the exercise can be done anyway. All that will be missing is the comparison of notes at the end.) The task is for each group to make a list of the ten qualities that a consensus finds to be the elements which define and characterize a man. Direct, honest feelings are encouraged, rather than social custom. Participants are urged to suggest anything that strikes them as being valid, no matter how silly or unconventional it may sound. It should not be assumed, for example, that anatomical considerations must (or must not) predominate. The whole idea is to confront the term "man" and try as sincerely as possible to zero in on the concept.

After each group has compiled its list, it should then begin the arduous process of putting the qualities in rank order, from one to ten. "Ten" will be that characteristic which, in the group's opinion, can most readily be sacrificed without losing the "essential man." Number "One" will obviously be the thing that is least dispensable.

When the rank ordering is completed, the community should convene for a sharing of the lists. The significance of the order should be analyzed in each instance. The following are some questions that may prove useful:

1. Was stereotyping evident?
2. Did the group seem to be making a conscious effort to avoid stereotyping? If so, how convincing did its list appear?
3. If the group was composed of males, did the qualities and the ordering of them appear to be what men or society demands?
4. If the group was composed of females, did the qualities and the ordering of them appear to be what men really think? What females really desire? What females think men want them to desire? And so on.
5. Did the list reflect any of the values of Christian Darling in Shaw's story?
6. If the answer to #5 is no, have times changed, or did the reading of the story perhaps make a difference?
7. Was the list typical of what society as a whole might have agreed upon?
8. If a person went out and attempted to live up to the ideals on the list, how would he fare in today's world?

If everyone is really interested in the implications of this assignment, and if time permits, it might be fun to try some role playing, whereby a male participant draws one of the lists (say from a hat) and then is given a situation—called out at random from the class—in which he may respond only in terms of the highest-ranked qualities. The feasibility and credibility of the qualities and the ordering can then be scrutinized more closely.

After the listing (and the role playing) an attempt should be made to tie it all together and reach some conclusions about the current state of the masculine sex role in American society and the likelihood of re-defining it.

Carson McCullers: *A Domestic Dilemma*

Assume that a bill is to be introduced before the Senate outlawing marriage as a legal institution. If it is passed, it will mean that husbands do not have the obligation to provide for the continuing support of their former wives and children, children over eighteen will be entirely on their own, and those under eighteen will become wards of the government to be educated at public expense provided they enter into public service. In the future, however, reproduction will be under federal control. Sexual relationships will be permitted for pleasure only, and those who bring unauthorized children into the world will be imprisoned.

The class is to conduct the Senate debate on this bill. A group of three or four volunteers should get together before class convenes and put the bill in a clear and coherent shape as well as decide how the bill is to be logically defended.

Others in the class should choose from a list of possible roles that can be drawn up by the instructor or by a student committee charged with working up the details of the Action. It is understood that everyone will play a senator. The following senatorial orientations are suggested for possible consideration:

1. A militant feminine liberationist who does not personally believe in marriage
2. A female senator who is happily married and wishes to save the institution
3. A male or female senator whose own childhood was spent shuttling back and forth between divorced parents
4. A male or female senator who is devoutly religious
5. A male or female senator of no religious connections
6. A male senator whose own wife continually complains that he has no time for his family
7. A male senator who secretly believes his philandering tendencies are kept under control by a stable family environment
8. A male or female senator who has many side interests
9. A female senator who feels that her political calling is more important than raising children
10. An unhappy female senator who wishes she had more time for her children
11. Two senators who are married to each other
12. A senator from a rural area
13. A senator from a highly industrialized area
14. A senator who is concerned over the population explosion
15. A Catholic senator who follows the letter of the papal law

Many other roles will doubtless come to mind. After each participant has selected the role he feels most comfortable playing, a set amount of time should be allotted for him to work up his defense or denunciation of the bill. Then let the Senate fight it out.

It might be fun to invite another class (if room permits) to listen to the arguments and then report back what they have observed. Did logic prevail? Emotions? Tradition? Confusion? Who was most convincing? Least? How would the observers have voted had they been senators?

After the debate is over, decide what has been learned. Is the family a necessary institution? Is it likely to survive in its present form? Is it the hope of the future or an albatross holding up progress? (If so, what is progress?)

Amiri Baraka: *Great Goodness of Life (A Coon Show)*

The conflict between Court Royal and his peers is by no means limited to the black experience. Regardless of ethnic background, nearly every one of us has had to weigh alternatives. Duties toward oneself or toward members of one's immediate family have to be measured against those exacted of him by some larger family to which he may belong.

Divide into small groups, each of which is presumed to be a family in the ordinary, strictest sense of that word. Members of the group may assign appropriate roles among themselves: mother, father, sons, daughters, aunts, uncles, in-laws living with them, etc. It is desirable to have as complex a web of dependency as possible. There should also be at least *one* person who represents the larger family and is visiting in order to prompt the choice.

One member of the family circle is to be the *Figure in Conflict*. That is, he must make a decision involving his own happiness, the needs of his family, and the higher loyalties demanded of him by virtue of membership in the larger circle. This might be an ethnic brotherhood, a revolutionary cause, a political constituency that wants him to run for an important office, or some other pressure-exerting group. If the outside pressure is urgent enough, if the cause is strong enough, and if the family circle is tight enough, a very explosive confrontation is quite possible.

Each group should, if conditions permit, retire to a secluded corner where it can act out the confrontation. Some basic setting should be decided upon. Possibly these can be written out beforehand on cards and either arbitrarily handed to the groups or drawn from a box.

Some suggestions:
1. A young black male must decide whether to stay with his family, who require his support, take a college scholarship, which will take him far away, or join the Black Panthers, who need his leadership abilities.
2. A young housewife must decide between an anti-marriage women's liberation group and her husband and children.
3. A middle-aged mother (college graduate) must choose between her intellectual peers and a husband who lacks talent and drive as well as teenage children, whose rebellious lives have forced them

to drop out of school and who appear to require strong parental guidance.

4. A husband and father of talent and foresight and philandering ways must choose between his exciting, creative friends (either sex) and a somewhat dull (to him) family, who he knows will not be able to manage very well on their own.

5. A young black female must decide between active participation in a revolutionary movement with militant peers and the stability of a well-established family and a boy friend whom she loves and who is eager to enter the family business. (To add more zest to the conflict, have the movement forbid marriage and the bearing of children.)

Once the particular setting is chosen, the group should act out the confrontation, with the visitor from the larger family trying to outweigh the various viewpoints set forth by those of the immediate family. If there are enough participants available, there should be one neutral observer to report back to the community what took place.

When time is called, reassemble as a class and discuss what happened in each group. Allow each Figure in Conflict to indicate what he decided and why. The observers, if any, may have much to add about the effect of this decision on the others. The resultant discussion should shed much light on the kinds of loyalties to which people tend to give priority.

Robert Frost: *The Death of the Hired Man*

Since the issue behind the poem relates to the general subject of whether people have responsibilities beyond immediate self-interest, it is interesting to test out various ways of approaching the problem. Furthermore, since the poem is by Robert Frost, who always takes a slight incident and gives it universal importance, the class can use the same technique. That is, it can begin with a simple situation and see how far it is able to carry the implications.

Step One: Divide into small groups. Each group is given a specified amount of time to devise a simple, everyday situation involving the issue of divided loyalties and higher responsibilities. It would be highly desirable if one group member could share a real and unresolved personal problem with the others and the group as a whole could embellish it. Or else let the group's problem be a composite of a number of personal ones. At any rate, the group should make no attempt to solve it. Rather, each person is assigned a specific role to play when the situation is acted out for the entire class, the role corresponding to a definite and unchangeable viewpoint in the matter.

Step Two: Present the situation.

Step Three: State the responsibility issue as clearly as possible. (This could be done by the central role-player, the person whose dilemma is being dramatized. If the situation were the one involved in the poem, the central character would be Warren.)

Step Four: The rest of the community solves—or attempts to solve—the problem.

Here's an idea of how it could work. Suppose Group One chooses the following situation:

> A student who has missed an important exam and is already in danger of flunking out of school is on his way to take a make-up which will mean the difference. He meets a member of the class who has taken the exam and pleads with him to reveal the questions.

A possible cast of characters would be the Student Who Missed Exam, the Student Who Took It, the Instructor, and the Department Chairman. The events might go like this:

1. Meeting in hall.
2. Student Who Took It decides to cooperate and writes out questions.
3. Student Who Missed Exam goes in and completes test in record time, incurring suspicion of Instructor.
4. Instructor reads exam and asks student who helped him.
5. Student admits getting help but points out that all he needs is to pass this course and he'll make it out of college. Besides, a good job is waiting for him, and anyway this subject is totally irrelevant.
6. Instructor says higher issues are involved.
7. Student pleads for consideration.
8. Instructor says as long as he had admitted receiving aid, he will be allowed to pass.
9. Department Chairman overhears the conversation and tells Instructor to pack his bags—he's through.
10. Instructor argues that he was doing the human thing.
11. Chairman says Instructor has betrayed the ideals and standards of higher education.
12. Instructor pleads for consideration.
13. Chairman says it isn't up to him.
14. Instructor says it is because the matter doesn't have to go any further.
15. Chairman asks what kind of Chairman he would be if he didn't do the right thing.
16. Instructor says the right thing is the human thing.
17. At this point the Chairman turns and asks the community to solve the problem for him.

Kahlil Gibran: *Jesus the Man*

The task is to test out the philosophy of love as Jesus taught it.

Divide into small groups, each of which is to select a specific situation in which a group problem is solved through a commitment to a certain form of action. The situation is then acted out three times:

1. One member of the group takes the approach of Jesus and solves the problem so as to benefit the group rather than himself.
2. Another member of the group takes what is commonly known as the realistic approach and solves the problem so as to serve his own needs.
3. The third time the group as a whole tries to work out the problem in a way that will benefit the most people without jeopardizing anyone's self-interest.

One or two neutral observers should watch the three different states of the action and then later report back to the total community on what transpired in each instance.

Some possible situations:

1. A family, about to go bankrupt, can stay together only if the only son (there are a number of daughters) drops out of school and takes a high-paying job as a plumber.
2. The survivors of a plane crash at sea realize there are too many people on the raft.
3. Trapped coal miners know that help is on the way but do not know how long it will take. An inventory of food and water reveals that the chances of rescue will be enhanced if there are fewer people to feed.
4. Somehow a copy of the final exam got into the hands of a number of people in the class. The teacher doesn't know who has benefited. Grades are running unusually high. He decides to fail everyone unless the culprit confesses and names the people who received the advance help. But no confession is forthcoming. One person, who did not utilize the exam, knows who stole it.
5. Prisoners of war, confined in one cell, are informed that their lives will be spared if one of them will reveal the nature of their mission. *Nobody knows for sure how important the information is to national security.*

After the situation is enacted three different times, convene as a total community and discuss the various approaches. Share feelings with each other about what has been learned.

1. Does the Jesus approach come easily or naturally? Is it believable when it is exhibited?
2. Is self-interest the way of the world?
3. Is cooperative problem solving more effective than a personal love-your-neighbor creed?
4. Does self-interest interfere with cooperative problem solving?

Plato: *A Classic Case for Injustice*

Glaucon's hypothetical case of the magic rings has remained one of philosophy's most intriguing puzzles, not to say one of the most embarrassing challenges to moral idealists who hold that there is a universal standard by which the rightness or wrongness of actions may be measured. It was ingenious of Plato to create his own opposition in order to forestall its impact. But many readers will wonder whether he succeeded only in raising a legitimate doubt about the human capacity for being motivated by anything other than self-interest.

Test out Glaucon's proposition that people act only out of selfish reasons unless they are forced to do otherwise.

Divide into role-playing groups. Each team has a specified amount of time to plan a situation, later to be acted out before the class, in which one member discovers that the ring he is wearing grants him the power to vanish. The discovery should occur at a crucial moment, a time when he is being propelled toward some very painful decision and the ability to disappear suddenly becomes very convenient. He must then decide whether to stay invisible and take advantage of this fact as a way out of his dilemma or to renounce the power of the ring in favor of an unselfish solution to the problem.

Two sample situations to get you started:

1. A fraternity member in dire need of money for some particular and pressing purpose asks one of his brothers for a loan but is turned down (though the brother is known to be affluent). Later the impoverished member is present during a meeting of fraternity officers at which the proceeds from a dance are being counted. He discovers the powers of the ring accidentally and, while invisible, he catches the affluent brother in the act of slyly pocketing three twenty-dollar bills.

2. A hungry man goes to the back door of an opulent restaurant and pleads for a meal. The owner angrily refuses. The man persists, reminding him of his responsibility toward his fellow human beings. The owner argues that he, the poor man, also has a responsibility not to force an honest person, struggling to get ahead in business, into incurring a loss of revenue. Why not go to an establishment with lower operating costs? The hungry man goes away, determined to get revenge. His plan: to don his one good suit, return via the front door pretend to be affluent, order the most expensive meal in the place, and then find a way to sneak out without paying the check. While dining, he has a change of heart and decides that the virtuous course is to admit the fraud and prepare to spend the night in jail. While such thoughts are running through his mind, he accidentally turns a ring he has found on the street. . . .

Bernard Williams: *The Amoralist*

The task here is to analyze a projected "amoral" deed and determine whether it succeeds in detaching itself from all moral boundaries or whether it still exists within the realm of morality and should be dealt with on that basis.

Let us begin by defining an amoral action as one which in no way exhibits

1. any concern for the welfare of others
2. any implication that the doer considers the deed to be universally appropriate
3. any idea that the doer expects similar behavior in return from other people

If the projected action pretends to be amoral but does not fulfill these requirements, then the alleged amoralist would deserve his own censure at the very least for his failure to be consistent. The purpose behind this Action is therefore to see whether an amoral position is possible or is easily attained.

Divide first into the following groups:

  I.   The Attempted Amoralists
  II. Rational Resisters
  III. Religious Resisters
  IV. Resisters in the Name of Society

After each person has drawn, selected, or been given his designation, there should be another grouping, this time into family units of equal numbers. Every family group should have one Attempted Amoralist and at least one representative of each of the other designations. (Hence the number of persons allowed to adopt the A.A. designation will be limited to the number of family groups the class will end up having.)

A specified period of time should then be allowed for the designation groups to meet. The A.A. people will project a list of possible deeds that each one will later seek to commit within his family circle. Some suggested amoral actions might be:

1. Hijacking an airplane as a means of defecting to a foreign power
2. Stealing an examination from an instructor's secret files
3. Cheating on a spouse who is out working to support the family
4. Signing an affidavit of conscientious objection on religious grounds but secretly having no religious beliefs

While the A.A. group is deliberating, the other designation groups will share their feelings about what "moral" means relative to their particular context. They will know that an A.A. person will soon be in their midst and their task will be to try to expose him as a fraud or at least a hypocrite.

Here's an example of how the Action might work:

Let us suppose that the A.A. arrives in his family group and announces that he plans to avoid military service for his country on the grounds that his religion is a pacifist one but that he really has no religion. Let us suppose that no other basis for conscientious objection is legally acceptable. The A.A. might then argue for the consistent amorality of his position because

1. he is being opportunistic
2. he is deliberately misrepresenting his beliefs

3. since he knows there is no God, he cannot see that lying about religion is a matter of any true consequence
4. not wishing to fight in a war is a matter of survival and the survival instinct a biological, not a moral, matter
5. he is not harming anyone else since, even if all refused military service on the same grounds and there were no armed forces and the nation fell to a foreign power, it would not matter to an amoralist *what* form of government prevailed

The Resisters would then have an opportunity to question the A.A., who must parry each thrust with a meaningful defense of his position. (Once again neutral observers for each family group are desirable.) Some sample thrusts are:

1. *Rational*: "Since you have no religious faith, you cannot know there is no God and so you are still within the realm of possible sacrilege by deliberately lying."
2. *Religious*: "If a foreign power should be aggressive and seek to enslave the free world, war *in the name of humanity* is moral; refusing to fight means refusing to serve humanity."
3. *Social*: "You are parasitic. You know that, if everyone refused to serve, the government would assume dictatorial powers. You know that the only reason conscientious objectors are granted immunity is that not enough people go this route to make that much difference. Therefore you are counting on the decency of other socially-minded people."

As the Resisters present their arguments, the A.A. will respond in ways that he spontaneously feels to be appropriate. After the session is over, there should be a community meeting either to hear the observers' reports or to discuss the general feeling about the strength of amoralism.

Frank O'Connor: *The Idealist*

The spectrum of moral values is so vast that one person in his lifetime would never be able to test out every possibility in the absolute/relative dispute. But since "The Idealist" deals specifically with the matter of truth telling versus expedient lying, why not take this opportunity to put this important moral issue to a test?

Have several small groups assigned (or choose volunteers) to get together outside of class for the purpose of working up a presentation which will be offered to the other members and which will involve giving *two* versions of the same incident. In the first, a person tells the absolute truth throughout; in the second, he plays it by ear, possibly telling the truth, possibly not, but in any case, doing the thing that he believes will benefit himself without deliberately harming anyone else. It will then be up to the "jury" to decide which version seems to represent the more admirable course, all things considered.

Some possibilities are:

1. A husband, who has developed outside interests, is asked by a desperate wife whether he is faithful.
2. A policeman has to testify under oath whether he has accepted a bribe or not.
3. A young couple would like to put the bride's widowed and handi-capped mother in a nursing home, knowing that she does not like such institutions.
4. A teacher has chosen between two needy students for a valuable scholarship, knowing that the loser will not be able to finish school.
5. A boy has decided that a very plain girl, whom he has dated out of pity, is becoming a distinct liability to him socially.
6. A girl has learned that she is to be awarded the Top Student award at graduation and that her steady date, who prides himself on his intellectual prowess, is runner-up.
7. A student who has invited his black roommate home for the holidays has had second thoughts, especially after learning about the social activities planned by his affluent parents.
8. A Black Power advocate has decided that his close white friend will be hard to explain to his black brothers and that he has to place his cause above a personal friendship.

If it could be arranged, invite a priest, a rabbi, or a minister to be on hand for the presentations. Invite other faculty members, or even another class, who have been told nothing about the Action. Get a variety of view-points to help decide whether moral absolutism or moral relativism is the desired approach.

John Steinbeck: *About Ed Ricketts*

There appear to be two main factors in the Ricketts life style which made it work: one, his devotion to science and his brilliance in that field; and two, his personal charisma, which obviously was very great. There are people who can literally do whatever they wish and seem to stay beyond reproach simply because they are who they are and nobody can question it. But it might be fun to test out the Ricketts life style and determine whether it could work for other people and in different kinds of situations.

Divide into groups, each of which is to represent a specific field or aspect of human activity. Examples are:

Religion
The law
Education
The family
A communal arrangement

The groups should be given some time to work out the details, deciding upon a particular situation that has arisen within the context of its activity, one involving a dilemma or a choice of directions that needs to be made. One member of each group will represent the Ricketts life style and respond to the dilemma in a way he deems true to the laws of his being. The others will represent alternate possibilities, such as a religious approach, a social-law-and-order approach, a purely rational approach, and so on. Each group will work out the problem as best it can and then later report to the entire community on whether the Ricketts approach proved a help or a hindrance. The Ricketts figure should report on whether the others proved to be obstacles to his self-fulfillment or whether a compromise was made and seemed satisfactory. If possible, there should be neutral observers to the deliberations of every group.

Here are some sample situations, showing how the Ricketts figure would be involved:

1. An ordained minister (Ricketts) owns and operates a bar where he attracts a huge following of young people, who hang out there evenings. A committee of concerned parents summons him to appear before them and explain how he can possibly look out for the spiritual life of their children by encouraging them to drink.

2. A group of young policemen and policewomen get together to try to decide how to curb an alarming rise in the crime rate of a particular town. One of them is Ricketts.

3. A PTA group asks for the resignation of a (Ricketts) teacher who is discovered to be sharing an apartment with one of his students— a girl twenty years younger than he.

4. A family faces a financial crisis, and each member is asked to make appropriate sacrifices, including the (Ricketts) elder son who has displayed a brilliant musical talent and doesn't want to go to work.

5. The officers of a commune call a meeting to map out ways of working out a more productive distribution of functions. One (Ricketts) member is a sculptor and cannot do heavy manual labor at the risk of damaging his hands.

II: BOUNDARIES

Niccolò Machiavelli: *The Prince as Fox and Lion*

Conduct a classroom experiment to determine which structural model will produce the best results for a society.

Divide into five groups, each of which is charged with the task of inventing, then drawing a detailed picture of a new product never before on the market, which will adequately symbolize the intent and spirit of this course. The only restriction is that the groups operate in different manners.

There should be one neutral observer to watch the deliberations and procedures of each group and then later report back to the entire community.

I. *The Power Figure Group.* The first person who thinks of an idea will automatically be selected as The Prince. He is then charged with carrying out the task and may utilize the resources of the others in any way he sees fit.

II. *The Majority Rule Group.* As the label implies, this unit will reach its decision after discussion and a vote.

III. *The General Will Group.* This model is based on the traditional *social contract* theory, meaning that "each member puts his person and all his power in common under the supreme direction of the general will." Majority rule is not in effect. The decision on the product must reflect the thinking of the group as a whole. No one must take charge or in any way attempt to influence the thinking of the others unless this can be accomplished in a manner that will not violate the social contract ideal.

IV. *The Holdout Group.* This will operate very much like Group III above, except that one member will play the role of the Holdout and refuse to cooperate with the general will no matter what its direction.

V. *The No-Rules Group.* This unit may enjoy itself in an atmosphere of spontaneity, hunches, instincts, and free argumentation. It may choose any method whatever for getting the job done.

A rigid time allotment should be set up and adhered to. When time is called, the group or groups which have not completed the assignment may be asked to pay a forfeit of some kind (perhaps designing the Action for the next class, erasing the blackboards, watering the plants, buying the instructor's lunch, and so forth). The reports from the observers should provide interesting input as the total community determines whether (1) societies need power people to function well; (2) the social contract ideal can work; (3) majority rule is the fairest method; or (4) lack of guiding principles and the absence of a vertical power structure of any kind brings out the best in people.

Walt Whitman: *American Democracy as Nature's Ultimate*

The task is to test out the following principles set forth by Whitman in this selection:

1. Whether a group, given unlimited freedom, can develop into an organized, efficiently operating unit, able to accomplish a task of some complexity

2. Whether a community of such groups can come together in the way Whitman thought possible for the nations of the earth

3. Whether those who lead such groups are ever forced to insist upon autonomous power in order to get certain jobs done

4. Whether the exercise of such power is freely granted by the group

When the groups are constituted by some method to be devised by the total class community, in collaboration with the instructor, each one is to be given an equal part of a large blank paper on which latitudes and longitudes have been drawn to give the idea that, when complete, the whole thing will be a map of some world. The group's job is to design and then draw a map of its own country—the terrain and natural features (oceans, bays, rivers, lakes, mountains, and so on) to serve the needs of the kind of nation the group sees as utopian. Thus, before the group's share of the world map is drawn, it should have carefully discussed the purpose of its nation, the kind of government it needs to have, where the capital should be, what resources the citizens should have. The utopian plan need not be an elaborate one, but it seems clear that the philosophy of the group will determine the way the country should ideally look. The one restriction is that only two borders of the country may be made up of bodies of water. Some portion of the land mass must extend to the other two borders, and obviously the group cannot know what the others will be doing with the same borders.

When the countries are designed and mapped, each group will select a leader to represent its interests in a summit conference to be held in the center of the room for the purpose of putting the world together.

Inevitably the pieces of the map will not make complete sense with respect to each other. Some land masses are bound to run together, while some bodies of water will not work well in connection with a land mass that is assumed to be extending onto somebody else's part of the map. To get a meaningful looking world, changes and compromises have to be made.

The nonleaders will observe the summit conference, but may not participate.

After the world map is finished, the leader should return to his group and listen to everyone's opinion of how he conducted himself.

At the conclusion of the Action there should be a community summary of what has been learned about how groups work and how leadership tends to operate.

Charles Reich: *Anatomy of the Corporate State*

The task is to determine whether the political or administrative model of the State works out better with respect to the well-being of the people as a whole. Or, to put the matter differently, whether Human Worth is enhanced or negated by either one.

Divide into two groups, or, if the class is a large one, into as many two-group units as seems feasible. (More than ten per group generally proves unwieldy.) One group represents the Political State, the other the Administrative State. Each is charged with the responsibility of making a playground-recreation area, using children's Tinkertoy sets.

The Administrative State is to operate in accordance with a rigidly observed power structure. That is, a leader must be chosen (supposedly the one who offers the best plan for the project). He in turn will delegate building responsibilities to individuals or groups of individuals. Some may be charged with building playground equipment; others with building a swimming pool; others with a tennis court, and so on. Since an Administrative State is always affluent, it is only right that this group be provided with many more building parts than the other group.

The Political State group will have no leader or doling out of responsibilities. Anybody's creative idea is welcomed. Unfortunately, it is likely to be furnished with an inadequate amount of materials and must therefore compensate for the oversight with two things: an outpouring of creative imagination, and a kind of *esprit de corps*.

Before the actual building takes place, there should be fifteen minutes or so allowed for planning and deliberation. Both groups need to examine their available resources and decide upon strategies, except that the Political State may only discuss the various possibilities suggested by the members. The Administrative State for its part will, of course, be organizing itself and getting into high gear.

When the signal "go" is given, both groups will proceed with the task for which a set amount of time is allotted and the limitation scrupulously observed.

When time is called, the participants may carefully inspect the labors of both groups or sets of groups. At a total-community meeting, the advantages and disadvantages of both systems can be analyzed in some detail.

1. Did the Administrative State in fact build a better physical plant? Was it good enough in view of its superior equipment?

2. Did the Political State show more ingenuity, considering its inferior equipment?

3. Which group members on the whole seemed to have had a better time? What does "better" mean in this context?

4. If the Administrative playground did indeed turn out to be better constructed and have more facilities, does such efficiency outweigh whatever positive things, if any, the Political group may claim to have accomplished?

5. To the neutral observers, did the Administrative group seem to have any problems? What about the Political group? Which group by comparison appeared to have had an easier time of it? What does "easier" mean in this context?

6. If the observers were asked to define Human Worth and to decide in which group this seemed most evident, what would their answer be?

7. How did the members of the respective groups feel about the question of Human Worth?

8. If the Administrative State *did* come up with a clearly superior performance, did the members of the Political State feel a sense of frustration? Did this in any way conflict with their feelings about their Worth as free citizens?

9. Did the members of the Administrative State feel a sense of pride in their superior achievement? Was this in any way countered by an awareness that they were being governed by a leader?

10. On the whole, does it appear that enthusiasm for a task is more likely when a group is running by some rational method of efficiency or when it is freely experimenting?

The Rockefeller Panel: *The American Economic Heritage*

This may work better if done outside of class. The problem is that it requires people working in groups, so that it is possible not everyone can participate. Perhaps groups of volunteers who have the time and the opportunity can get together and then report their findings back to the entire class.

The task is to use the game of "Monopoly" to determine whether the people of America fare better as a whole under an unlimited system of competitive economics or whether some checks are necessary against the possibility of rampant and uncharitable self-interest.

The groups should be so constituted:

I. *The Competitors.* The purpose of each player is to win by making more money and holding more real estate than the others. (In other words, this group plays it straight.)

II. *The Modified Competitors.* This group is bound by one added restriction: As soon as one player reaches an agreed-upon amount of capital (including the value of his real estate), he must split whatever he makes from that point on with the poorest player on the board.

III. *The Controlled Competitors.* This group is bound by a more rigid principle: Whenever any player wishes to buy any property, he must pay a surcharge of 20 percent of the stated value into a kitty, which is held by the bank. This fund will pay anyone whose capital falls below an agreed-upon figure an additional bonus every time that person passes "Go" and collects his regular $200.00. (To add further interest to this version: Graduate the surcharge each time a house is added and make the additional taxes for hotels very high. You might also have a neutral party acting as bank-and-government, a person to whom overtaxed millionaires may appeal in order to raise the amount of rent required by the deed.)

IV. *The Noncompetitors.* Have four persons play with the idea of splitting their economic resources equally at regular intervals. The motivation is to make the group as a whole as wealthy as possible.

The observers and the players should collaborate on the reports, so as to provide input from outside and inside sources. Some crucial questions that need to be answered are:

1. How did the losers in Group I feel? Would they change the system under which they played if they had to do it again?
2. Did the winner in Group I feel that he would have been willing to share his wealth with the others?

3. Did any variation in the rules of the straight game develop? What was it? Why did it happen?
4. Did those making substantial gains in Group II feel it was fair to have to split their money with the poor people?
5. Did this added rule take away from the enjoyment of the game?
6. Did the more rigorous restrictions placed upon capitalism in Group III dampen the enthusiasm of the players?
7. Did Group IV enjoy itself?
8. What system for playing "Monopoly" appeared on the whole to have been most successful? (This is to be answered by the total class community.)
9. Can valid applications be made of the results of this Action to real economic practices? What are they?
10. Which seemed more natural: competitiveness for its own sake, self-interest no matter what the system, or the pleasure of sharing? Why do you think this seemed natural?

Arthur C. Clarke: *Don't Forget Who Built Your Memory Banks!*

Bowman's willful murder of Hal may seem an exaggerated bit of human heroics, something that belongs in science fiction and makes a literary statement without being applicable to real life. Indeed all of us may be so thoroughly enslaved to the machine by now that no writer's myth of human affirmation will make much difference.

On the other hand, one does note a movement under way—an attempt, if only a symbolic one, to get back to human fundamentals and slide out from under technology's gleaming and steel-like grasp. In the communes, set up far from the cities, people live in tents or rustic cabins, often without electricity or running water. They try to live, as much as possible, on what they can grow themselves. Those who smile at such impractical behavior point to the disadvantages including the fact that even plague has reportedly broken out in some communes where living standards become "dangerously" primitive.

Without going quite so far, can you experiment, at least in imagination, with the possibility of living one day and doing without every mechanical device you can? This is the task set for you by this action.

Divide into small groups, each of which is presumed to be a family unit. Allow a given amount of time for discussion and planning, for making a list first of the mechanical things on which each of us depends from the moment he wakes up and then of some ingenious ways in which they can be sacrificed *with the least amount of inconvenience*. The deliberations should take into full consideration the degree of dependency that has been built up through years of using the machines. That is to say, a group shouldn't rush blithely into a statement like "We can use candles instead of electric lights" without exploring the full implications of the suggestion. The ingenuity which is the goal of the exercise, will be measured in terms of plausibility and careful analysis of all the consequences. The final report made by each group should aim at reasonable alternatives that are within human grasp.

After deliberation, the group reports should be given and each evaluated on its merits, using the rationale stated in the above paragraph. If possible, a panel of neutral observers should be invited in to decide which group provided the most feasible and realistic plan.

It may be that there will be several "best" reports or none at all. Whatever happens, the implications of the Action should be summarized after it is completed. *Are* we too deeply committed to technology to do anything about it? (If so, can anyone suggest a positive way of viewing the matter? Or is pessimism the only human response that makes sense?)

Plato: *The Last Days of Socrates*

The task is to test out three possible ways of dealing with an impossible situation, one that becomes untenable to you, one to which you cannot remain indifferent.

Divide into three groups: *Martyrs, Protestors,* and *Activists.* The first must find attitudinal and philosophical resources to help them deal with the situation but must remain static within it. They must, in short, endure and transcend but not try to do anything about it. The second must formulate an outcry and then do whatever is possible without going at least noticeably outside legal and social boundaries. This group must use the utmost ingenuity to try to bring about a change in the situation *short* of endangering the stability of the state in which they live. The third group may do whatever needs to be done, legal or otherwise, and whatever they think can and will work.

Two or three neutral observers, either from the class or from outside, should watch the proceedings and then report back to the total community after the Action is completed.

The situation(s) can be given by the instructor, suggested by the observers, or drawn from a pool of cards participants bring to class with them. Some possibilities are:

1. In order to save the college from losing the financial support of a foundation that deplores its liberal grading policies, the administration has decided the only fair way to handle the crisis is to hold a semester lottery and give failing grades to the "winners." The members of each group would be the winners of the first drawing, and some would be dropped from school because of it.

2. The local law enforcement people, in despair over a sharp increase in marijuana smoking among the younger generation, and sensitive to the growing discontent among the tax-paying parents, decide to round up a token group and confront them with circumstantial evidence designed for a quick and easy conviction. Everything has been rigged against the defendants, some of whom may have been guilty of smoking marijuana, some of whom may be innocent. After they have been jailed, town life becomes more stable and the mari-

juana traffic appears to decrease considerably. (The Martyrs ought to consider the pros and cons of trying to escape from jail.)

3. The federal government, alarmed at both crime statistics and the dangerous pollution levels in the heavily populated urban centers, has decided to distribute the people of America arbitrarily about the country, filling up millions of acres of unused land. The members of each of our three action groups are people who have been assigned to a desolate, arid area whose soil is all but useless for farming. It is understood that many Americans have suffered similar fates, while many others are now enjoying the advantages of life in the far less crowded metropolises. The national pollution level has also dropped, so that, at least from the point of view of a foreigner, the government's move might seem to have been wise indeed.

George Jackson: *Letter from a Soledad Brother*

This may seem a bit tame after the power and impact of the letter you have just read, but there are reasonable limits to what can be attempted in a classroom. The situation is that the college administration, after receiving many letters of protest from parents who feel that the experimental methods of both this book and the instructor represent a waste of time and money, has decided to reassign the instructor to nonteaching duties and to relocate the students in other, more traditional classes.

Divide into the following groups:

I. *Revolutionists.* Their task is to find ingenious undercover methods to prevent the change. These may include the use of disguise, falsified tapes, lying, editorials in the school paper with deliberate propaganda devices, or carefully managed (that is, nonviolent) confrontations. It must be assumed that overt radicalism would be met with stiff resistance and scuttle the entire plan.

II. *Moderates.* These are the students who wish to work within the established system to bring about rational and orderly change.

III. *Parents.* They should meet beforehand and draw up a list of what they consider to be reasonable grievances. Every possible effort should be made to emphathize with their views and to avoid overexaggeration.

IV. *Committee of Administrators and Faculty.* Their task is to investigate the teaching methods of the instructor by questioning students and parents. All of the considerations, both professional and personal (job security, envy, and so on), which *could* lie behind the roles taken by these committee members, should be involved. One member might even be sympathetic toward the instructor under fire, but inhibited from taking direct action on his behalf by a number of "delicate" concerns, such as being in line for a promotion.

Neutral observers should sit in on the deliberations of each group and the interaction between groups. Their task is to report back to the total community on the objective truth of the situation as they see it. Will the Revolutionists prove to be right? Or will they be found not to have accurately perceived the full problem? Will the establishment prove to have clung tenaciously to its power regardless of what reason appears to decree? Will they capitulate to the Parents through fear of attracting unfavorable publicity? Will the Moderates, guided as far as possible by reason, discover it is difficult, if not impossible, to effect a compromise between the extreme poles of revolution and establishment? Will they be defeated? Will those forces prevail who have power through hierarchy and economics? Will the instructor (played either by himself or a student) resign and become a martyr? Will that prove anything? Will the Revolutionists drop out of school in protest? Will they then fail to get good jobs and end up poor and wretched? What will the exercise teach us all about how change could or should occur?

Mohandas Karamehand Gandhi: *Love Versus War and Dictators*

The task is to determine through an experiment whether passive resistance or nonviolent noncooperation succeeds better than outright rebellion.

The class is divided into two major segments, each of which in turn is divided into an A group and a B group.

In Segments I and II, the A group represents the ruling party.

In Segment I, the B group is dedicated to nonviolence.

In Segment II, the B group is a revolutionary force.

Step One: Each A group is given a child's building toy set—the kind which has many component parts of all sizes, shapes, and functions. The assignment is for Segment I and Segment II to compete against each other and attempt to be the first to complete a library building *of testable sturdiness and reasonable design.*

Step Two: The instructor doles out the component parts indiscriminately to the A and B groups of both segments.

Step Three: The A group of Segment I, knowing its B group will refuse to cooperate, meets to determine how a competent structure can be built from the pieces it alone holds. It may plan but not begin building until the outcome of the Segment II revolution is decided.

Step Four: The B group of Segment II, holding its building parts, challenges its A group to a battle of wits. That is, members of B group will ask questions on current events or literature or some other category (the exact procedure to be decided by the segment beforehand). Every time a member of A group answers a question correctly, the questioner must surrender the building pieces he is holding. If a question is answered incorrectly, the pieces are considered lost forever to A group. In cases where an answer is declared incorrect but A group can successfully challenge the decision, the pieces will be forfeited to A group. The questioning continues until the fate of all the building parts has been determined.

If Segment II's A group wins more than half of B group's pieces, the revolution will be considered to have failed. All of the parts must be turned over, and members of the B group must help *honestly* in the building process. If, however, A group wins less than half the pieces, it may hold what it has attained and work from there with the cooperation of those B group members whose questions were successfully answered. Those whose questions were not answered will abstain from labor.

Step Five: At the signal "Go!" both segments will begin working on their buildings. Segment I with the noncooperative B group (who can act as neutral observers of all the deliberations) will have had the advantage of longer planning, but it will probably have far fewer component parts with which to work.

After the specified length of time (clearly announced in advance) has expired, both Segments immediately cease their labors, while the results are examined by the instructor and the observers.

Step Six: The entire class reconvenes in community to discuss the effectiveness of noncooperation as opposed to the risks of revolutionary activity. May serious application of the outcome of this game be made to real life?

Herman Melville: *The Trial and Death of Billy Budd*

Since Melville uses a ship in wartime as an example of how society must operate according to a principal of order, why not use the college campus to help you get at similar, but more modern, issues? Invite one or two college administrators into the class to participate in the experiment.

A group of volunteers (or people selected by the class) leave the room for a brief period. Each goes off by himself and thinks of something he will say he has just done before his return to the classroom. Whatever the deed, it must be a clear violation of some existing campus rule, such as hauling down the school flag, helping to stage a fraternity hazing in the foyer of the administration building, composing a folk song to guitar accompaniment in the reading room of the library, and so on.

The violators enter one by one and begin by saying "This is what I did." Then the class and the visiting administrators question him:

Why did you do it?

Did you realize it was wrong?

Do you disagree with the ruling?

Do you understand the reason for the rule?

What if every one did the same thing, especially at a time when it was inconvenient for you?

(Administrators may be counted upon to provide their own excellent questions.)

The violator's responses should be guided by an inner sense of having done no wrong; that is, the action must have some defensible integrity in terms of which to answer the questions and to provide enough input for a decision.

After the case has been argued, it would be interesting to have the class vote through secret ballot and then to have the administrators announce their own verdicts. It is assumed that their position will be that school policy must be upheld in each case. But, should their decision differ from the class verdict, they may be invited to explain why they believe it is sound to follow school policy rather than to make an exception in some circumstances. (If no administrator is available, the instructor may play the necessary role.)

After all the cases have been heard, there should be a general discussion of what has been learned from the Action. Will the principle of rule turn out to have been necessary in the majority of instances? Will the personal dignity of the violators prove to have been at stake and to have been more important than the rule? Does a decision always depend upon the individual situation? If so, what kind of procedure is to be followed in reaching a decision? For example, if an administrator decided to forget the incident despite the fact that it clearly deviated from campus policy, would he say he had been following the dictates of reason—or of the heart? How does an upholder of the principle of rule justify the role of the emotions? If "heart" is *never* a factor, why does the administrator believe it should not be?

In summarizing the exercise, the leader of the discussion should indicate whether the experiment showed that Human Worth is better served by a "tight ship" or a "flexible ship" model.

Henry David Thoreau: *Higher Laws*

The task is to determine, through role-playing, which life style is best suited to making people happy, given the conditions of living as they currently are.

Divide into three major groups, each of which is to pretend that it has decided to build a form of residence in the woods by Walden Pond and to live together for a period of two years. While the act itself is the same in every instance, the motives, purpose, and procedure will vary drastically.

Here are the groups:

I. *The "All the Way" Group.* This group wishes to build a cabin in order to forsake civilization altogether. It will allow itself no luxuries or even ordinary conveniences such as running water, inside plumbing, electricity, refrigeration, and articles of furniture carried in from the city. The residents, having read Thoreau, are confirmed vegetarians and also believe in abstinence from all sensual pleasures, including alcohol and sexual relationships.

II. *The "Semicivilized" Group.* These people have also read Thoreau but disagree that man can survive in the wilderness without taking any of the advantageous elements in city life. Accordingly, they propose to allow themselves minimal indulgence in the so-called necessities of life. They may or may not eat meat or drink alcohol. They may adopt any attitude toward sensual pleasures that the majority in the group believes is not inconsistent with their reason for being there, which is to at least meet nature half way.

III. *The "Totally Civilized" Group.* These people—all former residents of a large metropolitan area, all college graduates and advocates of a highly sophisticated way of life—have read Thoreau and decided it would be terribly chic to start a back-to-nature movement. Their purpose is to utilize the natural environment as a means of deriving even more pleasure from living than they may enjoy in the city. They have an unlimited budget, exquisite taste in eating, and drinking, and interesting ways of passing the time of day.

Here is the procedure:

1. Each group meets for a specified amount of time and discusses purpose, building plans, daily routine, and manner of living at Walden. In addition, it should select for role-playing some representative activity which it feels will best illustrate the strengths of wilderness living. It could be having its first meal, dividing up labors, spending its first evening at home in the woods, and so on.

2. When time is called, one or two neutral observers join each set of nature enthusiasts.

3. The groups begin to act out ten or fifteen minutes of their stay at Walden, utilizing the activity decided upon in Step 1 above. Each participant is to respond in a manner he feels is consistent with the general aims of his group. That is, even if he is secretly a gourmet, he must, if he belongs to the vegetarian group, try as hard as possible to convince himself that he despises meat. No one should try to disrupt the seriousness of the enterprise just to have fun. Every effort should be made to give the particular approach a fair test.

4. The observers should take notes on the proceedings, guided not by personal preferences but by what they actually see taking place.

5. When time is called, the class should convene as a community, listen to the reports, and then attempt to reach some conclusions regarding the human aptitude for living close to nature. Will it be found that the All the Way people floundered helplessly and had to borrow things from the others? that the Semicivilized people could not remain spartan but kept falling back increasingly on their city heritage? that the Totally Civilized people were much happier—or more bored—than the others?

Joseph Wood Krutch: *The Paradox of Humanism*

The essay appears life-denying in every possible sense. There is no way, according to the author, for humanity to live "safely and comfortably in the universe of nature." Still, this may be a drastic view, one which many readers will resist taking.

The author does not say so, but it could also be eminently human to hope for better things and plan for a better tomorrow.

The task here is to see whether the pessimism of Krutch can be utilized and converted into a positive blueprint for successful change. If it cannot, then we may have to concede that the author has a point and adjust ourselves to it accordingly.

Design either individually or in small groups a model for a future society in which man can utilize the most advantageous of his human strengths as well as imitate the animal traits which appear to be lacking at present in human society.

Some guidelines are:

1. Go through the essay and make a list like the following of animal versus human characteristics according to Krutch.

Animal	Human
Sex only for reproduction	Sex as an end in itself
Society-oriented	Individual-oriented
Mind exists for survival	Mind can exist for no practical ends

2. Decide for yourself or discuss among your group which traits you would like to encourage in your future society and which ones you would eliminate. For example, if you wish to avoid over-population, will you practice animal "chastity" and exercise strict controls over reproduction? Will you see that the sexual drive is diverted into another channel? Or will you continue to be "the only animal who loves all the year around"?

3. Decide upon some model for your society. Will it have the efficiency and complete species orientation of the anthill, where there will be no waste of manpower, no heedless pollution of the environment, but perhaps also no fun? Or will you have something more closely resembling the commune of today where there is a high degree of social orientation but at the same time a "do your thing" moral code in effect? Do you foresee some changes in the communal philosophy that will have to be made? Will you want to add more animal or more human characteristics?

4. Decide upon some unique manner of presenting your society to the rest of the class. Perhaps you will offer sketches of typical homes or community centers. Perhaps, if you are a small group doing the project together, you will present some improvised scenes that illustrate how your society operates and what its goals are.

John G. Neihardt: *Black Elk Speaks*

Revisiting the familiar legend of the "winning of the West" is a good idea if only to remind ourselves to be more sensible about such things—

and about history itself for that matter. For centuries white European culture has been history-oriented. Education based on European models has stressed the importance of "historical perspective." True, the more responsible scholars of history have attempted to reconstruct the past as objectively as possible, but deep-rooted cultural assumptions can "guide" the historian's objective vision. But the average American who has gone through a traditional curriculum probably forgets most of the complex efforts at historical fairness. He is likely to leave school with a few indelible impressions of the past stamped forever on his memory.

The task initially is to divide into groups and make a list of some of these indelible impressions. These can be labeled "Everyman's Storehouse of Neatly Packaged Ideas." For example: Columbus persuading Queen Isabella that the world is round; Columbus "discovering" America; the Pilgrims meeting with the Indians for the first Thanksgiving and so on. No one who has been through school can possibly fail to contribute to the ESNPI list.

The next step is to put down each person's recollection of how he came into possession of such knowledge. Was it from a particular class in school? What was the class like? What approach did the teacher take? Was it from a book? Does the title come to mind? What kind of book was it? Is the exact source of the information vague? Is it "common knowledge"?

The third step is for the class to meet in community so that each group may share its findings with the others. Discuss some conclusions that may be drawn from the Action thus far. What still seems valid about the aspects of history under discussion? What seems suspect? How should history be taught to bring it closer to reality? Is it possible to *have* "historical reality" at all? (If the answer to this last question is no, then what relationship, if any, to the past should we attempt to develop?)

Optional Follow-Ups:

It is possible that an Action like this will generate a good deal more concern than some of the others, and the class may well decide it wants to spend more time on it.

Something else that can be done following the community sharing, is to have each group select one specific historical conception (or misconception) and try to update it by going back and determining whether recent findings or new historical approaches are available to shed new light on the subject. Once again the information should be shared in community. To make the community session even more stimulating, each group may, on the basis of its research, offer a dramatized version of "what really happened."

R. Buckminster Fuller: *Towards a Better World Through Conscious Design*

Test out the future in advance. Pretend that the Fuller movement has won a worldwide following of architects, philosophers, and people-oriented politicians, who are desirous of implementing Fuller's world scheme immediately. But, as is to be expected, they meet much opposition. By role-playing the different viewpoints, you may be able to reach some interesting conclusions about the project's chances for success.

Divide into the following groupings:

I. *Fullerians.* Dome-designers and a variety of types the group feels would be interested in a consciously planned world, where the interest of all is more important than individual egos.

II. *World Leaders.* These are the heads-of-state, who have their own powers, responsibilities, and national integrities to protect.

III. *Professionalists.* These would be big businessmen, doctors, dentists, lawyers, and traditional politicians, who prefer to keep things as they are now. They believe that man is intended by nature to be competitive in a free society, that the whole tends to profit from the professional egoism of successful people much more so than if professionals were forced by some worldwide organization to conform to a global plan.

IV. *Scientific Realists.* These would represent a different kind of professionalism: people thoroughly trained in science and dedicated to the problems of ecology and population control. All are acutely concerned about the deterioration of the environment, the attainment of Zero Population Growth throughout the world, and the depletion of available resources. Like the Fullerians, they want a better world but disagree that so radical a change in the direction of human evolution can be brought about by a handful of people. They realize improvements have to be made gradually and realistically without upsetting the precarious balance of things as they stand. One example would be by trying experiments on the New York City water supply when this must take care of millions.

V. *Average Citizens.* People who do their jobs, want their paycheck on Friday, complain about rising food prices and the government, worry vaguely but not overmuch about the grim future. They tend to view proposals for change with suspicion and radical proposals with alarm and hostility.

The groups should be given a specified amount of time to jell—that is, to identify clearly the group identity as well as the roles each person will play when all five forces are brought together in confrontation.

The confrontation takes place in this manner. The Fullerians have prevailed upon the United Nations Assembly in New York to hold an emergency session on The State of the Earth. At this time they are going to try to persuade the World Leaders to unite in planning the future, which will include the eventual obliteration of nations as they currently exist. Other concerned parties—the Professionalists, the Scientific Realists, and the Average Citizens—have heard about the session and plan to attend in order to stop the Fullerians.

After the encounter is over, hold a community meeting to determine which group or groups "won" and whether everyone believes this is what would really happen. Also summarize what has been learned from the Action about people and their chances for a better life or even just for survival.

III: THE UNBOUNDED SELF

René Descartes: *A Piece of Wax*

Try an experiment in class to determine whether sensory observation or intellectualizing is more valuable to human beings.

Let five or six persons sit around a table. Give each member of this group an envelope containing some irregular shapes of plywood. The instructions are to make six squares of identical size out of the pieces. (The group is told that the pieces will, when put together correctly, make up the desired squares, but that they have been randomly placed in six different envelopes.) The rules are that no one may speak or take a piece of wood from another player; he may, however, give wood away.

Let the rest of the class act as observers of this group in the process of attempting to perform the task. One half of them will simply watch and report faithfully their sensory observations. They will make no effort to interpret or make sense of what they report.

The other half will try to understand what is happening between the players. Was there "hostility"? "co-operation"? "frustration"? "love"? "competitiveness"? and so on. The "intellectual" group will, in short, endeavor to put the events together into some kind of orderly sequence.

It should be enlightening for the two groups to compare notes. Will the "sense observation" group turn out to have seen more than the "intellectual" group? Will the players decide that the "intellectual" group perceived what was *really* happening? Or will they say that this group projected its own ideas?

If possible, the lesson of the experiment should be summarized at the end of the period and some conclusion reached.

Russell Maloney: *Inflexible Logic*

Test out the Law of Probability in the classroom.

Divide into two groups: A Thought Group and a Reality Group. The Thought people will be advocates of Reichenbach's law and will attempt to project the likelihood and frequency of certain actions that will be performed by the Reality people.

The Reality people, on the other hand, should embody a "hang loose" life style and be resolutely determined to remain unpredictable.

The Thought group deliberates, while the Reality group is allowed to take a walk outside. The deliberations should result in a checklist of probable things that the others will do when they are invited back into the room. For example, given the physical surroundings and the absurdity of the assignment, will

1. some of the group wander aimlessly about?
2. particular people engage in particular actions for which they are well known? (Will the girl with the long black hair start unconsciously combing it again? Will that boy keep pushing his hair away from his eyes? Will the trio from the back row who think the whole class is silly retreat to a corner and smirk?)
3. anyone begin to write nonsense words on the blackboard?
4. a number of people have soft drinks? about how many?
5. any of them enter with knowing, mysterious smiles as if they had just hatched a diabolic plot? which ones will do that?
6. some of them get into a conversation with the instructor? who? will he take part in it?

The information for the calculations will spring from the group's knowledge about the others and so will not be lacking in *any* rational basis.

Before they are asked to leave, the Reality people should be urged not to talk about the assignment among themselves, not to make a conscious effort to outfox the Thought group. To do such a thing would be to imply that Reality is rational in itself. To work at all, the Action must pit logic against whatever it is that exists "out there." Each Reality person should therefore behave in whatever way feels comfortable to him at the moment.

A variation on the procedure would be to have each Thought person make his own checklist in addition to there being a group-consensus checklist. In this way a more exact ratio between frequency of prediction and reality can be made. Whenever an action appears on the master checklist, it can be conceded as a triumph for mind over matter.

Crane Brinton: *The Role of Ideas*

The validity of intellectual history or, for that matter, most rational activities depends upon a meaningful and close relationship between reasoning and reality. Those who despair of the rational life deny that the mind's order can have any parallel in the "real" world. But those who adhere to the rational life point out that mind can affect reality, even if it may on occasion wander off into abstractions of its own devising. The cumulative body of scientific knowledge depends, after all, on the ability of the mind not only to discover nature's laws but to bring into existence things that nature never made and to make things happen that nature did not intend.

To test the strength of the human mind against the world of people and things as they are, divide the class into two groups, one representing

Thought, the other Reality. The purpose is to separate them and then to see whether one can indeed influence the direction of the other.

Send the Reality group out of the room, while the Thought group gets together and decides upon some specific action it wants Reality to perform. Some possibilities:

1. Force each person to write his name on the board.
2. Make the group as a whole sit in a circle for a discussion.
3. Get the group involved in searching for a missing article.

A logical plan must be devised. No direct communication will be permitted. Furthermore, the plan must be set down in writing so that it may later be compared with the way events worked out.

When the Reality group is readmitted to the room, its task will be to try to resist any efforts to direct its actions. This will force the Thought group to use the utmost subtlety, a fact which should be taken into consideration beforehand.

Alvin Toffler: *Overstimulation and the Breakdown of Reason*

Studies have indicated that people forced to absorb information under noisy and confused conditions take longer to learn but remember the material better. To test out this hypothesis, divide the class into two groups. One may be designated as the DQP group (Dwellers in the Quiet Past), and they will be allowed to absorb knowledge under the less frantic circumstances we nostalgically associate with yesterday. The other may be designated as the FSV group (Future Shock Victims), and their unhappy lot will be to try to absorb knowledge under accelerating stress.

The DQP group will be placed in a room made as quiet as possible. The steady hum of an airconditioner, the pleasant twittering of birds outside the window, soothing music from an FM station, and similar "gentle" distractions are permissible. The participants will be given a sheet of paper with a list of facts or other types of information to learn and told that they will be given a test at some indefinite time—perhaps in fifteen, perhaps in twenty minutes. At any rate, they are not to worry about the time factor. They are to concentrate on learning the material.

In contrast, the FSV group will be placed in a room made as noisy as possible. Several TV sets can be in operation, tuned to different channels. A stereo should be playing rock music. (The designers of the Future Shock room can take it from there.) The participants will be given the same facts or information to learn but told that there will be a test in a specified number of minutes, the time limit to be rigidly observed. (The time factor is essential to reproduce what Toffler calls "decision stress.")

The instructor will call time in the FSV room, remove the noise, administer the test, then saunter leisurely over to the DQP room and do the same thing. After the tests have been scored, the results as well as the feelings of the various participants can be analyzed.

Katherine Anne Porter: *Theft*

Role-playing helps us to derive more from fiction, especially when the emphasis has been on the illumination of character. By taking the main character(s) away from the story and into the three-dimensional world of the classroom, we are able to examine more closely all facets of complicated personalities. (Besides, it's fun.)

After you have read "Theft" a number of times, divide up into small groups, each of which will select one person to play the role of "she." The others will assume a variety of relationships, depending upon what the group chooses to do with the assignment. Ultimately all groups will report to the entire community what they have learned about the character from their mode of investigation.

Here are some suggestions:

1. "She" and her husband (assume she had one) appear before a group of marriage counselors.
2. "She" brings the janitress into court and charges her with the theft of an inexpensive purse with sentimental value.
3. "She" is hypnotized (simulated) by another member of the group, regresses to her childhood, and then is carried forward in time, revealing more and more of her life and her hangups.
4. "She" has made an impetuous call to Alcoholics Anonymous but has since decided she cannot face her life without her crutch. Nonetheless, an AA group arrives on the scene and attempts to straighten her out.
5. "She" is given a surprise birthday party by a recently acquired friend who unwittingly invites all of the people "she" has known and hurt. They are together in the same room, and "she" must face their accusations and try to defend herself.

Antoine de Saint Exupéry: *The Little Prince and the Proud Rose*

The form used by Saint Exupéry to house his enduring fable is a classic one: the marvelous journey, wherein the hero in quest of truth has many strange adventures and meets many strange people representing a variety of viewpoints and life styles. In this way Saint Exupéry analyzes what is wrong with the way different adults live and why they are unhappy (like the red-faced gentleman who had never looked at a star or done anything else except add up figures).

Divide up into small groups. Each one will map out an itinerary for a marvelous interplanetary journey designed to bring to light some of the problems (or evils?) to be encountered in the world of today. One person can be chosen to play the part of the traveler. For the sake of variety, try to create a personality other than a little prince. The others can provide his strange encounters and represent the group's version of mistaken dedications, hangups, and conditions of the adult world, these to be dramatized in front of the class.

Your traveler may run across things like the following:

1. An all-automated corporation where machines take coffee breaks and put coins into people
2. A tiny planet where live those whose eyes have become adapted to TV screens and can see nothing else, whose only knowledge of life derives from TV
3. A place where people live in fear of each other and carry hidden weapons always
4. A school where people learn only "matters of consequence"
5. A planet where a year is only five minutes and life spans are so brief the people are desperate to have as many pleasures as they can and perhaps miss out on so much

Thomas Merton: *Perfect Joy*

Oriental writings like this one usually sound very simple, yet, the more we read, the more complicated and profound they become. The same must surely be true of the musings of someone who, like Thomas Merton, spent twenty-seven years in meditation as a Trappist monk. In the effort to achieve an "existential grasp of reality in itself," language sometimes deserts one altogether. For this reason, much of the monastic life, both of the Christian and the Buddhist, is spent in silence.

More can be experienced and communicated in silence than we may at first suppose. Denying yourself words is sometimes the best way to get at things. Try to reproduce a monastic atmosphere in the classroom. Possibly someone in the class knows a relaxation exercise. You could draw the curtains and play some Oriental music or some sound-effects records with the gentle lapping of sea waves or the tolling of bells, and so on. When this is accomplished, begin to act and interact silently. Tell people things you have not been able to say. Ask questions you have not been able to ask. Experience what is happening about you. Point things out to people.

When time is called, the class should discuss what has just happened. Did it feel silly, or did some people really feel they had gotten into things that might otherwise have been impossible to reach? Did anyone communicate with anyone else for the first time? Did anyone gain fresh insight into someone else for the first time? How did the instructor feel? Did he experience the class differently? Did people in the class find out something new about him?

For ambitious groups: Arrange a silent party. There can be food and beverages and (certain kinds of) records, just as at a noise party. But no one is to speak on arriving or throughout the evening or on departure. The telephone is not to be answered. If a stranger comes to the door, he may not be spoken to, no matter how he responds. Every effort should be made to mingle with each other and to hold wordless conversations. Possibly even inaudible entertainment can be provided.

At the next class period the party can be discussed and analyzed as to the quality and intensity of the experiences people were able to have.

Did any positive decisions about changes in life style emerge from the evening?

Hermann Hesse: *Siddhartha's Enlightenment*

Not everyone can share the full experience of enlightenment which Siddhartha finds at last by the river. But it is not only possible but desirable that each of us learn some techniques for looking at the world and at our lives with new eyes. Even if it is a vain dream for some of us to think that we can transcend all the activities to which we have committed ourselves as personalities living in society, we have to admit we do get into ruts, do become entangled in circumstances that seem at times almost hopeless. In many cases the hopelessness can disappear if we would only back away long enough to achieve a new perspective.

The Action this time is a very simple, private one. The class should disperse, each member going his own way for an agreed upon period of time. Each should take a walk or find some attractive spot where he can simply sit. In either case he should make every effort to divorce himself from:

An inner awareness of himself as a separate person
Thinking about unresolved problems
Remembering what happened yesterday
Anticipating tomorrow.

This disconnection from the self can be achieved by really looking at everything. Everyone will discover that he usually half looks, that he is distracted by internal considerations. By opening up all of the senses he won't have time to be self-preoccupied.

When the class reconvenes, see what happens. Perhaps someone will want to describe what it was like to see with new eyes. Perhaps someone will have found that his problems are not so terrible after all and the solution to them is really very simple. Perhaps someone will share with the others some of the things he saw for the first time.

Optional: Write a paragraph or more indicating how this experience has led to some resolutions about the way you will conduct your life in the future.

Carlos Castaneda: *Peyote and Another World*

Divide up into small groups, each of which is charged with the task of creating a culture unheard of in America. It should be given a name, and, in the time allotted, a list of dominant characteristics should be drawn up to serve as the basis for the role-playing to follow. The following are some possibilities for inclusion.

Name: The Gnocchis, residents of the island of Gnocch off the southern coast of Sicily.
Mythology: All life began in the active volcano which stands in the center of the island; this is inhabited by Carlino, god of all creation,

whose symbol is the grape and whose worship includes endless wine drinking.

Morality: Because the volcano erupts every so often, the natives see physical pleasure as supreme among life's virtues. Marriage is outlawed, promiscuity is mandatory. Reproduction is held to a minimum. Those who desire children must receive a permit from the state. The family is an unknown institution, so that children are raised and educated by the state.

Rituals: Chief among them is the Volcania, held once a year, to honor the god of the volcano. The main purpose of the observance is to insure the perpetuation of their hedonistic philosophy by disrupting the operation of all institutions, such as the government, the schools, and the law.

When time is called by the instructor, each group pretends it has come to the United States to observe an alien culture and life style. Some members of the performing group should briefly introduce the culture, as if for an American audience played by the rest of the class, with possibly a short question-answer session allowed. Other members of the group should ask the Americans some questions about *their* odd customs and mores.

After all the groups have performed (which may take several days but could prove well worth the time) there should be a general discussion about what has been learned. Are moral values relative? Is the American life style superior? Is Western culture the best? Is it right for one culture to seek to enlighten or "civilize" another that it regards as primitive? What about bringing Christianity to "pagan" cultures? (James Michener's novel *Hawaii* shows how the happy life of the Polynesians was dimmed greatly by the introduction of Christian sin consciousness.) How about scientific advances? (Can countries with much disease and little medical knowledge be regarded as "backward"?) These and similar questions are guaranteed to produce lively sessions.

James A. Pike: *Voices from the Other Side*

Some few, like Bishop Pike, found what they considered incontrovertible evidence of life after death. Many others believe resolutely in such a thing even though they lack tangible proof. Still others of religious faith may accept the premise of immortality without knowing precisely what might be the nature of another world beyond this. Perhaps the majority of people are content to be open-minded on the subject, but know there is no "contact" available to *them* according to the laws of nature as these are understood.

Let us assume that the issue remains in doubt and that there may or may not be an after-life and that, if it does in fact exist in some dimensionality unimaginable to us, the souls who abide there may or may not retain their earthly identities. At any rate, our task here is to determine whether the human existence that we *do* know and in which all of us participate is better or worse for being all there is.

Divide into small groups. If you have been engaging in the group-oriented Actions up to this point and have kept your group's membership fairly stable, you should know one another pretty well by now. (Even if you haven't, the class as a whole should be on good speaking terms after all the community discussions.) Decide upon one person who seems to be liked by every one in the group, one person everyone can get along with, who has been the object of no hostility whatever. This is the person who will be imagined as having died.

The others should close their eyes while the "deceased" simply sits there and tries to achieve a state of euphoria and indifference. They should imagine what it is like not to have that person around anymore, *never to see that person again.* The eyes should remain shut until each "mourner" has convinced himself that the person is really gone forever and will not truly see him when he is once again able to look around him.

The deceased is presumed to be there with the group "in spirit," but for the time being, he may not communicate. The others for their part should handle the situation in the way they believe they would if death really had taken this popular figure from their midst. They may talk about his good qualities, how they wish to remember him, what they might do to perpetuate his memory, how they will get along without their friend, and so on.

But now a miracle takes place. One member of the group is imagined to have psychic powers and has made a successful attempt to establish contact with the departed in the spirit world. In a séance, the dead member is able to communicate—but only through the "medium" and in the most incomplete of terms. The others may ask questions, and the answers may be prophetic or betray other kinds of superhuman knowledge and powers of insight. The nature of the other world may be somewhat indicated, though nearly all records of such messages contain only the vaguest kind of information.

When time is called, the deceased in each group should leave the room to allow the others time to decide among them whether it is easier to adjust to the memory of a good friend or to the possibility of his continued existence in a different form and dimension.

Evan S. Connell, Jr.: *The Fisherman from Chihuahua*

If nothing else, a story like this one gives the reader a chance to steal a few minutes from the frantic rush of the day and slow his reactions down to a level where involvement becomes possible. In order to maintain his interest in the situation and the characters, the reader *has* to be willing to concentrate, and how often do we really do that? Think of how much of every day is lost to our sensibilities because there is too much happening to take it all in. How many people become so overwhelmed by sense impressions that they can never sort them out fast enough to keep pace with reality? (How much of our lives do we live in retrospect? And how much must our memories leave out in order to make even passable sense out of things?)

Assuming that the story has provided you with an exercise in involvement, why not extend the possibilities of this experience? A number of activities suggest themselves, but many others will doubtless occur to you. In each case, however, the recommended procedure is threefold: *narrowing down, involvement,* and *zeroing in.* For example:

1. Have the class go into the campus coffee shop—or wherever the largest concentration of students may be found—and disperse, each member wandering aimlessly about until he suddenly decides to narrow down his attention and carefully observe some particular action or interaction between two people or any kind of situation either developing or breaking down. After thoroughly absorbing himself, he may seek the quiet of the library and transfer the experience to paper.

2. A group of three or four volunteers can be chosen from the class and given some time to work up a situation. Each should provide himself with a personality (preferably cryptic, like that of the two Mexicans at Pendleton's) and with some inner thrust or purpose in the situation. The main ground rule is that the situation should not embody any readily identifiable controlling idea. Location and some intense purpose may provide enough of a context. (For example, four people find themselves trying to cram into the prow of a ship. For some reason, each one wishes to be foremost. Or four people come together at the end of a fishing pier to perform a strange annual ritual.) After the class has involved itself in the situation, they should discuss either orally or in writing, what was perceived. It should be clear, however, that there is no "right" or "wrong" in this case. The role-players are simply there to provide an object of perception.

3. If the classroom has a television set, turn it on without sound. Allow five minutes or so for intense involvement with what is happening on the screen. (Talk shows, soap operas, commercials, singers—the content is of no consequence.) Then have each person write down precisely what he experienced. The telling of it should have a sequence, like "Fisherman." A verbal situation should be the result, and the test will be to see whether others can become involved from the way in which it is presented.

Thomas S. Szasz: *The Ethics of Suicide*

The basic contention of Dr. Szasz is that to take physical steps against a suicide is to rob the person of his Human Worth. But it seems at least equally plausible that one who contemplates suicide is suffering from the lack of a positive self-concept and that it is better to give him one than to allow him to kill himself.

To test out both possibilities, play a game—call it Determination—in which one person, playing a potential suicide, matches wits against a group, representing society, with a neutral observer keeping score. The object of the game is for one side—the individual or the group—to amass the most points and thus win. A high score indicates the winning side has the right of Determination. If the suicide wins, it is assumed that, in theory, he has ended his life. If society wins, it is assumed that he cannot logically be allowed to do so.

Here's how the game works:

1. The potential suicide indicates that he has decided to take his own life and gives one basic reason.
2. Any member of the group may question him on the reason.
3. If the group, in the opinion of the observer, cannot logically dispute the reason, the suicide gets the point; if it can, the group does.
4. As in basketball, the one who did not make the point gets the "rebound" and asks the next question.
5. This continues until one side or the other reaches an agreed-upon number of points.
6. If the questioning side cannot think of a question or an answer, the other side wins the point by default.

A variation on the game would be to have two observers, each scoring as he sees fit, and to allow them time to debate their observations.

Another possibility is to have one group play the game with the majority of the class observing. There would still be a scorer or scorers, but the focus on one game would provide a better chance for a community discussion of the issue and the logic (or lack of it) of the scoring.

Now that you have opened up this matter for analysis, read the selection that follows, "A Summer Tragedy" by Arna Bontemps, using it as a test case.

Arna Bontemps: *A Summer Tragedy*

Does one achieve Human Worth by struggling against adversity, even with no real hope of triumph, or by taking one's own life?

To find at least a tentative answer, divide into two groups: Poor People and Well-Off People. (Those who have experienced real poverty or who have known poor people well enough to identify with the way life strikes them; and those who have never known such persons.) The reason behind the groupings is to allow economic factors to play as important a role as possible, in case a person's lack of Worth may be entirely or partially traced to lack of money or it should turn out that even money cannot make life seem worth living without other things.

Come up to the front of the room in pairs, one rich and one poor person. Using some method (such as picking a card or rolling the dice), have one pretend to be engaged in a suicide attempt and the other try to prevent it. It will not be known in advance who wishes to die and who wishes to preserve life. But as soon as the roles are decided, the attempted suicide must think of and advance every possible negative view of life he can think of, while the preventor should be totally positive. They should be allowed, say, three minutes for their life-and-death debate, at the conclusion of which the suicide will indicate *as honestly as possible* that he either still feels negative toward his life and wishes to end it or has now developed a more positive attitude and will go on living.

The class, acting as observers, should spend a few minutes discussing the decision relative to the facts of the case and the arguments that were presented on both sides. If intense controversy ensues, perhaps another pair can take over the same roles to see whether a different decision is possible or at least believable.

In going over each case, the class should be alive to such considerations as

1. Did money seem more of a factor for the "poor-negative" as opposed to the "rich-negative"?
2. Did money seem to make it easy for the "rich-positive" to affirm life to the "poor-negative"?
3. Did "poor-positive" people have some advantages that "rich-negative" people seemed to lack?
4. Did any pair of debaters leave money out of their consideration altogether? Did the situation seem believable without it? Which side—positive or negative—held the edge in decisions?
5. In summary: What possibilities for life-affirmation and reasons for life-denial appeared to come out of the exercise?
6. In summary: Is suicide life-affirming or life-denying? That is, does it represent the successful effort of a negative philosophy to makes its final assertion of negation? Or is it a positive act based on a positive attitude?

Elisabeth Kübler-Ross: *On the Fear of Death*

An unwillingness to talk about death is quite common among Americans— so goes the premise behind Dr. Kübler-Ross' book. But philosophers have been telling us for centuries that it's a good idea for a person to project himself ahead in his imagination to the moment at which his life terminates. Such "morbid" thoughts help us in the long run to see ourselves in better perspective. It is surprising, for example, how many of the "pressing" problems of the day seem to vanish when we try to view our life from beginning to end. We are more likely to understand what our values are— or should be. We are more likely to put the emphasis on the right things and relegate inconsequential matters to their proper place. But above all, the willingness to think about the act of dying may help to diminish our secret fears and give us the resources we need to enjoy life while we have it.

If the class is small enough to permit any degree of frank discussion, form one community circle. If not, divide into small groups. Think about your own deaths and share some feelings with each other. Some of the following questions and suggestions may prove useful:

1. Have you ever been close to death? What were the circumstances? How did you feel about life afterwards? Do you feel the same way now?

2. Do you want an after-life? If not, why? If you do, describe what you hope it will be like.

3. Make a list of the five most memorable experiences of your life thus far. Eliminate one experience after the other until you are left with the *single* experience you feel happiest about, the one you will remember most fondly at the moment of your death. Explain why it is so precious in your memory. Can you arrange your life so as to have this experience again? If not, what resources do you have to help you accept the fact that it will never happen again?

4. Suppose this is the day of your death. What opportunities for leading a fuller life will you regret having turned down? What missed opportunities that have disturbed you and caused you to be unhappy can you now feel unconcerned about?

5. Deliver a two-minute eulogy to be delivered over your grave. What will be the things for which you want most to be remembered? What has been really important about your life? (You will be surprised how this exercise almost immediately changes the complexion of things for you. Recognition, honors, material successes tend to seem less memorable than some "everyday" aspects of your life which you may be taking for granted.)

6. Sketch out your will, being as specific as possible on the disposition of your immaterial (and if you wish, material) possessions. Indicate why these things are important and why you intend to leave them to the people you have singled out.

7. As you die, what wishes do you leave behind for the other members of the group? What in *their* lives do you hope will change for the better?

8. You are to die shortly. But incomplete communication still bothers you. What will you tell any three persons (present or not) that you have been unable to say before? Now come back to reality. You are not really on the brink of death. Would you still try to say these things? Why can't you? How will you cope with the situation?

9. Thinking imaginatively about your death is also a good way to see your everyday identity in better perspective. Suppose for the moment that reincarnation were possible. Specify what species, style, or brand of the following you would be if you came back as

    a. an animal
    b. an automobile
    c. a building
    d. a bird
    e. a bar of soap
    f. an activity or event
    g. a piece of furniture
    h. a book
    i. a natural phenomenon

If you could come back as some other person, who would it be? If you could do something when you came back that you cannot do now, what would it be? (And why can't you do it now?)

10. Suppose you have a terminal illness and are given the chance to have your body frozen until a cure has been found. Will you take it? If the answer is yes, indicate what aspects of your life you would gladly give up as you start again perhaps fifty years hence. If the answer is no, indicate what aspects of your life are too precious to give up, even if death might be the price.

Albert Camus: *The Myth of Sisyphus*

The key to this exercise is the answer you gave to Response #4. (If you skipped the Responses, go back now and at least do that one.) Each participant in the class is to decide what activity he is presently engaged in that he considers futile—like the uphill rock-rolling—and that he wouldn't mind displaying before the others. (If he decides this is too personal, he may choose somebody else's activity which he is interested in analyzing.)

Everyone sits in a large circle. The first volunteer then rises and takes center stage. He asks this person or that one to play certain roles: such as his father or mother, a teacher he has had, the boss for whom he's working, perhaps even his fiancé or spouse. He will describe the nature of the role and the way it should operate with respect to making his activity an uphill rock-rolling and ostensibly futile one.

The participant suggests a situation, one that will illustrate the futility of the activity. He will then play himself, responding exactly as he normally would *without having read Camus*. The idea behind the Action is for each observer to decide whether

1. the activity is as futile as the person believes
2. his "mythic" expectations are based on a Cinderella or a Sisyphus pattern—that is, on some vague hope for which there is no realistic foundation, or on no hope of fulfillment whatever
3. his attitude is the right one for the condition (in other words, if it isn't futile but can be changed for the better, it would be foolish to be Cinderella-ish about is when positive action can be taken or to be an absurd hero when this isn't necessary)
4. the person is exhibiting as much control as he possibly can or is surrendering too easily
5. the whole approach can be called life-affirming or life-denying, assuming for the moment that Camus is right and that either one is within a person's powers to express

A certain amount of time should be allotted for a discussion of each situation, allowing the main performer to present his own views.

Viktor E. Frankl: *Experiences in a Concentration Camp*

Before logotherapy can help anyone discover meaning, purpose, and useful-ness in his life, it must first assist him to develop a more positive attitude. It must bring about the establishment of an "even keel," a person's willing-ness to cope with life's absurdity, cruelty, adversity, futility. It must cause him to see that a good deal of his unhappiness comes from frustrated expectations and that the search for personal meaning can only start from the point at which life's basic rules are accepted. So long as the individual requires that life assume certain dimensions and fulfill certain other obliga-tions, he will be hampered by anguish of his own making and over which he should be master. For example, what good would it have done for Dr. Frankl to have spent his days hating the Germans and dreaming of im-possible ways to overthrow the sadistic regime of the camp? To be realistic, to curtail unrealizable goals is not, for the logotherapist, to take the coward's way out. It is to harness one's powers rather than to dissipate them in futile, misguided anger.

It is not necessary to travel to Vienna to avail oneself of some of the advantages of logotherapy. At all events, it does no harm to test out some of the implications of the theory. It can be done right in the classroom.

Assume for the moment that each member of the class is part of a huge camp we might label "existence at large." Instead of barbed wire he is bounded by many of those very things with which this book has been concerned. Here's a quick list of possible "wires":

education	the Corporate State	the city
marriage	big business	technology
moral systems	legal machinery	logic

It doesn't matter how good or bad one thinks these "wires" may be. What counts is that somehow each of us is touched by these things in some way nearly every day of his life. If one wished, for example, to regard himself as a totally free, unencumbered human being, he wouldn't get very far before he found himself significantly confronted by one or more of the elements of "existence at large."

In order to harness one's powers, one's resources for living, then, it is necessary to decide what things are indeed beyond one's control and what things are not. It is necessary *to know what the rules are*. When you com-pare notes with others in the class, you will be amazed to discover how differently people perceive the rules and how confused some are about them.

Step One is to reach some consensus about the rules. An effective way to do it is to divide first into small groups, each of which is to discuss the matter in terms of

NEGOTIABLE   and   NON-NEGOTIABLE

aspects of living *as conditions appear to be today*. Each discussant should be given ample opportunity to make a case for his perceptions on any issue. Some may feel that there is nothing that can be done about the deterioration of the environment or the white middle-class power structure. Others may refuse to accept the non-negotiability of just about anything except the fact that, if one is alive, he has to breathe.

Step Two is for the groups to come together in community and share their lists of wires and freedoms. These can be written on large rolls of paper and taped to the wall for easy viewing.

Step Three is to find one or two non-negotiable wires on which all groups (or nearly all) have agreed. Perhaps it has been determined, for example, that the concept of the city is too deeply rooted to change it very substantially. What then shall one's attitude be? How can one effectively deal with an apparently hopeless situation? What resources suggested by Dr. Frankl can be borrowed in order to operate in accordance with this particular "rule"?

Step Four is to find one or two possible freedoms—things most people agree do not have to be accepted or regarded as wires—and to discuss how one approaches these matters in the coolest manner with his powers harnessed. What real opportunity for effective behavior does one have? What risks are involved? What expectations of success? What resources for coping with disappointment, even total failure?